THE EXECUTIVE AND PUBLIC LAW

The Executive and Public Law

Power and Accountability in Comparative Perspective

Edited by
PAUL CRAIG
and
ADAM TOMKINS

OXFORD
UNIVERSITY PRESS

OXFORD
UNIVERSITY PRESS

Great Clarendon Street, Oxford OX2 6DP

Oxford University Press is a department of the University of Oxford.
It furthers the University's objective of excellence in research, scholarship,
and education by publishing worldwide in Oxford New York

Auckland Cape Town Dar es Salaam Hong Kong Karachi
Kuala Lumpur Madrid Melbourne Mexico City Nairobi
New Delhi Shanghai Taipei Toronto

With offices in

Argentina Austria Brazil Chile Czech Republic France Greece
Guatemala Hungary Italy Japan Poland Portugal Singapore
South Korea Switzerland Thailand Turkey Ukraine Vietnam

Oxford is a registered trade mark of Oxford University Press
in the UK and in certain other countries

Published in the United States
by Oxford University Press Inc., New York

© the various contributors, 2006

The moral rights of the authors have been asserted
Database right Oxford University Press (maker)

Crown copyright material is reproduced under Class Licence
Number C01P0000148 with the permission of OPSI
and the Queen's Printer for Scotland

First published 2006

All rights reserved. No part of this publication may be reproduced,
stored in a retrieval system, or transmitted, in any form or by any means,
without the prior permission in writing of Oxford University Press,
or as expressly permitted by law, or under terms agreed with the appropriate
reprographics rights organization. Enquiries concerning reproduction
outside the scope of the above should be sent to the Rights Department,
Oxford University Press, at the address above

You must not circulate this book in any other binding or cover
and you must impose the same condition on any acquirer

British Library Cataloguing in Publication Data

Data available

Library of Congress Cataloging in Publication Data

The executive and public law : power and accountability in comparative
perspective / edited by Paul Craig and Adam Tomkins.
  p. cm.
Includes bibliographical references and index.
ISBN 0–19–928559–4 (hardback : alk. paper)
 1. Executive power. I. Craig, P. P. (Paul P.) II. Tomkins, Adam.
K3360.E97 2006
342'.06—dc22   2005023128

Typeset by Newgen Imaging Systems (P) Ltd., Chennai, India
Printed in Great Britain
on acid-free paper by
Biddles Ltd., King's Lynn

ISBN 0–19–928559–4

1 3 5 7 9 10 8 6 4 2

Contents

List of Contributors	vi
Table of Cases	vii
Table of Treaties and Legislation	xv
Introduction *Paul Craig and Adam Tomkins*	1
1. The Struggle to Delimit Executive Power in Britain *Adam Tomkins*	16
2. The Ambivalence of Executive Power in Canada *Lorne Sossin*	52
3. Continuity and Flexibility: Executive Power in Australia *Simon Evans*	89
4. New Public Management New Zealand Style *Janet McLean*	124
5. Taming the Most Dangerous Branch: The Scope and Accountability of Executive Power in the United States *Ernest A. Young*	161
6. The Domesticated Executive of Scotland *Chris Himsworth*	192
7. Executive Power in France *Denis Baranger*	217
8. The Growth of the Italian Executive *Giacinto della Cananea*	243
9. The Scope and Accountability of Executive Power in Germany *Eberhard Schmidt-Aßmann and Christoph Möllers*	268
10. The Executive and the Law in Spain *Daniel Sarmiento*	290
11. The Locus and Accountability of the Executive in the European Union *Paul Craig*	315
Index	347

List of Contributors

Denis Baranger, Professor of Public Law, University of Panthéon-Assas ('Paris II')

Paul Craig, Professor of English Law, St John's College, University of Oxford

Giacinto della Cananea, Professor of Administrative Law, University of Naples ('Federico II')

Simon Evans, Director, Centre for Comparative Constitutional Studies, Faculty of Law, University of Melbourne

Chris Himsworth, Professor of Administrative Law, University of Edinburgh

Janet McLean, Associate Professor, Faculty of Law, University of Auckland

Christoph Möllers, Professor of Public Law, University of Münster

Daniel Sarmiento, Advisor at the Spanish Ministry of the Presidency

Eberhard Schmidt-Aßmann, Professor of Public Law, University of Heidelberg, Director of the Institute for German and European Administrative Law

Lorne Sossin, Associate Professor and Associate Dean, Faculty of Law, University of Toronto

Adam Tomkins, John Millar Professor of Public Law, University of Glasgow

Ernest A. Young, Judge Benjamin Harrison Powell Professor of Law, University of Texas at Austin

Table of Cases

A. Australia

ABT v. Bond (1990) 170 CLR 321 .... 113, 116–7
Al-Kateb v. Godwin (2004) 208 ALR 124 97
Attorney General v. Breckler (1999) 197 CLR 83 98
Attorney General v. Quin (1990) 170 CLR 1 113
Austin v. The Commonwealth (2003) 195 ALR 321 97
Australian Communist Party v. Commonwealth (1951) 83 CLR 1 .... 95–6, 112, 114
Bank of NSW v. Commonwealth (1948) 76 CLR 1 112
Barton v. Commonwealth (1974) 131 CLR 477 .... 91, 93
Bennett v. HREOC (2003) 204 ALR 119 97
Bond v. The Queen (2000) 201 CLR 213 100
Brandy v. HREOC (1995) 183 CLR 245 98
Bropho v. WA (1990) 171 CLR 1 112
Brown v. West (1990) 169 CLR 195 94
Coal and Allied v. AIRC (2000) 203 CLR 194 114
Commonwealth v Grunseit (1943) 67 CLR 58 99
Cormack v. Cope (1974) 131 CLR 432 115
Craig v. South Australia (1995) 184 CLR 163 114
Davis v. Commonwealth 166 CLR 79 91
Deputy Commissioner of Taxation v. Richard Walter (1994) 183 CLR 168 112
Egan v. Chadwicke (1999) NSWLR 563 107
Egan v. Willis (1998) 195 CLR 424 90
Enfield v. Development Assistance Commission (2000) 199 CLR 135 114
FAI Insurances v. Winneke (1982) 151 CLR 342 .... 90, 101, 115
Federal Commissioner of Taxation v. Official Liquidator of E.O. Farley Ltd
  (1940) 63 CLR 278 93
General Newspapers v. Telstra (1993) 45 FCR 164 117
Greiner v. Independent Commission Against Corruption (1992) 28 NSWLR 125 102
Griffith University v. Tang [2005] HCA 7 118
Grollo v. Palmer (1995) 184 CLR 348 98
Hilton v. Wells (1985) 157 CLR 57 98
Horta v. Commonwealth (1994) 181 CLR 183 115
Huddart Parker & Co. v. Moorehead (1909) 8 CLR 330 98
Johnson v. Kent (1975) 132 CLR 164 93
Kable v. DPP (NSW) (1996) 189 CLR 51 100
Lange v. ABC (1997) 189 CLR 520 .... 89, 90, 97, 118
Lim v. Minister for Immigration (1992) 176 CLR 1 97
MIEA v. Wu (1996) 185 CLR 259 114
MIMIA, ex parte Applicant S20/2002 (2003) 198 ALR 59 114
MIMIA, ex parte Lam (2003) 214 CLR 1 113–4
MIMIA, ex parte Miah (2001) 206 CLR 57 113
MIMIA v. Al Khafaji (2004) 208 ALR 201 97
MIMIA v. Eshetu (1999) 197 CLR 611 113
MIMIA v. SGLB (2004) 207 ALR 12 113–4
Minister for Aboriginal Affairs v. Peko-Wallsend (1986) 162 CLR 24 114–5

Minister of Immigration v. Teoh (1995) 183 CLR 273 146
Mulholland v. AEC [2004] HCA 41 90
NEAT Domestic Trading Pty Ltd v. AWB (2003) 198 ALR 179 118
North Australian Aboriginal Legal Aid Service v. Bradley (2004) 206 ALR 315 100
NSW v. Bardolph (1934) 52 CLR 455 94
PMA Case (1975) 134 CLR 81 115
Petrotimor Companhia De Petroleos SARL v. Commonwealth (2003) 126 FLR 354 115
Plaintiff S157/2002 v. Commonwealth (2003) 211 CLR 476 .... 96, 99, 115–6
Precision Data Holdings v. Wills (1991) 173 CLR 167 99
R v. Davison (1954) 90 CLR 353 98
R v. Duncan, ex parte Australian Iron & Steel (1983) 158 CLR 535 100
R v. Hughes (2000) 202 CLR 535 .... 100, 101
R v. Joske, ex parte Australian Building Construction Employees and Builders'
  Labourers' Federation (1974) 130 CLR 87 98
R v. Kirby, ex parte Boilermakers Society of Australia (1956) 94 CLR 254 98
R v. Toohey, ex parte Northern Land Council (1981) 151 CLR 170 114–5
R v. Trade Practices Tribunal, ex parte Tasmanian Breweries (1970) 123 CLR 361 98
Re Becker (1977) 15 ALR 696 119
Re Drake (1979) 2 ALD 634 119
Re Patterson, ex parte Taylor (2001) 207 CLR 391 90
Re Residential Tenancies Tribunal (NSW), ex parte Defence Housing Authority
  (1997) 190 CLR 410 96
Ruddock v. Vadarlis (2001) 110 FCR 491 .... 2, 94–5
SAT FM v. ABA (1997) 75 FCR 604 117
Sue v. Hill (1999) 199 CLR 462 90
Vass v. The Commonwealth (2000) 96 FCR 272 94
Victoria v. Commonwealth (AAP) (1975) 134 CLR 338 91
Victoria v. Master Builders' Association of Victoria [1995] 2 VR 121 117
Victorian Stevedoring v. Dignan (1931) 46 CLR 73 95
Wilson v. Minister (1996) 189 CLR 1 98
Wishart v. Fraser (1941) 64 CLR 470 95

B. Canada

A.G. Ont. v. A.G. Can. [1912] AC 571 84
Auditor General of Canada v. Minister of Energy, Mines and Resources et al
  [1989] 2 SCR 49 59
Baker v. Canada (Minister of Citizenship and Immigration) [1999] 2 SCR 817 .... 80, 146
Beauregard v. Canada [1986] 2 SCR 56 64
Bertrand v. Quebec (A.G.) (1996) 138 DLR (4th) 481 84
Blaikie v. A.G. Quebec (No.2) [1981] 123 DLR (3d) 15–122 57
Brosseau v. Alberta (Securities Commission) [1989] 1 SCR 301 60
Canada (A.G.) v. PSAC [1993] 1 SCR 941 67
Canada (Director of Investigation and Research) v. Southam Inc. [1997] 1 SCR 748 79
Canadian Pacific Ltd v. Matsqui Indian Band [1995] 1 SCR 3 .... 60, 75
Cooper v. Canadian Human Rights Commission [1996] 3 SCR 854 .... 59, 61–4
Crevier v. Quebec (A.G.) [1981] 2 SCR 220 .... 67, 78
Cuddy Chicks Ltd v. Ontario (Labour Relations Board) [1991] 2 SCR 5 61
CUPE, Local 963 v. New Brunswick Liquor Corp. [1979] 2 SCR 227 79
Douglas/Kwantlen Faculty Association v. Douglas College [1990] 3 SCR 570 61
Eldridge v. British Columbia (A.G.) [1997] 3 SCR 624 81
Falkiner v. Ontario [2002] O.J. No. 1771 (CA) 80

Fraser v. Public Service Staff Relations Board [1985] 2 SCR 455...................................58, 71–3
I.W.A. v. Consolidated Bathurst (1990) 68 DLR (4th) 524 75
Little Sisters Book and Art Emporium v. Canada (Minister of Justice) [2000] 2 SCR 1120........82
McEvoy v. A.G. (Canada) [1983] 1 SCR 704..85
Mackin v. New Brunswick (Minister of Finance) [2002] 1 SCR 405..74
MacMillan Bloedel Ltd v. Simpson [1995] 4 SCR 725 67
New Brunswick Broadcasting Co. v. Nova Scotia (Speaker of the House of Assembly)
   [1993] 1 SCR 319...60, 67
Nova Scotia (Worker' Compensation Board) v. Martin; Nova Scotia (Workers'
   Compensation Board) v. Laseur [2003] 2 SCR 585 63
Ocean Port Hotels Ltd v. B.C. [2001] 2 SCR 781 76–7
Operation Dismantle v. The Queen [1985] 1 SCR 441 80
OPSEU v. Ontario [1987] 2 SCR 2..71–3
Osborne v. (Canada) Treasury Board [1991] 2 SCR 69 71–3
Paul v. British Columbia (Forest Appeals Commission) [2003] 2 SCR 585...............................63
Pezim v. British Columbia (Superintendent of Brokers) [1994] 2 SCR 557................................79
R v. Beare [1988] 2 SCR 387..80
R v. Lyons [1987] 2 SCR 309..80
R v. Morales [1992] 2 SCR 711...81
R v. Morgantaler [1988] 1 SCR 30..81
R v. Nova Scotia Pharmaceutical Society [1992] 2 SCR 606..81
R v. Oakes [1986] 1 SCR 103..65
Reference re Amendment of the Constitution of Canada [1981] 1 SCR 753....................54, 56
Reference re Provincial Judges Remuneration [1997] 3 SCR 3..62–3
Reference re Resolution to amend the Constitution ('Patriation Reference')
   [1981] 1 SCR 753..85
Reference re Same Sex Marriage [2004] SCC 79 ....83, 85–6
Reference re Secession of Quebec [1998] 2 SCR 486 ....62, 84–6
Slaight Communications v. Davidson [1989] 1 SCR 1038..82–3
Suresh v. Canada (Minister of Immigration and Citizenship) [2002] SCC 1 81
Tetreault-Gadoury v. Canada (Employment and Immigration Commission)
   [1991] 2 SCR 22..61
Union des Employes de Service, Local 298 v. Bibeault [1988] 2 SCR 1048 79
Valente v. The Queen [1985] 2 SCR 673 ....60, 74–5
Vriend v. Alberta [1998] 1 SCR 493 65
Weber v. Ontario Hydro [1995] 2 SCR 929...77
Wells v. Newfoundland [1999] 3 SCR 199..59

C. European Community

Case 11/70, Internationale Handelsgesellschaft [1970] ECR 1125 306
Case 22/70, Commission v. Council [1971] ECR 263 334
Case 57/72, Westzucker GmbH v. Einfuhr-und Vorratsstelle für Zucker
   [1973] ECR 321..338
Case 74/74, CNTA SA v. Commission [1975] ECR 533..338
Case 78/74, Deuka, Deutsche Kraftfutter GmbH, B.J. Stolp v. Einfuhr-und-Vorratsstelle
   für Getreide und Futtermittel [1975] ECR 421 338
Case 98/78, Firma A. Racke v. Hauptzollamt Mainz [1979] ECR 69 338
Case 44/79, Hauer v. Land Rheinland-Pfalz [1979] ECR 3727..339
Case 730/79, Philip Morris Holland BV v. Commission [1980] ECR 2671.........................338
Case 60/81, International Business Machines Corporation v. Commission
   [1981] ECR 2639..334

Case 205–215/82, Deutsche Milchkontor v. Bundesrepublik [1983] ECR 2633 284
Case 181/84, R v. Intervention Board for Agricultural Produce, ex p. E.D. & F. Man
  (Sugar) Ltd [1985] ECR 2889 .... 335, 340
Cases 62 and 72/87, Executif Regional Wallon and Glaverbel SA v. Commission
  [1988] ECR 1573 338
Case C-331/88, R v. Minister for Agriculture, Fisheries and Food, ex parte Fedesa
  [1990] ECR 4023 340
Case C-8/89, Vincenzo Zardi v. Consorzio Agrario Provinciale di Ferrara
  [1990] ECR I-2515 341
Case 6/90 and 9/90, Francovich [1991] ECR I-5357 .... 46, 310
Case-39/93P, Syndicat Français de l'Express International (SFEI) v. Commisson
  [1994] ECR I-2681 334
Cases C-46 and 48/93, Factortame (No.3)/Brasserie du Pecheur
  [1996] ECR I-1029 .... 46, 310, 312
Case T-358/94, Compagnie Nationale Air France v. Commission
  [1996] ECR II-2109 341
Case T-380/94, AIUFFASS v. Commission [1996] ECR II-2169 341
Case C-57/95, France v. Commission (Re Pension Funds Communication)
  [1997] ECR I-1627 334
Case C-390/95P, Antillean Rice Mills NV v. Commission [1999] ECR I-769 341
Case T-118/96, Thai Bicycle Industry Co Ltd v. Council [1998] ECR II-2991 341
Case T-30/99, Bocchi Food Trade International GmbH v. Commission
  [2001] ECR II-943 341
Case C-58/99, European Commission v. Italy [2000] ECR I-3811 251
Case C-353/99P, Council v. Hautala [2001] ECR I-9565 340
Case C-365/99, Portugal v. Commission [2001] ECR I-5645 340
Case C-50/2000P, Union de Pequenos Agricultores v. Council [2002]
  ECR I-6677 .... 45, 335
Case C-263/02P, Commission v. Jego-Quere & Cie SA [2004] ECR I-000 335

D. European Court of Human Rights

Bryan v. United Kingdom (1995) 21 EHRR 342 28
Stafford v. United Kingdom (2002) 35 EHRR 32 34–5
Thynne, Wilson and Gunnell v. United Kingdom (1990) 13 EHRR 666 34
V v. United Kingdom (1999) 30 EHRR 121 .... 31, 34
Wynne v. United Kingdom (1994) 19 EHRR 333 34

E. France

Du Graty case 226
Heyriès case 234–6
Jamart case 235–6
Syndicat General des Ingenieurs Conseils C.E., 26 June 1959, 394 237

F. New Zealand

Attorney-General v. New Zealand Maori Council [1991] 2 NZLR 129 143
Attorney-General v. Refugee Council [2003] 2 NZLR 577 144
Auckland Electric Power Board v. Electricity Corporation of New Zealand
  [1994] 1 NZLR 551 131–2
Burt v. Governor-General [1992] 3 NZLR 672 137
CIR v. Medical Council of New Zealand [1997] 2 NZLR 297 130–1
Daniels v. Attorney-General [2003] 2 NZLR 742 144

Table of Cases

Drew v. Attorney-General [2002] 1 NZLR 58 149
Electoral Commission v. Cameron [1997] 2 NZLR 421 135
Federated Farmers v. NZ Post Ltd [1992] 3 NZBORR 339 144
Fitzgerald v. Muldoon [1976] 2 NZLR 615 138
Huakina Development Trust v. Waikato Valley Authority [1987] 2 NZLR 188 145
Innes v. Wong [1996] 3 NZLR 241 137
KD Swan Familyn Trust v. Universal College of Learning (CA255/02) 138
Lumber Specialities v. Hodgson [2000] 2 NZLR 347 133
McInnes v. Ministry of Transport [2001] 3 NZLR 11 144
Mercury Energy Ltd v. Electricity Corporation of New Zealand [1994]
  1 WLR 521 132
Moonen v. Board of Film and Literature Board of Review [2000] 2 NZLR 9 148
New Zealand Licensed Resthomes v. Midland Regional Health Authority, unreported
  Hamilton High Court, 15 June 1999 151
New Zealand Maori Council v. Attorney-General [1987] 1 NZLR 641 142–4
New Zealand Maori Council v. Attorney-General [1992] 2 NZLR 576 143
New Zealand Maori Council v. Attorney-General [1994] 1 NZLR 513 133
New Zealand Maori Council v. Attorney-General [1996] 3 NZLR 140 143
Ngati Apa Ki Te Waipounamu Trust v. The Queen 128
Ngai Tahu v. Director-General of Conservation [1995] 3 NZLR 553 145–6
Ninety Mile Beach [1963] NZLR 461 146
Official Assignee v. Chief Executive of Ministry of Fisheries [2002] 2 NZLR 158 144
Petrocorp Exploration Ltd v. Minister of Energy [1991] 1 NZLR 1 135
Phipps v. Royal Australasian College of Surgeons [1999] 3 NZLR 1 135
Police v. Beggs [1999] 3 NZLR 615 ...... 136, 149
Power Co Ltd v. Gore District Council [1997] 1 NZLR 537 150
Pratt Contractors v. Transit New Zealand [2002] 2 NZLR 313 (CA) [2003]
  UKPC 83 150
Puli'uvea v. Removal review Authority (1996) 14 FRNZ 322 146
R v. Pora [2001] 2 NZLR 37 149
Rajan v. Minister of Immigration [1996] 3 NZLR 543 146
Rankin v. Attorney General in respect of the State Services Commissioner
  [2001] ERNZ 476 (No.2) 156
Ransfield v. Radio Network Ltd, unreported High Court Auckland Civ 2003-404-569 136
Schier v. Removal Review Authority [1999] 1 NZLR 703 146
Sellers v. Maritime Safety Inspector [1999] 2 NZLR 44 147
Simpson v. Attorney-General (Baigent's Case) [1994] 3 NZLR 667 137
Tavita v. Minister of Immigration [1994] 2 NZLR 257 146–7
Te Heu Heu v. Attorney-General [1999] 1 NZLR 978 133
Te Runanga o Muriwhenua v. Treaty of Waitangi Fisheries Commission
  [1996] 3 NZLR 10 143
Te Runanganui o te Ika Whenua Inc Society v. Attorney-General
  [1992] 2 NZLR 20 143
Te Weehi v. Regional Fisheries Officer [1986] 1 NZLR 680 145
Vector v. Transpower [1999] 3 NZLR 647 132
Waikato Regional Airport v. Attorney-General [2002] 3 NZLR 433 151
Wellington International Airport v. Air New Zealand (1993) 1 NZLR 671 144
Westhaven Shellfish Ltd v. Chief Executive of Ministry of Fisheries [2002]
  2 NZLR 158 144
Wolf v. Minister of Immigration HC Civ 2002 3485 106 147

G. United Kingdom

A v. Secretary of State for the Home Department [2005] 2 WLR 87 ....26, 47
Adams v. Scottish Ministers 2003 SC 171 210
Al Fayed v. Lord Advocate 2004 SC 568; 2004 SLT 319 210
Alconbury *see* R v. Secretary of State for the Environment, ex parte Holding and Barnes
Anufrijeva v. Southwark LBC [2004] 2 WLR 603 46
Associated Provincial Picture Houses v. Wednesbury Corporation
 [1948] 1 KB 223 ....43–4, 113, 141, 149
Begum v. Tower Hamlets LBC [2003] 2 AC 430 28
Bushell v. Secretary of State for the Environment [1981] AC 75 44
Campbell v. Hall (1774) Loftt 655; 98 ER 858 128
Carltona v. Commissioner of Works [1943] 2 All ER 50 .... 127, 195, 211
Council of Civil Service Unions v. Minister for the Civil Service
 [1985] AC 374 ....42–3, 74, 202
County Properties Ltd v. Scottish Ministers 2002 SC 79 210
Davidson v. Scottish Ministers (No.2) 2004 SLT 895 211
Dimes v. Proprietors of the Grand Junction Canal (1852) 3 HLC 759 44
Entick v. Carrington (1765) 19 St. Tr. 1029 ....41, 225
Ghaidan v. Godin-Mendoza [2004] 2 AC 557 26
International Transport Roth v. Secretary of State for the Home Department
 [2002] QB 1391 29
Lloyd v. McMahon [1987] AC 625 44
M v. Home Office [1994] 1 AC 377 211
McDonald v. Secretary of State for Scotland 1994 SC 234 211
Napier v. Scottish Ministers 2004 SLT 555 210
Padfield v. Minister of Agriculture, Fisheries and Food [1968] AC 997 42
Porter v. Magill [2002] 2 AC 357 44
Puhlhofer v. Hillingdon LBC [1986] AC 484 44
R v. Board of Visitors of the Maze Prison, ex parte Hone [1988] AC 379 44
R v. Bow Street Metropolitan Stipendiary Magistrate, ex parte Pinochet (No.3)
 [2000] 1 AC 147 44
R v. Broady (1988) 10 Cr App R (S) 495 36
R v. Director of Public Prosecutions, ex parte Kebilene [2000] 2 AC 326 ....27, 148
R v. Home Secretary, ex parte Northumbria Police Authority [1989] QB 26 201
R v. Inspectorate of Pollution, ex parte Greenpeace (No.2) [1994] 4 All ER 329 45
R v. Lord Chancellor, ex parte Witham [1998] QB 575 145
R v. Ministry of Defence, ex parte Smith [1996] QB 517 44
R v. Panel of Takeovers and Mergers, ex parte Datafin plc [1987] 1 QB 815 135
R v. Sargeant (1974) 60 Cr App R 74 36
R v. Secretary of State for the Environment, ex parte Holding and Barnes; R v. Secretary
 of State for the Environment, ex parte Alconbury; R v. Secretary of State for the
 Environment, ex parte Legal and General Assurance [2003] 2 AC 295 ....27–9, 36
R v. Secretary of State for Foreign Affairs , ex parte World Development Movement
 [1995] 1 All ER 611 45
R v. Secretary of State for the Foreign and Commonwealth Office, ex parte Rees-Mogg
 [1994] QB 552 47
R v. Secretary of State for the Home Department, ex parte Doody [1994] 1 AC 531 ....30, 44
R v. Secretary of State for the Home Department, ex parte Fire Brigades Union
 [1995] 2 AC 513 47
R v. Secretary of State for the Home Department, ex parte Northumbria Police Authority
 [1989] QB 26 41

Table of Cases

R v. Secretary of State for the Home Department, ex parte Pierson [1998] AC 539 30
R v. Secretary of State for the Home Department, ex parte Simms
   [1999] 3 WLR 328 145
R v. Secretary of State for the Home Department, ex parte Venables and Thompson
   [1998] AC 407 .... 30, 31, 32, 34, 35, 36
R v. Secretary of State for Transport, ex parte Factortame (No.2) [1991] 1 AC 603 26
R v. Somerset CC, ex parte Fewings [1995] 3 All ER 20, CA;
   [1995] 1 All ER 513, QBD 43
R (Anderson) v. Secretary of State for the Home Department
   [2003] 1 AC 837 .... 30–1, 35–6
R (Assn of British Civilian Internees: Far East Region) v. Secretary of State for Defence
   [2003] QB 1397 45
R (Daly) v. Secretary of State for the Home Department [2001] 2 AC 532 45
R (Farrakhan) v. Secretary of State for the Home Department [2002] QB 1391 29
Rederiaktiebolaget 'Amphitrite' v. The King [1921] 3 KB 500 134
Scottish House Builders Association Ltd v. Scottish Ministers 2002 SLT 1321 211
Secretary of State for the Home Department v. Rehman [2003] 1 AC 153 47
Somerville v. Scottish Ministers, unreported 8 February 2005 211
Starrs v. Ruxton (2000) JC 208 .... 200, 210
Town Investments Ltd v. Department of the Environment [1978] 1 AC 359 69
Westerhall Farms v. Scottish Ministers, unreported, 25 April 2001 211
Wheeler v. Leicester CC [1986] AC 240 44

H. United States

A.L.A. Schechter Poultry Corp. v. United States 295 US 495 (1935) 169
Alexander v. Sandoval 532 US 275 (2001) 174
Ange v. Bush 752 F. Supp. 509 (DDC 1990) 181
AT & T v. Iowa Utils. Bd. 525 US 366 (1999) 177
Bivens v. Six Unknown Named Agents of the Federal Bureau of Narcotics 403
   US 388 (1971) 174
Bowsher v. Synar 478 US 714 (1986) 168
Braden v. 30th Judicial Circuit Court 410 US 484 (1973) 185
Bush v. Lucas 462 US 367 (1983) 174
Campbell v. Clinton 203 F.3d 19 (DC Cir. 2000) 181, 191
Chevron USA v. National Resources Defense Council, Inc 467 US 837
   (1984) 9, 191, 337
Clinton v. City of New York 524 US 417 (1998) 188
Clinton v. Jones 520 US 681 (1997) 170
Commodity Futures Trading Comm'n v. Schor 478 US 833 (1986) 163
Dames & Moore, Inc. v. Regan 453 US 654 (1981) 167
Dellums v. Bush 752 F. Supp. 1141 (DDC 1990) 181
Doe v. Bush 323 F3d 133 181
Hamden v. Rumsfeld 344 F.Supp. 2d 152 (2004) 187
Hamdi v. Rumsfeld 124 S.Ct. 2633 (2004) 183–4, 187
Humphrey's Executor v. United States 295 US 602 (1935) 170
INS v. Chadha 462 US 919 (1983) 164, 168–9, 173
Jacobellis v. Ohio, 378 US 184 (1964) 269
Johnson v. Eisentrager 339 US 763 (1950) 184–5
J.W. Hampton, Jr & Co. v. United States 276 US 394 (1928) 168
Lowry v. Reagan 676 F. Supp. 333 (DDC 1987) 181
Marbury v. Madison 5 US (1 Cranch) 137 (1803) 173, 175, 190

Mathews v. Eldridge 424 US 319 (1976)	184
Mistretta v. United States 488 US 361 (1989)	164, 168–9
Morrison v. Olson 487 US 654 (1988)	163, 170
Motor Vehicle Mfrs. Ass'n of the US., Inc. v. State Farm Mut. Auto. Ins. Co. 463 US 29 (1983)	174, 178
Myers v. United States 272 US 52 (1926)	170
National Broadcasting Co. v. United States 319 US 190 (1943)	169
Nixon v. Fitzgerald 457 US 731 (1982)	170
Panama Refining Co. v. Ryan 293 US 388 (1935)	168–9
Rasul v. Bush 124 S.Ct. 2686 (2004)	184–5, 187
Schweiker v. Chilicky 487 US 412 (1988)	174
Seminole Tribe v. Florida 517 US 44 (1996)	189
Shields v. Utah Idaho Cent.R.R. 305 US 177 (1938)	173
United States v. Curtiss-Wright Export Corp. 299 US 304 (1936)	165
United States v. Lee 106 US 196 (1882); Ex parte Young 209 US 123 (1908)	173
United States v. Lopez 514 US 549 (1995)	165
United States v. Mathews 16 M.J. 354 (Ct. Mil. App. 1983)	185
United States v. Nixon 418 US 683 (1974)	170
Weiss v. United States 510 US 163	185
Whitman v. American Trucking Ass'ns 531 US 457 (2001)	168
Youngstown Sheet & Tube Co. v. Sawyer 343 US 579 (1952)	166–7

Table of Treaties and Legislation

A. Australia

Administrative Appeals Tribunal
    Act 1975 119
    s.25 119
    s.43(1) 119
    s.44 120
    s.45 120
    s.48 117
    s.51(1)(aa) 117
Administrative Decisions (Judicial
    Review) Act 1977 116–8
    s.3(1)(c) 117
    Sched 117
Auditor-General Act 1997 105
Australian Constitution
    Chapter I 97
    Chapter II 89, 97
    Chapter III 97
    s.1 97
    s.5 92
    s.6 90
    s.28 92
    s.32 92
    s.33 92
    s.49 90
    s.51(i) 96
    s.51(vi) 96
    s.57 92
    s.58 92
    s.61 .... 89, 90,
                                91, 94–5, 97
    s.62 90
    s.63 90
    s.64 90
    s.68 92
    s.71 97
    s.72 .... 92, 97
    s.75 .... 112, 114–5
    s.75(iii) 112–3
    s.75(v) 112
    s.83 90
    s.92 96
    s.99 96
Civil and Administration Tribunal
    Act 1992 (Vic) 113

Civil and Administrative Tribunal
    Act 1998 (Vic)
    s.57 119
Commonwealth Authorities and
    Companies Act 1997 105
Communist Party Dissolution
    Act 1950 96
    s.4 96
    s.5 96
Constitution Act 1902 (NSW) 107
Constitution Act 1975
    (Vic) 105, 120, 122
Employment Services (Consequential
    Amendments) Act 1994 121
Financial Management and
    Accountability Act 1997 105
Freedom of Information Act 1982 120–1
    s.8 121
    s.9 121
    s.10 121
    s.11 120
    s.15 120
    s.18 120
Legislative Instruments Act 2003 103
Migration Act 1958 95
    ss.245A-245H 95
    s.474 115
Ombudsman Act 1976 121
    s.5(1) 122
Public Service Act 1999
    s.16 122

B. Canada

Canada Labour Code 82
    s.21 82
    s.61.5(9) 82
Charter of Rights and Freedoms 52, 55,
              57, 62, 65–6, 72–3, 77, 81–3
    s.1 .... 65, 73, 80–2
    s.2 80
    s.4 65
    s.7 80–1
    s.15 .... 65, 80–1
    s.24(1) 60, 80–1
    s.24(2) 77, 80

Constitution Act 1867 .... 53–5, 58, 64–5, 68, 84
  s.11 53
  s.56 56
  s.91 86–7
  s.91(2) 87
  s.91(24) 87
  s.91(27) 87
  s.92 86–7
  s.92(7) 87
  s.92(13) 87
  s.92(16) 87
  ss. 96–100 .... 58, 64
  ss. 97–100 64
  s. 101 84
Constitution Act 1982 .... 55, 57, 65, 68
  s.33 65
  s.52 .... 66, 80
  s.52(1) 61
Liquor Control and Licensing Act 76
Public Service Act
  s.33 72–3
  s.33(1) 72
Supreme Court Act
  s.53 84–5
Unemployment Insurance Act 1971 61

C. European Union

Constitutional Treaty 316, 324, 328, 331, 344–5
  Art. I-21 320
  Art. I-21(2) 328
  Art. I-22(2) 320–1
  Art. I-24(2) 321
  Art. I-26(1) 320, 322
  Art. I-26(2) 320, 329
  Art. I-28 328
  Art. I-28(1) 328
  Art. I-28(4) 328
  Art. I-33(1) 324
  Art. I-36 324
  Art. I-36(2) 324
  Art. I-40(2) 324
  Art. I-40(3) 324
  Art. I-41 324
  Art. I-54(3) 328
  Art. I-55(1) 329
  Art. I-55(2) 329
  Art. I-55(3) 329
  Art. I-55(4) 329
  Art. I-56 329
  Art. III-295(1) 327
  Art. III-295(2) 327
  Art. III-297–298 327
  Art. III-365 334
  Art. III-365(1) 345
  Art. III-367 345
  Art. III-402(1) 329
  Art. III-404 329
Council Decision 87/373 [1987] OJ L197/33 323
Council Decision 93/731 [1993] OJ L340/43 340
Council Decision 99/468 [1987] OJ L184/23 323
Council Regulation 19/62 [1962] OJ 30/993
  Arts 25–26 323
Council Regulation 802/68 [1968] OJ L148/1
  Arts 12–14 323
Council Regulation 1605/2002 [2002] OJ L248/1 .... 328, 342, 345
  Art. 53(2) 342
  Art. 54 342
  Art. 54(1) 342
  Art. 54(2)(a) 342
  Art. 54(2)(b) 342
  Art. 54(2)(c) 342
  Art. 56(1) 342
  Art. 57(1) 342
  Art. 57(2) 342
  Arts 149–160 342
  Arts 163–71 342
EC Directives, 19, 20, 21 and 22/2002 250
European Convention on Human Rights 200
  Art. 6 .... 27–8, 34, 210, 285
  Art. 6(1) 27–8, 35
  Art. 41 332
EC Treaty 331, 336
  Art. 5 338
  Art. 12 336
  Art. 34(2) 336
  Art. 52 251
  Art. 59 251
  Art. 87(3)(a) 336
  Art. 90 336
  Art. 128 325
  Art. 130 325
  Art. 137 336

Art. 141	336
Art. 195(1)	331
Art. 195(2)	331
Art. 195(3)	331
Art. 201	329
Art. 202	317
Art. 208	321
Art. 211	317, 322
Art. 230	334, 336–7
Art. 230(2)	337
Art. 232	334
Art. 234	334–6
Art. 234(1)(b)	334–5
Art. 247(1)	332
Art. 247(3)	332
Art. 247(4)	332
Art. 248(1)	332
Art. 248(2)	333
Art. 248(3)	333
Art. 248(4)	333
Art. 249	275, 334
Art. 253	336
Art. 255	336
Art. 269	275, 328
Art. 272	328
Art. 274	328
Art. 276	328
Art. 279	328, 343
Art. 308	326
Rome Treaty	238, 315–6, 320–1
Treaty on European Union	265, 326
Art. 4	317, 320, 327
Art. 13(1)–(2)	327
Art. 13(3)	327
Art. 14	327
Art. 14(1)	327
Art. 15	327
Art. 17	327
Art. 18	327
Art. 18(3)	327
Art. 18(4)	327
Art. 21	327
Art. 26	327
Art. 27	327
Treaty of Nice	316

D. France

Act of Indemnity 1915	234
Charter 1814	239
Art. 14	225–6
Art. 19	225
Constitution 1787	217
Constitution 1791	217, 220–1
Titre III, section première, Art. 3	221
Titre III, section première, Art. 4	221
Constitution 1848	239
Constitution 1875	223, 239
Constitution 1946	228, 237, 239
Art. 3	232
Art. 13	228
Art. 47	226
Constitution 1958	226–7, 229, 237, 239
Art. 3	232
Art. 5	226
Art. 8	227
Art. 11	228, 240
Art. 12	228
Art. 14	227
Art. 15	227
Art. 16	226, 233
Art. 17	228
Art. 20	227, 241
Art. 21	227
Art. 27	239
Art. 34	229
Art. 35	227
Art. 37	233, 236–7
Art. 37(1)	227
Art. 37(2)	227
Art. 38	237
Art. 39	228
Art. 41	229
Art. 44	228
Art. 45	228
Art. 49	241
Art. 49(1)	241
Art. 49(2)	241
Art. 49(3)	241
Art. 50	241
Art. 53-2	239
Art. 61(2)	229
Art. 62	228
Art. 64	228
Art. 67	238
Art. 68	238–9
Art. 68-1	238
Constitutional Statute of 25 February 1875	
Art. 3	235
Declaration of the rights of man and citizen 1789	
Art. 5	232
Art. 6	219

Decree 96-520 of 16 June 1996
 Art. 5 228

E. Germany
Aarhus Convention 287
Administrative Procedure
 Act 1976 ....276, 278
Constitution 1919 271
Constitution 1949 (Grundgesetz) 280, 285
 Art. 1(3) 269
 Art. 10 273
 Art. 10(2) 272
 Art. 13 273–4
 Art. 17 287
 Art. 19(4) 269, 285
 Art. 20 ....269, 281
 Art. 20(2) 269
 Art. 28 270
 Art. 35 272
 Art. 44(1) 280
 Art. 80 276
 Art. 83 270
 Art. 103(1) 287
 Art. 104 274
 Art. 115 272
 Order of 1960 285

F. Italy
Budget Act 253
Constitution of 1948 ....243, 247, 265
 Art. 70 251
 Art. 74 264
 Art. 75 245
 Art. 76 251
 Art. 77 251
 Art. 87 ....245, 264
 Art. 89 264
 Art. 92 264
 Art. 113 263
 Art. 117 251
 Art. 134 261
 Art. 135 264
 Art. 138 ....247, 267
Finance Act 253
Law 400/1988 249
Law 241/1990 ....249, 252
Law 225/1992
 Art. 5 250
Law 249/1997 258
Law 443/2001 249
Law 145/2002 253

Law 215/2004 257
Decree 1092/1985 252
Decree 259/2003 250

G. New Zealand
Audit Act 2001 159
Bill of Rights 1688 137
Bill of Rights Act 1990 ....125, 128,
 130–1, 136, 142, 148–9, 151
 s.3 136
 s.3(a) 136
 s.3(b) 136
 s.3(1)(a) 130
 s.4 149
Broadcasting Act 1989 135
Commerce Act 1986 ....132–3, 139
Crown Entities Act 2004 ....129, 139
 s.17 139
 s.17(2) 139
 s.20 139
 s.21 139
Crown Organizations (Criminal
 Liability) Act 2002 140
 s.4 130
Crown Proceedings Act 1950
 s.2 130
Designs Act 1953
 s.2 130
Foreshore and Seabed Act 2004 146
Gas Amendment Act 2004 140
Judicature Act 1972
 s.3 130
Judicature Amendment Act 1972 135
Judicature Amendment Act 1977 130
Local Government Act 2002 139
 s.12(2) 139
Ngai Tahu Claims Settlement
 Act 1998 128
Official Information Act 1982 ....129, 131
 s.4 129
Ombudsmen Act 1962 131
Penal Institutions Act 1954
 s.41C-41G 136
 s.41E 136
Privacy Act 1993 139
Public Audit Act 2001
 s.5 130
Public Finance Act 1989 ....127, 129,
 131, 154–5
 s.14 154
 s.20–21 154

Public Finance Act Amendment
    2004 .... 129, 154
Public Works Act 1981 136
Regulations Disallowance Act 1989 150
State-Owned Enterprises
    Act 1986 .... 129, 131, 139, 142, 144
    s.9 142
State-Owned Enterprises Amendment
    Act 2004 129
State Sector Act 1988 .... 130, 156
    s.2 130
    s.28 127
    s.41 127
State Sector Amendment Act 2004
    s.57 129
State Sector Amendment Act (No.2)
    2004 129
Trespass Act 1954 136
Treaty of Waitangi 125, 127, 131,
    133, 142–5

H. Spain

Administrative Jurisdiction Act 1956 303
    Art. 1, section 1 300
    Art. 1, section 2 300
    Art. 1, section 3 301
    Art. 2, section (a) 301
    Art. 25 300
Administrative Jurisdiction Act 1997 303
    Art. 2 302–3
Administrative Jurisdiction Act 1998 305
    Art. 31, section 2 300
Citizen's Security Act 1992 306
Coastal Areas Act 1988 306
Conference for European Affairs
    Act 1997 297
Constitution of 1978 .... 290–3, 302,
    305, 309, 312–3
    Art. 9 302
    Art. 9.1 291
    Arts 14–52 306
    Art. 24 .... 298, 301
    Art. 24.1 302
    Art. 54 310–1
    Art. 55 298
    Art. 56 291
    Arts 56–65 291
    Art. 66.1 298
    Art. 76 299
    Arts 82–85 293
    Art. 86 294

    Art. 93 291
    Art. 97 291–4
    Art. 98.2 .... 291, 292
    Art. 103 .... 291, 292
    Art. 106, section 2 308–9
    Art. 109 299
    Art. 111 299
    Art. 116 298
    Arts 117–127 291
    Art. 122.2 300
    Art. 123 300
    Art. 136 311
    Arts 137–158 291
    Art. 148 295
    Art. 149 295
    Art. 149.15 295
    Art. 153 296
    Arts 159–165 291
Court of Auditors Act 1982 311
Health System Act 1986 306
    Title I, Chapter I 308
Judiciary Act 1985 300
    Arts 107–148 300
Legal Regime of Public Administrations Act
    s.3 307
Ombudsman Act 1981 310
State of Emergency, Exception and Siege Act
    Art. 1.2 298
    Art. 3 291

I. United Kingdom

Acts
Anti-terrorism, Crime and Security
    Act 2001 47
    Pt IV 47
Children and Young Persons Act 1933 31
Crime (Sentences) Act 1997 31
Criminal Injuries Compensation
    Act 1995 47
Crown Proceedings Act 1947 211
European Communities Act 1972 26
    s.2 202
    s.2(2) 200
Freedom of Information Act 2000 212
Freedom of Information (Scotland)
    Act 2002 212
Government of Ireland Act 1914
    s.4(2) 198
Government of Ireland Act 1920 194
    s.8 196
    s.8(2) 198

Government of Wales Act 1998 .... 16, 195, 198
Greater London Authority Act 1999 195
Human Rights Act 1998 .... 26–9, 42, 44, 46, 48, 148, 200, 210
   s.1 27
   s.2 28
   s.3 148
   s.4 .... 28, 48
   s.6 .... 27, 44
Indian Independence Act 1947 195
Local Government Act 1972 16
   s.120(1) 43
Local Government Act 1974 49
Local Government Act 2000 16
Ministers of the Crown Act 1975
   s.8(1) 197
Murder (Abolition of Death Penalty) Act 1965 30
Northern Ireland Act 1998
   s.23(1) 196
Northern Ireland Constitution Act 1973
   s.7 196
   s.7(2) 198
Parliamentary Commissioner Act 1967
   s.5(1) 50
Police Act 1996 16
Police and Criminal Evidence Act 1984 16
Public Finance and Accountability (Scotland) Act 2000 212
Race Relations Act 1976
   s.71 44
Royal Assent Act 1967 202
Scotland Act 1978 .... 193, 196, 199, 201–2
   s.20(1) 196
   s.21(1) 196, 199
Scotland Act 1998 .... 16, 196, 199, 204, 210, 212, 215
   s.1 192
   s.29(2) 200
   s.29(2)(e) 197
   s.30(2) 206, 213
   s.31(1) 206, 210
   ss.33–34 210
   s.35 213
   s.36(1) 206
   s.44 .... 192, 196
   s.44(2) 197
   s.45(2) 195, 205
   ss.45–46 197
   s.46 205
   s.47(2) 205
   s.47(3)(c) 195, 205
   s.48 197
   s.48(1) 205
   s.48(2) 205
   s.49 197
   s.49(3) 205
   s.49(3)(c) 205
   s.49(4)(c) 195
   s.51 .... 201, 214
   s.51(2) 203
   s.52(1) 197
   s.52(2) 198
   s.52(3) 198
   s.53(2)(a) 199
   s.53(2)(c) 198
   ss.53–54 200
   s.56 200
   s.57(1) 200, 213
   s.57(2) 200
   s.58 213
   s.63 .... 198–200, 213
   s.63(1) 206
   s.69(1) 210
   s.86 210
   ss.88–90 213
   s.98 210
   s.99 211
   s.108 .... 199, 206
   s.118 206
   s.126(1) 197, 200
   s.126(6)–(8) 203
   Sched.5 201
   Sched.5, Pt II 213
   Sched.6 .... 199, 210
   Sched.7 206
   Sched.8, para 7 211
   Sched.8, para 15(3) 202
Scottish Parliament (Constituencies) Act 2004 210
Scottish Public Services Ombudsman Act 2002 212
Secret Intelligence Services Act 1994 16
Security Service Act 1989 16
Statutory Instruments Act 1946 206
Terrorism Act 2000
   ss.2(4) 215

Statutory Instruments
Nigeria (Constitution) Order in Council, SI 1960/1652 196

Scotland Act 1998 (Transfer of Functions
  to the Scottish Ministers etc)
  Order 1999, SI 1999/1750 199
Scotland Act 1998 (Concurrent
  Functions) Order SI 1999/1592 200
Scotland Act 1998 (Transfer of Functions
  to the Scottish Ministers etc)
  (No.2) Order SI 1999/3321 199
Scotland Act 1998 (Transfer of Functions
  to the Scottish Ministers etc)
  Order SI 2000/1563 199
Scotland Act 1998 (Transfer of Functions
  to the Scottish Ministers etc)
  (No.2) Order SI 2000/3253 199
Scotland Act 1998 (Transfer of Functions
  to the Scottish Ministers etc)
  Order SI 2001/954 199
Scotland Act 1998 (Transfer of Functions
  to the Scottish Ministers etc)
  (No.2) Order SI 2001/3504 199
Scotland Act 1998 (Transfer of Functions
  to the Scottish Ministers etc)
  Order SI 2002/1630 199
Scotland Act 1998 (Transitory and
  Transitional Provisions) (Standing Orders
  and Parliamentary Publications)
  Order SI 1999/1095 208
Scotland Act 1998 (Transitory and
  Transitional Provisions) (Statutory
  Instruments) Order
  SI 1999/1096 206
Scottish Administration (Offices)
  Order SI 1999/1127 203
Transfer of Functions (Lord Advocate
  and Secretary of State) Order
  SI 1999/678 197
SI 2003/415 199

J. United States

U.S. Constitution
  Art. I 164, 167, 178, 188
  Art. I, § 1 .... 164, 166
  Art. I, § 8 165
  Art. II 164, 166, 168, 178
  Art. II § 1 .... 164, 166
  Art. II § 2 178
  Art. II § 2–3 164
  Art. III 178, 186
Federal Tort Claims Act 174
Independent Counsel Act 163
Indiana Constitution
  Art. 3, § 1 163
Massachusetts Constitution of 1780 162
Non-Detention Act 183

Introduction

Paul Craig and Adam Tomkins

1. Executive power and public law

Executive power is the power of governments. It is the legal authority vested in, and exercised by, for example, prime ministers, presidents, cabinets, and councils. It is the political power that all those who embark on a career in politics dream of wielding. It is the power to set policy, to take action, and to implement the law. In the great theory of the separation of powers that has hovered over western constitutional thinking since the mid eighteenth century, the preserve of the executive is to *do*. While the role of the legislature is to speak and that of the judiciary is to judge, governments *act*.

Few would deny that, at the opening of the twenty-first century, governments have become the most powerful organs of nation states. They determine the direction, if not always the detail, of domestic policy. They decide how public money should, and should not, be spent. Foreign policy is made almost entirely by governments. And control of military power is likewise the preserve of the executive. Whatever the truth of the claim that, in this era of apparent globalization, states are no longer the only or even the most powerful units of political power, within nation states governments still retain very considerable power. This is not to say that their power can never be checked. Governments may rule, but they do not always rule supreme. In democracies the personnel of the executive is subject to the verdict of the electorate; the policies of the executive may be subject to political or parliamentary accountability; and the legality of executive action may be reviewed by the courts of law.

It was not always the case that governments were so dominant. Dating the rise of the executive is a treacherous exercise, and differs substantially from jurisdiction to jurisdiction. In Britain and the United States executive power has been growing steadily for more than a century. In Italy and Spain, by contrast, it has ebbed and flowed, with periods of exceptionally strong (and undemocratic) government being relatively recently superseded by a more cautious approach. In both places, however, as chapters 8 and 10 of this volume show, executive power has started to grow once more, not least as a result of the workings of the European Union.

From a public law point of view what is immediately striking about the growth of executive power is how little constitutions appear to have to say about it. In the era generally seen as the time of great constitution writing—the late eighteenth century—it seems to have been the control of legislative power that most concerned revolutionaries and new constitutionalists. The US constitution, for example, contains in its opening Article a lengthy series of prescriptions setting out in detail the institutional structure and law-making powers of the two Houses of Congress. Article II, which deals with executive power, is less than half its length and provides, as Ernie Young explains in chapter 5, for only a small number of constitutional powers: the president is to be the commander in chief, is to make treaties (with the advice and consent of the Senate) and is to make certain ambassadorial appointments but, in the bare text of the constitution, that appears to be about it. The constitution says nothing at all about who, beyond the president and vice president, may exercise executive powers. As Professor Young observes, 'these enumerated powers are certainly non-trivial, but they hardly justify, in and of themselves, the frequent description of the American president as the most powerful individual in the world'. The Australian constitution, written more than a century after the American, is remarkably similar. Its section 51 enumerates forty specific areas in which the national parliament has power to legislate. Its section 61, dealing with executive power, states merely that 'The executive power of the Commonwealth is vested in the Queen and is exercisable by the Governor-General as the Queen's representative, and extends to the execution and maintenance of this Constitution, and of the laws of the Commonwealth.' As Simon Evans states in chapter 3, 'standing alone [this section] would provide an altogether misleading and incomplete picture' of the nature, the functions, and the institutional structure of executive power in today's Australia.

2. The nature of this book

This book was inspired by our desire, as British public lawyers, to learn something more about how executive power may be conceived. Before embarking on the project we knew that governments the world over had become extraordinarily powerful and we knew that constitutions around the world were struggling to define executive power, to delimit it, and to hold its exercise to account. Or at least, we knew these things for the jurisdictions on which and in which we had ourselves worked. We knew, for example, something about the recent Australian difficulties with executive power, exemplified by the *Ruddock v. Vadarlis* case that Simon Evans discusses in chapter 3, and by the fiercely controversial involvement of Australian troops in the 2003 Iraq war. From a British point of view what is striking about these experiences is how similar they are to the picture in the UK. What they suggest is that, like the British, the Australians had in 2001–2003 a government that seemed bent on extending the reach of its own power, with (again as in Britain) neither the courts nor parliament seeming able or willing effectively to check the executive's advance. Now, it may be that the similarity of experience is explained through constitutional likeness—after all, both Britain and Australia share problems in defining the prerogative powers of government and both counties have similar, parliamentary (rather than presidential) styles of democracy. Yet there are also important and, one might have thought material, differences: Australia has a written constitution whereas Britain's is unwritten, and Australia is a federal state whereas Britain is not. We also knew something about the difficulties faced by those who were attempting to draft a new constitution for the European Union. When it came to seeking to spell out what the executive powers of the EU are, what should the constitutional treaty say?

Upon considering these issues, it became clear to us that while we shared a sense that there was a common problem among the jurisdictions we happen to know best, it was more difficult to say whether it had causes in common, whether its consequences were the same everywhere, or whether the problem was more widely shared elsewhere. Was there a jurisdiction, we wondered, from which those legal systems which we knew something about could sensibly learn in terms of the way it had dealt with executive power? Was there a jurisdiction where the definition, delimitation, and accountability of executive power was *not* so problematic, or was *not* done so badly?

This book is the first result of our asking these questions. For this volume, we have selected an avowedly unrepresentative range of jurisdictions and have asked leading public lawyers from each the same questions about executive power. We chose the jurisdictions featured in this book on the basis of three principles. As British public lawyers, we wanted to look at places that had some obvious relationship with Britain; we wanted a mix of common law and European jurisdictions; and we wanted a mix of monarchies and republics, of unitary and federal states, and of presidential and parliamentary systems. We wanted to see whether any patterns emerged, whether (for instance) federal republics seem on the basis of these jurisdictions to have fewer problems of delimiting executive power than unitary monarchies do, or whether parliamentary systems find questions of accountability easier than do presidential ones.

To these ends, the essays in this book address three sets of questions concerning, respectively, the definition, delimitation, and accountability of executive power. The first asks how executive power is defined in public law. Is it defined in the text of the constitution (where there is such a text) and, if so, is the constitutional definition appropriate or adequate? If the formal, constitutional definition needs to be supplemented, who adds to it? Is it a matter for the executive itself to gloss, or is it something for the legislature or for the courts to address? Has administrative law been required (or able) to answer questions left unresolved by the constitution? Might it be that a system of public law can operate without a comprehensive definition of executive power; if so, does the absence of such a definition cause problems?

The second set of questions, closely related to the first, asks not how executive power may be defined, but how it may be confined. How does public law delimit the scope of executive authority? Is there a sense that certain issues fall within, and others outwith, the domain of the executive? If so, who decides? Might there be any conflict between what the executive deems to fall within its preserve and what another branch of the state deems to be a matter for the executive? With regard to those issues that are acknowledged to fall within the domain of the executive, how much freedom of manoeuvre does the executive have—to what extent, in other words, can its core activities be externally reviewed?

Consideration of these issues leads naturally on to the third set of questions, pertaining to accountability. In the British context, at least, these are the questions that are most frequently discussed by public lawyers thinking about executive power: how, and by whom, may the government be held to account? Most of the chapters distinguish political/parliamentary accountability from legal/judicial accountability, and most discuss in addition such further institutional mechanisms of accountability as may be provided through auditors, ombudsmen, and regulators.

These are big questions and answering them fully would take a good deal of space. In order to focus our inquiry and to make the book manageable, we have put some aspects of executive power to one side. Thus, the essays here consider central government but not local government and they do not, on the whole, consider police or military powers, although there are references in some chapters to emergency powers.

Having outlined the questions that are addressed in this book, what answers does it offer? No attempt will be made here to summarize the chapters that follow, but it may be helpful to draw out some of the main themes of the book.

3. Defining executive power

The inadequacy of formal, constitutional definitions of executive power is a widely shared phenomenon. All of the constitutions considered in this book have struggled to provide comprehensive definitions of executive power. The gaps and silences familiar in the US and Australian constitution are replicated in Canada, in New Zealand, in Scotland's new constitutional order—even in Germany, where the constitution's formally unitary conception of executive power, we are told in chapter 9, bears little relation to the reality of federally shared government. Lorne Sossin speaks for many when he writes of Canada that 'the executive represents the institution invested with the most power... and yet takes up the least space in [the] constitutional texts,' texts in which 'the most influential figure in the state, the prime minister, does not make an appearance'.

Constitutions' definitional difficulties with regard to executive power seem to have two aspects: first as regards defining executive functions and secondly as regards executive institutions. The extent to which the executive may make law is a point of contention in all of the jurisdictions considered here, for example. Whether it is delegated legislation made by government ministers or rule-making by independent administrative agencies, the performing of what is, classically, a legislative function by the executive appears everywhere to be simultaneously inevitable and bothersome. What seems to be less widespread a problem is the adoption of judicial roles by ostensibly executive actors, and *vice versa*. Whereas this is a matter that has detained Britain's highest courts on numerous occasions in recent years, albeit without apparently resulting in a coherent judicial account of where the line may be drawn between executive and judicial power (see chapter 1), and while this issue has also arisen, albeit in a different form, in Germany, difficulties in this regard do not seem to have been widely shared elsewhere. In Australia, for example, such work as the separation of powers has been able to perform has been quite sharply focused on maintaining the independence of the judicial role from legislative and executive actors (see chapter 3). A similar approach is evident in Canada, though not to the same extent. Where the executive does seem able more frequently to enter arenas traditionally reserved for the judiciary is in the context of emergency or counter-terrorist powers, powers to detain being perhaps the dominant example. The global reverberations of '9/11', the Iraq war, and the Madrid and London bombings can be felt throughout these chapters, as governments react to new (or newly perceived) threats to security by extending the reach of their own powers.

With regard to institutions, the public law regimes of many of the jurisdictions considered here have struggled to develop accounts of executive authority that match the structural complexity of modern executive power. Even the rather basic distinction between the political executive (government ministers and the like) and the permanent bureaucracy seems to have caused problems in some places, France being a notable example (see chapter 7). Britain has, of course, bequeathed its singularly unhelpful and inaccurately 'unified Crown' to a large number of Commonwealth countries, including those considered here. The substitution of the Crown for the executive is as daft, in the modern era, as constitutional law gets. The stymied understanding of the structure (even of the identity) of executive institutions in the public law of Britain, Canada, Australia, and New Zealand is a direct consequence of this particular piece of laziness. That a nation may be a monarchy and at the same time develop a sensibly independent understanding of executive power is illustrated by the case of Spain.

Both executive functions and institutions have undergone considerable change in recent years and constitutional law has often laboured to keep up. The move towards 'new public management', for example, has resulted in numerous formerly governmental functions being transferred to the private sector through processes of corporatization and privatization. This has been a recent feature of government in Britain and in Italy, as well as elsewhere, but is an especially prominent theme in the case of New Zealand, as chapter 4 makes plain.

4. Delimiting executive power

Confining or delimiting executive power seems to be almost as difficult a task for public law as defining it is. To the extent that this issue has been overtly addressed in the jurisdictions surveyed here, three distinct approaches have been taken. We will call these the 'subordinate' approach, the 'bits and pieces' approach, and the 'residual' approach. What is immediately apparent is that none of the jurisdictions has employed an enumeration strategy to deal with the scope of executive power. In none of them is there is a formal or constitutionally entrenched complete list of executive powers. This is a technique frequently adopted in the context of legislative powers, especially where they are federally divided: see, for example, the US and Australian constitutions, mentioned above; the UK devolution statutes such as the Scotland Act 1998, which lists in impressive detail the legislative powers reserved to the Westminster parliament; and the Constitutional Treaty of the EU, which enumerates the exclusive and the shared law-making competences of the EU, but does not expressly list those reserved to the member states. It is not the case, however, that the federal division of executive power necessarily follows the federal division of legislative power. Constitutionally enumerated lists of law-making powers are a misleading guide to the location of executive power. This is perhaps most obviously the case with regard to the EU (on which, see chapter 11). As is well known the EU possesses only a small bureaucracy. The bulk of EU law is executed not by the EU's institutions but by national or regional authorities within member states. Surveying the EU's law-making competences will offer little assistance in seeking to analyse the extent of its executive power.

The 'subordinate' approach conceives of the executive as the agent of the legislature. The legislature makes the law, which the executive is there simply to execute. This approach has been articulated in Canada (by the former Chief Justice, no less) but, as Lorne Sossin points out in chapter 2, it is difficult to reconcile this approach with the fact that the Canadian government possesses and uses prerogative powers as well as statutory ones, meaning that, as Sossin states, 'the precise nature of the relationship between the executive and legislative branches of government in Canada remains unclear'. The 'subordinate' approach has been taken furthest, perhaps, in French constitutional thinking, where the executive has been seen as subordinate to, and an agent of, the general will of the sovereign people. Denis Baranger argues in chapter 7 that such an approach to executive power, popular as it was in early republican France, was a mistake, as it failed to take account of the reality—indeed the necessity—that executive power 'could not be reduced to mere execution', as Baranger puts it.

Such an 'entrapment' of executive power, Baranger reports, never occurred in Britain or the US, where constitutional thinkers from Blackstone to Madison and Hamilton understood that executive power has the character of being a principal, not that of an agent.

The 'bits and pieces' approach sees the boundaries of executive power being set not by any governing principle but by the pragmatic choices of the legislature. For all the talk of executive privilege or prerogative power, in many of the jurisdictions considered here the most significant source of executive power is legislation. As such, the boundaries of executive power are for the most part set by the extent to which parliaments pass laws that confer powers on the government. On this approach the delimitation of executive power is less a matter of constitutional principle than it is the result of practical politics. Indeed, on this approach the analysis focuses not on executive power as a concept, but on executive powers. The issue is less the authority that inheres in the government than it is the specific powers that are for the time being conferred on the executive. This is a point that features in Simon Evans' chapter on Australia but is most clearly emphasized in Chris Himsworth's account of the Scottish Executive (chapter 6). Whereas the powers of the Scottish Parliament are defined at great length in the governing statute (the Scotland Act 1998), those of the Scottish Executive seem precariously dependent upon 'transfer of powers' orders issued by the British government. What the Scottish experience demonstrates is that the preoccupation with legislative powers that we saw in the making of the US and Australian constitutions has been carried on into very recent times, with executive power once again left playing catch-up.

The 'residual' approach sees executive power as that power which is not exercised by anyone else. It is what is left over. It approaches executive power almost in the negative—seeing it as that which is not legislative or judicial. Janet McLean suggests that aspects of New Zealand public law conceive of executive power in this way, with ministers being seen as 'the residual core of the state from which everything else is at arms length'. Giacinto della Cananea puts it more starkly. Writing of Italy he states that 'while legislative and judicial powers are identified and clearly attributed to parliament and the courts, the executive's jurisdiction is neither identified nor attributed'. 'Rather,' he says, 'it is a residual concept'.

A final point to make concerning the scope of executive power is that many of the chapters strongly argue that it is growing. What Janet McLean refers to as the 'increasing internationalization of domestic law' is seen as a process that enhances executive power within states. In Europe, of course, this development is most clearly seen through the lens of the EU. The chapters on Italy, Germany, and Spain all stress the extent to which national executive power has grown and is continuing to grow as a result of the transformation of European nation states into member states of the EU. From a public law point of view this is perhaps particularly the case with regard to governments' law-making powers, both in terms of the way in which European law is made and in terms of the way in which it must subsequently be transposed into domestic legal systems.

5. Holding executive power to account

Legal control through judicial review and actions for damages is a method for holding the executive to account in all of the jurisdictions represented in this book. It would be surprising if this were not so. Assessing the similarities and differences of these controls across eleven different systems is challenging to say the least.

Comparative law requires in-depth understanding of the formal legal rules that exist within the respective systems and also an appreciation of the socio-political context broadly understood in which those rules have evolved and developed. It involves judgment as to whether distinctions between the systems are merely formal, just different ways of expressing the same idea, or whether they are substantive, embodying real differences in underlying values expressed through the medium of legal rules. A middle way in this respect is advisable. We should be cautious about assuming that all 'developed' legal systems really contain the same principles if only we look hard enough behind the formal legal precepts. We should be equally mindful of straying too far to the opposite extreme of assuming that nothing can be learned from other systems because all is necessarily contingent on the particular social, legal, and political context in which such rules have evolved. In truth we can perceive significant commonality of approach, coupled with important variations.

The commonalities are foundational. There is a commitment to basic precepts of judicial review, normally conceptualized as based on the rule of law. The procedural principles share many common features, rights to notice, hearings, impartial adjudication and the like, combined with an increasing commitment to reasoned decision-making. We can see similar features when we turn the spotlight on substance. The tools of substantive review, including those of rationality, proportionality, legal certainty, and equality, are found in many of the jurisdictions represented in this book, although the extent to which they have been developed and their 'reach' still varies. At a slightly more abstract level there are also interesting points in common as to the mix between constitutional and administrative law as legal techniques for holding executive power to account. The constitutions represented in this book differ significantly in terms of detail and coverage. This clearly has some impact on the extent to which legal recourse against the executive is constitutional in nature, or whether the focus is on administrative law doctrine. This is *a fortiori* the case where there is no formal written constitution. Having said that, it is also apparent that even in systems with detailed constitutions, such as Germany, backed up by a strong constitutional court, administrative law is seen as equally if not more significant than constitutional law as a legal mechanism for holding executive power to account.

The variations between the countries studied are however equally interesting. While there is much common ground concerning procedural principles of review this tends to fall away once we move from the comfort of individualized adjudication to control over rulemaking. Nor does the legal landscape divide neatly between common law and civil law regimes. The USA has the most generalized and developed regime for according participation rights to those involved in rulemaking. In most other regimes such rights, if they exist at all, will be the result of statutory intervention in a specific area. The differences are in certain respects more far reaching, reflecting as they do the extent to which the executive in the particular political system is regarded as having its own rule-making power. It is clear moreover that the implications of such a power for procedural review will often be dependent on other precepts that underpin that system, as exemplified by France.

The common features that persist in the context of substantive review should not blind us to disparities. Yes it is true that most systems will maintain some distinction between legality and the merits coupled with a judicial injunction not to stray onto the latter, but where the distinction is drawn varies. This issue is exemplified in the debate about proportionality and the intensity with which it should be applied if and when it is recognized as a head of review. We should moreover be cautious about equating this technique for controlling executive power with other doctrinal tools, even where they might seem to be similar. Thus the ready assumption that there is, for example, little to choose between rationality review in the UK cast in terms of manifest unreasonableness and proportionality as used in the EU when framed in terms of manifest disproportionality misses the real differences concerning the extent to which the respective courts are willing to engage with the contested measure. The Community courts even when intervening through a test of manifest disproportionality will normally scrutinize the measure in far greater detail than their UK counterparts.

There are other significant differences in substantive review that cut across the civil law-common law divide. In most civil law regimes it is simply regarded as axiomatic that courts should decide issues of law, in the sense of substituting judgment on the meaning of the contested term for that of the primary decision-maker in the executive. The same approach underpins much of the jurisprudence in the UK, New Zealand, and Australia. The USA and Canada stand in marked contrast in this respect. The courts in those countries have been willing to accord a degree of autonomy over such matters to the initial decision-maker. The US courts achieve this through the medium of the two-part *Chevron* test, their Canadian counterparts through the more open-textured functional approach developed by the Supreme Court. This is not the place to pass judgment on which of these approaches is to be preferred. It is simply to note that developed legal regimes can still differ markedly over the degree of autonomy, if any, which can be allowed to rest with the executive when it makes such decisions. There are, to be sure, devices in all systems that serve to soften the force of this distinction. All lawyers will be familiar with the strategies courts use when they wish to afford more latitude to the views of the minister being reviewed. Playing with the distinction between fact and law is but one of the commonly used juridical techniques. That such characterization can be utilized in instrumental fashion does not however undermine the significance of the different starting points. Or to put the same point in another way, the foundational assumption as to whether courts should always substitute judgment on matters of law will itself affect the judicial readiness to manipulate the fact/law divide.

Differences between the systems are equally apparent when we reflect on the incidence and availability of monetary relief. It is clear that the criteria for recovery in countries such as France, Spain, and Italy are more generous than those in many of the common law jurisdictions. There are of course limits placed on such recovery in the civil law regimes which blunt the degree of difference between them and their common law neighbours. This should not however serve to mask the subsisting dissimilarities. Nor should it conceal the very real divergences in value and philosophy that underpin the respective regimes. The common law precept that monetary relief has generally to be based on private law causes of action, that there is no recovery for illegal action *per se* and scant chance of any relief for losses caused by lawful governmental action is expressive of a philosophy of state liability for executive action that is not shared by many civil law systems.

In discussing such doctrinal issues we should not moreover overlook the more general facets of review which differ as between the systems represented in this book. None is perhaps more significant than the debate about the legitimacy of review when juxtaposed to the democratic political process. This is a debate that takes centre stage in many—if not all—common law regimes. It is especially high profile where the courts engage in constitutional review leading to the striking down of primary legislation. But it is also salient when the courts review executive action within administrative law, whether this be under traditional common law heads of review, or under statutes such as the UK Human Rights Act 1998. In either context the courts will frequently take part in an explicit discourse about the proper scope of review of executive action and the extent to which they should show deference or respect for executive choices, either on pragmatic or principled grounds. The judicial discourse will normally be accompanied by lively academic debate, questioning the lines drawn by the courts, suggesting alternative criteria and taking issue with the views of academic colleagues. Opposing academic camps form, collapse, and formulate anew once more. Matters are rather different in civil law regimes. All generalizations are of course false, but this notwithstanding the debate concerning the boundary between the political and the legal, a debate to which the judiciary as well as academia join, does not appear to be central in civil law regimes or the EU in the way that it is within common law systems. Now this does not mean that the common law judiciary has produced convincing principled distinctions as to the divide between the political and the legal. The chapter on Britain throws into sharp focus difficulties in the courts' jurisprudence. It does mean that the legitimacy of review is an endemic feature of the common law discourse.

We should also reflect on the efficacy of legal controls as a method of rendering executive power accountable. This is a difficult matter to determine within any one legal order, let alone across eleven diverse systems. Views on this matter tend to diverge markedly. Some would regard the law and the panoply of doctrinal controls that comprise judicial review as the most important check on executive power relative to other methods that exist, and would also see such controls as being an effective restraint on the modern executive. Professionals in any discipline tend naturally to see the area covered by their own sphere of expertise as being especially significant. Lawyers are no different in this respect. It is therefore unsurprising that there will be legal scholars in all the systems studied that subscribe to this view. Those of the contrary persuasion tend to emphasize the specificity of legal intervention. The judicial focus will be on the particular legislative provision or administrative act contested before the court, with the consequence that the judgment will often not touch on the broader aspects of the executive's policy, whatsoever it might be. They also stress what might be termed the fortuity of legal intervention. Courts get involved at all only when a claimant decides to bring the case. The truth, as is often the case, lies somewhere between these two views. Yes, lawyers are prone to overestimate the importance of their own trade, and yes, it is difficult to come up with estimates as to the impact of judicial review that would pass social science scrutiny. The opposing view must however also be qualified. The fact that legal intervention is specific and fortuitous does not necessarily preclude it from having a broader impact on the general executive policy in issue. Nor does it prevent legal doctrine announced in a particular area from having a precedential impact on other areas where the executive wields significant power. We should not moreover forget that legal doctrine may come to be factored into decisions when initially made by the executive. The extent to which this occurs is difficult to measure, but this should not lead one to dismiss its impact. This is so whether the rationale is primarily 'defensive', designed to ensure that the executive decision satisfies the judge 'looking over one's shoulder', or whether the motivation is more 'positive', premised on the belief that mainstreaming of the relevant legal values within executive decision-making is a good thing.

The very fact that there are limits to legal controls does however mean that we should as lawyers always be mindful of the importance of the political as a way of checking and controlling the exercise of executive power. Political accountability continues to be of importance even in systems that are not parliamentary, such as the USA. This is more especially so given that political constraints are not bounded by any distinction between legality and the merits of the kind that characterizes legal intervention. It is clear from the essays in this volume that a variety of factors shape the nature and effect of political controls, some of which are relevant to all systems, others of which are more pertinent to some systems than others.

Thus similar difficulties in ensuring meaningful political control can be perceived in those parliamentary systems where the executive forms part of the legislature, more particularly where the electoral regime leads not infrequently to the dominant party having a significant overall majority within Parliament. Recourse to specialist committees designed to cast the spotlight on specific executive decisions is common. The efficacy of such committees will be affected by the extent to which they operate across party lines, or merely replicate party allegiances and hence continue adversarial politics in a smaller forum. Their effectiveness will also be markedly influenced by their power to get at the evidence, examine witnesses and the like, and on the political and legal impact of their findings.

The force of political control over the executive will also be shaped by less tangible factors, such as the degree of 'political capital' that the executive does or does not possess at the relevant time. Where the executive is strong it will often be able to ride out political criticism, whether voiced on the floor of Parliament or through committees. The strong executive with popular support can seek to rely on a combination of the response to strictures voiced by committees, coupled with the effluxion of time, confident that today's headlines will be rapidly overtaken by tomorrow's news. Where the executive's political capital is low the impact of political controls will, other things being equal, be more telling. Thus the forced resignation of the Santer Commission in the EU was precipitated by the report of the Committee of Independent Experts. This was however the culmination of more particular criticisms voiced by committees within the European Parliament and the Court of Auditors over a long period of time. The degree of support that the executive is able to muster will also be of relevance in determining whether it can survive wide-ranging political criticism. The critiques that led to the downfall of the Commission are again a case in point. Reform of the Commission may well have been warranted, but this should not mask the fact that the actual deficiencies revealed by the Committee of Independent Experts were less dramatic than might have been thought from a reading of some of the headlines that accompanied the report. There was scant evidence of any fraud by the Commission itself, and much evidence of bad line-management of projects that had been contracted-out. This is not to say that deficiencies of the latter kind are unimportant. It is to say that if the same criterion had been applied to the national executives considered in this book, there should have been many members seeking new jobs. The difficulty of ensuring adequate controls over projects contracted-out is an endemic one in all political systems. Reports of cost-overruns, fraud by contractors and bad value for money are a regular feature in the reviews conducted by audit offices and the like. The Santer Commission walked before it was formally pushed, whereas many national executives have survived the revelation of equally telling or greater executive error. This however has more to do with the degree of support and political capital that the executive can muster than the importance of the errors revealed.

The impact of the division of executive authority on political accountability is an issue of importance, albeit in different ways, for most of the systems represented in this book. The countries that form part of the EU face one dimension of this problem. Countries such as Britain, France, Spain, Germany, and Italy have to cope with the effect of the transfer of legislative power to the EU over an increasing range of subject-matter areas. This has, in one sense, increased the power of national executives over their respective legislatures. The latter may no longer have power to enact legislation in the areas where authority has been transferred to the EU, or legislative power may be shared between the EU and member states. In either eventuality the national executives will still be represented at the EU level through the Council of Ministers and the European Council. It has been difficult for national parliaments to have meaningful input into legislative initiatives passed by the EU. It is the national executives that are charged with implementation of EU legislation. It will moreover be the national executives and their bureaucracies that administer many of the important EU policies, such as Agriculture and the Structural Funds, jointly with the Commission. The very fact that administration is shared can make it difficult to apply the normal precepts of political accountability that operate in relation to domestic policy. This problem is exacerbated by the complexity of many of the schemes subject to shared administration.

The effect of more traditional divisions of authority within nation states on executive power and accountability is equally important. It seems clear from the analyses in this book that any generalization about the impact of federalism is problematic, since so much turns on the nature of the divide between federal and state authority. This is readily apparent from a reading of the chapters on Germany, Spain, Italy, Canada, Australia, and the USA. The formal legal precepts dividing authority differ markedly as between the systems, in terms of the relative specificity in the delineation of powers accorded to the respective branches of government. These legal precepts will then be subject to judicial interpretation that may result in a very different division of power from that envisaged by the drafters of the constitution. It is clear moreover, as stressed by Ernie Young, that the practical operation of a federal regime may be significantly affected by checks and balances as well as textual enumeration of respective powers.

It is therefore not easy to assess the influence of federalism on the political accountability of the executive. The very existence of some form of federalism will perforce limit the scope of federal power by assigning certain executive powers to states, regions, or municipalities. This is trite. But it tells one very little as to whether federalism serves to enhance political accountability of the federal executive. Nor does it offer any ready made conclusions about the accountability of executive power at the lower level, whether this be in states, regions, or municipalities. This is more especially so when experiments with federalism interact with other changes in the political regime in a way that could not be readily predicted. The story that Giacinto della Cananea tells about Italy is a classic example of this.

6. Conclusions

The public law regimes of all the jurisdictions considered in this book have found executive power to be a difficult and testing matter. An uneasy ambivalence about executive power may be detected in all of the chapters—a recognition, perhaps, that on the one hand the government must be allowed to govern but that on the other it is the role of public law to find ways of delimiting the government's reach and of holding the government's exercise of its power to account. Perhaps this is as far as public law research can take us into executive power: that what public lawyers can tell us about executive power is that, as Simon Evans puts it at the end of his contribution, 'there is no end-state to be reached, but an ongoing search for an accommodation'.

The definition, delimitation, and accountability of executive power have caused problems for public law everywhere. The problems are not always identical, of course, and they have been addressed differently in different places, but they do appear, at least from the evidence presented in these chapters, to have certain causes in common. Among these is a widely shared unwillingness to articulate precisely what it is that executive power is. This rather elemental failing, while true of executive power, is not a general feature of the way in which public law seeks to regulate legislative or judicial power. Law-making competences are, as we discussed above, commonly enumerated, often to great length and in considerable detail. Judicial power, while not generally enumerated as such, is easier to comprehend, albeit that there may be controversies at the borders. The judicial role is to adjudicate on the law in disputes which parties bring before them. Where there are advisory opinions (as in Canada and the EU, for example) and where judges are asked to chair politically sensitive public inquiries (as in Britain, for example) more difficult issues may be raised, but even with this in mind, the core judicial role is difficult neither to articulate nor to understand.

Executive power, by contrast, is not as straightforward. It may be said to be composed of at least four main elements, as follows: executives take responsibility for (1) setting legislative priorities, (2) implementing policy and legislation, (3) conducting foreign policy and defence, and (4) structuring and allocating the public budget. Even if this is an acceptable description of the variety of tasks entrusted to governments, two sorts of questions remain. First, why entrust such an apparently disparate range of activities to one power? Why, for example, should the same institution implement policy as the one which proposes it? Why not separate these powers? And secondly, why should it be to the executive that these powers are entrusted? Why is it, for example, that foreign policy is the domain of the head of government and the foreign minister rather than of (say) the chairman or chairwoman of the foreign affairs committees of parliament?

These are important questions, the answers to which may well be an interesting mix of principle and pragmatism. Whatever the answers, they will have to wait for another volume. Public law research into the nature of executive power is only just beginning. If one thing is for sure, it is that considerably more research and critical thinking will be needed in the future as governments around the world continue to extend their power.

1

The Struggle to Delimit Executive Power in Britain

Adam Tomkins*

1. Definition, composition, and structure

(a) Government and the law

British public law knows no definition of the executive as such. While public lawyers will happily talk and write about 'public administration', the 'government', or the 'executive', none of these terms has fixed or authoritative definitions in British constitutional or administrative law. This is not to say that the law is entirely ignorant of executive power. On the contrary, there are several sources and institutions of executive power that may be identified in legal terms. The 'Crown', 'ministers of the Crown', and 'secretaries of state' are all terms dealing with executive power that both common law and statute law make frequent use of, even if their precise meaning is not always clear.

It is to say, however, that the law's apparent knowledge of the executive is patchy. Neither the prime minister nor the cabinet are creatures of law. The 'core executive', a phrase much used in the contemporary political science literature on British government, is unknown to the law.[1] The employment of civil servants is a matter in respect of which there is only partial legal regulation (although, as we shall see, this is liable to be reformed in the near future). The further one moves from the core executive, the greater the degree of legal delimitation. The powers and functions of the police, of the security and secret intelligence services, of devolved government in Scotland and Wales, and of local government are all detailed in statute to a far greater degree than is the case with regard to central government, ministers, and the senior civil service.[2] This is a theme that will

---

* John Millar Professor of Public Law, University of Glasgow.
[1] See further on the core executive, below.
[2] See, e.g., the Police and Criminal Evidence Act 1984, the Police Act 1996, the Security Service Act 1989, the Secret Intelligence Services Act 1994, the Scotland Act 1998 (on which see Himsworth, this volume), the Government of Wales Act 1998, the Local Government Acts 1972 and 2000.

recur throughout this chapter: namely, the intermittent presence of law in the regulation of executive power in Britain.

The head of the government is the prime minister, an office on which British law is famously silent. There is no legal requirement that there be a prime minister. As with so much of the British constitution, the office of prime minister was not created out of constitutional principle. Rather, it emerged out of political convenience. It is often remarked that the first prime minister was Sir Robert Walpole (who held office from 1721 until 1742) and that there has continuously been a prime minister since William Pitt the Younger (who became prime minister in 1783). Today the prime minister is the leader of the political party which, for the time being, is able to command majority support in the House of Commons. He or (once)[3] she is appointed by the queen.[4] However, if the queen were to appoint someone other than the leader of the majority party in the Commons to the office, or indeed if she were to appoint no-one to the office, she would not be acting illegally. Improperly, perhaps, but not illegally.

The fact that the prime minister is now the person who leads the party with majority support in the Commons is, to the extent that it is a rule at all, a rule of constitutional politics, not a rule of law. Most constitutional commentators employ the term 'constitutional convention' to describe such rules. The very office of prime minister is a creation of constitutional convention, not of law. The status of constitutional conventions is contested. Some commentators insist that they are descriptive only and that to ignore or flout them means not that the constitution has been breached but that it has been changed. Others take a more prescriptive approach and hold that if someone refuses to follow a convention they are acting unconstitutionally ('acting unconstitutionally' being something different from 'acting illegally'). Even if this second view is preferred[5] the arbiter of whether or not behaviour contrary to a convention is unconstitutional is not a court of law but is, in this case at least, Parliament. All commentators agree that to the extent that conventions may properly be described as rules, they are rules that may not be judicially enforced. Insofar as they are enforced at all, they are enforced by political institutions such as the House of Commons. Thus, if the queen refused to appoint a prime minister she would not be acting illegally but she may well be acting unconstitutionally, albeit that the judge of her actions would be Parliament—and in particular the House of Commons—rather than the courts of law.

---

[3] Margaret Thatcher, Conservative prime minister from 1979–90 is, to date, the only woman to have held the office.

[4] The power of appointment is a legal one, vested in the queen as part of the royal prerogative. See further on the prerogative, below.

[5] Which, in my view, it should be: see A. Tomkins, *Public Law* (Oxford University Press, 2003), Chap. 1.

(b) Prime minister, cabinet, and core executive

While the head of government is the prime minister, the most common constitutional description of British government, in the twentieth century at least, was that it was an example of 'cabinet government'.[6] Like the prime minister, the cabinet is a creature of convention rather than of constitutional law, emerging in its modern form during the course of the eighteenth century.[7] Members of the cabinet are appointed by the queen on the advice of the prime minister. The prime minister determines who sits in his cabinet and which cabinet ministers are responsible for which areas of government policy. The cabinet usually comprises about twenty–twenty four senior government ministers, although the number is not fixed. It generally consists of the most senior minister from each government department, save that the most important departments (notably the treasury) usually have two ministers in the cabinet. The total number of ministers is normally about 110, the majority of whom are junior ministers who do not sit in the cabinet. All ministers are members of one of the two Houses of Parliament. In most administrations about ninety will be MPs in the House of Commons and about twenty will be peers in the House of Lords.

Government departments, unlike the prime minister and the cabinet, are creatures of law, created either by statute or under the prerogative.[8] That said, the prime minister may re-organize government departments and may reshuffle ministers at will. Thus, Mrs Thatcher merged trade and industry into one department and split the old department of health and social security into two. She abolished the department of energy and redistributed its functions elsewhere. Her successor, Mr Major, abolished the department of employment. Under his successor (Tony Blair), there is a new office of the deputy prime minister, a department which did not exist under either Mrs Thatcher or Mr Major, and the ancient lord chancellor's department was in 2003 replaced with a new department for constitutional affairs.

Most government departments are headed by a secretary of state, which, again, is a legal office. In legal terms, the major unit of executive power in Britain is the government department. When modern statutes confer powers on the executive they tend to do so by empowering 'the secretary of state'.[9] In British

---

[6] See, e.g., Sir Ivor Jennings' pioneering study, *Cabinet Government* (Cambridge University Press, 1936).

[7] Although with roots in the seventeenth: see C. Roberts, *The Emergence of Responsible Government in Stuart England* (Cambridge University Press, 1966).

[8] The prerogative is the power inherent in the Crown that the common law courts recognize as having legal force. Some Crown prerogative powers continue to be exercisable only by the queen (appointment of prime minister, dissolution of Parliament, royal assent to legislation, etc), but most such powers are now exercisable by ministers (making of treaties, defence of the realm, deployment of the armed forces, employment of the civil service, grant of honours, issuance of passports, etc.). See further on the prerogative, below.

[9] In law, the secretary of state is one office, meaning that each secretary of state may exercise the powers of any secretary of state. This has the advantage that, should the prime minister decide to

constitutional law, 'government is ministerial government. Powers and duties are laid on ministers, not on the prime minister' and not on the executive at large.[10] In law, if not in practice, the responsibility of a secretary of state for the policies pursued in his (or, more rarely, her) department rests with the secretary of state alone. No other minister, not even the prime minister, has the legal power to override him. The prime minister and the cabinet may encourage or discourage, but technically they cannot instruct individual ministers in the exercise of their powers.[11]

Such may be the legal position but the political reality is quite different. Ministers who fail to carry the support of the prime minister will quickly find themselves shuffled out of office. Moreover, while ministers cannot formally be told by prime minister of the cabinet to exercise their powers in a certain way, they are bound by what the prime minister and/or the cabinet decide is government policy. It is a constitutional convention that all ministers in the government (whether members of the cabinet or not) must take collective responsibility for all government policy. This gives the prime minister considerable strength (or, at least, it does for as long as the prime minister retains effective control over his government's policy-making), as any minister who finds himself unable to support and defend government policy in Parliament and in public will be expected to resign immediately from office.[12]

It used to be thought that the central unit of political power was the cabinet. Jennings opened his magisterial account of British government with the following words:

The cabinet is the core of the British constitutional system. It is the supreme directing authority. It integrates what would otherwise be a heterogeneous collection of authorities exercising a vast variety of functions. It provides unity to the British system of government.[13]

This was the standard view for much of the mid twentieth century.[14] Under the premierships of Margaret Thatcher and Tony Blair, however, it has become

---

transfer a particular area of government policy from one department to another, there is no need to make Transfer of Powers Orders for the secretary of state of the new department to have legal powers formerly exercised by the old one: see T. Daintith and A. Page, *The Executive in the Constitution: Structure, Autonomy, and Internal Control* (Oxford University Press, 1999), 32–3 and R. Brazier, *Ministers of the Crown* (Clarendon Press, 1997), 9–10.

[10] G.W. Jones, 'The United Kingdom', in W. Plowden (ed.), *Advising the Rulers* (Blackwell, 1987), 64.   [11] See Daintith and Page and the sources cited therein, n. 9, 30.

[12] See the Ministerial Code, para. 1. The Ministerial Code is issued by the prime minister to all ministers in the government. It contains the key rules and procedures governing ministerial conduct. It is not law, but many of its rules have the status of constitutional conventions. Parliament will expect ministers who fail to abide by such rules to resign from office. The Code is available online at http://www.cabinetoffice.gov.uk/propriety_and_ethics/ministers/ministerial_code/index.asp.

[13] See n. 6, 1.

[14] It was echoed by e.g., L.S. Amery, who wrote in his *Thoughts on the Constitution* (Oxford University Press, 1953) that 'the central directing instrument of government, in legislation as well as in administration, is the cabinet', 70.

customary to see the model of cabinet government as a relic. That cabinet government is 'dead' is, as one commentator recently expressed it, a 'common diagnosis'.[15] Indeed, even before Mrs Thatcher came to power there were those who argued that power—especially policy-making power—had effectively been transferred from the cabinet to the prime minister.[16] Numerous essayists, textbook-writers, and (no doubt) law teachers seem to revel in playing the game of determining whether British government is truly still one of collective cabinet decision-making or individual prime ministerial diktat.[17] On one side are lined up the prime minister's powers of patronage, his status as leader of his party, his unique relationship with the queen, his powers of hire and fire, his international standing, his media profile, and so forth. On the other are lined up the cabinet's apparent ability to remove the prime minister from office, the fact that cabinet continues to meet each week and that its meetings continue to take precedence over all other government and ministerial business, and the fact that serious disagreements among ministers continue to be resolved around the cabinet table.

Despite their continuing popularity in some quarters, however, these debates have become increasingly tired and unhelpful. Both political scientists and constitutional lawyers should move on from them. The reality is—as it has been for some time—that British government is neither government by prime minister nor government by cabinet. The cabinet continues to be important, but not (or at least not often) as an executive policy-maker. In a recent analysis Weller has suggested that its functions today are as follows: to allow for the exchange of information between senior ministers, to allow for the political temperature to be taken on sensitive issues of government policy, to gee up ministers, to provide a sense of solidarity, to set the tone, and to emphasize current issues and occasionally to resolve them where smaller groups of ministers have been unable to reach a resolution.[18] Weller concludes by observing that 'every government seems to still use cabinet for these political purposes, as insurance and to lock in support'.[19]

One task that cabinet clearly no longer undertakes, even if ever it did, is routinely to act as the highest level of policy-making within government. But this does not necessarily mean that policy is made only by the prime minister and his personal political advisers. The bulk of government policy is made by neither cabinet nor prime minister but by small groups of ministers, advisers, and civil servants working closely together. To seek to understand the operation of such

[15] See P. Weller, 'Cabinet Government: An Elusive Ideal?' (2003) 81 *Pub Admin* 701.
[16] See, e.g., R. Crossman's famous introduction, written in 1963, to Bagehot's *The English Constitution* [1867] (Fontana, 1993). See also P. Norton, *The Constitution in Flux* (Blackwell, 1982), Chap. 1.
[17] Recent examples are offered by A. Seldon, 'The Cabinet System', in V. Bogdanor (ed.), *The British Constitution in the Twentieth Century* (Oxford University Press, 2003), Chap. 4 and C. Foster, 'Cabinet Government in the Twentieth Century' (2004) 67 *MLR* 753.
[18] See Weller, n. 15, 716.   [19] *Ibid.*

groups, and to seek to move away from the cabinet versus prime minister debates, a number of political scientists have developed the model of the 'core executive'.[20] This term is designed to cover 'the small number of agencies at the very centre of the executive branch of government that fulfil essential policy setting and general business co-ordination and oversight functions above the level of departments.'[21] These agencies currently comprise the prime minister's office, the cabinet office, the treasury, the foreign office, central government law offices, and offices managing the governing party's parliamentary and mass support bases.[22]

This core executive—also frequently referred to, especially within the civil service, as 'the centre'—has grown considerably in both size and importance under the premiership of Tony Blair. As Burch and Holliday note in their valuable survey,

[T]he centre is far more substantial and integrated than in 1997. There are now 190 staff in the prime minister's office, compared to 130 in 1997... At the same time, the prime minister's office and cabinet office are more integrated and focused than before, with more staff working to the prime minister. The overall outcome is clearer lines of command and direction, and a strengthening of the position of the prime minister and his aides.[23]

The result is that 'the British core is increasingly co-ordinated and coherent' as well as being 'increasingly pro-active and performance-driven'.[24] Under the present prime minister it has tended to adopt an informal,[25] negotiating, and collaborative style 'designed to maximize its leverage over the rest' of government.[26] The growth of the core executive 'reflects a recognition on the part of central actors that highly departmentalized government is not an ideal model for effective administration in an age when policy problems and solutions frequently cross departmental boundaries'.[27] One of the expressions most frequently heard during Tony Blair's first term was 'joined-up government', it being recognized early on in the administration that a number of the problems it wished to tackle would require effective co-ordination across government departments. Addressing problems of 'social exclusion' was one notable example.

None of this is particularly contentious. Even commentators on British government who do not adopt the model of the core executive argue that under prime ministers such as Margaret Thatcher and Tony Blair the centre has

---

[20] See R.A.W. Rhodes and P. Dunleavy (eds.), *Prime Minister, Cabinet and Core Executive* (Macmillan, 1995) and M. Burch and I. Holliday, 'The Blair Government and the Core Executive' [2004] *Government and Opposition* 1.   [21] Burch and Holliday, *ibid.*, 3.
[22] *Ibid.*
[23] *Ibid.*, 12. They add the proviso that it is also 'worth noting that this has been coupled with a significant and expanding role for the Chancellor and his advisers in overseeing delivery'.
[24] *Ibid.*, 20.
[25] On the relative informality of Tony Blair's style of government, see Foster, n. 17, 764–71.
[26] Burch and Holliday, n. 20, 20.   [27] *Ibid.*

become significantly stronger.[28] This raises an acute question for constitutional lawyers with an interest in executive power. If the power of the centre has become stronger over recent years, to what extent has the accountability of the centre grown? When we come in part three of this essay to examine matters of accountability we shall see that it is true of numerous institutions (including the courts) that the nearer they come to seeking to hold the centre to account the more they struggle. This, then, can be seen as the second analytical theme of this chapter: namely, the tension between the structure of executive power in Britain (which, despite devolution, is largely centripetal) and the accountability of executive power in Britain (which is often centrifugal). We shall return to this theme later.

(c) Civil servants and advisers

Before we leave questions of the composition and structure of the executive there is one further aspect to be noted: the civil service. More than 450,000 civil servants are employed to assist ministerial government in the development of policy and in the delivery of public services.[29] The civil service is not party-political. The same civil servants serve ministers of all political persuasions. Civil servants are recruited, appointed, and promoted professionally on merit, on the basis of open competition. Civil service positions are not political appointments for ministers. This has been the case in Britain since the middle of the nineteenth century.

In addition to the civil service, a relatively small number of political advisers may be appointed by ministers to offer political advice. The number of such political appointees has been rising steadily (this is a matter of some concern in Britain) and currently stands at around eighty.[30] On the whole, advisers may not authorize public expenditure; they may not exercise line management supervision over permanent civil servants (although they may commission work from civil servants); and they may not discharge ministers' statutory powers (whereas, upon instruction to such effect, civil servants may do so). The only exceptions to these rules relate to a maximum of two special advisers appointed by the prime minister to work in senior positions in his office.

The vast majority of civil servants are concerned with service delivery rather than with policy development. In the most radical and important reform of the civil service in more than a century the Thatcher governments of the 1980s

---

[28] See, *e.g.*, Foster, n. 17.

[29] This number excludes those employed by the National Health Service (Britain's biggest single employer), those employed to teach in state (public) schools, and those employed as local government officers. It also excludes the military and the police. In this sense the 'civil service' comprises only one part of the public sector.

[30] See the report of the House of Commons Select Committee on Public Administration, *Special Advisers: Boon or Bane?*, HC (2000–01) 293, March 2001 and the government response, HC (2001–02) 463, December 2001.

re-organized the service, in effect splitting it into two. Those who were concerned with service delivery rather than with policy development were 'hived off' into so-called 'executive' or 'next steps' agencies. These agencies remained attached to their parent departments but were given chief executives, budgets, and performance targets of their own. The aim was to find ways of streamlining the civil service, to bring the Thatcherite values of economy, effectiveness, and efficiency—the so-called 'three Es' of value-for-money audit—into the heart of the civil service. The reform, which has not been reversed by the Labour government that came into power in 1997, was controversial among constitutional commentators mainly for its apparent undermining of the traditional lines of accountability of government to Parliament. As we shall see, the constitution imagines that ministers are accountable to Parliament for everything that happens within their departments. How the semi-autonomous next steps agencies would be made to fit within this paradigm was a matter that caused considerable difficulties.[31]

What is perhaps most remarkable about the development of next steps agencies, however, is that the government was able to effect their creation and growth without recourse to legislation. This is another example of our theme of patchy legal regulation of the executive that was introduced earlier. Civil servants are employed under the authority of the prerogative. Like ministers, they are servants of the Crown. Both the details of the terms and conditions of their employment and their broader constitutional position are governed not by statute but by Orders in Council (delegated rules made by ministers under the authority of the prerogative) and informal codes, the most important of which is the Civil Service Code, introduced in 1996.[32] It is this code—and no provision of law—that lays down, for example, that civil servants should act with 'integrity, honesty, impartiality and objectivity'.[33] Similarly, it is the code, and no provision of law, that governs what civil servants should do in the event that they are asked by their ministers to act inappropriately.[34] The current government has long promised to bring forward a draft Civil Service Bill for deliberation in Parliament but has dragged its heels. After persistent pressure from the House of Commons select committee on public administration, the government finally published its draft Bill in November 2004.[35] If, as now seems likely, a Civil Service Act is soon passed, it will place the civil service on a statutory basis for the first time.

---

[31] The difficulties were exemplified in the notorious rows over the prison service (a next steps agency within the home office) while Michael Howard was home secretary. For an account, see A. Tomkins, *The Constitution after Scott: Government Unwrapped* (Clarendon Press, 1998), 45–9 and 84–94.   [32] For discussion, see *ibid.*, Chap. 2.

[33] Civil Service Code, para. 1.   [34] *Ibid.*, paras 11–12.

[35] See, e.g., the committee's report, *A Draft Civil Service Bill: Completing the Reform*, HC (2003–04) 128, December 2003. For the government's draft Bill, see www.official-documents.co.uk/document/cm63/6373/6373.htm.

2. The functions of the executive

(a) No general principle

Just as in Britain there is no constitutional definition of the executive, neither is there an authoritative list of executive functions. It is a well-known feature of British public law that it is not based on any notion of the separation of powers that may be used to delineate executive functions from those of the other main constitutional powers (the legislature and the judiciary). While there is, at a rather basic level, a separately identifiable legislature, executive, and judiciary in Britain, both the personnel and the functions of the three 'branches' (to adopt the American term) overlap and blur into one another.

No constitutional or legal principle determines the functions that may be assigned to the executive by statute. The powers and tasks which Parliament confers by legislation upon the executive are determined, from statute to statute, in accordance with whatever requirements Parliament and government see fit. Legal restrictions exist in terms of EU and European human rights law, in that if Parliament were to confer on the executive a power that was in violation of EU law or that was in breach of a Convention right, the courts would have the jurisdiction to intervene. But such intervention takes the form of ex post judicial control, not ex ante legislative control.

Perhaps the nearest that domestic British law gets to an understanding of what are executive functions is its recognition of prerogative powers. These are the powers which the common law recognizes as vesting in the Crown. There are two forms of prerogative power. First there are the powers exercisable only by the monarch. These are now relatively few in number, although they remain important. Secondly there are the powers which would in earlier times have been exercised by the monarch him or herself but which are now exercised on the monarch's behalf by government ministers—that is, by ministers of the Crown. The first category comprises the following powers: the power to appoint the prime minister; the power to dissolve Parliament; the power to dismiss the government; and the power to grant (or withhold) the royal assent to legislation. It remains the case that only the reigning monarch may exercise any of these powers.[36]

There is no authoritative list of the prerogative powers which may be exercised by ministers, but these powers include the following: the making and ratification of Treaties; the conduct of diplomacy; the governance of British overseas territories; the deployment of the armed forces both overseas and within the United Kingdom; the appointment and removal of ministers; the appointment of peers; the grant of honours; the organization of the civil service; the granting and

---

[36] For discussion of their importance, see A. Tomkins, *Public Law* (Oxford University Press, 2003), Chap. 3.

revoking of passports; the granting of pardons; and the claiming of certain privileges and immunities, such as public interest immunity in the law of evidence.

For the common law, then, these are all matters for the executive. Significant though they undoubtedly are,[37] however, the list of legally recognized prerogative powers can hardly be taken as a complete list of matters which the law regards as falling within the purview of the executive. The list says nothing, for example, of the government's range of powers with regard to finance, social security, managing the welfare state, policing and criminal justice, and so on. All that can be gleaned from such lists of powers is that the executive acts in a bewilderingly wide array of policy arenas and subject matters. No general or over-arching principle that is defining or determinative of executive functions can be distilled by listing the powers that are conferred upon the executive by either statute or prerogative.

(b) Executive and legislative functions

Notwithstanding the fact that the British constitution is not based on the tripartite separation of powers between legislative, executive, and judicial functions, it may be that we can come slightly closer to unearthing a legal or constitutional understanding of executive functions if we examine cases or instances that lie at the borders of executive authority, on the basis that it is in hard cases where definitions become most pressing. Accordingly, we shall approach this in two ways. First we shall consider the border between executive and legislative powers. We shall then consider the border between executive and judicial powers.

Of these two, it is the close relation, indeed frequent overlap, between executive and legislative powers that has traditionally been the more notorious in Britain. In terms of personnel the extent of the overlap is clear: as we saw above, constitutional convention requires that every one of the 110 or so ministers in the government should simultaneously be members of one of the two Houses of Parliament. The functional overlaps between legislature and executive are just as stark. Perhaps the classic example is the making of legislation by the executive. Processes and practices of delegated legislation, of the making of statutory instruments, Orders in Council, and the like, have been the subject of sustained and critical analysis for the best part of a century.[38]

For all the concern and criticism, however, it seems that rule-making by the executive is here to stay. There is nothing in the Blair government's programme of constitutional reform to lessen the need for or the extent of executive

---

[37] See, e.g., A. Tomkins, *Our Republican Constitution* (Hart Publishing, 2005), Chap. 4.
[38] See G. Ganz, 'Delegated Legislation: A Necessary Evil or a Constitutional Outrage?', in P. Leyland and T. Woods (eds.), *Administrative Law Facing the Future: Old Constraints and New Horizons* (Blackstone, 1997), Chap. 3 and E. Page, *Governing by Numbers: Delegated Legislation and Everyday Policy-Making* (Hart, 2001).

legislation. On the contrary, there is a sense in which government rule-making has grown (both in volume and in constitutional importance) since 1997.[39] One of the most significant constitutional reforms to have been undertaken by the Blair government is devolution. Under a series of enactments, executive and in some instances also legislative powers have been devolved to newly created bodies in Scotland, Wales, and Northern Ireland.[40] The devolution legislation sets out in detail such matters as the legislative competence of the Scottish Parliament and the procedures according to which devolution matters may be judicially reviewed, and so forth, but one issue on which the legislation is virtually silent is the way in which the various UK administrations will deal and interact with one another. Inter-governmental relations in the post-devolution United Kingdom are governed almost entirely by informal arrangements made within the executive branch. Moreover, these are arrangements in respect of which neither the Westminster nor the devolved parliaments were consulted, and they are arrangements in respect of which there can be no judicial review. This is another example of a theme introduced in part one of this chapter: namely the patchy, intermittent legal regulation of British government. It is also a striking example of the extent to which the executive is self-regulatory within the British constitutional system.[41]

(c) Executive and judicial functions

While the overlap between executive and judicial powers has been the subject of less longstanding concern in Britain than has that between executive and legislative powers, it is with regard to the executive/judicial border that there has been most activity in recent years. One striking feature of the reforms witnessed in Britain since 1997 has been the growth in the constitutional authority of the judiciary. The powers of the courts have grown both with regard to the legislature[42] and also—and more importantly for our purposes—with regard to the executive. This is particularly notable in the case of the Human Rights Act 1998

---

[39] See N. Barber and A. Young, 'The Rise of Prospective Henry VIII Clauses and their Implications for Sovereignty' [2003] *PL* 112.

[40] See the Scotland Act 1998, the Government of Wales Act 1998 and the Northern Ireland Act 1998. At the time of writing devolution to Northern Ireland is suspended, on account of continuing political disagreement as to the security situation there. For an overview of the various devolution arrangements, see N. Burrows, *Devolution* (Sweet and Maxwell, 2000). For an assessment of the impact thus far, see A. Trench (ed.), *Has Devolution Made a Difference? The State of the Nations 2004* (Imprint Academic, 2004).

[41] See R. Rawlings, 'Concordats of the Constitution' (2000) 116 *LQR* 257 and House of Lords Select Committee on the Constitution, Second Report of 2002–03, *Devolution: Inter-Institutional Relations in the UK*, HL (2002–03) 28, December 2002.

[42] The courts' powers with regard to legislation have been extended by two enactments: the European Communities Act 1972 and the Human Rights Act 1998. On the former, see *R v. Secretary of State for Transport, ex parte Factortame (No. 2)* [1991] 1 AC 603. On the latter, see *Ghaidan v. Godin-Mendoza* [2004] 2 AC 557 and *A v. Secretary of State for the Home Department* [2005] 2 WLR 87.

(HRA), section 6 of which provides that 'It is unlawful for a public authority to act in a way which is incompatible with a Convention right'. This means that the courts may quash any government action or decision they rule to be incompatible with a Convention right.[43]

As the extent of the executive's legal accountability has grown through enactments such as the HRA the question arises as to what (if anything) the courts have had to say about what they consider the appropriate tasks or functions of the executive to be. In order to address this question, two sets of cases will be contrasted with each other. The first concerns judicial review and the reach of the HRA in the context of executive decisions which the courts recognize to be far-reaching in their political and economic consequences. The second concerns judicial review of executive decisions in the context of criminal sentencing.

Our first case is *Alconbury*,[44] which concerned a series of challenges to British planning laws. The challenges centred on Article 6(1) of the European Convention on Human Rights, which provides that 'In the determination of his civil rights and obligations... everyone is entitled to a fair and public hearing... by an independent and impartial tribunal...'.[45] British planning laws provide for an intricate decision-making process. Most planning applications are dealt with routinely by local authorities but a small number—those which raise particularly complex, delicate, or contested issues—may under the relevant legislation be 'recovered' or 'called-in' by the secretary of state (that is, by the minister in central government with responsibility for the environment). To give an indication of scale, in the region of 500,000 planning applications are considered each year in Britain, of which about 250 annually are recovered or called-in.[46] When the secretary of state recovers or calls-in a planning application, the application will be considered by a planning inspector who will conduct a public inquiry and will then make recommendations in a report to the secretary of state. The secretary of state makes the final decision on the application. He or she is not bound by the recommendations contained in the inspector's report, although in practice the secretary of state will follow the recommendations of the planning inspector in about 95 per cent of cases. The issue in *Alconbury* was

---

[43] As Lord Hope put it in one of the first Human Rights Act cases to reach the House of Lords: 'the incorporation of the European Convention on Human Rights into our domestic law will subject the entire legal system to a fundamental process of review and, where necessary, reform by the judiciary'. See *R v. Director of Public Prosecutions, ex parte Kebilene* [2000] 2 AC 326, 374–5.

[44] *Alconbury* is, in fact, three conjoined appeals: *R v. Secretary of State for the Environment, ex parte Holding and Barnes*, *R v. Secretary of State for the Environment, ex parte Alconbury* and *R v. Secretary of State for the Environment, ex parte Legal and General Assurance*. The appeals to the House of Lords were heard together and the speeches (judgments) in the three appeals are reported as one case at [2003] 2 AC 295.

[45] Article 6 is domestically incorporated into UK law by force of HRA, s. 1.

[46] Additionally, in the region of 13,000 appeals from local authorities are considered each year by the secretary of state through the planning inspectorate.

whether this decision-making process was compatible with Article 6(1) given that the final decision-maker, the secretary of state, is a government minister rather than an 'independent and impartial tribunal'.

At first instance, the Divisional Court held that Article 6 was violated. It granted a declaration under the HRA that the relevant provisions of Britain's town and country planning legislation were incompatible with a Convention right.[47] The appeal to the House of Lords was successful, their Lordships unanimously ruling that Article 6(1), while engaged,[48] was not violated.

Two main reasons underpinned the Lords' decision. The first related to the case law of the European Court of Human Rights, case law which under the terms of the HRA the domestic courts are required to take into account (although having taken it into account they are not required to follow it).[49] The key case, *Bryan v. United Kingdom*,[50] offered authority for the proposition that even where a decision-maker is lacking in independence and impartiality, Article 6(1) will not necessarily be breached if the decision-maker is subject to a certain degree of judicial review or other scrutiny by a sufficiently independent and impartial supervisory body. Applying *Bryan*, the House of Lords held that, as the decisions of the secretary of state were fully subject to judicial review, the requirements of Article 6 were satisfied.[51]

The second reason underpinning their Lordships' ruling is one that raises issues of particular interest in the context of this chapter. All five Law Lords who heard the appeals in *Alconbury* gave speeches. All five spoke about the need to ensure that the HRA did not undermine the essential democratic requirement that, as Lord Hoffmann expressed it, 'decisions as to what the general interest requires are made by democratically elected bodies or persons accountable to them'.[52] The kind of complex, contested planning application that is recovered or called-in by the secretary of state is one that is likely to raise acute questions of policy. Should a fifth terminal be constructed at London's Heathrow airport? Should an additional motorway be constructed between Birmingham and Manchester? Should a new high-speed rail-link be developed to reduce travelling time between London and the Channel tunnel? These are the sorts of questions that fall to be addressed in the biggest planning applications.

All the Law Lords stressed the delicate political nature of such decisions. And they all emphasized the importance in a democracy of having political decisions such as these made by political actors who are democratically answerable for their decisions, rather than by independent and impartial courts. In other words, the court stressed that planning decisions were principally matters for the executive

---

[47] See HRA, s. 4.
[48] The House of Lords rejected the argument that decision-making in the context of planning applications did not amount to the determination of a 'civil right' within the meaning of Art. 6(1).
[49] See HRA, s. 2.   [50] (1995) 21 EHRR 342.
[51] See further on this issue, *Begum v. Tower Hamlets LBC* [2003] 2 AC 430.
[52] *Alconbury*, n. 44, para. 69.

rather than the judiciary. Lord Slynn expressed it in the following terms:

> The adoption of planning policy and its application to particular facts is quite different from the judicial function. It is for elected members of Parliament and ministers to decide what are the objectives of planning policy, objectives which may be of national, environmental, social or political significance...[53]

Lord Nolan agreed, stating that while electoral accountability alone would be 'plainly insufficient to satisfy the rule of law',[54] in the context of the making of planning decisions which have 'acute social, economic and environmental implications,... to substitute for the secretary of state an independent and impartial body with no electoral accountability... would be profoundly undemocratic.'[55] Lord Hoffmann spoke in similar terms, declaring that such cases

> [I]nvolve general social and economic issues. They concern the rights of individuals to use, enjoy and own their land. But the number of persons potentially interested is very large and the decisions involve the consideration of questions of general welfare, such as the national or local economy, the preservation of the environment, the public safety, the convenience of the road network, all of which transcend the interests of any particular individual.[56]

Lords Clyde[57] and Hutton[58] spoke in virtually identical terms.

What emerges from these dicta is a strong sense that, even in a constitutional order with no formal separation of powers between legislature, executive, and judiciary, and even in a constitutional order in which the judicial power has recently been strengthened through reforms such as the passing of the Human Rights Act, the courts are careful to demarcate an area of constitutional competence which belongs to the executive. This is not, it should be noted, a matter of 'deference' to the executive. Since the coming into force of the HRA there has been considerable attention focused on the question of what deference the courts should show to the institutions of parliamentary government when reviewing their decisions and actions against human rights standards. This issue arises in the context of proportionality review, when courts are required to consider whether an interference with a Convention right is 'necessary in a democratic society'.[59] The judges showing deference to the policy choices arrived at by the institutions of parliamentary government is quite different from the House of Lords' concern in *Alconbury*. Here the judges were concerned not with the latitude that should be accorded to Parliament or government but with the very tasks that should properly fall to the executive rather than to the judiciary.

---

[53] *Ibid.*, para. 48. [54] *Ibid.*, para. 61. [55] *Ibid.*, para. 60. [56] *Ibid.*, para. 68.
[57] See, e.g., *ibid.*, paras. 139–40. [58] See, e.g., *ibid.*, para. 198.
[59] Leading case law on 'deference' includes *International Transport Roth v. Secretary of State for the Home Department* [2003] QB 728 and *R (Farrakhan) v. Secretary of State for the Home Department* [2002] QB 1391.

Getting to the heart of the reason why the law lords considered planning decisions to be matters for the executive rather than for the judiciary, however, is not so simple. Three discrete factors are relied on in the passages from Lords Slynn, Nolan, and Hoffmann cited above. The first is that planning decisions may have implications for 'national', 'environmental', 'social', or 'economic' policy. The second is that Parliament has entrusted such decisions to the government, which is then liable to be held to account both in Parliament and electorally for the decisions it makes. The third is that even though individuals' property rights may be directly affected by planning decisions, such rights are not necessarily determinative of planning applications, which may be resolved in the public or general interest even where such resolution infringes individuals' interests in property usage or ownership.

It may be that a theory of executive power could be developed from these factors: the executive is responsible for policy, for which it is accountable to Parliament, and which it should develop in what it considers to be the public interest. No doubt there are countless problems of detail in this formulation as an understanding of executive power. (What do we mean by 'policy'? How should the 'public interest' be determined? And so forth.) Despite its incompleteness, however, what we have here is at least a start in developing a coherent judicial account of executive power. It will not work as a general account, however, for the reason that away from the planning context the courts have fashioned quite different—and incompatible—conceptions of executive power, as we shall now see.

A second area that has in recent years been the subject of intense judicial scrutiny and in which questions of executive functions have been raised is that of the sentencing, punishment, and detention of persons convicted under English law[60] of murder. The House of Lords has been required to revisit this area of law numerous times in recent years.[61] For our purposes its two most important decisions are the cases of *Venables and Thompson*,[62] which concerned child offenders and *Anderson*,[63] which concerned adults. In order to understand these cases and, in particular, to understand what they say about executive power, some background is needed.

Since 1965 adults convicted of murder have been sentenced to life imprisonment.[64] This sentence is mandatory upon a conviction for murder. 'Life imprisonment' does not mean that the person convicted will necessarily spend the rest of his life in prison. Mandatory life prisoners may, after certain

---

[60] The positions in Scotland and Northern Ireland are different.
[61] See, e.g., *R v. Secretary of State for the Home Department, ex parte Doody* [1994] 1 AC 531 and *R v. Secretary of State for the Home Department, ex parte Pierson* [1998] AC 539, as well as the cases considered here.
[62] *R v. Secretary of State for the Home Department, ex parte Venables and Thompson* [1998] AC 407.   [63] *R (Anderson) v. Secretary of State for the Home Department* [2003] 1 AC 837.
[64] The death penalty for murder was abolished by the Murder (Abolition of Death Penalty) Act 1965.

requirements have been met, be released from imprisonment, albeit that after release they may for the remainder of their life be recalled to prison if the conditions attached to their release are broken.[65] Such conditional release was, until *Anderson*, a matter for the home secretary's discretion.[66]

In 1983 the then home secretary announced in the House of Commons the details of government policy with regard to mandatory life prisoners.[67] The effect of the policy is as follows. The sentence is broken down into component parts: retribution and deterrence on the one hand and protection of the public on the other. The trial judge makes a recommendation as to the period of years required to satisfy the requirements of retribution and deterrence. This period is known as the 'tariff'. All such recommendations are seen by the Lord Chief Justice (the senior criminal law judge in England and Wales), who may agree with or may vary the recommended tariff. In the light of, but not bound by, the advice he has received from the trial judge and from the Lord Chief Justice the home secretary makes his own decision as to the minimum period that will have to be served as the tariff. The home secretary will not refer the prisoner's case to the Parole Board (who advise on matters of conditional release and such like) until three years before the tariff period expires. The home secretary will not exercise his discretion to allow conditional release until the tariff period has expired.

The position with regard to child murderers is similar but not identical. Since the early twentieth century English law has distinguished between the sentencing of adult prisoners and the sentencing of children. The age of criminal responsibility in English law is ten years, which, in comparative European terms, is low.[68] With this in mind legislative schemes governing the sentencing of child offenders have sought since 1908 to incorporate appropriate consideration of the interests of the welfare of the child into the sentencing process. Both the sentence (known as 'detention during Her Majesty's pleasure') and the legislation governing it (the Children and Young Persons Act 1933, as amended) are different from those concerning adult offenders.

In the 1990s the home secretary adopted the same tariff policy for child offenders as was used for adults but a three-to-two majority of the House of Lords ruled in *Venables and Thompson* that such a policy was unlawful.[69] Detention during Her Majesty's pleasure, the majority ruled, was not to be equated with mandatory life imprisonment for the reason that the former

---

[65] For a good account, see J. Schone, 'The Hardest Crime of All: Myra Hindley, Life Sentences, and the Rule of Law' (2000) 28 *Int J of the Soc of Law* 273.
[66] The relevant legislation was the Crime (Sentences) Act 1997. See now the Criminal Justice Act 2003. [67] See HC Deb., 30 Nov. 1983, cols. 505–7, WA.
[68] The age of criminal responsibility is seven in Ireland and Switzerland, eight in Scotland, thirteen in France, fourteen in Germany, Austria, and Italy, fifteen in the Scandinavian countries, sixteen in Portugal and Poland, and eighteen in Spain and Belgium: see *V v. United* Kingdom (1999) 30 EHRR 121, para. 50.
[69] Lords Browne-Wilkinson, Steyn, and Hope; Lords Goff and Lloyd dissented on this point.

required the secretary of state to consider from time to time whether the continued detention of the child offender was justified. While the secretary of state might set a provisional tariff as to the period of detention to be served by the child offender by way of punishment and deterrence, a policy whereby that period could not be varied by reason of matters occurring subsequently to the commission of the offence was unlawful as it failed adequately to take into account the interests of the child.

Venables and Thompson concerned the sentencing of two boys who were convicted of murdering two-year-old James Bulger. At the time of the murder, Venables and Thompson were themselves only ten-and-a-half years old. The crime caught the attention of both the media and the public, with the offence itself and the subsequent trial, conviction, and sentencing being the subjects of intense media and public scrutiny. A tabloid newspaper campaign was launched advocating particularly severe punishment and the home office received a series of petitions, signed by hundreds of thousands of members of the public, urging that the killers be detained for the whole of the rest of their lives. Following conviction, the trial judge stated that, had the defendants been adults, he would have recommended a tariff of eighteen years as the minimum period of detention to be served as retribution and deterrence but that taking into consideration the defendants' age this should be reduced to eight years. The Lord Chief Justice advised that the penal element should be ten years. The home secretary, expressly taking into account the widespread public concern in the case, increased this to fifteen years.

There were two legal issues in *Venables and Thompson*. The first was whether the policy of fixing a tariff was lawful in the case of child offenders—and we have seen the verdict of the House of Lords on this point. The second was concerned with whether, and if so how, the secretary of state may take into consideration the views of the public when deciding how long offenders should remain in detention. It is in relation to this question that the case is of interest to us, as in addressing it the law lords made a series of observations about the nature of executive power. Their observations centred on the question of whether sentencing is an executive or a judicial function. There was a marked division of opinion among their lordships on this issue—as there was on the first.

A majority of judges (Lords Goff, Steyn, and Hope) considered that in making decisions concerning the length of detention the secretary of state, as Lord Goff expressed it, was 'exercising a function which is closely analogous to a sentencing function with the effect that, when so doing, he is under a duty to act within the same constraints as a judge will act when exercising the same function'.[70] 'In particular,' Lord Goff continued, should the secretary of state 'take into account public clamour directed towards the decision in the particular case which he has under consideration, he will be having regard to an irrelevant

[70] [1998] AC 407, 490.

consideration which will render the exercise of his discretion unlawful.'[71] Lord Goff was anxious to draw a distinction between what he called 'public concern of a general nature with regard to, for example, the prevalence of certain types of offence, and the need that those who commit such offences should be duly punished' and 'public clamour that a particular offender whose case is under consideration should be singled out for severe punishment'.[72] A sentencing authority (whether a minister or a judge) may take the former, but not the latter, into account, according to Lord Goff. Lord Steyn spoke in similar terms, although unlike Lord Goff he expressed himself directly in constitutional terms. For Lord Steyn, when the home secretary was fixing a tariff he was

[C]arrying out, contrary to the constitutional principle of separation of powers, a classic judicial function.... Parliament must be assumed to have entrusted the power to the home secretary on the supposition that, like a sentencing judge, the home secretary would not act contrary to fundamental principles governing the administration of justice.[73]

Against these remarks Lord Browne-Wilkinson sounded what he called 'a word of caution'.[74] For him it was critical that Parliament had entrusted the decisions under review in the case not to the judiciary but to the executive. As such, 'the court should be careful not to impose judicial procedures and attitudes on what Parliament has decided should be an executive function.' Given that, as all the law lords agreed, the home secretary, when exercising his discretion in this area, was entitled to have regard to broad considerations of the public interest, including public attitudes to criminal sentencing, how, Lord Browne-Wilkinson asked,

[I]s the secretary of state to discover what those attitudes are except from the media and from petitions? To seek to differentiate between the secretary of state discovering public feeling generally (which is proper) and taking into account distasteful public reactions in a particular case (which is said to be unlawful) seems to me too narrow a distinction to be workable in practice. Public attitudes are ill-defined and are usually only expressed in relation to particular cases.[75]

To the question 'is sentencing an executive or a judicial function?' three different answers are offered in these passages. For Lord Goff, the question was immaterial, perhaps even misconceived. For him, it made no difference whether the function was classified as executive or judicial: the material consideration was, whoever it was that performed the function (and it could apparently be anyone to whom Parliament conferred the power), certain considerations would be relevant (and therefore lawful) and others would be irrelevant (and therefore unlawful).[76] For Lord Steyn, sentencing is a classic judicial function and whenever it is performed by anyone other than a judge the constitutional

[71] *Ibid.*, 490–1.   [72] *Ibid.*, 491.   [73] *Ibid.*, 526.   [74] *Ibid.*, 503.
[75] *Ibid.*, Lord Lloyd spoke in very similar terms, 517.
[76] Lord Goff gave no reasons to justify his ruling that taking into account general public concern is lawful whereas taking into account public concerns about a particular case is unlawful.

principle of the separation of powers is violated. Because it is a judicial function, all sentencing authorities, whether judges or not, must act judicially. Lord Steyn ruled that it would be an 'abdication of the rule of law' for a judge to take into account a newspaper campaign designed to encourage him to increase a particular sentence and

[T]he same reasoning must apply to the home secretary when he is exercising a sentencing function. He ought to concentrate on the facts of the case and... like a judge the home secretary ought not to be guided by how popular a particular decision might be... The power given to him requires, above all, a detached approach.[77]

For Lord Browne-Wilkinson, the key issue was one of parliamentary sovereignty: Parliament had legislated so as to confer on the executive, not on the courts, the powers in question and they were, accordingly, to be treated as executive and not as judicial powers, such that the courts should take care not to impose undue judicial constraints on the decision-maker.

As *Venables and Thompson* was decided before the Human Rights Act was passed, the House of Lords gave no consideration to matters concerning Convention rights. The claimants took their cases to the European Court of Human Rights, where they successfully argued, among other issues, that their sentences were contrary to Article 6(1) of the Convention.[78] The Court held that the home secretary's fixing of the tariff 'amounts to a sentencing exercise'[79] and that, because the home secretary is not an 'independent and impartial tribunal', Article 6(1) was breached.[80]

In previous case law the European Court of Human Rights had ruled that the home secretary's role in fixing the tariff for adult mandatory life prisoners was not in violation of Article 6. The Court's reasoning was that the sentence, which was imposed by the criminal court, was one of life imprisonment and that the secretary of state's role was not one of determining the sentence, but merely of administering it.[81] However, the Court revisited its earlier authority on this point in *Stafford v. United Kingdom*.[82] In *Stafford*, the Court described its case law on this issue as 'evolving' and stated that the home secretary's role 'has become increasingly difficult to reconcile with the notion of separation of powers

---

[77] [1998] AC 407, 526.   [78] See *V v. United Kingdom*, n. 68.
[79] *V v. United Kingdom, ibid.*, para. 111.
[80] *Ibid.*, para. 114. The fact that the home secretary's decision was open to challenge by way of judicial review was deemed to be irrelevant in the context of sentencing. This contrasts with the position with regard to the determination of planning applications (see above). Quite why the availability of judicial review means that Art. 6 is not violated in that context whereas it is in this is unclear.
[81] See, e.g., *Wynne v. United Kingdom* (1994) 19 EHRR 333. The Court had taken a different view of the secretary of state's role in decision-making in the context of (adult) discretionary life prisoners—i.e., of those convicted of offences other than murder who were sentenced to life imprisonment. In this context the Court ruled that the secretary of state's role was unlawful: see, e.g., *Thynne, Wilson and Gunnell v. United Kingdom* (1990) 13 EHRR 666.
[82] (2002) 35 EHRR 32.

between the executive and the judiciary, a notion which has assumed growing importance in the case law of the Court.'[83] Holding that it could no longer be maintained that there was any material distinction between the mandatory life sentence, discretionary life sentences, and sentences of detention at Her Majesty's pleasure, the Court went on to rule that the home secretary's fixing of the tariff in any of these contexts was 'a sentencing exercise', not merely an administrative one, and was therefore incompatible with the requirements of Article 6(1).[84]

In *Anderson* the House of Lords followed the European Court's line in *Stafford*. A panel of seven Law Lords unanimously agreed that the role of the home secretary in fixing the tariff of a mandatory life prisoner was a sentencing function, that it was incompatible with the independence and impartiality requirement of Article 6(1) of the ECHR, and that it was therefore unlawful. Three Law Lords gave substantive speeches. Of these only one—Lord Steyn—addressed the general issue of whether determining the length of a custodial sentence is an essentially judicial function which should be performed only by a court of law. On this issue Lord Steyn echoed what he suggested in his speech in *Venables and Thompson*. He stated that the British constitution has 'never embraced a rigid doctrine of separation of powers' as 'the relationship between the legislature and executive is close'. But he continued: 'on the other hand, the separation of powers between the judiciary and the legislative and executive branches of government is a strong principle of our system of government.'[85] Turning to Article 6(1), his lordship ruled that its purpose was clear:

First, only a court or an independent tribunal may decide on the guilt or otherwise of an accused person. The executive have no role to play in the determination of guilt. Secondly, only a court or independent tribunal may decide on the punishment of a convicted person. Again, the executive have no role to play in the determination of punishment.[86]

Lord Steyn then conceded that 'it is sometimes difficult to categorize a particular function as judicial or non-judicial'.[87] But aside from the singular exception of Parliament's historic ability to punish for contempt, Lord Steyn noted that it has been 'the position in our legal system since at least 1688' that 'a decision to punish an offender by ordering him to serve a period of imprisonment may only be made by a court of law'.[88]

Commentators on the law and policy of sentencing were overwhelmingly critical of the home secretary's roles in setting tariffs for life prisoners. Schone,

---

[83] *Ibid.*, para. 78. [84] *Ibid.*, para. 79. [85] *Anderson*, n. 63, para. 39.
[86] *Ibid.*, para. 49. [87] *Ibid.*, para. 50.
[88] The grammatically pedantic may insist that Lord Steyn expressed himself less than perfectly here. Courts may do more than only make such decisions: they may also amend, modify, rescind, or unmake such decisions. What Lord Steyn presumably meant was that only courts could make such decisions, in which case he should have said that 'a decision to punish an offender by ordering him to serve a period of imprisonment may be made only by a court of law.'

typical of such authors, described it as an 'anomaly' that was 'nothing more than a historical accident' and equated its removal with the reassertion of 'the importance of the rule of law in our constitution'.[89] Shute similarly bemoaned the 'anomalous' fact that 'the law allows any sentencing decision to be taken by such a person' as a government minister.[90] Valier referred to it as 'yet another saga in the sorry tale of the politicization of sentencing policy'.[91] In a scathing account of the last fifty years of government policy in sentencing, Wasik identified the 'highly politicized way in which sentencing issues are now characterized' as being a 'real problem', the home secretary's role in life sentences being one notable example.[92]

Yet, as all five Law Lords in *Venables and Thompson* recognized, it is neither inappropriate nor unlawful for a sentencing authority—whether a minister or a judge—to take into account public opinion when making decisions as to length of sentence. In his excellent analysis, 'The Place of Public Opinion in Sentencing Law', Shute surveyed such (somewhat sparse) authorities as exist on this issue[93] and demonstrated how they showed public opinion to be 'an entirely legitimate consideration for sentencing judges'.[94] If this is so, what is it, precisely, that makes sentencing a task which only the judiciary may perform? Why should there be no role at all for the executive? Following *Anderson*, this is what English law now requires: Lord Bingham ruled in that case that 'it must now be held that the home secretary should play no part in fixing the tariff of a convicted murderer, even if he does no more than confirm what the judges have recommended.'[95] Even if it is conceded that the executive should not determine the length of sentence, why should the government have no voice at all in recommending a certain period of detention in respect to serious crimes such as murder? After all, did the House of Lords not rule in *Alconbury* that it is for the government, not the judiciary, to make determinations affecting the public interest? If, as everyone accepts, the public have an interest in sentencing and if, as the law acknowledges, public opinion is a relevant consideration for a sentencing authority to bear in mind, what is the difference between planning decisions (which are for the executive) and sentencing decisions (which are for the judiciary)?

It is not that the one involves fundamental human rights whereas the other does not. Both do. Rights to property are directly affected by executive decisions such as those made in the *Alconbury* appeals, just as the right to liberty is

---

[89] Schone, n. 65, 287.

[90] S. Shute, 'The Place of Public Opinion in Sentencing Law' [1998] *Crim LR* 465, 473.

[91] C. Valier, 'Minimum Terms of Imprisonment in Murder, Just Deserts and the Sentencing Guidelines' [2003] *Crim LR* 326.

[92] M. Wasik, 'Going Round in Circles? Reflections on Fifty Years of Change in Sentencing' [2004] *Crim LR* 253, 253–4.

[93] Principally, before *Venables and Thompson, Sargeant* (1974) 60 Cr App R 74 and *Broady* (1988) 10 Cr App R (S) 495.   [94] See n. 90, 473.

[95] *Anderson*, n. 63, para. 28, emphasis added.

obviously affected by decisions concerning detention. Neither is it that the one concerns general policy whereas the other particular decisions. Again, both are concerned with individual decisions. The issue in *Alconbury* was not 'who should set the general parameters of national planning policy?', but 'who should have the last word in determining individual planning applications?'. And nor is it that the one concerns matters of public interest whereas the other does not—as we have seen government, courts, and academic commentators all support the view that the public is legitimately interested in sentencing and criminal justice.

What we have here, it seems, are two lines of authority that simply pull in different directions. There is nothing in the planning cases to explain why sentencing is a judicial matter and there is nothing in the sentencing cases to explain why planning applications should sometimes be determined by ministers. The law, it appears, has no general conception of what is an executive function and what is not. Context is everything: in the planning context we have one conception of executive power and in the sentencing context quite another.

3. Accountability

In comparison with the powers and functions of the executive, matters of government accountability are more widely understood in Britain and they can, accordingly, be considered here more briefly.[96] As with most of the jurisdictions examined in this book, the accountability of the executive can be divided into three forms: political, legal, and other.

(a) Political accountability

It is arguably the paramount rule of the British constitutional order that the government of the day may remain in office for only as long as it commands the confidence of the House of Commons. The moment that the government loses the confidence of the House it must resign. What is true of the government as a whole is also true for individual ministers. All ministers in the government must have the confidence of whichever House of Parliament they are members of. Once such confidence is lost the minister concerned will be expected to resign from office (although he or she will normally be able to remain a member of Parliament). The rules of collective and individual ministerial responsibility to Parliament are constitutional conventions. As such, their enforcement is political, rather than legal, and takes place in Parliament, rather than in the courts of law.

---

[96] This section draws on the chapters on accountability in my *Public Law* (Oxford University Press, 2003), Chaps. 5–6.

Because the 'first-past-the-post' electoral system used for elections to the House of Commons usually generates results that give the governing party very large majorities of seats in the Commons,[97] and because of Britain's political tradition of strong party discipline, the obligations of both collective and individual ministerial responsibility are generally straightforward for the government. The last time that a British government lost a vote of confidence in the House of Commons was in 1979, which was also the last time in Britain that the governing party did not enjoy an absolute majority in the Commons. That said, however, the prime minister will from time to time make it clear that if he does not obtain majority support in the Commons on a particular issue he will resign from office. Tony Blair, for example, stated that this would have been his course of action had the Commons failed to support his war policy in Iraq in 2003.

More routinely, the government will require majority support in both Houses of Parliament whenever its policies can be realized only through primary legislation. In terms of such major planks of public policy as taxation and the economy, trade and industry, transport, criminal justice, education, health, social security, and so forth, the need for primary legislation will be the norm. In this sense, the government needs to maintain majority support in Parliament as a matter of political routine. No government can rule effectively nor survive in office for long without Parliament's active support.

Individual ministers are responsible to Parliament for their own and for their department's actions, policies, and decisions. Such individual ministerial responsibility has a dual character. On the one hand, ministers are required to come to Parliament to account for (that is, to explain) government actions, policies, and decisions. On the other hand, it also requires them to be politically liable for the government's actions, policies, and decisions. It follows (particularly from the first of these) that any minister who misleads Parliament must apologize and must set the record straight at the earliest opportunity. Any minister who deliberately misleads Parliament (that is, who lies) will be expected to resign.

During the 1990s there was considerable controversy and disquiet about the operation of these principles, as a series of ministers in John Major's government were seemingly permitted by Parliament to avoid taking responsibility for various government failings. Thus, home secretary Michael Howard argued that he was responsible to Parliament only for failures of policy and not for operational failings. For operational failures, it was civil servants who were responsible to ministers, not ministers to Parliament. A second minister, William Waldegrave, argued that ministers were responsible only if they

---

[97] Of the last five general elections, only two (1992 and 2005) have failed to deliver to the victorious party a majority of more than 100 seats in the House of Commons. The Conservatives had a three-figure majority following the 1983 and 1987 elections; the Labour party enjoyed majorities of more than 160 after both the 1997 and 2001 elections. The Conservatives' majority following the 1992 election was twenty one; the current Labour majority, following the 2005 election, is sixty six.

deliberately misled Parliament. If they inadvertently misled Parliament, they were not responsible—not even where (as was the case with regard to Waldegrave's particular circumstances) they should have realized that what they were telling Parliament was untrue.[98]

These controversies contributed to the Conservatives' devastating electoral defeat in 1997. More pertinently, they also spurred Parliament into action. Part of the reason why they were allowed to occur in the first place was because, at the time, the most authoritative written version of the rules of ministerial responsibility were contained in a document, known as Questions of Procedure for Ministers, which the government itself produced. This gave the impression that, as the government wrote the document that contained the rules, the rules were themselves in the ownership of the government. If Mr Howard wished to clarify (or re-write) the rule as to where the dividing line between ministerial and civil service responsibility should be drawn, he could. Likewise, if Mr Waldegrave wished to clarify (or re-write) the rule concerning the misleading of Parliament, he could.

By 1996 Parliament recognized the danger inherent in giving to the government the power to set the limits to its own constitutional responsibility, and took ownership of the rules of ministerial responsibility for itself, removing them from the government of the day. It did this by passing two resolutions (one in each House) setting out what Parliament expected ministers to do and not to do. These parliamentary resolutions were subsequently written in to Tony Blair's revised version of Questions of Procedure for Ministers, which he renamed the Ministerial Code.[99] The effect of the resolutions was threefold. First, it tightened the rules, clarifying (contrary to the Howard/Waldegrave positions) that ministers are responsible both for policy and for operational matters and also that ministers should not mislead Parliament in any circumstances—a resignation from office may be required only when ministers have actually lied, but even inadvertent errors need to be acknowledged, corrected, and apologized for. Second, it clarified the dual nature of individual ministerial responsibility (accountability on the one hand and liability on the other) referred to above. Finally, it removed the possibility from future administrations of repeating the attempts made by John Major's ministers to re-write the rules. Ministers have no competence to re-write what is decreed in a parliamentary resolution: only Parliament itself may do that.

It has often been thought that big government majorities in the House of Commons are bad news for advocates of political accountability. Whereas the Conservative majority was twenty one following the 1992 election, the Labour majority was in excess of 160 seats following both the 1997 and the 2001 elections. Yet despite this, the principles of individual ministerial responsibility have actually

---

[98] For the full story, see Tomkins, *The Constitution after Scott*, n. 31, Chap. 1.
[99] The text of the revised Ministerial Code is available online: see n. 12.

operated much more satisfactorily under the Blair government than they did during the time of the Major administration. In terms both of ministerial responses to departmental failures and in terms of resignation from office, the constitutional requirements of ministerial responsibility have—thus far—proved to be an effective and robust means of holding the Blair government to account.[100]

The House of Commons has three principal means by which it holds ministers to account: through the staging of parliamentary debates, through the asking of parliamentary questions (both oral and written), and through the work of select committees. All of these are capable of making significant contributions to the project of holding the government to account. The asking of parliamentary questions—particularly written questions, which require a written answer that will be published in Parliament's official report, known as Hansard—is perhaps the principal means by which parliamentarians may obtain information from government departments. The regulation of ministerial answers to parliamentary questions has been significantly strengthened in recent years (again, in reaction to abuses that occurred during the Thatcher and Major governments).[101]

Select committees are small groups of backbench (that is, non-ministerial) MPs that conduct inquiries into the 'policies, administration and expenditure' of government departments. There is one select committee for each major government department. The committees determine for themselves what, within their terms of reference, they should investigate. They have extensive powers to call for persons, papers, and records. They take both written evidence and—in open, public hearings—oral evidence, from a wide range of ministers, senior civil servants, and others. Both the evidence and the reports which the committees draw up are published, on paper and on the Internet.

The committees do not lack for powers. While they are nothing like as well resourced as the big Congressional committees in the United States, the select committees of the House of Commons regularly produce reports of high quality into a broad range of areas of government policy. The principal restraint on committees is the ambition of the MPs who sit on them. Where there is the political will, select committees are able to be high-profile, vocal, informed, and effective critics of government policy. The health committee in the 1980s, the social security committee in the early 1990s, and the transport committee in the later 1990s are three of the best known examples. In each case these committees made substantial contributions to the reshaping of critical aspects of government policy.[102]

---

[100] For a detailed appraisal, see D. Woodhouse, 'The Reconstruction of Constitutional Accountability' [2002] *PL* 73 and 'UK Ministerial Responsibility in 2002: The Tale of Two Resignations' (2004) 82 *Pub Admin* 1.

[101] See Tomkins, *The Constitution after Scott*, n. 31, 96–103. See also, B. Hough, 'Ministerial Responses to Parliamentary Questions: Some Recent Concerns' [2003] *PL* 211.

[102] See further on the powers, performance, and reform of select committees, A. Tomkins, 'What is Parliament for?', in N. Bamforth and P. Leyland (eds.), *Public Law in a Multi-Layered Constitution* (Hart Publishing, 2003), Chap. 3.

(b) Legal accountability

The constitutional doctrine of the rule of law provides that the executive may do nothing without clear, direct legal authority.[103] The rule of law is a doctrine of the common law, created, shaped, and enforced by judges. At its most basic, it provides that if the government does something which it has no legal authority to do, its action is illegal and the court may quash it. Taken alone, this is not a particularly difficult obstacle for the government to overcome. This is for two reasons. First, even where the government does not have statutory authority for doing something, it may claim that it has prerogative authority. The courts have sometimes been alarmingly lax in their policing of the boundaries of the prerogative.[104] Secondly, if the government lacks statutory authority for something which it considers it needs the power to do, all the government has to do in order to obtain such authority is to steer the appropriate legislation through Parliament. It is not the case that the government is always able to secure through Parliament exactly the legislative powers which it would like, but it is almost always the case that the government gets pretty much what it wants.

The bulk of the powers exercisable by the government are conferred upon it by legislation, either primary or secondary. In reviewing the exercise of such powers, courts will have a further constitutional fundamental in mind, in addition to the doctrine of the rule of law. They will also have in mind the sovereignty of Parliament. This doctrine—like the rule of law a doctrine of the common law—provides that Parliament may make or unmake any law and that no-one may override or set aside the properly enacted legislation of Parliament.[105] In reviewing the exercise of powers which Parliament has by legislation conferred upon the executive, the courts are anxious to ensure that the executive has acted in a way which is consistent and compatible with what Parliament enacted. Suppose, for example, that Parliament legislates so as to confer a discretionary power on a minister, that in circumstances a or b, he (or she) may do x, but that in circumstances c or d the minister may not do x. When reviewing the legality of the minister's doing x, the courts will be anxious to ensure that he or she did so while circumstances a or b, and not circumstances c or d, pertained. This concomitant of sovereignty is known as the doctrine of ultra vires. It means that the courts will ensure that government ministers (and others on whom statutory powers are conferred) act within the limits of the powers conferred upon them—that they act within and not beyond the four corners of their

---

[103] The authority usually given is *Entick v. Carrington* (1765) 19 St. Tr. 1029. Not all writers accept this definition. An alternative view is that the government, like ordinary people, has the freedom to do anything that is not prohibited by law. For defence of this view, see B. Harris, 'The "Third Source" of Authority for Government Action' (1992) 108 *LQR* 626.

[104] See, e.g., *R v. Secretary of State for the Home Department, ex parte Northumbria Police Authority* [1989] QB 26.

[105] It may be that both of these aspects of the sovereignty of Parliament now need to be read in the light of EU and European human rights law, but happily these issues are immaterial here.

jurisdiction. On the basis of the twin constitutional principles of the rule of law and the sovereignty of Parliament the courts have fashioned a complex body of case law governing the legality of executive decision-making. This is the law of judicial review.

At common law there are three principal grounds of review—illegality, irrationality, and procedural impropriety. In addition, the Human Rights Act 1998 must be read as providing new grounds which supplement these three, as we shall see. The tri-partite distinction between illegality, irrationality, and procedural impropriety was adopted by Lord Diplock in his seminal speech in the so-called *GCHQ* case in 1984.[106] It is not the only way in which the common law grounds of judicial review may be classified, but for our purposes it serves as a useful starting point.[107] Both illegality and irrationality relate closely to the doctrine of ultra vires. An executive decision-maker will have acted illegally when he or she fails to have proper regard to, or fails properly to give effect to, the law that regulates his or her decision-making competence. This is relatively straightforward where the legislation conferring the power upon the decision-maker is clear. Suppose, for example, that a statute provides that the secretary of state may issue directives to the broadcasting authorities as to the times and the circumstances in which they may broadcast obscene material. Suppose further that the secretary of state purports to rely on this power when he issues directives to the broadcasting authorities as to the number of party political broadcasts that may be broadcast. Such action by the secretary of state would be clearly illegal, as the statutory power on which he has purported to rely does not empower him to issue directives concerning party political broadcasts: it empowers him to issue directives which relate only to obscene material.

Matters are not always so simple, however. At least two sorts of problems may arise with the doctrine of illegality. The first is the issue of apparently subjective discretion. Suppose that Parliament confers on a decision-maker (such as a government minister) the power to do something 'if he shall so direct', or 'if he should deem it reasonable'. Under what circumstances can the courts review the exercise (or non-exercise) of such a power on the basis of the doctrine of illegality? In a controversial extension of the law, the House of Lords held in *Padfield* that even where Parliament had legislated to confer what appeared to be subjective discretion on a minister, the exercise of such a power was amenable to judicial review.[108] The Lords, led by Lord Reid, ruled that ministers and others on whom apparently subjective discretion is conferred must exercise that discretion in such a way as is in conformity with the aims and policy objectives of the statute read as a whole. What such aims and policy objectives are in any particular case is a matter of law for the courts to determine.

---

[106] *Council of Civil Service Unions v. Minister for the Civil Service* [1985] AC 374.
[107] For a comprehensive analysis, see P. Craig, *Administrative Law* (Sweet and Maxwell, 5th edn., 2003). [108] *Padfield v. Minister of Agriculture, Fisheries, and Food* [1968] AC 997.

The second problem that may arise concerns the ambiguity or openness of legislative language. This issue is best illustrated with an example concerning local government. Somerset County Council, a democratically elected local authority, wished in the early 1990s to ban stag hunting on its land. The power on which it sought to rely was section 120(1) of the Local Government Act 1972. This provided that decisions by local authorities with regard to use of land had to relate to the 'benefit, improvement or development' of the land. The question for the court was whether a decision to ban stag hunting related to the 'benefit', 'improvement' or 'development' of land. At first instance Laws J held that the banning of stag hunting was a 'moral' consideration which fell outside the scope of the local authority's power under section 120(1).[109] On appeal the Court of Appeal upheld Laws J's verdict (that the decision was unlawful), but on substantially different grounds. In direct contra-distinction to Laws J, two of the three appeal court judges opined that the language of section 120(1) was sufficiently broad to enable the local authority lawfully to take into account considerations based on their moral viewpoint on hunting.[110]

The doctrine of irrationality, also known as *Wednesbury* unreasonableness, is more difficult. There are two authoritative definitions. The first, which comes from the *Wednesbury* case, provides that it is unlawful for an executive authority to act in a way which is so unreasonable that no reasonable authority would have acted in that way.[111] The second, which is Lord Diplock's definition of irrationality in the *GCHQ* case, provides that an irrational decision is one which is 'so outrageous in its defiance of logic or of accepted moral standards that no sensible person who had applied his mind to the question to be decided could have arrived at it'.[112] What exactly the difference is between something which is merely unreasonable (and therefore not unlawful) and something which is so unreasonable that no reasonable authority would have done it (and therefore unlawful), is left for individual judges to determine from case to case. Likewise, Lord Diplock's phrases 'accepted moral standards' and 'sensible person' are left undefined, for judges to interpret from case to case.

Given the open-ended nature of the 'tests' (if they may be called that) of unreasonableness/irrationality, it is perhaps unsurprising that the courts have found it impossible to create much in the way of clear guidance or consistent principle. There are numerous examples, but for present purposes two House of Lords cases will serve to illustrate the point. In the first the Lords held that it was irrational for Leicester City Council to disallow Leicester Rugby Football Club from using one of the Council's recreation grounds for practice in response to the fact that a number of the club's players had participated in a rebel tour of apartheid South Africa, notwithstanding the fact that the Council was under a

---

[109] *R v. Somerset CC, ex parte Fewings* [1995] 1 All ER 513.
[110] *R v. Somerset CC, ex parte Fewings* [1995] 3 All ER 20.
[111] *Associated Provincial Picture Houses v. Wednesbury Corporation* [1948] 1 KB 223.
[112] n. 106, 410.

statutory duty 'to promote good race relations'.[113] In the second case, the House of Lords dismissed an application for judicial review brought by a family of four who were living in a single room in a guesthouse, with no laundry or cooking facilities and with no meal provided apart from breakfast. The family had applied to the local council for housing but were denied on the basis that they were already reasonably housed, in the guesthouse. Their Lordships ruled that for the family to succeed in their judicial review they would have to have shown that the council acted 'perversely' in rejecting their application for housing and this, apparently, they had failed to do.[114]

In the 1990s—during the last few years before the Human Rights Act—the courts tried to sharpen the bite of *Wednesbury* review, particularly in the context of fundamental rights. In *R v. Ministry of Defence, ex parte Smith*,[115] for example, the Court of Appeal ruled that 'the more substantial the interference with human rights, the more the court will require [from the government] by way of justification'. How far this common law jurisprudence remains important, and how far it has now been overtaken by the Human Rights Act, is a matter that is not entirely clear.

Lord Diplock's third ground of review, procedural impropriety, concerns matters of administrative procedure rather than substance. There are two established principles of procedural propriety: the rule against bias and the duty to act fairly (also known as the duty to hear the other side). Thus, if a decision-maker falls within one of the categories of bias,[116] or has failed to act fairly in making a decision, the courts may annul the decision. What 'acting fairly' requires depends considerably. Sometimes it will be necessary for the decision-maker to conduct an oral hearing, sometimes legal representation will have to be permitted, sometimes the parties will have the right to cross-examine one another, sometimes it will be necessary for the decision-maker to give reasons, and so forth, but none of these features of 'acting fairly' will be required in all circumstances.[117]

So much for the common law grounds of review. To these we must now add the reforms effected by the Human Rights Act 1998 and by subsequent judicial interpretation of it. Section 6 of the Act provides that 'It is unlawful for a public authority to act in a way which is incompatible with a Convention right.' The House of Lords has held, in its ground-breaking judgment in the *Daly*

---

[113] See *Wheeler v. Leicester CC* [1986] AC 240. For the statutory duty, see Race Relations Act 1976, s. 71.   [114] See *Puhlhofer v. Hillingdon LBC* [1986] AC 484.
[115] [1996] QB 517.
[116] The leading authorities include *Dimes v. The Proprietors of the Grand Junction Canal* (1852) 3 HLC 759, *R v. Bow Street Metropolitan Stipendiary Magistrate, ex parte Pinochet (No. 3)* [2000] 1 AC 147, *and Porter v. Magill* [2002] 2 AC 357.
[117] Authorities on these issues include, respectively, *Lloyd v. McMahon* [1987] AC 625. *R v. Board of Visitors of the Maze Prison, ex parte Hone* [1988] AC 379, *Bushell v. Secretary of State for the Environment* [1981] AC 75, and *R v. Secretary of State for the Home Department, ex parte Doody* [1994] 1 AC 531.

case,[118] that when reviewing the legality of executive action under section 6 the intensity of review will often be stronger than it would under the common law doctrine of irrationality. The rule in *Daly* is that, in the context of Convention rights, domestic courts should apply a test of proportionality rather than one of mere unreasonableness or irrationality. Lord Steyn, giving the leading speech in *Daly*, gave a three-pronged definition of the new proportionality test. He ruled that, when applying the principle of proportionality, a court should ask itself whether '(i) the legislative objective is sufficiently important to justify limiting a fundamental right; (ii) the measures designed to meet the legislative objective are rationally connected to it; and (iii) the means used to impair the right or freedom are not more than is necessary to accomplish the objective'.[119]

These, in outline, are the principal grounds of judicial review in English public law.[120] The availability of judicial review is limited by numerous factors. Two are particularly relevant in the context of the executive: standing to seek judicial review, and the remedies available in judicial review. With regard to the first of these, English law has, in recent years, taken a relatively liberal view of standing, at least when compared with courts such as the Court of Session in Scotland or the European Court of Justice.[121] The underlying principle is that applicants will be able to seek judicial review if they can show that they have a 'sufficient interest' in the matter. While there are exceptions, the general thrust of the courts' interpretation of this condition has been generous both to individual applicants and to pressure and lobby groups. Organizations such as Greenpeace and the World Development Movement have been permitted to seek judicial review of government decisions in which their interest can be described only as public or political rather than as personal or deriving from property law.[122] Unlike in some other jurisdictions—especially, perhaps in the EU—overly restrictive rules of standing do not seem to have presented too high an obstacle to effective legal accountability in English law.

Only certain remedies are available in judicial review. All public law remedies are discretionary. This means that even if an applicant is successful on the merits of his or her case, the court may decline to grant the remedy sought. The

---

[118] *R (Daly) v. Secretary of State for the Home Department* [2001] 2 AC 532.

[119] *Ibid.*, para. 27. The Court of Appeal has held that the proportionality test applies in English law only in the context of Convention rights (and, where appropriate, also in the context of EU law): see *R (Assn of British Civilian Internees: Far East Region) v. Secretary of State for Defence* [2003] QB 1397. For analysis of the application, thus far, of proportionality under the HRA, see Craig, n. 107.

[120] That is to say, in the public law of England and Wales. The grounds of judicial review in Scotland and Northern Ireland are largely the same, although there are some differences of detail. There are more significant differences with regard to the procedure for applying for judicial review and the remedies available in judicial review.

[121] On the former, see L. Hope, 'Mike Tyson comes to Glasgow: A Question of Standing' [2001] *PL* 294; on the latter, see Case C-50/00P, *UPA v. Council* [2002] ECR I-6677.

[122] See *R v. Inspectorate of Pollution, ex parte Greenpeace (No. 2)* [1994] 4 All ER 329 and *R v. Secretary of State for Foreign Affairs, ex parte World Development Movement* [1995] 1 All ER 611.

remedies typically available are an order to quash an unlawful decision, an order to require a duty to be performed, an order to prohibit an unlawful decision from being made, and a declaration (which is declaratory of the law and has no coercive effect). It is to be noted that compensatory remedies such as an award of damages are not generally available in public law.[123] This restriction is currently under some strain, however, as the effect of both EU law and the Human Rights Act has in recent years been to extend the circumstances in which damages may be awarded against the state.[124]

Summing up the legal accountability of the British government is not easy. Nearly fifty years ago de Smith, in what was the first major treatise on English administrative law, famously suggested that judicial review was 'sporadic' and 'peripheral'.[125] In the mid 1990s the editors of the latest edition of de Smith's book argued that, such had been the transformation in the law from the 1960s on that, by the final decade of the century, judicial review had become both 'constant' and 'central'.[126] De Smith's editors are surely correct in at least two respects. The possibility of being judicially reviewed is now a constant thought in the back of the government's mind, at least in some departments. In areas of government policy dealt with by the home office, by the department of social security, by the inland revenue, and by the department of the environment, among others, judicial review has had a significant impact on administrative procedure and, to a lesser degree perhaps, also on aspects of substantive policy.[127] It has also had an impact on the polity at large. Judicial review is now a prominent feature of the British political landscape, with both politicians and journalists taking a greater interest in it than ever before.

In other respects, however, we should be cautious about claims that judicial review is either a constant or a central check on the exercise of government power. This is for several reasons.[128]

First, there continue to be large slices of government that judges leave virtually untouched. Foreign affairs, diplomacy, and military matters, among others, are

---

[123] That said, however, damages are available in private law proceedings against public authorities, such as in actions for negligence and breach of statutory duty. This area of the law has been much revised through recent decisions of the House of Lords and remains both complex and fast moving. For an excellent commentary, see C. Harlow, *State Liability: Tort Law and Beyond* (Oxford University Press, 2004).

[124] See, on EU law, Cases C-6/90 and 9/90, *Francovich* [1991] ECR I-5357 and Case C-48/93, *Factortame (No. 3)/Brasserie du Pêcheur* [1996] ECR I-1029 and, on human rights law, HRA s. 7 and *Anufrijeva v. Southwark LBC* [2004] 2 WLR 603.

[125] S. de Smith, *Judicial Review of Administrative Action* (Stevens, 1959).

[126] S. de Smith, L. Woolf and J. Jowell, *Judicial Review of Administrative Action* (Sweet and Maxwell, 5th edn., 1995), vii.

[127] For an overview, see G. Richardson, 'Impact Studies in the United Kingdom', in M. Hertogh and S. Halliday (eds.), *Judicial Review and Bureaucratic Impact: International and Interdisciplinary Perspectives* (Cambridge University Press, 2004), Chap. 4.

[128] Only a brief account can be given here. For fuller analysis of the limitations inherent within legal models of accountability, see A. Tomkins, *Our Republican Constitution* (Hart Publishing, 2005), Chap. 1.

almost never reviewed. On the rare occasions when they are, applications for judicial review are not successful.[129]

Secondly, a range of factors may take decisions which ordinarily would be reviewable beyond the scope of judicial review. For example, decisions the government claims to have made in the interests of national security remain largely beyond the scope of judicial review, even when they directly affect an individual's fundamental rights.[130] Similarly, the commercial confidentiality exclusion has significantly impaired the courts' ability to find ways adequately of reviewing the range of activities subject to government by contract.[131]

Thirdly, it is important to remember the particularity of judicial review as a mechanism of executive accountability. The courts can never (and nor should they be able to) review government policy as such. All that can be reviewed are particular instances, decisions, or applications of government policy. Let us take as an example the recent case in which the House of Lords held that the indefinite detention without trial of suspected international terrorists was unlawful.[132] It was not the government's post 9/11 counter-terrorism strategy per se that was impugned. Nor was it the centre-piece of that strategy, the Anti-terrorism, Crime and Security Act 2001. Nor was it even the whole of the notorious Part IV of that Act. All that was challenged was the legality of one particular power contained in Part IV of the Act: namely, the government's power to detain without trial. This is, let us recall, but one section in an Act of 128 sections, which in turn is but one legislative instrument in a number of Acts concerned with counter-terrorism, which legislation in turn covers only a fraction of the government's activities with regard to terrorism. Even in a high profile instance such as the *A* case, judicial review can hardly be said to be a constant and central avenue for securing government accountability.

A final reason to be cautious about the constancy and centrality of judicial review as a constraint on the executive concerns remedies. The government losing a case in court does not necessarily mean that the government will be unable to do what it wished to do. Indeed, it only very rarely means this. If the court holds that the government lacks a power, all the government has to do is to steer legislation through Parliament which, when enacted, will give it the power.[133] If the court holds that the government has acted unfairly in

---

[129] See, e.g., *R v. Secretary of State for the Foreign and Commonwealth Office, ex parte Rees-Mogg* [1994] QB 552. It is possible that one impact of the Human Rights Act may be to encourage courts to enter these arenas more boldly; it is still too soon to know whether this will be so.

[130] See, e.g., *Secretary of State for the Home Department v. Rehman* [2003] 1 AC 153. *A v. Secretary of State for the Home Department*, n. 42, may be a rare exception to this, although we should be careful not to exaggerate the courts' achievements in that case: see A. Tomkins, 'Readings of *A v. Secretary of State for the Home Department*' [2005] *PL* 259.

[131] See C. Harlow and R. Rawlings, *Law and Administration* (Butterworths, 2nd edn., 1997), Chap. 9. [132] *A v. Secretary of State for the Home Department*, n. 42.

[133] This was the result, e.g., following the government's narrow defeat in the House of Lords in *R v. Secretary of State for the Home Department, ex parte Fire Brigades Union* [1995] 2 AC 513: see the Criminal Injuries Compensation Act 1995.

reaching a particular decision, the government may well be able to make the same decision again, albeit the second time around adopting a procedure that satisfies the requirements of procedural propriety. Even where the court rules, as in the *A* case, that statutory powers are incompatible with Convention rights, under the scheme of the Human Rights Act all that the court can do is issue a declaration of incompatibility, a remedy which the Act is careful to specify does not affect the continuing validity, operation, or enforcement of the impugned legislation.[134]

None of this is to say that judicial review is unimportant. But it is to remind us that, just as there are significant limitations to how the courts have defined executive power, so too are there limitations to the ways in which the courts may hold the exercise of executive power to account.

(c) Other mechanisms of accountability

Law and politics comprise the principal disciplines through which the executive may be held to account. In addition to the core institutions of law and politics—the courts on the one hand and Parliament on the other—there exist in the contemporary British state a range of further institutions and processes through which executive accountability may be realized. All of these, in one way or another, are designed to support and to supplement the core means of legal and political accountability that we have explored in the preceding two sections. Three such supplementary processes may be briefly outlined here. They are audit, public inquiries, and ombudsmen.

In the British constitution it is Parliament, and in particular the House of Commons, that has the power of the purse. The Bill of Rights 1689 confirmed that only Parliament may authorize the raising of revenue through taxation. As such, Parliament has a special responsibility to scrutinize government expenditure, so as to ensure that the moneys voted by Parliament for a particular purpose are used by the government for that purpose. Since the 1860s the House of Commons has employed an officer of the House, known as the Comptroller and Auditor General, to assist it in these tasks. The Comptroller and Auditor General is now supported by the National Audit Office (NAO), a body which employs a staff of several hundred.[135] The NAO is responsible for auditing the accounts of all government departments, along with a number of non-departmental public bodies. In addition, it prepares for Parliament in the region of sixty reports each year examining the 'value for money' provided by various government activities. Value-for-money audit was introduced in the 1980s as a way of seeking to ensure that public expenditure is economic, effective, and

---

[134] HRA, s. 4.

[135] The NAO maintains an excellent website: see www.nao.org.uk. For a valuable overview, see I. Harden, 'Money and the Constitution: Financial Control, Reporting and Audit' (1993) 13 *LS* 16.

efficient.[136] The reports of the NAO are considered by the Public Accounts Committee of the House of Commons, a committee which is generally considered to be among Parliament's most powerful committees. Like all select committees of the Commons, the Public Accounts Committee has extensive powers to call for persons, papers, and records. It uses the reports of the NAO to subject ministers and senior civil servants to rigorous scrutiny in terms of public expenditure.

Public inquiries are from time to time conducted into particular scandals, blunders, natural or political disasters, or other broad areas of political difficulty. Such inquiries are often, but do not have to be, chaired by senior judges. Recent years have seen a good number of high profile inquiries. The Scott inquiry examined government policy with regard to covert arms trading during the 1980s between Britain and Saddam Hussein's Iraq.[137] The Phillips inquiry examined the outbreaks of BSE ('mad cow disease') and new variant CJD in the UK in the 1990s.[138] The Hutton inquiry, ostensibly concerned with the circumstances surrounding the death of government scientist Dr David Kelly, focused in large part on the BBC's handling of its story, obtained principally from Dr Kelly, that the government had effectively lied in putting to Parliament and the public its case for war against Iraq in 2002–03.[139] And the Butler inquiry examined the intelligence on which the government's case for the Iraq war was based.[140]

While public inquiries are normally established by the government itself, and while the government will have a substantial say in the inquiry's terms of reference and sometimes also in its resources and procedures, in doing so the government will be acting under close and intense media scrutiny, as it is in the nature of the stories that lead to public inquiries that they attract significant media attention. Public inquiries serve two main purposes. First, by taking and considering extensive oral and written evidence they seek to establish exactly what did, and what did not, happen. Secondly, they publish (sometimes very lengthy) reports which contain recommendations for reform or for further action. While inquiries lack coercive powers to ensure that their recommendations are put into effect, because of their high media profile the government will often find itself under considerable pressure to act.[141]

The first ombudsman introduced in Britain was the Parliamentary Commissioner for Administration, as it was initially called—now more generally known as the Parliamentary Ombudsman. This office was created by Act of Parliament in 1967.[142] Like the Comptroller and Auditor General, the

[136] For critical commentary of the rise of audit as a technique of accountability, see M. Power, *The Audit Society: Rituals of Verification* (Oxford University Press, 1997).
[137] See HC (1995–96) 115, February 1996.   [138] See www.bseinquiry.gov.uk.
[139] See www.the-hutton-inquiry.org.uk.   [140] See www.butlerreview.org.uk.
[141] For an overview of a number of concerns arising out of recent public inquiries in Britain, see I. Steele, 'Judging Judicial Inquiries' [2004] PL 738.
[142] Ombudsmen for local authorities were introduced by the Local Government Act 1974.

Parliamentary Ombudsman is an officer of the House of Commons. This reflects the fact that the office was designed to assist MPs in holding government to account. The Ombudsman is a fact-finder, who investigates complaints of 'injustice' arising out of 'maladministration',[143] and who reports on the investigations he (or, now, she) undertakes. Borrowing again from the model of audit, the Ombudsman reports to Parliament where a committee of the House of Commons (now the Public Administration Committee) will, where appropriate, subject instances of maladministration to further scrutiny. The Ombudsman performs two principal tasks. On the one hand the office is used by complainants to seek redress (including sometimes financial redress) for administrative wrongs they have suffered. In this aspect the Ombudsman bears some similarities to a small claims tribunal, offering a cheaper avenue for review of administration than is available through the courts. On the other hand the Ombudsman—and even more so the Public Administration Committee—use investigations of maladministration in the past as the basis to seek reform for the future. A major goal for the Ombudsman is to try and make public administration better in the future, as well as to compensate individuals for the administrative wrongs they have suffered in the past.[144]

4. Conclusions

Three main conclusions may be drawn from the preceding analysis. The first is that, in the British constitution, law plays only an intermittent role in delimiting executive power and in holding its exercise to account. We have seen how key players (including the prime minister, no less) are not defined in law, how there is no general legal account or coherent conception of executive power, and how the law is but one of several means by which the executive may be held to account.

The second is the tension, alluded to in the introductory section, between power and accountability. We saw in the opening section that, notwithstanding devolution, power within British government has been intensified at the centre. The political authority, the sheer size, and the level of detailed work undertaken by the prime minister's office and by the cabinet office have grown markedly in recent decades—particularly under prime ministers Margaret Thatcher and Tony Blair. Yet the structure of executive accountability in Britain has not changed to reflect this. It is certainly not true that there is no accountability at the centre but it is, on the whole, weaker than the accountability often found elsewhere. This is particularly the case with regard to legal accountability. It remains extremely

---

[143] See Parliamentary Commissioner Act 1967, s. 5(1).
[144] For evaluation of both of these aspects of the Ombudsman's role, see Harlow and Rawlings, n. 131, Chaps. 12–13.

unusual for politically sensitive decisions made by the highest office holders (prime minister, chancellor of the exchequer, and foreign secretary) to be judicially reviewed. The Ombudsman, similarly, tends to focus on allegations of maladministration away from the centre. There are all sorts of reasons for this—some jurisdictional or to do with standing, others concerned with a reluctance to enter into political waters best reserved to Parliament. It is in Parliament (and perhaps also in public inquiries) where the greatest degree of accountability of the centre may be found.

A final observation is that the British constitution has done considerably more to create mechanisms and institutions of executive accountability than it has to set clearly defined limits to executive power. British public law has strikingly little to say about what the executive should do. There is no general principle which may be applied to determine whether a particular function is, or is not, best left to the executive. This is not because such questions have not come before the courts: they clearly have. But when the courts have had to grapple with these issues they have struggled—and thus far failed—to construct a coherent account of executive power.

2

The Ambivalence of Executive Power in Canada

*Lorne Sossin**

Canada's constitutional order is sometimes referred to as a study in institutionalized ambivalence.[1] This ambivalence is captured in the very premise of Canada as a 'constitutional monarchy'. Canada's Charter *of Rights and Freedoms*, entrenched as part of the repatriation of Canada's constitution from the United Kingdom in 1982, reflects fidelity both to individual and to group rights. While Canada's constitutional framework is organized around a legislative, executive, and judicial branch of government, Canada until recently was said not to have a 'separation of powers' doctrine. Ambivalence, I will suggest below, also provides a window into the centrifugal and centripetal forces which characterize Canada's executive branch of government. Because Canada has a Westminster system of Parliamentary government inherited from the United Kingdom, the executive branch also exercises effective control over the legislative process. The result is that a very small group of very powerful individuals shape the policy and politics of the country. The power of the executive is qualified by two significant and often countervailing forces: the first is a robust and independent judiciary with extensive powers to review and reverse executive action; and the second is a dynamic system of federalism which balances most significant areas of governmental authority between federal and provincial levels of government, who often differ profoundly in their ideological orientation and their goals. The tensions of federalism generally are accentuated in the special case of Quebec, Canada's lone francophone province, in which a system of civil law governs.

There are two central questions I seek to address in this chapter. First, I will examine the scope of executive authority in Canada. In this regard, I will elaborate two distinctive challenges which arise when demarcating the scope of executive power in Canada. Both relate to questions of intra-executive relations

---

* Associate Professor and Associate Dean, Faculty of Law, University of Toronto. I am grateful to Leslie Zamojc for her superb research assistance.

[1] See, e.g., C. Tuohy, *Policy and Politics in Canada: Institutionalized Ambivalence* (Temple University Press, 1992).

and the tension between independence and interdependence within the organs of government which constitute the executive branch. First, I briefly explore the interdependent relationship between the political executive and the civil service. Second, I examine the relationship between the executive and quasi-independent administrative agencies, boards, and tribunals. The second part of the chapter explores how executive authority is held to account in Canada and evaluates the effectiveness of the Canadian constitutional system in that regard. Specifically, I explore the role of judicial review in this regard (including the courts' advisory functions to the executive) and the role of federalism.

1. Scope of the executive

(a) 'Executive power' as defined in the constitution

The executive represents the institution invested with the most power in Canada's political system and yet takes up the least space in Canada's constitutional texts. Moreover, the description of the executive in those texts bears virtually no relation to the actual scope and nature of executive authority. If not a further reflection of Canada's institutionalized ambivalence, it certainly remains a puzzle.

The Constitution Act 1867 devotes a mere eight sections to the definition and description of executive authority in Canada.[2] Those eight sections, however, are not an exhaustive delineation of the executive's role because the Act's purpose was simply to outline the distinctions between the Canadian constitution and the constitution of the United Kingdom. The Preamble to the Constitution Act 1867 states that Canada is to have a constitution 'similar in Principle to that of the United Kingdom'.[3] As the constitutional law scholar Cheffins notes, the Constitution Act 1867 was 'a statute of the British Parliament passed for the purpose of bringing together into one political unit some of Britain's colonies in North America'.[4]

The sections that the Act does devote to executive power declare that executive authority in Canada continues to be vested in the Queen, making Canada a constitutional monarchy.[5] Specifically, section 11 establishes the Queen's Privy Council, members of which would be chosen by the Governor General on behalf

---

[2] The following discussion relates to the federal executive. Each of Canada's ten provinces has its own constitutionally established executive (Canada's three territories, Nunavut, the Northwest Territories, and the Yukon are in effect federal protectorates without constitutionally rooted executive authority but have been delegated much of that authority from the federal government).

[3] *A Consolidation of the Constitution Acts 1867 to 1982* (Department of Justice Canada, 2001) preamble.

[4] R. I. Cheffins, *The Constitutional Process in Canada* (McGraw-Hill Ltd, 1969), 9.

[5] *A Consolidation of the Constitution Acts 1867 to 1982* (Department of Justice Canada, 2001), s. 9.

of the Queen for the purpose of aiding and advising in the Government of Canada. Further, the powers of the Governor General are formally limited by section 13, which states that any provisions of the Act which refer to the Governor General are to be interpreted as requiring the advice of the Queen's Privy Council for Canada. The frequency with which the Governor General appears in the part of the Constitution outlining executive power is interesting considering that nowhere in the Act is this office actually created and further it is silent on any direction as to how and when the role is to be filled.[6] Hogg explains that the reason for this deficiency is that at the time, it was assumed that the position would be filled in the same manner as it had always been filled; by the Queen acting on the advice of the British Colonial Secretary.[7] At present, the role continues to be filled by the Queen, however now she acts on the advice of the (Canadian) Cabinet. This effectively leaves the federal executive in the hands of the prime minister, who appoints and controls the cabinet.

It is important to note not what these sections do explain with regards to the role of the executive in Canada, but rather what is missing in these eight sections. The most influential figure in the state, the prime minister, does not make an appearance in the Act. Other important actors in the Canadian political system are also conspicuously absent. The cabinet and the leader of the opposition, along with the prime minister all receive, maintain, and fulfill their roles without guidance from any constitutional text:

> To read the British North America Act [the Constitution Act, 1867] would be to get a totally misleading impression of the constitution, leading the untutored observer to conclude that the country was, in fact, ruled by the Governor General, seeking the advice of the Privy Council.[8]

In fact, a search of all of the documents and statutes mentioned in the Constitution Act 1982 also reveals no mention of the prime minister or the cabinet.[9] This is one of the most perplexing features of the Canadian constitutional system, note scholars Cheffins and Johnson. They find interesting the 'subtle line distinguishing the formal executive, the monarch and her representatives, from the purely informal executive, the cabinet,'[10] which, as we have seen, is absent from constitutional documents. They do, however, go on to note that the Supreme Court of Canada suggested in *Reference Re Amendment of the Constitution of Canada*[11] that the reference to the United Kingdom's constitution in the preamble of the Constitution Act 1867 entrenches the principle of responsible government. This principle will be discussed further in a later section. However, because this principle is not explicitly articulated, there are others

---

[6] P.W. Hogg, *Constitutional Law of Canada* (Carswell Thomson Canada Ltd, 3rd edn., 1992), 6.   [7] *Ibid.*
[8] Cheffins, n. 4, 12.
[9] R. I. Cheffins and P. A. Johnson, *The Revised Canadian Constitution: Politics as Law* (McGraw-Hill Ryerson Ltd, 1986), 77.   [10] *Ibid.*
[11] [1981] 1 SCR 753.

who suggest that this 'principle' mentioned in the preamble may instead refer to the concept of parliamentary supremacy or civil rights.[12]

As a result of having a constitution which situates the Queen at the head of the executive, Canada's system is termed a 'constitutional monarchy.' The role of the Queen, and her representative in Canada, the Governor General (and provincial counterpart Lieutenant Governors) is entirely formal, however the term 'the Crown' has persisted in reference to the executive branch.[13] Thus, the Canadian Constitution varies widely from other constitutions because of its purpose. It did not codify all of the nation's rules, rather it codified only what was necessary to accomplish confederation.[14] The framework established through the Constitution Act 1867 allowed for continuous adjustment and refinement without actual constitutional amendment. This ability was reduced through the enactment of the Constitution Act 1982 and the Canadian Charter of Rights and Freedoms, which imposed new constraints both on the legislative branch and the executive.[15] Nonetheless, the importance of Canada's common law constitution remains.

In practice, executive authority is exercised by the prime minister and the cabinet under the principle of responsible government. This principle is comprised of conventions or rules that are seldom strayed from but legally unenforceable. Ultimately the enforcement mechanism is the expectation of the Canadian public that their elected leaders will conform to these rules or risk facing political damage.[16] Conventions dictate the actual composition of the executive, its powers, and its relationship to the legislative branch, exactly as it was in the United Kingdom.[17] These unwritten rules govern much of the workings of the Canadian political system. For example, legislative power is in practice controlled by the cabinet which, as we have seen, is not mentioned in the formal constitution although it is the 'dominant force by which executive power is put in practice.'[18] This domination is exemplified by the following process: when the Constitution or a statute states that a certain decision should be made by the Governor-General, in practice the cabinet makes the decision without even meeting with the Governor-General and sends him or her the minutes of the meetings, which by convention, are automatically approved.[19] Further, it is by convention that political parties choose their leader and if they are successful in obtaining a majority of seats in the Parliament, that leader will be called upon by the Governor General to form the administration. It is also convention for the leader to select members of his own party in the House of Commons and the Senate to fill the cabinet.[20]

[12] Cheffins and Johnson, n. 9, 86.
[13] P. W. Hogg and P. J. Monahan, *Liability of the Crown* (Carswell Thomson Canada Ltd, 3rd edn., 2000), 11.   [14] Hogg, n. 6, 5.
[15] P. J. Monahan, *Essentials of Canadian Law: Constitutional Law* (Irwin Law, 1997), 17.
[16] *Ibid.*, 20.   [17] Hogg, n. 6, 6.
[18] J. E. Magnet, *Constitutional Law of Canada* (Juriliber Ltd, 7th edn., 1998), 160.
[19] Hogg, n. 6, 235.
[20] Cheffins, n. 4, 12. As a practical matter, the cabinet will be drawn entirely from the elected House of Commons and only from the appointed Senate where it is necessary to achieve regional representation.

Certainly, a central feature of Canada's approach to the Westminster system of parliamentary sovereignty is ministerial responsibility.[21] The civil service and all government departments and agencies are organized with a minister of cabinet at their apex. It is the minister who is accountable for the activities of the executive to Parliament and by extension to the public. Traditionally, ministerial responsibility has been viewed as the 'most important and most contentious' of constitutional conventions.[22] As Kernaghan has observed, ministerial responsibility is rarely defined and this lack of a shared understanding of its requirements 'permits confusing, creative, and misleading interpretations of its meaning.'[23] For example, while ministerial responsibility is often tied to the anonymity of the civil service, it is rare for a minister to resign over the misdeeds of a civil servant in her or his ministry and quite common for individual civil servants to be singled out for political (and legal) sanction.[24]

Conventions have also had the effect of nullifying some of the provisions in the Constitution Act 1867. For example, section 56 of the Act gives the monarch the power to disallow Canadian legislation although by convention this power shall never be exercised.[25] One of the most important unwritten principles that guide the Canadian constitutional system is the principle of responsible government. This principle requires that Crown powers be exercised in accordance

---

[21] As Andrew Heard has observed, 'The principles of individual and collective ministerial responsibility take form mostly in the informal rules that have arisen to modify the positive legal framework of the constitution. The importance of these rules of responsible government cannot be overstated; without them the nature of our system of government would be fundamentally transformed.' A. Heard, *Canadian Constitutional Conventions: The Marriage of Law and Politics* (Oxford University Press, 1991), 48.

[22] K. Kernaghan, 'The Future Role of a Professional Non-Partisan Public Service in Ontario' (2003) Panel on the Role of Government, Research Papers (No. 13), 3.

[23] *Ibid*. He cites as illustration the comments of Brenda Elliot, a former Environment Minister under the Conservatives in Ontario who testified at the Walkerton Inquiry in June of 2001 into deaths and illness in a rural Ontario town caused by contaminated drinking water, and replied when asked about her responsibility as Minister for the actions of the ministry, 'Well, we're now into a very complex discussion about responsibility, which ... has been debated for centuries as part of the Westminster Parliamentary tradition' (quoted at 4). Kernaghan also canvasses the various jurisdictions which do attempt to spell out the requirements of ministerial responsibility and the distinction between an official being 'answerable' and 'accountable' for her or his actions (4–11).

[24] The constitutional texts say nothing of the obligation of ministers to resign in the face of maladministration or the obligation of ministers to defend the actions of their ministries to Parliament, but these are nonetheless core requirements of Canada's constitutional democracy. In the 'Sponsorship Affair', which refers to the alleged mismanagement of funds directed by the Canadian federal government to sponsor events in Quebec following the 1995 Referendum as part of a national unity strategy, and has led to Parliamentary committee hearings, a public inquiry headed by Justice Gomery and a series of civil and criminal legal proceedings, no minister was called on to resign (though a former minister responsible for the impugned programme, was summarily dismissed from his subsequent post of ambassador to Denmark). By contrast, the lead civil servant involved in the programme was called before a legislative committee, the resulting public inquiry, and is subject to criminal allegations of fraud.

[25] For judicial discussion of constitutional conventions which restrict Crown prerogative authority, see *Re Resolution to Amend the Constitution* [1981] 1 SCR 753. For academic commentary, see Heard, n. 21.

Scope of the executive

with the guidance of elected officials in Parliament.[26] Conventions also dictate who will form the executive,

> There are carefully defined conventions of the Constitution which determine who is called upon to form a government. Normally the leader of the party with the largest number of seats in the House of Commons is given by the governor general the queen's commission to form a government. It is then the responsibility of this person to submit to the governor general a list of ministers, to which the governor general will give his approval. Thus, legally, the first minister and cabinet are appointed by the governor general acting under the prerogative authority of the Crown. Those persons who can be designated as the first minister and ministers of the Crown are, of course, determined by convention.[27]

Thus, a cabinet is formed, and it remains in power until the first minister is no longer in office. The governor general's discretionary power to appoint is critical in a situation where a prime minister passed away while in office, as that would result in the extinction of the cabinet. Only the prime minister can give binding constitutional advice, and hence a replacement must be chosen as quickly as possible.[28]

The Crown also derives power through the royal prerogative, which was described by Dicey as 'the residue of discretionary or arbitrary authority, which at any given time is left in the hands of the Crown.'[29] It consists of the powers and privileges accorded to the executive by the common law.[30] Courts delineated this power by stating that there was no prerogative power to legislate, nor was there authority for the Crown to administer justice. Further, executive action could not impede individual liberty without the specific limitation being enshrined in a statute. Finally, any statute which occupied the field of a former prerogative power overruled that power.[31] On balance, it is fair to say that the powers of the executive stem from the sum total of statutory, constitutional, and common law sources, all of which have received the imprimatur of the Supreme Court.[32]

(b) Does Canada have a separation of powers?

One of the facets of Canada's institutionalized ambivalence is what might be termed its separation anxiety, in which the British Westminster model lives uneasily with an American style concern for appropriate checks and balances. The separation of powers is an emerging but poorly understood facet of Canada's legal and political system, and has only recently received formal recognition as a feature of Canada's political and legal system.[33]

---

[26] Monahan, n. 15, 58. [27] Cheffins and Johnson, n. 9, 86. [28] *Ibid.*
[29] Hogg and Monahan, n. 13, 15. [30] Hogg, n. 6, 13. [31] *Ibid.*, 14.
[32] Magnet, n. 18, 147. See also, *Blaikie v. A.G. Quebec (No. 2)* [1981] 123 DLR (3d) 15–122.
[33] The separation of powers only attracted significant attention after the Constitution Act 1982 and the enactment of the Charter of Rights giving courts the power to strike down

The separation of powers is as much a normative as a functional exercise in dividing the labour of governmental authority. Investing separate branches of government with insuperable powers is intended to protect against tyranny, just as federalism prevents the concentration of power by dividing local and national powers between two levels of government. James Madison, one of the architects of the US Constitution, referred to the separation of powers as a central 'auxiliary precaution' against oppression by the government.[34] It is intended to preserve freedom through diffusing power. Diffusing power requires not just dividing government authority between different branches but also ensuring that no single branch is invested with sufficient power to dominate the others. For example, according authority to the judiciary to supervise legislative and executive activities to ensure they comply with the rule of law would not curb the potential for oppression if one or the other of those branches could appoint or dismiss judges at will. Thus, the separation of powers and the balance of powers emerge as two interdependent principles of liberty.[35]

Neither the Constitution Act 1867 (formerly the BNA Act), nor the Constitution Act 1982 which includes the Charter), contains any explicit reference to a separation of powers, although the Constitution Act 1867 does recognize certain executive, legislative, and judicial powers, and in some cases, infers institutional relationships between the branches of government. There are even rudimentary checks and balances to be found if one takes the time to look. For example, by virtue of sections 96–100 of the Constitution Act 1867, discussed in greater detail below, the executive branch in Canada has the power to appoint judges, but the legislature is given the power to set their salaries. In lieu of clear constitutional boundaries, such as the first three articles of the US Constitution, however, where should one search for Canada's separation of powers? An analysis of the separation of powers in Canada must take into consideration three central dynamics of Canada's political and legal framework: (1) the dynamic of the parliamentary system; (2) the dynamic of the administrative state; and (3) the dynamic of judicial independence. Below, I discuss each of these dynamics, as well as the relationship between them.

---

legislation and invalidate executive action. The first clear articulation of the separation of powers as a feature of Canada's legal and political system was made by Dickson CJ in *Fraser v. Public Service Staff Relations Board* [1985] 2 SCR 455, 469–70, ironically a case which did not feature the Charter, where he observed that: 'There is in Canada a separation of powers among the three branches of government—the legislature, the executive and the judiciary. In broad terms, the role of the judiciary is, of course, to interpret and apply the law; the role of the legislature is to decide upon and enunciate policy; the role of the executive is to administer and implement that policy.'

[34] J. Madison, *The Federalist Papers*, No. 51, cited and discussed in H. Mansfield, 'Separation of Powers in the American Constitution', in B. Wilson and P. Schramm (eds.), *Separation of Powers and Good Government* (Rowman & Littlefield, 1994), 3.

[35] B. Knight, 'Introduction', in B. Knight (ed.), *Separation of Powers in the American Political System* (George Mason University Press, 1989), 11.

(i) The dynamic of the parliamentary system

The Canadian doctrine of separation of powers is premised on a hierarchy of governmental functions. One could argue that the executive branch of government in Canada is intentionally subordinate to the legislative branch because executive authority flows from statutory grants of power.[36] However, a residue of Crown prerogatives also remain which do not depend on statutory authority (e.g. the granting of honours, the granting of mercy, decisions relating to foreign affairs, including the sending of peacekeeping and other troops abroad).

The precise nature of the relationship between the executive and legislative branches of government in Canada remains unclear. The Supreme Court has expressed some ambivalence regarding the constitutional relevance of the fact that the leading party in the legislative branch of government will control the executive branch in a Westminster, parliamentary system. In *Canada (Minister of Energy, Mines and Resources) v. Canada (Auditor General)*, Dickson CJ observed:

> It is of no avail to point to the fusion of powers which characterizes the Westminster system of government. That the executive through its control of a House of Commons majority may in practice dictate the position the House of Commons takes on the scope of Parliament's auditing function is not, with all respect to the contrary position taken by Jerome A.C.J., constitutionally cognizable by the judiciary. The grundnorm with which the courts must work in this context is that of the sovereignty of Parliament. The Ministers of the Crown hold office with the grace of the House of Commons and any position taken by the majority must be taken to reflect the sovereign will of Parliament.[37]

More recently, in *Wells v. Newfoundland*,[38] however, the Court held that:

> The separation of powers is not a rigid and absolute structure. The Court should not be blind to the reality of Canadian governance that, except in certain rare cases, the executive frequently and *de facto* controls the legislature.

Notwithstanding some ambivalence on the constitutional significance of the entanglement between the legislative and executive branches in a parliamentary system, the sovereignty of Parliament remains an important feature of Canada's system of government. Not only does this mean that, absent a constitutional infringement, neither a court nor a minister can interfere with the legislative process, but also that Parliament alone has the authority to adjudicate its internal

---

[36] Lamer CJ elaborates on this point in *Cooper v Canadian Human Rights Commission* [1996] 3 SCR 854, 878. 'The justification for this hierarchical relationship, in present-day Canada, is a respect for democracy, because legislatures are representative institutions accountable to the electorate. A respect for democracy is also at the heart of those aspects of administrative judicial review which seek to ensure that administrative bodies do not exceed the boundaries of the powers granted to them by the legislature. The hierarchical relationship between the executive and the legislature is also another aspect of the separation of powers, since the separation of powers inheres in Parliamentary democracy.'

[37] *Auditor General of Canada v. Minister of Energy, Mines and Resources et al.* [1989] 2 SCR 49, 103.   [38] *Wells v. Newfoundland* [1999] 3 SCR 199, para. 54.

disputes.[39] While Parliament may assume adjudicative duties over a limited number of internal disputes, far more anxiety arises from the spectre of administrative tribunals undertaking a full range of adjudicative functions, including constitutional interpretation. It is to this dynamic that I now turn.

(ii) The dynamic of the administrative state

In its most basic form, the relationship between the legislative and executive branch of Canadian government is mutually reinforcing. The legislature enacts the laws which the executive branch implements. All bureaucratic officials are responsible to a minister of the cabinet, who in turn is responsible to Parliament. The growth of the administrative state in the post-war era has complicated the relationship between the executive and legislative branches. Hundreds of administrative boards, agencies, commissions, and tribunals, appointed by the executive branch, and given a statutory mandate by the legislative branch, decide thousands of applications, disputes, and appeals. Ministers no longer exercise any meaningful supervision over the affairs of government, nor do they take responsibility very often for the errors of government.[40]

As a consequence of the administrative state, judicial functions, including the interpretation of law, have been vested in non-judicial bodies such as tribunals.[41] At least in their adjudicative capacity (and to a more limited extent in their policy making capacity), these administrative bodies are protected from political interference and required to be independent (this independence often requires an internal separation of powers between the adjudicative, political, and policy-making departments of a single branch of government, which is discussed below).[42] Adjudicative independence typically includes the provision for security of tenure, financial security, and control over the administration of the adjudicative process.[43]

The precise constitutional status of these executive agencies, boards, and commissions has been further complicated by the introduction of the Charter. Section 24(1) of the Charter provides that 'anyone whose rights or freedoms...have been infringed or denied may apply to a court of competent jurisdiction to obtain such remedy as a court considers appropriate and just in the circumstances.' Can the many executive bodies of the administrative state constitute 'courts of competent jurisdiction' for the purpose of giving remedies under the Charter, remedies which might include invalidating legislative

---

[39] See *New Brunswick Broadcasting Co. v. Nova Scotia (Speaker of the House of Assembly)* [1993] 1 SCR 319. See also, A. Heard, 'The Expulsion and Disqualification of Legislators: Parliamentary Privilege and the Charter of Rights' (1995) 18 *Dalhousie Law Journal* 380.

[40] For further discussion of this position, see S. Sutherland, 'Responsible Government and Ministerial Responsibility: Every Reform Is Its Own Problem' (1991) 24 *Canadian Journal of Political Science* 91.   [41] *Re Residential Tenancies Act, 1979*, [1981] 1 SCR 714, 728.

[42] See, e.g., *Brosseau v. Alberta (Securities Commission)* [1989] 1 SCR 301.

[43] This standard was established in *Valente v. The Queen* [1985] 2 SCR 673, and applied to the field of executive agencies in *Canadian Pacific Ltd. v. Matsqui Indian Band* [1995] 1 SCR 3 per Lamer CJ.

provisions? Can a tribunal which is the creature of the executive branch invalidate part of the statute which created and empowers it to act?

These questions were first considered in a trilogy of cases by the Supreme Court in the early 1990s: *Douglas/Kwantlen Faculty Association v. Douglas College*,[44] *Cuddy Chicks Ltd v. Ontario (Labour Relations Board)*,[45] and *Tétreault-Gadoury v. Canada (Employment and Immigration Commission)*.[46] Faced with a stark opportunity to draw firm boundaries between executive and judicial functions, the Court once again reflected Canada's ambivalent posture toward its constitutional order. In each of the cases of the trilogy, an administrative tribunal was asked to rule on a challenge under the equality protection in section 15 of the Charter and, in each, La Forest J wrote the opinion of the Court on this issue.

In *Douglas/Kwantlen Faculty Association v. Douglas College*, the Court held that an arbitrator had jurisdiction to consider the validity of a provision in a collective agreement that provided for mandatory retirement. In *Cuddy Chicks Ltd v. Ontario (Labour Relations Board)*, the Court held that the Ontario Labour Relations Board had jurisdiction to determine the constitutional validity of a statutory provision that excluded farm workers from collective bargaining. Finally, in *Tétreault-Gadoury v. Canada (Employment and Immigration Commission)*, the Court held that a Board of Referees under the Unemployment Insurance Act 1971 did not have jurisdiction to determine the constitutional validity of a provision that restricted certain benefits to those under the age of 65. The separation of powers issue, that is the possibility that an executive body would have the power to invalidate legislative action, was not squarely addressed in the trilogy. Significantly, the Court in the trilogy did not find a constitutional source for the executive bodies' power to apply the Charter; rather, the Court in each case held that the intent of the executive body's empowering statute was determinative. Therefore, the key question for the Court was whether the legislature had intended for the executive body at issue to have the power to apply the Charter.

The implication of the trilogy for the separation of powers was considered in *Cooper v. Canada (Human Rights Commission)*.[47] Writing a concurring judgment, Chief Justice Lamer described the separation of powers as nothing less than 'the backbone of our constitutional system'.[48] In *Cooper*, the Supreme Court was asked to consider whether the Canadian Human Rights Commission had jurisdiction to decide the constitutional validity of its empowering statute. The Canadian Human Rights Commission is an executive body, established to screen and investigate human rights complaints and determine which should be referred to a hearing before a human rights tribunal. Allowing the Commission to review its empowering legislation, and possibly to strike down portions of that legislation as unconstitutional, would effectively result in the executive branch being able to reverse the legislative branch (although in the trilogy of cases noted

---

[44] [1990] 3 SCR 570. [45] [1991] 2 SCR 5. [46] [1991] 2 SCR 22.
[47] *Cooper*, n. 36. [48] *Ibid.*, 867.

above the Court had established that the extent of an administrative body's remedial reach would be to hold a statutory provision 'inoperative' in the case before it, with no binding effect as a precedent even internal to the administrative body in question).

The majority of the Court once again approached the problem from the standpoint of interpreting legislative intent. Writing again for the majority on this issue, La Forest J held that, while some executive boards, commissions and tribunals could invalidate the legislation that created them (labour boards, for example), the Human Rights Commission did not have such jurisdiction. As there was no provision in its empowering legislation which explicitly gave the Commission power to determine questions of law and nothing in the scheme of the Act which implied that the Commission had this power.

Lamer CJ, wrote concurring reasons in *Cooper* on his own behalf, and reached the same result as the majority but for different reasons. He argued that no board, tribunal or, commission appointed by the executive should ever have the power of overturning legislative action, and therefore, even if the Commission had been given the power to determine questions of law, it would not have authority under the Constitution to challenge the validity of legislation. This was due to two defining and related features of the Constitution: parliamentary supremacy and the separation of powers. Lamer CJ maintained that the Human Rights Commission and other executive agencies are 'mere creatures of the legislature'. They are created by statute and can be modified or even eliminated by statute as well. For them to declare a statute constitutionally invalid would invert the hierarchical relationships between the executive and the legislature in a parliamentary democracy in which the executive's role is to implement the laws of the legislature. Only the courts, as a consequence of the separation of powers, have the necessary independence to declare invalid an act of the legislature under the Constitution of Canada, he reasoned, including the Charter of Rights.

In *Cooper*, Lamer CJ acknowledged the earlier case law of the Court, which had held the separation of powers not to be 'strict' in the sense of prohibiting non-judicial tribunals from assuming some judicial powers or prohibiting judges from assuming some non-judicial powers.[49] However, he cautioned that 'the absence of a strict separation of powers does not mean that Canadian constitutional law does not recognize and sustain some notion of the separation of powers.'[50] He concluded that while the separation of powers doctrine in Canada may not be 'strict', it nonetheless required that some functions be exclusively reserved to particular bodies.[51] On the basis of the judiciary's need to be free from interference in its constitutional decision-making, Lamer CJ held that only courts and not executive bodies like the Commission or a human rights tribunal had jurisdiction to consider the constitutionality of legislation. In the result, of

---

[49] *Cooper*, n. 36, A similar point was made by the Supreme Court in *Reference re Secession of Quebec* [1998] 2 SCR 486, para. 15.   [50] *Ibid*.
[51] *Cooper*, n. 36, 871. See also, *Reference re Provincial Judges Remuneration* [1997] 3 SCR 3, 90.

course, the majority of the Court in *Cooper* disagreed and upheld the Court's earlier finding in the trilogy that the Canadian constitution did not prevent executive bodies from applying its terms to legislation within their jurisdiction. A dissent in *Cooper* authored by McLachlin J (as she then was) would have gone further than the majority and extended the authority to apply the Charter to any administrative body with the statutory power to make legal findings.

The Court revisited its divided stance from *Cooper* in *Nova Scotia (Workers' Compensation Board) v. Martin; Nova Scotia (Workers' Compensation Board) v. Laseur*, which once again raised the question of when a tribunal had jurisdiction to apply the Charter to a provision of its empowering statute.[52] The case concerned a Worker's Compensation Board's determination of whether the exclusion of 'chronic pain' from the list of regular worker's compensation benefits violated the equality guarantee of the Charter of Rights.

By a unanimous decision, the Court upheld the tribunal's jurisdiction to hear Charter arguments.[53] The Court effectively overruled its earlier position in *Cooper* and adopted the dissenting perspective from that case which greatly expanded the number of tribunals that would presumptively have the jurisdiction to apply the Charter. Gonthier J, writing for the Court, reiterated the view articulated by McLachlin J (as she then was) in her dissenting reasons in *Cooper* that the Charter 'belongs to the people of Canada,' and as such, Canadians should be able to access it in the most effective and efficient manner, without being forced into duplicate proceedings before the courts.[54] Gonthier J further asserted that concerns regarding tribunals extinguishing rights were unfounded, since such decisions would be given no deference if judicially reviewed and would be subject to a standard of correctness.[55] Gonthier J articulated the new test in the following terms:

Administrative tribunals which have jurisdiction—whether express or implied—to decide questions of law arising under a legislative provision are presumed to have concomitant jurisdiction to decide the constitutional validity of that provision. This presumption may only be rebutted by showing that the legislature clearly intended to exclude Charter issues from the tribunal's authority over questions of law.[56]

As a result of this jurisprudence, executive bodies (which, as discussed below, may or may not be free of political interference from the government of the day) may hold both statutory provisions and government action to account on constitutional grounds. What saves this scheme from hopeless incoherence (at least in the eyes of the courts) is the availability of judicial review to correct any errors of constitutional interpretation. It is to the dynamic of judicial independence that I now turn.

[52] See also the companion case released the same day, *Paul v. British Columbia (Forest Appeals Commission)* [2003] 2 SCR 585, which considered a tribunal's power to apply constitutional guarantees relating to aboriginal rights and applied the framework developed in *Martin*.
[53] [2003] 2 SCR 504.   [54] *Ibid.*, paras. 28–9.   [55] *Ibid.*, para. 31.
[56] *Ibid.*, para. 3.

(iii) The dynamic of judicial independence

Unlike the relationship between the executive and the legislative branches, which are entangled in a variety of ways, the judicial branch of Canadian government appears to stand apart. Assuming the judicial branch has its own constitutional authority, the source of that authority is neither uniform nor self-evident.[57] Sections 96–100 of the Constitution Act 1867, provide for the creation of courts and the appointment of judges, but do not set out limitations on the scope of judicial review, nor provide any mechanism for judicial accountability. Nonetheless, the Supreme Court has interpreted these provisions as implying a regime of judicial independence in Canada. In *Cooper*, for example, Lamer CJ affirmed that the primary source for the judiciary's independence is sections 96–100 of the Constitution Act 1867.[58] A secondary source for judicial independence was found to be the preamble to the Constitution Act 1867, which states that Canada is to have a constitution similar in principle to that of the United Kingdom.[59] While not necessary to the dispute at issue, Lamer CJ proceeded to assert that these provisions of the Constitution are not merely concerned with judicial independence but also with the judiciary as a constitutionally separate branch of government.[60]

In *Reference re Remuneration of Judges of the Provincial Court of Prince Edward Island*,[61] Lamer CJ again considered the nature of Canada's separation of powers, writing on behalf of the majority of the Court, with La Forest J dissenting. The *Provincial Remuneration Reference* considered a number of provinces' attempt to curtail or cut the salaries of provincially appointed judges (federally appointed judges have their salary fixed by the federal government). Lamer CJ, referring to the requirement that the financial security of courts be free from political interference, stated,

These different components of the institutional financial security of the courts inhere, in my view, in a fundamental principle of the Canadian Constitution, the separation of powers. As I discussed above, the institutional independence of the courts is inextricably

---

[57] See W.R. Lederman, 'The Independence of the Judiciary', in *Continuing Constitutional Dilemmas—Essays on the Constitutional History, Public Law and Federal System of Canada* (Butterworths, 1981).

[58] *Provincial Remuneration Reference*, n. 51, in which Lamer CJ. explained, 'Although the wording of this provision suggests that it is solely concerned with the appointment of judges, through judicial interpretation—an important element of which has been the recognition that s. 96 must be read along with ss. 97–100 as part of an integrated whole—s. 96 has come to guarantee the core jurisdiction of the superior courts against legislative encroachment.' See also, R. Elliot, 'Rethinking Section 96: From a Question of Power to a Question of Rights', in D. Magnusson and D. Soberman (eds.), *Canadian Constitutional Dilemmas Revisited* (Institute of Intergovernmental Relations, 1997), 17–30.

[59] *Cooper*, n. 36, 871. Lamer CJ cited the following passage from Dickson CJ.'s reasons in *Beauregard v. Canada* [1986] 2 SCR 56, 72: 'Since judicial independence has been for centuries an important principle of the Constitution of the United Kingdom, it is fair to infer that it was transferred to Canada by the constitutional language of the preamble.'   [60] *Ibid.*, 872–3.

[61] [1997] 3 SCR 3.

bound up with the separation of powers, because in order to guarantee that the courts can protect the Constitution, they must be protected by a set of objective guarantees against intrusions by the executive and legislative branches of government.[62]

Lamer CJ held that the remuneration of provincial judges could not be subject to government-wide cuts because to do so would compromise the independence of the judiciary, contrary to the unwritten guarantee of judicial independence incorporated into Canada's Constitution through the preamble of the Constitution Act 1867.[63]

While judicial independence is an enduring feature of the Canadian constitutional landscape, it has taken on new and significant dimensions with the enactment of the Constitution Act 1982 and entrenchment of the Charter. The question of judicial power in Canada now embodies a new approach to the separation of powers, more influenced by American than Westminster values. While section 52(1) of the Constitution Act 1982 empowers courts to render laws and government action of no force or effect, there is a balancing mechanism built into section 1 of the Charter, which permits infringements of Charter rights to be 'saved' where they are found to be reasonable limits 'demonstrably justified in a free and democratic society.' Furthermore, the legislative branch is given an override by virtue of section 33 to enact laws notwithstanding the Charter.[64]

The post-Charter nature of the judiciary's relationship to the other branches of government was discussed in *Vriend v. Alberta*.[65] In *Vriend*, the Supreme Court found that the omission of sexual orientation from the protected grounds of discrimination in the Alberta Individual Rights Protection Act infringed the protection against discrimination under section 15 of the Charter. Having found section 15 to have been violated by the Alberta's statute, the majority proceeded to determine whether the violation was justifiable under section 1 of the Charter.[66] In the majority's section 1 reasons, Justice Iacobucci reviewed the Court's relationship to the legislative and executive branches of government.[67] Rather than simply affirming the Court's role as an equal and coordinate branch

---

[62] *Ibid.*, 90.   [63] *Ibid.*, 64–9.

[64] The override itself is of limited application. It does not apply to the democratic rights contained in the Charter, nor to mobility rights or language rights protection, and where it does apply, it must be renewed every five years. The effect of this limitation is to ensure an election is held before an override can be renewed as elections can be no later than five years apart pursuant to section 4 of the Charter (which, of course, is a section which cannot itself be overridden by Parliament). The override applies only to legislation, not to government action (e.g. exercise of administrative discretion, etc.).   [65] [1998] 1 SCR 493.

[66] Under the section 1 analysis, the Court must consider whether the law being challenged has a pressing and substantial objective, and whether the law is rationally connected to that objective, infringes the constitutional rights as minimally as possible and is proportionate given the importance of the right at issue and the objective of the law. See *R v. Oakes* [1986] 1 SCR 103.

[67] n. 65, 564–5, in which Iacobucci J stated, 'Because the courts are independent from the executive and legislature, litigants and citizens generally can rely on the courts to make reasoned and principled decisions according to the dictates of the constitution even though specific decisions may not be universally acclaimed. In carrying out their duties, courts are not to second-guess legislatures and the executives; they are not to make value judgments on what they regard as the proper policy

of government, Iacobucci J focussed on the development of a Canadian version of the American 'checks and balances,' intended to ensure the accountability of each branch of government to the other.[68] Adopting the idea of the courts and the other branches engaged in a 'dialogue',[69] Iacobucci addressed the issue of accountability in the following terms:

> To my mind, a great value of judicial review and this dialogue among the branches is that each of the branches is made somewhat accountable to the other. The work of the legislature is reviewed by the courts and the work of the court in its decisions can be reacted to by the legislature in the passing of new legislation (or even overarching laws under s. 33 of the Charter). This dialogue between and accountability of each of the branches have the effect of enhancing the democratic process, not denying it.[70]

The aspiration to a dialogue is indicative of the Canadian approach to the separation of powers. It reflects a genuine ambivalence toward the sovereignty of Parliament and the guardianship over the Constitution accorded to the judiciary by virtue of section 52 of the Constitution Act 1982. Many remain sceptical, however, about the mutuality of the dialogue. Morton and Knopff, for example, have asserted that the Charter era is characterized not by a beneficial dialogue but rather by a judicial 'monologue,' which has resulted in a deleterious weakening of the legislative branch's power.[71] The notion of a dialogue also reflects the entangled relationship between the branches of Canadian government and the lack of exclusivity as a model for the balance of powers. It is in the context of this lack of exclusivity that the contrast to the American model is drawn most starkly. The separation of powers question in Canada has become intertwined with questions surrounding the proper scope of judicial intervention, and the public's uneasy embrace of the Charter of Rights and Freedoms. To cite but one recent example, proposals have surfaced in Canada to have Supreme Court judges submit to some form of parliamentary confirmation.[72]

---

choice; this is for the other branches. Rather, the courts are to uphold the Constitution and have been expressly invited to perform that role by the Constitution itself. But respect by the courts for the legislature and executive role is as important as ensuring that the other branches respect each others' role and the role of the courts.'

[68] *Ibid.*, 565.

[69] See P. Hogg and A. Bushell, 'The Charter Dialogue Between Courts and Legislatures (Or Perhaps the Charter *of Rights* Isn't Such a Bad Thing After All)' (1997) 35 *Osgoode Hall LJ* 75. See also, K. Roach, *The Supreme Court on Trial* (Irwin, 2001). [70] n. 65, 566.

[71] F.L. Morton and R. Knopff, *The Charter Revolution & The Court Party* (Broadview Press, 2000), 166.

[72] Jacob Zeigel, 'Merit Selection and Democratization of Appointments to the Supreme Court of Canada,' Choices 5(2) June 1999: 4. In 2004, the federal government referred to a Parliamentary committee the question of reforming the appointments process to the Supreme Court of Canada to include a 'Parliamentary role'. The committee failed to reach a consensus on a new approach, and when two appointments to the Supreme Court were made in the summer of 2004, the Minister of Justice appeared before the committee to defend the appointments. No new process has been announced and the appointments remain, from a constitutional perspective, within the unfettered discretion of the federal executive.

It is the striking lack of exclusivity that has led some leading Canadian constitutional observers to conclude that Canada's constitution simply does not provide for a separation of powers.[73] This is debatable.[74] Perhaps it would be more accurate to describe Canada's Constitution as establishing a separation of *institutions*.[75] Others characterize the Canadian separation of powers as functional rather than constitutional.[76] However one defines the nature of the separation, it is the extent of the overlapping responsibilities and collaborative possibilities that perhaps sets Canada apart. While both the legislative and the judicial spheres have some exclusive domains, the executive appears the most porous. For this reason, it is possible to see the executive at once as the most powerful branch of government and the branch of government whose power is the least well articulated. Not only is the power of the executive diffuse, but the very scope of the executive is also difficult to ascertain. While the membership of the legislative and judicial branches is highly circumscribed, the make-up of the executive is anything but clear. Not only is there some question of who forms part of the executive (ministers, civil service departments, agencies, tribunals, crown corporations, hospitals, universities, etc.), there is also a question as to the relationship between various components of the executive—in particular the relationship between the government and the civil service on the one hand and the relationship between the government and administrative tribunals on the other. It is to these relationships that I now turn.

---

[73] According to Peter Hogg, for example, 'The [Constitution] Act does not separate the legislative, executive and judicial functions and insist that each branch of government exercise only "its own" function. As between the legislative and executive branches, any separation of powers would make little sense in a system of responsible government; and it is clearly established that the Act does not call for any such separation. As between the judicial and the two political branches, there is likewise no general separation of powers.' Hogg, n. 6, 7–24. This description received judicial approval in *MacMillan Bloedel Ltd v. Simpson* [1995] 4 SCR 725, para. 52. See also, P. Russell, *The Judiciary in Canada: The Third Branch of Government* (McGraw-Hill Ryerson, 1987), 75–103; W. Mackay, 'The Legislature, the Executive and the Courts: The Delicate Balance of Power or Who is Running this Country Anyway?' (2001) 24 *Dalhousie LJ* 37.

[74] At a minimum, judicial review functions are constitutionally exclusive to the judiciary. For example, in *Crevier v. Quebec (A.G.)*, the Supreme Court held that judicial review of executive action, at least to ensure the executive official acted within his or her statutory mandate, is constitutionally protected and cannot be ousted by even the most clearly worded statute by the legislative branch purporting to insulate an executive agency from supervision by the courts. See *Crevier v. Quebec (A.G.)* [1981] 2 SCR 220. See also, *Canada (A.G.) v. PSAC* [1993] 1 SCR 941, 961.

[75] It is worth noting that there is a strain in the American separation of powers literature that similarly holds the US constitution to have separated institutions rather than powers. See R. Neustadt, *Presidential Power: The Politics of Leadership* (John Wiley & Sons, 1960), 33.

[76] In *New Brunswick Broadcasting Co. v. Nova Scotia (Speaker of the House of Assembly)* [1993] 1 SCR, Justice Beverley McLachlin (as she then was) described this concept in the following terms: 'Our democratic government consists of several branches: the Crown, as represented by the Governor General and the provincial counterparts of that office; the legislative body; the executive; and the courts. It is fundamental to the working of government as a whole that these parts play their proper role. It is equally fundamental that no one of them overstep its bounds, that each show proper deference for the legitimate sphere of activity of the other.'

(c) Defining the boundaries of the executive

(i) The Interdependence of cabinet and the civil service

The symbolic apex of the executive is the governor-general and the Queen. The functional apex of the executive branch of government is the prime minister and cabinet. The actual exercise of executive authority, however, depends on the civil service. As Willis once wrote, 'Parliament is the heart, the civil service, the head and hands, of government.'[77] The civil service and what I term the political executive (i.e. cabinet) in Canada have a nuanced and complex relationship. I characterize this relationship as one of interdependence. This relationship both addresses a key question regarding the scope of the executive branch, and as discussed below, also addresses a key check on executive power.

In his thought-provoking study of Canadian bureaucracy, Savoie takes as his point of departure that the relationship between bureaucrats and politicians is not subject to constitutional rules and therefore has developed around mutually acceptable practices, or in his words, a 'bargain'.[78] While it is true, as Savoie observes, that the Canadian Constitution Acts of 1867 and 1982 contain virtually no references to the civil service, this overlooks a rich constitutional tradition in Canada in locating many of our most important constitutional principles (judicial independence, the primacy of the rule of law, and so forth) largely outside the formal text of the Acts. I have argued that the civil service is subject to a dense network of constitutional provisions, conventions, and principles, and that our democratic institutions and practices would be meaningfully enhanced if these rules, principles, and conventions were more fully elaborated.[79] Civil servants are the guardians of a public trust underlying the exercise of all public authority.[80] Their ability to maintain the integrity of that trust and, when

---

[77] J. Willis, *The Parliamentary Powers of English Government Departments* (Harvard University Press, 1933), 171.

[78] D. Savoie, *Breaking the Bargain: Public Servants, Ministers and Parliament* (University of Toronto Press, 2003), 4–16. Savoie elaborates, 'In the absence of formal rules, politicians and public servants some time ago struck a "bargain"... Under the arrangement, public servants exchanged overt partisanship, some political rights and a public profile in return for permanent careers, or at least indefinite tenure, anonymity, selection by merit, a regular work week, and the promise of being looked after at the end of a career... Politicians meanwhile exchanged the ability to appoint or dismiss public servants and change their working conditions at will for professional competence and non-partisan obedience to the government of the day.' (5–6).

[79] This section is adapted from L. Sossin, 'Speaking Truth to Power: The Search for Bureaucratic Independence in Canada' (2005) 55 *University of Toronto Law Journal* 1.

[80] Under this approach, public officials are 'entrusted' with authority subject to the condition that it be exercised fairly, reasonably and justly. See P. Finn, 'The Forgotten "Trust": The People and the State', in Malcolm Copp, (ed.), *Equity Issues and Trends* (The Federation Press, 1995), Chap. 5. See also, D.K. Hart, 'Social Equity, Justice and the Equitable Administrator' (1974) *Public Administration Review* 34 and L. Sossin, 'Public Fiduciary Obligations, Political Trusts and the Evolving Duty of Reasonableness in Administrative Law' (2003) 66 *Saskatchewan Law Review* 129–82. For discussion of 'public trust' in the public service context, see J. Tait, 'A Strong Foundation: A Report of the Task Force on Public Service Values and Ethics (Government of Canada: 2000) (www.ccmd-ccg.gc.ca/research/publications/pdfs/tait.pdf) (last accessed February 20, 2004), 47.

called upon, to 'speak truth to power,' depends on a measure of independence from undue political influence. Neutrality, integrity, professionalism, and trust, on this view, are inextricably linked to the norm of bureaucratic independence. The consequence of reaffirming the critical role played by the civil service in discharging the public trust is not to erode or undermine Parliamentary supremacy. Rather, it is to recognize that the separation of powers doctrine, as it has developed in Canada (and elsewhere), has failed to come to terms with the complexities of the executive branch. As Daintith and Page have observed:

> While the trinity of executive, legislative and judicial functions may be the most powerful rationalization of the specialization process that has yet been offered, it cannot by itself capture the overall significance of any given structure of government for constitutional values such as democracy and accountability... We should therefore resist the easy assumption that the allocation of powers and functions within each of the organizational blocs identified by the separation of powers are less significant to the protection of constitutional values than are the relations between those blocs.[81]

In embarking on this inquiry into bureaucratic independence, the first question to address is: independence from whom? Public servants work for the Crown. In most cases, civil servants take instruction from the government of the day. Indeed, some would suggest that any distinction between the Crown and the government of the day is itself a legal fiction?[82] To what extent and in what circumstances does their duty to the Crown to uphold the public interest permit or even require public servants to refuse instructions from the government of the day? What constitutional doctrines enable bureaucrats to remain protected from the undue interference of their ministers? What safeguards ensure civil servants cannot use their positions to partisan ends? Is bureaucratic independence, to the extent it is safeguarded, consistent with democratic principles? Could it be used to frustrate the legitimate goals of democratically elected governments who rely on the civil service to implement their policies? I attempt to address these questions below.

The boundary between the partisan interests of ministers and the impartial duties of civil servants represents the defining, internal dynamic within the executive branch of government. When one speaks of the separation of powers in Canada, one tends to consider the relationship between the executive, legislative, and judicial branches of government. From this vantage, the relationship

---

[81] T. Daintith and A. Page, *The Executive in the Constitution: Structure, Autonomy and Internal Control* (Oxford University Press, 1999), 12. In discussing the dynamics within the executive branch in particular, the authors observe with puzzlement the lack of attention by constitutional scholars: 'The executive governs us; it comprises the individuals—mostly ministers and civil servants—who actually control, from day to day, the state's instruments of coercion, wealth and information. The idea that it might not be constitutionally important would seem too bizarre to mention, were it not for the fact that the literature on constitutional law is remarkably reticent on the subject.' (2).

[82] See, e.g., R. Watt, 'The Crown and its Employees', in M. Sunkin and S. Payne (eds.), *The Nature of the Crown* (Oxford University Press, 1999), 288. See also, *Town Investments Ltd v. Department of the Environment* [1978] 1 AC 359, 361 per Lord Diplock.

between ministers and bureaucrats appears straightforward. The executive branch is headed by the premier or prime minister and the cabinet composed of the ministers, who in turn are in charge of the bureaucracy. Bureaucrats are accountable directly to ministers and ministers are accountable directly to the legislative branch, which in turn is accountable to the people. The concept of bureaucratic independence as a constitutional norm challenges this traditional, one-dimensional view of the executive branch of government. It implies that the executive branch of government must be seen in pluralistic terms, as a complex web of political arrangements, institutional relationships, constitutional obligations, and legal duties. For the purposes of this analysis, the key dynamics include the roles of the 'political executive' (premier/PM and cabinet, drawn from the political party which controls the legislature),[83] and the roles of the 'civil service.' The political executive directs the 'government of the day' while the civil service, like the Crown itself, enjoys continuity through transitions of government.[84] Under this approach, the political executive and civil service may be seen at once as interdependent and independent entities within government.[85]

If it is to remain coherent, bureaucratic independence must be a concept that is elastic enough to encompass highly adjudicative administrative tribunals and highly independent officials such as Crown prosecutors on the one hand, and a range of policy analysts, line departmental staff members, and bureaucrats on the other hand. It must be capable of adapting to what is sometimes referred to as the 'post-bureaucratic era' of change-oriented, citizen-centred forms of public service-delivery and restructuring within the public service which may include public-private partnerships, outsourcing tasks, and a variety of 'new public management' initiatives.[86] These new pressures create confusion and dislocation in terms of the roles and responsibilities of the bureaucratic and political spheres of executive government.[87] This sense of uncertainty about boundaries and

[83] It is worth noting that in at least two territories, Nunavut and the Northwest Territories, there are no political parties in the legislature. A separate aspect of this research, to be published in a subsequent paper, will consider the significance of the relationship between the political executive and the civil service in settings without partisanship between political parties. Other political consideration tends to replace party affiliation in such settings, such as political groupings along regional and ethnic lines, so that the potential for political pressures on the civil service is not substantially reduced in such settings.

[84] The continuity of the Crown itself is a constitutional postulate, once elegantly described by Frank MacKinnon in the following terms: 'The Crown is the symbol of government which remains throughout any difficulty. The existing administration may fall and the new administration might not yet be in control. But governmental authority itself remains ...' F. MacKinnon, *The Crown in Canada* (Glenbow-Alberta Institute, 1976), 51.

[85] There are other dynamics within the executive branch of government which are not addressed at length in this study but which reflect the diversity and complexity of Canada's constitutional system—these include most notably the range of executive boards, tribunals, and agencies with fixed term appointments.

[86] For discussion, see K. Kernaghan, 'The Future Role of a Professional Non Partisan Public Service in Ontario'(2003) Panel on the Role of Government, Research Paper Series No. 13, 31–3.

[87] See the discussion of the 'fault line' in bureaucratic-political relations in J. Tait, 'A Strong Foundation: A Report of the Task Force on Public Service Values and Ethics (Government of

concern for the integrity of the civil service is exacerbated by the diversity of state action. Unlike constitutional principles such as judicial independence or parliamentary supremacy which operate mostly on the basis of bright lines, bureaucratic independence must operate on the basis of a spectrum of duties and obligations applicable across often disparate governmental settings.

Bureaucratic independence is so elusive precisely because it must be sufficiently practicable to be capable of application across diverse administrative settings, yet sufficiently principled to provide clear standards as to appropriate and inappropriate influence and conduct between the political executive and the civil service. The success or failure of this argument rests on its ability to resolve the fundamental tensions which underlie the constitutional status of the civil service, tensions which emerge from reconciling the constitutional convention of political neutrality on the part of the civil service with the right of free expression to which individual civil servants are entitled, and between the duty of loyalty owed by civil servants to the government of the day and the duty owed by civil servants to the Crown to ensure government acts in accordance with the rule of law and not contrary to the public interest.

Three Supreme Court cases have addressed (at least, in *obiter*) these tensions in the context of interpreting the convention on the political neutrality of the civil service: *Fraser v. Public Service Staff Relations Board*,[88] *OPSEU v. Ontario*,[89] and *Osborne v. (Canada) Treasury Board*.[90]

Fraser involved a gadfly who worked at Revenue Canada, but whose hobby appeared to be publicly criticizing the government's policies, especially on metrification, (he was photographed in the Whig-Standard with a placard that read 'your freedom to measure is a measure of your freedom').[91] Mr Fraser was sanctioned for his conduct and challenged this sanction on the grounds that civil servants should be free to criticize the government of the day if they disagree with their policies or practices. In the course of finding that Mr Fraser enjoyed no legal protection against being sanctioned for his behaviour, the Supreme Court held that '[A] public servant is required to exercise a degree of restraint in his or her actions relating to criticism of government policy, in order to ensure that the public service is perceived as impartial and effective in fulfilling its duties.'[92] Dickson CJ characterized the civil service as built around values such as 'knowledge ... fairness ... and integrity' and emphasized that its duty of loyalty was to the government of Canada, not to any political party that might enjoy power at the time.[93]

Canada, 2000) (www.ccmd-ccg.gc.ca/research/publications/pdfs/tait.pdf) (last accessed 20 February 2004), 45–6.

[88] [1985] 2 SCR 455.   [89] [1987] 2 SCR 2.   [90] [1991] 2 SCR 69.
[91] *Fraser* n. 88, 458.   [92] *Ibid.*, 466.
[93] *Ibid.*, 470. This duty of loyalty is discussed in greater depth in the second section of the paper. Like the requirement of political neutrality, this duty does not appear to have an express foundation in the written Constitution but arguably is implied. Dickson CJ simply declared that the public interest in impartiality 'dictates a general requirement of loyalty on the part of the public servant'. (456).

While finding no bar to the sanctions in the case before him, Dickson CJ asserted that it would be inappropriate to penalize a civil servant for opposing government policy in public where the government was involved in illegal acts; or where the government's policies jeopardized the life, health or safety of public servants or others; or where the public servant's criticism has no impact on his or her ability to perform effectively the duties of a public servant or on the public perception of that duty.[94] In other words, if this logic is followed, all civil servants enjoy a measure of legal protection should they decide to become 'whistleblowers' whether or not specific whistle-blower legislation exists to protect them. The implications of this case, I argue, may be broader still. The Court in *Fraser* recognized that a civil servant's duty of loyalty to the Crown, and through the Crown to the public interest, must in some circumstances be a higher obligation than the duty of loyalty owed to the government of the day. The civil service, in other words, may itself hold the executive to account in egregious circumstances.

Dickson CJ is less clear about the legal basis for this distinction between when the public servant's duty of loyalty governs her conduct, and when the higher duty to the government trumps the duty of loyalty. In other words, when Dickson CJ characterizes the sanction of public servants for legitimate whistleblowing or for criticism of government which does not impair the neutrality of the civil servant, as 'inappropriate', does he mean that such sanctions would be inadvisable, unlawful or unconstitutional? Dickson CJ does not resolve this ambiguity. He refers instead to the 'tradition' in the Canadian public service which 'emphasizes the characteristics of impartiality, neutrality, fairness and integrity'.[95] Again, this raises questions. Is a tradition distinct from a constitutional convention? These are among the important issues which the Court in *Fraser* left for another day. What *Fraser* did accomplish was a principled application of a constitutional norm regarding the status of the civil servant which was alert to the operational realities of government.

Following *Fraser*, a public sector union in Ontario sought to invalidate certain statutory provisions in public service acts which restricted political activity on the part of civil servants. The union argued both that *Fraser* guaranteed a form of political speech as a matter of constitutional principle and that the province should not be able to restrict political activities through ordinary legislation. In *OPSEU v. Ontario*,[96] the Supreme Court rejected both propositions and upheld the legislation. Because *OPSEU* involved a challenge which was initiated before the Charter of Rights came into effect, the Court declined to consider the effect of the freedom of expression of the Charter on the legislative restrictions on political activities. This issue came before the Supreme Court shortly thereafter in *Osborne*, which involved a direct challenge to a legislative provision (section 33 of the federal Public Service Act),[97] which circumscribed the political activities

---

[94] *Fraser* n. 88, 470.   [95] *Ibid.*, 471.   [96] [1987] 2 SCR 2.
[97] R.S.C. 1985, c.P-33. S. 33 provided: 33(1) No deputy head and...no employee shall (a) engage in work for or against a candidate; engage in work for or against a political party; or (c) be a

in which a civil servant could engage. The challenge was brought by several civil servants whose partisan activities ranged from participating in a leadership campaign for a political party, to stuffing envelopes on behalf of the party. *Osborne* is discussed below with respect to its treatment of the 'freedom of expression' of civil servants under the Charter and so here I leave the substantive outcome of the challenge to one side.

The constitutional convention of political neutrality arose in *Osborne* in two ways. First, the federal government argued that one part of the Constitution, the Charter, could not invalidate another part, a statute encapsulating a constitutional convention. Second, the federal government argued that the legislation constituted a reasonable infringement on the freedom of expression of civil servants under section 1 of the Charter by virtue of the fact that the provision reflected a constitutional convention. Both submissions were rejected by the Court, which struck down the impugned legislation. But in the course of their analysis, the existence of the convention on political neutrality was affirmed and discussed at some length (particularly in the lower courts).

While *Fraser, OPSEU*, and *Osborne* leave the existence of the convention on political neutrality for the civil service unquestioned, these decisions reflect a variety of approaches toward the convention's rationale and purpose. The Federal Court of Appeal in *Osborne* characterized the convention as 'a right of the public at large to be served by a politically neutral civil service'.[98] In *Osborne*,[99] Sopinka J described the convention as an 'essential principle' of responsible government.[100] In *Fraser*, this convention was characterized as a matter of the 'public interest in both the actual, and apparent, impartiality of the public servant.'[101] Can a convention be simultaneously a 'right' of the people, an 'essential principle' of responsible government and a 'policy' in the public interest? The answer is undoubtedly that conventions can and do have multiple rationales and serve multiple ends. This is consistent with what I have characterized as the plural nature of the executive branch in Canada's constitutional system.

The Court in *OPSEU* characterized the convention in terms of a duty owed by the civil service as an 'organ of government'.[102] While not necessarily more definitive an account than the others, it is this characterization which strikes me as best suited to addressing the delicate boundary between independence and interdependence which shapes the relationship between the civil service and the political executive. The convention on political neutrality does not turn the civil service into the fourth branch of government; it does suggest, however, that the

---

candidate.' The provision also provided for an unpaid leave of absence should a civil servant wish to undertake political activities.

[98] *Ibid.*   [99] n. 90, 69.

[100] *Ibid.*, 88. Sopinka J. rejected the government's argument that section 33 of the Public Service Act was immune from Charter scrutiny because it codified a constitutional convention, but did observe that the fact a provision reflects this convention 'is an important consideration in determining whether in s. 33, Parliament was seeking to achieve an important political objective'.

[101] *Fraser*, n. 88.   [102] n. 89, para. 93.

executive branch contains distinct organs of government—notably cabinet and the civil service—which must maintain at least some separation from one another under our constitutional system. It is in this sense that political neutrality presupposes a measure of bureaucratic independence.[103] Thus, to accept bureaucratic independence as a constitutional norm is to challenge the traditional view that the regulation of the civil service is a matter for the political executive alone to resolve.[104] This not only points to further indication of Canada's constitutional ambivalence toward the power and authority of the executive but also highlights the importance of intra-executive relationships and not just the traditional separation of powers concern for relationships between the three branches of government.

(ii) The independence of administrative tribunals

In light of the discussion of bureaucratic independence and the earlier discussion of the highly adjudicative role of certain administrative tribunals, the problem of the independence of such tribunals from the political executive presents a distinct challenge to Canada's constitutional framework. I wish briefly to focus on this question as it also shows a counterexample of one area in which the Court has attempted to defend formal institutional distinctions notwithstanding evidence of functional entanglement.

It should be stated at the outset that the 'right' of institutional independence is not a right enjoyed by a tribunal but rather a right enjoyed by those whose claims and disputes are adjudicated by that tribunal.[105] Tribunals do not constitute a separate branch of government with jurisdictional integrity to guard. Much of the particularity and the peculiarity of institutional independence in Canadian administrative law, however, arise because the institutional independence protection at common law has been modeled on the constitutional norm of judicial independence. In *Valente v. The Queen*,[106] the Supreme Court of Canada noted that, broadly speaking, the test for independence in the judicial setting is 'the one for reasonable apprehension of bias, adapted to the requirement of independence'.[107] The Court further noted that, although there is obviously a close relationship between independence and impartiality, they are nevertheless separate and distinct values or requirements:

The word 'impartial'... connotes absence of bias, actual or perceived. The word 'independent' in s. 11(d) reflects or embodies the traditional constitutional value of judicial independence. As such, it connotes not merely a state of mind or attitude in the actual

---

[103] The content of tribunal independence is discussed below, but in the context of administrative law, courts have approached independence as a precondition for the appearance of impartiality of administrative decision-makers.

[104] For a discussion of this view, see Daintith and Page, n. 81, 62–3. See also, *Council of Civil Service Unions v. Minister of the Civil Service* [1985] AC 374 (HL).

[105] Once again, in this sense, the analogy to judicial independence holds. See Binnie J (in dissent) in *Mackin v. New Brunswick (Minister of Finance)* [2002] 1 SCR 405.

[106] (1985), 24 DLR (4th) 161 (SCC).   [107] *Ibid.*, 168.

exercise of judicial functions, but a status or relationship to others, particularly to the Executive Branch of government, that rests on objective conditions or guarantees.[108]

While administrative tribunals are viewed as part of the executive branch in a separation of powers context,[109] the Court chose to adopt the framework of institutional independence for administrative bodies directly from this judicial framework.[110] According to that framework, there are three essential conditions of judicial independence: security of tenure, financial security, and administrative independence.

In *Canadian Pacific Ltd v. Matsqui Indian Band*,[111] the Supreme Court of Canada held that the test for institutional independence enunciated in *Valente* applied, with added flexibility, to administrative tribunals as a component of the rules of natural justice, more colloquially referred to in Canada as the duty of fairness.[112] Lamer CJ concluded that the *Valente* principles apply to administrative tribunals on the basis of natural justice principles, but that the test for institutional independence may be less strict than for courts:

Therefore, while administrative tribunals are subject to the *Valente* principles, the test for institutional independence must be applied in light of the functions being performed by the particular tribunal at issue. The requisite level of institutional independence (i.e., security of tenure, financial security and administrative control) will depend on the nature of the tribunal, the interests at stake, and other indices of independence such as oaths of office.

In some cases, a high level of independence will be required. For example, where the decisions of a tribunal affect the security of the person of a party (such as the immigration adjudicators in *Mohammad, supra*), a more strict application of the *Valente* principles may be warranted. In this case, we are dealing with an administrative tribunal adjudicating disputes relating to the assessment of property taxes. In my view, this is a case where a more flexible approach is clearly warranted.[113]

The analogy between tribunal independence and judicial independence cuts at least two ways. First, it reflects an understanding of the functional similarity of adjudication between courts and tribunals. On this view, whether a dispute is adjudicated before a tribunal or a court should be less important than that the adjudication, in whichever venue it occurs, comports with the rules of natural

---

[108] *Ibid.*, 169–70.
[109] As Katrina Wyman put it, 'The doctrine of tribunal independence is not concerned with establishing administrative tribunals as a fourth branch of government': K. Wyman, 'The Independence of Tribunals in an Era of Ever Expanding Judicial Independence' (2001) 14 *Canadian Journal of Administrative Law & Practice* 61, 100. See also, J. M. Brown and J. M. Evans, *Judicial Review of Administrative Action in Canada* (Canvasback, 1998, Looseleaf), 11: 4120, who note that where an executive body appears before an executive tribunal, a conflict does not inherently arise.
[110] In earlier cases, such as *I.W.A. v. Consolidated Bathurst* (1990), 68 DLR (4th) 524, 561 (SCC), the term 'judicial independence' was used by this Court to characterize the common law standards applicable to a labour tribunal. [111] (1995), 122 DLR (4th) 129 (SCC).
[112] While Sopinka J appeared to write for the greatest number of judges on this point, it is Lamer CJ's decision which has become the predominant articulation of institutional independence in Canada. See paras. 75–80. [113] *Ibid.*, 83–5.

justice. The second dimension of the analogy is to the methodology employed to assess whether the requisite standard of independence has been breached. The Court has pursued the methodological analogy to judicial independence while downplaying the functional similarity between the two.

This trend was cemented in a controversial judgment of the Supreme Court, *Ocean Port Hotels Ltd v. B.C.*, in which the Court confirmed that the guarantee of institutional independence in adjudicative tribunal settings is not a constitutional right, but rather a common law protection, and as such, is vulnerable to the government overriding it through ordinary statutory language at any time for any reason.[114] In other words, even where a tribunal is engaged in adjudication that is functionally indistinguishable from a court, the court proceedings will be governed by the constitutionally entrenched protections of judicial independence while the tribunal proceeding will not.

Ocean Port involved an investigation by a Senior Inspector with the Liquor Control and Licensing Branch, which led to allegations that Ocean Port Hotel Ltd ('Ocean Port') the operator of a hotel and pub, had committed five infractions of the Liquor Control and Licensing Act and Regulations. Ocean Port alleged, inter alia, that the Liquor Appeal Board lacked the requisite institutional independence. Pursuant to the relevant legislation, the chair and members of the Liquor Appeal Board 'serve at the pleasure of the Lieutenant Governor in Council'. In practice, members were appointed for a one-year term and served on a part-time basis and on a per diem basis. The Supreme Court of Canada held that, even if the tribunal did not meet the common law natural justice requirements for institutional independence, this was not fatal to its ability to function:

It is well-established that, absent constitutional constraints, the degree of independence required of a particular government decision-maker or tribunal is determined by its enabling statute. It is the legislature or Parliament that determines the degree of independence required of tribunal members. The statute must be construed as a whole to determine the degree of independence the legislature intended.[115]

The Court went on to assert that, confronted with silent or ambiguous legislation, courts generally infer that Parliament or the legislature intended the tribunal's process to comport with principles of natural justice. In *Ocean Port*, the Court concluded that the provincial legislature 'spoke directly to the nature of the appointments to the Liquor Appeal Board'; under its enabling legislation, the chair and members of the Board were expressly stated to 'serve at the pleasure of the Lieutenant Governor in Council',[116] leaving the Court no room to infer procedural protections such as institutional independence.

---

[114] [2001] 2 SCR 781. For a more detailed appraisal of *Ocean Port*, see P. Bryden, 'Structural Independence of Administrative Tribunals in the Wake of *Ocean Port*' (2003) 16 *Canadian Journal of Administrative Law & Practice* 125; L. Sossin, 'Developments in Administrative Law: the 2001–2002 Term' (2002) 18 *Supreme Court Law Review (2nd)* 41–74.   [115] *Ibid.*, para. 20.
[116] *Ibid.*, para. 25.

In *Ocean Port*, McLachlin CJ does not distinguish administrative independence from judicial independence on any other than formal grounds. In *Ocean Port*, McLachlin CJ characterized tribunals as spanning 'the constitutional divide between the judiciary and the executive'.[117] This very metaphor suggests a set of institutions which, functionally at least, operates within both the judicial and executive spheres. While conceding that courts and tribunals may share similar functions, McLachlin CJ stressed that it is the constitutional status of each that was at issue in this case. Of tribunals, she stated, 'while they may possess adjudicative functions, they ultimately operate as part of the executive branch of government, under the mandate of the legislature.'[118] It is not at all clear why an element of natural justice as fundamental as institutional independence should flow from the categorization of a decision-maker, rather than from her function. It is easy to say that courts are courts and tribunals are tribunals, but far more difficult to say that the adjudication which occurs in courts is any more significant, either for the parties involved or for the public interest, than the adjudication which occurs in tribunals. For example, consider that, as indicated above, most tribunals may now decide Charter issues.[119] Indeed, the Court has confirmed that a range of tribunals constitute 'courts of competent jurisdiction' pursuant to section 24(2) of the Charter.[120] The effect of *Ocean Port* would be that a tribunal member appointed at the pleasure of cabinet, who decided a Charter issue may be dismissed if a government is unhappy with the interpretation given, but a judge who decided the very same Charter issue would be protected from any political interference. Thus, while the relationships within the executive branch and the functions given to executive bodies are diverse and multifarious, there remains an undercurrent of formalism to the Canadian constitutional approach.

2. Checks on executive power

While policy-making and policy implementing power in Canada is highly centralized in the executive branch, there are several significant checks on executive power. I discussed above the self-regulatory role played by the civil service as a check on executive action. In addition, Canada has several Parliamentary officers who are created in part so as to act as a check on executive action—for example, Canada has a robust tradition of Auditors General who issue annual report highlighting government mismanagement and questioning administrative practices. This catalyst function gives the Auditor General no power to interfere in executive action but unfettered access to the public through Parliamentary reports. The potency of this function was recently demonstrated

---

[117] *Ibid.*, para. 22. [118] *Ibid.*, para. 12. [119] See *Martin*, n. 53, and *Paul*, n. 52.
[120] See *Weber v. Ontario Hydro*, [1995] 2 SCR 929. The Court justified this finding, in part, due to the French version of s. 24(2) which refers to 'tribunal' rather than 'cour'.

in the Sponsorship Affair.[121] Public inquiries, in turn, represent a further form of executive accountability, even though they can only be launched by an executive act. Ombudsman and Information and Privacy Commissioners represent yet other mechanisms which have the effect of constraining executive action or providing accountability to those affected by that action. While the activities of these independent legislative offices have a constraining effect on executive action, and serve an important function in rendering transparent what would otherwise remain government secrets, only the courts have the power to quash, modify, compel, or impose conditions on executive decision-making.

I wish to focus on the two most significant external checks on executive power which serve as an accountability counterweight: the role of judicial review and the role of federalism. Below, I discuss the various ways in which each of these constrains executive action.

(a) Judicial review

There are several ways in which judicial review may constrain executive action. Administrative law remedies are available against the Crown (whether provincial or federal) where there has been a breach of the duty of fairness or where there has been an error of sufficient seriousness to warrant judicial intervention. The substantive review of administrative decision-making depends on a preliminary finding by a court of which 'standard of review' applies to the executive action.[122]

The standard of review doctrine in administrative law raises a deceptively simple question—on what grounds may a court interfere with the decision of an administrative body? The answer to this question must start first from the principled proposition that no administrative act may lay absolutely outside the purview of judicial interference or there would be no mechanism by which to ensure the rule of law is respected by the executive,[123] and second, from the practical proposition that courts do not have the institutional competence, capacity, or legitimacy to intervene in any administrative setting as they wish. The standard of review thus represents the search for a constructive relationship between courts and administrative decision-makers which reflects respect for the rule of law, parliamentary supremacy, judicial capacity, administrative expertise, and the complex decision-making environments of the modern state.

The framework for determining the degree of curial deference appropriate for particular administrative settings remains as elusive and critical a question today

---

[121] The 'Sponsorship Affair' refers to the alleged mismanagement of funds directed by the federal government to sponsor events in Quebec following the 1995 referendum as part of a national unity strategy, which has led to parliamentary committee hearings, a public inquiry headed by Justice Gomery and a series of civil and criminal legal proceedings.

[122] For a review of the development of Canada's standard of review jurisprudence, see L. Sossin, 'Empty Ritual, Mechanical Exercise or the Discipline of Deference?: Revisiting the Standard of Review in Administrative Law' (2003) 27 *The Advocate's Q* 478.

[123] A further constitutional foundation for this proposition is discussed in *Crevier v. Quebec (A.G.)* [1981] 2 SCR 220. See also, D. Mullan, *Administrative Law* (Irwin, 2001), 43.

as ever, notwithstanding (or perhaps in part because of) the steady stream of judicial thinking on the matter flowing from the courts for the past quarter-century or so. The Supreme Court has been clarifying, rationalizing, and harmonizing its approach to the standard of review of administrative decision-making almost continuously since its watershed 1979 decision in *CUPE, Local 963 v. New Brunswick Liquor Corp.*[124] With *CUPE*, the Supreme Court sought to leave behind the Diceyan legacy of active judicial intervention in administrative decision-making and to recognize that administrative tribunals possess greater institutional competence and legislative authority than courts to decide certain issues.[125] While *CUPE* established that the purpose of the standard of review analysis is to ensure an appropriate degree of deference is paid to administrative decision-making, the method of analysis for determining just what degree of deference was appropriate to particular decision-making settings was not fully elaborated until *Bibeault*.[126] What became known as the 'pragmatic and functional' approach emerged from that decision and reflected the Court's concern that deference not be determined as a result of a formal or technical calculation but rather should flow from a contextual analysis of the legislation governing an administrative decision-maker and the legislative and institutional environment in which that decision-making takes place. The pragmatic and functional approach has come to consist of four parts: (1) the wording of the statute (i.e. the presence or absence of a privative clause or statutory right of appeal); (2) the expertise of the decision-maker; (3) the purpose of the provision and the Act as a whole; and (4) the nature of the problem (i.e. is it a question of fact or law, or mixed fact, etc.).

What emerged from this early case law was a choice for courts between two standards: patent unreasonableness, which meant the highest deference, and correctness, which meant the lowest deference. The 'all or nothing' stakes for deference seemed inappropriate to settings where the signals emerging from the pragmatic and functional analysis were mixed. For example, a privative clause typically signals deference, while a statutory right of appeal typically signals stricter scrutiny. Some statutes, especially in sphere of economic regulation, contain partial privative clauses, partial rights of appeal and sometimes the legislation is silent on the matter of review altogether. To address these middle-group situations, the Supreme Court recognized in the mid-1990s a middle-ground standard of review, termed reasonableness *simpliciter*.[127] Administrative law review has proven particularly helpful in challenges to improper exercises of

[124] [1979] 2 SCR 227.
[125] On the pre-*CUPE* state of the law, see H. Arthurs, 'Rethinking Administrative Law: A Slightly Dicey Business' (1979) 17 *Osgoode Hall LJ* 1. See also, D. Dyzenhaus, 'Constituting the Rule of Law: Fundamental Values in the Administrative State' (2002) 27 *Queen's LJ* 445, 454–7.
[126] *Union des Employés de Service, Local 298 v. Bibeault* [1988] 2 SCR 1048, 1088–9.
[127] *Pezim v. British Columbia (Superintendent of Brokers)* [1994] 2 SCR 557; *Canada (Director of Investigation and Research) v. Southam Inc.* [1997] 1 SCR 748.

ministerial discretion,[128] notwithstanding a recent trend toward more deference where the discretion engages issues of national security.[129] Judicial review of administrative decision-making, both on procedural and substantive grounds, remains a frequently invoked and effective as a check on executive power. In addition to judicial review of discretion on traditional administrative law grounds, courts in Canada have also been asked to apply the Charter of Rights as a check against executive action in discretionary contexts.[130]

(i) Judicial review of administrative discretion under the Charter

Early in its Charter jurisprudence, the Supreme Court affirmed that all executive action would be subject to the constraints of the Charter, including cabinet itself exercising a Crown prerogative.[131] In that era of Charter jurisprudence, however, the Court's concern for discretion was rooted in the context of criminal justice.[132] Section 24(2) of the Charter provides a specific remedy (the exclusion of evidence) as a means of regulating and remedying the unconstitutional exercise of prosecutorial or police discretion. The basis for judicial remedies in the context of administrative discretion and the application of section 24(1) of the Charter, which empowers a court to remedy a breach of the Charter by means it considers 'just and appropriate', are less clear. The Charter would appear to justify intervention in administrative discretion in at least four different ways (in most cases, a violation of either section 2, 7 or 15 will provide the grounds for a Charter challenge, but the unconstitutional exercise of discretion would certainly not be limited to these rights).

First, a law granting discretion may be facially unconstitutional. For example, a law which granted a discretionary benefit to heterosexual spouses would create a distinction which, by its very terms, could violate section 15 of the Charter, as it necessarily excludes a group from a benefit based on marital status. Where this cannot be justified as a reasonable limit under section 1, this discretionary authority would be struck down pursuant to section 52 of the Constitution Act 1982. This was the case, for example, in *Falkiner v. Ontario*,[133] in which the Ontario Court of Appeal struck down a Regulation issued under the Ontario Works Act which empowered ministry officials to determine whether two people living in the same location were 'spouses' for the purposes of the Act. Because the 'spouse in the house' discretion extended even to relationships of very short duration, which had a disproportionately harsh effect on unmarried women on

---

[128] For the high water mark, see *Baker v. Canada (Minister of Citizenship and Immigration)*, [1999] 2 SCR 817 and the collection of essays on the significance of Baker, D. Dyzenhaus, (ed.), *The Unity of Public Law* (Hart, 2004).   [129] See *Suresh*, n. 139.

[130] The following analysis of discretion and the Charter relies on 'Discretion Unbound: Reconciling the Charter and Soft Law' (2003) 45 *Canadian Public Administration* 465. See also, N. Lambert, *The Impact of the Charter of Rights and Freedoms on Canadian Administrative Law* (D.C.L. Dissertation, McGill University Faculty of Law, 2004).

[131] *Operation Dismantle v. The Queen* [1985] 1 SCR 441.

[132] See, e.g., *R v. Lyons* [1987] 2 SCR 309, 347–8; *R v. Beare* [1988] 2 SCR 387, 410–11.

[133] [2002] O.J. No. 1771 (CA).

social assistance, the Ontario Court of Appeal found the Regulation violated section 15 of the Charter and could not be saved under section 1.

The second circumstance involves a law granting discretion which is not facially unconstitutional, may nevertheless be *applied* in an unconstitutional manner. This approach was adopted in *Eldridge v. British Columbia (A.G.)*.[134] In *Eldridge*, a law authorizing the Medical Services Commission to fund certain health services was not found to violate the Charter, but the exercise of discretion by that Commission, deciding not to fund interpreters for deaf patients, was found to violate section 15 of the Charter and not to be upheld under section 1. This gave rise to a remedy under section 24(1) of the Charter directing the British Colombia government to administer the medical funding legislation in a fashion consistent with the Charter.

In the third circumstance, a law granting wide discretion authority without sufficient guidance as to its application, or without safeguards against arbitrary conduct, could violate the procedural component of section 7 of the Charter. This basis for challenging discretion was relied upon by the majority of the Supreme Court in *R v. Morgantaler*.[135] In *Morgantaler*, the impugned provision was a law prohibiting abortion unless a physician determined that the life or health of a woman was endangered. The procedures which therapeutic abortion committees established in hospitals to decide whether this threshold was met in individual cases were found by the majority to lack coherence, predictability, and fairness. Here again, the remedy would be to strike down the legislation or read in sufficient procedural guarantees.

Fourth, and finally, a law granting a discretion that is too vague to provide sufficient notice to those who might infringe it could violate the substantive component of section 7, which would render the legislative provision invalid.[136] As Mullan observes, 'where the line is actually to be drawn between overly broad discretionary power and permissible undefined discretion, nonetheless, remains a highly speculative exercise.'[137] In *R v. Morales*,[138] for example, the Court held that a provision granting pre-trial detention where it was justified in 'the public interest' was unconstitutionally vague. However, in *Suresh v. Canada (Ministry of Citizenship and Immigration)*,[139] the Court found that a discretion to issue a ministerial certificate against a non-citizen believed to be engaged in terrorist activities or believed to pose a danger to the security of Canada was not unconstitutionally vague notwithstanding the absence of a statutory definition of 'terrorism', 'danger', or 'security' in the Immigration Act.

These four bases on which administrative discretion may be attacked under the Charter are by no means exhaustive. Further, the line dividing a precise

---

[134] *Eldridge v. British Columbia (A.G.)* [1997] 3 SCR 624.
[135] *R v. Morgantaler* [1988] 1 SCR 30.
[136] See generally *R v. Nova Scotia Pharmaceutical Society* [1992] 2 SCR 606.
[137] Mullan, n. 123, 127. [138] *R v. Morales* [1992] 3 SCR 711.
[139] *Suresh v. Canada (Minister of Immigration and Citizenship)* [2002] SCC 1.

discretion from an imprecise one is by no means clear. The Supreme Court's most detailed examination of the Charter's relationship with administrative discretion was in *Slaight Communications v. Davidson*.[140] At issue in that case was a remedial discretion provided to adjudicators to resolve grievances under collective agreements under the Canada Labour Code.[141] The grievance in *Slaight* concerned an allegation of wrongful dismissal. The adjudicator found that the dismissal had been wrongful and ordered the company to provide the employee with a factual reference. The adjudicator also ordered the company to respond to any inquiries about the employee by providing the reference but prohibited any other views about the employee to be expressed. The adjudicator thus compelled the company to express certain facts and prohibited it from expressing other opinions. The majority found that neither aspect of the adjudicator's order violated the Charter.

Justice Lamer (as he then was) dissented in part in the case, holding that recourse to the Charter was unnecessary since the impugned order preventing the company from expressing an opinion other than providing the reference letter was patently unreasonable and therefore should be quashed on administrative law grounds. However, writing for the Court on the issue of the proper approach to discretionary decision-making under the Charter, he identified two kinds of discretion, each of which led to a different section 1 analysis under the Charter:[142]

1. The exercise of discretion was made pursuant to legislation which confers, either expressly or by necessary implication, the power to infringe a protected Charter right.

    —It is then necessary to subject the legislation to the test set out in s. 1 by ascertaining whether it constitutes a reasonable limit that can be demonstrably justified in a free and democratic society.

2. The legislation pursuant to which the exercise of administrative discretion was made confers an imprecise discretion and does not confer, either expressly or by necessary implication, the power to limit the rights guaranteed by the Charter.

---

[140] *Slaight Communications v. Davidson*, [1989] 1 SCR 1038. On the significance of *Slaight*, see June M. Ross, 'Applying the Charter to Discretionary Authority' (1991) 29 *Alberta Law Review* 382. See also, *Little Sisters Book and Art Emporium v. Canada (Minister of Justice)* [2000] 2 SCR 1120, and for additional commentary, Sujit Choudhry and Kent Roach, 'Racial and Ethnic Profiling: Statutory Discretion, Democratic Accountability and Constitutional Remedies,' (2003) 40 *Osgoode Hall LJ* 1.

[141] *Canada Labour Code*, R.S.C. 1970, c. L-1, as amended by S.C. 1977–78, c. 27, s. 21. section 61.5(9) of the Code provided: 'Where an adjudicator decides pursuant to subsection (8) that a person has been unjustly dismissed, he may, by order, require the employer who dismissed him to

   (a) pay the person compensation not exceeding the amount of money that is equivalent to the remuneration that would, but for the dismissal, have been paid by the employer to the person;
   (b) reinstate the person in his employ; and
   (c) do any other like thing that it is equitable to require the employer to do in order to remedy or counteract any consequence of the dismissal.

[142] *Slaight Communications*, n. 140, para. 91.

—It is then necessary to subject the <u>order</u> made to the test set out in s. 1 by ascertaining whether it constitutes a reasonable limit that can be demonstrably justified in a free and democratic society;

Lamer J assumed without any detailed examination that discretionary acts which could be tied to statutory authority met the 'prescribed by law' threshold under section 1 of the Charter. This aspect of the constitutional analysis is discussed in more detail below.

The central holding of *Slaight* was that no public official could be authorized by a statute to breach the Charter and therefore, all discretionary authority had to be read down only to authorize decision-making which is consistent with Charter rights and guarantees. Hogg articulates this principle in the following terms:

Action taken under statutory authority is valid only if it is within the scope of that authority. Since neither Parliament nor a Legislature can itself pass a law in breach of the Charter, neither body can authorize action which would be in breach of the Charter. Thus, the limitations on statutory authority which are imposed by the Charter will flow down the chain of statutory authority and apply to regulations, by-laws, orders, decisions and all other action (whether legislative, administrative or judicial) which depends for its validity on statutory authority.[143]

Thus, discretionary authority exercised by executive officials always comes with an implied condition, which is that they be exercised in a manner consistent with all the applicable Charter rights. Review under both administrative law and Charter grounds provides a significant recourse for parties aggrieved by executive decision-making.

(ii) Advisory opinions, references and the executive functions of judicial review

The focus of judicial review of the constitutionality of legislation or the reasonableness and fairness of government action typically is holding the executive to account. In Canada, it is also possible for the Court to undertake this function not at the behest of an adversarial party to the Crown but at the behest of the Crown itself. This is accomplished through the reference power by which the executive can seek advisory opinions from the Court.

While these opinions are not binding, and can only be issued on questions posed by the government, they nonetheless have become significant constraints on executive action. In the context of the recent reference on proposed same-sex marriage legislation, for example, the government chose not to appeal a lower court ruling which struck down the definition of marriage as excluding same sex couples. Rather, it launched a reference to the Supreme Court on the issue.[144]

Reference decisions involve the Court acting almost as a check on the executive from within rather than from without. For this reason, there was initially

---

[143] Hogg, n. 6, para. 34–11. [144] *Reference re Same Sex Marriage* [2004] SCC 79.

uncertainty in Canada as to whether this advisory function of courts was consistent with the separation of powers.[145] The separation of powers, and the legitimacy of the Court's role in the partisan struggles between the Canadian and Quebec governments, emerged as a defining feature of the *Reference re Secession of Quebec*.[146] This case confronted the Supreme Court with an explosive political dispute between the federal government and the province of Quebec, one which raised issues of fundamental importance to Canada's constitutional make-up. As McRoberts observed, the *Secession Reference* 'had become the central element in a public debate over the future of Canada—indeed whether Canada was to have a future.'[147]

On September 30, 1996, the federal government referred three questions for consideration by the Court regarding the possibility of Quebec seceding from Canada.[148] The Government of Quebec declined to participate in the reference.[149] As a result, the Court took the unusual step of appointing Andre Joli-Coeur, a well respected Quebec lawyer, as *amicus curiae* (friend of the Court) to present arguments on Quebec's behalf. The *amicus curiae* first challenged the constitutionality of section 53 of the Supreme Court Act, which authorizes the Court to respond to reference questions posed by the Governor-General-in-Council. The basis of this challenge is the separation of powers doctrine, under which the legislative, executive, and judicial branches are prohibited from

---

[145] The constitutionality of these advisory opinions first was considered in a 1912 decision, *A.G. Ont. v. A.G. Can.* [1912] AC 571 (the 'Reference Appeal') in which the Judicial Committee of the Privy Council ('JCPC'), then the highest court of appeal for Canadian cases, considered whether the Constitution Act 1867 prevented Parliament from amending the Supreme Court Act to provide for reference questions to be answered by the Court. The provinces challenged the federal government's power to seek advisory opinions from courts. They argued that section 101 of the Constitution Act 1867 empowered Parliament to establish and maintain a 'Court,' which by definition limited such a body to judicial tasks. The provinces contended that advisory opinions on legislation or policies not yet in force did not qualify as a judicial task. The JCPC rejected this view and held that the reference power was a legitimate exercise of the adjudicative function.

[146] [1998] 2 SCR 486.

[147] Kenneth McRoberts, 'In the Best Canadian Tradition' (January–February 1999) 7 *Canada Watch* 11.

[148] These questions were: Question 1: Under the Constitution of Canada, can the National Assembly, legislature or government of Quebec effect the secession of Quebec from Canada unilaterally? Question 2: Does international law give the National Assembly, legislature or government of Quebec the right to effect the secession of Quebec from Canada unilaterally? In this regard, is there a right to self-determination under international law that would give the National Assembly, legislature or government of Quebec the right to effect the secession of Quebec from Canada unilaterally? Question 3: In the event of a conflict between domestic and international law on the right of the National Assembly, legislature or government of Quebec to effect the secession of Quebec from Canada unilaterally, which would take precedence in Canada? See Order in Council P.C. 1996–1497.

[149] Quebec previously had withdrawn from a private suit brought by lawyer Guy Bertrand, which alleged his constitutional rights would be violated in the event of Quebec's secession. In the Bertrand litigation, the government of Quebec took the position that the secession of Quebec was a political matter for the people of Quebec to determine, not a legal question for judges to decide. Therefore, Quebec withdrew from the litigation after a Quebec Court dismissed its attempt to strike out the suit *Bertrand v. Quebec (A.G.)* (1996), 138 DLR (4th) 481 (Que. S.C.).

infringing each other's powers. Advisory opinions such as the *Secession Reference*, for example, would be clearly unconstitutional in the United States on this basis.[150] The Supreme Court gave this argument relatively short shrift. First, the Court noted that some American states had passed legislation authorizing state courts to issue advisory opinions and that a number of European states similarly authorized advisory opinions (i.e. Germany, France, Italy, Spain, Portugal, and Belgium) as well as international tribunals (i.e. European Court of Human Rights, European Court of Justice, and the Inter-American Court of Justice). The Court concluded:

> There is no plausible basis on which to conclude that a court is, by its nature, inherently precluded from undertaking another legal function in tandem with its judicial duties... Thus, even though the rendering of advisory opinions is quite clearly done outside the framework of adversarial litigation, and such opinions are traditionally obtained by the executive from the law officers of the Crown, there is no constitutional bar to this Court's receipt of jurisdiction to undertake such an advisory role. The legislative grant of reference jurisdiction found in s. 53 of the *Supreme Court Act* is therefore constitutionally valid.[151]

However, while the constitutional validity of advisory opinions was confirmed in the *Secession Reference*, the Court also affirmed that the judiciary retains an inherent discretion to decline to answer reference questions, should they fail to raise any concrete or justiciable issues, or should insufficient or inadequate material be put before them. In other words, even an advisory opinion to the executive must have judicially enforced boundaries.[152] In *Reference re Resolution to amend the Constitution ('Patriation Reference')*,[153] the majority of the Supreme Court characterized its discretion bluntly:

> The scope of the [reference] authority in each case is wide enough to saddle the respective courts with the determination of questions which may not be justiciable and there is no doubt that the courts, and this Court on appeal, have a discretion to refuse to answer such questions.[154]

More recently in the *Same Sex Marriage Reference*, the Court acknowledged that it had exercised its discretion to decline to answer reference questions in the past rarely which reflected 'its perception of the seriousness of its advisory role.'[155] The Court declined to address one of the four questions put to it in the *Same Sex*

---

[150] See J. Choper and R. Fallon, 'Opinion on the Ripeness Doctrine in Relation to the Quebec Secession Reference' in supplément au dossier, Rapperts d'Experts de l'amicus curiae, *Secession Reference* Materials, 4. [151] *Secession Reference*, n. 146, paras. 14–15.
[152] See *McEvoy v. A.G. (Canada)* [1983] 1 SCR 704. [153] [1981] 1 SCR 753.
[154] *Ibid.*, 768. Former Chief Justice Laskin and Justices Estey and McIntyre, concluded, however, that the *Patriation Reference* should be heard notwithstanding concerns regarding the concreteness of the questions posed: 'While we deprecate the practice of bringing before the Court as important constitutional questions as are raised in this case on extremely flimsy material, we would not abort the appeal on this ground. We believe for the reasons which follow that the Court has enough of the essential features of the proposed scheme to be compelled to the conclusion that all three questions must be answered in the negative.' *Ibid.*, 851. [155] n. 144, para. 61.

Marriage Reference regarding the constitutionality of opposite sex only definitions of marriage both because the government had stated that it would proceed with the proposed legislation recognizing same sex marriage in any event and because the government had already conceded that the opposite sex only marriage provisions violated the equality guarantee of the Charter before lower courts. In this way, the Court deftly navigated between the shoals of its executive advisory role and its aversion to being used to provide political cover to the government of the day about to embark on a risky initiative on a divisive issue. In other words, the Court was able both to give effect to its advisory role to the executive while also fulfilling its accountability function over executive action. The position of the Court is more complicated where the issue before it is one not of executive accountability but of dispute resolution between two or more governments. In the *Secession Reference*, for example, the Court was confronted with an apparent zero sum game. Recognizing the authority of either the federal government or Quebec in relation to the question of secession would have meant curtailing the authority of the other branch. In a deft compromise, the Court concluded that the constitution required, in the event of a clear majority vote of on a clear question of secession in Quebec, the two executives to negotiate a political solution. As the next section examines, federalism represents a pervasive dynamic of executive action in Canada and one in which the Court is a critical, if sometimes reluctant participant.

(b) Federalism

The ambivalence of executive power in Canada is reflected in Canada's federal structure with its centralizing and decentralizing forces working to keep each level of government beholden to the other for its success. Canada's federal constitution parcels all sovereignty and legislative authority between the federal government and the provinces. It is important to note that in this system the enumeration and delegation of powers is exhaustive, and the judiciary acts as a supervisor of the distribution of power, ensuring that the two levels of government share power in a coherent and principled fashion.[156]

The central and local or regional legislative powers are formally separated in sections 91 and 92 of the Constitution Act 1867 and as we have seen, the distinction between legislative and executive power is far from clear. Section 91 states that the formal central executive, the Queen with the advice of the Senate and the House of Commons, shall 'make laws for the Peace, Order, and good Government of Canada, in relation to all Matters not coming within the Classes of Subjects by this Act assigned exclusively to the Legislatures of the Provinces.'[157] For clarity, a list of subjects exclusive to the central authority follows

[156] Monahan, n. 15, 21.
[157] *A Consolidation of the Constitution Acts 1867 to 1982* (Department of Justice Canada, Ottawa, 2001) s. 91.

which includes such issues as: the regulation of Trade and Commerce, Indians and Lands reserved for the Indians and the Criminal law.[158] Section 92 enumerates sixteen subjects which are exclusive to the provincial legislatures, notably the management of hospitals, property and civil rights and 'Generally all Matters of a merely local or private Nature in the Province.'[159]

It is important, however, to note that regardless of this enumeration, the part of section 91 that states that the central authority make laws for the 'Peace, Order and good Government' operates as a residual power. In circumstances where the subject does not fall under any of the specified groups in section 91 or section 92, it is up to the central power to create the appropriate legislation. Further, even where the subject falls under a certain category, there may be legitimate interests dealing with another category that overlaps. Smiley gives this example:

> [P]arliament has the exclusive power to enact laws in respect to unemployment insurance; but the levels of unemployment benefits and the conditions under which those are paid have a direct and immediate impact on the demands for social assistance provided by the provinces and their constituent municipalities ... [160]

Given this state of affairs, interaction and cooperation between the central and regional governments is critical to effective and efficient functioning of the executive and legislative powers. As such, a custom has developed whereby the federal or central executive meets with provincial authorities in order to maintain a relationship of collaboration. Some commentators have described these meetings as 'the most important new phenomenon in our constitutional life.'[161] These collaborations have tended to blur the distinctions between the jurisdictions as outlined in the constitution. Agreements often lead to shared and overlapping responsibilities.[162] One example of such collaboration is the federal funding of health care, postsecondary education, and social programmes run by the various provinces.[163] Through this exercise of its 'spending power' the federal government is able to influence areas of provincial jurisdiction and provide a *de facto* check on the policy choices available to provincial governments. By the same token, because only provincial governments can implement policy priorities of the federal government in area such as health care, education, and social policy, those provincial governments constitute a *de facto* check on the policy choices available to provincial governments. Intergovernmental agreements, intergovernmental competition, and intergovernmental dispute resolution all fetter the discretion which would otherwise be open to the executive.[164] In this

---

[158] Sections 91(2), (24) and (27) respectively.
[159] *A Consolidation of the Constitution Acts 1867 to 1982* (Department of Justice Canada, Ottawa, 2001) ss. 92 (7), (13) and (16) respectively.
[160] D. V. Smiley, *The Federal Condition in Canada* (McGraw-Hill Ryerson, 1987) as quoted in J. E. Magnet, *Constitutional Law of Canada* (Juriliber Ltd, 7th edn., 1998), 109.
[161] Cheffins, n. 4, 15.   [162] Monahan, n. 15, 18.   [163] *Ibid*.
[164] This is true in the international realm as well, where the federal executive may negotiate, sign, and ratify treaties and conventions, but only the provinces have the power to implement the terms of such agreements domestically if they touch on provincial areas of jurisdiction.

fashion, federalism acts as a significant but often intangible executive constraint, because it is often tied to intergovernmental negotiations across a wide range of areas, so that a provincial executive's desire for greater access to natural resource revenues might lead it to agree to a federal health initiative which it otherwise might have opposed.

3. Conclusion

The purpose of this chapter has been to elaborate on the scope of the Canadian executive and to explore how the executive is held to account. I have used the characterization of ambivalence to capture the competing values and tensions animating executive power in Canada. I have argued that this ambivalence is reflected in the very scope of the executive branch, and particularly in the tension between the political executive and the civil service, and in the tension between the government of the day and quasi-independent executive tribunals. This ambivalence is also apparent in the mechanisms by which the executive is held to account in Canada, and particularly in the tensions surrounding judicial review and federalism. As a result of this ambivalent posture toward the executive, it is possible to say that Canada has one of the most centralized and powerful executive branches in the common law world, and that the executive in Canada is subject to greater internal and external constraints than most other common law jurisdictions. While ambivalence may easily bleed into incoherence, these countervailing tendencies in the Canadian context, I would suggest, have had a mostly salutary effect, allowing the executive to govern according to its democratic mandate while at the same time ensuring the executive remains subject to rule of law constraints and a measure of accountability.

3

Continuity and Flexibility: Executive Power in Australia

Dr Simon Evans[*]

1. Executive power under a system of responsible government

Section 61 of the Australian Constitution provides:

The executive power of the Commonwealth is vested in the Queen and is exercisable by the Governor-General as the Queen's representative, and extends to the execution and maintenance of this Constitution, and of the laws of the Commonwealth.

Standing alone, section 61 would provide an altogether misleading and incomplete picture. Executive power under the Australian Constitution is shaped by its origins in the English system of responsible government[1] and section 61 and the remainder of Chapter II of the Constitution ('The Executive Government') must be read in this context.[2]

The system of responsible government may be described in various ways. At its most abstract, the system contains principles identifying who exercises executive power and principles relating to accountability for its exercise. The constitutional text concentrates on the accountability principles. It establishes a 'formal relationship between the Executive Government and the Parliament'[3] that enables 'the Parliament to bring the Executive to account' and ensures that 'the Executive's primary responsibility in its prosecution of government is owed

---

[*] Director, Centre for Comparative Constitutional Studies, University of Melbourne. I gratefully acknowledge research assistance provided by Beth Midgley and Rowan McRae and comments by Leighton McDonald, Graeme Hill, and Geoff Lindell.

[1] Responsible government was introduced into Australia from 1855 with the self-government Acts for the various Australian colonies. On executive power generally see G. Winterton, *Parliament, The Executive and the Governor General* (Melbourne University Press, 1983); for a constitutional analysis of responsible government, see G. Lindell, 'Responsible Government', in P.D. Finn (ed), *Essays on Law and Government* (Law Book Co, 1995), Vol. 1.

[2] *Lange v. ABC* (1997) 189 CLR 520, 557.   [3] *Ibid*, 558.

to Parliament'.[4] The constitutional expression of this relationship can be found in:

- section 6, which requires that there be a session of the Parliament in every year and that no more than 12 months intervene between the sittings;
- section 83, which entrenches legislative control over supply;
- section 64, which provides for ministers to administer the Departments of State[5] and requires that they be or become a member of the Parliament within three months of appointment;
- sections 62 and 63, which provides for a Federal Executive Council (of which ministers are members: s. 64) to advise the Governor-General in the government of the Commonwealth;
- section 49, which gives the legislature power to regulate the 'powers, privileges and immunities' of the Houses.[6]

The principles of responsible government that identify by whom executive power is exercised are not expressed in the Constitution but rest instead on conventions.[7] According to those conventions, the Governor-General exercises the executive power of the Commonwealth on the advice of his or her ministers and those ministers hold office for only so long as they have the confidence of the lower house of Parliament. As a result, and notwithstanding the language of section 61, in all but exceptional circumstances the roles of the Queen and Governor-General are purely formal.[8] The conventions ensure that, again notwithstanding the language of section 61, executive power is exercised at the initiative of ministers who are accountable for its exercise to the democratic organs of government.[9]

The remainder of this chapter considers the scope of executive authority and the mechanisms for holding its exercise to account that presently operate in Australia. It focuses principally on the Commonwealth position, noting the State position only where it diverges significantly.[10]

---

[4] *Egan v. Willis* (1998) 195 CLR 424, 451 quoting D. Kinley, 'Governmental Accountability in Australia and the United Kingdom: A Conceptual Analysis of the Role of Non-Parliamentary Institutions and Devices' (1995) 18 *UNSWLJ* 409, 411.

[5] The High Court has accepted that two or more ministers may administer the one department, a result described as an an instance of 'development and adaptability' made possible by 'the deliberate lack of specificity on the part of the framers of the Constitution concerning the functioning of the Executive': *Re Patterson, ex parte Taylor* (2001) 207 CLR 391, 402–3, 459–60; *Mulholland v. AEC* [2004] HCA 41 (8 September 2004) [9]. [6] *Lange*, n. 2, 558–9.

[7] In contrast, the ACT self-government act and the South Australian, Victorian, New South Wales, and Queensland State constitutions refer expressly to conventional aspects of responsible government.

[8] The Queen's role is now formal and symbolic. The only power she exercises is to appoint the Governor-General (and State Governors) and she does so on the advice of Australian ministers. See *Sue v. Hill* (1999) 199 CLR 462.

[9] Cf. *FAI Insurances v. Winneke* (1982) 151 CLR 342, 364 (Mason J).

[10] On the position in the States more generally, see the magisterial recent work, A. Twomey, *The Constitution of New South Wales* (Federation Press, 2004), Ch 5.

2. Scope of executive authority

The Constitution provides no definition of executive power other than section 61's enigmatic statement that Commonwealth executive power 'extends to the execution and maintenance of this Constitution, and of the laws of the Commonwealth' and a handful of other provisions that vest specific powers in the Governor-General. The principles governing the scope of executive authority must for the most part be found in academic commentary and judicial decisions.

(a) The federal division of executive power

Executive authority is divided between the Commonwealth and the States along the same lines that the Constitution expressly divides legislative authority. Commonwealth executive power 'enables the Crown to undertake all executive action which is appropriate to the position of the Commonwealth under the Constitution and to the spheres of responsibility vested in it by the Constitution'.[11] In addition, Commonwealth executive power extends to matters that are appropriate to 'the character and status of the Commonwealth as a national polity'[12] or can be 'deduced from the existence and character of the Commonwealth as a national government'.[13] This is clearest where there is 'no real competition with State executive or legislative competence'.[14] This power has been held or assumed to authorize celebration of Australia's bicentenary, the designation and protection of national emblems and anthems, the establishment of research institutes, and to support legislation prohibiting sedition.[15]

(b) Scope of powers

What the Commonwealth executive may do within this federally-determined field of competence is determined by:

1. the specific constitutional powers conferred on the executive;
2. the scope of the prerogative (unwritten) powers of the executive;
3. the statutory powers conferred on the executive and the constitutional constraints on such conferral.

(i) Constitutional powers

The Constitution confers specific powers, exercisable in accordance with the advice of ministers, on the Governor-General or the Governor-General in

---

[11] *Barton v. Commonwealth* (1974) 131 CLR 477, 498.
[12] *Davis v. Commonwealth* (1988) 166 CLR 79, 93.
[13] *Victoria v. Commonwealth (AAP Case)* (1975) 134 CLR 338, 397; cf. *ibid.*, 362, 406, 412–3.
[14] *Davis*, n. 12, 93–4.   [15] *Ibid.*, 94–5, 111; *AAP Case*, n. 13, 362.

Council.[16] These powers include the power to summon, prorogue, and dissolve the Parliament (ss. 5, 28, 57); to issue writs for elections (ss. 32, 33); to convene joint sittings of the two Houses (s 57); to assent to legislation (s. 58);[17] and to appoint and remove judges (s. 72).[18] Although these powers must remain vested in the Governor-General, the better view is that the Parliament can validly regulate their exercise and thus subject the potentially arbitrary exercise of executive power to democratic control.[19]

Four exceptional powers, the reserve powers, are exercisable in accordance with constitutional conventions but without the advice of ministers.[20] These powers are the power to appoint a prime minister; to dismiss a prime minister; to refuse to dissolve Parliament; and (most controversially) to force a dissolution of Parliament. The reserve powers give the Governor-General the capacity to protect the Constitution and ensure that the rule of law is maintained by the government.[21] It is debatable whether this is an adequate justification for vesting these powers in an unelected Head of State.[22] Moreover, the infrequency with which the reserve powers have been exercised means that the extent of the powers and the conventions governing their exercise is unclear. The power to dismiss a prime minister or premier, for example, has only been exercised on two occasions, both of which remain controversial.[23] Since the dismissal of the Whitlam government in 1975, an ongoing area of controversy (both political and academic) has been the Governor General's power to dismiss a prime minister who maintains the confidence of the lower house but who lacks support in the Senate and, because of the Senate's power to reject money bills, is unable to obtain supply.[24] In part reflecting this controversy, the 1988 Final Report of the Constitutional Commission declined to adopt the recommendation of its Advisory Committee on the Executive that Parliament codify the reserve powers;[25] similarly the (ultimately unsuccessful) 1999 referendum proposal

[16] The distinction between the executive powers conferred on the Governor-General, and those conferred on the Governor-General in Council is purely 'historical and technical, rather than practical or substantial': J. Quick and R. Garran, *The Annotated Constitution of the Australian Commonwealth* (Legal Books, 1901 (1976 reprint)), 707.

[17] The power under s. 58 to reserve legislation for the Queen's assent is obsolete.

[18] Additionally s. 68 s vests '[t]he command in chief of the naval and military forces of the Commonwealth' in 'the Governor-General as the Queen's representative'.

[19] See generally *Report of the Advisory Committee on Executive Government to the Constitutional Commission*, (Commonwealth of Australia, 1987), 57–9 and the works cited there; L. Zines, *The High Court and the Constitution* (Butterworths, 4th edn, 1997), 271–2.

[20] The conventions are non-justiciable norms derived from historical practice. For a survey, see Republic Advisory Committee, *An Australian Republic: The Options* (Commonwealth Government Printer, 1993), Vol 2, 242–73, 290–5.   [21] Winterton, n. 1, 153–4.

[22] See *ibid.*, 155; Republic Advisory Committee, n. 20, Vol. 2, 246.

[23] The first was the dismissal of the NSW Premier John Lang in 1932 and the second was the dismissal of Prime Minister Gough Whitlam in 1975.

[24] Surveyed in Republic Advisory Committee, n. 20, Vol. 2, 256–63.

[25] Constitutional Commission, *Final Report of the Constitutional Commission*, (Australian Government Publishing Service, Canberra, 1988), Vol. 1, 344–5. The Constitutional Commission was established by the Commonwealth government in 1985 to enquire into and report on revision

that Australia become a republic and the Governor-General be replaced by a President would have preserved but not codified the reserve powers as well as the constitutional conventions governing their exercise.[26] Codification therefore seems unlikely; it is also doubtful that any codification could completely address the complex situations that would call for the exercise of these powers. Though the status quo may be difficult to justify, it is difficult to discern an alternative that is politically feasible.

(ii) The prerogative

In British constitutional theory, the executive government, personified in the Crown, possesses prerogative powers—unwritten powers—that are recognized by the common law. The Commonwealth executive is the creature of the Constitution and its powers are conferred by the Constitution, not the common law.[27] However, as the Republic Advisory Committee wrote:

> In the light of the Constitution's background in British constitutional history and the common law, section 61 has been treated as a shorthand prescription for incorporating the prerogative in the Crown in right of the Commonwealth; so that the full range of executive prerogatives relevant to Commonwealth legislative power is vested in the executive government of the Commonwealth, and the executive power of the Commonwealth, like the (common law) prerogatives, is subject to control by legislation.[28]

In *Federal Commissioner of Taxation v. Official Liquidator of E.O. Farley Ltd.*, Evatt J distinguished three branches of the prerogative: the royal or executive prerogatives, such as the power to declare war or make peace; preferences and immunities, such as the right to be paid in preference to all other creditors; and the proprietary prerogatives, such as the right to escheats and the ownership of the foreshore.[29] In a later case, Brennan J explicitly distinguished between two distinct foundations for executive action, the prerogative powers that are possessed by the executive government alone (such as the power to enter treaties) and the capacities that are also possessed by ordinary citizens (such as the power to enter contracts).[30] That analysis appears to be orthodox in Australia.

Prerogative powers and capacities can be legislatively implemented or, indeed, abrogated or displaced by statute. Accordingly, it is often necessary to identify whether a claimed prerogative power exists and whether it has been relevantly affected by statute.[31] For example, the High Court has held that the executive

---

of the Constitution to reflect Australia's status as an independent national and federal parliamentary democracy, to recognize an appropriate and effective division of federal responsibilities, and to ensure that democratic rights were guaranteed. The Commission was assisted by five Advisory Committees which reported in particular areas of the Constitution.

[26] Constitutional Alteration (Establishment of Republic) Bill 1999 (Cth).
[27] *Johnson v. Kent* (1975) 132 CLR 164, 169 (Barwick CJ); *Barton*, n. 11, 498.
[28] Republic Advisory Committee, n. 20, Vol. 1, 146.   [29] (1940) 63 CLR 278, 320–1.
[30] *Davis*, n. 12, 107–9.
[31] See, e.g. *Johnson v. Kent*, n. 27 (power to build on Crown land); *Barton*, n. 11 above (power to arrange extradition without a treaty).

does not need statutory authority in order to enter into contracts, or at least those contracts that arise 'in the ordinary course of administering a recognized part of the government of the State'.[32] It requires statute only to appropriate the funds necessary to perform the contract. The absence of an appropriation does not prevent judgment being entered against the government.[33] However, the power to enter into contracts may be regulated or displaced by statute, either in relation to particular subject matters or more generally. Then, following the general principles of statutory abrogation, the executive must comply with the terms of the statute.[34]

The most recent and significant case on the existence of an alleged prerogative power and statutory abrogation is *Ruddock v. Vadarlis*.[35] On 26 August 2001, the MV Tampa, a Norwegian commercial vessel, rescued 433 people from a sinking vessel between north-western Australia and Indonesia. Most of these people were asylum seekers from Afghanistan and had been attempting to enter Australia in the vessel from which they were rescued. The Australian government determined that they should not do so and dispatched members of the armed services to board the Tampa. A civil liberties organization and a solicitor commenced proceedings in the Federal Court alleging, in part, that the government's actions amounted to an unlawful detention of the asylum seekers. The government argued in response that its actions were a lawful exercise of its prerogative (non-statutory) executive power to exclude and expel aliens and to detain them for that purpose. In particular, it argued that the detailed statutory provisions regarding the exclusion, expulsion, and detention of aliens had not abrogated the non-statutory executive power and that it was not obliged to rely on the statute to support its actions. (If it were obliged to rely on the statute, it would have had to bring the asylum seekers to Australia and to consider their claims.)

The first question for the Full Court on appeal was whether the prerogative power to exclude and expel aliens (and to detain them in order to do so) still existed or had become obsolete. The majority concluded that the power did exist. French J, who wrote the leading judgment, did not confine himself to the historical record but reasoned that '[t]he scope of the Executive power conferred by s 61 of the *Constitution* is to be measured by reference to Australia's status as a sovereign nation and by reference to the terms of the *Constitution* itself' and that therefore a power to determine who enters Australia must exist and be held directly by the executive.[36] As I have argued elsewhere, the importance to sovereignty and national self-definition of the power to exclude may demonstrate that the power is held by *some* branch of government but it does not demonstrate that it is held by the executive government acting without statutory

---

[32] *NSW v. Bardolph* (1934) 52 CLR 455, 508.   [33] *Ibid.*, 502, 510.
[34] *Brown v. West* (1990) 169 CLR 195; *Vass v. The Commonwealth* (2000) 96 FCR 272.
[35] (2001) 110 FCR 491.   [36] *Ibid.*, 542–3.

authorization.[37] Section 61 cannot be an unlimited reserve of power for the executive to do whatever is in the national interest.[38] There has been some debate as to whether section 61 confers a separate power to maintain the Constitution that is beyond the scope of the prerogative and that, unlike other aspects of executive power, cannot be controlled by Parliament.[39] The preferable view is that it does not.[40]

The second question was whether this power had been abrogated by the *Migration Act 1958* (Cth) or any other legislation. French J concluded that this aspect of the prerogative had not been abrogated by the Migration Act.[41] It appears that, for French J, only direct inconsistency between the statutory regime and the prerogative power would abrogate the prerogative.[42] The better view is rather that the prerogative is abrogated here because the Parliament has 'covered the field'; it has purported to regulate in detail the topic of interdiction, exclusion, and expulsion of unlawful non-citizens.[43] The legitimacy of the exercise of government power depends on its commitment to the forms of legality inherent in the rule of law. It is hardly likely that the Parliament intended that the prerogative continue to operate alongside the statutory regime as an alternative but inconsistent source of power, particularly when the existence and extent of the prerogative power was controversial. The courts should approach questions regarding the prerogative with a view to enhancing rule of law values, including clarity and prospectivity, and democratic accountability rather than executive unilateralism in the service of an ill-defined concept of the national interest.

---

[37] S. Evans, 'The Rule of Law, Constitutionalism and the *MV Tampa*' (2002) 13 *PLR* 94. The text draws on this article. [38] Compare *Ruddock*, n. 35, 501 (Black CJ dissenting).

[39] Winterton, n. 1, 31–4, 95–8.

[40] The Constitution does not contain any provision for its own suspension or abrogation in time of war or public emergency. Nor does it provide explicitly for any expansion in the scope of executive authority or for any greater 'executive unilateralism' at such times. However, members of the Court have been willing to countenance a wider statutory delegation of legislative power to the executive during war time: e.g. *Victorian Stevedoring* (1931) 46 CLR 73, 99, 120–1; *Australian Communist Party v. Commonwealth* (1951) 83 CLR 1, 194–5, 257; *Wishart v. Fraser* (1941) 64 CLR 470. Nonetheless, the *Communist Party Case* shows that even in these periods the High Court regards itself as the ultimate guardian of the federal division effected by the Constitution and of the separation of powers: below, text at n. 44. However, that is little safeguard against overreaching by state executives and a slender safeguard against the Commonwealth.

[41] *Ruddock*, n. 35, 544–6.

[42] *Ibid.*, 545. The judgments use analogies drawn from the Australian constitutional jurisprudence relating to inconsistency between Commonwealth and State laws. See generally Peter Hanks, *Constitutional Law in Australia* (Butterworths, 2nd edn., 1996), 263–82. French J's reasoning was strongly influenced by his view of the prerogative as an aspect of the Executive power of the Commonwealth vested in the Queen under s 61 and not as '[t]he residue of discretionary or arbitrary authority which at any given time is legally left in the hands of the Crown'. As 'a power conferred as part of a negotiated federal compact expressed in a written Constitution' there was 'no place ... for any doctrine that a law made on a particular subject matter is presumed to displace or regulate the operation of the Executive power in respect of that subject matter': *Ruddock*, n. 35, 540.

[43] See especially Migration Act, ss. 245A to 245H, discussed by Black CJ: *Ruddock*, n. 35, 506–8.

(iii) Executive power arising from statute

By far the most important contemporary source of Commonwealth executive power is statute. Nonetheless, the Constitution does impose significant constraints on the powers that can be conferred on the executive by statute.

Some constraints derive from constitutional prohibitions on the substantive content of Commonwealth laws: for example, the requirements that interstate trade and commerce be absolutely free (s. 92) and that the Commonwealth not discriminate between States or parts of States in certain laws (ss. 51(i) and 99).

There is also the federal constraint: Commonwealth executive power is limited (subject to nationhood matters) to the subject matters within the Commonwealth's legislative competence. This is coupled with a constraint derived from the separation of powers[44]: the executive cannot conclusively determine the scope of its own powers.[45] These constraints led the High Court to strike down the Communist Party Dissolution Act 1950 (Cth) in *Australian Communist Party v. Commonwealth*.[46] The nine recitals to the Act aimed to demonstrate that the Act's operative provisions were necessary for 'the security and defence of Australia and for the execution and maintenance of the Constitution and the laws of the Commonwealth' and thus to establish a sufficient link between the Act and the legislative powers with respect to defence (s. 51(vi)) and matters incidental to the execution of the powers vested in the executive government (s. 51(xxxix)). Section 4 of the Act declared the Communist Party to be an unlawful association and provided for it to be dissolved and its property managed by a receiver. Section 5 provided for similar consequences for organizations in various ways linked with the Communist Party where the 'Governor-General [was] satisfied that... the continued existence of [such a body of persons] would be prejudicial to the security and defence of the Commonwealth or to the execution and maintenance of the Constitution or the laws of the Commonwealth'. The Court held that neither the legislative recitals nor the Governor-General's subjective satisfaction could provide the objective link to a constitutional head of power that was required to sustain the legislation.

Other constraints derive from constitutional implications, the most significant of which are the intergovernmental immunities necessary to sustain a federal system of government, the implied freedom of political communication and the doctrine of the separation of powers.

Intergovernmental immunities. State laws cannot validly affect the executive capacities of the Commonwealth though they may affect the exercise of those capacities.[47] Conversely, Commonwealth laws cannot validly single out State

---

[44] See text, n. 48.   [45] *Plaintiff S157/2002 v. Commonwealth* (2003) 211 CLR 476, 505.
[46] *Australian Communist Party*, n. 40.
[47] *Re Residential Tenancies Tribunal (NSW), ex parte Defence Housing Authority* (1997) 190 CLR 410. The distinction between legislation affecting capacities and legislation regulating the exercise of those capacities is rather elusive.

governments or discriminate against them in such a way as to threaten the continued existence of the Commonwealth and the States as constituent entities of the federal compact.[48]

Implied freedom of political communication. The constitutional provisions establishing the system of representative and responsible government 'necessarily imply a limitation on legislative *and executive* power to deny the electors and their representatives information concerning the conduct of the executive branch of government [including public bodies that report directly or through a minister to the Parliament] throughout the life of a federal Parliament'.[49] The limitations on executive power have not yet been explored in any detail. However, in *Bennett v. HREOC*, the Federal Court held that a public service regulation prohibiting disclosure of information of which a public servant has official knowledge was unconstitutional under this principle because it was not appropriate and adapted to a legitimate governmental purpose.[50]

Separation of powers. Sections 1, 61, and 71 of the Constitution (the opening provisions of Chapters I, II, and III of the Constitution) respectively vest legislative, executive, and judicial powers in separate arms of government.[51] On the basis of this structural arrangement, the High Court has inferred a constitutionally entrenched separation of powers. Notwithstanding the constitutional symmetry that is its foundation, the Australian separation of powers doctrine operates asymmetrically and is most concerned to separate the exercise of judicial power from the exercise of executive and legislative powers. That aspect of the doctrine has two limbs:

- First, federal judicial power can only be vested in the courts identified in section 72 of the Constitution (the High Court and courts established by the Commonwealth Parliament—whose members have tenure guaranteed by the Constitution—and certain State courts). Although it has been suggested that the doctrine may develop to provide a substantive guarantee of due process,[52] it seems unlikely to do so except in isolated pockets.[53] For example, the High Court has held that imprisoning people for the purpose of punishment is an essentially judicial function and can only be exercised by the courts.[54] But the executive can imprison aliens as an incident of excluding them from the Australian community and removing them overseas; and this extends to mandatory *indefinite* detention if it is not possible to remove the person from Australia.[55]

[48] See most recently *Austin v. The Commonwealth* (2003) 195 ALR 321.
[49] *Lange*, n. 2, 561 (emphasis added). [50] (2003) 204 ALR 119.
[51] For a general account, see C. Saunders, 'The Separation of Powers', in B. Opeskin and F. Wheeler, *The Australian Federal Judicial System* (Melbourne University Press, 2000), 3.
[52] M. McHugh, 'Does Chapter III of the Constitution Protect Substantive as well as Procedural Rights?' (2001) 21 *Australian Bar Review* 235.
[53] And moreover, with very limited exceptions, the doctrine only applies to the federal level of government. [54] *Lim v. Minister for Immigration* (1992) 176 CLR 1.
[55] *MIMIA v. Al Khafaji* (2004) 208 ALR 201; *Al-Kateb v. Godwin* (2004) 208 ALR 124.

- Secondly, the High Court and other federal courts cannot exercise executive (or legislative) functions, unless they are 'incidental or ancillary' to the exercise of judicial power.[56] However, federal judges can perform executive functions that are conferred on them as persona designata, that is, in their personal capacity rather than as members of a court.[57] There are two provisos. First, the judicial officer must consent to undertake the non-judicial role. And, secondly, the non-judicial function must be constitutionally compatible with the individual judge's judicial function and the operation of the judiciary as an institution.[58] The latter proviso was applied in *Wilson v. Minister*,[59] to invalidate the appointment of a federal judge to prepare a report for the minister under indigenous heritage protection legislation. The majority noted that public confidence in the judiciary is dependent on a strict separation of judicial function from the *political* functions of government.[60] The writing of the report was distinguished from the work of a Royal Commissioner who, although providing advice to the executive, was required to act independently and in accordance with the terms of the legislation authorising the Royal Commission. By contrast, the judge appointed under the heritage legislation became '*part of* the process of the Minister's exercise of power'.[61] And yet the High Court has upheld legislation that empowered judges to grant warrants authorizing investigators to intercept telephone calls.[62]

The doctrine has attracted significant criticism.[63] It has been tested by the growth in tribunals and administrative bodies in response to demands for more accessible, less formal, and less expensive dispute resolution mechanisms. For example, the High Court has held that the Human Rights and Equal Opportunity Commission could validly determine complaints under anti-discrimination legislation; however, as enforceability was a hallmark of judicial power, those determinations could not be made enforceable.[64] And it has proven difficult to identify the scope of judicial power with precision.[65] Judicial power has traditionally been said to involve a binding and authoritative determination of rights by reference to law.[66] However, more recently courts have stated that it is impossible to refer to any 'essential or constant characteristic' of judicial power[67] and have turned to historical practice and conventions for guidance.[68] Some powers take their character from the person or body exercising them and

---

[56] *R. v. Kirby, ex parte Boilermakers Society of Australia* (1956) 94 CLR 254, 296.
[57] *Hilton v. Wells* (1985) 157 CLR 57, 68.
[58] *Grollo v. Palmer* (1995) 184 CLR 348, 364–5. [59] (1996) 189 CLR 1.
[60] *Ibid.*, 16. [61] *Ibid.*, 18 (emphasis added). [62] *Hilton v. Wells*, n. 57; *Grollo*, n. 58.
[63] See, e.g. *R. v. Joske, ex parte Australian Building Construction Employees and Builders' Labourers' Federation* (1974) 130 CLR 87, 90 (Barwick CJ); *Wilson* (1996) 189 CLR 1, 42, 49–50 (Kirby J). [64] *Brandy v. HREOC* (1995) 183 CLR 245.
[65] See, e.g. the balancing of factors approach in *Attorney General v. Breckler* (1999) 197 CLR 83.
[66] *Huddart Parker & Co. v. Moorehead* (1909) 8 CLR 330, 357. [67] *Brandy*, n. 64, 267.
[68] See, e.g., *R v. Davison* (1954) 90 CLR 353, 381–2; *R. v. Trade Practices Tribunal, ex parte Tasmanian Breweries* (1970) 123 CLR 361, 387, 394.

may therefore be exercised by the executive or the courts.[69] Nonetheless the doctrine is well entrenched and precludes (at least at federal level) what might be efficient allocations of power to executive and mixed tribunals.

The asymmetry of the doctrine of the separation of powers is in part a concession to the pragmatic needs of modern government. Few limits have been placed upon the extent to which legislative power can be delegated to the executive. In *Victorian Stevedoring v. Dignan*, the High Court upheld a statutory provision empowering the Governor-General to make regulations with respect to the employment of transport workers.[70] Certain aspects of the employment of transport workers were particularized but the power was not confined to those aspects. The authorizing legislation provided that the regulations 'shall have the force of law' 'notwithstanding anything in [almost] any other Act'. The principle that a delegate may not delegate its powers did not prevent delegation because the legislature is not the delegate of the Australian people or of the Imperial Parliament.[71] And the principle of the separation of powers did not prevent delegation of legislative power, notwithstanding the asymmetry this produces in Australian separation of powers jurisprudence, for pragmatic reasons and because the Constitution was framed against the background of British constitutional practice in which such delegation was accepted.[72] Suggestions that a delegation may be so broad or extensive as to amount to an impermissible abdication of legislative power do not appear likely to operate as a real constraint.[73] However, in a recent case, five members of the High Court have suggested that a provision conferring an open-ended decision-making power on a minister 'would appear to lack [the] hallmark of the exercise of legislative power..., namely, the determination of "the content of a law as a rule of conduct or a declaration as to power, right or duty" '.[74] These comments have perhaps opened the way for reconsideration of the constitutional validity of extensive or wholesale delegation of legislative power to the executive and a strengthened adherence to the doctrine of separation of powers.[75]

(c) Executive power at the state and territory level

The principles relating to the scope of the executive power of State and territory governments are broadly similar. In particular, all operate under the conventions

---

[69] *Precision Data Holdings v. Wills* (1991) 173 CLR 167, 189.   [70] (1931) 46 CLR 73.
[71] G. Lindell, 'Why is Australia's Constitution Binding?—The Reasons in 1900 and Now, and the Effect of Independence' (1986) 16 *FLR* 29 argues that this is not affected if the authority of the Constitution now rests on popular sovereignty. On the authority point, see S. Evans, 'Why is the Constitution Binding? Authority, Obligation and the Role of the People' (2004) 24 *AdelLR* 103.
[72] Evans, n. 71, 100–2, 118–19.   [73] *Ibid.*, 101, 119–20.
[74] *Plaintiff S157/2002*, n. 45 above, 513, quoting *The Commonwealth v. Grunseit* (1943) 67 CLR 58, 82.
[75] See further, D. Meyerson, 'Rethinking the Constitutionality of Delegated Legislation' (2003) 11 *AJAL* 45.

of responsible government. The State constitutions and the self-government legislation of the Northern Territory have the effect that executive power is exercisable by the Governor or Administrator; however, in the Australian Capital Territory, executive power is vested directly in the executive comprised of the chief minister and ministers.[76] The State constitutions and territory self-government acts do not entrench a separation of powers that prevents executive powers from being exercised by their courts;[77] however, the federal doctrine prevents the exercise of executive and legislative powers by State and territory courts where that would be incompatible with the exercise of federal judicial power by the same courts, and in particular where it would be incompatible with appearance of independence and impartiality required for the exercise of such power.[78]

An issue of contemporary significance is the effect on national and cooperative schemes of the distinction between the federal and State executives.[79] In *Duncan*,[80] the High Court upheld Commonwealth and State legislation that established a joint tribunal for settling disputes in the coal industry. The tribunal could exercise powers derived from the Commonwealth legislation or from the State legislation as was appropriate in any particular case. More recently, the Court's decision in *R v. Hughes* indicated some limits to such joint appointments. The Commonwealth can consent to officers who hold Commonwealth statutory appointments also performing State functions and accepting State appointments in addition to their Commonwealth functions and appointments.[81] However, where a Commonwealth law not only expresses the Commonwealth's consent to such an appointment but also imposes a duty to perform functions created and conferred on the officer by State law, the Commonwealth law must be supported by a Commonwealth head of legislative power. But that may not be possible—the very point of the cooperative scheme, such as the corporations scheme considered in *R. v. Hughes*, may be to fill gaps in the Commonwealth's legislative competence. The decision in *Hughes* was based on a formal analysis of Commonwealth legislative power but the pattern of joint appointments clearly raises the possibility of unclear lines of authority and political accountability through the principles of responsible government. That issue has not been fully explored by the High Court, although it was noted in passing in the judgment in *Bond v. The Queen*.[82] Zines has argued that this is a political risk that the Parliaments of the federation are competent to undertake and the courts should not invalidate such schemes on the basis of a rigid conception of responsible government.[83] But that is a view that the High Court

---

[76] Australian Capital Territory (Self-Government) Act 1988 (Cth), ss 36–9.
[77] *Kable v. DPP (NSW)* (1996) 189 CLR 51.
[78] *North Australian Aboriginal Legal Aid Service v. Bradley* (2004) 206 ALR 315.
[79] G. Hill, 'Will the High Court "*Wakim*" Chapter II of the *Constitution*?' (2003) 31 *FLR* 445.
[80] *R v. Duncan; Ex parte Australian Iron & Steel* (1983) 158 CLR 535.
[81] *R v. Hughes* (2000) 202 CLR 535, 553. [82] (2000) 201 CLR 213, 219.
[83] Zines, n. 19, 271.

might be unwilling to adopt if the legislation is as complex and impenetrable as that considered in these cases[84] so that it is implausible to assume that each Parliament has a clear understanding of what it has enacted. Parliamentary scrutiny may also be attenuated in such cases if the legislation is presented to the various Parliaments as the outcome of an agreement between the executive governments of the federation which each Parliament may accept, or reject (at the cost of losing transfer payments from the central government), but not amend.[85]

3. Accountability through Parliament

Under the doctrine of responsible government, ministers are individually and collectively responsible to the Parliament and can only retain office while they have the 'confidence' of the lower House.[86] The doctrine provides a mechanism by which ministers are held accountable through Parliament to the people for the governmental powers they exercise and the public funds they spend.[87]

On all but one occasion, in accordance with the conventional principles of *collective* responsibility, votes of no confidence in the prime minister or government as a whole have resulted in the resignation of the government.[88] However, as the Constitutional Commission pointed out, the power balance between Parliament and the executive is clearly weighted in favour of the latter:[89] party discipline ensures that in all but extraordinary circumstances,[90] the lower house will support the executive drawn from the ranks of the party or parties controlling that house. While political parties may be the 'only machinery we have for the formulation of policies that can be presented to the people for democratic choice',[91] their existence also tends to limit the effectiveness of responsible government.

---

[84] E.g. *Hughes*, n. 81, 576.
[85] Working Party of Representatives of Scrutiny of Legislation Committees throughout Australia, *Scrutiny of National Schemes of Legislation* (Position Paper), (Commonwealth of Australia, 1996).
[86] *FAI Insurances*, n. 9, 364 (Mason J); Constitutional Commission, n. 25, [2.185].
[87] On accountability through the Parliament, see generally J. Uhr, *Deliberative Democracy in Australia: The Changing Place of Parliament* (Cambridge University Press, 1998).
[88] Lindell, n. 1, 77. The exceptional case followed the Governor-General's dismissal of the Whitlam Labour government and the appointment of the caretaker Fraser Conservative government in 1975. The Labour opposition retained a majority in the House of Representatives and secured passage of a no confidence motion in the hours before the minority Fraser government advised the Governor-General to dissolve the House. The Fraser government was returned at the ensuing election. See I. Harris (ed), *House of Representatives Practice* (Department of the House of Representatives, 4th edn, 2001), 316. [89] Constitutional Commission, n. 25 [2.233].
[90] Which might include the breakdown of a coalition or independent members withdrawing their support for a minority government. The latter is more likely in State Parliaments.
[91] Constitutional Commission, n. 25 [2.236].

Individual ministerial responsibility holds that ministers are individually responsible to Parliament for their own acts and omissions in the administration of their departments, including those of government officials acting on their behalf, and requires that they must resign if they lose the confidence of the House.[92] However, this is an idealization of a political practice that is more complex and pragmatic.[93] Ministers have resigned on a number of occasions over personal misconduct, their inability to support government policy or their failure to supervise their department—even these cases are relatively infrequent.[94] But as Thompson and Tillotsen's analysis shows, 'ministerial resignation is not expected for departmental maladministration';[95] rather, they argue, resignation is primarily a political damage limitation strategy.[96]

It is sometimes argued that this reflects a diminution of the Parliament's capacity to function as an accountability mechanism, perhaps brought on by the size and complexity of modern government and a more general debilitation of Parliament under a rigid party system,[97] and that this requires the creation of extra-parliamentary accountability mechanisms. Harry Evans, clerk of the Senate since 1988, disagrees. For him, 'accountability is essentially a political process' that consists of 'public exposure of matters that affect the public perception of government'; extra-parliamentary mechanisms can only be successful 'to the extent that they expose matters that threaten to turn the public perception of governments':[98]

In spite of its debilitation, ... parliament is the key to maintaining accountability, even through extra-parliamentary bodies, because it is the principal forum of the political process and because accountability relies ultimately on the political process.[99]

---

[92] In practice, votes of censure in the Senate have not led to ministerial resignations.

[93] Compare R. Mulgan, 'On Ministerial Resignations (and the Lack Thereof)' (2002) 61 *AJPA* 121.   [94] Lindell, n. 1, 95.

[95] It is debatable whether it ever did, outside of the tidy rules formulated by constitutional theorists, or was ever appropriate once departments grew beyond an extension of the minister. But the current approach raises the risk of an accountability vacuum in those cases where the failure is neither solely the department's nor the minister's but represents the failure of a large, complex system caused by multiple (perhaps trivial) errors: compare in another field entirely C. Perrow, *Normal Accidents* (Princeton University Press, 1984).

[96] E. Thompson and G. Tillotsen, 'Caught in the Act: The Smoking Gun View of Ministerial Responsibility' (1999) 58 *AJPA* 48, 57. An emerging practice is of ministerial advisers being sacked in a way that was 'not consistent with normal performance management or disciplining of an employee, but was being imposed as a substitute for sanctions against a responsible minister': The Senate, Finance and Public Administration References Committee, *Staff Employed Under the Members of Parliament (Staff) Act 1984* (2003) 21 (Advisers Report).

[97] H. Evans, 'Parliament and Extra-Parliamentary Accountability Institutions' (1999) 58 *AJPA* 87, 87.   [98] *Ibid.*, 88.

[99] *Ibid.*, 89. Several governments have promulgated codes of ministerial conduct: see, e.g. Department of Prime Minister, *A Guide on Key Elements of Ministerial Conduct*, (Canberra, 1998). *Greiner v. Independent Commission Against Corruption* (1992) 28 NSWLR 125 revealed the lack of clear standards by which the Commission could determine that ministerial conduct was corrupt; the relevant legislation was amended to provide that a prescribed code of conduct could provide such standards. A code of conduct for parliamentarians has been prescribed; no separate code for ministers has been prescribed. On codes for public servants, see Kinley, n. 4.

There are three principal parliamentary mechanisms in which this political process is played out: Question Time, the work of parliamentary committees, and the exercise of the power to require the executive to produce documents.[100]

(a) Question Time

Question Time is a period of approximately one hour set aside on most sitting days in both Houses to allow questions without notice to be put to ministers. In principle, it represents the principal opportunity for the Parliament to obtain the information needed to keep the executive accountable to the Parliament. All available ministers attend Question Time.[101] In the House of Representatives, the Speaker alternates the call between non-government and government Members.[102] In the Senate, the President is expected to allocate the call as proportionally as is practicable amongst the various parties, groups, and independent senators.[103]

Many commentators doubt the ability of Question Time to hold the executive accountable. For example, Jaensch claims that the practice of 'confrontation politics' in Australian parliaments means that Question Time has become 'less a process of seeking and giving information than a chance for scoring partisan points'.[104] Instead of providing an opportunity for members to scrutinize, criticize, and press for government action, it becomes a time for 'political opportunism'.[105] As Prime Minister Keating famously observed, Question Time is 'a courtesy extended to the House by the Executive branch of government'.[106]

Opposition parties have joined commentators in proposing that the presiding officers, and in particular the Speaker, follow the British tradition and resign from their political party when they are chosen as presiding officer and that they

---

[100] The work of the Senate in scrutinizing delegated legislation is less often political. Most delegated legislation must be tabled in both Houses of Parliament. The Senate Regulations and Ordinances Committee scrutinizes each instrument to ensure (Standing Order 23(3)):

(a) that it is in accordance with the statute;
(b) that it does not trespass unduly on personal rights and liberties;
(c) that it does not unduly make the rights and liberties of citizens dependent upon administrative decisions which are not subject to review of their merits by a judicial or other independent tribunal; and
(d) that it does not contain matter more appropriate for parliamentary enactment.

The scrutiny process may lead the Senate to disallow delegated legislation: see the Legislative Instruments Act 2003 (Cth). On occasions, government has resorted to delegated legislation when it has been unable to persuade the Senate to pass primary legislation only to have the Senate disallow the delegated legislation, sometimes repeatedly: e.g. G. Sawer, *Australian Federal Politics and Law 1929–1949*, (Melbourne University Press, 1963), 30–1.

[101] A rostering system was briefly observed in the House under Sessional Orders in 1994. [102] Harris (ed.), n. 88, 518.

[103] H. Evans (ed.), *Odgers' Australian Senate Practice* (Canberra Department of the Senate, 10th edn., 2001), 503.

[104] D. Jaensch, *The Politics of Australia* (South Melbourne, 2nd edn, 1997), 110. See also Uhr, n. 87, 198–9. [105] Harris (ed), n. 88, 515.

[106] Quoted in Uhr, n. 87, 198.

not be challenged at subsequent elections.[107] However, these parties have unsurprisingly lost enthusiasm for the proposal when they have won government. There is little prospect of the current practice changing, except perhaps to the extent of presiding officers no longer attending meetings of their parliamentary party. Australian parliaments are significantly smaller than the Westminster Parliament and reserving a seat for an independent Speaker could affect the ability of a party to form government and, in any event, would be of doubtful constitutionality. Moreover, it is unlikely that such a change would significantly affect the capacity of Question Time in the House to contribute to executive accountability. The real barriers to Question Time performing a meaningful accountability function are the prevailing political culture, government control of the House, and to some extent the Standing Orders that are 'specifically designed to enable the governing party to maintain the initiative and facilitate its control over the business of the House and debate'.[108]

Until recently, there has been a greater likelihood for executive accountability to be achieved through Question Time in the Senate. The governing party rarely has control of the Senate and the President is often a member of a non-government party. The Senate's Standing Orders place a time limit on questions and answers. But even in the Senate there is no obligation on ministers to *answer* questions.[109] And as a result of the November 2004 election, the government will control the Senate from July 2005, for the first time since 1981.

(b) Committees

In contrast to Question Time, the parliamentary committee system, particularly in the Senate,[110] remains an important and reasonably effective mechanism for ensuring executive accountability.

---

[107] E.g. B. Snedden, 'Ministers in Parliament—A Speaker's Eye View', in P. Weller and D. Jaensch (eds), *Responsible Government in Australia* (Drummond Publishing, 1980), 68, 82; P. Cotton, 'Masters of the House' (2002) 11 *About the House* 8. For a survey see M. Healy, *The Independence of the Speaker* (1997) Parliament of Australia, Parliamentary Library, Research Paper No. 38, 1997–98, available at http://www.aph.gov.au/library/pubs/rn/1997-98/98rn38.htm at 28 July 2004.

[108] Snedden, n. 107, 68, 69, citing B. Snedden, 'The Speaker of the Australian House of Representatives' (1978) 59(4) *Parliamentarian*.

[109] Moreover there is nothing to prevent a minister in one House refusing to answer a question on the basis that it is more appropriately directed to a minister in the other House or to officials who will be appearing at a Committee of the other House. See, e.g. House of Representatives, Hansard. 15 February 2005, 1–5, where the Prime Minister referred a series of questions concerning the interrogation of Iraqi prisoners to the Defence Minister Senator Robert Hill.

[110] The House of Representatives and Joint Committees should not be overlooked, notwithstanding their government majorities. The principal House of Representatives Committees are the (currently thirteen) standing Committees established by resolution of the House in each Parliament and allocated particular subject matters (from Aboriginal and Torres Strait Islander Affairs to Transport and Regional Services). They have power to enquire and report into matters referred to them by the House or a minister. There are also the usual committees responsible for the workings of the House (e.g. the Procedure Committee and the Privileges Committee). The most important Joint

The most visible aspects of committee work, and among the most important for executive accountability, are the enquiries conducted by the Senate's eight standing legislation committees into budget estimates and the annual reports of agencies.[111] Estimates Committees base their work on the proposed expenditure items listed in the Budget Statements and the Additional Estimates Statements (produced in May and November respectively) and on the Annual Reports of agencies that must be tabled by 31 October each year.[112] The responsible minister, or his or her representative in the Senate, and officers of the relevant agencies appear before public meetings of the Committees to answer questions. Questions must be relevant to estimates of expenditure but this is interpreted as allowing questions relating to past performance, particularly as revealed by annual reports. Estimates Committees can only seek explanations for particular items of expenditure or proposed expenditure; the Standing Orders prevent them from conducting a more open-ended enquiry into agency programmes and performance. They can (at least in principle) call particular officers as witnesses and do not have to depend on ministers making officers available. The Auditor-General and officers of the Australian National Audit Office can brief committees on audit matters or comment on audit reports raised in committee hearings.[113] And the Committees have resisted attempts to limit scrutiny of statutory authorities.[114]

Committees include the Joint Committee of Public Accounts and Audit, established under statute and responsible, amongst other things, for examining the financial affairs of Commonwealth authorities: reviewing reports of the Auditor-General; considering the operations and resources of the Australian National Audit Office; and approving or rejecting the appointment of the Auditor-General; and the Joint Standing Committee on Treaties which interposes some measure of parliamentary scrutiny of international treaties between the otherwise purely executive acts of signature and ratification.

[111] Standing Order 25 establishes eight pairs of committees, a references committee and a legislation committee responsible for particular subject areas. In addition to their estimates and other accountability-oriented work, the legislation committees enquire into proposed legislation before the Senate. This paragraph draws on Evans (ed), n.103, 379ff. See also Uhr, n. 87, 178–90, on the contribution of the Joint Public Accounts and Audit Committee.

[112] The annual report accountability framework is established by the Commonwealth Authorities and Companies Act 1997 (Cth) and the Financial Management and Accountability Act 1997 (Cth).

[113] The Auditor-General is an independent officer of the Parliament, appointed under the Auditor-General Act 1997 (Cth) whose statutory responsibilities include:

- auditing financial statements of agencies, Commonwealth companies, and authorities and their subsidiaries;
- conducting performance audits of agencies, Commonwealth companies, and authorities (other than GBEs unless requested to do so);
- reviewing 'a particular aspect of the operations of the whole or part of the Commonwealth public sector'.

The Constitution Act 1975(Vic) was amended in 2003 to entrench the independence of the Victorian Auditor-General, in response to threats to the independence of the office under earlier governments: for context see C. Clark and M. De Martinis, 'A Framework for Reforming the Independence and Accountability of Statutory Officers of Parliament: A Case Study of Victoria' (2003) 62 *AJPA* 32.

[114] Evans, n. 103, 498, 512 ('there are no areas of expenditure of public funds where these corporations have a discretion to withhold details or explanations from Parliament or its committees' summarizing a 1971 committee resolution).

While the committee system in general, and Estimates Committees in particular, clearly have enormous potential to hold the executive to account, they also suffer a number of significant limitations.

• First, the most effective committee system is located in the Senate, primarily because the governing party usually does not control this House and (in most cases) parties are represented on committees in proportion to their representation in the House or Houses from which the Committee is drawn. However, the lack of governing party control is simultaneously the source of the principal weakness of the Senate committee system. No matter how thorough or detailed Senate committee scrutiny of government activity is, there is no obligation upon the government to take committee reports into account, let alone abide by committee recommendations. And, as already noted, from July 2005, for the first time since 1981, the government will control the Senate. The implications for the structure, membership, financing and work of Senate Committees remain to be seen.

• Secondly, the Parliament and hence its committees are predominantly made up of members of major political parties. Given the strength of party discipline, some committees replay the confrontational politics that typifies Question Time in the House.[115]

• Finally, there are restrictions on committees' power to compel ministers, staff, and officers to attend and answer questions. Ministers who are members of the House of Representatives (and former ministers who were members of the House) have asserted that they are not obliged to appear before committees of the Senate.[116] More controversially, this immunity has been asserted to extend to ministerial staff.[117] Officers may not be asked to give opinions on matters of policy, other than (with the minister's consent) to explain its background.[118] They may invoke an executive or Crown privilege against disclosing certain sensitive material.[119] And ministers can direct officers and agencies not to appear at or make submissions to committee enquiries.[120] Unless the Senate is willing

---

[115] The tradition in some Committees (particularly the Scrutiny of Bills and Regulations and Ordinances Committees) is different.

[116] Select Committee on a Certain Maritime Incident, Senate, *A Certain Maritime Incident* (Commonwealth of Australia, 2002) ('CMI Report'), 180–1. Lindell has argued in support of this immunity, in so far as the Senate seeks to investigate matters connected with the minister's membership of the House *or in respect of which the Minister could be held to account in the House*, on the basis that the two Houses are equal and independent: (2002) 17 *Australasian Parliamentary Review* 111–30.   [117] CMI Report, n. 116, 180–1.

[118] Department of Prime Minister and Cabinet, *Government Guidelines for Official Witnesses before Parliamentary Committees and Related Matters—November 1989*, available at http://www.pmc.gov.au/pdfs/OfficialWitness.pdf at 19 August 2004.

[119] See G. Lindell, 'Parliamentary Inquiries and Government Witnesses' (1995) 20 *MULR* 383. A minority party Bill that would have given the Federal Court to arbitrate on such immunity claims was not supported by government or opposition: see Uhr, n. 87, 202–3.

[120] E.g. CMI Report, n. 116, 193.

to confront the executive directly and impose its blunt powers to hold officers in contempt,[121] its enquires may be thwarted or rendered politically irrelevant.

(c) Document production

Both the Senate and the House have the power to make an order requesting that documents be tabled.[122] The power is regularly exercised by the Senate[123] and constitutes one of the 'most significant procedures available to the Senate to deal with matters of public interest giving rise to questions of ministerial accountability'.[124] Of particular interest for executive accountability are the standing requests by the Senate that the government table regularly (a) a list of all statutory provisions that have not been proclaimed and come into operation, reasons that those provisions have not been proclaimed, and a timetable for when they will come into effect; (b) up-to-date indexes of departmental and agency files, facilitating requests for specific documents by the Senate and under freedom of information legislation; and (c) details of government contracts worth more than $100,000 including the reasons for any confidentiality provisions contained in each contract. Refusals by the government to comply with such orders are relatively rare.[125] However, to date, the Senate has not taken measures beyond censure of the government for failure to produce documents. It is unclear whether the Senate might be prepared to punish the government for not tabling a document, or to consider refusal as a contempt of the Senate. The willingness of opposition parties to extend parliamentary accountability mechanisms is often subject to the calculation that those mechanisms might be turned on those parties when in government.[126]

(d) Obstacles to responsible government and accountability through Parliament

The traditional doctrine of responsible government rests on a hierarchical but tightly coupled conception of governmental power and accountability. Under

---

[121] *Ibid.*, 181–2.
[122] House of Representatives, Standing Order 316; Senate, Standing Order 164.
[123] Evans, n. 103, 454.
[124] *Ibid.*, 460. All State parliaments with the exception of New South Wales have legislated to prescribe the privileges of their houses, including orders for documents to be produced. The lack of a statutory power in New South Wales led to the decision in *Egan v. Willis*, n. 4, in which the High Court held that the Constitution Act 1902 (NSW) gave effect to the (evolving) principles of responsible government such that it was reasonably necessary for the discharge of the Legislative Council's functions that it have the power to require a minister to produce documents to the House. *Egan v. Chadwick* (1999) NSWLR 563 held that that power extended to documents subject to legal professional privilege but not to cabinet documents. See generally Bradley Selway, 'Mr Egan, The Legislative Council and Responsible Government', in A. Stone and G. Williams (eds), *The High Court at the Crossroads* (Federation Press, 2000), 35.   [125] Evans, n. 103, 454.
[126] E.g. Selway, n. 124, fn 4. Some state governments now publish significant contracts as a matter of course: see, e.g. http://www.contracts.vic.gov.au at 2 September 2004.

this conception, ministers are the agents of the state (personified in the Crown) and they act through hierarchically organized Departments of State that have no separate legal existence from the minister. Ministers are in turn responsible to the Parliament for their own actions and those of their departments; through the Parliament they are ultimately responsible to the people. The political mechanisms of accountability described above that rest on this conception of government face challenges from changes in the structure and operation of government. Here, I consider three such changes: what I shall call government-at-arm's-length, the increasing number and role of ministerial advisers, and the use of inter-departmental task forces.

(i) Government-at-arm's-length

Australia, following a worldwide trend, has attempted to reduce the size of government and to improve the quality of government services by increased use of independent statutory authorities and government business enterprises (GBEs) and through 'outsourcing' the provision of services to contractors. Government retains the responsibility for policy development—and of course funding—but independent government agencies or private sector bodies deliver the actual services. One impact is a shift from the traditional process-oriented government accountability measures to the outcomes-oriented ('bottom-line') accountability measures associated with the private sector. This tracks other changes in public sector accountability measures, in particular the shift to accrual accounting and appropriations of funds to support the delivery of particular outcomes, in place of the traditional cash accounting and appropriations of funds to support budgeted expenditures.[127] There is also an almost inevitable (and intentional) reduction in the scope of ministerial accountability corresponding to the reduction in the minister's capacity to direct the operations of the authority or GBE or the performance of the contract. This might lead to a bifurcation of responsibility under which ministers are responsible to Parliament, for example, for the decision to contract and the terms of the contract and the contractor is responsible for decisions taken under the contract. In practice, however, this bifurcation is not clearly observed, in part, as Mulgan observes, in the case of outsourcing because the contracts themselves are often 'open-ended, relational contracts of the partnership style'[128] that 'rely on building shared values and shared responsibility for outcomes'.[129] Equally, governments have

---

[127] See generally Commonwealth Parliament, Joint Committee of Public Accounts and Audit, *Review of the Financial Management and Accountability Act 1997 and the Commonwealth Authorities and Companies Act 1997* (Commonwealth of Australia, 2000).

[128] R. Mulgan, 'Accountability Issues in the New Model of Governance', ANU Asia Pacific School of Economics and Government, Discussion Paper No. 91, April 2002, http://apseg.anu.edu.au/pogo/pogo_pub.php at 14 August 2004, 10.

[129] *Ibid.* See, e.g. the Commonwealth Ombudsman's comments on the immigration detention centre management relationship between the Department of Immigration and Multicultural Affairs and Australasian Correctional Management: Commonwealth Ombudsman, *Report of an Own*

found it difficult to avoid political responsibility for the operational activities of GBEs.

The two further changes that I noted above in government structure noted above came to the fore in the Children Overboard affair. On 7 October 2001, at the beginning of an election campaign, the Minister for Immigration claimed publicly that 'a number of children had been thrown overboard' from a vessel carrying asylum-seekers after it had been intercepted by the Australian Defence Force. The claim was in fact untrue. Soon after it was first made, it was known to be untrue (or not positively known to be true) by public servants, defence force officers, and ministerial advisers. Nonetheless, the claim was repeated by other senior ministers during the election campaign (apparently for political advantage). It was not withdrawn until much later. The Report of the Senate Select Committee into the affair (the Certain Maritime Incident (CMI) Report) found that this incident demonstrated that traditional mechanisms for ensuring executive accountability no longer operated adequately, in particular, given the increase in numbers and responsibilities of ministers' personal advisers and the workings of inter-departmental task-forces.[130]

(ii) Ministerial advisers

The number of ministerial staff has roughly doubled in the past thirty years and each minister today generally employs around six to eight advisers, as well as a number of additional support staff.[131] Advisers were traditionally regarded as facilitating the relationship between department and minister. More recently they have come to play key roles in policy development and implementation. Three aspects of the role and behaviour of advisers in communicating with departments and officials drew attention in the CMI Report.

First, the instructions given by advisers to officials and defence force officers compromised the political impartiality of the public service and defence force:

[R]ather than ministerial advisers serving as a political buffer limiting the risk of politically partisan activity on the part of the public service, they are increasingly interventionist in ways that embroil agencies improperly as means to advisers' politically partisan ends.[132]

Secondly, advisers were communicating directly with officials outside the hierarchical lines of authority and accountability within the public service.

Thirdly, rather than acting as conduits for information between the public service and the minister, advisers were actively filtering the information that minister received from the public service and making decisions that were not

Motion Investigation into The Department of Immigration and Multicultural Affairs' Immigration Detention Centres, (2001), 24–5.

[130] CMI Report, n. 116 above.   [131] *Ibid.*, 173–5; Advisers Report, n. 96 above, 11.
[132] CMI Report, n. 116 above, 177.

necessarily known to or approved by the minister.[133] Officials could not rely on the previously safe assumption that information given to (and instructions received from) an adviser would reach (or ultimately come from) the minister.

The latter changes are perhaps necessary given 'the number and urgency of demands for information', as a former head of the Public Service put it.[134] But it does point towards a 'serious accountability vacuum',[135] particularly if advisers are 'wielding executive power in their own right'.[136] In that case, it would be appropriate that they be required to give an account of their conduct to the Parliament even if the ultimate responsibility remains with ministers. The government has asserted that ministerial advisers do not have to appear before Senate committees to fulfil such an accountability obligation because, first, it would dilute the responsibility of ministers if advisers had their own accountability obligations and, secondly, it would undermine the confidential relationship that exists between a minister and his or her staff and is essential to the provision of frank advice.[137] Such assertions of immunity become particularly problematic when ministers maintain that they were not provided with accurate information by their advisers (and thus cannot themselves be called to account) and yet refuse to allow their advisers to be questioned.[138] In the case of the Children Overboard affair, the relevant ministers took no action to hold advisers accountable for providing inaccurate information.[139]

The CMI Report noted the similarities between current debates over the appearance of ministerial advisers before Senate committees and debates twenty-five years ago over the appearance of public servants.[140] The appearance of public servants before committees is 'now quite routine'[141] and does not attenuate ministerial responsibility providing that it is understood that public servants (and advisers) appear only to provide information relevant to holding ministers responsible for their actions and not to be held independently to account.[142] The Senate Finance and Public Administration References Committee has recently recommended that a code of conduct for ministerial advisers be developed and that the government make ministerial staff available to appear before parliamentary committees where:

(a) A minister has renounced, or distanced him or herself from, a staff member's action that is relevant to the committee's Terms of Reference;
(b) A minister has refused to appear to answer questions regarding the conduct of a member of their staff;

---

[133] A particularly dangerous development given the precarious tenure of Departmental Secretaries (see J. Richardson, 'Defenceless Secretaries' (2000) 97 *Canberra Bulletin of Public Administration* 5) and the risk of group-think exposed in the The Butler Report: *Review of Intelligence on Weapons of Mass Destruction*, (The Stationery Office, 2004), 16, 110.
[134] Michael Keating, 'In the Wake of "A Certain Maritime Incident": Ministerial Advisers, Departments and Accountability' (2003) 62 *AJPA* 92, 94.   [135] CMI Report, n. 116, 173.
[136] *Ibid.*, 180.   [137] *Ibid.*, 177–8.   [138] Keating, n. 134, 92, 92–3.
[139] Cf. earlier decisions to sack advisers: CMI Report, n. 116, 193.   [140] *Ibid.*, 178.
[141] *Ibid.*   [142] Advisers Report, n. 96, 40.

(c) Critical or important information or instructions have emanated from a minister's office but not from the minister;
(d) Critical or important information or instructions have been received by a minister's office but not communicated to the minister; or
(e) A government program is administered to a significant extent by [advisers].[143]

(iii) Joined up government

While there has always been some degree of cooperation between government agencies, there is now growing demand for departments to adopt 'whole of government' or 'joined up' approaches, involving inter-departmental committees, taskforces, and so on. These approaches, which draw on multiple lines of authority, present challenges for the traditional model of accountability, which tracks a single line of authority upwards through the bureaucratic hierarchy and ultimately through the minister to Parliament.

One commentator, Considine, has argued that accountability must now be exercised horizontally, between government departments, as well as vertically so that accountability involves 'the appropriate exercise of a navigational competence: that is, the proper use of authority to range freely across a multi-relationship terrain in search of the most advantageous path to success'.[144] He urges replacing 'lines of accountability' with a 'culture of responsibility'.[145] I find this prescription rather opaque. However, Considine's language was adopted by the CMI Report in its analysis of the People Smuggling Taskforce (PST), an inter-departmental committee formed in response to the arrival of several boatloads of asylum seekers in mid-2001,[146] which was instrumental in passing on inaccurate information regarding the 'children overboard' incident.

What might a 'culture of responsibility' have contributed to the work of the PST? Some of the matters identified by the CMI Report reflect a simple failure to implement risk management and accountability procedures for the PST that were well established within the individual departments that contributed to the PST: '[b]asic record-keeping, monitoring and risk management procedures'.[147] Others reflect a failure to agree on 'a clear governance framework which ... defines accountability and reporting arrangements'[148] before the PST embarked on its substantive business. The CMI Report argued futher that the proper accountability arrangement for the PST was 'not simply a line ... to the Prime Minister' but 'should have embraced the departments who both informed the PST and had to implement the decisions which arose from its advice'.[149] This is what it saw as a

---

[143] *Ibid.*, 40, 59.
[144] M. Considine, 'The End of the Line? Accountable Government in the Age of Networks, Partnerships and Joined-Up Services' (2002) 15 *Governance* 21, 22.   [145] *Ibid.*, 23.
[146] The CMI Report also discussed how in practice the dual leadership of the Australian Defence Organisation by the Secretary of the Department and the Chief of the Defence Force cut across traditional distinctions between operational and bureaucratic responsibilities and led to confusion of responsibilities: n. 116, 151–8.   [147] *Ibid.*, 172.
[148] *Ibid.*, 171.   [149] *Ibid.*

'culture of responsibility'. But what this arrangement involves is rather unclear. In order to make the 'culture of responsibility' real, it is necessary to specify the nature of the accountabilities involved[150]—not least, who is accountable, to whom, for what, and by what mechanism—and to recognize that there may be different strands within the bundle of accountabilities to which different answers apply.[151]

4. Accountability through the courts

In this section I outline the extent to which the exercise of executive power can be held to account by means of judicial review.[152]

(a) Judicial review under the Constitution

Section 75 of the Constitution confers original jurisdiction on the High Court in matters in which any of three named administrative law remedies (writs of mandamus, prohibition, or an injunction[153]) are sought against an officer of the Commonwealth (s. 75(v)) and in matters 'in which the Commonwealth, or a person suing or being sued on behalf of the Commonwealth, is a party' (s. 75(iii)). The framers thus guaranteed 'that there is an entrenched jurisdiction to deal with the validity of Commonwealth legislation and executive action'.[154] In *Bank of NSW v. Commonwealth*, Dixon J said that section 75(v) was drafted 'to make it constitutionally certain that there would be a jurisdiction capable of restraining officers of the Commonwealth from exceeding Federal power'.[155]

Section 75(v) jurisprudence, and Australian administrative law more generally, is profoundly influenced by this rule of law reasoning (to which I return below) and by the doctrine of the separation of powers.

The Australian separation of powers doctrine results in a sharp demarcation between judicial review, which addresses only the legality of executive

---

[150] See generally R. Mulgan, *Holding Power to Account: Accountability in Modern Democracies* (Palgrave Macmillan, 2003), in particular Ch 1.

[151] For example, accountability by the provision of information might be diffused while accountability by way of remedies and sanctions might remain within one hierarchical line.

[152] Two other points about accountability through the courts should be noted. First, s. 75 of the Constitution removes the Commonwealth executive's immunity from suit. Legislation does so in each of the States. Secondly, in *Bropho v. WA* (1990) 171 CLR 1, the High Court overturned the presumption that legislation does not bind the Crown.

[153] Mandamus is an order compelling a decision-maker to perform a duty; prohibition prevents a decision-maker from acting in excess of jurisdiction; public law injunctions can perform either function and unlike the constitutional writs of mandamus and prohibition may be available in cases of non-jurisdictional error.

[154] L. Zines, 'Federal, Associated and Accrued Jurisdiction', in B. Opeskin and F. Wheeler (eds), n. 51, 265, 269. The rule of law was identified as an implied constitutional assumption by Dixon J in *Australian Communist Party*, n. 40, 193. For later citations, see D. Kerr and G. Williams, 'Review of Executive Action and the Rule of Law under the Australian Constitution' (2003) 14 *PubLR* 219.

[155] (1948) 76 CLR 1, 363. See also *Deputy Commissioner of Taxation v. Richard Walter* (1994) 183 CLR 168, 178–9.

decision-making, and administrative review, which in addition addresses the merits of executive decision-making. The principal manifestation of this demarcation is the obvious one of allocation of functions to institutions.[156] The federal courts perform judicial review and cannot perform administrative review. Brennan J's dictum in *Attorney General v. Quin* is often quoted:

The duty and jurisdiction of the court to review administrative action do not go beyond the declaration and enforcing of the law which determines the limits and governs the exercise of the repository's power. If, in so doing, the court avoids administrative injustice or error, so be it; but the court has no jurisdiction simply to cure administrative injustice or error. The merits of administrative action, to the extent that they can be distinguished from legality, are for the repository of the relevant power and, subject to political control, for the repository alone.[157]

The demarcation also carries over into the *manner* in which the courts perform judicial review and have developed the common law grounds of judicial review.

• Courts have continued to distinguish between jurisdictional and non-jurisdictional errors made by executive decision-makers—jurisdictional errors raise issues of legality whereas non-jurisdictional errors go to the merits and are not the concern of the courts.[158]

• Courts are markedly reluctant to expand the grounds of judicial review in ways that might undermine the demarcation. Thus, for example, there is little scope for a decision-maker to commit a reviewable error in the course of fact-finding.[159] The 'no evidence' ground of review is strictly applied.[160] The High Court continues to adhere to the *Wednesbury* standard of review on the ground of unreasonableness—a decision is reviewable on this ground only if it is so unreasonable that no reasonable decision-maker could have made it.[161] Gleeson CJ and McHugh J observed that this formula could be used merely as an 'emphatic [way] of saying that the reasoning is wrong', in which case it 'may have no particular legal consequence'.[162] Moreover, this ground focuses only on the outcome of discretionary decision-making powers—it does not provide a basis for review of the decision-maker's prior reasoning process or his or her fact

---

[156] At least at the federal level. At the state level, the separation of powers does not operate as a constitution rule and mixed tribunals exist, such as that established by the Victorian Civil and Administrative Tribunal Act 1992 (Vic).   [157] (1990) 170 CLR 1, 35–6.

[158] See *Re MIMA, ex parte Lam* (2003) 214 CLR 1, 24–5, where the persistence of the distinction is put explicitly on separation of powers grounds. Some justices have hinted that injunctions and relief under s. 75(iii) might be available for non-jurisdictional error: e.g. *Re MIMA, ex parte Miah* (2001) 206 CLR 57, 123. Justice Kirby favours doing away with the distinction: *ibid*.

[159] E.g. *ABT v. Bond* (1990) 170 CLR 321, 341 (noting the risk of turning judicial review into merits review).

[160] *Ibid.*, 355–6 (requiring literally no evidence). (The position may be different under the ADJR Act: see M. Aronson et al., *Judicial Review of Administrative Action*, (Butterworths, 3rd edn, 2004), 239–45.) Moreover, there must be no evidence of a matter that the statute makes a precondition to the exercise of jurisdiction: *MIMIA v. SGLB* (2004) 207 ALR 12.

[161] *Associated Provincial Picture Houses v. Wednesbury Corp* [1948] 1 KB 223.

[162] *MIMA v. Eshetu* (1999) 197 CLR 611, 626.

finding.[163] The High Court has recently acknowledged that a high degree of irrationality or illogicality in a decision-maker's fact finding process could constitute a basis for judicial review but has not had occasion to articulate what level of irrationality or illogicality was required.[164] Nor has it adopted the emerging English principles of substantive legitimate expectations, substantive abuse of power, or substantive unfairness[165] or the the proportionality ground of review (though a handful of justices have been receptive to it).[166] Judicial review on the ground that the decision-maker failed to take into account relevant considerations (or conversely on the ground that he or she took into account irrelevant considerations) is only available in respect of matters that the decision-maker was required to consider (or conversely forbidden from considering).[167] Inappropriate weighting of considerations is a matter for the administrative decision-maker and not the court (unless the inappropriateness reaches the reviewable level of irrationality).[168] A decision-maker's failure to consider evidence presented to him or her (as opposed to failure to take into account considerations made mandatory by statute) usually will not constitute reviewable error.[169]

• Courts do not scrutinize the reasons given by decision-makers 'minutely and finely with an eye keenly attuned to the perception of error' lest they venture into 'a reconsideration of the merits of the decision.'[170] But they do not defer to executive decision-makers' interpretation of the law—the separation of powers means that the courts are the only authoritative interpreters of the law.[171] Consistently with this approach, they have adopted a wide test for determining when an administrative decision-maker (but not an inferior court) commits a jurisdictional error.[172]

The second major influence on judicial review in Australia has been the rule of law. I referred above to judicial observations concerning the intended function and practical capacity of section 75 to uphold the rule of law in Australia. The *specific* contributions of the rule of law as a constitutional norm to Australian administrative law include the following:

• Rule of law reasoning has produced some expansion in the availability of judicial review. The traditional view that judicial review was not available against the Crown[173] was overturned in *R v. Toohey, ex parte Northern Land Council*[174] at least in relation to decisions made under statutory powers where review is

---

[163] *Re MIMA, ex parte Applicant S20/2002* (2003) 198 ALR 59.
[164] *Ibid., SGLB*, n. 160, [38].   [165] *Lam*, n. 158, 21–5.   [166] *Ibid.*, 23.
[167] *Minister for Aboriginal Affairs v. Peko-Wallsend* (1986) 162 CLR 24.   [168] *Ibid.*
[169] Aronson et al., n. 160, 251.   [170] *MIEA v. Wu* (1996) 185 CLR 259, 272.
[171] *Enfield v. Development Assistance Commission* (2000) 199 CLR 135.
[172] *Craig v. South Australia* (1995) 184 CLR 163, 179. This appears to be a presumption of statutory interpretation rather than an inflexible rule. Some tribunals may fall into legal errors that are non-jurisdictional: *Coal and Allied v. AIRC* (2000) 203 CLR 194.
[173] This view was expressed by Dixon J in *Australian Communist Party*, n. 40 above, 179, 222, 257–8.   [174] (1981) 151 CLR 170.

sought on the grounds of improper purpose.[175] Judicial review is also now available against the Crown on the basis of breaches of the requirements of procedural fairness;[176] it is unclear whether review may also be available on the grounds of bad faith,[177] or (ir)relevant considerations.[178] The scope for judicial review under the Constitution is further reinforced by the High Court's narrow approach to non-justiciability. Although accepting that some matters are purely political and beyond the scope of judicial review,[179] the courts have not always abstained from reviewing matters that are policy driven or politically controversial.[180]

- Rule of law reasoning precludes the Parliament from validly enacting a privative or ouster clause that deprives the High Court of jurisdiction to grant the remedies mentioned in section 75 in relation to a decision that is affected by jurisdictional error. Thus in *Plaintiff S157 of 2002 v. Commonwealth*,[181] section 474 of the Migration Act (which provided that most decisions under the Act were 'not subject to prohibition, mandamus, injunction, declaration or certiorari in any court on any account') was read down in accordance with rule of law principles to exclude decisions affected by jurisdictional error.[182] Although a

---

[175] It remains unclear whether review is available of decisions taken under common law or prerogative powers: see generally F. Wheeler, 'Judicial Review of Prerogative Power in Australia: Issues and Prospects' (1992) 14 *SydLR* 432; C. Horan, 'Judicial Review of Non-Statutory Executive Power' (2003) 31 *FLR* 551. In *R. v. Toohey, ex parte Northern Land Council* (1981) 151 CLR 170, Mason J commented that 'the prerogative discretions of the Attorney-General to enter a *nolle prosequi*, to grant or refuse a fiat in relator action and to file an ex officio information', and it seems the royal prerogatives relating to war and the armed services: at 218, 219–20. Although it seems that he was unwilling to exclude review of prerogative action a priori, he argued that the exercise of statutory power often possessed attributes making it susceptible to review, attributes lacked by the exercise of the prerogative: the exercise of statutory power 'very often affects the right of the citizen; there may be a duty to exercise the discretion one way or another; the discretion may be precisely limited in scope; it may be conferred for a specific or an ascertainable purpose; and it will be exercisable by reference to criteria or considerations express or implied. The prerogative powers lack some or all of these characteristics. Moreover, they are in some instances by reason of their very nature not susceptible of judicial review.'

[176] *FAI Insurances*, n. 9, 366.   [177] *R. v. Toohey* (1981) 151 CLR 170, 191, cf. 255.

[178] The breadth of the discretions usually conferred on a Governor-General may often limit the potential for a court to rule on what constitutes a relevant or an irrelevant consideration: Wheeler, n. 175, 469.

[179] See, e.g., *Minister v. Peko-Wallsend* (1987) 15 FCR 274, where Cabinet decisions were held to be beyond the scope of judicial review. Other examples include 'national security; the making of treaties; the defence of the country; the prerogative of mercy; the grant of honours; the dissolution of Parliament and the appointment of Ministers' (*Minister for Arts, Heritage and the Environment v. Peko-Wallsend* (1987) 15 FCR 274, 277) and the recognition of foreign governments (*Horta v. Commonwealth* (1994) 181 CLR 183). See also *Petrotimor Companhia De Petroleos SARL v. Commonwealth* (2003) 126 FCR 354.

[180] See G. Lindell, 'The Justiciability of Political Questions: Recent Developments', in H.P. Lee and G. Winterton, *Australian Constitutional Perspectives*, (Law Book Co, 1992), 180–250. For example, some justices have contemplated that judicial review may be available of the decision to dissolve both Houses of Parliament under the special procedure that s 57 of the Constitution provides for resolving deadlocks between the Houses (*Cormack v. Cope* (1974) 131 CLR 432, 454, 466; *PMA Case* (1975) 134 CLR 81, 157, 183–4).   [181] n. 45.

[182] n. 45, 513.

judicial review *jurisdiction* is entrenched as a result of section 75(iii) and (v), the Constitution does not, entrench any particular *grounds* of review; nor does it confer any substantive rights 'except in so far as the [constitutional] grant of jurisdiction [in s 75] necessarily recognises the principles of general law according to which the jurisdiction to grant the remedies is exercised'.[183] And although the Parliament is able to define the jurisdiction of decision-makers so that the errors they commit are non-jurisdictional, it cannot confer on a decision-maker the authority to determine the extent of their own jurisdiction[184] and it seems cannot expand the jurisdiction of a decision-maker by giving them an arbitrary discretion.[185] As a result, the extent of the protection provided by section 75(v) remains uncertain and ambiguous.

Notwithstanding this recent expansion, judicial review under the Constitution is a partial, complex, and limited avenue of accountability: it is necessary to identify a jurisdictional error; review under section 75(v) is only available in relation to decisions of 'officers of the Commonwealth'; and there are divergent time limits and procedures for the different writs and remedies. Statutory reforms of judicial review took place in the 1970s. However, because of statutory exclusion of judicial review in a number of areas, section 75(v), complete with its procedural complexities, has survived as a distinct avenue of judicial review.

(b) Judicial review under statute

The Administrative Decisions (Judicial Review) Act 1977 (Cth) (ADJR Act) was intended to simplify the grounds and procedures for judicial review of Commonwealth decisions.[186] It enables persons aggrieved by decisions[187] 'of an administrative character' that are 'made...under an enactment' to seek review of those decisions.[188] It does away with the distinction between jurisdictional errors and non-jurisdictional errors and it creates a statutory entitlement to reasons for administrative decisions that are reviewable under the Act.[189] However, many complexities remain.

The unified standing requirement, that the applicant be a person aggrieved by a decision (one whose interests are adversely affected by the decision),[190] is simpler than the multiple common law standing rules. But it is no clearer. The leading work observes: 'There are many statements to the effect that the *ADJR's*

---

[183] A. Mason, 'The Foundations and Limitations of Judicial Review' (2001) 31 *AIAL Forum* 1, 4.
[184] *Plaintiff S157/2002*, n. 45, 505–6.   [185] See text, n. 74.
[186] Similar legislation now exists in Queensland, Tasmania, and the ACT. More limited reforms were made in Victoria. See generally Aronson et al., n. 160, 15–24.
[187] A 'decision' is final and substantive and not procedural: *ABT v. Bond* (1990) 170 CLR 321.
[188] It also allows review of conduct engaged in for the purpose of making a decision (ie of the conduct of proceedings) and of failure to make a decision: ss. 6 and 7.   [189] Section 13.
[190] Section 3(4).

test is "at least" as generous as the common law's special interest test, but no definite pronouncement that it is more generous.'[191]

The Act excludes decisions of the Governor-General, reflecting the state of the common law at the time it was enacted, but not reflecting the more recent developments described above.[192] It also excludes review of a wide range of decisions listed in the Schedule to the Act. (The Administrative Review Council is currently investigating further options for limiting the scope of judicial review to 'achieve an appropriate balance between providing individuals with a means of testing the legality of administrative action and preventing litigation from frustrating government policies'.[193])

The requirement that a decision be of an administrative character will usually preclude review of the making of delegated legislation but it also precludes review of an ill-defined class of decisions that enunciate a rule of general rather than specific application.[194]

The requirement that a decision be 'made under an enactment' entails that the decision must be required, authorized, or be given effect by the enactment.[195] As a result, intermediate decisions are usually not reviewable.[196] Decisions made under non-statutory schemes are also not reviewable,[197] even where the decision involves the expenditure of public funds.[198] (The Administrative Review Council has recommended that the scope of the ADJR Act be expanded to include decisions under a 'non statutory scheme or program, the funds for which are authorised by an appropriation made to Parliament' but that recommendation has not been accepted.[199]) Nor are decisions that derive their effect from a general power to administer an Act, or decisions made under the executive's common law or prerogative powers. For example, decisions made under internal guidelines and policy documents will not be reviewable because the guidelines do not derive their force from statute. Importantly, in an era of increased outsourcing, the decisions of private sector bodies will also often lie

---

[191] Aronson et al., n. 160, 684.

[192] ADJR Act, s. 3(1)(c). The Administrative Review Council has recommended that the ADJR Act be amended to remove the exclusion of decisions of the Governor General made under an enactment: Administrative Review Council, *Review of the Administrative Decisions (Judicial Review) Act: The Ambit of the Act* (Report No. 32, 1989) 49, recommendation 2 ('*Ambit*'). (The Administrative Review Council was established by s. 48 of the Administrative Appeals Tribunal Act 1975 (Cth) 'to keep the Commonwealth administrative law system under review, monitor developments in administrative law and recommend to the Minister improvements that might be made to the system': s. 51(1)(aa).)

[193] Administrative Review Council, *The Scope of Judicial Review: Discussion Paper* (2003) 8 ('*Scope*').   [194] See generally *SAT FM v. ABA* (1997) 75 FCR 604 and the cases cited there.

[195] *General Newspapers v. Telstra* (1993) 45 FCR 164; *Bond*, n. 187.   [196] *Bond*, n. 187.

[197] Compare in a non-ADJR Act context, *Victoria v. Master Builders' Association of Victoria* [1995] 2 VR 121.

[198] Decisions by service providers about eligibility for services funded by the Commonwealth will similarly be excluded.

[199] Administrative Review Council, *The Contracting Out of Government Services* (Report No. 42, 1998) 84 ('*Contracting Out*'); *Ambit*, n. 192, 40–1.

outside the scope of the ADJR Act because the decision-maker derives its capacity from the general law (relating to the powers of natural persons or corporations) and not statute.[200] The decisions of contractors will only be subject to judicial review if the decision-maker is directly authorized under an enactment, or acts as the delegate of a decision-maker under an enactment.[201]

(c) Judicial review—assessment

The principal challenge for Australian judicial review under the general law is to work through the implications of the rule of law and the separation of powers, both as limits on the scope of judicial review and as potential guarantors of a minimum scope for judicial review. The difficulty is that both concepts are fluid and, although they are clearly presupposed by the constitutional text, the text provides little concrete guidance on what particular conception is applicable. With the reluctance of the High Court to travel beyond the text and structure of the Constitution and rely openly on extra-constitutional political concepts,[202] the leverage that these concepts provide (in particular the rule of law, which has not yielded a well-developed body of case law[203]) may be limited.

A secondary challenge, particularly under the statutory avenues of judicial review, is to identify the proper scope of judicial review of non-governmental decision-making. The High Court has not been receptive to review of private sector decision-making even where the decision is an element in a regulatory scheme. In *NEAT*, the majority refused to superimpose administrative law obligations on the profit-maximising obligations of the corporate decision-maker notwithstanding the corporation's central role in the public decision-making process and its immunity from certain private law accountability mechanisms.[204] The Court's reasons are not persuasive[205] and it is to be hoped that the Court has the opportunity to revisit this area.

Embracing both these challenges is the wider question of the proper scope of judicial review. The Parliament's ongoing attempts to restrict review of migration decisions[206] reflects the commonplace observations that accountability through judicial review has financial costs and that accountability is but one public good among many competing goods.[207]

---

[200] *NEAT v. AWB* (2003) 198 ALR 179 (holding that a private body's statutory power to prevent its competitors from exporting wheat did not involve it in making reviewable decisions); see also *Griffith University v. Tang* [2005] HCA 7 (3 March 2005). And they will lie outside the scope of s. 75 because the corporate decision-maker cannot be an officer of the Commonwealth.

[201] *Contracting Out*, n. 199, 81.   [202] *Lange*, n. 2.

[203] But note the recent observations in *Lam*, n. 158, 23 ('It may be said that the rule of law reflects values concerned in general terms with abuse of power by the executive and legislative branches of government. But it would be going much further to give those values an immediate normative operation in applying the *Constitution*.').   [204] *NEAT*, n. 200.

[205] See, e.g., C. Mantziaris, 'A "Wrong Turn" on the Public/Private Distinction: *NEAT Domestic Trading Pty Ltd v. AWB Ltd*' (2003) 14 *PLR* 197.   [206] See text, n. 181.

[207] See *Scope*, n. 193.

5. Other accountability mechanisms

The administrative law reforms of the 1970s went beyond the introduction of the ADJR Act. They also included the establishment of a broadly based and independent merits review tribunal, the introduction of freedom of information legislation, and the appointment of an ombudsman. More recently, several States have adopted anticorruption commissions and whistle-blowing legislation.

(a) Independent merits review

One of the key aspects of the reforms was a broad (but not universal) avenue of merits review in which an independent decision-maker reconsidered the facts, law, and policy to determine the correct and preferable decision.[208] The Administrative Appeals Tribunal (the AAT) was established in 1976 under the Administrative Appeals Tribunal Act 1975 (Cth) (AAT Act) as the principal independent merits review tribunal. In appearance, structure, and operation, the AAT resembles a court rather than an administrative body.[209] In *Re Drake*, Brennan J, acting in the capacity of President of the AAT, noted that the AAT 'is rightly required to reach its decisions with the same robust independence as that exhibited by the courts'.[210] And in *Re Becker*, he observed:

> The Legislature clearly intends that the Tribunal, though exercising administrative power, should be constituted upon the judicial model, separate from, and independent of, the Executive.... Its function is to decide appeals, not to advise the Executive.[211]

There is no automatic right of review of federal administrative decisions in the AAT. The right only exists where it is specifically provided for by the legislation that confers power to make the decision.[212] Where a right of review does exist, it confers on the AAT Member all of the discretions and powers of the original decision-maker,[213] including the power to affirm, vary, or set aside a decision, to substitute a new decision, or to remit a decision back to the original decision-maker. The AAT is not obliged to give effect to government policy but does so (in particular policy determined at the political level and for which the principal accountability remains through the minister to Parliament) as far as is consistent with its obligation to reach the correct and preferable decision on the facts of the case.[214]

---

[208] Cf. Administrative Review Council, *What Decisions Should be Subject to Merits Review?* (1999), 1–2.
[209] P. Cane, 'Merits Review and Judicial Review: The AAT as Trojan Horse' (2000) 28 *FLR* 213, 215; G. Brennan, 'The Administrative Appeals Tribunal: Early Issues' (2001) 9 *AJAL* 5, 6–7.
[210] (1979) 2 ALD 634, 643.   [211] (1977) 15 ALR 696, 699.
[212] AAT Act, s. 25. For the relevant principles, see *What Decisions Should be Subject to Merits Review?*, n. 208.   [213] AAT Act, s. 43(1).
[214] *Re Becker*, n. 211; *Re Drake*, n. 210. The Victorian Civil and Administrative Tribunal, whose role and functions partly correspond with those of the AAT, is bound to give effect to certain government policies: Victorian Civil and Administrative Tribunal Act 1998 (Vic) s. 57.

An 'appeal' lies from the AAT to the Federal Court on questions of law and the AAT can refer questions of law to the Federal Court.[215]

In the 2002–2003 financial year, 7,762 applications were lodged with the AAT.[216] In addition to the AAT, a number of specialist merits review tribunals have been established, including the Social Security Appeals Tribunal[217] and Veterans Review Board, the Migration Review Tribunal, and the Refugee Review Tribunal. Government attempts to reform and simplify the tribunal system—by amalgamating most of the existing tribunals to create a single Administrative Review Tribunal (the ART)[218]—failed in the Senate, principally due to concerns that the proposed ART would lack much of the independence of the AAT (and most of the other existing tribunals) from the departments whose decisions it was reviewing.[219]

(b) Freedom of information

The Freedom of Information Act 1982 (Cth) (FOI Act) contains three mechanisms for promoting government accountability[220]:

- It provides for an enforceable right of access to documents in the possession of ministers and agencies (ss. 11, 15 and 18) subject to exemptions (Part IV) and subject to fees and charges (s. 29).

- It requires agencies to publish information concerning their functions, their consultation procedures, the categories of documents that they maintain, and the facilities for accessing them (s. 8). It requires agencies to make their

---

[215] AAT Act, ss. 44, 45. The 'appeal' is strictly an application to the Federal Court in its original jurisdiction for judicial review of the AAT's decision. In accordance with separation of powers principles, the Federal Court is limited to determining the lawfulness of the AAT's decision. It cannot exercise for itself the administrative power that is vested in the AAT. See text at n. 157.

[216] AAT, *Annual Report 2002–2003*, (2003), appendix 4, table 4.3.

[217] During the 1990s, government job-training and job-finding services were contracted out to private providers. This led to a bifurcation of decision-making about eligibility for government benefits (and therefore diffused responsibility for decision-making and increased the complexity of merits review) and reduced the systemic effects of merits review (because private providers were more interested in bottom-line financial performance): see R. Bacon, 'Rewriting the Social Contract? The SSAT, the AAT and the Contracting Out of Employment Services' (2002) 30 *FLR* 39.

[218] Administrative Review Council, *Better Decisions: Review of Commonwealth Merits Review Tribunals* (Report No. 39, 1995); Australian Law Reform Commission, *Managing Justice: A Review of the Federal Civil Justice System* (Report No 89, 2000).

[219] See Senate Legal and Constitutional Committee, *Inquiry into the Provisions of the Administrative Review Tribunal Bill 2000 and the Administrative Review Tribunal (Consequential and Transitional Provisions) Bill 2000* (Commonwealth of Australia, 2001); and the symposium in (2000) 27 *AIAL Forum* 1–49. More recently, the same Senate Committee has commented adversely on aspects of more limited reform proposals, in particular proposals to limit the tenure of members of the AAT: *Inquiry into the Administrative Appeals Tribunal Amendment Bill (2004)* (March 2005).

[220] Similar legislation was enacted in each State and Territory between 1982 and 1992. The Victorian Constitution Act 1975 was amended in 2003 to entrench a requirement that there be a state FOI Act.

internal policy manuals and interpretive guidelines available for inspection and purchase (s. 9). And it provides that information and procedures contained in such documents must not prejudice members of the public if the documents are not published (s. 10).

- It provides mechanisms by which individuals can require ministers and agencies to correct their records of personal information about individuals (Part V).

The Australian Law Reform Commission and Administrative Review Council reported on the FOI Act in 1995.[221] They identified an ongoing 'culture of secrecy that still pervades some aspects of public sector administration' and recommended among other things that an FOI Commissioner be appointed 'to monitor and improve the administration of the FOI Act and to provide assistance, advice, and education to applicants and agencies about how to use, interpret and administer the Act'.[222] These and other recommendations have gone largely unimplemented.

One set of recommendations, in relation to the application of the FOI Act to government contractors under outsourcing arrangements, are of particular interest. The 1995 review concluded that accountability principles required access to documents held by contractors but it did not recommend a particular mechanism for achieving this. The Act was amended to extend rights of access to documents held by one specific set of contractors (those that provide job-training and job-finding services for unemployed people).[223] In 1998 the Administrative Review Council recommended that FOI Act be amended, first, to deem that all documents in the possession of contractors, and that related directly to the performance of contractual obligations, were in the possession of the government agency and, secondly, to require that contractors be required to provide these documents to the agency on request.[224] Those recommendations have not been implemented. Instead, access continues to depend on whether the contract itself provides for a right of access. It remains to be seen whether any government is willing to take up the wider recommendations in the 1995 report and these particular recommendations about contractors.

(c) Ombudsman

The Ombudsman, an independent tenured office established under the Ombudsman Act 1976 (Cth), faces similar difficulties.[225] The Ombudsman

---

[221] Australian Law Reform Commission, *Open Government: A Review of the Federal Freedom of Information Act 1982* (Report No. 77, 1996). The same report is published as Administrative Review Council, *Open Government: A Review of the Federal Freedom of Information Act 1982* (Report No. 40, 1995).

[222] They did not recommend that receipt of government funding should be sufficient to make FOI obligations attach to private sector bodies: *ibid.*, [15.14].

[223] See Employment Services (Consequential Amendments) Act 1994 (Cth).

[224] *Contracting Out*, n. 199, 60.

[225] See A. Stuhmcke, 'Privatisation and Corporatisation: What Now for the Commonwealth Ombudsman' (2004) 11 *AJAL* 101. State and Territory Ombudsmen were established under

investigates and reports on actions that relate to a matter of administration taken by a department (not by a minister) or by a prescribed authority (a term that extends to the job-finding and job-training contractors noted above in relation to FOI; it does not extend to other contractors).[226] The Ombudsman's capacity to investigate the implementation of outsourcing contracts is therefore limited. Thus, the Ombudsman wrote in his *Report of an Own Motion Investigation into The Department of Immigration and Multicultural Affairs' Immigration Detention Centres*:

> While I do not see the role of my Office as participating in the assessment of the [contractor's] performance in meeting the detention standards, my Office does respond to complaints about administrative issues and provides feedback to [the Department] where we see an underlying cause that is capable of correction. I have raised the issue of the need to have a clear framework for [the Department] to produce some public reporting arrangement of its own to indicate where performance targets were not being met.... [The Department] has stated that it will explore what opportunities exist for public reporting against the Immigration Detention Standards. It also proposes to strengthen performance monitoring of [the contractor] by increasing operational meetings at [immigration detention centres].[227]

(d) Anticorruption commissions and whistle-blowing

Finally, the role of commissions of inquiry and whistle-blowing legislation should be noted. In the late 1980s and early 1990s, wide ranging enquiries were held in Queensland, Victoria, and Western Australia in relation to government corruption.[228] New South Wales, Queensland, and Western Australia have standing independent anti-corruption commissions.[229] There is whistle-blowing legislation in six jurisdictions but not at Commonwealth level, although some protection is available under section 16 of the Public Service Act 1999 (Cth).[230]

---

legislation between 1971 and 1978. There are also industry ombudsmen who act in areas in which government was previously the monopoly provider (for example, telecommunications at Commonwealth level and transport in the States) and in which the government has moved from a regulatory to a self-regulatory model (for example, banking). The Victorian Constitution Act 1975 was amended in 2003 to entrench the independence of the Ombudsman.

[226] However, the Ombudsman may, with the consent of the minister, agree to act as ombudsman under schemes that established 'in accordance with the conditions of licences or authorities granted under an enactment': Ombudsman Act 1976 s. 5(1).

[227] *Report of an Own Motion Investigation into the Department of Immigration and Multicultural Affairs' Immigration Detention Centres*, n. 129, 25.

[228] See generally A. Peachment (ed.), *Westminster Inc: A Survey of Three States in the 1980s* (Federation Press, 1995).

[229] See generally S. Donaghue, *Royal Commissions and Permanent Commissions of Inquiry* (Butterworths, 2001).

[230] See generally D. Lewis, 'Whistleblowing Statutes in Australia: Is it Time for a New Agenda?' (2003) 8 *Deakin LR* 318.

6. Conclusion

The Australian experience with executive power demonstrates one of the familiar tensions inherent in constitutionalism, namely, the tension between continuity and flexibility. The Westminster system of responsible government may have been more or less appropriate for the United Kingdom at the end of the nineteenth century. Australia at the start of the twenty-first century is dramatically different: not least in that it is a federal state with a written constitution, an entrenched separation of powers, an elected second parliamentary chamber, rigid party discipline, and a large bureaucracy supporting a (reduced but still extensive) welfare system.

The institutional innovations and adaptations described in this chapter have responded to these differences. In particular they have attempted to address the weakness of parliamentary accountability and its inability to provide rectification of individual grievances. They have done so by diffusing and multiplying lines of accountability. Those lines no longer track lines of authority back to a single minister responsible to, and holding the confidence of, the Parliament. Instead, those who exercise executive power are accountable through the general FOI disclosure obligation and the specific obligations to provide reasons for their decisions; they are accountable through tribunals and courts for their individual decisions; and they are accountable through the Ombudsman both for individual decisions and systemic failures of the bureaucracy. Nonetheless, the traditional principles of responsible government provide a reference point for courts and commentators analysing the design and adequacy of Australian accountability mechanisms.

These innovations and adaptations have not yielded an end-state of optimal accountability. This chapter has outlined arguments that accountability ought to be extended (for example, to embrace ministerial advisers and government contractors) and noted government arguments that it ought to be restricted (for example, to restrict the scope of judicial review of migration decisions and to reform tribunals in the interests of economy and administrative efficiency). It is impossible to arbitrate here on these arguments. They present a quintessentially political question, namely, how to reconcile the costs and benefits of accountability with other public goods. There is no end-state to be reached, but an ongoing search for an accommodation of one of the other tensions inherent in constitutionalism, that between the need to hold the exercise of public power to account and the need to allow it to be exercised effectively for the public good.

4
New Public Management New Zealand Style

*Janet McLean**

The New Zealand political system, and the role of the executive within it, has been the site of fundamental change during the last twenty years. The period 1984–2004 saw both major electoral reform—mixed member proportional representation replacing the first past the post system—and the adoption of a radical version of the New Public Management. State sector and financial management reform has been programmatic and thoroughgoing. Many formerly government activities have been corporatized and privatized while private and corporate models of governance have been adopted for those activities that have remained under government management. There has been a perceived internationalization of the legal system as the importance of international law has been increasingly recognized in domestic law. Simultaneously there is an emerging (though sometimes fragile) self-confidence about New Zealand's indigenous legal culture. The period has seen the adoption of an interpretative Bill of Rights and the replacement of the Judicial Committee of the Privy Council with the New Zealand Supreme Court as the final appellate court. Discussions about the proper role of the judges vis à vis the executive and legislature have prompted fierce public and scholarly debate. Changes to understandings of the place of the indigenous Maori people within the unwritten constitution have taken place in the legislature, the bureaucracy, and the courts. Maori victories in fishing and other litigation have provoked broader constitutional controversies. The 2005 election may be the first to be fought on constitutional issues.

Various trends have emerged that cut across each other in interesting ways. New Zealand's version of the New Public Management focused on clarifying

---

* Thanks to Chong Lim, David V Williams, Sir Kenneth Keith, Mike Taggart, Treasa Dunworth, Paul Rishworth, Richard Mulgan, and Penelope Stevenson. Special thanks to Sue Newberry for patiently explaining the intricacies of accrual accounting. All errors, misunderstandings, and distortions remain the responsibility of the author.

political and managerial accountability through the ex ante specification of policy outputs and outcomes. Its architects sought to achieve this by fragmenting the executive branch into separate units that were to focus on clear and unified objectives. Large departments were disaggregated into policy, service delivery and monitoring agencies; and arm's-length agencies (including commercial ventures) were created to operate outside direct ministerial control.

The new managerial focus on *ends* in preference to *means* necessitated the increased *legal* autonomy of various parts of the state sector. Entities should have the flexibility to meet policy objectives by whatever lawful means they choose. The powers of the core state sector and of the separate entities at its periphery were, accordingly, conceived as analogous to those of natural persons of full legal capacity. Legislation no longer conferred specific powers on the executive to be policed by the courts through the ultra vires rule. Instead, the focus of legislation was to confer on government entities those special powers that they sometimes require over and above those enjoyed by ordinary people.

There are obvious tensions between the new intra-government emphasis on *ends* and reporting rather than on process and outputs, and the work of the courts in their exposition of public and administrative law doctrine. Administrative law doctrine has been traditionally, even paradigmatically, concerned with *means* rather than ends. Supervising process and keeping public actors within their statutory powers has been central to the courts' role in judicial review cases. The period has seen the courts continue to contribute requirements by way of process. Where the executive has changed its means of regulation and delivery from traditional command and control to contractual modes, however, the courts have, to a large extent, been reluctant to interfere with executive flexibility. In other areas, they have continued to define, and therefore confine, executive power, not only by reference to statutory schemes, but, increasingly, by reference to values extrinsic to legislation, such as, human rights instruments, Maori custom, and administrative law norms.

At the same time as legal autonomy has apparently increased, internal administrative controls and reporting within the executive have become more onerous. Traditional hierarchical political controls through ministers have continued to operate, despite fragmentation.[1] Notwithstanding their distance from day to day decision-making, ministers are held politically accountable for the activities of chief executives of government departments and even, sometimes, for those of separate statutory bodies. Indeed, the unified Crown is increasingly conceived as the fount for legal redress for government failures. It is the Crown that is liable to fulfil obligations under the Treaty of Waitangi and for damages under the New Zealand Bill of Rights Act 1990. These developments have prompted, since 2001, calls for a 'whole of government approach' to public

---

[1] R. Mulgan, 'Public Sector Reform in New Zealand—Issues of Accountability' (forthcoming) *International Journal of Public Administration*.

management that is at odds with the New Zealand version of New Public Management as originally conceived.[2]

This essay is divided into three parts. The first will focus on legislative and executive attempts to define the executive and judicial responses to those attempts. The second part will focus primarily on legislative and executive attempts to define executive *power*. Finally, in Part three, a range of judicial and non-judicial accountability and control mechanisms will be considered.

1. Who is the executive?

The period in question has seen many self-conscious attempts by the executive-dominated legislature[3] to define what executive government should do and to provide effective incentives and flexible means for actors within and outwith the executive to perform such functions.

Defining 'the executive', as it has emerged as a result of these attempts, is no easy task and is not entirely meaningful. It is the relationships between the various parts and the whole, and the mechanisms by which they are subject to control and accountability, that tend to matter.

(a) Political notions of the executive

The executive comprises the Ministers of the Crown and the departments they head. Traditional constitutional understandings about the executive focus on political relationships. The political relationship between Her Majesty in Right of New Zealand and her responsible ministers is central and defining. Except for legislative references to a particular minister in constitutional terms as 'the responsible Minister', however, these relationships are treated largely as matters of convention rather than law. Conventional understandings also define the relationship between the public service and ministers. Government departments are conceived as 'extensions of the Minister acting in the Minister's name and in accordance with the Minister's wishes'.[4] Constitutionally at least, the public service is conceived as the primary *means* by which the government acts, rather than as a separate actor. Ministers are ultimately responsible through Parliament

---

[2] This has been an ongoing problem. One strategy that sought to coordinate the different agencies, has been the adoption of a broad planning framework (since 1994) that specified Strategic Results Areas and Key Results Areas across the whole of the government sector. More recently, the Labour government has introduced departmental 'statements of intent' which refer to outcomes as well as outputs.

[3] There has been minority government for much of the period, but nevertheless the executive has enjoyed much of its former (pre-mixed member proportional representation) dominance on some issues.

[4] State Services Commission, *Responsibility and Accountability: Standards Expected of Public Service Chief Executives* (State Services Commission, 1997).

for the conduct of their departments. For the most part, these understandings remain central to the *political* (as opposed to the legislative) business of Parliament.

(b) Legislative definitions of the executive

A number of different and sometimes competing conceptions of the place and role of executive government find expression in legislation. The extensive general delegation provisions in the New Zealand statute book tend to reinforce the conventional view of the relationship between ministers and the public service. Ministers may delegate their statutory functions and powers to Chief Executives of government departments,[5] and a Chief Executive may also delegate her (and with his consent, the minister's) functions and powers.[6] The delegation provisions make clear that the delegate exercises such powers as if they were conferred on her directly. When the delegate acts, it is as if the minister himself has acted.[7]

A rival understanding of the executive emerges out of other legislative provisions that represent the relationship between ministers and their Chief Executives and departments as either an arm's length one or one in which the department acts as an agent for the minister. For example, while the Public Finance Act 1989, consistently with the traditional constitutional analysis, defines the 'Crown' to include 'ministers and their departments', its core provisions conceive of departments as the suppliers of outputs to ministers. Ministers are defined as purchasers of goods and services on behalf of the public. Under this view ministers tend to be conceived as the residual core of the state from which everything else is at arm's length. The Crown is the entity in which government assets are vested, and which exercises ownership and purchaser interests throughout the state sector. The 'contractual' (so called) relationships that specify expectations and objectives as between ministers and Chief Executives are a further example of this conception at work. These accountability devices are at odds with the traditional constitutional framework, which would conceive of the state sector as the *means* by which the Crown is able to act, rather than as a discrete entity responding to various incentives. The newer conception was intended to clarify where political responsibility resides but may have (further) obscured it, as we shall see below.

Yet another conception operates where the Treaty of Waitangi, between the Crown and the indigenous Maori people of New Zealand, is concerned.

---

[5] State Sector Act 1988, s. 28. [6] State Sector Act 1988, s. 41.

[7] It is controversial whether the *Carltona v. Board of Works* [1943] 2 All ER 560 doctrine applies in New Zealand. There is a longstanding practice of including extensive delegation powers in individual statutes and recognition in the case law that the Minister does not have personally to perform the whole of a statutory power or duty so long as she exercises control and properly directs her mind to the matter. Their Lordships were not prepared to determine what effect, if any, the generous delegation provisions in the State Sector Act 1988, s 41 may have had on the principle in *Carltona* at [2004] 3 NZLR 1 [64] (PC).

Legislation, in this area, invariably refers to the government's obligations as attaching to the Crown (otherwise undefined).[8] This usage has presumably arisen not only because Queen Victoria was a party to the 1840 Treaty, but also because government assets, on which Maori grievances have been focused, vest in the Crown. References to the Crown, in this context, also serve other rhetorical and political purposes. The Crown is represented as a permanent unified whole that transcends the particular government of the day. Maori tend to appeal for redress of grievances to the Crown as if it were an apolitical entity. This view, that the Crown commitments under the Treaty of Waitangi are pre-political and constituent of the state itself, and that in fulfilling such commitments the Crown neither engages with nor is bound to engage with democratic processes, is understandable when viewed against the colonial conception of the Crown.[9] How is such a Crown to be reconciled with a modern executive operating within a democratic system of Parliamentary sovereignty? And whom does the Crown represent here: the United Kingdom; the New Zealand Government of the Day; or all the present citizens of New Zealand—Maori and non-Maori?

References to 'the Crown' in relation to the Treaty of Waitangi may have had more than rhetorical effect. Legislative procedures adopted by the House of Representatives when giving effect to Treaty Settlements are another way in which Parliament defines the relative powers of the executive and Parliament. Settlements negotiated between ministers and Maori tribes, such as, for example, the Ngai Tahu Claims Settlement, have been urged on Parliament effectively to be enacted as agreed without amendment.[10] Negotiating ministers have argued that for Parliament to do otherwise would undermine the Crown's (ministers') obligation to negotiate with Maori in the utmost good faith. Up until now, Parliament has acquiesced (even when one Maori Member from another affected tribe raised serious objections to the content of the agreement).[11]

Quite apart from these different conceptual understandings, the executive is commonly defined for the pragmatic purpose of determining whether and which internal government accountability and control mechanisms should apply. A number of legislative accountability frameworks include mechanical lists of the entities that are considered to be part of the executive government for particular purposes. The list of departments of the public service attaching to the State Sector Act 1988 is the most narrowly focused of these and has the effect of determining who should be regarded as a public servant whose political

---

[8] 'The Crown' is not only the entity identified by legislation as the repository of legal redress in relation to things Maori. It has also been identified by the judiciary as the source of financial remedies under the New Zealand Bill of Rights Act 1990, see pp. 136–7.

[9] See e.g. *Campbell v. Hall* (1774) Loftt 655; 98 ER 858. Some Maori would also argue that the Crown should be viewed as an international legal person who continues to treat with Maori, and that Maori are themselves a collective entity in international law.

[10] Ngai Tahu Claims Settlement Act 1998.

[11] These controversies resulted in litigation, *Ngati Apa Ki Te Waipounamu Trust v. The Queen* [2000] 2 NZLR 659 (CA).

neutrality should be protected and who is directly answerable through a responsible minister. The Official Information Act 1982, which promotes disclosure of official information in order to 'enhance respect for the law and promote the good government of New Zealand' is much broader in its application and includes, for example, all of the state owned enterprises and many other statutory (and non-statutory) entities alongside the core state departments.[12] The financial reporting regime administered under the Public Finance Act 1989 applies not only to the Crown but also to a broad variety of 'Crown entities' including statutory and non-statutory boards, corporations and other enterprises in whom the Crown has a financial interest but which may otherwise operate at arm's length from government. It categorizes entities in terms of how much financial independence from central government they ought to enjoy.

The new Crown Entities Act 2004 is a further attempt to categorize these diverse bodies according to their perceived need for political as well as financial independence from central government. There are five broad categories that are supplemented by scheduled lists of entities. They are: *crown agents* that must *give effect to* government policy when directed by a minister (e.g. the Pharmaceutical Management Agency which is the monopsony purchaser of pharmaceuticals); *autonomous crown entities* that must *have regard* to government policy (e.g. the Broadcasting Commission that scrutinizes standards and balance in Broadcasting); *independent crown entities* that are not subject to direction (e.g. the Electoral Commission); *crown entity companies* (with commercial or partly commercial goals); and *crown entity subsidiaries*. The explanatory note to the omnibus Bill, which introduced these changes, perpetuates the 1990s ideology that emphasized the independence of such bodies from ministers, stating 'Crown entities form part of the government reporting entity, but are not part of the Crown itself'.[13] The overall thrust of the Act and related amendments, however, is to further extend the scope of central government control. So, for example, while employees of Crown entities do not enjoy the same conditions of employment as public servants, they are now subject to the same 'minimum standards of integrity' issued and enforced by the State Services Commissioner.[14] Given that the new raft of legislation[15] strengthens central government control over Crown entities, the distinction between the Crown and the entities that report to it that the Act purports to effect, is progressively reduced.

---

[12] Official Information Act 1982, s. 4. The same section also states that the Act 'promotes accountability of Ministers and Crown officials'. State owned enterprises were originally included in the schedule by the State-Owned Enterprises Act 1986, but the provision was subject to a sunset clause. A Parliamentary select committee issued a strong report that the State-Owned Enterprises should continue to be subject to the information regime notwithstanding fierce opposition from the state enterprises themselves and, consequently, coverage has remained.

[13] Public Finance (State Sector Management) Bill 2003 explanatory note.

[14] State Sector Amendment Act 2004, s. 57.

[15] Public Finance Amendment Act 2004, State Sector Amendment Act (No. 2) State Owned Enterprises Amendment Act 2004, Crown Entities Act 2004.

Given the variations between them, and the pragmatic inclusions and exclusions they often contain,[16] references to these various mechanical lists for guidance on the question of who is the executive, should be undertaken with caution. All depends on the purpose for which one is asking the question: is this actor part of the executive?

Other statutory references to the executive more explicitly invite normative judgment.[17] Some statutes refer to the executive in generic terms such as 'an instrument of the Executive Government of New Zealand' or 'instruments of the Crown in respect of the government of New Zealand'.[18] Application of the New Zealand Bill of Rights Act 1990, for example, depends on whether an entity is part of the 'executive branch' (s 3(1)(a)) or is otherwise 'any person or body in the performance of any public function, power, or duty conferred or imposed on that person or body by or pursuant to law'. The Judicature Amendment Act 1977 sets out a series of different, but perhaps even broader, tests for who may be susceptible to a judicial review action. Judicial review is available both under the Act and at common law by way of prerogative order.[19]

(c) Judicial definitions

How then has the judiciary responded to these more open ended provisions? The leading judicial authority on the scope of the executive branch is *CIR v. Medical Council of New Zealand*.[20] It concerned whether the Medical Council, a statutory body, could be considered an 'instrument of the Executive Government of New Zealand' for the purposes of enjoying tax immunity. The Court of Appeal rejected a functional test and opted instead for a control test.[21] Conceding that the promotion of public health care was a 'state responsibility', Keith J, in particular, relied on the legislative characterizations of the executive as providing essential guidance as to how the courts should proceed saying: 'It is not for the Courts to second-guess the political judgment made by the legislature'.[22]

Keith J characterized the public sector into three groups. The first is the group of bodies serving ministers and the Governor-General who make up the public service.[23] Such bodies are lead by Chief Executives who have direct

---

[16] The Governor-General, for example, is regularly omitted from such lists, and sometimes officers of parliament such as the Controller and Auditor-General and the Clerk of the House are included for limited purposes, Crown Organisations (Criminal Liability) Act 2002, s. 4.

[17] The Public Audit Act 2001 includes a control test, s. 5. See the Audit office web site for a statement of how it is defined. The web site also contains an opinion about whether it has statutory authority to audit private non-governmental organizations that provide tax-payer funded public services. It concludes that the audit should focus on the contract for such services rather than be drawn into the internal operations of such NGOs.

[18] See, e.g. Crown Proceedings Act 1950, s. 2 ; Designs Act 1953, s. 2; New Zealand State Sector Act 1988, s. 2.

[19] Section 3 of the Judicature Act 1972, as amended, broadly defines 'statutory power' and 'statutory power of decision', see further *McGechan on Procedure* (Brooker's Wellington) (on-line).

[20] [1997] 2 NZLR 297 (CA).   [21] *Ibid.*, 327.   [22] *Ibid.*

[23] Defined by the State Sector Act 1988.

responsibilities to ministers and who tender advice to ministers. The second group comprises government trading enterprises that are characterized by placing greater accountability on boards and managers and by the greater distance of ministers from their day-to-day operations. The third group of bodies is much more diverse and the different entities enjoy varying degrees of independence from ministerial and other controls. It includes administrative tribunals, funding bodies, advisory bodies, trading corporations that are not state enterprises, and control and supervisory bodies. The Court decided that while the Council was a distinct statutory entity and the responsible minister had a role in the appointment of its members, the minister had no control over the matters it considered, no direct access to its funds, and no power to give directions as to policy. In addition it was not subject to the reporting or auditing requirements of the Public Finance Act 1989, Official Information Act 1982, or Ombudsmen Act 1962. It was, therefore, not part of the executive.

Of course this analysis is a response to the question of whether the Medical Council should enjoy the Crown's immunity from taxation—a fiscal privilege rather than the application of an accountability regime. As such, the *Medical Council* decision cannot be the last word on the matter.

(d) The application of judicial accountability regimes

The judiciary has frequently been asked to define the executive for the purposes of deciding whether *judicially* based accountability regimes should apply. Should judicial review, the New Zealand Bill of Rights Act 1990, or Treaty of Waitangi principles relating to the nature of the Crown's obligations to Maori, operate as a restraint on power? Such cases have drawn different responses from those articulated in the *CIR v. Medical Council* case.

(i) Judicial review

In the 1980s, the first cases to raise the question of whether judicial review would apply to the disaggregated parts of the executive were those involving entities that had formerly been part of the core state sector but had been converted by the State-Owned Enterprises Act 1986 to state-owned enterprises. Such entities operate in response to commercial incentives at arm's length from ministers.

The Court of Appeal (over which President Richardson presided from 1996–2001) refused to extend judicial review to these bodies. In *Auckland Electric Power Board v. Electricity Corporation of New Zealand*, the Court of Appeal characterized state-owned enterprises as performing commercial *functions* and exercising commercial contractual *powers* over which government had no direct control.[24] The Court, in this context, regarded the presence of legislated mechanisms of accountability such as ministerial directions through statements

---

[24] *Auckland Electric Power Board v. Electricity Corporation of New Zealand* [1994] 1 NZLR 551.

of corporate intent, reporting requirements, and the coverage by the Official Information regime as indicative that judicial review was unnecessary and ought *not* to be available. According to the Court, the only public law mechanisms to operate should be internal bureaucratic and political controls—not external ones such as judicial review. Private law rules of general application should be the primary means for external accountability.[25] In this approach we can see a convergence between the executive's and judiciary's understanding of the nature and character of the state sector reforms, and a shared desire that the law should provide a 'level playing-field' as between publicly owned and other commercial enterprises.

The case, renamed after Auckland Electric Power Board acquired a new corporate livery as Mercury Energy Ltd, was appealed to the Judicial Committee of the Privy Council *(Mercury Energy Ltd v. Electricity Corporation of New Zealand*[26]*)*. The Committee did not agree with the Court of Appeal's approach. It regarded the presence of internal political controls as an indication of the public status of state-owned enterprises and of their susceptibility to judicial review. Having surmounted that initial hurdle, the Judicial Committee then focused its inquiry on the nature of the power in order to determine which grounds of judicial review should apply. In the context of the power to enter a commercial transaction, it found that only the very narrowest rationality and bad faith grounds of judicial review would be available. This restriction on the available grounds of challenge was enough effectively to quell future challenges of state-owned enterprises by way of judicial review.

What followed should be briefly mentioned here. Given that Richardson P, in the Court of Appeal, had posited in *Auckland Electric Power Board* that the principal mechanism of external control (other than political control) ought to be private and not public law—subsequent litigation involving state owned enterprises understandably centred on whether monopoly suppliers of essential services were under *common law* obligations to supply customers at fair and reasonable prices as a matter of private law.[27] The Court of Appeal later rejected this approach as 'judicial review in another guise' in yet another case about electricity pricing, involving the same parties as before, and reported in the new names of their respective corporate successors *Vector v. Transpower*.[28] The Court once again used the availability of political mechanisms of control as a reason not to develop the common law. The government's ability to set policy goals through statements of corporate intent agreed with the state-owned enterprise (Transpower) and its power to regulate prices over the electricity sector as a whole under the Commerce Act 1986 combined with its restraint in exercising these

---

[25] *Auckland Electric Power Board v. Electricity Corporation of New Zealand* [1994] 559, 560–1.
[26] *Mercury Energy Ltd v. Electricity Corporation of New Zealand* [1994] 1 WLR 521 (PC).
[27] *Auckland Electric Power*, n. 24, 559 cf. *Vector v. Transpower* [1999] 3 NZLR 647, discussed in J. McLean, 'The Ordinary Law of Tort and Contract and the New Public Management' (2001) *Common Law World Review* 387. [28] *Vector*, n. 27, 667.

regulatory powers, was read by the Court as a reason for the common law too, to pursue a 'lighted-handed' approach in relation to regulating particular transactions.[29] Given that Transpower never threatened to discontinue electricity supply, and what was really at issue in the dispute was whether the electricity supplier to Auckland (New Zealand's largest city) should have the advantage of a discount for bulk, the facts of the case fell well short of establishing that an abuse of power had occurred. The majority of the Court of Appeal went further to suggest that the Commerce Act 1986 had completely covered the field and there was no room for the common law to operate or develop.[30] This had the effect of quelling future challenges by way of the common law of essential services. It seems that, in the end, politicians and not the courts, would regulate the new corporate monopolies—or not, as the case may be.

Some judicial review cases have raised more directly the question of whether state-owned enterprises should be treated as part of the executive or at arm's length from it. This has been important, for example, in the context of the Treaty of Waitangi. Obligations under the Treaty of Waitangi have been taken to reside in the Crown (used here in a unified central government sense) rather than in its instruments or emanations.[31] In one of these cases, the critical question was whether the relationship between the Crown and corporatized and privatized broadcasting entities was sufficiently arm's length, that the government had effectively put it beyond its powers to fulfill its obligations under the Treaty of Waitangi to promote the Maori language. Lord Woolf in *New Zealand Maori Council v. Attorney-General* remarked that '[a]lthough, under the Act, a state enterprise is structured so that it is separate from the Crown ... it remains very much the Crown's creature'.[32] In that case it was important to the government that the state enterprise should be treated as *its* 'creature' in order that the government should be found *not* to have breached its Treaty of Waitangi obligations to promote the Maori language. The government successfully argued that the transfer of broadcasting assets to separate corporate entities did not compromise its ability to regulate such bodies. It suited the government here to argue that it retained control.

In another case, *Lumber Specialities v. Hodgson*,[33] it was crucial to both the government and the state-owned enterprise that they be treated as *separate* creatures, though for the same reason as in the previous case, in order to preserve the government's regulatory role. Timberlands (a state-owned enterprise) had entered into contracts with Lumber Specialities Ltd (a private logging company)

---

[29] *Ibid*.

[30] Thomas J dissented on the question of whether the common law could still develop for modern conditions to control the worst abuses of power.

[31] See *Te Heu Heu v. Attorney-General* [1999] 1 NZLR 98 (HC) which decided that a statutory obligation to act consistently with the Treaty of Waitangi was only binding on the Crown and not on State Owned Enterprises.

[32] [1994] 1 NZLR 513, 520 (PC). This was acknowledged in *Lumber Specialities v. Hodgson* [2000] 2 NZLR 347, para. 77.   [33] [2000] 2 NZLR 347, 363, para. 77.

to supply virgin indigenous forest. The incoming government, concerned about the environmental impact of such logging, reversed the previous government's policy and announced that no further such contracts would be entered and that existing beech logging would cease. Ministers communicated the policy change to Timberlands through the statement of corporate intent. Timberlands then successfully invoked *force majeure* clauses in the existing contracts on the basis that the change of government policy was beyond its control. It was thereby freed from its contractual obligation to supply timber for logging. The Court treated the state-owned enterprise as separate from the minister despite the fact that formally the statement of corporate intent was agreed between the two entities. This allowed the government to take the role of regulator rather than contracting party, influencing matters at arm's length and on general public policy grounds.

Had the government and Timberlands been treated as a single entity, the result would likely have been much worse for the government. It is unlikely that the doctrine of 'executive necessity', that would allow the government to escape its contractual obligations because of pressing matters of state, applies in New Zealand, or indeed would apply in this factual scenario, though there is no case law directly on the point.[34] Governments sometimes attempt to achieve a similar outcome by including 'termination for convenience' clauses in contracts. Such clauses typically recognize that the government may have to break contracts because of changes in policy and other exigencies and provide for compensation for work that has been performed under the contract up until the point of termination but not for loss of profits in the future. Courts tend strictly to construe them, though again there is no New Zealand case law directly on point.[35] Clearly, the inclusion of such a clause would have made both the contract itself and the consequences of not performing it more expensive for government. It was much cheaper, and more effective for central government to interfere with the contractual obligations of its separate creature, the state-owned enterprise.[36]

Both these cases demonstrate unexpected results for those who may have thought that creating corporate entities at arm's length from central government makes control by ministers more difficult. In fact such a structural separation provided more options for government. In the first case, the government could retain the appearance of control without having to do anything actively to fulfill its Treaty of Waitangi obligations (it had no control over the day to day operation of entities). In the second case, the perceived separation enabled both the government and the state-owned enterprise to avoid paying damages to the logging companies as a consequence of the government's decision to reverse

---

[34] *Rederiaktiebolaget 'Amphitrite' v. The King* [1921] 3 KB 500.

[35] See N. Seddon, *Government Contracts* (Federation Press, 2nd. ed, 1999), 5.4–5.9.

[36] Hadfield, discusses the limitations the United States courts have imposed on the application of 'termination for convenience clauses' see G. Hadfield, 'Sovereignty and Contract' (1999) 8 *Southern California Interdisciplinary Law Journal* 467, 492–3.

logging policy.[37] A crucial factor in both these cases is how the juristic personality of the government is conceived. We can discern in these cases, too, the judicial recognition of a functional separation of powers within the executive branch as between the government as regulator and the government as commercial actor.

(ii) Private regulatory bodies

While the judges may have been unclear about how much to apply judicial review doctrine to outsourced activities and privatized and corporatized enterprises, they have been more willing to extend judicial review to *private* regulatory bodies. In *Electoral Commission v. Cameron*, the Court of Appeal reviewed the Advertising Standards Complaints Board on the basis that it had misinterpreted its own rules.[38] The Advertising Standards Complaints Board is a private unincorporated body constituted by the Advertising Standards Authority Incorporated. Membership of the society comprises the representative organizations of the major industry interest groups. The Board was set up to hear complaints based on the Authority's code of conduct. The Complaints Board's regulatory jurisdiction does not depend on statute but is recognized as an integral part of regulatory scheme by the Broadcasting Act 1989.

A member of the public brought a complaint to the Board against the Electoral Commission (a statutory body) on the basis that its campaign promoting public awareness of the new Mixed Member Proportional Electoral System was misleading and therefore in breach of the code. The Board found against the Electoral Commission. In a nice reversal of the usual scenario in judicial review cases, the Electoral Commission (a public body) subsequently sought judicial review of the decision of the Advertising Standards Complaints Board (a private body) on the basis that it had misunderstood its powers. The Court of Appeal found that as a body exercising 'public power' the Board was amenable to judicial review, both on the basis of the wording of the Judicature Amendment Act 1972 and on the reasoning of the English Court of Appeal in *R v. Panel of Takeovers and Mergers, ex parte Datafin plc*.[39] The Court found that the Board had no authority to make rulings in relation to advertisements of the Commission published in the exercise of its statutory public awareness functions.

In the later case of *Phipps v. Royal Australasian College of Surgeons*[40] the Court of Appeal was again prepared to review a private regulatory body this time for erroneous findings and procedural errors in a report on the professional conduct and standards of a surgeon (who was not a member of the College) commissioned

---

[37] Cf. *Petrocorp Exploration Ltd v. Minister of Energy* [1991] 1 NZLR 1 (CA) 641 (PC) that further illustrates the distinction between governments acting as regulators and as contractors.
[38] [1997] 2 NZLR 421 (CA).   [39] [1987] 1 QB 815.
[40] [1999] 3 NZLR 1, 11–12. The case was appealed to the Judicial Committee but remains authoritative on these issues.

at the contractual behest of his employer. The Court characterized this 'exercise of power' as having a sufficiently public character and consequences to attract the supervision of judicial review. The non-commercial context of the case was emphasized. The focus was on the actual exercise of the power and on whether the particular grounds of review had been made out.[41] One wonders if this is really another functional test masquerading as a 'power' test.

(iii) Application of New Zealand Bill of Rights Act 1990

Another test that mixes function and source of power or authority appears in the New Zealand Bill of Rights Act 1990. Section 3 states:

This Bill of Rights applies only to acts done—
By the legislative, executive, or judicial branches of the government of New Zealand; or
By any person or body in the performance of any public function, power, or duty conferred or imposed on that person or body by or pursuant to law.

This provision has not been the subject of extensive judicial discussion so far and is unlikely to be so in the future because the breadth of section 3(b) makes it unnecessary to determine the scope of section 3(a). Where rights are at stake one would imagine that an expansive view of the public sector ought to be taken. Some legislation has made explicit that the Bill of Rights applies (to private prisons, for example).[42] At least two matters remain unsettled in relation to the coverage of the Bill of Rights framework.

First, should a private actor, exercising power under legislation, be subjected to the same degree of control as a public actor exercising power under statute? Should a private shopkeeper issuing a trespass notice under the Trespass Act 1954 against political protestors, for example, be under the same obligations to observe the Bill of Rights freedoms of expression and association as the Speaker of the House of Representatives?[43] By what calculation ought the private shopkeeper's autonomy rights be taken into account when interpreting the Trespass Act?

The second issue concerns who is liable to provide a remedy for breaches of the Bill of Rights. This is not a problem when the remedy can be effected by the exclusion of evidence, invalidation of a decision, or interpretation of the power. It becomes an issue when the remedy sought is damages. In *Simpson*

---

[41] Rule 626 of the High Court Rules assisted in this approach by including a reference to 'A person exercising a power that affects the public interest'.

[42] See ss. 41C–41G Penal Institutions Act 1954, amended in 1994 to extend public law accountability mechanisms (and the Public Works Act 1981) to private prisons. Section 41E deems acts done by a 'contract penal institution' to be acts of the 'executive branch of the government of New Zealand'. Randerson J helpfully sets out the criteria for determining whether an entity is performing a public function in *Ransfield v. Radio Network Ltd*, unreported High Court Auckland Civ 2003-404-569, 11 June 2004, para. 69.

[43] Consider *Police v. Beggs* [1999] 3 NZLR 615, HC involving a warning notice issued under the Trespass Act by the Speaker to political protestors on the grounds of Parliament.

v. *Attorney-General (Baigent's Case)*,[44] the Court of Appeal founded a new public law remedy of damages for breach of the Bill of Rights. It established that the Crown is *directly* liable for breaches of the Bill of Rights as a matter of public law. McKay J said 'where the right is infringed by a branch of government or a public functionary, the remedy under the Act must be against the Crown'. As with the Treaty of Waitangi, the Crown is to be the fount of redress. Notice the asymmetry here: the Bill of Rights applies to bodies however much they are disaggregated from central government; the government is treated as a unified whole for the purposes of the damages remedy.

The Law Commission argued, in response to the *Baigent* decision, that the availability of damages claims directly against the Crown is inconsistent with the financial and other autonomy of public sector bodies.[45] It advocated a control test.[46] In a privatized environment, however, it is exactly when central government does not exercise close supervision or control that the threat to constitutional values may be greatest. The real issue here is how best to create proper incentives for the upholding of such values: is it by encouraging closer supervision by central government or by letting costs lie where they fall.[47] This is a difficult question to answer as an empirical matter, as we shall see from the subsequent discussion.

The executive is the subject of differing definitions both in terms of how it is fundamentally conceived and depending on which accountability mechanisms are to apply. Relationships between the different disaggregated entities to the core are of primary importance, as are the mechanisms for control by the centre.

2. What is the nature of executive power?

(a) Legislative definitions

Under traditional constitutional understandings, the executive power is based on the ancient prerogative.[48] Statute may limit or supplement such prerogative powers. The Bill of Rights 1688, which is part of New Zealand law, places

---

[44] [1994] 3 NZLR 667.

[45] NZ Law Commission, *Crown Liability and Judicial Immunity: A Response to Baigent's Case and Harvey v Derrick* (Report No. 37, 1997), para 38. Sir Kenneth Keith, now Rt. Hon Justice Keith of the Supreme Court, was President of the Law Commission at the time of the writing of this report.

[46] See P. Rishworth, et al., *The New Zealand Bill of Rights* (Oxford University Press, 2003), 819–20 for the discussion of *Innes v. Wong* [1996] 3 NZLR 241–2 in which the High Court allowed a damages claim against a separately incorporated Crown Health Enterprise.

[47] See further, for the US experience, G. Metzger, 'Privatization as Delegation' [2003] 103 *Col L Rev* 1367.

[48] For completeness, it should be noted that in *Burt v. Governor-General* [1992] 3 NZLR 672, the Court of Appeal accepted that the prerogative was potentially subject to judicial review. See also rule 626(c) High Court Rules.

important constraints on the executive's power to act without Parliament,[49] as do many ordinary statutes. But the powers of executive government are not restricted to those given by statute. It enjoys numerous special prerogative powers that only the government can enjoy (such as to enter treaties, make wars, grant pardons, and confer honours). Importantly too, the executive is generally understood to be capable, like an ordinary citizen, of doing anything that is not prohibited.[50]

Throughout the 1990s it was this latter notion, which came to be referred to as the executive's 'natural person' power, which achieved a certain degree of prominence in executive and legislative attempts to define executive power.[51] As we discussed earlier, such an approach is consistent with a government management strategy that focuses on ends and encourages flexibility around means. This idea contains within it a number of separate concepts. It identifies 'the Crown' as the single unified legal person representing the core of government, usually as owner of government assets or purchaser of government services. It suggests that not only public law, but private law, will operate as a discipline on government, and it emphasizes the capacity of the executive to act without statutory authorization.

This 'private law model of public law' has manifested itself in a number of legislative practices. In 1989, an influential opinion restated the long held legal position that statutes *need not* set out the functions of government departments. It went on to recommend that statutes *should not* do so in the interests of efficiency and flexibility.[52] Her Majesty may seek advice from whomsoever she pleases, including private consultants. This systematic change in practice made the myriad restructurings of the years that followed much easier to effect. And while Parliamentary scrutiny was not necessarily reduced (a newly constituted standing select committee of the House had around that time been given significant powers of investigation into the conduct of the state sector) the likelihood of legal challenges based on ultra vires arguments has been reduced.[53] At

---

[49] See for a modern application, *Fitzgerald v. Muldoon* [1976] 2 NZLR 615.

[50] For the orthodox view in New Zealand see B.V. Harris, 'The "Third Source" of Authority for Government Actions '[1992] *LQR* 626 cf. A. Tomkins, *Public Law* (Clarendon, 2003), 78–9 who states 'Whereas the rule of law provides that the executive may do nothing without clear legal authority, individuals may conversely do anything unless expressly prohibited by law'.

[51] See, e.g. the approach of Keith J in *KD Swan Family Trust v. Universal College of Learning* (CA255/02) where he determinedly finds that a lease granted without the legislatively required consent is valid. He relies in part on the fact that there is a range of internal legal mechanisms for ensuring accountability of educational institutions (see paras 9–11).

[52] See the legal opinion of the New Zealand Legislation Advisory Committee, '*Departmental Statutes: Report No 4*' (Department of Justice, 1989) and especially the appendix by F.M. Brookfield. Though not explicit about this, the advice would seem to adopt the United Kingdom position expressed in the so-called Ram doctrine which took the form of a memorandum from Glanville Ram, First Parliamentary Counsel 2 November 1945 referred to in A. Lester and M. Weaitt, 'The Use of Ministerial Powers without Parliamentary Authority': the Ram Doctrine' [2003] *PL* 415.

[53] Government Administration Committee. The new legislative practice is also sometimes at odds with the 'listing technique' adopted in the various accountability regimes. Why should it

the same time as the practice of establishing departments by statute changed, the inconsistent practice of conferring statutory power to enter contracts for certain purposes was eliminated. The power to contract, including the power to dispose of Crown assets, was assumed to be part of the executive's natural person powers.[54]

Drafting practices that discourage ultra vires arguments and aim to encourage flexibility and efficiency have persisted, and not merely for the core state sector. The Local Government Act 2002, for example, has conferred powers of general competence on local authorities.[55] The Crown Entities Act 2004 states explicitly in section 17 'that a statutory entity may do anything that a natural person can do'.[56] Section 20 of that Act creates an exception to classical ultra vires doctrine to ensure that the non-governmental party to an ultra vires transaction can still enforce it, provided the party does not know of the absence of authority.

Not only are there intended to be efficiency and flexibility gains through this means of characterizing government power, the analogy between the executive and a natural person has also been portrayed as establishing a level playing field, not only of powers but also of liabilities. Another component of the private law model of public law as adopted in New Zealand was the expectation that the main form of regulation ought to be effected through the ordinary principles of private law. Particularly in the 1990's, such was the Diceyan confidence in the power of the ordinary common law to constrain public power that it was considered as *a*, if not *the*, primary means of regulation. Moreover, somewhat oddly, the ordinary common law was regarded as a 'market' mechanism of regulation.[57] The law of contract was intended to be an important part of such regulation. Sometimes 'contracts' were used in non-legal settings to refer to economic and managerial relationships. In many cases, however, under the New Zealand version of the new public management, contracts were fully intended to have legal status, and different parts of the former state sector were established as separate legal persons so that contracts between them would have full legal effect. So, for example, purchasers and providers, separately incorporated, entered into fully enforceable legal contracts for health care (unlike in the United Kingdom where NHS 'contracts' were political and administrative but not *legal* devices for

---

matter which department of government holds official information if they are all part of one unified legal entity? It may matter for the purposes of the Privacy Act 1993 in that information collected for a particular purpose must be used for that purpose.

[54] The usual practice for the disposal of assets was to confer a general power to be effected in a particular instance by an order in council. See, e.g. the State Owned Enterprises Act 1986.

[55] A local authority is a body corporate with perpetual succession. Local Government Act 2002, s. 12(2) provides: '(a) For the purposes of performing its role, a local authority has—full capacity to carry on or undertake any activity or business, do any act, or enter any transaction; and (b) ... full rights, powers and privileges.' [56] There are provisos in s. 17(2) and s. 21.

[57] The Commerce Act 1986 was considered to be the other primary mechanism for market regulation.

accountability).[58] Corporate methods of accountability were adopted where possible, most notably in the state-owned enterprises model. For those state owned enterprises that have now passed into private ownership, competition and contract law are still intended to be the main forms of regulation. Industry specific self-regulatory regimes for gas and electricity are only now being established.[59]

The desire to make the Crown susceptible to the criminal law is part of the same impulse to achieve a level playing field between the state and the ordinary citizen. In a reaction to the tragic collapse of a viewing platform on Department of Conservation land that killed a number of students, Parliament passed the Crown Organizations (Criminal Liability) Act 2002. It treats Crown organizations as having separate legal personality for the purpose of enabling their prosecution for criminal liability under the building and health and safety legislation (which prescribes fines). It has not yet been tested judicially.

The longstanding technical legal understanding that (subject to legislation) government has all the powers of a natural person was given new, ideological, resonance in the era of the new public management. Natural person powers came to variously represent: devolution and empowerment; freedom, equality, and the rule of law; efficiency; and neo-liberal politics (depending on one's political perspective).

The focus of the legislature and executive has been to enlarge the means by which government may pursue its policies and to focus on internal bureaucratic mechanisms of accountability (as we shall see below). Indeed, changes to drafting practices may have also been intended to minimize less predictable external juridical forms of accountability, especially those fashioned for the public sector in particular.

(b) Judicial responses

The relatively open-ended terms under which modern legislation confers power on the executive has been effective in conferring greater flexibility over the means by which the executive may operate than formerly and in limiting certain kinds of judicial intervention. Traditional ultra vires type claims to the courts have become increasingly rare. The reluctance of the Court of Appeal to judicially review state owned enterprises when exercising their commercial functions, discussed above, is further evidence that the attempts on the part of Parliament to achieve a level playing field between the government and ordinary corporations have been reasonably successful. As this also demonstrates, the courts have been reluctant to

---

[58] See J. McLean and T. Ashton, 'Quasi-Markets and Pseudo Contracts in the New Zealand Public Health System' (2001) 10 *Otago Law Review* 17, cf. A.C.L. Davies, *Accountability: A Public Law Analysis of Government by Contract* (Clarendon, 2001), and P. Vincent-Jones, 'Regulating Government by Contract: Towards a Public Law Framework' (2002) 65 *MLR* 611.

[59] See, e.g. the Gas Amendment Act 2004. The new electricity regime remains a Bill at the time of writing.

develop special common law doctrines as a means to regulate formerly public utilities, preferring instead to maintain one unified ordinary law. They have also been reluctant to impose onerous procedural requirements on public agencies when they are exercising commercial or quasi-commercial functions.

While certain kinds of judicial intervention have sometimes been restricted, or at least constrained, by the way in which contemporary legislation confers executive power, other traditional forms of judicial response have been relatively unaffected and new more substantive forms of intervention have been developing. Despite the executive's desire to achieve more flexibility, judicial review has continued its traditional role in controlling the means by which the government pursues its policies, tending to leave the ends as a matter for politics and legislation.

The procedural controls of judicial review may limit the executive's flexibility in *how* it exercises its power without necessarily limiting its ultimate power. Such judicial supervision serves to ensure increased participation and greater transparency in executive decision-making. It is a mechanism by which to call the executive to account.

The more substantive controls of judicial review (e.g. *Wednesbury* review, requiring that certain considerations be taken into account, ensuring that statutory powers are interpreted consistently with 'fundamental' or 'constitutional' values) do potentially confine and limit executive power as well as the way in which it is exercised. These more substantive challenges extend the availability of ultra vires challenges beyond the now more limited traditional forms which focused on whether the powers of the executive had exceeded those conferred explicitly by statute, to more open-textured questions about whether the powers of the executive have been exercised consistently with 'constitutional values' broadly defined. Such substantive challenges call and hold the executive to account and also have the potential to define and confine executive power.

Despite the differences between these two kinds of judicial review, one limiting power and the other limiting the manner in which power is exercised, they are both examples of public bodies being held to different standards than private bodies. For ease of reference we shall discuss both kinds of judicial review below under the head of judicial forms of accountability.

3. Accountability

As Mulgan observes, 'accountability' is a concept of relatively recent currency. Its application used to be restricted to financial accountability and audit but has come to be used as a general model for management processes—public as well as private.[60] In this section we shall first consider 'external' modes of accountability,

---

[60] R. Mulgan, *Holding Power to Account* (Palgrave, 2003), 6.

focusing on judicial review. We shall then consider 'internal' accountability mechanisms within the state sector and the extent to which accountability mechanisms have been integrated with, and affected by, the financial management system.

(a) Judicial forms of accountability

(i) General themes in judicial review

Judicial review is the primary legal means of calling the executive to account. It has not only tested whether broad aspirational statutory language is justiciable, but has also been increasingly informed by the substantive values embodied in the Treaty of Waitangi and Maori customary law, international conventions, common law values, and is potentially informed by the New Zealand Bill of Rights Act 1990.

There are no leave requirements, wide standing rules, and liberal discovery practices in applications for judicial review in New Zealand. It is a small jurisdiction, which produces a small number of judicial review cases even relative to its size.[61] Even so, we shall need to be selective here. *New Zealand Maori Council v. Attorney-General*,[62] (hereafter the *Lands* case) is representative of a number of different trends that have emerged in the courts and been represented in the reported cases. It is arguably the most important case of the last two decades in terms of its constitutional significance. The case involved the successful judicial review of the government's attempts to transfer Crown land to state-enterprise ownership without providing any process by which the executive could take account of the principles of the Treaty of Waitangi. The transfer was to be effected by an order in council. Once transferred from Crown ownership, the Crown's ability to give effect to Waitangi Tribunal's recommendations for redress of historical grievances relating to such land and interests in land would be seriously diminished.[63]

The State-Owned Enterprises Act 1986 contains a number of broadly aspirational provisions, or legislative statements of objectives, section 9 among them. That section, as it turned out, imposed the only constitutional legal impediment on the transfer of state assets by the executive during this period. Section 9 states:

Nothing in this Act shall permit the Crown to act in a manner that is inconsistent with the principles of the Treaty of Waitangi.

---

[61] There are an estimated 120–130 judicial review cases annually—see M. Taggart, 'Introduction to Judicial Review in New Zealand' [1997] *Judicial Review* 236, fn 14.

[62] [1987] 1 NZLR 641 (hereafter the *Lands* case).

[63] It should be noted that Cooke P did not defer to the Waitangi Tribunal as an expert body set up to decide the content of the principles of the Treaty of Waitangi, claiming that that was ultimately a question of law to be decided by the courts.

In all probability, the framers of the Act did not mean this provision to be justiciable or to operate as any kind of legal constraint on executive power. The Solicitor-General's response to an interlocutory that the executive had done 'nothing' to give effect to this provision, however, was the crucial admission that effectively prevented the transfer of assets pending the establishment of a process by which to take Treaty of Waitangi principles into account. Consequently, it was left primarily to the parties to negotiate the substantive content of the 'principles of the Treaty of Waitangi'. Aspirational, formerly non-justiciable, legislative provisions could now conceivably operate to constrain executive power.

The broader effects of the case are various. The unprecedented political success of the *Lands* case encouraged the strategic use by Maori of the courts to further their political aims. It was the first in a large number of judicial review actions by Maori challenging government action.[64] Some would see this as part of a Maori renaissance, or, more pejoratively, as evidence of an emerging 'Treaty Industry'. It is important to understand these developments, however, against the background of systematic privatization and corporatization. It was a time during which private rights were being created over formerly public goods. Every time the government created new private rights, it provided an opportunity for Maori to claim a share as first occupants of the territory. This was not only the case with land, but also with the creation of private property rights in fishing quota, coal, and the airwaves. These cases can be viewed as a direct, if unintended, by-product of a public policy that was committed to the use of property rights as a regulatory device.

Although the legislation said nothing about the relationship between Maori and the Crown or about processes for consultation required between them, the Court in the *Lands* case made some general statements about the procedural obligations owed by the Crown to Maori including the duty to consult, and to act honestly and with the utmost good faith. One of the most important of the immediate effects of the decision, in terms of defining how the executive is required to exercise its power, was the government's embrace of this procedural approach in the development of its future Treaty relationship with Maori.[65] Successive governments have developed extensive consultation processes with Maori that have become an established part of doing the business of government.[66]

---

[64] See, e.g. *Attorney-General v. New Zealand Maori Council* [1991] 2 NZLR 129; *New Zealand Maori Council v. Attorney-General* [1992] 2 NZLR 576; *New Zealand Maori Council v. Attorney-General* [1996] 3 NZLR 140; *Te Runanganui o te Ika Whenua Inc Society v. Attorney-General* [1992] 2 NZLR 20 ; *Te Runanga o Muriwhenua v. Treaty of Waitangi Fisheries Commission* [1996] 3 NZLR 10.

[65] Department of Justice, Principles for Crown Action On the Treaty of Waitangi, (Department of Justice, 1989) were produced as a direct result of the *Lands* decision.

[66] A comprehensive reference produced for the government policy analysts is Te Puni Kokiri. *He Tirohanga o Kawa ki te Tiriti o Waitangi (A Guide to the Principles of the Treaty of Waitangi as expressed by the Courts and Waitangi Tribunal)* (Te Puni Kokiri, 2001).

Consultation practices have not been restricted to Maori. Courts began to wonder aloud whether duties to consult should be read into other statutory regimes, and to flesh out what the existing statutory duties to consult might require in particular contexts. At the same time, governments began to realize that consultation with 'stake-holders' could forestall litigation. Extensive consultation procedures became the preferred *means* of doing business under the New Public Management New Zealand-style. The strategy would spawn some of the over 400 'duties to consult' in the statute book.[67] This factor is very important given that in New Zealand there was no equivalent to the UK Citizens' Charters. In many respects the largest contribution that judicial review may have made to accountability has been to require greater participation and transparency in governmental processes by *sometimes* interpolating duties to consult where the statute has been silent. This has indirectly led to the enactment of explicit provisions requiring notification and consultation. How effective such processes are, is quite another matter that this essay does not attempt to assess.[68]

New Zealand has been slow to develop a tradition of public interest litigation beyond the Maori cases. Many of the trends illustrated by the *Lands* case have, however, had effects beyond Maori.[69] The other aspirational provisions in the State-Owned Enterprises Act 1986 imposing social goals alongside commercial ones on newly created state-owned enterprises (such as to be 'socially responsible' and 'good employers') would also come to be litigated (in these cases unsuccessfully).[70] The practice of including legislated statements of objectives and other aspirational provisions, especially references to the Treaty of Waitangi, would subsequently dwindle. The creation of private rights over formerly public property would give rise to numerous fishing quota cases and challenges to other allocation regimes.[71]

In many ways the *Lands* decision was the first New Zealand case to give effect to the 'constitutionalisation of judicial review'.[72] It was the constitutional significance of the Treaty of Waitangi that provoked the Court of Appeal to impose significant procedural requirements in the *Lands* case and to stop any privatization taking place until such processes were put in place. It was the first case

---

[67] There was an initial period of litigation to determine how extensive such duties would be, see *Wellington International Airport v. Air New Zealand* [1993] 1 NZLR 671 (CA); *McInnes v. Ministry of Transport* [2001] 3 NZLR 11 (CA).

[68] Sometimes general consultation is afforded when more onerous procedural duties may be more appropriate. Moreover, consultation as to population needs can sometimes lead to difficult conflicts of interests when the consequent services are put to tender (and the stakeholders who were consulted become providers).

[69] This is notwithstanding broad standing rules and few threshold tests for bringing actions. Recent examples are *Daniels v. Attorney- General* [2003] 2 NZLR 742 and *Attorney-General v. Refugee Council* [2003] 2 NZLR 577.

[70] See, e.g. *Federated Farmers v. NZ Post Ltd* [1992] 3 NZBORR 339.

[71] See, e.g. *Official Assignee v Chief Executive of Ministry of Fisheries* [2002] 2 NZLR 158 (CA); *Westhaven Shellfish Ltd v. Chief Executive of Ministry of Fisheries* [2002] 2 NZLR 158 (CA).

[72] See P. Joseph, 'Constitutional Review Now' [1998] *NZ Law Review* 86.

overtly to integrate certain substantive constitutional values (heretofore undefined) about the constitutional relationship between Maori and the Crown, with traditional ultra vires and procedural remedies. In the years that followed, many other substantive and especially human rights values would come to find expression in otherwise traditional judicial review causes of action. The means by which government achieves its goals would be supervised by the courts. Would the goals of government also be affected?

(ii) Maori custom as a constraint on executive power

Much of the Treaty of Waitangi litigation already discussed depended on the incorporation of Treaty principles in domestic legislation. Such provisions have become highly politically contested and, consequently, increasingly rare. While Maori have tended to prefer to frame claims in terms of the Treaty of Waitangi, to a certain extent the Treaty is a codification of common law customary rights.[73] Article Two, for example, confers a right of preemption on the Crown, and guarantees to Maori their traditional rights over lands, forests, fisheries, and other treasures. The capacity of non-statutory Maori custom law to impose legal impediments on executive power is a controversy of long standing.

Is custom part of the common law, a legal impediment on government action unless and until such rights are clearly extinguished by statute, or is it merely a moral claim that needs legislation for legal effect? There is conflicting New Zealand authority on this point. In *Te Weehi v. Regional Fisheries Officer*,[74] however, the High Court made strong and influential statements to the effect that custom does constrain executive power unless and until it is clearly extinguished by statute.[75] If that is the case, then it may be easier to make arguments based on custom than on the Treaty itself.[76]

In a later decision, perhaps the high water mark of cases in terms of the content of Maori custom and its effect on traditional judicial review actions, the Court of Appeal was prepared to recognize that a Maori operated tourist whale-watching venture could be a modern manifestation of a customary use. In *Ngai Tahu v. Director-General of Conservation*,[77] the Court of Appeal found that such customary rights not only required the Maori tribe in question to be consulted about the licensing process but also entitled it to 'a reasonable degree

---

[73] On the relationship between Treaty and customary rights see: P. McHugh, 'What a difference a Treaty makes—the Pathway of Aboriginal Rights Jurisprudence in New Zealand Public Law' (2004) 15 *PLR* 87.   [74] [1986] 1 NZLR 680 (HC).

[75] Strictly speaking this was obiter as the statute in question did preserve the status of Maori fishing rights.

[76] The methodology is similar to that adopted in *R. v. Lord Chancellor, ex parte Witham* [1998] QB 575 and *R. v. Secretary of State for the Home Department, ex parte Simms* [1999] 3 WLR 328. There remains a question of whether the Treaty of Waitangi can be used to constrain executive power. In *Huakina Development Trust v. Waikato Valley Authority* [1987] 2 NZLR 188, the High Court considered the Treaty to be a mandatory relevant consideration.

[77] [1995] 3 NZLR 553 (CA).

of preference'[78] within the licensing process. The contribution of judicial review appears to have gone beyond process here and toward the constitutionalization of rights themselves (to ends rather than means).

Most significant of all, as a political matter, has been the seabed and foreshore controversy. One of the questions raised in *Ngati Apa v. Attorney-General*[79] was whether the radical title that passed to the Crown with sovereignty over the territory was to be held consistently with and burdened by native customary rights. The Court of Appeal held that it was, and that whatever rights to the seabed and foreshore as may be found to exist (yet to be proved in the Maori Land Court) had not been clearly extinguished by statute or by cession of sovereignty. In so holding, it overruled a 1963 judgment that had found that for Maori property to exist, it had first to be converted into land held in fee from the Crown.[80] The Foreshore and Seabed Act 2004 has since been enacted. It restricts the Maori Land Court's jurisdiction and prescribes procedures for proving territorial title and customary rights. It renders *executive* action inconsistent with customary rights capable of extinguishing such rights, thereby reducing them to moral rather than legal claims.[81] Matters of redress have been left to the discretion of the executive.

(iii) International treaties

The other major trend by which judicial review cases have been constitutionalized is through the use of international conventions to constrain the way in which executive power is exercised. Most of these cases have arisen in the immigration context, traditionally a highly discretionary area into which judges have been slow to enter. The *Tavita* line of cases[82] demonstrates the Court of Appeal's willingness to treat international human rights conventions as mandatory relevant considerations, that is, as matters that must be considered in government decision-making even though the statute does not refer to them. The relevant legislation empowered the decision-maker to exercise discretion on humanitarian grounds not to deport a person illegally in New Zealand. In each case, the person subject to the removal order was the parent of a New Zealand born child who was a New Zealand citizen, who sought to rely on the UN Convention on the Rights of the Child as a factor that had to be taken into account in deciding whether humanitarian grounds existed. The Convention itself states that the best interests of the child should be 'a primary consideration'.

---

[78] [1995] 3 NZLR, 562.   [79] [2003] 3 NZLR 643.
[80] *Re the Ninety Mile Beach* [1963] NZLR 461 (CA).
[81] Foreshore and Seabed Bill. For a recent discussion of New Zealand developments see M.P. Belgrave et al., *Waitangi Revisited* (Melbourne, Oxford, 2004).
[82] *Tavita v. Minister of Immigration* [1994] 2 NZLR 257; *Puli'uvea v. Removal Review Authority* (1996) 14 FRNZ 322; *Rajan v. Minister of Immigration* [1996] 3 NZLR 543 [CA]; *Schier v. Removal Review Authority* [1999] 1 NZLR 703 (CA), cf. *Baker v. Canada (Minister of Citizenship and Immigration)* [1999] 2 SCR 817; *Minister of Immigration v. Teoh* (1995) 183 CLR 273 (HCA).

However, while the Court consistently has found that the interests of the children are relevant to the exercise of the humanitarian discretion, it has not been prepared to determine the weight to be given to the children's interests in the overall decision, or to engage in a proportionality calculus.[83] The approach has the effect of enhancing transparency—calling the executive into account— but not necessarily rectifying the original decision. (In fact, while the *Tavita* case did not compel this result, the minister ultimately decided to allow Mr Tavita to stay in New Zealand.)

In another case, the international law of the high seas was used, not merely as a factor to be weighed by the executive, but to confine the actual scope of the power itself as an interpretative (and jurisdictional) matter. In *Sellers v. Maritime Safety Inspector*[84] the Court of Appeal found that a discretionary power conferred on the Director of Maritime Safety could not be exercised to require safety equipment to be carried on craft on the high seas.[85] The Director did not have the power to give a direction that was inconsistent with the freedom of the high seas and the freedom of navigation.

One way of viewing these controversial cases is to regard them as *holding*[86] the executive to account domestically for the commitments it has made internationally. Indeed, Cooke P explicitly framed his *Tavita* judgment in these terms.[87] To put it in another way, the executive in its internal persona is unified with the executive in its domestic persona. It is the executive that is imposing constraints on itself, even if those constraints are enforced by the courts.

However, these cases do not directly *call* the executive into account for entering into international obligations in the first instance. Inevitably these developments have lead to parliamentary pressure for greater openness about the treaty making process itself—traditionally the exclusive preserve of the executive. In a new procedure, trialed in 1998, and subsequently adopted in Standing Orders,[88] Parliament's internal rules have required that post-signature but pre-ratification, all multilateral treaties should be presented to the House of Representatives for a select committee to report on a national interest analysis, the extent of the social, cultural, and economic obligations imposed, the consultations undertaken, and how the agreements should be implemented. The government agrees not to take any further steps in relation to the Treaty during the reporting period. The major political parties have been concerned to achieve a balance between enhancing Parliament's consideration of treaties without

---

[83] *Wolf v. Minister of Immigration* HC Civ 2002 3485 106 Wild J discusses the applicability of the proportionality test.   [84] [1999] 2 NZLR 44.
[85] For an excellent discussion of the contrast between methods see C. Geiringer, '*Tavita* and all That: Confronting the Confusion Surrounding Unincorporated Treaties and Administrative Law' (2004) 21 *NZULR* 66.
[86] I adopt Mulgan's distinction between calling to account (transparency) and holding to account (rectification) here, Mulgan, n. 60, 9.
[87] *Tavita v. Minister of Immigration* [1994] 2 NZLR 257, 266.
[88] *Standing Orders of the House of Representatives* 2004 SO 382–5.

derogating from the Crown's ultimate power to become party to a particular treaty.[89]

This has not satisfied some of the smaller parties. A private member's Bill proposed that Parliament should have a power to approve treaties rather than simply enjoy a right to be consulted. This would have meant a fundamental break with the constitutional tradition. The concern of the Bill was not only to stop economic treaties having force but may also have applied to the attempts by the courts to incorporate treaty norms into administrative exercises of power. The Bill provided that:

No treaty, or provision in any treaty, has the force of law in New Zealand by virtue of approval given . . .

The Bill was defeated by a coalition of the major parties (the parties most likely to lead the governing majority). Executive power has been preserved. While incorporation into domestic legislation is not always necessary before treaties may have domestic effect, Parliament does, of course, retain some control through ordinary legislative processes.

(iv) New Zealand Bill of Rights Act 1990

Apart from minor differences, that have been overstated, the New Zealand Bill of Rights Act 1990 has served as the model for the United Kingdom Human Rights Act 1998.[90] Perhaps as a consequence of case numbers and intellectual and geographical distance from Strasbourg, the New Zealand jurisprudence has been less bold than that of the United Kingdom. The judicial impact of the New Zealand Bill of Rights Act 1990 so far has tended to be focused on the conduct of the police, criminal trials, and the prison service.[91]

Academic commentators, this author among them, had predicted that the New Zealand Bill of Rights Act would have had a great impact on administrative law in its first fourteen years.[92] The direct and explicit effect of the Bill of Rights on the executive is not yet apparent, whether in the form of a direct constraint on

---

[89] T. Dunworth, 'Public International Law' [2000] *NZ Law Review* 217–21; T. Dunworth, 'Public International Law', [2002] *NZ Law Review* 255; M. Chen, 'A Constitutional Revolution? The Role of the New Zealand Parliament in Treaty-making' (2001) 19 *NZULR* 448.

[90] The force of the interpretative direction contained in s. 6 of the NZ Bill of Rights and s. 3 of the Human Rights Act 1998, appears to be similar despite the comments of Lord Cooke in *R. v. Director of Public Prosecutions, ex parte Kebeline* [2002] 2 AC 326, 362. Moreover the New Zealand Court of Appeal developed a 'declaration of compatibility' out of the structure of the New Zealand Bill of Rights Act in *Moonen v. Board of Film and Literature Board of Review* [2000] 2 NZLR 9. The Court derived this from the structure of the Act.

[91] For a compendious and valuable comparative account of the Act's operation see, P. Rishworth et al., *The New Zealand Bill of Rights* (Melbourne, Oxford, 2003). See also, J. McLean, 'Legislative Invalidation, Human Rights Protection and s. 4 of the New Zealand Bill of Rights Act' [2001] *NZ Law Review* 421.

[92] J. McLean, M. Taggart and P. Rishworth, 'The Impact of the New Zealand Bill of Rights on Administrative Law', in *The New Zealand Bill of Rights Act 1990* (Auckland, Legal Research Foundation Inc, 1992); D. Mullan, 'A Comparison of the Impact of the New Zealand Bill of

the scope of executive power,[93] as a mandatory relevant consideration, as affecting the *Wednesbury* standard of review or as giving rise to legitimate expectations.[94] However, a new focus on 'acts' performed and particular rights-infringing applications of statutory provisions may see the Bill of Rights have greater impact on the executive in the future. It is likely that the emerging United Kingdom 'principle of legality jurisprudence' will have an effect here.[95]

Drew v. Attorney-General[96] is illustrative. Drew had been charged under the Penal Institutions Act 1954 with drug offences and sought to defend himself on complex medical grounds. A regulation made under the Act stated in absolute terms that prisoners could not have legal representation in the hearing of disciplinary charges before the Prison Visitor. The Court of Appeal held that 'this empowering provision cannot have been intended by Parliament to authorize a regulation, which, in its operative effect, results in some hearings that may be conducted in a manner contrary to the principles of natural justice'.[97] It was the particular *application* of the regulation, to disallow legal representation in a complex proceeding involving the cross-examination of medical experts that was ultra vires. The application of the rule, rather than the rule itself, was inconsistent with the Bill of Rights. While this case can be explained in orthodox terms as reinforcing existing controls on the executive in relation to regulations, primary legislation could be susceptible to the same analysis. If primary legislation can be applied consistently with the Bill of Rights, but is applied in a particular instance in a way that breaches the Bill of Rights, the provision may be read down to exclude that particular application. *Drew* did not depend on the Bill of Rights given that the right protected also existed at common law, but it did clarify that the analysis under the Bill of Rights would be the same.[98]

(v) Regulations

In many ways it is unsurprising that there have not been more judicial challenges to executive made regulations. There is relatively extensive parliamentary scrutiny of regulations, to which individuals have easy access. In response to the overuse by the executive of regulation-making power in the early 1980s, a number of control mechanisms were put in place. The Parliamentary Regulations Review

---

Rights Act and the Canadian Charter of Rights and Freedoms on Judicial Review of Administrative Action' (2003) 1 *NZJPIL* 115.

[93] *Police v. Beggs* [1999] 3 NZLR 615 gets close to this but is not articulated in these terms.

[94] The most constitutionally interesting case concerns Parliament's ability to impliedly repeal earlier provisions that protect human rights see *R v. Pora.* [2001] 2 NZLR 37.

[95] See *R. v. Pora.* [2001] 2 NZLR 37. Elias CJ's judgment invokes the UK 'principle of legality' jurisprudence. The methodology may also be likened to the UK cases, n. 76.

[96] [2002] 1 NZLR 58 (CA).   [97] At para. 66.

[98] The case clarified that s. 4 NZ Bill of Rights Act did not protect regulations from invalidation on ultra vires grounds, para. 68. This view had been embraced by some government advisors until the *Drew* challenge.

Committee was granted extensive powers to inquire into the content of both empowering provisions and regulations. This may be at the instigation of individuals[99] and includes grounds such as that the regulation 'trespasses unduly on personal rights and liberties'.[100] Other grounds go beyond what would normally be contemplated in an action before a court.[101] In addition, the Regulations Disallowance Act 1989 provides a procedure by which the opposition dominated Committee can make a motion to the House that a regulation should be disallowed. If the motion is passed or is not withdrawn or disposed of within a prescribed time, the regulation lapses. Thus far, this process has never been used. Nevertheless, it is an important constraint on regulation-making power and shifts power back to Parliament. New hybrid forms of legislation are the new source of challenge to these processes.[102]

(vi) Contract law

We have been discussing public law constraints on executive power. The executive itself took the view that private law would be an important constraint on public actors. Indeed, it may have preferred the constraints of the general law to those of public law. What effect have such constraints had?

There are very few reported cases involving contracts with government. That does not indicate much either way on the question of whether contract law has proved an effective tool of accountability. The courts have, on the rare occasions they have been called upon to rule in this area, tended to focus on the contracting process.[103] As the experience in the health sector has shown, contracts between government purchasers and providers have primarily been successful in imposing internal rather than external disciplines. Purchasers and providers have, through the contracting process, enhanced internal planning processes, information gathering and priority setting. Contract has been less successful as an external accountability mechanism. The contracting cycles have been such that it has been rare for contractors to measure what had been done against the original contract. In some cases the contractual agreement would only be completed in time to begin negotiating the contract anew. As a political mechanism of accountability contracts have scarcely, if ever, been referred to. Purchaser-provider contracts have tended to have the reduction of costs rather than the

---

[99] *Standing Orders of the House of Representatives* 2004. SO 379.
[100] *Standing Orders of the House of Representatives* 2004, SO 378(2)(b).
[101] For example, SO 378(b)(f) 'Contains matters more appropriate for parliamentary enactment'. The Regulations Review Committee has investigated, among other things, the level of fees charged by Disputes Tribunals.
[102] Regulations Review Committee, *Interim Report on the Inquiry Into Affirmative Resolution Procedures* IJHR I.16 F (12/7/2004); *Inquiry Into the Principles Determining Whether Delegated Legislation is Given the Status of Regulations* I.16E (30/6/2004).
[103] This is particularly true of the tendering cases where a two-contract approach has been adopted, see *Pratt Contractors v. Transit New Zealand* [2002] 2 NZLR 313 (CA) [2003] UKPC 83. See also the closing obiter statements in *Power Co Ltd v. Gore District Council* [1997] 1 NZLR 537.

general public as their focus, and have not tended to focus on quality. In this respect purchasers and providers have not always been good proxies for patients. As one judge explained, the rationing of public funds that was achieved by this process had the effect of:

[L]eaving] more elderly people in their homes who may previously have been admitted to residential care. The lesson is salutary: it is the public who suffer when the contractors in this sector fall out.[104]

Importantly, in the New Zealand context, there has been no equivalent of a Citizen's Charter. Health is unusual in that it has had the nearest thing to an external regulator to protect the patients' interests in the Health and Disabilities Commissioner who can enquire into the quality (though not the availability) of health care in individual cases.[105] Tort law mechanisms of accountability are not available where there has been a 'personal injury by accident' in New Zealand.[106]

(vii) Summary: judicial forms of accountability

This section has discussed the ability of the judiciary to define the way executive power is exercised and sometimes even to confine the extent of executive power itself. The ability of the judiciary to call and hold the executive to account tends to be more assumed than proven. Undoubtedly the case law has had an impact on procedural modes of operation by the executive branch and has encouraged the transparency of many governmental processes in ways not necessarily contemplated by New Public Management. The advent of the New Zealand Bill of Rights Act and the increasing domestic role of unincorporated treaties has given rights some prominence in the policy making process, and not just the property rights favoured by New Public Management. Maori customary rights and rights under the Treaty of Waitangi ambiguously straddle both the traditional property concerns of New Public Management and the new human rights movement. Maori aspirations to 'separatism' may indeed have been fostered by the disaggregating aspects of the reforms.

By their nature, however, judicial mechanisms of accountability are sporadic, unpredictable, and prone to be limited in their impact beyond the parties, by legislative change. Where judicial review is concerned, remedies are discretionary.[107] The effectiveness of financial remedies in improving government systems (rather than in vindicating rights and compensating for loss) is also frequently presumed rather than proven, as we shall consider in the next section.

---

[104] *New Zealand Licensed Resthomes v. Midland Regional Health Authority*, unreported Hamilton High Court, 15 June 1999 per Hammond J, 32, and 17.
[105] The Commissioner has at times made damning judgments about the overall system—for example in Health and Disability Commissioner, *Canterbury Health Limited: A Report by the Health and Disability Commissioner* April 1998 (Auckland, Health and Disability Commissioner, 1998).
[106] Owing to New Zealand's Accident Compensation regime. Exemplary damages actions are sometimes available.
[107] See, e.g. *Waikato Regional Airport v. Attorney-General* [2002] 3 NZLR 433.

(b) Financial accountability and control

In previous sections, we have emphasized that New Zealand-style public management sought to minimize external (by which we mean judicial) accountability mechanisms and to enhance internal control, even if such control was itself envisaged as something of an arm's length affair. Public finance reforms have been crucial, although for the most part they have not received much attention from lawyers. The public finance system is central to strategic planning processes and performance measurement and defines relationships between ministers, civil servants, and crown entities. It operates as the executive's single most important, pervasive, and effective mechanism of centralized control.

Under the former system, appropriations and estimates processes reported bank account transactions.[108] The Public Finance Act 1989 applies private sector accrual accounting methods to public financial reporting. The new system is more 'transparent' in this sense: it reports the total cost of the government's activities as a return on its assets. This, its architects argue, gives a better indication of the government's net worth than formerly, at least as far as the financial markets and ministers are concerned.[109] It is not obvious, however, that transparency has been increased as far as Parliament and all but the most experienced and senior ministers are concerned.

The estimates set out different classes of appropriations, for example operating flows, and capital flows. Operating flows are allocated into different output classes such as 'Policy advice and ministerial support' or 'Specific crime prevention or maintenance of public order.' Supporting documentation is required to show the links between various output classes and key government goals. The estimates are, therefore, at the very centre of the system for specifying the desired direction of government.

'Appropriation', however, is not defined in the Act. Some voted appropriations are no more than a permission to incur expenses.[110] They do not necessarily allocate public money for such spending. It is a notional 'book entry' that is being appropriated. So, for example, while appropriation for 'other expenses' includes such things as the cost of restructuring, in practice a department will never receive money for the actual costs of restructuring.[111] Cash and accrual ideas can be used selectively in the absence of a legislative definition. Neither

---

[108] Public Finance Act 1977.

[109] See generally, G. Scott, *Public Sector Management in New Zealand* (Canberra, Centre for Law and Economics, 2001).

[110] S. Newberry, 'Intended or Unintended Consequences? Resource Erosion in New Zealand's Government Departments' (2002) 18(4) *Financial Accountability and Management* 309, 317; S. Newberry, ' "Sector Neutrality" and NPM "Incentives": Their Use in Eroding the Public Sector' (2003) 13 *Australian Accounting Review* 28, 32.

[111] S. Newberry, *New Zealand's Public Sector Financial Management System: Financial Resource Erosion in Government Departments* PhD Thesis submitted at the University of Canterbury 2002, 156 (on file with author).

does appropriation necessarily indicate activity. So, for example, a naval frigate already owned by the government would be required to receive a separate appropriation for the cost of its depreciation regardless of whether it were to leave port. On the other hand, departments are entitled to incur costs in order to earn 'trading revenue' (in competition with other suppliers) without Parliamentary approval.[112]

While public management New Zealand-style purports to be neutral about means, critics have argued that the Public Finance reforms are far from neutral.[113] The process of valuing assets and assessing the returns on such investments had obvious relevance at a time when governments were seeking to privatize assets as they were in New Zealand in the 1980s and 1990s.[114] An on-going system of accrual accounting may create continuing incentives to privatize even after the political willingness to do so has dissipated.[115]

Accrual accounting favours methods of providing services that do not require direct capital investment by government. If the public sector retains capital capacity to produce something for which there are not economies of scale, or from which it cannot recover revenue, there is a negative effect on the balance sheet. Contractual and rental-type arrangements, and public-private partnerships will almost always look better on the balance sheet than outputs produced in-house.[116] Presuming such private providers have other sources of revenue, government will not be funding the whole of the depreciation of their assets. On top of the depreciation effects of accrual accounting, the Treasury also levies a capital charge (according to its discretionary formula). This, in its own words, 'encourages departments to sell under-used or non-essential assets and thus reduce their level of capital and their capital charge'.[117] If one starts with the presumption that the public sector is always less efficient than the private sector, such a method of accounting will often make it so.[118] The incentive effect will operate regardless of whether assets are really surplus. Capital charging and

---

[112] The Treasury, *Putting It Together*, Ch 4, 'Authority from Parliament', 30 (The Treasury. 1996).

[113] S. Newberry, 'Intended or Unintended Consequences? Resource Erosion in New Zealand's Government Departments' (2002) 18(4) *Financial Accountability and Management* 309ff.

[114] Between 1987–93, a privatization agenda was openly pursued by both Labour and National governments. [115] Newberry, 'Sector Neutrality', n. 110, 28ff.

[116] The debt incurred in public-private partnerships, for example, does not need to be reported as public debt and is dealt with in practice as an off-balance sheet financing arrangement. Guarantees have to be registered with Treasury.

[117] The Treasury, *Putting It Together* Ch 5, 42 (http://www.treasury.govt.nz/). Moreover, chief executives may use proceeds from selling a departmental asset to buy or develop a new capital asset provided the department's total asset value does not increase as a result (which would require appropriation) (43). Such transactions can be operated through departmental bank accounts as opposed to the crown Bank account.

[118] Newberry suggests that this system of 'competitive neutrality' explains why direct intervention to force private sector involvement as occurred in the United Kingdom has not been necessary in New Zealand, Newberry, 'Sector Neutrality', n. 110, 32.

appropriation of depreciation also give the appearance of greater public spending than is actually taking place.

In theory, accrual accounting, which requires the voting of appropriation for depreciation, should automatically provide for asset replacement. The various discretionary powers entrusted to Treasury (over which there appears to be little oversight) render this uncertain. Reported surpluses must be paid to the 'Crown as owner'.[119] Reported deficits, on the other hand, are not governed by the Act but are, in practice, treated as indicating poor performance and required to be borne by the department.[120] In addition, Treasury enjoys broad discretionary power to manipulate money between departmental and Crown bank accounts and to decide from which fund payments should be made.[121] At the point at which they may seek additional capital funding, departments are often required to be in severe financial crises. Moreover, there is little or no parliamentary, or other, control of government borrowing under the Public Finance Act 1989.[122] Treasury, by delegated power, operates a derivatives market far from public scrutiny. Treasury has enormous flexibility and capacity to control the operation of the system.

Given the extent of such Treasury discretions, the controversies surrounding how they operate in practice,[123] and the difficulties of applying independent scrutiny, it is very difficult to predict the necessary incentive effects of damages awards on departments. Much will tend to depend on the size and power of the relevant department and its general financial position. Damages awards are usually met out of operating budgets. A recent employment compensation award of one million dollars to a senior Police Officer for wrongful dismissal, for example, was met out of a Police regional operating budget. But for the publicity surrounding the particular case, it would not have received Parliamentary or public scrutiny. Given the size of the Police budget, a new appropriation was not required.[124] Had the amount not been able to have been met from existing funds, the Police would have been able to seek supplementary assistance. Such assistance would normally be treated as a loan that Treasury would have sought to recover in later years.

Cabinet has set up procedures for the authorization of damages and compensation claims according to monetary value.[125] Apart from this blunt

---

[119] Public Finance Act 1989, s 14. Initially, in addition, 'efficiency dividends' were removed from funding baselines each year.

[120] Newberry, 'Intended or Unintended Consequences', n. 110, 322–3.

[121] Public Finance Act 1989, ss. 20–21.

[122] Public Finance Amendment Act 2004 adds more by way of codification but not much by way of control: see Part 6 and especially s 65F and s 65G.   [123] Ss 79–81.

[124] Thanks to DSS Gary Davey for this information. In 2002 compensation awards under Vote:Justice were large enough relative to the size of the budget to require separate appropriation.

[125] As at 2004, (Cabinet Office Circular 99/7) decision-making authority is vested in the Chief Executive for damages or compensation payments up to $100,000, the responsible minister up to $500,000 and over that the matter is referred to the Crown Law Office.

technique, and an obligation to report potential liabilities to Treasury as fiscal risks, there is no apparent system through which to assess whether compensation awards may indicate systemic problems. The incentive to spend money on systemic problems may be greatest for those departments who have the least capacity to do so. More work needs to be undertaken on these issues given the increasing availability of, and propensity for parties to seek, financial redress for government failures.

Crown entities have not escaped these financial disciplines despite enjoying separate legal identity. Indeed some entities, such as hospitals, were at one time required to pay dividends to the Crown on top of capital charges and the like. (This never actually transpired because of the parlous financial condition of the health sector.) Again the centre exercises coercive, if arm's length, financial and reporting controls. The case of the universities is illustrative. Government has consistently reduced its grant contributions to universities. The shortfall is to be made up by efficiency gains, student fees, and private funding. At the same time, government has imposed a cap on fees. Universities' much vaunted independence from government has never been more under threat.

The Public Finance Act has increased transparency for some purposes and drastically reduced it for others. It is not neutral about the preferred means of delivery of government programmes. It imposes multiple reporting requirements on departments including forecast, In-Year, and annual financial reporting. Most of all it confers huge, unchecked, control powers on Treasury. Efficiency issues are given priority over capacity and quality controls.

(c) Political accountability

The Public Finance regime embeds the idea of the Crown acting as owner and purchaser of 'outputs' from departments, notwithstanding that the 'Crown' is defined by the Public Finance Act to include 'Ministers and their departments'. How much, however, has political accountability been affected by these conceptions?

(i) *Ministers' relationships with the Civil Service*

The relationship between ministers and their advisors has been the subject of a great deal of state sector reform. Under the reforms, ministers were to be responsible for ex ante specified *outcomes* and chief executives of departments were to be responsible for ex ante specified *outputs*. These were specified in performance agreements between ministers and Chief Executives, reflected in the public financial reporting documentation and integrated with the government's strategic goals. All is pervaded by an underlying and fundamental ambiguity about what the proper role of politics should be under the new public management. Thus, at the very time that the Parliament was being made more representative, by the introduction of Mixed Member Proportional Representation, politicians themselves were attempting to put matters beyond their direct control. Public choice arguments have figured in much of this analysis. Ministers were to leave the day to day operation of departments to chief executives and to focus on deciding direction and priorities. The difficulties of achieving this separation, both managerially and politically, are illustrated by the Christine Rankin case.

Prior to the State Sector Act 1988, the strict legal position was that State Services Commission had the sole input into the appointment of Chief Executives (then known as Permanent Secretaries). As the former name suggests, one could retain such a position indefinitely. The 1988 Act gave cabinet a power to refuse the State Services Commission's appointment recommendation and input into the conditions of appointment. It also restricted the term to five years (renewable). This was recognition of the need for greater bureaucratic responsiveness to political goals.[126]

In the case of Mrs Rankin, the Chief Executive of the Department of Work and Income, the State Services Commissioner refused to renew the contract against the background of the government's warning that it would refuse a recommendation to reappoint. Mrs Rankin had performed admirably as far as achieving the efficiency and productivity measures set for her department by ministers. It was her mode of delivery that was at issue. Her lavish corporate spending on staff retreats, her response to the loss of confidential records, and her flamboyant personal style (large earrings, décolletage and mini skirts) attracted a great deal of adverse media and Parliamentary comment. She embarrassed the minister.

Mrs Rankin sued the State Services Commission in the Employment Court for failing to renew.[127] Such action in itself bespeaks a certain obtuseness about the political environment in which she was operating.[128] It emerges from the case that she viewed the Department as her own organization rather than as part of the government as a whole, and had lost the minister's confidence. Though procedural errors were found to have been made, unsurprisingly her contract was not renewed. Mrs Rankin has since found herself a role on a television agony-aunt show.

---

[126] The anticipated control over the over-politicization of such decisions is that any refusal to appoint a named person must be published.

[127] *Rankin v. Attorney General in respect of the State Services Commissioner* [2001] ERNZ 476 (No. 2).

[128] In the course of the litigation, ministers and senior members of the public service were called to give evidence about their interactions with the plaintiff—including some potentially embarrassing matters that would, under normal circumstances, never be publicly disclosed. Although she was employed by the State Services Commissioner on behalf of her Majesty, all the interactions of her seniors, including ministers, were treated by the Court as actions of her employer. This is interesting given the statutory power in the Governor-General in Council to refuse to follow the State Service Commissioner's recommendation.

Since this case, it is fair to say that chief executives have been appreciably less visible.[129] The distinctions between outputs and outcomes, ends and means, have proved unrealistic and unworkable in practice.[130] As a mechanism of political accountability, outputs have rarely, if ever, been referred to.[131] Political responsibility has remained with ministers. They remain answerable in Parliament and to the media for the successes and failures of their departments and for putting mistakes to right. Parliamentary question time, the powers of select committees to undertake inquiries[132] and the use by the parliamentary opposition and the public of information accessed under the Official Information Act 1982—all enhance the operation of this convention. Ministers frequently appear before select committees to defend their bills and policies.

The existence of ministerial responsibility surely does not depend on the frequency with which ministerial offers of resignation are accepted. Most commonly, resignations are proffered and accepted for personal failings, such as in recent years, allegations of fraud pending their proper investigation, drunk driving, or intemperate and inappropriate comments in relation to particular immigration cases. In some cases ministers have even resigned in the face of failings for which they are not personally to blame.[133] The most controversial case involved the collapse of a viewing platform erected by the Department of Conservation killing fourteen young people. A Commission of Inquiry found that the primary cause of the collapse was that the platform had not been properly constructed, clearly an operational matter for which the Chief Executive was responsible and not the minister. The Commission also found that there was a culture of under-funding in the department that created an incentive to do more with less. That was not necessarily a matter for which the minister alone was to blame, but rather a matter for which Cabinet as a whole was in some part responsible. As a response to the tragedy, the Minister (the Hon Denis Marshall) took steps to improve safety systems and the budget of the department. Having taken responsibility for correcting the failures of his department, he then resigned. The government accepted his resignation.[134] Despite the greater visibility of senior public servants, and the attempts to clarify respective accountabilities, this example may well show that traditional

---

[129] The State Services Commissioner said in his Annual Report in the relevant year: 'I do not think a system of public management could stand more than one such a case without seriously undermining the ability of the government and civil service to operate effectively'. Annual Report of the State Services Commissioner for the year ended 30 June 2001. Part One [2001] *AJHR* G3, 4.

[130] A. Schick, *The Spirit of Reform* (State Services Commission 1996), 87.

[131] Mulgan, n. 1, IV ff.

[132] Backbencher and opposition members have gained greater power in the select committee processes. In recent years high profile select committees have conducted enquiries into cannabis use, genetic engineering, weatherproofing of homes, and fisheries allocations.

[133] See further G. Palmer and M Palmer, *Bridled Power: New Zealand's Constitution and Government* (Oxford University Press, 2004), 71–7.

[134] As it happened, the Chief Executive followed the same course.

constitutional lines of responsibility as between ministers and their civil servants have been retained and perhaps even strengthened.

Ministers have not escaped political accountability for the actions of some Crown entities either. In the 1990s there were various scandals about lavish payouts to board members at the expiry of their terms. One employee of a state owned timber corporation was fired after organizing a political lobbying campaign against (as it transpired) the incoming government's policies to restrict native logging (notwithstanding that employees of state owned enterprises are not formally public servants). Recently, the government was called to account in Parliament, in relation to the conduct of the chief executive of a Crown entity. The chief executive of the Maori Language Commission had made a submission to a parliamentary select committee considering the Foreshore and Seabed Bill. A government-appointed statutory board employs the Chief Executive. The government urged the board to take action against the chief executive and to consider its own position (one of the Board members was himself reported to have taken part in a public protest against the Bill). Effective de facto, political control is evident here notwithstanding the legal separation of such bodies. The new Crown Entities Act 2004 will to some degree align the de jure position of such employees with the de facto political position and will undoubtedly increase central control. The looming question is how much are these political challenges and the changes to the operation of the model mere tinkering or an abandonment of the model itself?[135]

The current emphasis is on results and coordination. Under a new policy, ministers express their desired outcomes in statements of intent (for which they have promised legislative backing). These must cover areas such as capability, risk management, and coordination with other agencies. Departments, in turn, produce output plans but are now intended to pay greater attention to the link between outputs and outcomes. The current emphasis is on results and coordination. Departments are being reconsolidated and the purchaser-provider split is regarded as having failed as a management device.

(d) Other forms of audit and investigation

In comparison with the sharp-edged coercive fiscal controls of the Public Finance Act, and the potent political accountabilities of traditional ministerial responsibility, other external devices for investigation tend to take 'softer' forms that depend on reputation effects and the stature of various officers.

The role of the Controller and Auditor-General is illustrative. Unlike Treasury, the Auditor-General is an officer of Parliament and does not serve the executive. His controller function has been drastically diminished in that it only operates in relation to the transactions concerning the Crown's bank accounts.

---

[135] See J. Kelsey, *At the Crossroads: Three Essays* (Bridget Williams, 2002).

Thus Treasury effectively can decide whether funds are to reside in the Crown's or departmental accounts. On the other hand, the office has been given expanded powers to make recommendations about quality issues. The Public Audit Act 2001 gives the Office expanded powers to investigate public entities. There are three basic kinds of audit: the traditional financial report audit that must take place, the traditional inquiry into the misspending of public moneys that the Auditor-General can undertake on his own initiative or on request, and the new idea of a 'public audit' that is undertaken on the auditor's own volition. Under the public audit power, the Auditor-General may investigate the effectiveness and efficiency of an entity, its compliance with statutory obligations, and its acts and omissions. The array of performance audits that have so far been undertaken is revealing[136] and follow very much the UK model.

In 2003, for example, a performance audit was undertaken of the management of hospital-acquired infection. League tables of rates of infection were not published. However, each District Health Board received a report on their comparative standing in the sector. A similar approach has been followed in relation to public procurement standards. The Auditor-General publishes a series of good practice guides that includes a public procurement standard. The publication carries this statement:

This publication is a statement of good practice. It is not a set of rules. We suggest that each public entity used the statement as a benchmark for its own procurement policies and procedures, and as a guide to what its own procurement manual should contain. In our role as the auditor of public entities, we would expect to find that an entity's procurement polices and procedures compare favourably with this statement. The statement is also not a guide to a public entity's legal obligations. Each entity should supplement the statement with legal advice if necessary.[137]

The potentially more demanding requirements of New Zealand's procurement policies are contained in trade agreements with Singapore and Australia.[138] This is another sign of the increasing significance of the international environment.

There are a number of other mechanisms for investigation and audit. Officers of Parliament include the Ombudsman who has been a central investigatory body since 1962 with powers to inquire into 'matters of administration'. The Ombudsman may undertake inquiries at his own motion, has virtually unrestricted access to government information, can, unlike a judge, decide that a

---

[136] Performance audits include State Services Commission: 'Managing Threats to Domestic Security' 1983; State Services Commission: 'Capability to Recognise and Address Issues for Maori' 2004; New Zealand Defence Force 'Deployment to East Timor—Performance of Health Sector Support' 2003; Bringing Down the Road Toll: The Speed Camera Programme 2002.

[137] Auditor-General, *Procurement: A Statement of Good Practice* (Office of Controller and Auditor-General, June 2001), Introduction 'How should this statement be used?', http://www.oag.govt.nz/.

[138] See http:/www.med.govt.nz/ for the Australia New Zealand Government Procurement Agreement, NZ Singapore Closer Economic Partnership Agreement, Asia-Pacific Economic Cooperation and World Trade Organisation requirements.

decision is just 'plain wrong', and can identify and address systemic issues.[139] The office has only a recommendatory power but such is its status that it is taken very seriously in governmental processes. The office of Ombudsman also has jurisdiction over access to official information and may investigate refusals to disclose. The potency of its recommendations, as with the Auditor-General, and less so with other officers such as the Human Rights Commissioner, however, depends on its ability to maintain a delicate mixture of independence and quasi-insider status. One Ombudsman who was a strident public critic of government policies during the early days of privatization and corporatization pointedly did not have her term renewed.

4. Conclusion

This essay paints a complex picture of a strong, but fragmented, executive, employing coercive, if arm's length, mechanisms of control and subject to traditional hierarchical forms of political accountability. New Zealand style New Public Management has attempted to emphasize ends over means by the grant of legal autonomy to entities at both the core and on the periphery of the public sector. The courts have brought a nuanced functional approach to bear on such entities: maintaining as much as possible a level-playing field between public and private commercial actors; preserving the capacity of government to perform a regulatory role; and preserving the courts' own regulatory role over private regulatory bodies. Legislative techniques, that aimed to limit external judicial control of the executive by way of ultra vires arguments, have been effective on their terms. Courts have, however, continued to impose procedural disciplines on the executive and have increasingly brought human rights, international agreements, and Maori Treaty and customary rights to bear on executive decision-making. The overall impact of such developments has not been necessarily to constrain the executive. The executive's reaction has been to attempt to neutralize Maori Treaty and customary claims, to preserve its Treaty making powers albeit with increased, but limited, scrutiny from Parliament, and to embrace proceduralism while maintaining substantive decision-making power. The increasing internationalization of domestic law does not necessarily constrain executive power, indeed, it may enhance it. Finally, the executive has embraced soft-law forms of external bureaucratic control combined with enhanced command and control and highly discretionary internal controls over the public purse.

---

[139] See further K. J. Keith, 'Development of the Role of the Ombudsman with Reference to the Pacific', in 22nd Australasian and Pacific Ombudsman Regional (APOR) Conference, Parliament House, Wellington, NZ 9–11 February 2005.

5

Taming the Most Dangerous Branch: The Scope and Accountability of Executive Power in the United States

*Ernest A. Young**

Alexander Hamilton famously said that the judiciary is the 'least dangerous' branch of American government.[1] For the Founders, the *most* dangerous was the legislature; they constructed their draft constitution at Philadelphia, after all, against a backdrop of runaway state legislatures running roughshod over creditor rights. Most observers today, however, tend to reserve that title for the national executive.[2] Although fears of an 'Imperial presidency'[3] have been tempered by post-Watergate reforms and assertive Congresses during periods of divided government, it seems likely that the executive would be the modern branch of government least recognizable to the American Founders. The twin imperatives of constant national security concerns abroad and demand for a large administrative state at home have radically expanded the executive's bureaucratic establishment, and the nationalization of American culture has enhanced the stature of the President's 'bully pulpit.' As the events of the past year illustrate, the election of a President is now viewed—rightly—as the most critical event in American politics.

American law has struggled to accommodate these changes. This essay undertakes a brief descriptive account of executive power—both its scope, and the means that American law has developed to hold the executive to account for its actions. By adopting the phrase 'most dangerous branch,' I do not wish to express any normative view as to whether the present prominence of executive

---

   * Judge Benjamin Harrison Powell Professor of Law, the University of Texas at Austin. I am grateful to David Han for research assistance, and to Adam Tomkins for comments on the manuscript.
   [1] The Federalist No. 78, at 522 (J. Cooke, ed., Wesleyan 1961) (Alexander Hamilton).
   [2] See, e.g., Martin S. Flaherty, 'The Most Dangerous Branch' (1996) 105 *Yale LJ* 1725, 1727–8; Michael Stokes Paulsen, 'The Most Dangerous Branch: Executive Power to Say What the Law Is' (1994) 83 *Geo. LJ* 217, 220–1.
   [3] Arthur M. Schlesinger, Jr., *The Imperial Presidency* (Houghton Mifflin, 1973).

authority is a good or bad thing. A strong case can be made for presidential leadership, and it is not at all clear that the challenges of the twentieth century could have been met in any other way. American law has been suspicious of executive authority ever since the Declaration of Independence, however, and my focus here will be on the means that survive for limiting that authority's scope and enhancing the accountability of its exercise.

The chapter proceeds in five parts. Part 1 offers a brief theoretical overview of the American separation of powers. Part 2 describes the scope of executive authority. In Part 3, I discuss legislative, judicial, and political mechanisms for holding the executive to account. Part 4 then illustrates how some of those mechanisms play out in three distinct contexts: the exercise of delegated powers, the President's 'war power,' and the contemporary problem of executive detention. Finally, Part 5 advances some brief conclusions about the comparative efficacy of separated powers and checks and balances models, and the relation of those modes to judicial review.

1. Separation of powers in American law

American separation of powers theory finds its roots in the older notion of 'mixed government,' which envisioned mutually-checking governmental institutions reflecting the different social groups composing society. Aristotle's 'the one,' 'the few,' and 'the many' became, in the widely-admired British Constitution, the King, the aristocracy, and the Commons.[4] The American revolutionaries inherited this enthusiasm for dividing power without the stark social divisions that undergirded the British Constitution; they thus gravitated to different notions of division, prominent in thinkers like Montesquieu and Locke, that rested on governmental function rather than social station.[5] James Madison described Montesquieu as 'the oracle who is always consulted and cited on this subject,' and he accepted the notion that '[t]he accumulation of all powers legislative, executive and judiciary in the same hands...may justly be pronounced the very definition of tyranny.'[6]

This commitment—at least in theory—to sharp separation of government functions is reflected in early state constitutions, such as the Massachusetts Constitution of 1780. That instrument specifically provided that 'the legislative department shall never exercise the executive and judicial powers...; the executive shall never exercise the legislative and judicial powers...; the judicial shall never exercise the legislative and executive powers.'[7] Some state

---

[4] See generally, Gordon S. Wood, *The Creation of the American Republic, 1776–87* (W.W. Norton & Co., 1969), 197–200.

[5] Jack N. Rakove, *Original Meanings: Politics and Ideas in the Making of the Constitution* (Knopf, 1997), 245–8; Wood, n. 4, 150–7, 244–55; Flaherty, n. 2, 1756–65.

[6] The Federalist No. 47, n. 1, 324 (James Madison).

[7] Mass. Const. of 1780, pt. I, Art. XXX.

constitutions retain similar provisions to this day.[8] But from the beginning this notion of separated powers has coexisted with a distinct principle of checks and balances, which holds that 'the degree of separation ... essential to a free government, can never in practice, be duly maintained' unless 'these departments be so far connected and blended, as to give to each a constitutional controul over the others.'[9] The Constitution thus assigns the President a role in legislation through the veto power, for example, and the Senate a role in the ratification of treaties and the confirmation of executive appointments. Checks and balances fits comfortably with the broader institutional strategy articulated in Federalist 51, which counted on 'opposite and rival interests' to maintain both the horizontal separation of powers among the branches of the national government and the vertical separation of powers between the national government and the states.[10] '[T]he great security against a gradual concentration of the several powers in the same department,' Madison wrote, 'consists in giving to those who administer each department, the necessary constitutional means, and personal motives, to resist encroachments of the others.'[11]

These two principles—separated powers and checks and balances—have tended to correlate strongly with two distinct jurisprudential approaches to separation of powers questions in the courts.[12] Decisions emphasizing the separation of functions have often employed a 'formalist' approach that draws bright lines between the branches. These decisions typically seek first to characterize the power being exercised, is it legislative, executive, or judicial, then ask whether that power is being employed by the right branch.[13] Decisions emphasizing checks and balances, by contrast, have displayed a more 'functionalist' commitment to general norms of balance among governmental institutions. Opinions in this vein typically assess innovative governmental arrangements by asking whether they 'aggrandize' one branch at the expense of another to an extent sufficient to unbalance the system as a whole.[14] Perhaps not

---

[8] See, e.g., Indiana Const. Art. 3, § 1 ('The powers of the Government are divided into three separate departments; the Legislative, the Executive including the Administrative, and the Judicial; and no person, charged with official duties under one of these departments, shall exercise any of the functions of another, except as in this Constitution expressly provided.').

[9] The Federalist No. 48, n. 1, 332 (James Madison); see also Wood, n. 4, 547–53. Madison was at pains to show that, notwithstanding strong separation provisions like that in Massachusetts, the state constitutional practice in 1789 featured frequent instances of overlapping and checking functions. Federalist No. 47, n. 1, 327–31.   [10] The Federalist No. 51, n. 1, 349.

[11] Ibid.

[12] See generally, Peter Strauss, 'Formal and Functional Approaches to Separation of Powers Questions—A Foolish Inconsistency?' (1987) 72 *Cornell L Rev* 488; M. Elizabeth Magill, 'The Real Separation in Separation of Powers Law' (2000) 86 *Va L Rev* 1127, 1136–47.

[13] See, e.g., *Bowsher v. Synar* 478 US 714 (1986) (striking down the Gramm-Rudman Act's delegation of power to cancel spending items to the Comptroller of the Currency); *Clinton v. New York* 524 US 417 (1998) (striking down the Line Item Veto Act).

[14] See, e.g., *Commodity Futures Trading Comm'n v. Schor* 478 US 833 (1986) (upholding a provision allowing agency adjudication of state law claims); *Morrison v. Olson* 487 US 654 (1988) (upholding the Independent Counsel Act).

surprisingly, the functionalist approach has been far more forgiving than the formalist one: employing the former tends to lead to upholding the arrangement in question, whereas the latter tends to bring the arrangement to grief.[15] These two strands have existed side by side in the case law for decades, and developing a principled explanation why the Supreme Court takes one approach in some cases and a different one in others is one of the great puzzles of separation of powers jurisprudence.[16]

I attempt no such explanation here. Nonetheless, the competing principles of separated powers and checks and balances, as well as the jurisprudential tendencies they have engendered, will be relevant to many of the issues concerning the scope and accountability of executive power that I discuss in the balance of this essay.

2. The scope of Executive authority

Controversies about the scope of executive authority in America have tended to fall into three different categories. The first concerns the propriety of executive action taken on the President's own initiative, either in the absence of Congressional action or in opposition to some policy expressed by the legislature. These disputes focus on the scope of the President's own powers, enumerated, implied, or residual in nature. The second class of case involves attempts by Congress to confer power on the executive branch pursuant to a scheme of administrative regulation. These cases implicate the doctrine of non-delegation. A third category concerns executive privileges and immunities, such as the President's immunity from personal liability and his right to control his subordinates. I consider each class of cases in turn.

(a) Enumerated and residual powers

Article II of the American Constitution creates the Presidency and delimits its powers. At first glance, Article II's structure is similar to that of Article I, which deals with the structure and powers of Congress. Each article features a 'vesting clause' that instils the executive and legislative powers in the President and Congress respectively.[17] The vesting clauses are then followed by a list of specific powers: Congress can regulate commerce among the several states and spend

---

[15] Compare, e.g., *Mistretta v. United States* 488 US 361 (1989) (using a functionalist analysis to uphold the US Sentencing Commission), with *INS v. Chadha* 462 US 919 (1983) (using a formalist analysis to strike down the legislative veto).

[16] For an effort to find a pattern in this carpet, see, e.g., Bradford R. Clark, 'Separation of Powers as a Safeguard of Federalism' (2001) 79 *Texas L Rev* 1321, 1391–3.

[17] US Const. Art. I, § 1; Art. II, § 1.

money to promote the general welfare, for example; the President can make treaties and command the armed forces.[18] Both articles have engendered controversy over the existence and extent of 'implied' authority beyond these enumerated powers. The crucial difference is that while Congress's list of enumerated powers is quite extensive (and supplemented by an express provision for such implied powers as are 'necessary and proper' to carry the enumerated functions into execution),[19] the President's enumerated list is considerably less impressive. That list includes the power:

- to be 'Commander in Chief' of the armed forces;
- to require opinions of his cabinet officers;
- to pardon offences against the US;
- to make treaties (with the 'Advice and Consent' of the Senate);
- to appoint ambassadors, judges, and other officers to fill offices created by law;
- to address Congress and propose legislation;
- to convene Congress and (in certain rare cases) to adjourn it;
- to receive ambassadors; and
- to 'take Care that the Laws be faithfully executed.'[20]

These enumerated powers are certainly non-trivial, but they hardly justify, in and of themselves, the frequent description of the American President as the most powerful individual in the world.[21]

It is not surprising, then, that while debate about Congress's authority has focused on the scope of its enumerated powers,[22] many executive power disputes emphasize the question whether the relatively meagre list in Article II exhausts the President's authority. In foreign affairs law, for example, one camp contends that the limited powers expressly granted to the President confirm that Congress is to have the upper hand in foreign affairs.[23] The opposing camp claims extensive non-textual powers for the President grounded in his role as representative of the national sovereignty in foreign affairs.[24] More generally, recent academic debates have focused on whether the Vesting Clause of

---

[18] US Const. Art. I, § 8; Art. II, §§ 2–3.   [19] US Const. Art. I, § 8.
[20] US Const. Art. II, §§ 2–3.
[21] See, e.g., Saikrishna B. Prakash and Michael D. Ramsey, 'The Executive Power over Foreign Affairs' (2001) 111 *Yale LJ* 231, 233 ('[T]he President's enumerated powers [in the field of foreign affairs] do not seem to convey anything approaching even the minimum powers everyone assumes the President to enjoy.').
[22] See, e.g., *United States v. Lopez* 514 US 549 (1995) (discussing the scope of Congress's enumerated power to regulate interstate commerce).
[23] See, e.g., John Hart Ely, *On Constitutional Ground* (Princeton, 1996), 149 ('The Constitution gives the president no general right to make foreign policy. Quite the contrary.... [V]irtually every substantive constitutional power touching on foreign affairs is vested in Congress.').
[24] See, e.g., *United States v. Curtiss-Wright Export Corp.* 299 US 304, 318–20 (1936); H. Jefferson Powell, 'The President's Authority over Foreign Affairs: An Executive Branch Perspective' (1999) 67 *Geo Wash L Rev* 527.

Article II vests a more general 'executive power,' of which the enumerations in the Article are simply examples.[25]

Prakash and Ramsey recently articulated a nuanced version of this 'vesting clause thesis,' grounded in a close textual reading of Article II.[26] They read the vesting clause of that Article—'The executive Power shall be vested in a President of the United States of America'—as reflecting a broad category of powers understood to be 'executive' in nature at the time of the Founding.[27] The specific grants in Article II are thus simply illustrative of that category. Prakash and Ramsey note, however, that many of the powers expressly granted to *Congress* in Article I, such as the power to declare war, would likewise have been understood to be 'executive' in nature in 1789. Hence, the President's implied or 'residual' executive authority does *not* include those powers carved out and delegated to Congress.[28] This approach seems readily generalizable to executive authority questions outside the realm of foreign affairs, although in domestic policy the broad authority that the text allocates to Congress may leave little room for residual executive power. Even this nuanced approach to unenumerated executive power is not without difficulties,[29] but it better fits the text than the polar positions and also conforms reasonably well to current practice.

Whether or not one views the President as having residual powers not listed in Article II, further questions arise concerning the potential overlap between executive and legislative authority. Congress's authority to declare war, to raise troops, and to make rules to govern the armed forces, for example, may well overlap with the President's Commander-in-Chief authority. And many assertions of implied or residual executive authority occur in areas the Congress has—or at least could—regulate. That was the issue in the famous *Steel Seizure Case* of 1952,[30] in which President Harry S. Truman temporarily nationalized the nation's steel mills in order to avert a strike by the steelworkers' union and thereby to ensure the flow of war material to American troops fighting in Korea. Justice Black's majority opinion took a sharply formalist approach, categorizing the seizure as legislative in nature and therefore rejecting it on the ground that 'the President's power to see that the laws are faithfully executed refutes the idea that he is to be a lawmaker.'[31] But the more influential concurrences of Justices Frankfurter and Jackson took a more functionalist tack, construing executive

---

[25] Compare, e.g., Prakash and Ramsey, n. 21 (arguing that Article II's Vesting Clause confers unenumerated executive authority on the President); John C. Yoo, 'War and the Constitutional Text' (2002) 69 *U Chi L Rev* 1639, 1676–8 (making a similar argument in the context of war powers), with Curtis A. Bradley and Martin S. Flaherty, 'Executive Power Essentialism and Foreign Affairs' (2002) 102 *Mich L Rev* 545 (rejecting the Vesting Clause as a font of unenumerated presidential powers). [26] See generally, Prakash and Ramsey, n. 21.

[27] This reading draws support from the contrast between the vesting clause of Article I, which vests in Congress only those legislative powers 'herein granted,' see US Const. Art. I, § 1, and the vesting clause of Article II, which simply vests '[t]he executive Power' in the President, *Ibid.*, Art. II, § 1. [28] Prakash and Ramsey, n. 21, 234–5.

[29] See, Bradley and Flaherty, n. 25, 551–2 (summarizing criticisms of the vesting clause thesis).
[30] *Youngstown Sheet & Tube Co. v. Sawyer*, 343 US 579 (1952). [31] *Ibid.*, 587.

authority as at least in part a function of congressional action in any given case. Without deciding what might be permissible in the absence of legislation, both justices emphasized that Congress had enacted a variety of statutory mechanisms for dealing with labour disputes and military supply crises, and that all these mechanisms were limited in ways suggesting that President Truman's action was contrary to congressional policy.[32]

Justice Jackson's *Steel Seizure* concurrence laid out a tripartite framework that has proven influential in many subsequent cases.[33] The first category includes cases '[w]hen the President acts pursuant to an express or implied authorization of Congress.' In these cases, Justice Jackson wrote, 'his authority is at its maximum, for it includes all that he possesses in his own right plus all that Congress can delegate.' Such actions are 'supported by the strongest of presumptions and the widest latitude of judicial interpretation.'[34] The second category arises '[w]hen the President acts in absence of either a congressional grant or denial of authority.' In this area, 'he can only rely upon his own independent powers, but there is a zone of twilight in which he and Congress may have concurrent authority, or in which its distribution is uncertain.' Such cases are likely to turn 'on the imperatives of events and contemporary imponderables.'[35] Finally, the third category occurs '[w]hen the President takes measures incompatible with the expressed or implied will of Congress.' Here, Justice Jackson concluded, 'his power is at its lowest ebb,' and presidential action 'must be scrutinized with caution.'[36] These categories, of course, leave many unanswered questions. The crucial point for present purposes, however, is that presidential power questions will generally not be answered in a vacuum, but rather by paying attention to the relationship between executive and legislative action in any given situation.

Justice Jackson's opinion in the *Steel Seizure* case is also important for its recognition that the President's 'paper powers' hardly exhaust his *political* authority as Chief Executive:

Executive power has the advantage of concentration in a single head in whose choice the whole Nation has a part, making him the focus of public hopes and expectations. No other personality in public life can begin to compete with him in access to the public mind through modern methods of communications. By his prestige as head of state and his influence upon public opinion he exerts a leverage upon those who are supposed to check and balance his power which often cancels their effectiveness. Moreover, rise of the party system has made a significant extra constitutional supplement to real executive power.[37]

However the ongoing debate about the scope of executive authority plays out, it is well to remember Justice Jackson's point: no substantive power accorded to the

---

[32] *Ibid.*, 597–603 (Frankfurter, J, concurring); *Ibid.* 639 (Jackson, J, concurring).
[33] See, e.g., *Dames & Moore, Inc. v. Regan* 453 US 654 (1981) (employing Justice Jackson's framework). [34] *Youngstown*, n. 30, 636–7 (Jackson, J, concurring).
[35] *Ibid.*, 637. [36] *Ibid.*, 637–8. [37] *Ibid.*, 653–4.

President in Article II is so significant as the political leverage afforded by the White House's position at the centre of American political life.

(b) Delegation of powers to the executive

The other broad class of separation of powers cases in American constitutional law involves the delegation of legislative power. The paradigm case concerns the extent to which Congress may delegate its lawmaking authority to federal administrative agencies, which are empowered to promulgate regulations, or secondary legislation in British terms, to implement the broad directives of federal statutes. Related problems arise when Congress attempts to 'self-delegate'—that is, to confer legislative authority on subsets of itself. Legislative veto mechanisms like the one struck down in *INS v. Chadha*,[38] for example, may confer the power to override executive branch action on a single House of Congress, or both Houses without Presidential approval, or even on a single congressional committee. Still other cases have involved conferring aspects of legislative power on entities, like the Comptroller of the Currency, or the Federal Sentencing Commission, whose branch allegiance is ambiguous.[39]

I want to focus here on the basic problem of delegation, for it is the transformation of the executive branch into the primary font of American law that has most threatened, some would say disrupted, the Founders' initial separation and allocation of powers. The problem of holding the executive to account becomes less serious, at least in ordinary domestic contexts, to the extent that the executive has not controlled the *content* of the law that it enforces. For that reason, Congress 'is not permitted to abdicate, or to transfer to others, the essential legislative functions with which it is ... vested.'[40] At the same time, American courts have never denied that modern regulation requires flexibility in implementation, and the doctrine has permitted Congress to 'leav[e] to selected instrumentalities the making of subordinate rules within prescribed limits and the determination of facts to which the policy as declared by the legislature is to apply.'[41] The line between these two imperatives has been defined by the requirement that 'when Congress confers decisionmaking authority upon agencies *Congress* must "lay down by legislative act an intelligible principle to which the person or body authorized to [act] is directed to conform." '[42]

Although they have adhered to the 'intelligible principle' requirement in theory, American courts have basically conceded that it is not judicially enforceable in practice. Justice Scalia has explained the problem.

---

[38] 462 US 919 (1983).
[39] *Bowsher v. Synar* 478 US 714 (1986); *Mistretta v. United States*, 488 US 361 (1989).
[40] *Panama Refining Co. v. Ryan* 293 US 388, 421 (1935).   [41] *Ibid.*
[42] *Whitman v. American Trucking Ass'ns*, 531 US 457, 472 (2001) (quoting *J.W. Hampton, Jr. & Co. v. United States* 276 US 394, 409 (1928)).

Once it is conceded, as it must be, that no statute can be entirely precise, and that some judgments, even some judgments involving policy considerations, must be left to the officers executing the law and to the judges applying it, the debate over unconstitutional delegation becomes a debate not over a point of principle but over a question of degree.[43]

Unable to draw principled lines between those delegations that go too far and those that do not, American courts 'have almost never felt qualified to second-guess Congress regarding the permissible degree of policy judgment that can be left to those executing or applying the law.'[44] Only twice in our history has the US Supreme Court struck down a federal statute on delegation grounds,[45] and the courts have upheld incredibly broad grants of authority to federal agencies. The courts have found an intelligible principle, for example, in broad grants of authority to the Federal Communications Commission to regulate the airwaves 'in the public interest.'[46] It is thus commonplace to speak of the 'complete abandonment of the nondelegation principle,'[47] at least as a matter of enforceable doctrine.

The demise of the straightforward delegation doctrine has left a gap in American constitutional law. As Justice White observed in *Chadha*, '[t]here is no question but that agency rulemaking is lawmaking in any functional or realistic sense of the term,' and '[f]or some time, the sheer amount of law—the substantive rules that regulate private conduct and direct the operation of government—made by the agencies has far outnumbered the lawmaking engaged in by Congress through the traditional process.'[48] The question is thus not so much how to hold the executive to account for *violating* the law, but rather how to connect law that is to all intents and purposes *made* by the executive with the wellsprings of legitimacy generally reserved for legislative output. As I discuss in Part 4, efforts to fill this gap have taken a number of different forms: some have emphasized that executive agencies are themselves democratically accountable, either through the person of the President, who unlike Members of Congress is elected by the whole People, or through Congress's powers of oversight. Others have tried to develop an independent claim to legitimacy based on the inclusiveness of the agency's own proceedings. Finally, many have stressed the role of judicial review in ensuring that agencies adhere to whatever strictures and guidelines Congress does choose to impose on their activities.

---

[43] *Mistretta*, 488 US at 415 (Scalia, J, dissenting).   [44] *Ibid.*, 416.
[45] *A.L.A. Schechter Poultry Corp. v. United States* 295 US 495 (1935) (striking down a provision of the National Industrial Recovery Act authorizing the President, in conjunction with industry representatives, to promulgate regulations governing the poultry industry); *Panama Refining Co. v. Ryan* 293 US 388 (1935) (striking down another NIRA provision authorizing the President to regulate petroleum production).
[46] *National Broadcasting Co. v. United States* 319 US 190, 225–6 (1943).
[47] Gary Lawson, 'The Rise and Rise of the administrative State' (1994) 107 Harv L Rev 1231, 1241.   [48] *INS v. Chadha* 462 US 919, 985–6 (1983) (White, J., dissenting).

(c) Executive privileges and immunities

A final set of issues have focused more directly on the accountability and independence of the executive. I include in this category both cases recognizing and refusing to recognize particular defences to liability or scrutiny, but also cases considering the President's control over other members of the executive branch. *United States v. Nixon*,[49] which recognized a strong presumption that presidential communications and correspondence are privileged from disclosure, would fall in the first group; *Myers v. United States*,[50] recognizing the 'unitary executive' principle that all executive officers must be subject to presidential removal, comes within the second.[51] It is important to recognize that this latter set of cases, concerning presidential control, has valued that control not simply as a means of protecting the executive against encroachments by the other branches, but also as a way of ensuring that every executive officer is accountable, through the elected President, to the People. In any event, I will have more to say about both of these lines of cases in the next section, which considers the mechanisms of executive accountability in the American system.

3. How executive authority is held to account

I have divided this survey of accountability mechanisms into three categories entailing legislative, judicial, and political mechanisms, respectively. Both the first and third of these categories fit into what some English scholars have called the 'political' constitution, that is, mechanisms by which 'those who exercise political power... are held to constitutional account through political means, and through political institutions.'[52] The legislative checks, however, rely on processes that are themselves established by law, such as the approval of executive budgets or the confirmation of nominees to executive positions; the purely political mechanisms, on the other hand, rely on mechanisms such as political parties that are generally not prescribed by legal mandate. The category of judicial mechanisms, of course, corresponds to the definition of a 'legal

---

[49] 418 US 683 (1974).   [50] 272 US 52 (1926).

[51] For other examples of the first category, see *Clinton v. Jones* 520 US 681 (1997) (holding that the President is not immune from private damages suits for conduct unconnected with his official duties); *Nixon v. Fitzgerald* 457 US 731 (1982) (holding that the President *is* immune from damages liability for his official acts). Additional examples of the second category include *Humphrey's Executor v. United States* 295 US 602 (1935) (holding that Congress may insulate the commissioner of the Federal Trade Commission from presidential removal); *Morrison v. Olson* 487 US 654 (1988) (upholding the Independent Counsel Act, which created an independent prosecutor not subject to presidential removal).

[52] Adam Tomkins, *Public Law* (Clarendon, 2003), 18–19; Dawn Oliver, *Regionalism in a Political Constitution: The UK Experience*, in Basil Markesinis and Jorg Fedtke (eds.), *Patterns of Regionalism and Federalism* (forthcoming Hart, 2005).

constitution' as one 'through which the government is held to account [by] the law and the court-room.'[53]

It is worth noting, if only in passing, that executive accountability has a second dimension in America's federal system. Most of the executive officials, such as police officers, who come in contact with citizens in the ordinary course of life will be minions of state and local governments.[54] Extensive mechanisms exist in both federal and state law for holding these officers to account, the most prominent being 42 USC §1983, the federal statutory mechanism for private suits to redress violations of federal law by persons acting 'under color of state law.'[55] These mechanisms are probably best considered in the context of federalism doctrine, however. The discussion here will focus on the accountability of the *national* executive.

(a) Legislative mechanisms

Legislative checks on executive power are one of the distinguishing features of separation of powers in a presidential system, as the chief executive cannot count on legislative majorities to implement his policies.[56] Such checks are obviously most effective during periods of 'divided government', that is, when the same political party does not control all three institutions of the House, Senate, and Presidency. But these mechanisms may be effective even in a period of unified government due to a combination of unreliable party discipline and procedural mechanisms in the Congress that allow minorities to block legislation and appointments under certain circumstances.

The federal executive depends on Congress for the funding of its initiatives and, in many instances, for the confirmation of its personnel. The annual appropriations cycle provides an opportunity for congressional review of executive activities, and congressional committees have shown themselves willing to punish executive agencies that act in opposition to Congress's preferences.[57] Likewise, confirmation hearings may permit Congress to exert pressure on an executive official's future policies, as when senators were able to extract a promise to appoint a special Watergate prosecutor at the confirmation hearings of Attorney General Elliott Richardson.[58] Or such hearings may provide an

---

[53] Tomkins, n. 52, 18–19.

[54] See, e.g., William J. Stuntz, 'Terrorism, Federalism, and Police Misconduct' (2002) 25 *Harv J L & Pub Pol'y* 665, 665.

[55] For a good introductory discussion, see Erwin Chemerinsky, *Federal Jurisdiction* (Aspen, 4th edn., 2003), 463–586.

[56] But see, Tomkins, n. 52, 44–54 (arguing that the British parliamentary system nonetheless features a vital separation of powers by which Parliament checks the national executive).

[57] Harold H. Bruff, 'Presidential Power and Administrative Rulemaking' (1979) 88 *Yale L J* 451, 457–8.

[58] Beth Nolan, 'Removing Conflicts from the Administration of Justice: Conflicts of Interest and Independent Counsels under the Ethics in Government Act' (1990) 79 *Geo LJ* 1, 14 n.53.

occasion for review and criticism of the nominee's performance in a prior executive post. The recent confirmation hearings of Alberto Gonzales as Attorney General and Condoleezza Rice as Secretary of State, for example, provided a forum for senatorial debate over those officials' prior positions, respectively, on interrogation of suspected terrorists and the war in Iraq.[59]

Congress may also, in certain instances, seek to hold the executive to account by investigating its activities. Individual committees often hold congressional hearings as a means of drawing public attention to particular policies that some Members of Congress may oppose. Less frequently, Congress may conduct investigations of alleged misconduct with an eye toward facilitating the filing of criminal charges.[60] Even more rarely, the House of Representatives may vote to impeach executive officials for 'high crimes and misdemeanors,' resulting in a trial in the Senate.[61] Only two Presidents in American history have been impeached, and neither one was convicted by the required two-thirds Senate majority.[62] It remains to be seen whether the Clinton impeachment in 1998 will go down as a harbinger of increased willingness to use the impeachment mechanism or a cautionary tale deterring similar episodes in the future.

In prior years, the possibility of investigation by Congress itself was augmented by the Independent Counsel statute, which provided for appointment of an investigator and prosecutor within the executive branch, but largely independent of presidential control.[63] The statute expired in 1999 and has not been renewed, largely owing to perceived excesses in Kenneth Starr's investigation of President Clinton. But the President has, in the past, agreed to appoint special prosecutors to investigate certain allegations and accorded them substantial autonomy. The appointments of Archibald Cox and, later, Leon Jaworsky as special prosecutor during the Watergate scandal, for example, occurred as a result of political agreement prior to the enactment of the Independent Counsel law.[64]

Legislative veto mechanisms form a final important set of legislative checks on executive authority. The classic legislative veto was a procedure by which Congress would delegate broad authority to an executive agency or officer, but

---

[59] On congressional oversight mechanisms, see generally Louis Fisher, *The Politics of Shared Power: Congress and the Executive* (Texas A&M, 1998), 71–82; Matthew D. McCubbins and Thomas Schwartz, 'Congressional Oversight Overlooked: Police Patrols versus Fire Alarms' (1984) 28 *Am J Pol Sci* 165.

[60] Fisher, n. 59, 73–5; Harold Hongju Koh, *The National Security Constitution: Sharing Power after the Iran-Contra Affair* (Yale, 1990), 16–22 (discussing the congressional investigation of the Iran-Contra scandal). [61] US Const. Art. II, § 4.

[62] See generally, William H. Rehnquist, *Grand Inquests: The Historical Impeachments of Justice Samuel Chase and President Andrew Johnson* (Morrow, 1992), 143–248; Richard A. Posner, *An Affair of State: The Investigation, Impeachment, and Trial of President Clinton* (Harvard, 1999).

[63] *See* 28 USC §§ 591–9 (1994 & Supp. 1996).

[64] Abraham Dash, 'Bidding Adieu to the Clinton Administration: Assessing the Ramifications of the Clinton 'Scandals' on the Office of the President and on Executive Branch Investigation' (2001) 60 *Md L Rev* 26, 33–4 (describing the hiring and firing of Cox—and the subsequent hiring of Jaworski—by the Nixon administration); Thomas W. Merrill, 'Beyond the Independent Counsel: Evaluating the Options' (1999) 43 *St Louis L J* 1047, 1078–9.

then provide in the relevant statute that particular exercises of that authority might be nullified by subsequent Congressional action short of a new statutory enactment. Such action might take the form, for example, of a resolution by a single House of Congress disapproving the measure. The Supreme Court struck down the legislative veto in *INS v. Chadha*,[65] holding that the subsequent disapproval amounted to legislative action but did not satisfy the constitutional requirements of bicameral action and presentment to the President. Even immediately after *Chadha*, however, observers predicted that 'the old veto might re-emerge in new legal clothes.'[66] Congress may still, for example, provide that executive agency actions become effective only after a time delay, in order to afford Congress an opportunity to review the action and legislate if necessary. Or Congress may provide by internal rule that the Appropriations Committee will not approve funding for particular sorts of agency action unless the legislative committee that oversees the relevant agency approves those actions. And notwithstanding the fact that a court will not enforce a legislative veto after *Chadha*, Congress may sometimes exercise such a veto as part of an informal agreement with the executive, with adherence compelled by the threat of Congressional retaliation rather than judicial mandate.[67] Reports of the legislative veto's death may thus have been greatly exaggerated.

(b) Judicial mechanisms

The American system confers on private litigants relatively broad rights to judicial review of executive action. This has been true at least since *Marbury v. Madison*,[68] when Chief Justice John Marshall asserted the right of the courts to review the failure of even high executive officials—of the primary author of the Constitution, for goodness sake—to perform nondiscretionary duties. The availability of prospective relief against federal officials for violation of constitutional rights was recognized in *United States v. Lee* and extended in *Ex parte Young* even to cases not involving interests recognized at common law.[69] Both these cases relied on a long tradition holding that suits against government officials are not subject to sovereign immunity. But Section 702 of the Administrative Procedure Act confirmed the availability of such remedies by waiving sovereign immunity for suits against the United States for relief other than money damages.[70]

---

[65] 462 US 919 (1983).
[66] Stephen Breyer, 'The Legislative Veto After Chadha' (1984) 72 *Geo L J* 785, 785.
[67] Fisher, n. 59, 102–4.   [68] 5 US (1 Cranch) 137 (1803).
[69] *United States v. Lee* 106 US 196 (1882); *Ex parte Young* 209 US 123 (1908). *Ex parte Young* actually involved a suit against a *state* government official, but 'its principle has been easily absorbed in suits challenging *federal* official action.' Richard H. Fallon, Jr., Daniel J. Meltzer, David L. Shapiro, *Hart and Wechsler's The Federal Courts and the Federal System* (Foundation, 5th edn., 2003), 959 (citing *Shields v. Utah Idaho Cent. R.R.*, 305 US 177, 183–4 (1938)).
[70] 5 USC § 702. The APA's waiver was explicitly qualified, however, by preserving any other specific statutory restrictions on relief against the United States.

Damages relief is also available against federal officers, or against the United States itself, in a variety of circumstances. For constitutional violations, the Supreme Court recognized an implied private right of action under the Constitution itself in *Bivens v. Six Unknown Named Agents of the Federal Bureau of Narcotics*.[71] The *Bivens* remedy has been substantially limited by the Court in later cases, in part because of general hostility to implied private rights of action and in part because Congress has, in many circumstances, provided alternative means of redress.[72] Moreover, the available data indicates that *Bivens* plaintiffs are rarely successful in the lower courts.[73] Plaintiffs have fared better under statutory schemes that waive sovereign immunity and permit private suits. The Federal Tort Claims Act permits suits against the United States for torts committed by federal employees, so long as the United States would be liable under the applicable state law if it were a private entity.[74] And the Tucker Act generally permits damages suits against the United States for claims involving the taking of private property, breach of contract, and other non-tort theories.[75]

Finally, the Administrative Procedure Act broadly provides for judicial review of executive agency action, including both agency rulemaking and adjudicatory decisions. Such review may focus on whether agency implementation measures comply with the underlying statutory enactments,[76] whether the agency's policy-formation process conformed to a wide array of procedural requirements,[77] whether the agency actually applied its expertise in a demonstrable way to the problem at hand,[78] and even whether the substantive decision reached by the agency was 'arbitrary or capricious.'[79] The nature and mechanics of such review form virtually their own field of specialization, and they are accordingly outside the scope of my discussion here. The point is simply that the exercise of executive power by agencies of the administrative state is subject to fairly rigorous judicial review, on both substantive and procedural grounds.

All of these avenues for holding executive power to account through the courts are subject to important and complex limitations. As Fallon and Meltzer have noted, 'the law of [judicial] remedies is inherently a jurisprudence of deficiency' in which the rights asserted will almost inevitably fall short of complete vindication.[80] But although John Marshall's dictum that there must be a remedy for

---

[71] 403 US 388 (1971).

[72] For judicial skepticism of implied rights of action, see, e.g., *Alexander v. Sandoval* 532 US 275 (2001). For cases deferring to Congress's provision of an alternate remedy, *Bush v. Lucas* 462 US 367 (1983); *Schweiker v. Chilicky* 487 US 412 (1988).

[73] Perry M. Rosen, 'The Bivens Constitutional Tort: An Unfulfilled Promise' (1989) 67 *NC L Rev* 337, 343–4. [74] 28 USC §1346(b).

[75] 28 USC §§1346(a)(2), 1491(a)(1). [76] 5 USC §706(2)(C).

[77] 5 USC § 706(2)(D).

[78] *Motor Vehicle Mfrs. Ass'n of the U.S., Inc. v. State Farm Mut. Auto. Ins. Co.*, 463 US 29, 43 (1983) (interpreting the 'arbitary and capricious' standard as requiring the agency to 'examine the relevant data and articulate a satisfactory explanation for its action'). [79] 5 USC §706(2)(A).

[80] Richard H. Fallon, Jr. and Daniel J. Meltzer, 'New Law, Non-Retroactivity, and Constitutional Remedies' (1991) 104 *Harv L Rev* 1731, 1778; see also, *Ibid.*, 1777–91 (offering a general account of American remedies for constitutional violations).

every right has not always been honoured in every case, it remains reasonably clear that '[t]he Constitution... contemplates a judicial 'check' on the political branches... to ensure that government generally respects constitutional values.'[81]

(c) **Political mechanisms**

Finally, executive power is almost always subject to significant purely political constraints. Although the American President is elected for a fixed term and can be removed only by impeachment, a considerably higher standard than would ordinarily be required for a parliamentary vote of 'no confidence', the most prominent concern in recent years has been that Presidents are *too* responsive to public opinion, rather than insufficiently so.[82] Moreover, given the relatively narrow list of enumerated executive powers in Article II, Presidents are generally dependent on Congress to either delegate power in different policy areas or support particular policy initiatives through legislation. Presidents must therefore take account of how any given exercise of executive power will be viewed both inside and outside of Washington, DC.

What is somewhat less apparent is the extent to which political parties both empower and constrain the exercise of executive authority. The Framers of the Constitution seem not to have anticipated the development of strong political parties, which has undermined the Framers' assumption, made clear in Federalist 51, that Congress and the President each would jealously guard their institutional prerogatives against encroachment by the others. Once parties unite politicians across the institutional boundaries of the separation of powers, legislators in one party may well be willing to cede power to a President of the same party. At the same time, however, parties may also constrain executive action by creating a focused constituency to whom the President is accountable. Many observers believe, for example, that Richard Nixon's ability to resist calls for his resignation collapsed at the point that the leaders of his party in Congress withdrew their support.[83]

---

[81] *Ibid.*, 1788. For Chief Justice Marshall's statement, *Marbury v. Madison* 5 US (1 Cranch) 137, 163 (1803) ('The government of the United States has been emphatically termed a government of laws, and not of men. It will certainly cease to deserve this high appellation, if the laws furnish no remedy for the violation of a vested legal right.').

[82] See, e.g., Daryl J. Levinson, 'Empire-Building Government in Constitutional Law' (2005) 118 *Harv L Rev* 915, 930 ('Even second-term presidents evidently care so much about staying in line with public opinion that their approach to governing often seems indistinguishable from an ongoing political campaign.'); Mimi Hall, *New White House, New 'War Room' for Strategizing*, USA Today, July 5, 2001, at 4A (observing that 'Clinton's reliance on opinion polls was derided by Republicans who said he followed polls, not principles or convictions').

[83] See, e.g., Michael J. Gerhardt, 'Chancellor Kent and the Search for the Elements of Impeachable Offenses' (1998) 74 *Chi-Kent L Rev* 91, 114 ('By early August, Nixon lost the support of all of his fellow Republicans in Congress.... The willingness of prominent and loyal Republicans to join in acknowledging President Nixon's impeachability and in encouraging him to resign obviously helped to precipitate his resignation.').

Similarly double-edged considerations arise from the President's control over his subordinates. Early in the last century, Congress strove to limit presidential authority by creating 'independent' executive agencies, such as the Interstate Commerce Commission or the Federal Communications Commission, whose members would serve for fixed terms rather than at the pleasure of the President. These sorts of arrangements have been challenged under the theory that the executive branch is 'unitary', that is, that every executive officer must be subject to presidential direction and removal. This unitary theory obviously enhances the President's power over the branch that he heads; it also, however, renders executive officers accountable to the people, albeit indirectly, through the elected President they serve. By clarifying the President's responsibility for the acts of every executive officer, the unitary executive may facilitate the operation of political checks on executive power.[84] And while it seems highly unlikely that a subsequent presidential election will actually turn (even for individual voters) on a particular act of a subordinate official,[85] the accountability advantages of unitary executive authority have loomed large in these debates for many years.[86]

4. Key issues of executive accountability

In this section I want to take up in more detail three questions concerning executive accountability. These are by no means the *only* questions, but they are both particularly salient at the present time and may serve to illustrate some of the broader themes already sketched. The first is the long-term problem of controlling the executive's exercise of legislative authority delegated by Congress. The other two—the control of the war power and the President's authority to detain suspects in the War on Terror—have taken on special significance as a result of recent events.

(a) The control of delegated authority

I have already recounted how the death of the delegation doctrine as a judicially-enforceable principle has created a problem of both executive accountability and democratic legitimacy: Much of American law is not made by the People's elected representatives, but rather by faceless bureaucrats with no direct mandate

---

[84] On the unitary executive principle, see generally Lawrence Lessig and Cass R. Sunstein, 'The President and the Administration' (1994) 94 *Colum L Rev* 1; Steven G. Calabresi and Kevin H. Rhodes, 'The Structural Constitution: Unitary Executive, Plural Judiciary' (1992) 105 *Harv L Rev* 1153.

[85] Peter Shane, 'Political Accountability in a System of Checks and Balances: The Case of Presidential Review of Rulemaking' (1995) 48 *Ark L Rev* 161, 199–200.

[86] See, e.g., Federalist No. 70, n. 1, 476–7 (Alexander Hamilton); see also, sources cited in n. 97.

from or accountability to the voters.[87] The original notion of administrative action, predicated on precise and narrow delegations of power from Congress, envisioned the executive agency 'as a mere transmission belt for implementing legislative directives in particular cases.'[88] With the advent of much broader delegations, American administrative law has progressed through a series of different justifying theories that have sought to re-legitimate the national administrative state. For a time, the agencies' role rested on 'the need for professional administrators, applying a neutral and impartial expertise, to set themselves the direction and terms of regulation.'[89] As administrative decisions came to be seen as political rather than objective or scientific, however, this technocratic ideal gave way to theories that stressed the openness of the administrative process to participation by affected groups. Under this view, which flourished in the 1960s and 1970s, 'the full and fair participation of these interests in agency processes would serve as the principal check on administrative discretion.'[90]

Interest group pluralism had its own problems, however. Much more recently, some scholars have urged a new paradigm of 'presidential administration,' under which the President both exercises greater internal control over administrative policymaking and takes broader external ownership of those policies by presenting them to the public as his own.[91] This direct involvement of the President, in turn, allows administrative lawmaking to be grounded more plausibly in the President's own electoral mandate.

The story that I have just told, in which one administrative law paradigm follows another in neat succession, needs serious qualification. In particular, as Kagan has noted, '[e]ach kind of administrative control...—congressional control, self-control (through bureaucratic experts), and interest group control—...survives in some form today, well past its purported demise.'[92]

One can, moreover, match each paradigm with particular doctrines enforced through judicial review of agency action. Congressional control continues to be enforced through judicial review mechanisms that purport to ensure that administrative regulations and actions conform to the authorizing statute;[93] likewise, canons of statutory construction enforce some vestige of the non-delegation doctrine itself by construing delegations narrowly in certain

---

[87] See generally, Lisa Schultz Bressman, 'Beyond Accountability: Arbitrariness and Legitimacy in the Administrative State' (2003) 78 *NYULRev* 461 (linking the legitimacy problem to the 'counter-majoritarian difficulty' in constitutional law, and tracing different approaches to administrative legitimacy).

[88] Richard B. Stewart, 'The Reformation of American Administrative Law' (1975) 88 *Harv L Rev* 1667, 1675.

[89] Elena Kagan, 'Presidential Administration' (2001) 114 *Harv L Rev* 2245, 2253.

[90] *Ibid.*   [91] *Ibid.*, 2250–2.   [92] *Ibid.*, 2254.

[93] *AT&T v. Iowa Utils. Bd.* 525 US 366, 392 (1999) (invalidating a regulation promulgated by the Federal Communications Commission on the ground that it was inconsistent with the underlying statute).

circumstances.[94] Respect for bureaucratic expertise survives in judicial review doctrines that seek not so much to evaluate the substance of agency decisions but instead to ensure that the agency has in fact applied its expertise by considering all relevant data, evaluating feasible alternatives, compiling a thorough evidentiary record, and explaining its conclusions.[95] And judicial enforcement of participation rights continues to vindicate theories of administrative legitimacy that rely on the openness of the administrative process to participation by interested groups.[96] The same is true of contemporary theories of presidential administration. Most broadly, the notion of the unitary executive seeks to promote the accountability of all agency officials to the President, thereby both facilitating not only his control over those officials but also the voters' ability to hold *him* electorally accountable for their actions.[97] In any event, as these examples demonstrate, the intellectual history of *justifying* agency authority provides a helpful set of organizing principles for understanding the different ways in which bureaucratic authority is held to account in our system today.

(b) Control of the war power

While control of delegated authority goes to the day-to-day operation of the administrative state, controversies over control of executive war powers implicate decisions made only infrequently, but with wide-ranging implications for the nation and the world. The Constitution contains no 'war power' in terms; instead, it identifies a number of different war powers and allocates them between the executive and legislative branches. Article I confers on Congress the power 'to declare war'; 'to grant letters of Marque and Reprisal, and make Rules concerning Captures on Land and Water'; to 'raise and support Armies,' and to 'provide and maintain a Navy'; 'to make Rules for the Government and Regulation of the land and naval Forces'; as well as certain powers pertaining to the militia.[98] Article II, in turn, says that the President 'shall be Commander in Chief of the Army and Navy of the United States, and of the Militia of the several States, when called into the actual Service of the United States.'[99] Even the Judiciary is not entirely left out: In the early Republic, one of the most important aspects of the admiralty jurisdiction conferred in Article III was the decision of prize cases arising from hostile military operations.[100] The

---

[94] Cass. R. Sunstein, 'Nondelegation Canons' (2000) 67 *U Chi L Rev* 315.
[95] *Motor Vehicle Mfrs. Ass'n of the U.S., Inc. v. State Farm Mut. Auto. Ins. Co.*, 463 US 29 (1983).
[96] Jonathan T. Molot, 'An Old Role for a New Litigation Era' (2003) 113 *Yale LJ* 27, 102 (describing the judicial expansion of the basic notice and comment provisions in § 553 of the APA and stating that courts have 'secured for interested parties elaborate participation rights in the agency rulemaking process').
[97] Steven G. Calabresi, 'Some Normative Arguments for the Unitary Executive' (1994) 48 *Ark L Rev* 23, 42–5; Lessig and Sunstein, n. 84, 102–3. [98] US Const. Art. I, §8.
[99] US Const. Art. II, §2.
[100] William Casto, 'The Origins of Federal Admiralty Jurisdiction in an Age of Privateers, Smugglers, and Pirates' (1993) 37 *Am J Leg Hist* 117.

boundaries between these powers are not self-defining, however. In particular, debate has focused on when the initiation of military hostilities falls within the President's powers of command, and when such action requires a declaration of war by Congress.

These debates have been with us since the beginning of the Republic. The Founders plainly intended to create an executive power—entirely lacking under the prior Articles of Confederation—with sufficient energy, initiative, and unity of purpose to respond to foreign threats in a dangerous world. 'Of all the cares or concerns of government,' Alexander Hamilton wrote in Federalist 74, 'the direction of war most peculiarly demands those qualities which distinguish the exercise of power by a single hand.'[101] At the same time, there was also considerable distrust of executive authority in this area. James Madison declared that '[w]ar is in fact the true nurse of executive aggrandizement,' and that consequently 'the executive is the department...most distinguished by its propensity to war.'[102] Substantial evidence thus suggests that the Founders meant to divorce the powers (which had been combined in the British monarch) of *conducting* a war from that of initiating it. This history forms the core of the 'strong Congress' position in contemporary war powers debates, which would deny the President the authority to initiate military hostilities without authorization from Congress.[103]

The case for strong congressional primacy has encountered two major difficulties. Ramsey has identified 'a serious textual embarrassment' arising from the fact that 'Congress...has the power 'to declare war,' not the power 'to authorize hostilities,' and it is not immediately clear why the two should be equated.'[104] Indeed, some scholars have argued that 'declaring war' was historically understood simply to trigger legal consequences arising from a state of war under international law, a determination existing entirely separate from the practical

---

[101] The Federalist No. 74, n. 1, 500 (Alexander Hamilton).

[102] 'Helvidius' No. 4 (14 Sept. 1793), *in* 15 *The Papers of James Madison* (Thomas A. Mason et al. eds., 1985), 106, 108–9.

[103] See, e.g., Louis Fisher, *Presidential War Power* (Kansas, 1995), 3–12; John Hart Ely, *War and Responsibility: Constitutional Lessons of Vietnam and Its Aftermath* (Princeton, 1993), 3–5; Charles A. Lofgren, 'War-Making under the Constitution: The Original Understanding' (1972) 81 *Yale L J* 672, 677–88. As Michael Ramsey's recent survey of the academic literature explains:

The academic case for Congress stands, in main, upon three points. First, during the drafting and ratifying debates, and in the years immediately following, a number of key Framers and other leading figures made statements heavily implying that Congress had complete control of the decision to initiate hostilities.... Congressional advocates also point to the records of the Philadelphia convention regarding the drafting of the Constitution's Declare War Clause.... Third, congressionalists draw comfort from the exercise of war powers in the years immediately following ratification. Though Washington, as President, was fairly aggressive in exercising unilateral foreign affairs powers, he did not unilaterally commit the nation to hostilities, even though opportunities to do so arose on several occasions.

Michael Ramsey, 'Textualism and War Powers' (2002) 69 *U Chi L Rev* 1543, 1549–51.

[104] Ramsey, n. 103, 1552.

decision to employ military force.[105] Perhaps more seriously, practice since the Founding has departed substantially from the strong Congress ideal. Although the Congress has declared war in connection with only five conflicts in American history,[106] one study found '234 instances in which the United States has used its armed forces abroad in situations of conflict or potential conflict or for other than normal peacetime purposes.'[107] Although many of these instances were authorized by Congress in a form other than a declaration of war, many, such as the 1999 air campaign in the former Yugoslavia, were not. The 'strong Executive' position thus emphasizes that congressional control of war powers would require departures from both the constitutional text and more recent practice.

Ramsey has recently offered an intermediate reading grounded in the original understanding of the 'Declare War' Clause. The key point is his finding of a widespread eighteenth century practice that war may be 'declared' either by word or action. As one British admiralty court put it,

Where is the difference, whether a war is proclaimed by a Herald at the Royal Exchange, with his trumpets, and on the Pont Neuf at Paris, and by reading and affixing a printed paper on public buildings; or whether war is announced by royal ships, and whole fleets, at the mouths of cannon?[108]

It follows that any action that 'declares war', that is, any act that initiates a state of war under international law, must be authorized by Congress.[109] On the other hand, uses of military forces short of war, such as the re-flagging and escort of tankers in the Persian Gulf, or the deployment of peacekeepers, need not be authorized by Congress. Moreover, Congress's authority extends only to the *initiation* of hostilities. If some *other* actor creates the state of war, then the President as Commander-in-Chief is entitled to prosecute the war to its conclusion without needing to seek Congress's approval.[110] Ramsey's approach has the virtues of hewing closely to the constitutional text *and* history, and while it is not consistent with all of subsequent practice it may well fit most people's intuitions about the 'right' allocation of authority better than its competitors. That is because it places the responsibility for major commitments to force in legislative hands, while preserving important executive authority

---

[105] John C. Yoo, 'The Continuation of Politics by Other Means: The Original Understanding of War Powers' (1996) 84 *Cal L Rev* 167. Emmerich Vattel, for example, held that 'publication of a declaration of war is necessary for the instruction and guidance of a State's own subjects, and in order to fix the date from which certain rights belonging to them in virtue of war are to begin, and in order to settle certain effects which the voluntary Law of Nations attributes to formal war.' Emmerich de Vattel, *The Law of Nations or the Principles of Natural Law Applied to the Conduct and to the Affairs of Nations and of Sovereigns* (trans. Charles G. Fenwick, Carnegie Inst. 1916), 255.

[106] They are: the War of 1812; the Mexican-American War of 1846–48; the Spanish-American War of 1898; World War I; and World War II.

[107] Ellen C. Collier, *Instances of Use of United States Forces Abroad, 1798–1993* (Congressional Research Service, 1993).

[108] *The Maria Magdalena* 165 Eng Rep 57, 58 (Adm 1779) (quoted in Ramsey, n. 103, 1586).

[109] Ramsey, n. 103, 1609–10.   [110] *Ibid.*, 1619–35.

in situations involving lesser commitments and/or calling for particularly expeditious action.

Congress sought to resolve some of these questions in the 1970s by enacting—over President Richard Nixon's veto—a framework statute governing the use of military forces. The War Powers Resolution[111] purports to state Congress's own interpretation of the constitutional allocation of war powers by declaring that the President may use military force 'only pursuant to (1) a declaration of war, (2) specific statutory authorization, or (3) a national emergency created by attack upon the United States, its territories or possessions, or its armed forces.'[112] The Resolution requires the President to consult with and report to Congress when he introduces American armed forces 'into hostilities or into situations where imminent involvement in hostilities is clearly indicated,' and its 'clock' provisions require the withdrawal of those forces if Congress does not authorize their use within sixty days.[113] Most commentators have not viewed the Resolution as a successful curb on the President's actions. By effectively authorizing the initial use of force, for up to sixty days, the statute both permits the President to conduct short-term operations and, in situations where longer involvement is required, allows him to present Congress with a *fait accompli*.[114] An unbroken line of Presidents, on the other hand, have taken the position that the War Powers Resolution is both unconstitutional and unwise: unconstitutional because it unduly restricts the President's ability to use military force, and unwise because it causes both adversaries and allies to question whether any given military commitment will endure past sixty days.[115]

The courts have come close to an absolute refusal to resolve these disagreements. In *Campbell v. Clinton*,[116] for example, the US Court of Appeals for the District of Columbia Circuit dismissed a lawsuit by several congressmen challenging President Clinton's use of American forces to support the NATO campaign in Yugoslavia. The Court's dismissal for lack of standing was typical of many decisions using justiciability, standing or ripeness to avoid deciding war powers cases.[117] Others have relied upon the political question doctrine to reach the same result.[118] It seems clear that the American judiciary has little interest in inserting itself in a constitutional clash between the President and Congress on this issue, and the opinions typically stress the availability of other means by

---

[111] Pub. L. No. 93–148, 87 Stat. 555 (1973), codified at 50 USC §§1541–1548.
[112] *Ibid.*, §1542(c). [113] *Ibid.* §§1543, 1544(b).
[114] Ely, n. 103, 117 (noting 'Congress's gift to the president of sixty (actually ninety) free days to fight any war he likes').
[115] See, e.g., President Nixon's Message Vetoing the War Powers Resolution (24 Oct. 1973), in Curtis A. Bradley and Jack L. Goldsmith, *Foreign Relations Law: Cases and Materials* (Aspen 2003), 199. [116] 203 F.3d 19 (DC Cir. 2000).
[117] See, e.g., *Doe v. Bush* 323 F.3d 133 (1st Cir. 2003); *Dellums v. Bush* 752 F. Supp. 1141 (DDC 1990).
[118] See, e.g., *Ange v. Bush* 752 F. Supp. 509 (DDC 1990); *Lowry v. Reagan* 676 F. Supp. 333 (DDC 1987).

which Congress may limit or punish what it deems the improper use of military forces without resorting to the courts.[119]

Notwithstanding the inherent limitations of the War Powers Resolution and the unwillingness of the courts to enforce what it *does* require, it would be a mistake to conclude that the President has escaped the need to seek congressional support when he wishes to use military force. The two most important uses of American military force in the past fifteen years were the Gulf War of 1991, fought to evict Saddam Hussein from Kuwait, and the Iraq War of 2003. In both those instances, as well as in Afghanistan in 2001, the President sought—and received—congressional authorization for his actions. The requests for such authorization, in each instance, were couched in the customary language of being 'consistent with' the War Powers Resolution, rather than in compliance with it, in order to avoid conceding the Resolution's binding force. But the fact remains that American Presidents feel far more secure in using force with congressional authorization than without it.

It is hardly difficult to see why this would be true. A President who goes to war without a show of congressional support will be doubly liable to political recriminations should the venture go awry; for that reason, he has an interest in forcing his potential critics to go on record before hostilities commence. Likewise, a President who *does* have a formal demonstration that Congress is behind him confronts both adversaries and potential allies from a position of strength. Potential coalition partners, for example, can infer from a successful authorizing vote that the President's initiative has substantial popular support and that they are unlikely to be left high and dry should they choose to participate in the venture. Although President George W. Bush's attempt to garner United Nations support for the Iraq War was ultimately unsuccessful, he would have been in a far weaker bargaining position if he had failed first secure the support of his own legislature. And Senator Kerry faced an excruciating dilemma, in the 2004 presidential election, when he sought to criticize the President once events in Iraq seemed to go badly, since he had earlier voted to authorize the expedition.[120] None of these reasons mean that Presidents will *never* use force without congressional approval; President Clinton, after all, employed American air forces in the former Yugoslavia without formal congressional authorization.[121] But it does seem clear that Presidents have strong incentives to seek congressional approval for military ventures, and these 'political safeguards' may push practice

---

[119] See, e.g., *Campbell*, 203 F.3d at 23 (noting that Congress may cut off funds, enact a statute barring the action, or even impeach the President).

[120] Katharine Q. Seelye, *The 2004 Campaign: The Advertising Campaigns; Both Sides' Commercials Create Brew of Negativity, at a Boil*, NY Times, 23 Sept. 2004, at A23 (describing a Bush campaign ad criticizing Kerry for 'vot[ing] for the Iraq war, oppos[ing] it, support[ing] it, and now oppos[ing] it again.').

[121] John C. Yoo, *Applying the War Powers Resolution to the War on Terrorism* (2003) 6 *Green Bag* 2d 175, 180 ('President Clinton deployed U.S Armed Forces in Haiti and Bosnia without prior congressional authorization.').

to conform to the best interpretation of constitutional authority despite the difficulty of judicial enforcement. In this area, the legal constitution has had relatively little influence, but the political constitution seems to have considerable vitality.

(c) Limiting executive detention

The legal constitution has played a greater role in recent controversies over executive detention of suspected terrorists. Since the attacks by Al Qaeda terrorists on the World Trade Center and the Pentagon on 11 September 2001, the government has moved aggressively to identify, detain, and interrogate suspected terrorists both at home and abroad. These efforts have raised a host of issues, most of which I cannot hope to canvass here. But three particular controversies—over the detention within the United States of American citizens suspected of terrorism, the detention of aliens suspected of terrorism at the US naval base at Guantanamo Bay, Cuba, and the trial of suspected terrorists before military commissions rather than civilian courts—will give some sense of the extent to which, and the means by which, the executive is being held to account in the context of the War on Terror.

Yaser Esam Hamdi was captured in Afghanistan in 2001, where US military authorities believed he was fighting on the side of the Taliban and Al Qaeda forces. When they discovered that Hamdi was an American citizen (he had been born in the United States but grew up in Saudi Arabia) those authorities returned him to the United States and held him in a naval brig in Norfolk, Virginia. Hamdi's father filed a petition for a writ of *habeas corpus* on his son's behalf, challenging his son's detention under the Due Process Clause of the Fifth Amendment and the Non-Detention Act, which provides that '[n]o citizen shall be imprisoned or otherwise detained by the Untied States except pursuant to an Act of Congress.'[122] The government responded aggressively, arguing that the President had inherent power to detain suspected terrorists and that the Non-Detention Act only applies to civilian detention. The Supreme Court accepted that the President had power to detain Hamdi, but on far narrower grounds: it concluded that Congress's authorization to use military force to pursue the parties responsible for the September 11 attacks included the authority to detain suspected terrorists, thereby satisfying the Non-Detention Act and avoiding any need to consider an inherent powers theory.[123]

The Court went on to consider, however, the extent of Hamdi's right to challenge the factual basis of his detention—that is, the government's contention that Hamdi was an 'enemy combatant' rather than, as Hamdi claimed, a humanitarian relief worker who found himself in the wrong place at the wrong time. The government conceded that the writ of *habeas corpus* was available to

[122] 18 USC §4001(a). [123] *Hamdi v. Rumsfeld* 124 S. Ct. 2633, 2639–42 (2004).

challenge the detention of an American citizen held within the United States, but insisted that its burden to justify the detention could be met simply by providing a written declaration from an executive officer setting forth the facts surrounding Hamdi's capture. The Court rejected this argument for extreme deference, applying the traditional balancing test from its procedural due process jurisprudence.[124] Weighing the government's strong security interests against the basic due process rights at issue, the Court concluded that 'a citizen-detainee seeking to challenge his classification as an enemy combatant must receive notice of the factual basis for his classification, and a fair opportunity to rebut the Government's factual assertions before a neutral decisionmaker.'[125] The Court was unwilling, however, to require anything approaching the safeguards associated with a normal trial: '[T]he exigencies of the circumstances may demand that... enemy combatant proceedings may be tailored to alleviate their uncommon potential to burden the Executive at a time of ongoing military conflict.'[126] Although the Court did not lay out a definitive set of procedures for future proceedings, it suggested that,

> [H]earsay, for example, may need to be accepted as the most reliable available evidence from the Government in such a proceeding. Likewise, the Constitution would not be offended by a presumption in favour of the Government's evidence, so long as that presumption remained a rebuttable one and fair opportunity for rebuttal were provided.[127]

Hamdi seems to indicate a Supreme Court that is deferential to executive assertions of national security imperatives, but nonetheless willing to stake out a meaningful judicial role in policing the exercise of executive power.

The same pattern was evident in *Rasul v. Bush*,[128] which considered whether detainees being held at Guantanamo Bay, Cuba, could seek judicial review of their detention by means of a writ of *habeas corpus*. Prior precedent had suggested they could not: In *Johnson v. Eisentrager*, a World War II case involving German nationals prosecuted by a military tribunal sitting in China for aiding the Japanese after the German surrender, Justice Jackson's somewhat murky opinion had suggested that enemy aliens being held and tried outside the United States, for war crimes committed outside the United States, had no right under the Constitution to any sort of judicial process.[129] In *Rasul*, however, the

---

[124] *Mathews v. Eldridge* 424 US 319 (1976). As the *Hamdi* court explained,

Mathews dictates that the process due in any given instance is determined by weighing 'the private interest that will be affected by the official action' against the Government's asserted interest, 'including the function involved' and the burdens the Government would face in providing greater process. The *Mathews* calculus then contemplates a judicious balancing of these concerns, through an analysis of 'the risk of an erroneous deprivation' of the private interest if the process were reduced and the 'probable value, if any, of additional or substitute safeguards.' S. Ct. 2646 (quoting *Mathews*, 424 US at 335). [125] 124 S. Ct. 2648.
[126] *Ibid.*, 2649.   [127] *Ibid.*   [128] 124 S. Ct. 2686 (2004).
[129] 339 US 763, 776–81 (1950).

majority avoided *Eisentrager* by noting that the prior case considered only whether the Constitution *required* a right to judicial process, as all had assumed that the *habeas* statute did not independently grant such a right. By the end of the twentieth century, however, the *habeas* statute had been interpreted more broadly to reach persons held outside a particular federal court's territorial jurisdiction, so long as the court in question had jurisdiction over the *custodian* of the prisoner or someone higher up in the custodian's chain of command.[130] In light of these intervening developments in the construction of the *habeas* statute, the *Rasul* majority found that the statute covered the Guantanamo detainees, whose custodians at the Cuban base were ultimately subject to the command of the President, who was in turn within the geographical jurisdiction of the federal district court for the District of Columbia. The Court thus had no occasion to revisit the question, at issue in *Eisentrager*, of whether the Constitution itself would require such access if the statute had not conferred it.

Because *Rasul*'s holding is statutory in nature, Congress would be free to amend the *habeas* statute and confine the federal courts' jurisdiction more narrowly. The decision was thus deferential in that it left the ultimate say up to Congress, and there is no guarantee that, if the Congress did amend the statute to exclude foreign detainees, the Court would overturn *Eisentrager*'s narrow interpretation of the underlying constitutional entitlement. Likewise, the Court did not explore what *sort* of review enemy aliens detained abroad would be entitled to under the *habeas* procedure, and there is reason to believe that such review might be narrow.[131] At the end of the day, however, *Rasul* represents a remarkable willingness to construe the federal courts' jurisdiction broadly so as to permit them an opportunity to hold executive power to account, *wherever* such power is exercised. Again, the recent cases suggest a Court that is deferential to the political branches in many respects but nonetheless determined to play a meaningful supervisory role.

Finally, there is the question of trials of alleged enemy combatants by military commissions rather than in the ordinary federal courts. Debate about this question has been plagued by a number of misconceptions, particularly among some foreign observers. It is important to recognize that the American armed forces encompass a military justice system—developed primarily for the purpose of trying military personnel for crimes—that is extremely well-developed and that incorporates elaborate institutional safeguards designed to guarantee independence on the part of counsel and decision-makers.[132] The safeguards in that

---

[130] See, e.g., *Braden v. 30th Judicial Circuit Court* 410 US 484 (1973).

[131] Erwin Chemerinsky, 'Three Decisions, One Big Victory for Civil Rights' Trial, Sept. 2004, 74, 74–5 ('The *Rasul* Court did not address what type of hearing must be accorded to the Guantanamo detainees, but the courts will probably say that a meaningful factual hearing before a military tribunal is sufficient.').

[132] See, e.g., *Weiss v. United States* 510 US 163, 166–9 (1994) (outlining the structure of the military justice system); *United States v. Mathews* 16 M.J. 354 (Ct. Mil. App. 1983) (applying civilian Eighth Amendment precedents limiting the imposition of the death penalty to military

system, and especially the quality of counsel provided for defendants, compares favourably with what exists in many of the *state* jurisdictions that try the overwhelming majority of criminal cases in the United States. Indeed, the professionalism and independence already displayed by military lawyers assigned to defend suspected enemy combatants before military commissions has been remarkable; those lawyers have not, for example, been content merely to rebut the charges against their clients; rather, they have filed pre-emptive challenges to various aspects of the commission procedures themselves and have felt free to criticize those procedures publicly outside the courtroom.[133] Moreover, the procedures developed by the Defense Department for use in military commission proceedings—procedures developed, in part, in response to an initial wave of constitutional criticisms of the proposed process—generally have been more generous to the accused than most observers anticipated. Those procedures include, for example, a requirement of proof 'beyond a reasonable doubt,' as well as familiar rights to counsel, cross-examination of witnesses, and the like.[134] Widespread perceptions that the military commissions have been set up to administer summary justice ignore the actual process that has been developed.

Nonetheless, the federal courts have not been content to stand by and watch this process play out. The administration has conceded, notwithstanding an apparently categorical prohibition on judicial review of commission proceedings in the President's initial order establishing those commissions, that the commissions are subject to review by writ of *habeas corpus* in the Article III courts.[135] Although no cases have yet reached the US Supreme Court, the lower federal courts have been fairly aggressive in overseeing the commission process. In *Hamdan v. Rumsfeld*, for example, the District Court for the District of Columbia held that the Geneva Convention's requirement that a 'competent

---

cases); see generally, Lt. Col. James B. Ross and Capt. Cynthia Buxton, 'The American Military Justice System in the New Milennium' (2002) 52 *Air Force L Rev* 185.

[133] Pamela Hess, *Military Lawyers Criticize Tribunal*, United Press International, 15 Jan. 2004, available at http://www.upi.com/view.cfm?StoryID = 20040114-072539-7001r (reporting the filing of an amicus brief, prepared by five U.S. military lawyers assigned to defend prisoners before a military tribunal, that 'argu[ed] against the tribunal's legitimacy, the detainees' inability to appeal to a U.S. civilian court and the Bush administration's attempt to have the judicial branch "usurped."').

[134] Jennifer Elsea, *The Department of Defense Rules for Military Commissions: Analysis of Procedural Rules and Comparison with Proposed Legislation and the Uniform Code of Military Justice*, Congressional Research Service Report for Congress (updated 18 Jan. 2005) (available at http://www.fas.org/irp/crs/RL31600.pdf).

[135] Compare, Alberto R. Gonzales, *Martial Justice, Full and Fair*, NY Times, 30 Nov. 2001, at A27 ('Under the order, anyone arrested, detained or tried in the United States by a military commission will be able to challenge the lawfulness of the commission's jurisdiction through a habeas corpus proceeding in a federal court.'), with, Detention, Treatment, and Trial of Certain Non-Citizens in the War Against Terrorism, §7(b)(2), 66 Fed. Reg. 57,833, 57,835–36 (13 Nov. 2001) ('[Any individual subject to this order] shall not be privileged to seek any remedy or maintain any proceeding, directly or indirectly, or to have any such remedy or proceeding sought on the individual's behalf, in (i) any court of the United States, or any State thereof, (ii) any court of any foreign nation, or (iii) any international tribunal.').

tribunal' determine which detainees are 'unlawful combatants' subject to trial by military commission was incorporated in the Uniform Code of Military Justice—the statutory source of authority for creation of the commissions in the first place.[136] The same court also held that denial of the accused's right to be present when portions of the case against him were presented would also violate the UCMJ.[137] In consequence, the initial set of commission trials has been held up while the government appeals and, if necessary, the relevant procedures are altered to conform to the District Court's requirements.[138] Other lower courts have likewise been willing to intervene in the commission process. Whether or not these particular rulings ultimately stand up on appeal, the examples of *Hamdi* and *Rasul* strongly suggest that the Supreme Court will be unwilling simply to give the government *carte blanche* in this area. Rather, the likelihood seems to be that the Court will, in line with *Hamdi*, interpret the Due Process Clause to require certain basic procedures in military commission cases, and that it will interpret the UCMJ generously to provide such rights—and therefore avoid the constitutional question that would otherwise arise—wherever possible.

5. Separated powers, checks and balances, and judicial review

So what does this highly summary survey of executive power in the United States tell us about the dynamics of the separation of powers? My primary purpose has been descriptive in the most basic sense—that is, to provide a general introduction to the system for people to whom it may be unfamiliar, rather than to develop a sophisticated new theory of executive authority. But I do want to advance two more general points.

First, the dynamics of American separation of powers at the outset of the twenty-first century may tell us something about the efficacy of enumeration strategies in comparison with strategies that rely on the creation of countervailing centers of power. Second, those dynamics, and particularly the three more specific examples I discussed in Part 4, permit a few more general comments about the role of courts and the legal constitution in holding executive authority to account.

As I discussed early on, American separation of powers doctrine has always encompassed a tension between notions of 'separated powers' and 'checks and balances.' Separated powers tends to rely on a strategy of textual enumeration: powers are identified and allocated between the branches of the government, and the system is maintained in place by adherence to—and perhaps judicial enforcement of—the boundaries on each branch's authority described in the initial enumeration. Checks and balances, on the other hand,

---

[136] 344 F.Supp. 2d 152, 159–61 (2004). [137] *Ibid.*, 167–72.
[138] Elsea, n. 134, 1 and n.4.

creates countervailing centres of power and institutional mechanisms, like the presidential veto or the Senate's power over executive officers, that give each branch both some supervisory authority over the others and weapons by which to defend its own turf. The actual allocation of powers and functions may turn out to be somewhat fluid under this latter conception, but the hope is that a rough 'equality of arms' will maintain the overall balance of the system.

These two approaches may be complementary in many instances. The Senate, for instance, may punish executive agency action that it believes to cross the separated-powers line between enforcement and legislation by exercising its check-and-balances authority to reject nominees for executive positions. Both approaches, moreover, may be enforced through both a 'political' and 'legal' constitution. Fear of adverse political reactions may encourage the President to respect Congress's authority to declare war, and the Supreme Court has struck down legislation that would restructure the institutional mechanisms of checks and balances.[139] Nonetheless, it seems possible to identify correlations. When one branch is confronted with an encroachment by another, check-and-balance mechanisms provide means to force compromise or retreat without resort to the courts; these mechanisms, in other words, strengthen the political constitution and tend to avoid resort to the legal. Separated-powers arrangements, on the other hand, seem more likely to require judicial enforcement where they are not paired with institutional checks.

Perhaps the best way to illustrate this dynamic is to compare the *horizontal* separation of powers dynamics on which I have focused here with *vertical* separation of powers—that is, the division of authority between the states and the nation in the American federal system. At least since the Seventeenth Amendment transferred the power to select Senators from the state legislatures to the People in 1913,[140] our federal system has relied on the equivalent of a separated powers arrangement. Article I allocates particular enumerated powers to Congress, and the Tenth Amendment reserves the rest to the states. There are political checks on national authority, such as the fact that Members of Congress remain at least somewhat responsive to the interests of state governments.[141] But the states have no countervailing authority in the direct check-and-balances sense. At least since the Civil War, it has been clear that the states lack any institutional mechanism to 'nullify' or otherwise block the exercise of national power.[142]

---

[139] See, e.g., *Clinton v. City of New York* 524 US 417 (1998) (striking down the Line Item Veto, which allowed the President to veto independent provisions of tax and spending bills, rather than having to accept or reject the entire bill).

[140] See US Const. amend. 17 ('The Senate of the United States shall be composed of two Senators from each State, elected by people thereof. . . . ').

[141] See generally, Herbert L. Wechsler, 'The Political Safeguards of Federalism—The Role of the States in the Composition and Selection of the National Government' (1954) 54 *Colum L Rev* 543.

[142] See, e.g., Garry Wills, *A Necessary Evil: A History of American Distrust of Government* (Simon & Schuster, 1999), 123–78 (discussing nullification and 'interposition' by state governments in

The trajectory of American federalism can thus tell us something about how enumeration or separated-power strategies work when not paired with checks and balances. The clear answer is 'not very well.' Judicial enforcement of limits on Congress's enumerated powers in the federalism context has been highly controversial, and the Rehnquist Court's limited revival of such enforcement is unlikely significantly to constrain the continuing consolidation of national power.[143] Although it is also true that executive power vis-à-vis the other branches at the national level has expanded considerably over the last century, it seems far easier to say that meaningful balance continues to exist in our horizontal separation of powers than in the vertical relationship between the national government and the states. That, I submit, is because horizontal separation of powers has long relied on centers of countervailing power with institutional checks on one another's powers, rather than a purely separated powers model. This history ought to be at least somewhat instructive for institutional design projects in other systems around the world, although one should not discount the particular pitfalls of comparative analysis of institutional structures.[144]

The specific examples discussed in Part 4 suggest some similar conclusions about the use of judicial mechanisms for holding executive power to account. Although it is too early for definitive conclusions, judicial review of executive detention has been at least somewhat aggressive, while courts have been considerably less willing to get involved in limiting executive war powers. This set of outcomes seems attributable, at least in part, to the presence or absence of countervailing power centers, as well as more overtly political checks, in these respective contexts. When the President uses military force in opposition to the will of Congress, that body has any number of mechanisms for asserting its displeasure: It may limit or cut off funding for the venture, investigate the underlying basis for it, mobilize public opinion to oppose the President's policy, or even consider impeachment. Individuals detained or prosecuted by executive authority, on the other hand, have no institutional mechanisms available to them other than the procedural safeguards afforded by judicial process, and they are likely to be sufficiently unpopular to make political intervention on their behalf unlikely. It is not hard to see why courts have felt the need to intervene more

---

defiance of national law). The states do have certain mechanisms to resist national authority when it is applied *to them*. They may assert sovereign immunity, for example, against damages claims brought by individuals to enforce federal law. See, e.g., *Seminole Tribe v. Florida* 517 US 44 (1996). Even that right is qualified by the existence of many other remedies against states and their officers for federal law violations.

[143] Ernest A. Young, 'The Rehnquist Court's Two Federalisms' (2004) 83 *Texas L Rev* 1 (surveying the Court's federalism jurisprudence).

[144] Vicki C. Jackson, 'Narratives of Federalism: Of Continuities and Comparative Constitutional Experience' (2001) 51 *Duke L J* 223, 272–4. For an example of such a comparative argument, see Ernest A. Young, 'Preserving Member State Autonomy in the European Union: Some Cautionary Tales from American Federalism' (2002) 77 *NYULRev* 1612, 1677 (arguing that the EU should not primarily rely on an enumerated powers strategy for limiting central power).

frequently and aggressively in cases of detention than in controversies over the authority to use of military force.

The record in the third area that I canvassed, judicial review of power delegated to executive agencies, is more complex. On the one hand, the courts have been completely unwilling to enforce the basic limitation on agency authority, that is, the delegation doctrine. On the other hand, judicial review is a pervasive presence in this area. That review, however, is basically *collaborative* in character, in the sense that it operates to strengthen political and institutional checks on executive agency action that are imposed by other actors. So, for instance, the courts enforce the substantive statutory limits on agency authority that Congress *has* imposed, and they enforce adherence to the procedures that Congress has mandated in statutes like the Administrative Procedure Act. Likewise, the courts enhance outside political checks on agencies by enforcing rights of interested groups to participate in agency policy formation.

As the term 'collaboration' suggests, of course, the American law of judicial review leaves considerable room for judicial creativity. The important point is simply that courts have not stood alone, fashioning purely (or even primarily) substantive constraints on executive authority. Rather, they have situated judicial review as part of a broader system of institutional checks and balances, and they have devised doctrines to enhance the overall ability of that system to hold executive actors to account. Although one could identify any number of defects and inefficiencies in the present system of judicial review of agency action, as a very general matter it seems fair to say that the courts have been relatively successful in this role of enhancing political and institutional checks. Given the perils and limitations of direct confrontations between the courts and the political branches—as illustrated, perhaps, in continuing controversy over the judicial role in the terrorism cases[145]—this collaborative role may be a preferable approach in cases where it is available.

One should also not discount the importance of institutional competence considerations in explaining where courts are willing aggressively to hold executive power to account, where they are not, and where they take a more nuanced role. The executive detention cases find courts operating in the unfamiliar context of the War on Terror, to be sure, but the rights they are being asked to enforce are familiar criminal procedure protections, asserted by the venerable mechanism of *habeas corpus*. The cases involve, moreover, what John Marshall called 'the province of the court ... to decide on the rights of individuals.'[146] The war powers cases, by contrast, concern the competing prerogatives of institutions, and they require unfamiliar judgments of military necessity. As one judge recently noted,

---

[145] See, e.g., Robert H. Bork and David B. Rivkin, Jr., *A War the Courts Shouldn't Manage*, Wash. Post, Jan. 21, 2005, A17 (arguing that 'judicial micromanagement of America's war against radical Islamic terrorists' is 'constitutionally illegitimate and, in practical terms, potentially debilitating'). [146] *Marbury v. Madison* 5 US (1 Cranch) 137, 169 (1803).

If the President may direct U.S. forces in response to third-party initiated war, then the question any plaintiff who challenges the constitutionality of a war must answer is, who started it? The question of who is responsible for a conflict is, as history reveals, rather difficult to answer, and we lack judicial standards for resolving it.[147]

Competence concerns have likewise dictated the form of much judicial review of executive agency action. Unable to develop workable standards for judging overly broad delegations of legislative power to agencies, and unwilling to second-guess the substantive judgments of expert bureaucrats, courts have largely confined themselves to enforcing limits imposed by determinate statutory texts and ensuring that agencies conform to prescribed procedures for applying their expertise.[148]

6. Conclusion

Much more could be said, of course, but it will not be said here. After decades in which American constitutional scholars were overwhelmingly concerned with issues of individual rights, we have seen a renaissance of interest in the structural arrangements of federalism and separation of powers, including path-breaking new scholarship on the nature and limits of executive authority. I have tried here only to convey a sense of the basic issues that are in play. Nor do I wish to be read as suggesting that American law has always answered these questions correctly or, what would be even more obnoxious, that other systems should necessarily take our resolutions as a model. I do think that the American separation of powers, with its emphasis on countervailing centers of power and relatively extensive judicial review of executive action, provides a useful counterpoint to more prevalent Parliamentary models. In that spirit, I hope it will be of interest to the readers of this volume.

---

[147] *Campbell v. Clinton* 203 F.3d 19, 27 (DC Cir. 2000) (Silberman, J, concurring).
[148] See, e.g., *Chevron, U.S.A. v. National Resources Defense Council, Inc.* 467 US 837 (1984) (holding that courts will defer to reasonable agency interpretations of ambiguous statutory meaning, but will enforce Congress's intent where it is clear).

6
The Domesticated Executive of Scotland

*Chris Himsworth**

1. Introduction

' "There shall be a Scottish Executive..." I like that.'[1] No, it's true. The late Donald Dewar was never known to have viewed with the same affection the institution created by section 44 of the Scotland Act 1998 as the Scottish Parliament created by section 1. He was the proud father not of the Scottish Executive but of the Parliament. The Labour government's White Paper of 1997 had been called *Scotland's Parliament*.[2] The Scottish people, in the referendum held on 11 September 1997, had voted in favour of the proposition that 'there should be a Scottish Parliament'. Earlier, the final report of the Scottish Constitutional Convention, published as *Scotland's Parliament: Scotland's Right* in 1995 had been, in the tradition of the century-old campaign for home rule, almost exclusively focused on the proposed Parliament, with hardly a mention of any new executive arrangements for Scotland. There were only passing references to an 'administration' headed by a chief minister; the need for a reorganization of the Civil Service in the Scottish Office; and the need for provisions for 'the Parliament to recruit suitable staff for the various departments so as to ensure that the Parliament works effectively'.[3]

This near exclusive reference to the Parliament, with virtually nothing on the new Scottish government, is not very surprising. It was the new Parliament with its new democratic legitimacy and its new legislative powers which would be the symbolic focus of the new Scottish political autonomy. Talk of executive institutions and functions and the more technical issues they would raise would, at best, be a distraction from the principal campaign and, at worst, might tend to undermine it through its reminder of the negative connotations of the continuing need for politically driven ministers and the civil servants still required.

---

* University of Edinburgh.
[1] It was at an event to launch the Scotland Bill at a meeting in Glasgow on 18 December 1997 that Donald Dewar MP declared: 'Clause 1 states there shall be a Scottish Parliament—I like that!'. See *The Herald*, 19 December 1997.   [2] Cm 3658.
[3] pp. 25–26.

Away from the campaign, however, the more dispassionate observer of constitutional change would recognize the need for a much greater focus on executive matters. In ways that do not, in the context of this book as a whole, need to be explained, the executive branch has a capacity to dominate the constitutional order. The rules which govern executive formation, the allocation of executive powers, and the procedures for executive accountability to the legislature and others are, of course, of the highest importance. And, to be fair, these issues did achieve a higher profile in the immediate run-up to devolution and especially in the work of the Consultative Steering Group appointed by Donald Dewar as Secretary of State for Scotland in November 1997. The Group's report, published in December 1998, concentrated largely on recommendations for the future working of the Parliament itself but many of these were also directed towards the need for 'power-sharing' between the Parliament and the Executive and the accountability of the Executive to the Parliament.[4]

Nor indeed was the need for provision for a Scottish Executive wholly ignored in the UK government's White Paper, although the principal emphasis was necessarily on the Parliament. Within chapter 2 on 'What the Scottish Parliament can do', there were two paragraphs explaining that there would be a Scottish Executive accountable to the Scottish Parliament and exercising executive responsibility in relation to devolved matters. The relationship between the Scottish Executive and the Scottish Parliament would be similar, the government said, to the relationship between the UK government and the UK Parliament. It would consist of the First Minister with a team of Scottish Ministers including Law Officers. As well as having responsibility for the devolved matters transferred to them, the Executive would have additional functions in certain reserved areas.[5] And, if this treatment were thought a little skeletal, it was known by 1997 that inspiration for the new Scotland Bill would derive not only from the political initiative of the Scottish Constitutional Convention in the 1980s and 1990s but also from the Bill's legislative forerunner, the Scotland Act 1978. The memories of the fate of that Act in the referendum of March 1979 and the subsequent banishment of devolution from the political agenda during the Thatcher years may, on the whole, be negative. In many respects, the Act's provisions were overtaken by the new thinking in the Convention about the Parliament and the means by which its powers would be defined. But much of the 1978 Act, including provisions on the Executive, needed only slight adjustment before reincorporation into the 1997 Bill. The Scotland Act 1978 itself drew heavily upon the White Paper of 1975—*Our Changing Democracy: Devolution to Scotland and Wales*[6]—which, in turn, owed much to the Report of the Royal Commission on the Constitution[7] in which some consideration had

---

[4] *Shaping Scotland's Parliament: Report of the Consultative Steering Group on the Scottish Parliament*. [5] *Scotland's Parliament*, paras 2.6–2.7.
[6] Cmnd 6348. The White Paper was followed initially by the ill-fated Scotland and Wales Bill (1975–76). [7] Cmnd 5460, 1973.

been given to the structure of the devolved governments it proposed and their relationship to the central government in London.[8] Nor, of course, was the Kilbrandon report the first opportunity for serious discussion of devolved executives within the United Kingdom. For the fifty years from 1922 to 1972, the Government of Ireland Act 1920 had provided the framework for the Stormont system of government in Northern Ireland. Despite the political peculiarities of that system, it remains the most substantial single example of functioning devolution in the constitutional history of the United Kingdom.

Devolved government on the Scotland Act model raises some, but not all, of the questions about executive power and its accountability posed in relation to (nation) state level governments elsewhere in this book. Although complicated by the distinctive relationship between the Scottish Executive and the UK government, most of the accountability questions are, on the face of it, as aptly raised in relation to the Scottish Executive as other governments. The principal issue has tended to be framed in terms of whether the Scotland Act structures have created the conditions for the better containment of executive power than those which, too feebly for most, operate at the UK level. Does the spectre of unrestrained executive authority, especially that available to the prime minister, have its counterpart in Scotland despite the institutional restraints thought to have been installed? Accountability is the focus of section 3 below.

As to the 'proper scope' of executive power, this is an issue of more limited proportions in relation to the domesticated condition of the Scottish Executive. Confined within the statutory framework of the Scotland Act, the position of the Executive raises few of the threats of the use and abuse of new executive power posed by government at the UK level or by national governments elsewhere. That is not to say, however, that questions about the sources and extent of the powers of the Scottish Executive are of no constitutional significance. They are, of course, important and they are of some difficulty and complexity. They are the subject-matter of section 2.

2. Powers for the Scottish Executive[9]

It is easily said[10] that the Scottish Executive 'will consist of the First Minister plus a team of Scottish Ministers'; that it 'will exercise executive responsibility in relation to devolved matters'; that the statutory powers and duties of UK ministers in relation to devolved matters 'will be transferred to Ministers of the Scottish Executive'; and that additional responsibilities for reserved matters will also be transferred. But how does one arrive at an executive consisting of the

---

[8] Paras 803–808, 1143–6.
[9] For a general account of the arrangements for Scottish government under the Scotland Act, see C.M.G. Himsworth and C.M. O'Neill, *Scotland's Constitution: Law and Practice* (Butterworths, 2003), hereafter Himsworth and O'Neill.   [10] *Scotland's Parliament*, Cm 3658, para. 2.6.

ministers mentioned? How will the transfer of powers to the Scottish Executive be effected? Will the Scottish Ministers not need non-statutory as well as statutory powers to be transferred to them? Who will have the legal authority to exercise the powers vested in the Scottish Ministers? Which ministers? And civil servants? Would the '*Carltona* principle' extend to civil servants in the devolved administration? What, in general, would be the status of the civil service in that administration?

Some of these questions may appear to have a merely 'technical' aspect, with the answer to be provided by legislative provision to appropriate effect. It is the very stuff of much legislation to create new institutions; to prescribe the manner of their formation; to create *ab initio* or to transfer from other bodies an appropriate package of responsibilities (often further defined in other legislation); and to prescribe some of the new entity's methods of working. Much of our local government legislation and the statutes to create other forms of governmental body have this character, including the legislation to create 'regional' forms of government such as the Greater London Authority Act 1999. Even the Government of Wales Act 1998 takes a similar form as it creates the National Assembly for Wales on a model of executive devolution.

In UK practice, however, additional problems have been associated with projects to recreate at the 'regional' or 'sub-national'[11] level an expressly 'parliamentary' form of government with a law-making parliament or assembly and a separate executive formed from and accountable to it. In principle, the aim has been to produce by statute a modified form of government on the 'Westminster model' and this prompts a number of questions. The first relates to convention. There will probably be an initial wish to adapt or replace some rules which are merely conventional at Westminster with new statutory rules to similar effect. It may, for instance, be desirable to make more explicit the rules requiring a governmental resignation when parliamentary confidence is lost.[12] But, thereafter, there are real questions about how far it is necessary or desirable to recreate conventional rules on a statutory basis—or instead to leave the new governmental actors with an assumption that some conventional rules will indeed need to emerge but also the freedom to superintend that process themselves and without statutory guidance or regulation. Supplementing the 'internal' Northern Ireland experience, in this respect, is that succession of 'external' projects starting with the Indian Independence Act 1947 and continuing through the other independence Acts of the 1950s to 1980s which conferred new Westminster-model written constitutions on the formerly dependant members of the Commonwealth.

Although those constitutions did, in addition to resolving questions of the survival of conventions, have to address the general composition of the

---

[11] There are, of course, perils lurking in the terminology used here. Many would prefer to use the term 'national' rather than the generic 'regional' in relation to Scottish government but this can cause ambiguities when distinctions are sought between Scottish and UK 'national' governments.
[12] See Scotland Act 1998, ss. 45(2), 47(3)(c), 48(2) and 49(4)(c).

executive—whether retaining the Queen as head of state, or establishing a kingdom with a local monarch or a republic with presidency—they are less directly useful as a model for executive-creation at the sub-national level within the United Kingdom.[13] Here, the starting question has been the role, in the devolved government, of the Queen. Different practices have emerged. In both the unimplemented Government of Ireland 1914 and then in section 8 of the Government of Ireland Act 1920, it was stated that the executive power in Northern Ireland[14] should continue to be vested in the King. The same formula was used in section 7 of the short-lived Northern Ireland Constitution Act 1973 and now, in section 23(1) of the Northern Ireland Act 1998, the same formula has again been retained. The section goes on to say that, in relation to the powers transferred to the Assembly, 'the prerogative and other executive powers of Her Majesty in relation to Northern Ireland shall be exercisable on Her Majesty's behalf by any Minister or Northern Ireland Department'.

For some reason, this pattern of stating that primary executive power is vested first in the Queen but then exercisable on her behalf, in relation to devolved matters, by members of the devolved executive, has not been adopted in the Scottish legislation. Gladstone's Scottish Government Bill of 1892 *did* contain the formula 'The Executive Government of Scotland shall continue to be vested in Her Majesty'.[15] But, by the time of the Scotland Act 1978, there was no express provision declaring that executive authority would be vested in the Queen. Instead the Scottish Executive, consisting of the First Secretary and other Secretaries, would have been created[16] and it was then stated that '[s]uch of Her Majesty's executive powers as would otherwise be exercisable on behalf of Her Majesty by a Minister of the Crown shall, if they relate to devolved matters and are exercisable in or as regards Scotland, be exercisable on behalf of Her Majesty by a Scottish Secretary'.[17] The power-conferring language was modified in the Scotland Act 1998 and this will be considered below. The 1998 Act does, however, maintain the 1978 Act's general style. Section 44 creates the Scottish Executive consisting of the First Minister, other ministers and the two Law Officers and, again without any general statement that the executive power of government in Scotland lies with the Queen, the Act moves on to provisions transferring functions (some of which are stated to be exercisable on behalf of Her Majesty) to the Scottish Executive.

It may or may not have any practical consequences but it is clear that Scotland has gone down a different track from that adopted in Northern Ireland and the

---

[13] It should be noted, however, that the Nigerian Constitution of 1960 (created by the Nigeria (Constitution) Order in Council 1960, S.I. 1960/1652) is one of those which was federal in character, with regional executive authority vested in the Queen and exercisable by Governor, Premier and ministers. [14] Originally also 'Southern Ireland'.
[15] Cl. 8. The clause went on to state that that Government should be 'carried on by the Secretary of State on behalf of Her Majesty, with the aid of such officers and such council as may be provided by the Scottish Legislature'. [16] s. 20(1).
[17] s. 21(1).

Commonwealth independence constitutions. Whilst powers exercisable on behalf of the Queen are transferred to the Scottish Executive, there is no overarching concept of the Queen's being the ultimate repository of executive authority in Scotland. This does not mean, however, that there is a total disengagement of the Queen from Scottish government. The First Minister is appointed by the Queen, following the recommendation by the Presiding Officer of the person nominated by the Scottish Parliament, and is stated to hold office at Her Majesty's pleasure.[18] Other ministers are appointed, with the approval of Her Majesty, by the First Minister and again hold office at Her Majesty's pleasure[19] although they do not thereby become 'Ministers of the Crown'.[20] The Law Officers (the Lord Advocate and the Solicitor General for Scotland[21]) are appointed by the Queen on the recommendation of the First Minister.[22] It is to be assumed that, in these matters of appointment and dismissal, the formal powers vested in the Queen are exercisable subject to the conventional constraints which have operated at the UK level. Equally, steps have been taken to ensure that the Queen receives copies of the papers of the Scottish Cabinet[23] and, although there is no direct equivalent of the weekly meeting with the prime minister, the present First Minister has said that he has 'audiences with Her Majesty the Queen from time to time'.[24]

Although the principal institution[25] created by the Scotland Act is the Scottish Executive, the Act also instructs that the members of the Scottish Executive are to be 'referred to collectively as the Scottish Ministers'[26] and it is under this name that 'statutory functions' are to be conferred on them[27]. On its face, this creation

---

[18] ss. 45–46.   [19] s. 47. See also junior/deputy ministers in s. 49.

[20] Although that term is not formally defined in the Scotland Act except (in s. 126(1)) to include the Treasury, it is defined by s. 8(1) of the Ministers of the Crown Act 1975 as 'a holder of an office in *Her Majesty's Government in the United Kingdom*' and the logic of the Scotland Act is to distinguish clearly UK ministers (as 'Ministers of the Crown') from the Scottish Ministers. For discussion of other interpretations, see P.P. Craig, *Administrative Law* (Sweet & Maxwell, 5th edn., 2003), 212–13. Informally, of course, members of the Scottish Executive may, from time to time, be referred to as Ministers of the Crown—see, for instance, First Minister Rhodri Morgan, distinguishing the current status of ministers in Scotland and Wales, at Record of Proceedings (NAW) 6 October 2004.

[21] The incorporation of the Lord Advocate and the Solicitor General into the Scottish Executive (to be replaced as Scottish Law Officer to the UK Government by the Advocate General for Scotland) involved some quite sophisticated two-stage transfers of powers—see the Transfer of Functions (Lord Advocate and Secretary of State) Order 1999 (S.I. 1999/678)—and the entrenchment of prosecution and other powers: Scotland Act s. 29(2)(e). There may be questions left unanswered by this reinvention of an ancient office in new statutory trappings. Whilst, for instance, the Lord Advocate as UK Law Officer was one of the historic 'Officers of State' (on which see *Stair Memorial Encyclopaedia*, Vol 7 'The Crown', paras 790–810) does that continue to be the case in post-devolution Scotland?   [22] s. 48.

[23] *Guide to Collective Decision Making* (Scottish Executive), para. 4.34. The *Guide*, which has been issued in successive editions since 1999, supplements the *Scottish Ministerial Code*.

[24] SPOR. S2W-1283, 28 July 2003.

[25] For the creation of the 'Scottish Administration' and the 'Officers of the Scottish Administration' see p. 203 below.   [26] s. 44(2).

[27] s. 52(1).

of the Executive as a collective body with powers, also allocated collectively in the main, stands in contrast to the UK model in which powers are conferred on individual ministers.[28] On the other hand, the tendency at the UK level to allocate powers to the generic 'Secretary of State', enabling them to be exercised as a matter of law by any Secretary of State, creates a 'collective' government of its own sort. In Scotland, despite the collective *allocation* of functions, they are expressly stated to be *exercisable* by any member of the Scottish Executive and on behalf of Her Majesty.[29] Since the Scottish Parliament first acquired legislative competence on 1 July 1999 there have been many Acts of the Scottish Parliament (ASPs) which do indeed confer powers on the Scottish Ministers and, over time, ASPs will, as they create new legislative provision or consolidate older Westminster measures, doubtless become the principal source of the Scottish Executive's powers. Of much greater initial significance in quantitative terms, however, have been the powers directly transferred to the Scottish Ministers from UK ministers under the Scotland Act itself or by virtue of orders made under the Act. In addition, powers have been conferred on the Scottish Ministers since 1999 by the Westminster Parliament either directly in that name or indirectly by reference to the Secretary of State but in such a way as to ensure transfer to the Scottish Ministers.[30]

A detailed exposition of these powers cannot be undertaken here[31] but, because they raise questions about techniques for the repackaging of the bundle of powers of UK ministers for the purpose of their transfer to a devolved government, some consideration should be given to the provision for their initial transfer to the Scottish Ministers. Stage one of the transfer of functions was done by reference to those 'within devolved competence', a term defined by section 54 of the Scotland Act to include, in short, those functions within the legislative competence of the Parliament.[32] Most of the powers previously exercisable by UK ministers in the area now defined as within devolved competence are, of course, of statutory origin. Their transfer is straightforwardly done by reference to functions conferred on a Minister of the Crown by a 'pre-commencement enactment'.[33] The means of transferring prerogative powers and other powers of non-statutory origin has to be different. In earlier legislation there has been a reference to the 'prerogative or other executive powers of Her Majesty'.[34] The

---

[28] See T. Daintith and A. Page, *The Executive in the Constitution* (Oxford University Press, 1999), 29.   [29] s. 52(2), (3).

[30] Either by declaring the Westminster Act to be a 'pre-commencement enactment' or by use of an order under s. 63 of the Scotland Act. See below.

[31] For a fuller account, see Himsworth and O'Neill, n. 9, 244.

[32] This method of transferring functions generically by reference to devolved competence is to be distinguished sharply from the technique of transfer of specific named functions under the Government of Wales Act 1998. See R. Rawlings, *Delineating Wales: Constitutional, Legal and Administrative Aspects of National Devolution* (University of Wales Press, 2003).

[33] s. 53 (2)(c). The term can be adopted by 'post-commencement' Acts of Parliament to render them also 'pre-commencement' Acts for the purposes of these transfer provisions.

[34] See Government of Ireland Act 1914, s. 4(2), Government of Ireland Act 1920, s. 8(2), Northern Ireland Constitution Act 1973, s. 7(2).

Scotland Act 1978 dropped the reference to prerogative powers and transferred '[s]uch of Her Majesty's executive powers as would otherwise be exercisable on behalf of Her Majesty by a Minister of the Crown'.[35] The original wording of the Bill had referred to 'prerogative and other executive powers' but, after successive amendments in the House of Lords first to remove the reference to the prerogative and then to remove non-statutory powers from the transfer process altogether,[36] the formula 'executive powers' without reference to the prerogative was adopted. There seems little doubt, however, that the excision was without any noticeable legal consequence. 'Executive powers' would include prerogative-based powers. At all events, this question does not arise in relation to the Scotland Act 1998 which reinstates the formula 'prerogative and other executive functions' and also transfers to the Scottish Ministers 'other functions conferred on a Minister of the Crown by a prerogative instrument'.[37]

A second principal transfer of functions to the Scottish Ministers was achieved by Orders in Council under section 63 of the Scotland Act. It had always been the intention that the competence of the Scottish Executive should be permitted to extend beyond the legislative competence of the Parliament and these Orders in Council have achieved this.[38] It might be that these extensions of executive power beyond the scope of the Parliament's own competence could be viewed as converting the Executive into a mere agent of the UK government but there is no sign that the Executive's accountability to the Parliament is affected.

A feature common to the transfer to the Scottish Ministers of both statutory and 'prerogative and other executive functions' is that, except where there are clear words to the contrary, these functions are transferred in their entirety. There is no sense in which a residual power to exercise the functions is left also in the hands of the UK ministers. In the case of devolved functions, it would be unlawful for the Secretary of State to purport to exercise them.[39] There is neither a reason in general constitutional principle nor in the language of the Scotland Act for any executive equivalent of the continuing (supreme) power of the Westminster Parliament to legislate for Scotland on all matters, whether reserved or devolved. Nor is there any equivalent, therefore, of a 'Sewel motion' procedure by which the Scottish Parliament consents to Westminster legislation in the devolved areas.[40] Even with the consent of the Scottish Ministers, the purported exercise by the Secretary of State of their transferred powers would be

---

[35] s. 21(1).
[36] See annotation of s. 21(1) by A.W. Bradley and D.J. Christie in *Current Law Statutes*.
[37] s. 53 (2)(a), (b).
[38] See, in particular, the Scotland Act 1998 (Transfer of Functions to the Scottish Ministers etc) Order 1999, S.I. 1999/1750 and also S.I.s 1999/3321, 2000/1563, 2000/3253, 2001/954, 2001/3504, 2002/1630, 2003/415. It should also be noted that, under s. 108 of the Act, powers may be transferred in the reverse direction from the Scottish Ministers to UK ministers.
[39] This might raise a 'devolution issue' under Sched. 6 to the Scotland Act.
[40] On which, see, in particular A. Page and A. Batey, 'Scotland's Other Parliament' [2002] *PL* 501.

unlawful. All this has, of course, to be read subject to the terms of the Scotland Act and that Act has created a number of exceptions to the general rule of exclusivity of transfer. A short list of powers transferred to the Scottish Ministers are expressly stated to be exercisable concurrently by the Secretary of State.[41] A number of powers transferred by orders under section 63 are stated to be exercisable either concurrently or with the consent of the Secretary of State. Very importantly in practice, there is also express provision in section 57(1) of the Act that functions of UK ministers to implement Community law obligations under section 2(2) of the European Communities Act 1972 continue to be exercisable by them, as well as by the Scottish Ministers. The use of that power is monitored by the Scottish Parliament's European and External Relations Committee.

Questions of concurrency apart, it is reasonably clear, in the case of transferred statutory powers, what the extent of those powers is. Such powers have to be read, of course, within the same interpretative environment as at the stage before they left the Secretary of State. In the case of a challenge to their misuse, however, there may be a need to resolve the additional question of whether the exercise of a particular power does indeed fall within 'devolved competence'.[42] That, in turn, may raise questions of whether the exercise of a function might 'relate to a reserved matter' and also of compatibility with Convention rights[43] and with Community Law.[44]

In the case of prerogative and other non-statutory executive powers transferred to the Scottish Ministers, rather different questions arise. Three may be briefly considered. There are, in the first place, some important questions about what exactly these powers are, questions which are wholly unanswered on the face of the Scotland Act or, by definition, in any of the statutory sources incorporated by that Act. The starting point has, instead, to be the text book accounts, of varying authoritative status,[45] of the powers exercisable by UK ministers and then judgments have to be made on the extent to which they have been transferred according to the criteria and under the procedures already mentioned. Among the truly prerogative-based powers, rapid decisions may be made on those

---

[41] Scotland Act, s. 56 and S.I. 1999/1592.   [42] *Ibid.*, ss. 53–54.

[43] i.e. rights guaranteed by the European Convention on Human Rights and 'incorporated' by the Human Rights Act 1998. See Scotland Act 1998, s. 126(1). The suggestion has been made that, in the case of a function held to be incapable of being exercised without breach of the Convention, the function does not transfer *at all* to the Scottish Ministers but (in a process of 'washing') remains with the Secretary of State. See *Starrs v. Ruxton* (2000 JC 208 at 251–252. And see Lord Reed and J. Murdoch *A Guide to Human Rights Law in Scotland* (Butterworths, 2001), para. 1.31.

[44] s. 29(2) defines the limits of the legislative competence of the Parliament and thus of devolved competence in these respects. That is reinforced in respect of acts of a member of the Scottish Executive, thus including powers outwith devolved competence but exercisable under orders made under s. 63, by s. 57(2) of the Scotland Act 1998.

[45] See also 4th Report of the HC Public Administration Select Committee, *Taming the Prerogative: Strengthening Ministerial Accountability to Parliament* (HC 42, 2003–04). For an earlier account, specific to Scotland, see J.D.B. Mitchell, 'The Royal Prerogative in Modern Scots Law' [1957] *PL* 304.

relating to treaty-making, other aspects of foreign affairs, and the defence of the realm. Clearly, those remain exclusively with UK ministers.[46] On the other hand, the prerogative of mercy may, in principle, be presumed to have been transferred. The home civil service is a reserved matter but many managerial powers are transferred to the Scottish Ministers.[47] A controversial prerogative-based power, presumably devolved, is the power to supply arms to police forces.[48] It has, in addition, to be assumed that any relevant non-statutory but non-prerogative powers within devolved competence such as powers to contract have also been transferred to the Scottish Ministers and are being exercised by them.[49]

All these 'non-statutory' powers transferred to the Scottish Ministers in 1999 were in the form in which they had been previously exercisable by UK ministers. Their content may, however, vary over time. In particular, they are subject, one assumes, to variation by Act of the Scottish Parliament. The Westminster Parliament may clearly repeal or otherwise modify prerogative powers and it seems wholly acceptable that the Scottish Parliament's general authority to make laws, which includes the power to amend Acts of the UK Parliament also includes the power, within the limits of its legislative competence, to modify prerogative powers. The Scottish Parliament could remove the power to supply arms to police authorities. The Scottish Parliament's powers do not, of course, formally restrict those of the Westminster Parliament which could also legislate in respect of those powers exercisable by the Scottish Ministers, but presumably with the accompanying need for a Sewel motion. When the House of Commons Select Committee on Public Administration reported on their proposals for the statutory regulation of prerogative powers,[50] they showed no sign of having considered the position of devolved prerogative powers or of the possible need for the consent of the Scottish Parliament for their draft Bill which explicitly extended to the whole of the United Kingdom. An alternative would be a Bill which did not extend to Scotland or, whilst extending to Scotland, expressly excluded powers exercisable by the Scottish Ministers, thus leaving their prerogative-based powers untouched.

A second, more technical, question also arises in relation to the transfer by statute of non-statutory powers. Have the powers, because of their new basis in a statutory transfer, themselves become statutory powers? It is not clear that, whatever the formal answer to that question, it has any practical consequences but it was apparently concerns along these lines that so exercised the House of Lords in their consideration of the Scotland Bill of 1977–78 that they were inclined to modify the Bill and ensured the exclusion from the 1978 Act of any

---

[46] Save to the extent that Sched. 5 to the Scotland Act 1998 provides otherwise, e.g. Pt. I, para. 7(2) 'observing and implementing international obligations'.   [47] Scotland Act 1998, s. 51.
[48] *R v. Home Secretary, ex parte. Northumbria Police Authority* [1989] QB 26.
[49] Unsurprisingly, no formal record is kept of the extent of use of the prerogative-based and non-prerogative powers. See S2W-7345 (5 May 2004).   [50] 4th Report (HC 422, 2003–04).

reference to the transfer of prerogative powers. Members of the House of Lords objected to subsuming prerogative powers into statute because, they argued, the courts would subsequently be obliged, in cases of doubt, to look only at the general terms of the Act rather than considering what the prerogative otherwise consisted of. This view received short shrift from the learned commentators on the Scotland Act 1978.[51] All that the section did, they said, was 'to declare that certain powers which have in the past been exercised by a minister on behalf of the sovereign will in future, in certain limited areas, be exercised on behalf of the Crown by a Scottish Secretary. Therefore it only affects the manner of the exercise of the prerogative, and leaves untouched the scope, and the form, of the prerogative powers themselves. A useful parallel can be found in the Royal Assent Act 1967, which merely regulates the manner of notification of the Royal Assent to a Bill, but does not affect the nature of that particular prerogative power'.[52] It may be the case that the approach of the courts to the interpretation of a prerogative power will be unaffected by the statutory manner of its transfer to the Scottish Ministers. If anything, the intervention of the *GCHQ* case[53] may have diluted the distinction between the two sources of authority and freed the hands of the courts. On the other hand, it may still be doubted, with respect, whether the comparison with the Royal Assent Act is wholly apposite. That Act did regulate only the manner of notification of Assent. It did not reallocate the power to exercise the prerogative. It does seem possible that the transfer of prerogative-based powers by the devolution Acts is of different effect.

Thirdly, there was yet another group of powers which had to be transferred from UK ministers to their Scottish counterparts on devolution but which, because of their conventional rather than legal nature, could not appropriately be the subject of measures taken by or under the Scotland Act. These are the powers of ministers to advise the Queen on, for instance, appointments or on the Scottish business of the Privy Council.[54] To the extent that these advisory and other powers related to devolved matters, they were declared by Prime Ministerial statement to have passed to the First Minister and other members of the Scottish Executive.[55]

A further note on executive structures. The Scottish Executive was earlier introduced as the principal governmental institution created by the Scotland Act. The position is, however, more complicated than this. For one thing, the Executive decided, from the start, to work through a 'Scottish Cabinet', consisting latterly of all members of the Executive with the exception of the Law

---

[51] See Bradley and Christie, n. 36.   [52] *Ibid.*
[53] *CCSU v. Minister for the Civil Service* [1985] AC 374.
[54] Despite its conventional character, legal recognition is given to 'an Order in Council made on the recommendation of the First Minister' by s. 2 of the European Communities Act 1972 as amended by the Scotland Act 1998, Sched. 8 para. 15(3).
[55] HC Debs 30 June 1999, cols 215–216 (WA). The announcement was repeated in the House of Lords at HL Debs 1 July 1999, cols WA 50–51.

Officers.[56] Secondly, whilst the Cabinet is non-statutory, the Scotland Act itself creates the Scottish Administration consisting of the ministerial office-holders in the Scottish Executive and junior/deputy Scottish Ministers, non-ministerial officeholders and the Administration's staff.[57] All members of the Administration with the exception of ministers are members of the home civil service.[58]

3. Accountability

Turning now to the question of accountability, the Scottish Executive is quickly seen to join the broad family of governments on the parliamentary model. Despite its sub-national status its situation raises all the familiar questions of how a government whose very existence is defined by reference to the support it has from a majority of members of the Parliament can be held to account by that parliament; and how far that parliamentary accountability can or should be supplemented by other forms of accountability owed to the courts and to other institutions such as ombudsmen and auditors. A distinguishing feature of the Scottish Executive as a subordinate government is the relationship, in part a relationship of accountability, which it maintains with the central government in London. This section of the chapter is divided into four substantive parts. The first deals with accountability to the Scottish Parliament; the second with accountability to the courts; the third with ombudsmen and others; and the fourth with the relationship with Whitehall.

(a) Accountability to the Scottish Parliament

It was the intention of the architects of the new Parliament that a very different relationship should be established between it and the Scottish Executive than between the equivalent UK institutions. When it was said in the White Paper that the Executive should be accountable to the Parliament and that the relationship between the Scottish Executive and Scottish Parliament would be similar to that between the UK government and the UK Parliament,[59] it was nevertheless widely assumed that this accountability and the mechanisms by which it was assured at Holyrood could achieve a vitality only dreamed of at Westminster. If not much prior attention had been given to the Executive itself, attention *had* been given to what the Parliament would need to do in order to secure and maintain its own primacy on behalf of the people of Scotland. If this was to be achieved, it would be, in part, the result of specific provision made in

---

[56] *Guide to Collective Decision-Making* (Scottish Executive). At the start, the Lord Advocate was also included.

[57] Scotland Act 1998, s. 126(6)–(8). Section 126(8) identifies certain non-ministerial officeholders including the Keepers of the Registers and Records. Others have been designated by Order of Council. See, e.g. S.I. 1999/1127.   [58] Scotland Act 1998, s. 51(2).

[59] *Scotland's Parliament*, para. 2.6.

the Scotland Act itself and then, in part, the result of the Parliament's own efforts. The latter were aided by a process which had begun in the Constitutional Convention and continued by the Consultative Steering Group, already mentioned, including that Group's formulation of some 'Founding Principles' subsequently adopted by the Parliament itself and whose progress towards realisation on the ground was monitored by the Procedures Committee of the Parliament towards the end of the first session in 2002–03.[60]

But to start with the Scotland Act itself, two fundamental characteristics were built into the Scottish Parliament which would produce conditions there which were abruptly different from those at Westminster—the electoral system and the Parliament's fixed term.

The additional member system of proportional representation adopted in the Scotland Act has produced at Holyrood political conditions very different from those at Westminster. There are possible dangers inherent in the creation of two 'classes' of MSP—the constituency members and the regional members—especially given that the politics of the situation largely produces a Parliament of constituency Executive MSPs and regional Opposition members. There is little doubt nevertheless that the system of moderating the initial effect of the first-past-the-post constituency voting by the addition of the second vote to elect the regional members by a list system creating greater overall proportionality of outcome has produced more 'fairness' in the system overall. What the system also created, however, were the conditions for the near inevitability of coalition government leading, in turn, to the negotiated partnership agreements on policy and the added complexity of relationships both within government and between ministers and their backbenchers which have characterized the Labour-Liberal Democratic administrations of the first two sessions of the Parliament. It is uncomfortable for parties compelled to fight each other south of the border to join in government in Scotland. The electoral system has also led to a much more diverse range of parties and individuals on the opposition benches of the Parliament. The SNP are the nearest to an 'official' opposition but the opposition parties as a whole produce a much more variegated response to government than at Westminster.

The impact of the parliamentary fixed terms incorporated into the Scotland Act,[61] subject only to limited exceptions, also has an important effect not only on relationships within the Executive, in the absence of a First Ministerial power to demand a general election at a time of the office-holder's choosing, but also on the dynamic of relations between the Executive and opposition parties in the Parliament and thus on the dynamic of accountability itself. Short of the use of the emergency power to terminate the Parliament early, the Executive has to live with the Parliament as elected through to the end.

---

[60] *The Founding Principles of the Scottish Parliament*, 3rd Report 2003 (SP Paper 818). See note 83 below.   [61] s. 2.

As with so much else, it is too early to draw conclusions about how these constitutional relationships will actually develop. Quite apart from the statutory backdrop, much may come to depend in practice on emerging relationships within the dominant political party (so far, the Labour Party) and between that party and its coalition partner; and then between the Scottish Executive, the Parliament and, perhaps most importantly, the media. It is, as yet, unclear how Scottish governance will come to be located on the scale reaching from cabinet government properly so called into first ministerial government or a quasi-presidential form of government so often invoked in descriptions of the UK government.

The Scotland Act contains other provisions which, whilst not of such fundamental importance, do also have the possibility of reshaping accountability in the Scottish Parliament. They are designed to strengthen the Parliament's role, at least symbolically but also to some instrumental effect. In the first place, the Parliament is given an express role in government formation which the Westminster Parliament does not enjoy. The First Minister is appointed following nomination by the Parliament.[62] The appointment of other ministers, deputy ministers, and the Law Officers requires the approval of the Parliament before they can be formally made by the sovereign.[63] Even though the results of votes so far held may have been politically predetermined, these requirements have at least ensured that, in the case of nominations of First Ministers, there has been the opportunity for the Parliament to consider a range of candidates and, for the rest, there has been the need for time to be set aside for First Ministerial nominations to be debated, in ways which would be wholly unfamiliar at Westminster. In assessing these procedures, we have, of course, to remember that the one elected chamber in Scotland has to be relied upon to provide the entire ministry. For better or for worse, there is not the option of recourse to an equivalent of the House of Lords with its pool of additional politicians who have ceased to face, or have never faced, the electorate directly.[64] The democratic instinct, especially in the context of a 'new politics', demands direct electoral accountability. Equally, however, there can be little doubt that the lack of access to an additional pool of talent may come to be a matter of regret for some First Ministers and perhaps for the political system as a whole.

Another novelty in the Scotland Act version of the Westminster model is the express statutory requirement imposed on all categories of minister that their resignation is required in the event of the Parliament's resolving that 'the Scottish Executive no longer enjoys the confidence of the Parliament'.[65] In other

---

[62] *Ibid.*, s. 46.   [63] *Ibid.*, ss. 47(2), 48(1), 49(3).

[64] For a proposal by Lord Sewel that powers be conferred to appoint ministers who are not MSPs, see HL Debs 29 November 2004 col 345.

[65] *Ibid.*, s. 45(2), s. 47(3)(c), s. 48(2) and s. 49(3)(c). Motions of no confidence in the Parliament so far (both unsuccessful) have been directed towards individual ministers—SPOR 13 December 2000, col 841 (Galbraith, management of SQA), SPOR 15 February 2001, col 1279

respects too, the Scotland Act contains provisions which contribute to ensuring a measure of executive accountability. Adjustments to the powers of the Scottish Parliament or of the Scottish Executive by Order in Council require the express consent of the Parliament.[66] In relation to legislative procedures, there is the requirement that the relevant member of the Scottish Executive certifies the competence of Executive Bills;[67] the Scotland Act, whilst not laying down parliamentary procedural requirements in detail, does itself stipulate the need for stages of Bills to ensure the opportunity for MSPs to vote on the general principles, the details and the final passing of all Bills.[68] In relation to delegated legislation made by the Scottish Ministers, section 118 of the Act translates existing statutory requirements of approval by one or both Houses at Westminster into the need for approval (or absence of rejection) by the Scottish Parliament. Thus far the Parliament has not passed its own version of a Statutory Instruments Act[69] and, in its place, there operates an Order made on a temporary basis by the Secretary of State.[70] On the whole, that Order tracks the terms of the Statutory Instruments Act 1946, although it does also make express provision for the 21-day rule on laying prior to implementation[71] which is merely conventional at Westminster. The Parliament's Subordinate Legislation Committee has been vigorous in its technical scrutiny of Scottish statutory instruments, as it has also been in its other principal function—the scrutiny of Bills from the perspective of delegated powers.[72]

In the area of financial administration, the Scotland Act contains extensive provision for the involvement of the Parliament in financial matters generally,[73] in audit (including the need for the Auditor General for Scotland to be appointed on the nomination of the Parliament[74]), and in relation to the tax-varying power.[75] As a general aid to openness in the Parliament, the Scotland Act provides that the Parliament's standing orders must include provision for the proceedings of the Parliament normally to be held in public.[76] Provision is made for the Parliament to compel the attendance of witnesses and the production of documents.[77]

(Boyack, transport policy). See also SPOR 30 September 2004, col 10747 (Chisholm, health service).

[66] s. 30(2), s. 63(1), s. 108 and Sched. 7. Guidance on the use of s. 30(2) has been given in Devolution Guidance Note 14.   [67] s. 31(1).
[68] s. 36(1).
[69] The Parliament's Subordinate Legislation Committee has, however, included a review of procedures in its future programme.
[70] Scotland Act 1998 (Transitory and Transitional Provisions) (Statutory Instruments) Order 1999, S.I. 1999/1096.   [71] *Ibid.*, art. 10(2).
[72] See C. Himsworth, 'Subordinate Legislation in the Scottish Parliament' (2002) 6 *Edin LR* 356. See also, C. T. Reid (2002) 6 *Edin LR* 380 and (2003) 24 *Stat LR* 187.   [73] Part III.
[74] s. 69(1).   [75] *Ibid.*, Pt. IV.   [76] *Ibid.*, Sched. 3, para. 3(1).
[77] Scotland Act 1998, ss. 23–26. For reluctance, however, to use these powers in relation to the (Fraser) Holyrood Inquiry, see SPOR 31 March 2004, cols 7227–56.

It has already been explained that the wish to create the Scottish Parliament as a body different from its Westminster Parliament, especially in its relationship with the executive branch, materialised not only in the Scotland Act itself but also in the work of the Consultative Steering Group and then in the adoption by the Parliament itself of the principles promulgated by that Group—especially in the Parliament's own standing orders. The four key principles which were adopted by the Group both to guide its own work and as a manifestation of the 'new politics' intended to operate in devolved Scotland were that (1) the Parliament should embody and reflect the sharing of power between the people of Scotland, the legislators and the Scottish Executive; (2) the Scottish Executive should be accountable to the Scottish Parliament and the Parliament and Executive should be accountable to the people of Scotland; (3) the Parliament should be accessible, open, responsive, and develop procedures which make possible a participative approach to the development, consideration, and scrutiny of policy and legislation; and (4) the Parliament in its operation and its appointments should recognize the need to promote equal opportunities for all.

To an extent, the adoption of these new principles does also accommodate the transmission to the Scottish arrangements of the historically acknowledged fundamental principle at Westminster of the individual responsibility of ministers to Parliament. One should be cautious in a convention-dependent field such as this to assume that the principle of ministerial responsibility (already highly problematic, of course, at the UK level) will, in fact, turn out to develop in precisely the same way in Scotland.[78] The collective vesting of powers in the Scottish Ministers, in addition to reinforcing collective responsibility as such, might tend to dilute individual responsibility. The tendency to allocate portfolios to ministers which cut across departmental boundaries within the Scottish Administration may come to affect the accountability relationship between ministers and civil servants. There have been first ministerial undertakings, in the wake of the (Fraser) Holyrood Inquiry[79] to re-examine minister/civil servant relationships more widely. Already, it appears that civil servants are accompanying ministers in public fora much more commonly than their Whitehall counterparts. It may be that a different balance between political, legal and other accountabilities will produce a culture overall in which individual ministerial responsibility will take a different form. In the meantime, however, it does have to be conceded that there are many indications that the UK assumptions are being broadly replicated. Ministers have had to take the consequences of

---

[78] c.f. D. Woodhouse, 'The Reconstruction of Constitutional Accountability' [2002] *PL* 73, 82–3 where discussion of events in Scotland appears to take little account of the possibility of different constitutional relationships.

[79] Formally reinforced by Andy Kerr MSP, Minister for Finance and Public Services, in the debate on the Fraser Report—SPOR 22 September 2004, cols 10413–6.

personal errors of judgment.[80] Ministers have been compelled to accept responsibility for the activities of themselves and their departments when under pressure from parliamentary questions, parliamentary committees, or when confronted by motions of no confidence.[81]

It was on the basis of the principles it had articulated that the Consultative Steering Group developed its proposals across the entire range of the future work of the Parliament which were published in December 1998, and which were highly influential in the making of the Parliament's standing orders, first on a temporary basis by the Secretary of State[82] and then on a permanent footing by the Parliament itself from December 1999. As an introduction to an assessment of how far the Parliament has been successful in living up to the CSG principles—its 'Founding Principles'—it may be useful, as a starting point, to take selective account of the views of the Parliament's own Procedures Committee which reported in March 2003,[83] and especially on the principles of accountability and power-sharing.[84] Under the head of accountability itself, the principal focus of the report was on acknowledged failings of the processes of legislative scrutiny in the Parliament, especially in the allocation of sufficient time during and between the stages of Bill procedure.[85] There would be more reviews to follow in the Parliament, of both primary and secondary law-making procedures. There was also substantial critical comment on the Parliament's discharge of its administrative scrutiny responsibilities. Financial and audit procedures were criticized;[86] as were parliamentary question procedures[87] (which had been subject to Procedures Committee scrutiny on earlier occasions as well); and the improvement of opportunities for subject debates and Members' business in the Parliament[88] was proposed. Under the head of power-sharing, there was some consideration of openness and transparency in the working of committees, including the Parliamentary Bureau which, as the Executive's vehicle for ensuring its leading role in the organisation of the Parliament's business, has a special role; and a substantial section on the work of the Public Petitions Committee. Despite

---

[80] See, e.g. the resignation of Dr Richard Simpson on 26 November 2002, after making disparaging remarks about striking firefighters. [81] See n. 65.

[82] Scotland Act 1998 (Transitory and Transitional Provisions) (Standing Orders and Parliamentary Publications) Order 1999, S.I. 1999/1095.

[83] *The Founding Principles of the Scottish Parliament*, SP Paper 818 (2003). The report is long and unwieldy, even when reduced to its 135 recommendations.

[84] Recommendations on access and participation related largely to questions of public access to the Parliament itself. Clearly the final principle of equal opportunities is also of importance but it is, for present purposes, less relevant.

[85] *Founding Principles* n. 83, paras 295–362. The Procedures Committee has since published a report on *Timescales and Stages of Bills* (SP Paper 228, November 2004).

[86] *Ibid.*, paras 401–403. See also the review conducted by the Parliament's Finance Committee—SP Paper 784 (2003).

[87] SP Paper 818, para. 485. A corollary to the 'collective' allocation of functions to the Executive is that (with the exception of questions directed to the First Minister and the Law Officers) parliamentary questions are addressed to the Scottish Ministers, with answers provided by the minister administratively responsible. [88] SP Paper 818, para. 499.

any lingering concerns that an additional procedure for handling complaints by citizens might be considered superfluous in a Parliament in which the Executive is directly represented and held to account, the Petitions Committee was established as a flagship of the accessibility of the Parliament. Certainly many grievances have received an airing but the Committee has been in danger of being overwhelmed and the significance of actual outcomes is difficult to assess.

The Procedures Committee also commented generally on Executive-Parliament relations:

> More generally, we think it will be very important to the continued drive for co-operative government between the Executive and the Parliament and the development of better government, for the work plans of the Executive and the Parliament, to be co-ordinated where possible in order to ensure that opportunities for consensus working across all areas of government, policy and legislation, are identified. We recommend that the Scottish Executive and the Parliamentary authorities should discuss how this might be taken forward.[89]

At points such as this, the Procedures Committee demonstrates a loyalty to the 'Founding Principles' and it was at pains to urge that the Parliament retains its dedication to the task of matching its performance against the Principles.[90] Equally, there can be no doubting the diligence with which the Committee addressed this initial review. A very substantial quantity of evidence was gathered in and commented on. The Committee was appropriately critical in its report, in response to observations made to it and especially the frustrations of MSPs themselves.

It would, however, be unwise to rely on the Committee's report as an objective commentary on Executive-Parliament relations. The Committee is, to a large degree, a captive of the rhetoric of the 'Founding Principles'. It is a party to the undoubted collusion between Parliament and the Executive on the prospects for the new relationship, the 'new politics', which the Principles assert. There is an inevitable lack of a sceptical edge which might penetrate more deeply both the content of the Principles themselves and the Parliament's adherence to them. The Committee could make sensible suggestions for procedural reform but it was unlikely to offer a sharply critical challenge to present arrangements. It was, for instance, unlikely to doubt the capacity of the Parliament and especially its committees to confront the Executive. It would not mount a serious challenge to the rationale of the Public Petitions Committee. It did not really get a grip on the proper role of the Parliamentary Bureau. It had no real answer to the swamping of the committee system with business. It is one of the ironies that, in a system of devolution designed to allocate Scottish business to a body with more time and resources at its disposal, and to give a leading role to committees, those committees have themselves been subject to disabling pressures. It was, in large part, these pressures which produced the case for maintaining the Parliament at

[89] Rec. 131.   [90] Rec. 135.

its present size rather than suffer a reduction as originally heralded in section 86 of the Scotland Act.[91]

(b) Accountability to the courts

In the closing years of the twentieth century, the tide was running strongly in favour of the restraint of governmental power by its accountability to the courts. The expansion of the grounds of judicial review and the adoption of explicitly rights-based review on the passing of the Human Rights Act 1998 provided, for better or for worse, a new legitimacy for the role of the courts. And the devolution project was a child of these times. In Scotland this was most prominently reflected in the provision made for Bills in the Parliament to be subject to review by the Judicial Committee of the Privy Council[92] and for Acts of the Parliament also to be reviewable under the procedures prescribed for 'devolution issues' under the Scotland Act.[93] This policing of the Parliament's competence has important consequences for the Executive. All Executive Bills have to be certified on introduction as legislatively competent.[94] It is, in effect, the Executive's legislative programme which is subject to judicial scrutiny and it is the risk of possible challenge that has occasionally compelled the Executive to seek statutory powers by the Sewel convention procedure from the Westminster Parliament.[95] It is the Executive's principal Law Officer, the Lord Advocate, who will normally be the appropriate contradictor in a case challenging the validity of an Act of the Scottish Parliament.[96]

The Executive's own acts and failures are also challengeable as devolution issues on grounds, for instance, of breach of human rights and encroachment into reserved areas. There have been intermittent instances of the Scottish Ministers being challenged on human rights grounds, the most significant of which was *Napier v. Scottish Ministers*[97] in which a challenge based on the practice of 'slopping out' in Scottish prisons was upheld.[98] Much the biggest concentration, however, has so far been on devolution issues where it has been the Lord Advocate as prosecutor whose actions have been under scrutiny—most famously in *Starrs v. Ruxton*[99] where the system of temporary sheriffs in Scotland was condemned on the basis that the prosecution was unlawfully brought before a court which contravened Article 6 of the ECHR.[100] One may speculate as to

[91] Scottish Parliament (Constituencies) Act 2004. [92] Scotland Act 1998, ss. 33–34.
[93] See s. 98 and Sched. 6.   [94] s. 31(1).
[95] A. Page and A. Batey, 'Scotland's Other Parliament' [2002] *PL* 501, 517.
[96] *Adams v Scottish Ministers* 2003 SC 171, para. 31.   [97] 2004 SLT 555.
[98] Other prominent human rights based cases have included *County Properties Ltd v. Scottish Ministers* 2002 SC 79 (planning procedures). See C. Himsworth, 'Planning Rights Convergence: A Note on *County Properties and Alconbury*' (2002) 6 *Edin LR* 253.
[99] 2000 JC 208, 2000 SLT 42.
[100] Another principal focus has been on delay. See C. Himsworth, 'Jurisdictional Divergences over the Reasonable Time Guarantee in Criminal Trials' (2004) 8 *Edin LR* 255. In *Al Fayed v. Lord Advocate* 2004 S.C. 568; 2004 SLT 319 one of the reasons for the rejection of the petition seeking a

why there has been so little sign of challenges to Scottish Executive decisions on the grounds that ministers have strayed beyond devolved competence. As already mentioned, delegated legislation is subject to technical scrutiny by the Parliament's Subordinate Legislation Committee but, in the early days at least, deviation into reserved matters was not a great concern.[101] It is unclear, in what might appear to be a potentially fruitful area for challenge by private litigants, why there has been so little activity.

In most other respects, there has been no radical change. Judicial scrutiny of the Scottish Executive has tracked that of the scrutiny of UK government departments. This includes an apparent recognition of the extension of the *Carltona*[102] principle (competence of civil servants to act on behalf of ministers) to the Executive.[103] In civil proceedings the Lord Advocate acts on behalf of the Executive[104] and recognition has been given to the need to accommodate litigation between the Scottish Executive and the UK government by section 99 of the Scotland Act which provides that rights and liabilities may arise between the Crown in right of the UK government and, on the other hand, the Crown in right of the Scottish Administration. A feature which has been continued into the devolutionary period has been the probable divergence of Scots law and English law in the remedies against the Crown. Whereas the English courts have held that, in judicial review proceedings, ministers may be vulnerable to injunctions,[105] a succession of Scottish decisions has, until very recently, held that the Crown Proceedings Act 1947 denies the possibility of equivalent orders against ministers in Scotland.[106] It seems that the opportunity has now been created for a final view on remedies against the Crown in Scots law to be taken by the House of Lords.[107]

(c) Accountability to ombudsmen and others

Just as devolution has provided the opportunity for a repackaging of governmental accountability to the new Parliament and to the courts, there has also been some necessary redesign of accountability to other external agencies.

---

fatal accident inquiry was that an inquiry into a foreign death was not within the competence of the Lord Advocate but was a reserved matter. See paras 29–30.

[101] C. Himsworth, 'Subordinate Legislation in the Scottish Parliament' (2002) 6 *Edin LR* 356, 373.   [102] *Carltona v. Commissioner of Works* [1943] 2 All ER 50.

[103] *Scottish House Builders Association Ltd v. Scottish Ministers* 2002 SLT 1321; *Westerhall Farms v. Scottish Ministers* (25 April 2001, unreported). This is a position recently reinforced in *Somerville v. Scottish Ministers* (8 February 2005, unreported), paras 63–82.

[104] Scotland Act 1998, Sched. 8 para. 7 (amendments to Crown Proceedings Act 1947).

[105] *M v. Home Office* [1994] 1 AC 377.

[106] See, in particular, *McDonald v. Secretary of State for Scotland* 1994 SC 234. But see also now *Beggs v. Scottish Ministers* (First Division unreported 15 March 2005) in which, following reasoning analogous to that in *M*, the Scottish Ministers were held to be in contempt of court and civil servants ordered to appear on their behalf.

[107] *Davidson v. Scottish Ministers* (No. 2) 2004 SLT 895, para. 76.

Although the Freedom of Information (Scotland) Act 2002 passed by the Scottish Parliament broadly tracks in respect of the Scottish Executive and other Scottish public bodies[108] the provision made by the Freedom of Information Act 2000, it may be that the Scottish Act's greater insistence on a test of 'substantial prejudice' will provide for a greater penetration into the affairs of government. Separate provision has been made for the Auditor General for Scotland, reporting to the Scottish Parliament[109] and, although it is early days, there have been signs that the Auditor is prepared to flex his muscles.[110] Structurally most interesting, however, although it is again too early to assess the actual impact of the office, has been the establishment of the Scottish Public Services Ombudsman.[111] A desire to create a 'one-stop shop' for complaints led to the new Ombudsman assuming a 'central government' role in relation to the Scottish Administration (as well as the Parliamentary Corporate Body) together with the functions of the ombudsmen formerly supervising local government, the national health service and housing associations in Scotland. The core responsibilities of the Public Services Ombudsman remain the same as in previous models save that her[112] jurisdiction includes investigations of service failure and hardship (rather than injustice as such) and, in certain circumstances, investigations at the request of the affected public authority itself. There is no MSP filter standing between citizen and ombudsman. The combined effect of the merger of powers and the other adjustments has probably been the creation of a more 'free-floating' and less 'parliamentary' model of ombudsman. It is unclear how far, if at all, the Parliament will give direct support to the investigative role of the new Scottish ombudsman.

(d) The Scottish Executive's relationship with Whitehall

As we have seen, there are some respects in which the accountability of the Scottish Executive to the courts is shaped by the overall subordination of the Executive and the Scottish Parliament as well, to the institutions of government at the UK level. Devolution is about the opportunity for difference but it is an opportunity regulated by the terms of the constitutional settlement. This is a feature which is also more widely reflected in the overall pattern of intergovernmental relationships. Although the rhetoric of partnership between the two levels of government (as well as within the wider family of devolved administrations) is frequently used, there is no doubt that the terms of any such partnership are largely formed by the statutory background of the Scotland Act. This confers quite extensive powers of control on UK ministers and, with that control,

---

[108] Including the Parliament itself.
[109] Scotland Act 1998, s. 69(1) and the Public Finance and Accountability (Scotland) Act 2000.
[110] See, e.g. his report on the Parliament's Holyrood project of 29 June 2004.
[111] Scottish Public Services Ombudsman Act 2002.
[112] Professor Alice Brown is the first holder of the office.

a measure of subordination and a form of accountability—beyond that owed to the Scottish Parliament—which has no direct parallel in a (nation) 'state-level' executive. It is, of course, a subordination and accountability which is shared with the Scottish Parliament itself and keeping the two institutions conceptually distinct will be important for many purposes but a primary focus on the Scottish Executive reveals a list of ways in which the potential for UK-level controls may be asserted. The list will be briefly considered:

1. Overarching the whole central-devolved relationship is the fact that neither the Scottish Executive nor the Scottish Parliament is formally immune from the unilateral adjustment of their powers by primary legislation in the UK Parliament. So far, such adjustments have been made by consent following consultation but there is a vulnerability here. The powers of both the Executive and Parliament are also subject to a degree of adjustment by Order in Council, again by consent.[113]

2. The Secretary of State has available powers under the Scotland Act to intervene, on specified grounds, to prevent the passing of laws by the Parliament or to prevent the exercise of executive powers by the Scottish Ministers.[114] Neither of these powers has so far been invoked.

3. There are other ways too in which the powers of the Scottish Executive and the ways in which they may be used can be affected by UK ministerial intervention. One is in relation to EC law. Not only does UK membership of the EU affect the devolution settlements by enabling UK ministers to control the content of UK (including Scots) law in the areas of strong EC competence such as fisheries through their membership of the Council of Ministers but, as earlier mentioned, the power of UK ministers as well as the Scottish Ministers to exercise powers of implementation under section 57(1) of the Scotland Act does provide the opportunity for important UK-level interventions. Quite separately, the Scotland Act arrangements for shared control of 'cross-border public authorities', even though not formally encroaching on the power of the Scottish Parliament to arrange things differently in the longer term, provide for a substantial level of central intrusion and an adjustment of the general model of devolved powers.[115]

4. Of great importance to the practice of devolved government in Scotland is the near-complete financial dependence of the Executive on the UK government. There is a potential for limited flexibility deriving from the Parliament and Executive's control over the *local* taxation system.[116] There is the possibility of limited charging for services. But, otherwise, the Executive is almost entirely dependent upon grants from the UK government. It is true that the Parliament's

---

[113] Scotland Act 1998, ss. 30(2), 63.   [114] *Ibid.*, ss. 35 and 58 respectively.
[115] *Ibid.*, ss. 88–90.
[116] *Ibid.*, Sched. 5, Pt II, S.AI, producing the possibility of shifting some of the Executive's financial burden on to the local taxpayer.

tax-varying power is of some constitutional significance but it has little practical impact so long as coalition governments in Scotland commit themselves to refraining from its use. The effects of the resulting dependence on UK government grants are, of course, moderated by the system of distribution based on the Barnett formula—both in the stability which it provides and also the relative generosity with which Scotland has been treated.[117] It is also important to note that, in contrast with some devolved governments elsewhere, the Scottish Executive does receive a 'block' grant, without specification of particular forms of expenditure.

5. The civil service. The report of the Royal Commission on the Constitution in 1973 expressed the view that the only way in which Scottish devolved government could operate autonomously would be, as at Stormont, with its own, separate civil service.[118] That has, however, been denied by the Scotland Act which reserves the civil service and provides that civil servants in the Scottish Administration are members of the general UK home civil service.[119] So far, this is judged not to have been to the detriment of Scottish Executive autonomy, and indeed to have contributed to harmonious relations with the UK departments.

6. Concordats. Whilst the features just described may be the principal formal determinants of the relationship between the Scottish and UK governments, a significant investment has also been placed by the UK government in the creation of departmental 'concordats' under an overarching 'Memorandum of Understanding'.[120] These are the agreements between the Scottish Executive (and the other devolved administrations) and the different UK departments designed to ensure that, on matters of mutual concern—for instance proposed legislation in common areas of interest—there will be consultation and a degree of confidentiality of communication. The concordats are expressly stated to be not binding in law but in honour only. Different views have been expressed on the overall constitutional and political significance of the concordats.[121] Whilst acknowledging that there might be a case for giving them a more formal status especially if they are to withstand the greater pressures of a more markedly different political complexion of the parties to the concordats at some future point, the House of Lords Constitution Committee had also to take account of the view that the process of their making in the first place was more important than their operation in practice.[122] It is certainly the case that one effect of the concordats entered into by 'partners' of such differing power and influence may, despite the rhetoric of the desirability of harmonious relations, be to constrain further the autonomy of the weaker (devolved) party. What the concordat

---

[117] See M. Keating, *The Government of Scotland* (Edinburgh UP, 2005), Ch 6. See also, Himsworth and O'Neill, n. 9, Ch 10.   [118] Cmnd 5460 (1973) paras 807 and 1146.
[119] Scotland Act 1998, s. 51.
[120] Cm 4444 (1999), subsequently reissued as Cm 4806 (2000) and Cm 5240 (2001).
[121] Himsworth and O'Neill, n. 9, 265–8.
[122] *Devolution: Inter-Institutional Relations in the United Kingdom* (HL Paper 28, 2002–03), para. 40.

regime does, at least, reflect is the overall political character of the relationship between the two tiers of government. The Scotland Act provides a statutory framework but no more than that.

4. Conclusions

When it was alleged and then officially denied[123] in January 2001 that 10 Downing Street had taken umbrage at the use by First Minister Henry McLeish of the term 'Scottish Government' in relation to the Scottish Executive[124] the story was widely treated as a storm in a teacup. Whatever the formal terminology in the Scotland Act and whatever the possible sensitivities in Whitehall and indeed among Scottish MPs at Westminster, the substance of the matter was that, functionally at least, the Scottish Executive was every bit as much the Scottish Government in respect of its devolved responsibilities as the body headed by Prime Minister Blair was the British Government.[125] What was in a name?!

It was indeed on the basis that Scotland would have a 'government' on the London model that much of the discussion of the Scottish Executive and its powers and accountabilities has been conducted. Technical aspects of how powers were to be conferred on the Executive would need, as we have seen, to be treated differently from their Whitehall comparators. But, once clothed with these powers, the Scottish Executive should be viewed as occupying the same constitutional territory as any other based on the model of parliamentary government. It was, however, at this point that opinions divided. The UK government's White Paper spoke of a relationship of the Scottish Executive to the Parliament as similar to the equivalent relationship at Westminster. Others, in the tradition of the Scottish Constitutional Convention and the 'Founding Principles' of the Parliament have sought a very different relationship between the two.

On whether such a different relationship has indeed been established, reasonable people may disagree. Some formal distinctions have been compelled by the rules (including the electoral rules and the resulting coalition governments) of the Scotland Act itself. Beyond those, other claimed differences may be viewed more sceptically. Party discipline, even though exercised within the context of a coalition, may eventually be proved to have the capacity to prevail over those who would wish to substitute another model.

---

[123] Downing Street Lobby Briefing, 10 January 2001.
[124] See, e.g. SPOR 11 Jan 2001, cols. 164–166.
[125] In s. 2(4) of Terrorism Act 2000, 'the government' is defined to mean 'the government of the United Kingdom, of a Part of the United Kingdom or of a country other than the United Kingdom'.

The truth of the matter may, however, lie elsewhere. Perhaps the initial shared assumption that executive government in Scotland and at the UK level are very similar constitutional phenomena and raise the same questions of accountability was simply misplaced. Perhaps there is something categorically different about an executive which, although in formal terms similarly located, is an executive which can never go to war, never conduct relations with foreign states, never has to protect its borders with an immigration policy, and can hardly tax its own population. The Scottish Executive could never have threatened to exercise the raw executive powers of a national government. Even responsibility for the management of the welfare state in Scotland falls only partially to the Executive. It was always to be a much more restrained and domesticated constitutional animal—a phenomenon which is also perhaps reflected in its emerging reputation for multiple consultation prior to decision.

This being the case, it may be possible to draw two conclusions which appear to be rather paradoxically opposed. On the one hand, the Scottish Executive may be found to escape many of the new forms of parliamentary accountability which were intended by its founding fathers. On the other hand, it may be that, given its much more confined powers, those additional parliamentary and legal accountabilities were, in any event, a step too far.

We shall see. Stuff will happen. In the United Kingdom we have been used to the assessment of constitutional practice within the dynamic of a functioning polity. We have to be much more cautious about developments on the relatively green field site of Scottish devolved government. Whilst there have been some continuities, it has broadly been a picture of *both* new politics *and* a new constitutional design. In ways that may be much more reminiscent of the early experience of independence constitutions than of more routine constitutional adjustments, there will be a need over time for the critical assessment of the functional interaction of the politics and law of Scottish devolution. It will be only at a much later stage that we shall be able to make an assessment of how the devolution settlement has itself settled down, assuming that it is permitted to do so. We shall be better placed to work out how the complex of inter-dependent factors—some legal, some political—will come to bear upon the powers and accountability of the Scottish Executive.

7

Executive Power in France

*Denis Baranger**

At the end of the eighteenth century, Bentham expressed the hope that a universal grammar of powers would one day make national political arrangements commensurable or, in other words, reducible to a common measure. Bentham's own categories did not gain universal currency but, with the process usually called 'constitutionalism', a set of terms and ideas regarding political arrangements came to be shared between several countries. 'Executive power' is one of these terms: first coined in seventeenth century England in the context of the civil wars, it later gained currency in America and France. In both countries, it was marked with a distinguished stamp of authority by being used in the Constitutions of 1787 and 1791. Does that mean that, from that time onwards, the words 'executive power' have belonged to a universal language of constitutional law? Is there a 'golden metwand' with which constitutional lawyers can compare the scope of executives in different countries and design the best means to bring them to account?

The notion that there is an executive power, for which it is possible to define a certain scope, relies on a logical precondition: that there are several 'powers'. Separation of powers, as a normative doctrine, implies that power *ought* to be divided. This in turn implies that power, as a phenomenon, *can* be partitioned. Considered as a process, separation of powers implies either that power was at a certain time undivided or has, at all times, a natural tendency to be united in the same hands. In the view of French monarchical absolutism, power was not to be divided. Certainly, this overlooked the fact that power was, in a sense, already shared: with the Church, and, within the temporal realm, with such institutions as parliaments. The legal description of the monarchical status could, from time to time, identify certain 'powers', such as the legislative one. But it did not attempt to reduce governmental activity to a limited set of functions. For whatever purpose, French lawyers carefully drew a list of the king's rights ('*droits du roi*') at the forefront of which stood the power to defend the kingdom, to declare war and peace, 'police' (and later 'administration'), and the levying of taxes.[1]

---

* Professor of Public Law, Université de Paris II (Panthéon-Assas).
[1] F. Olivier-Martin, *L'absolutisme Français* (LGDJ, 1997), 121 *et seq.*

In the brave new world of separation of powers, enumeration of existing powers, immunities, or revenues has ceased to be the main intellectual instrument. In his celebrated chapter on the English constitution,[2] Montesquieu distinguishes between three '*pouvoirs/puissances*' which, he says, belong to all states. The definition of these powers can be seen under two, not mutually incompatible, lights: one is as an intellectual attempt to convey the abstract meaning of these separate powers, under the premise that they exist everywhere if only one has eyes to see them. Another is as an attempt to pick up some of the items listed in the enumerations made by pre-modern lawyers and to fit them forcibly into three larger boxes, and three only. The king's rights ('*droits du roi*') are drawn out of their natural environment and immersed into a new setting. The impact of this move is very significant, as Montesquieu will thus define some of the most central categories of modern constitutionalism. But he did not write a work of technical legal literature, and was therefore not forced to confront all the consequences of this attempt to make ancient law (the old wine) fit into 'modern' political theory (the new bottle).

But this is precisely the problem with which Blackstone was faced when he drafted the chapters of his *Commentaries* on the king's powers. Before Blackstone, there was in England a legal literature focusing on prerogative, and a political literature using the phrase 'executive power'. Blackstone did not fully merge them. He did not attempt to use 'executive power' as an all-encompassing category, into which it was possible to subsume the entirety of the existing law. Instead, he devoted several chapters to the prerogative, and drew on existing typologies. Of 'executive power' he certainly spoke, but most of the time with a view to putting the legal study of prerogative in the context of political liberty. Ever since Blackstone wrote his *Commentaries*, British law has been wavering between the discourse of prerogative and the modern language of executive power.

French law, it seems, is not in the same position: there has been a revolution, which has had legal as well as other aspects, and it has swept away all previous legal categories. In the language of French public law, the word 'now' refers to an imaginary day (something like the single day during which, according to a legal fiction, every British parliament is supposed to legislate) which began on 17 June 1789, and has not yet come to an end.

1. Definition and scope

(a) Sovereignty and government in Revolutionary France

This is where the language of constitutionalism ceases to be universal. The French attempt to delimit the province of the executive power is very specific.

---

[2] *The Spirit of the Laws* (Trans. by Thomas Nugent, revised by J. V. Prichard, Bell & Sons, 1914), Bk IX, Ch VI.

It is based on a doctrine of sovereignty. However important separation of powers is in the French tradition, it has always been subjected to a higher principle of political legitimacy which has been expressed in institutional terms. Most British lawyers accept that Britain is a democracy but, in Britain, 'the people' is not an institution which the constitution knows of and to which it grants legal capacities. There is an electorate which votes to elect Members of Parliament. But the only sovereign institution which the British constitution will know of is Parliament.

In France, the sovereignty of the political community has been transposed into an institution (the 'nation') which is at the same time a political and a legal sovereign. Establishing the nation as political sovereign was the central move of a process which led to the creation of separated 'powers' in French constitutionalism. In this sense, this process is foundational. At the same time, in harmony with the very concept of 'revolution', it is a process of destruction. What was being brought to the scaffold was the traditional understanding of authority. Monarchical authority did not lend itself to a separation into two or three functions, but rather to analytical distinctions of the type that old regime lawyers attempted with the '*droits du roi*'. The dividing line along which modern constitutionalism, in France as well as everywhere else, attempted to tear apart monarchical authority was the distinction between sovereignty and government. It is precisely the distinction on which representative regimes are based, as we could define a representative regime as one in which sovereignty and government are separated and allocated to distinct institutions.

With the establishment of the 'nation' as sovereign, revolutionary constitutionalism (or at least its driving force) preserved some central features of monarchical authority: its unity, and to some degree, its incarnation, namely its ability to be at the same time transcendent and immanent. The establishment of the nation is the central move of French constitutionalism, just as the establishment of a constitution-making 'people' was the central move of American constitutionalism. This move, however successful in terms of defining *sovereignty* (at least insofar as national sovereignty remains a defining feature of French constitutionalism up to this day), also limited the extent to which French legal culture could be made to understand *government*. With the sovereignty of the nation, the emphasis was consciously put on the unity of power ('power' as opposed to 'powers'). The concept of nation showed the political community as the bearer of a political will ('*volonté générale*'). The national will was thereby identified in the constitution as the *primum mobile* from which all other actions were to flow.

While the first tenet of revolutionary constitutionalism was the sovereignty of the nation, the second was that '*la loi est l'expression de la volonté générale*': acts of the national assembly express the general will.[3] Therefore, despite belonging

---

[3] Art. 6 of the Declaration of the rights of man and citizen of 1789.

to the sphere of government, the assembly was the only legitimate mouthpiece of the nation. In the most radical formulations of the early revolutionary period, the nation existed only in the assembly. The sovereign nation was first and foremost a legislator. But the reverse was also true: only through legislation could the nation be brought to expression. This went some way towards blurring the newborn distinction between sovereignty and government. There was in the sphere of government an institution, the legislative body, which was the mouthpiece of the sovereign. This also restored something of ancient authority—a quaint taste for unity—within the new pattern of (separated) powers. This generated a bias in the French understanding of separation of powers. While Montesquieu had spoken of the executive as a 'power to administrate things' ('*puissance exécutrice des choses*') French public law will see it primarily as a power to execute acts of parliament. The meaning of the word 'execution' was thus decisively reoriented: it moved away from a general effort to describe the relationship between government and the sphere of reality (as it could be found in Machiavelli or in Locke) and was later held to mean only a subordinate function of carrying into effect a superior and more abstract (i.e. more remote from the sphere of facts) expression of will.

In this new pattern, the executive was put in a strange position. It retained a monarchical form in the first French Constitution of 1791 (we may call it a 'king-as-executive'). But it was denied monarchical authority. 'Sovereignty' went to the nation. The king-as-executive was further denied the right to speak in the name of the nation. Certainly, the Feuillant party revised the 1791 Constitution to make it say that the king was, with the national assembly, a 'representative' of the nation. But the king was not granted this representative function insofar as he was entrusted with the executive function: he was a representative because his veto power gave him a share in legislation.[4] The notion that statutes were an 'expression of the general will' created a hierarchy within the sphere of government. The king-as-executive was not a primary actor in the governmental sphere. He was granted only a subordinate position.[5] It is not therefore surprising that the revolutionary doctrine was dominated by a vision of the executive as a power whose function was to carry into execution the legislative will of the nation. Where the nation had spoken, what else could an executive do? French constitutionalism restricted its understanding of the concept of an executive to the meaning which was most immediately conveyed by the word

---

[4] See G. Burdeau, F. Hamon and M. Troper, *Droit constitutionnel* (LGDJ, 28th edn., 2003), 319 ; G. Glénard, *L'exécutif et la constitution de 1791* (Thèse pour le doctorat en droit, Paris II, 1999), 168 *et seq.*

[5] It is this idea of a hierarchy between the legislature and the holders of the executive function which was conveyed by Raymond Carré de Malberg in his influential *Contribution to a General Theory of the State* (Recueil Sirey, 1920–2). Carré de Malberg directly deduced this principle from the revolutionary principle of the law (*loi*) being the expression of the general will. He saw the legislative power as essentially defined by its superiority and ability to initiate decisions. As a result the executive was defined by its ancillary position, and its normative inferiority.

used to express it. The executive was meant to execute, not to govern in the sense of being a primary source of political decision.

Despite the fact that the word 'executive' was coined in England, such an entrapment never took place in Britain. Blackstone had foreseen that the executive was dangerous to liberty and thus had to be contained. But at the same time, with this sense of creative self-contradiction which happens to be his trademark, he insisted that 'strength and despatch' were the virtues which the monarchical executive contributed to the mixed regime. Blackstone thus expounded an important truth about the executive power, a lesson which would be remembered in the Federalist Papers.[6] This truth, namely that the executive could not be reduced to mere 'execution', was almost consciously ignored in France. The king-as-executive was essentially defined as a 'weak' executive.

As far as legislation was concerned, it is the immanent (or institutionalized) side of the sovereign *nation* that was visible. '*Corps législatif*' and '*loi*' were endowed with its supernatural qualities (unity and unquestionable supremacy) while providing the *nation* with a tangible cloak. The reverse is true as far as the executive power is concerned. Ever since the word 'executive' has been thrown in the constitutional debate, it has been clouded with ambiguity. In the French context at least, this ambiguity lies in the understanding of the executive power as the authority whose function it is to *execute*, to carry into effects the superior orders of the legislature. France has not been the only country in which that misunderstanding of the role of the 'executive' has been made. But it might be the place where the consequences of this mistake have been most systematically developed. It is not surprising that an attempt to reconstruct political arrangements from first principles should lead to the notion that it is one thing to make a decision, and another to put it into effect. Therefore, it seems only logical to devolve those distinct functions to two separate institutions, each of them being endowed with adequate powers and internally arranged to discharge its duties. The political role of the houses was thus enhanced, but by no means was it claimed that only they could express the 'will of the *nation*'. French revolutionaries disliked executives as much as their English or American contemporaries. But that hatred, mingled as it was with a passion for constitutional unity, led French constitutionalism towards a long misunderstanding about the nature of executive power. In the 1791 Constitution, executive power was only 'delegated to the king'[7] who only derived his authority from statutes (*lois*).[8]

It is not only that absolute kingship could not be recast into constitutional monarchy by the sole virtue of a written constitution. There lay here a deeper misunderstanding. The word 'executive' might incorporate the notion that there is in the constitution an entity which is confronted to a certain sort of reality, no

---

[6] A. Hamilton, J. Madison, J. Jay, *The Federalist Papers* (C. Rossiter ed., with an introduction by C. R. Kesler, Mentor, 1999), letter 70.

[7] Titre III [*preliminary articles*], Art. 4 : ' *le pouvoir exécutif est délégué au roi*'.

[8] Titre III, Ch II, section première, Art. 3.

less real, maybe, than the facts presented to a court of justice or those justifying new legislation, but with a certain quality of immediateness, which calls for a rapid and practical response (*reality* as *necessity*). It might be also that this entity is the one who should be in charge of the most direct sort of relations with individuals. For that entity, the term 'immediate power', coined by J. S. Mill, might have been more appropriate than 'executive power', as in its province lie, not only the execution of statutes, but also capacities not provided for in any enactment. To a certain extent, the term 'executive' implied a denial of this ability. French constitutionalism pushed this tendency very far. The foundation of executive power in France is indistinguishable from a process of voluntary oblivion: a veil was thrown on government. Because of the destruction of traditional authority, sovereignty was from then on understood as something to be distinguished from action: sovereignty, Sieyès thought, is pure thought and not at all action. But because of the emphasis on sovereignty, governmental action could only mean the execution of a superior will. Little room was left in the constitutional scheme for a power to confront the sort of reality which does not lend itself to full determination by the positive law enacted by the sovereign, or in his name.[9] There was a tendency to reduce concrete reality to 'facts' which could be understood only as the minor of a syllogism, and which could be fully subsumed under legislative enactments.

(b) The executive as administration

This vision not only had philosophical implications, but also deeply influenced public law. The central phenomenon which has to be elucidated in order to understand how French public law defines the scope of the executive is the assimilation of the executive function to a function of administration.[10] What we have apprehended (so far) as the executive power has been frequently described in France as the accomplishment of an administrative function.[11] The term function means several things. First, the scope of the executive power is defined in terms of boundaries rather than in terms of goals. The second implication is that the executive power is a part of the state. In British law, the major constitutional institutions exist by themselves. The classical description of the Crown, Parliament, etc., does not treat them as parts of a larger, all-encompassing, body.

---

[9] The matter of foreign affairs stands as an exception to this general attitude: Ch IV (*De l'exercice du pouvoir exécutif*), section III (*des relations extérieures*) acknowledges the autonomy of the king-as-executive in this field, see Glénard, n. 4, 214.

[10] That this should be a direct consequence in the field of constitutional law of philosophical rationalism can be seen in the fact that, in a very different context, Bentham, in his constitutional theory, reached very similar results: his 'executive' was composed of the 'administrative [authority] and the judiciary'. *Constitutional Code*, (F. Rosen and J. H. Burns eds., Clarendon Press, 1984), Vol. I, 26.

[11] This identification seems to date back to the July Monarchy, G. Guglielmi, *La notion d'administration publique dans la théorie juridique Française* (LGDJ, 1991), 253.

There is no need to assume the existence of 'a state' which would be the primary bearer of all legal powers and within which several agencies would have been created in order for these powers to be exercised. In France, conversely, the existence of the state is implied in all parts of public law. The separation of powers is over-determined, politically by the concept of nation, and legally by the concept of state. It is a theory of how powers belonging to a single and superior entity are distributed between several state authorities. Therefore, power is at the same time apprehended as being united (politically in the nation, legally in the state) and distributed (according to the principle of separation of powers). As a result, no constitutional authority can be said to be initial: it is always an agent of the nation and an arm of the state.

Let us now turn to the move by which executive power has been made to collapse into an administrative function. It amounts to interpreting the frequent references in French written constitutions to the 'executive power' as referring to what is really an administrative function and the agencies in charge of it. This move is primarily to be found in academic writing, especially during the third republic (1875–1940) but in this case, it is probable that academic writing reflected the viewpoint of a larger legal community. Not all lawyers agreed with this interpretation, but those who disagreed were in a minority. The majority opinion itself was far from being unanimous. But, beyond those differences, one can identify a common understanding of the legal framework of executive action. In the theory of the state, 'power' was an ambiguous term. It could mean an 'agency' (in French: *organe*). But to say that some state agencies were labelled as 'executive' in the constitution did not amount to saying why, and for what purpose.

'Power' could also refer to a certain function. Despite many differences, the major lawyers of the period tended to express the activity of the state in functional terms. A legal theory of the state was supposed to identify some specific activities taking shape in specific legal forms: the legislative function corresponded to the enactment of legislative measures (even if they were enacted by an 'executive' authority); the jurisdictional function took shape through judicial decisions. This orientation led the majority opinion to analyse the functional province of the executive in terms of administration. The reasoning of Carré de Malberg, one of the major public lawyers of the third republic, exemplifies this attitude. In his *Contribution to a general theory of the state*,[12] he began by identifying an administrative function, along with a legislative and a judicial (*juridictionnelle*) one. He then undertook to explain why the Constitution of 1875 was justified to call this function 'executive', despite the fact that, since the revolution, the notion that the administrative organs were only authorized to execute legislative enactments in a subordinate and mechanical fashion had fallen into general disrepute. However, Carré de Malberg was unwilling to give up some sort of dependence between 'executive' action and

---

[12] *Contribution à la Théorie générale de l'Etat* (Sirey, 1920–2).

written law: every executive action had to be based on a statutory authorization. Duguit, another prominent supporter of the majority opinion, could only see, alongside the legislative function and the judicial one, an administrative function. The executive was thus shown as what it really was from a legal point of view: nothing but administration.

> I use the expression ['*attributions exécutives*'] to follow general usage, but in fact there is no executive function belonging to the State ... One means by this a series of acts which, at the end of the day, happen to be either physical operations, legislative measures, or administrative measures.[13]

This tendency to make the executive power collapse into an administrative function was based on different justifications, and formulations could vary widely. But, despite those disagreements, the majority opinion relied on a set of common denominators.

First, the doctrine meant that the agencies to which the administrative function was devolved had no share in sovereignty. The use of the term 'administration' implied that those agencies were subordinate ones. The growing importance of the principle of legality in French public law gave ample justification to this view. For instance, the *Conseil d'Etat* eventually decided that all the regulatory powers (*pouvoir réglementaire*) of the *Président de la République* were administrative in nature. This was already well established with regard to traditional '*règlements*' based on Article 3 of the '*loi constitutionnelle*' of 25 February 1875 (one of the three constitutional statutes of the third republic). But in 1907, the *Conseil d'Etat* extended this solution to the *règlements d'administration publique*, a type of regulation which could be enacted only on the basis of a legislative authorization. The court decided that those regulations were administrative in nature. More precisely, the court said that they were enacted by an administrative authority and that, as a result, they came under the judicial review of administrative courts. The *Commissaire du Gouvernement*, a magistrate who is expected to express an independent point of view on the legal issues at stake in each case, but does not take part in the court's decision, explicitly based this solution on the idea that the *règlements d'administration publique* were not to be mistaken for a legislative enactment.[14]

Secondly, this doctrine of the executive as administration meant that the legal capacities granted to executive agencies were neither inherent nor initial. These two features were in fact two sides of the same coin. Administrative functions were not inherent. They were always derived from a superior legal enactment: statute and/or constitution. An inherent power is one which is derived, not from a legal enactment, but from the nature of the institution. This is why it is a normal feature of a customary constitution, in which legal reasoning can deduce rules from the nature of institutions, the king can do no wrong, or the king is

---

[13] *Traité de droit constitutionnel* (De Boccard, 1926), Vol. IV, 586.
[14] C.E., 6 December 1907, *Chemins de Fer de l'Est*, Sirey 1908, III, 1.

fountain of justice. Administrative functions are therefore not primary ones: if we take the functioning of the state to be a chain of successive actions, administrative action is never the *primum mobile*. It is always ignited by the enactment of a constitutional or legislative measure. The vocabulary with which one can describe this varies considerably, sometimes with significant theoretical implications. But the result is always the same: what is called 'executive power' in the constitution is interpreted to be deprived both of the faculty to initiate state action and of the ability to use legal capacities which would not be granted from above. To put it in other terms, to say that the executive power must be understood as an administrative function is to deny that it can be interpreted as a prerogative.

(c) The executive in the constitution

We may safely assert as a general principle of French public law that an executive authority cannot act except on the basis of a power granted by a written enactment. This is the French law equivalent, in a legal culture where a greater importance is attached to the written rule, of *Entick v. Carrington*.[15] As for the authorities which the written constitution calls 'executive', this grant must normally come either from the written constitution or from acts of Parliament. However, it is not easy to find enabling clauses defining in broad terms the executive task. In fact, it was precisely the reverse which was attempted: not to reflect the actual variety of the executive organ's activity, but to restrict this activity to a subordinate task of administration.

It took either a different philosophy of power, as in Article 14 of the 1814 Charter, or extraordinary circumstances for a broader acknowledgement of the scope of executive action to take place. Thus, the constitutional decree of 17 February 1871, adopted after the fall of the Second Empire and before the enactment of the three constitutional statutes of 1875, gave to Adolphe Thiers the title of 'head of the executive power' (*chef du pouvoir exécutif*) and empowered him to 'provide immediately for the necessities of government and the conduct of negotiations' with the Prussian invader. Barthélémy believed that this was the best definition of executive power ever given in French history.[16] It is surprisingly reminiscent of the words used by the Lords' and Commons' *Declaration in Defense of the Militia Ordinance* (27 May 1642) in order to justify their taking over of some of the king's legal powers: in their view, the High Court of Parliament was a council 'to provide for the necessities, prevent the imminent dangers, and preserve the public peace and safety of the kingdom'.[17]

[15] (1765) 19 St. Tr. 1029.
[16] J. Barthélémy, *Le rôle du pouvoir exécutif dans les républiques modernes* (Giard et Brière, 1907), 479.
[17] *The Constitutional Documents of the Puritan Revolution 1625–1660* (Clarendon, S. R. Gardiner ed., 3rd edn., 1906), 254 *et seq*. The 1871 clause covers diplomatic powers, which makes the French definition a bit more general and adequate.

In fact, one would probably find other statements with a similar content in the history of many countries. But with the exception of Article 14 of the 1814 Charter, the 1871 clause is far from being typical of the definition of the scope of executive action to be found in French constitutions before 1958.[18] Most of the time, the executive organs' task has been defined as one of carrying statutes into execution, (Article 3 of the constitutional statute of 25 February 1875 which, in the view of the public lawyer Moreau, 'embraced all the executive attributions';[19] Article 47 of the 1946 Constitution).

The Constitution of 1958 stands out in this context. It does not restrict the competence of the executive organs to the execution of statutes. The task of the cabinet ('*le gouvernement*') is to 'define and conduct the nation's policy'. But it is the President who is the core institution of the 1958 system. It is the institution which serves the constitution's ultimate purpose: to regenerate the state. Of the President, De Gaulle said that the entirety of the state's authority is devolved to him. While it did not suppress the role of the houses in expressing the general will, this vision placed above Parliament and the ministers (gathered in a '*gouvernment*') a superior sort of legitimacy: Articles 5 and 16 are evidence of the President's ultimate power to represent the country. He is granted a '*pouvoir d'arbitrage*'[20] by which he ensures the 'regular functioning of public services' and the 'continuity of the state'. Article 16 entrusts him with a loosely defined power to act in times of emergency: the decisions he takes must be rendered necessary by circumstances, and they must aim at restoring as quickly as possible the state authorities' capacity to discharge their mission in a context where this mission has suffered an interruption. When the powers granted by Article 16 have been used (only once in 1961, but for five months) they have enabled the President, *inter alia*, to enact legislative measures. As such, Article 16 allows a temporary breach of the principle of separation of legislative and executive functions. They also indicate that the President's powers go beyond the executive sphere and the traditional sphere of a parliamentary head of state's powers. This is not only a question of scope, but also on the nature of these powers: the 1958 Constitution has isolated a category of powers which are not subject to ministerial countersign

---

[18] At least as a constitutional enactment. Case law has, from time to time, embodied similar statements about the nature of executive action. See, for instance; the *Du Graty case* (referring to the government's power 'to protect France's territorial security, to be in charge of national defence, to exercise in time of war police powers regarding foreigners as it deems it necessary'); C.E. 4 January 1918, *Du Graty, Revue du Droit Public*, 1918, 212–19. Jèze noted that this solution, as it justified the C.E.'s decision to deny its jurisdiction, offended the lawyer's 'sentiment of legality' and shed light on 'the lacunas of our war legislation', the French Parliament having not, at the time, established a 'legal state of war' (*un régime légal de guerre*), 217.

[19] *Précis élémentaire de droit constitutionnel, 4/organisation des pouvoirs publics* (Librairie de la société du recueil général des lois et des arrêts, 1897), 281. Moreau, however, distinguishes himself from the majority opinion by his definition of the executive power as 'government', 285–6.

[20] It has come to be generally agreed that the word 'arbitrage' means here that the President is an '*arbiter*' in the sense either of 'one whose opinion or decision is authoritative in a matter of debate; a judge' (*O.E.D.*, definition No 1) or of 'one who has power to decide or ordain according to his own absolute pleasure; one who has a matter under his sole control' (*O.E.D.*, No 3).

(*contreseing*). This category, enumerated in Article 19, is traditionally labelled '*pouvoirs propres*', a term which does not mean (as in the *Labonne* case)[21] inherent powers, but powers which, being not subject to ministerial countersign, are exercised under the President's exclusive authority and responsibility, or absence of the latter. As a result, the President has appeared as more than simply an 'executive' authority. He has been defined as the holder of a 'state power' (*pouvoir d'Etat*).[22] In fact, it would have sufficed to acknowledge that executive organs are traditionally in charge of the safeguarding of the commonwealth. But this was next to unthinkable in the French tradition: to say that an executive organ has acquired a power of sovereignty in order to protect the community requires, in the French context, to depict him as something other than the holder of a mere executive function: for instance the representative of the state as a non-specialized constitutional entity.

In any event, there is only a limited degree of functional separation of powers in the Constitution, as the prominence of the executive in the 1958 Constitution means that it has been granted powers to intervene in all of the main state functions. Like any other written constitution, the 1958 enactment devolves legal capacities to the different 'executive' agencies. Some of these are traditionally identified as executive: the President nominates the Prime Minister and the other ministers, Article 8. He is head of the armed forces, Article 15, although Article 20 also states that the government 'has authority over the armed forces'. Similarly, the power to enact regulations is also shared between the President and the Prime Minister. The President only enacts 'ordinances', subordinate legislation adopted on the basis of an enabling Act of Parliament, and 'decrees discussed in *Conseil des ministres*'. The other central regulatory powers belong exclusively to the Prime Minister, Article 21, but normally not to the ministers. Ministers do not normally have an inherent power to enact regulations: they must be empowered by a statute. In the absence of such a statute, and if courts are unwilling to acknowledge the existence of an 'inherent power' (a topic to which I shall turn later) they act incompetently, and their decisions can be annulled judicially. There are also some executive powers which are neither legislative nor judicial, although they do not fall in the category of 'administrative powers'. This is especially the case of the executive powers in the field of international relations and national security: for instance, the President nominates ambassadors and gives letters of credit to foreign diplomats, Article 14; he is head of the armed forces, Article 15. A declaration of war, however, must be authorized by Parliament, Article 35, although, in recent cases, some military interventions of a more limited kind have not been subjected to that constraint. Other major military powers are not discussed in the Constitution: it is a mere

---

[21] C.E., 8 August 1919, *Labonne*, 737.
[22] See J.M. Denquin, 'Georges Burdeau et le pouvoir d'Etat dans la constitution de 1958' (1991) *Droits* 14, 141–52.

decree which empowers the President, and the President alone, to decide that France will make use of its nuclear weapons.[23]

The executive is also granted constitutional means to intervene in the functioning of Parliament and in the legislative function. Let us take only a few examples of this category of powers. The Prime Minister may initiate legislation, Article 39, and the *gouvernement* can lay down amendments, Article 44. The *gouvernment* can arbitrate a conflict between the two houses by submitting a bill on the text of which both houses have failed to agree to a special body which will try to broker a settlement, Article 45. To the President belongs the power to dissolve the national assembly, Article 12. The President and the Prime Minister are among the authorities empowered to bring a bill before the *Conseil Constitutionnel*, France's constitutional court, Article 62. The President can also decide to ask the electorate to pass a bill on a limited set of subject-matters, enumerated in Article 11, by way of a referendum. This is an exception to Parliament's monopoly over legislation. Finally, the executive is devolved some powers belonging to the judicial function. The President is, according to Article 64, 'the guardian of the judicial power', ('*pouvoir judiciaire*' which in French means only the ordinary courts, deciding private and criminal law cases, not the administrative courts and the *Conseil Constitutionnel*). To the President also belong some traditional judicial prerogatives of a head of state, such as pardon, Article 17.

This broad sketch does not exhaust the scope of executive powers. Defining this scope in more precise terms has proved difficult for theoretical reasons. The majority opinion, which identified executive power with an administrative function, was not easily reconciled with the view that the administrative function could lend itself to a substantial definition, or in other words that its scope could be defined by a set of subject-matter which would by essence be 'executive' or 'administrative'. Such an undertaking was effectively dismissed by Carré de Malberg, who established, convincingly in the logic of the majority opinion, that no specific sphere of attributions could adequately be described as the executive's province. The very assertion that executive agencies ought to act, if not always with a view to carrying into execution a statute, at least under statutory or constitutional authorization, made it impossible to assert that there was a special field of administrative or executive matters: any matter touched by the legislature became, as such, one in which the administration could intervene.

In fact, attempts were made to move in the opposite direction, namely to define restrictively a special sphere of legislative matters. During the third republic, the executive was enabled by statutes to enact regulations in fields previously covered by legislation. During the fourth republic, this attempt was reiterated, under stronger constitutional pressure, since Article 13 of the 1946 Constitution explicitly prohibited any delegation of its legislative power by the

---

[23] Decree 96–520 of 16 June 1996 (esp. Art. 5).

national assembly. In 1953, the *Conseil d'Etat*, acting in its consultative capacity, advised the government that this method was, in its view, constitutional only if the delegation did not extend to a certain set of subject-matters belonging exclusively to the legislature's competence. This set of reserved matters was delimited by reference to a 'republican constitutional tradition' and to the constitution.[24] This pattern was reproduced in the 1958 Constitution, which restricted the province of the legislature to a limited number of subject-matters.

Conversely, the scope of the regulatory power of the executive (*'pouvoir réglementaire'*) is residual. As such, it covers all the subject-matters not mentioned in Article 34, and in other enabling clauses scattered throughout the Constitution. As a result, Article 37(1) describes an omnicompetent executive, with the exception of the matters expressly devolved to the legislature. The *Conseil Constitutionnel* has interpreted Articles 34 and 37(1) as creating a distinction which the executive could use quite freely: it is able to prevent Parliament from encroaching upon the executive's ground by using two specific constitutional procedures, Articles 41 and 37(2).[25] But the use of these procedures is optional: an encroachment upon the field of 'autonomous' regulations does not make a statute incompatible with the Constitution. It will not be quashed, at least for this reason, by the *Conseil Constitutionnel* under Article 61(2).

We may sum up the state of the law as follows: the executive is at liberty to create law by way of autonomous regulations or by initiating, or letting representatives initiate, parliamentary legislation. If this legislation encroaches upon the field of autonomous regulations, the executive may or may not close its eyes to it. A greater freedom one can hardly imagine.

2. Control of executive action

(a) Judicial review

The French system of judicial review of administrative action is based on a principle of autonomy: a specific body of public law rules are being adjudicated by a specialized hierarchy of administrative courts, at the top of which stands the *Conseil d'Etat*. These courts are competent regarding 'administrative litigation': *'le contentieux de l'administration'*. What was meant by this was difficult to ascertain, as administration can mean either 'public authorities' or 'public services' in a functional sense. One must put the question this way: is the decision an administrative one? If it is so, administrative courts will be competent to examine its legality according to public law rules. Normally, the decision of a

---

[24] The C.E. had already anticipated this reasoning in a 1906 case (C.E., 4 May 1906, *Babin*). See B. Stirn, note No 2 (*avis du 6 février 1953*) in Y. Gaudemet et al., *Les Grands Avis du Conseil d'Etat* (Dalloz, 2nd. edn., 2002), 75.

[25] C.C., DC 82–143, 30 July 1982, *'blocage des prix et des revenues'*.

public authority is subject to administrative law courts, while the matter is more complex when public services are being devolved, as they frequently are, to private persons. For the sake of simplicity I will focus on unilateral decisions, setting aside public contracts and the question of non-contractual liability.

When the decision is identified as an *'acte administratif'*, it is subjected to control for legality. This framework of judicial review does not grant a specific status to executive decisions: as far as administrative courts are concerned, either they are administrative decisions, and if so it is as if they had been adopted by the humblest of civil servants, or they are not, and administrative courts will decline jurisdiction. In many cases, the fact that a minister or even the head of state is the author of the decision will not be relevant. This is a normal feature of a legal system in which the rule of law applies to all authorities. Having said this, it is nonetheless the case that the treatment of executive action in the framework of judicial review has some specific features. The fact that a decision was adopted by the President, the Prime Minister or an individual minister has an impact on the administrative court which will be competent to hear an application for judicial review. As a general rule, *the Conseil d'Etat* is the court of first instance of executive decisions. This may either be because of their form, the decree of 30 September 2003 making the *Conseil d'Etat* competent to hear applications against 'décrets' and 'ordonnances', the highest type of executive decisions. It may alternatively be because of their content: the *Conseil d'Etat*, in its capacity as a court, is competent to hear first instance applications against the administrative decisions of ministers when they have a regulatory content, *'actes réglementaires'* as opposed to nominative measures,[26] or when the law states that they must be adopted with the advice of the *Conseil d'Etat*, in its capacity as the *gouvernement's* legal counsel.[27] However important those peculiarities are, I will not attempt to draw an exhaustive picture of the law of judicial review as it applies to executive authorities. Rather, I will focus on some specific problems.

(b) Executive action and administrative action: the theory of *'actes de gouvernement'*

The first question that an administrative court has to resolve is that of its own competence. The question at stake is that of the nature of each decision: if labelled an 'administrative decision', it will be potentially subject to judicial review. Conversely, the label *'actes de gouvernement'* refers to a type of decision which the courts refuse to review. Only rarely is it possible to conclude that administrative courts have denied their jurisdiction on that basis. But this category is of particular interest for several reasons. In the twentieth century, public lawyers have been little concerned with traditional questions of political theory. They abandoned to others the question of the elucidation of such concepts as

---

[26] Decree of 30 July 1963. [27] Decree of 13 June 1966.

'government' or 'executive power'. Despite their rarity, *actes de gouvernement* exemplify the way in which these problems bounced back into public law litigation. They also show how the question of which decisions are liable to be judicially reviewed interacts with the scope of executive action. In other words, in a litigation-based science of public law, 'accountability', and 'scope' are not entirely distinct questions.

Actes de gouvernement are decisions whose authors are, with only a few exceptions, higher executive authorities, mainly the President, Prime Minister and other ministers. Some belong to the sphere of constitutional interactions between the executive and Parliament, such as a decree of dissolution, decisions taken by executive authorities in the course of the public bill procedure, and promulgation of statutes. Others belong to the sphere of international relations, such as use of the President's treaty-making power and diplomatic interventions of various kinds.[28] These decisions are not justiciable. The existence of *actes de gouvernement* is probably justified by the acknowledgement, on the part of courts and academic writers, that executive agencies have powers which are not 'administrative' by nature. When the President decides to dissolve the National Assembly, or makes use of his treaty-making power, it cannot be said that this is an administrative kind of action: 'they are not administrative decisions as they are not made in order to carry statutes into execution.'[29] But the problem lies in the definition of the activity. It is far from certain that all the decisions labelled as *actes de gouvernement* belong to the same 'function'. Some could be linked to the legislative function, such as when, for instance, the Prime Minister lays down a bill before one of the houses. But others do not fit nicely into one of the 'functions' traditionally identified in state activity. This led some authors to identify new functions such as a 'diplomatic' one.

A more general approach, favoured by many distinguished authors, was to identify a 'governmental function' corresponding to the *actes de gouvernement*. Legal analysis, says Chapus, forces us to acknowledge that governmental activity can have a character which is not administrative.[30] However, it is more difficult to define positively this 'non-administrative yet governmental' function. Some lawyers have argued that the governmental function could not be defined in legal terms, as it corresponds to no specific type of decision. They seem to bring this point home, but this may just mean that government is not a function. It is an activity which can manifest itself through a large variety of legal forms. Some happen to be '*actes administratifs*': they are justiciable before administrative courts. Some can be subsumed under another legal category: the use of the President's prerogative of pardon used to be labelled as an *acte de gouvernement*.

---

[28] These paragraphs owe a great deal to the work of Pierre Serrand, 'Actes de Gouvernement', in *Dictionnaire de la Culture Juridique* (P.U.F., 2002), 14–17; and *L'acte de gouvernement (contribution à la théorie des fonctions juridiques de l'Etat)* (Thèse de doctorat en droit, Paris II, 1996).   [29] R. Capitant, quoted by P. Serrand, *L'acte de Gouvernement*, n. 28, 434–5.
[30] R. Chapus, '*L'acte de gouvernement, monstre ou victime*' (Dalloz, 1958), 5–10.

But since 1947, it is considered to be a judicial measure: administrative courts still decline jurisdiction, but this is because the nature of the decision, as it is now characterized, falls under the jurisdiction of the other 'order': the judiciary (*juridictions judiciaires*). But when none of these existing legal characterizations, being themselves litigation-based concepts meant to define a certain court's field of jurisdiction, applies to a governmental decision, it is likely that it will be called, negatively, an *acte de gouvernement*, although it should more appropriately be called an '*acte de gouvernement* which cannot be characterized at the same time as an *acte administratif*'.

Analysis in terms of legal forms stops here, and the further study of the *acte de gouvernement* would, I think, require another type of reasoning. *Actes de gouvernement* are not unlike the trail of air bubbles which a charged particle leaves when it passes through a bubble chamber. They are a trace that something has happened. The thing itself (*die Sache selbst*) courts are ill-equipped to observe. Government is often a legally shapeless phenomenon. It exists independently of legal or even constitutional enactments. Moreover, it does not fit easily into a legal 'function': *actes de gouvernement* pop up at the contact point between the activity of constitutional agencies and the sphere of sovereignty. They are traces of a phenomenon to which modern public law was blind from birth: the possible fusion of government and sovereignty, or rather the moment at which sovereignty cannot remain in the calm sphere of legislation where it has been relegated by democratic constitutionalism. There are times at which the sovereign nature of the ruler's action has to be acknowledged—for instance by a judicial grant of non-justiciability, as immunity has traditionally been an appendage of sovereignty—despite the care taken by democratic constitutionalism to prevent rulers from appropriating sovereignty.[31] Diplomatic *actes de gouvernement* exemplify this situation where sovereignty is repatriated in the sphere of governmental action. Similarly, the declaration of an 'Article 16' state of emergency by the President can certainly be explained in terms of a constitutional authority taking over sovereignty in order to confront a peril. It is a matter of sovereignty because the very existence of the body politic is at stake, and because this forces a (partial and temporary) merger of (normally separated) state functions: the President is empowered, or at least this power is acknowledged to belong to him, to take measures which would belong to other 'powers', such as the legislature, in normal times. It is also a matter of sovereignty because the ruler's action is based on necessity.

This analysis of *actes de gouvernement* as instances of governing sovereignty (*souveraineté gouvernante*) does not aim at explaining away all the occurrences of the phenomenon in case law. It is not an administrative law theory, a theory of what administrative courts do with the words that administrative courts use or could use, but rather a tentative interpretation of the phenomenon in terms of

---

[31] A warning to the effect that sovereignty belongs to the nation only and cannot be appropriated by a man or a body of men is inserted in the 1789 declaration of rights (Art. 5) and repeated in the 1946 (Art. 3) and the 1958 (Art. 3) Constitutions.

political theory. It is not meant to deny, either, that the frontier between *actes de gouvernement* and *acte administratif* is a fuzzy and a moving one, precisely because it is the result of a joint venture between courts who deny jurisdiction for various, often opaque, motives, and technical academic writing. As a matter of fact, there has been a tendency on the part of administrative courts to shrink the area of *actes de gouvernement* and extend their review. In 1962, the *Conseil d'Etat* refused to extend the immunity from judicial review to executive regulations adopted, not in the context of Article 16, but on the basis of a legislative measure enacted by way of a popular referendum.[32] The court decided that, though the President was enabled by the act to enact '*ordonnances*' which, in terms of subject-matter, intervened in the field covered by Article 34 in which Parliament is normally competent, he was not thereby granted a capacity to 'legislate',[33] but only to act as an administrative authority enacting regulations. As a result, the President's measures were subject to a full control of legality. The regulation, which created a special court in order to judge offences committed in Algeria, contained a very general ouster clause which was deemed a breach of 'the general principles of criminal law'. It was thus annulled.

Less spectacularly, the same result is often reached by distinguishing between a core non-justiciable decision and other measures which are detached from it in order to be subjected to judicial review. This is emphatically the case with the special powers granted to the President by Article 16 of the 1958 Constitution. The President's decision to use these powers is a non-justiciable *acte de gouvernement*. But the measures taken by the President in the use of the extended powers he is granted in the period during which, as French lawyers have it, 'Article 16 is declared' are themselves fully justiciable if they happen to be administrative decisions, as in the case of a regulation adopted in the field of Article 37 of the 1958 Constitution, the so-called 'autonomous regulations'.[34] The field of justiciable measures in the sphere of diplomatic relations has vastly increased in recent times: decisions are made justiciable by the acknowledgement that they are 'detachable' from foreign relations. Thus, what we observe is not abandonment of the category of *actes de gouvernement*, but simply an increasing recognition by courts of their ability to identify elements of legality in executive action, in a way which empowers them to judicially review new aspects of this action.

(c) Defining executive powers in the context of judicial review

If the administrative court identifies the existence of an administrative decision, it may subject this decision to several tests of legality, depending on the

---

[32] C.E., 19 October 1962, *Canal, Robin et Godot*, 552.

[33] In French, the word '*législation*' is only used in the context of primary legislation: what would be called in English 'subordinate legislation' is called in French '*pouvoir réglementaire*', a term which bears no analogy with parliamentary legislation.

[34] C.E., 2 March 1962, *Rubin de Servens*, rec. 143.

arguments contained in the statement of claim and, more rarely, on questions of legality which the court has to raise even if they have been omitted by the claimant (*moyens d'ordre public*). They are traditionally (and with some procedural consequences, notably as to the time limit applying to the statement of claim) divided into two categories: 'external legality', namely tests regarding the form of the decision and the competence of its author; and 'internal legality', namely the fact that the content of the decision conforms to the superior norm's content. Some rules are specific to executive measures. This is especially the case with questions of competence. The importance of executive decisions is such that the *Conseil d'Etat* takes a strict view of the procedural requirements for their enactment. For instance, the requirement, for some decrees or other regulations, that the *Conseil d'Etat* itself should be consulted as an advisory body, has been treated by the *Conseil d'Etat* acting as a court not as a matter of mere procedure but, more strangely, as one of competence: decrees adopted without consulting the *Conseil d'Etat*, in a case where this advice was compulsory, are said to be incompetently adopted, and therefore illegal. Procedurally, this move enables the *Conseil d'Etat* to raise the issue even if the claimant has not pointed to it in the statement of claim (*moyen d'ordre public*). But there is more to it than mere procedural convenience. In so doing, the *Conseil d'Etat* raises its own participation in the making of the decision from that of an advisory body to that of a co-author.

But, apart from those peculiarities, the judicial treatment of executive decisions raises questions of principle about the legal status of executive action in French public law. The dearth of indications regarding the foundation and scope of executive action in the French constitutions would not have been a serious problem if it had not been for the view that everything the executive did had to be based on either statute or constitution. It took a lot of skill, or maybe of faith, systematically to relate executive action to a written enactment. The *Heyriès* case[35] is a good example of these difficulties. The First World War and the extension of executive powers during the time of hostilities generated a certain amount of litigation before administrative courts. In most cases, special acts of Parliament with a retrospective effect had validated wartime administrative measures which would have otherwise been bound to be annulled, as they were obviously *ultra vires* at the time at which they had been adopted. A legislative draftsman's slip of the pen caused a *décret*, a regulation enacted by the *Président de la République*, to be omitted from the scope of a 1915 Act of Indemnity. The decree's purpose was to suspend some procedural rights granted by statute to civil servants, notably the right to access their administrative file before a disciplinary sanction is issued against them. Suspension of Acts of Parliament is normally not a power which belongs to the *Président de la République*, not because of an explicit prohibition of the type contained in the British Bill of

---

[35] C.E., 28 June 1918, *Heyriès*, 651.

Rights of 1689 but, implicitly, because of the hierarchy of norms in the French legal system. There is in French administrative law a 'fundamental rule', namely the principle of legality, according to which 'regulations and decrees are subordinate to Acts of Parliament and cannot undertake anything against them'.[36] At the same time, this hierarchy of norms reflects a hierarchy of state agencies and functions: how can one expect that the holder of a subordinate, 'administrative' function, should be enabled to set aside statutes passed by the 'representative of the national will', namely Parliament?

The *Conseil d'Etat* nevertheless managed to rescue the decree from illegality by deciding that Article 3 of the constitutional statute of 25 February 1875 put the President at the head of the French administration and mandated him to carry laws into execution. As a result, it was incumbent upon him to make sure that, at all times, public services would be in working order. Wartime necessities certainly played a part in the reasoning which led to affirming the legality of the decree. But the *Conseil d'Etat* was careful to ground this decision, in want of an appropriate statute, on a constitutional basis. The decision was welcomed by Hauriou as a break with the unhealthy habit of defining the executive power only by the duty to carry statutes into execution. The executive's mission, he said, was twofold: firstly to ensure the proper functioning of the administration and also of government; secondly to carry statutes into execution. This truth, said Hauriou, was now unveiled: 'it took the war. But, under such a light, some truths are glaring'.[37] Hauriou stood first among the holders of the minority view on the executive. He believed that it could not be made to collapse into an administrative function. Especially, he did not see it as subordinate. He saw it as the primary activity in the state. As a result, he welcomed the *Heyriès* case. One could have taken another view of the same matter. Indeed, if justified by necessity, executive suspension of procedural rights had not been deemed illegal, or more precisely, its illegality had been covered up by a reference to a constitutional authorization. But one could also analyse the *Conseil d'Etat*'s solution as a rather unconvincing attempt to find at any cost a legal basis for a decision otherwise doomed to be annulled. In other words, the notion that all executive actions have to be authorized by written law either statutory or constitutional was stretched to the extent of becoming entirely fictional. Under appropriate construction, Article 3 of the constitutional act of 25 February 1875, which made no reference to war powers or necessity, could be made to justify almost anything.

Also at issue in the *Heyriès* case was the '*pouvoir d'organisation du service*': the power belonging to the heads of administrative/executive agencies to make arrangements, by way of regulations, for the proper functioning of their service. It is in this field that one finds a rare instance of inherent administrative powers in French public law: the *Jamart* case. In 1936, the *Conseil d'Etat* began a line of

---

[36] M. Hauriou, *Notes d'arrêt sur décision du Conseil d'Etat et du Tribunal des Conflits publiées au recueil Sirey de 1892 à 1928* (Sirey, 1929), Tome 1, 81.   [37] *Ibid.*

cases in which ministers, who are normally not enabled to enact regulations except under statutory authorization, are nevertheless granted a power, as heads of service, to 'take the necessary measures with a view to the proper functioning of the services under their authority'. It is no surprise that such a power should be justified by 'the necessities of service'.[38] In other words, necessity, big (as in the *Heyriès* case) or small (as in *Jamart*), is a mark of government. When, in 1969, she (unsuccessfully) defended the view that ministers should be granted an autonomous power to enact regulations in the sphere of tax incentives to businesses, the *Commissaire du Gouvernement* Questiaux said that this power was justified in the light of 'the necessities of the guarantee of citizens' rights [and] the necessities of modern administrative action'.[39] The term 'necessity' indicates the moment at which the tasks of executive agencies cannot be subsumed under the administrative function, with its subordinate legal status, and must be justified, not by written law, but by 'the pressure of facts'. In such circumstances, courts are forced to acknowledge that 'facts' may have an inherent force to generate legal action: they empower the rulers to act without prior textual authorization. But it is only exceptionally that courts have acknowledged the existence of inherent executive powers. This was emphatically the case of the police powers of the third republic President, whose duty it was 'in the absence of any legislative delegation and as a part of his inherent powers (*pouvoirs propres*) to determine those police measures which must in any case apply on the whole territory'.[40]

(d) Constitutional review of executive action

In the course of judicial review of executive action by administrative courts, the hierarchy of norms can take a specific profile. As a rule, the *Conseil d'Etat* is the judge of legality, in the sense that it will only enforce legislative rules and principles of equal force. It is not, as a matter of principle, a constitutional court. There are situations, however, in which the executive acts without being authorized by an Act of Parliament, and without being subjected to existing legislative measures. This is especially the case of the 'autonomous regulations' of Article 37. As a result, the 'legality' of the decision is not so much constrained by measures of a legislative nature as by higher, constitutional, rules. To use the analogy familiar to French lawyers, it is as if the 'screen' of legislative norms which normally constrain administrative action had been 'lifted'. As a result, the courts are enabled, and indeed compelled, to check the validity of administrative

---

[38] See *Commissaire du Gouvernement* Bernard's *'conclusions'*, on the 'UNAPEL' case, C.E., 6 October 1961, *Revue du Droit Public*, 1961, 1279.

[39] *'conclusions'* on the *Société Distilleries Brabant* case, C.E., 23 May 1969, 272 (footnote). The court did not follow the *commissaire*'s recommendation on this point.

[40] C.E., 8 August 1919, *Labonne*, 737. This solution has been transposed to the Fifth republic's *gouvernement* (C.E., 4 June 1975, *Bouvet de la Maisonneuve*, 330).

decisions with regard to constitutional norms. In the key case '*Syndicat Général des Ingénieurs Conseils*'[41] an engineers' union applied for judicial review of a decree regulating their profession in the French overseas territories. The decree widened the scope of a monopoly granted to architects with regard to the construction of buildings, as a result of which the ability of engineers to work in that field was hampered. Because of the peculiarity of overseas legislation, the decree was not an ordinary one. It did not implement a statute; in that case, the executive authority was a primary legislator. As a result, the 'legislative screen' was lifted. The territory was one in which metropolitan statutes had no force except when incorporated into local law by an executive regulation. But the *Conseil d'Etat* stated that, even though the minister could legislate by decree for those departments, he was compelled to act constitutionally. The 'legality' to which the decree was submitted included norms of constitutional force, such as the general principles ('*principes généraux du droit*') contained in the preamble to the 1946 Constitution. Expressed with regard to the law as it resulted from the 1946 Constitution, the solution flourished under the fifth republic. Article 37 of the 1958 Constitution created a category of regulations which did not rely on a prior legislative authorization: as far as '*réglements autonomes*' are concerned, the legislative screen is lifted at all times, as they operate in a field (a set of subject-matters) distinct from that of parliamentary legislation.

The *Conseil d'Etat* was thus brought to examine the constitutionality of executive measures, although it is not normally a constitutional court. Symmetrically, the *Conseil Constitutionnel*, the constitutional court created by the 1958 Constitution, is a judge of legislative measures, and does not normally review executive measures. But it has a say on the constitutionality of the legislative process, in which the fifth republic's executive takes an important part. As a result, the constitutional court's interpretation of the Constitution binds the executive, as exemplified by the jurisprudence on legislative delegations. In Article 38 of the Constitution, the delegation given by Parliament to the executive in order to enact regulations in legislative matters is delimited by the government's 'programme': the *Conseil Constitutionnel* has interpreted this clause as 'compelling the *gouvernement* to indicate with precision...what is the purpose of the measures it intends to take'.[42] Similarly the *Conseil Constitutionnel* has set limits to the *gouvernement*'s use of its power to lay down amendments in the course of the public bill procedure. There are, says the court in a bout of creative writing, 'inherent limits to the amending power' and if the *gouvernement* (or, indeed, members of parliament) exceeds these limits, this could result in the quashing of the corresponding clause in the bill. This development of constitutional review is far from negligible. It targets one of the core aspects of governmental activity: the initiation of legislation, and through it, the ability to trigger state action.

[41] C.E., 26 June 1959, 394.   [42] C.C. DC 76–72, 12 January 1977.

(e) Criminal liability of executive authorities

Like many other democracies, fifth republic France has witnessed the rise of the ideology of the rule of law. For better or worse, the reshaping of executive activity in the Constitution was paralleled by an extension of judicial review of executive action, based on internal sources and also on international law. In general, submission of the executive to 'the rule of law' means submission to what is meant to be the ordinary law (*le droit commun*). It does not, as a result, consist in an attempt better to define the meaning and scope of executive action. It is precisely this gap between the philosophy of the 1958 text and the ideology of the rule of law which is visible in the question of the criminal liability of executive authorities. As far as ministers are concerned, Article 68-1 of the Constitution, introduced by a constitutional statute of 27 July 1993, makes ministers liable for offences committed during their time in office, which were defined by positive law either as crimes or as misdemeanours at the time they were perpetrated. This has been interpreted as a move towards a greater submission of officials to the ordinary law of the land.

The status of the President is more complex. Article 68 states that he is not liable for offences committed in the course of his functions, except if he has committed a 'high treason', a term that the Constitution does not define. The distinct question of the President's liability for crimes or misdemeanours detachable from his constitutional duties has recently come to the fore. In a context where the present head of state has been involved in several criminal inquiries regarding his behaviour as Mayor of Paris and head of a political party before his presidential term, the *Conseil Constitutionnel* and the *Cour de Cassation* (the top court of the judiciary) have reached different conclusions about the state of the law. In 1999,[43] the constitutional court decided that the President was not covered by an immunity, but only by a '*privilège*': only a special court, the *Haute Cour de Justice* (Articles 67 and 68 of the Constitution) was competent to judge him during his term as President. In a later case,[44] the *Cour de Cassation* decided firstly that it was not bound in this matter by the *Conseil Constitutionnel*'s *res judicata*; secondly that the *Haute Cour de Justice*'s competence extended only to high treason and not to acts detachable from his office; and thirdly that the President could be tried by ordinary courts for this category of offences only after the end of his term.

These difficulties spring from the necessity to strike a balance between the need to grant a legal immunity to those in charge of executive action, and the growing hostility against the impunity of rulers. Nowhere is this hostility more evident than in the 1998 Treaty of Rome creating the International Criminal Court. There was an obvious incompatibility between some of the clauses of the

---

[43] C.C., D.C. No 98–408 du 22 janvier 1999, traité portant statut de la cour pénale internationale,
[44] Cour de Cassation, arrêt No 481, 10 October 2001, M. Michel Breisacher.

Treaty, notably Article 27 insofar as it denied that 'official capacity as head of state' exempted a person from criminal liability under its provisions, and the immunities granted by the French Constitution to the President, the ministers, and other office-holders. The Constitution has been revised in order to make the ratification of the Treaty possible. Significantly, this has been done, in a blunt and somewhat inelegant way, by inserting a clause (Article 53–2) to the effect that 'the republic is allowed to acknowledge the jurisdiction' of the International Criminal Court. It was decided not to amend Article 68 in order to restrict the President's constitutional immunity. In a non-technical sense, the substantive conflict between the rule granting immunity and the rule denying immunity has not been removed: it has been set in constitutional stone.

(f) Political accountability

In France, the parliamentary model is only one of several traditions which must be taken into account in order to understand the relationship between the executive and Parliament. The early republican tradition of *'gouvernement d'assemblée'* was based on the notion that the legislature was the only legitimate mouthpiece of the general will. As a result, the executive was not equal in dignity to the house, but a mere agent. An instance of this is the Constitution of the fourth republic. At other times in French constitutional history, there developed a different view which insisted on the political autonomy of the executive. This was the case under the 1814 Charter, as it restored a divine right king who did not owe his throne to the nation. The head of state could also be autonomous from the houses in a democratic context. This was the case in the 1848 Constitution where the *Président de la République* was, for the first time, elected directly by the people.

These two foundations of executive legitimacy have, strangely enough, managed to co-exist at certain times with the parliamentary tradition. It is not the purpose of this chapter to study in depth the roots of this latter tradition in France. Suffice it to say that it developed during the 1814–1848 period, during the Restoration and the July Monarchy. After a period of non-parliamentary regimes, the Second Republic and the Second Empire, the 1875 Constitution restored cabinet responsibility and the principle that ministers needed a majority in parliament to support their policies and measures. The 1946 (fourth republic) and 1958 (fifth republic) Constitutions retained this parliamentary character and 'rationalized' parliamentarism by entrenching its core mechanisms, motions of censure, votes of confidence at the initiative of the cabinet, and dissolution, in detailed constitutional clauses which imposed specific majorities, time limits, and other procedural requirements.

The orientation of this 'rationalization' was however very different in 1946 and 1958. In 1946 it was meant to provide securities for the National Assembly's primacy while limiting the rapid turnover of ministries falling victim to votes of no confidence. In 1958, conversely, the new philosophy of institutions, which aimed at consolidating 'the state' by giving sufficient authority to the executive and especially to the *Président de la République*, was oriented in the opposite direction, since the executive was given means to force its will upon the two chambers. 1958 witnessed the end of what had been, quite ironically, called in France the 'supremacy of Parliament'. This was not, as in the UK, a legal principle proclaiming the supremacy of acts of parliament, but the assertion of the houses' political primacy in the régime, at the expense of both the executive and the people. Examination of the nature of the regime established in 1958 can provide other insights into the French understanding of 'executive power'. For the reasons already mentioned, it was possible to analyse the new Constitution as removing, at least in part, the cover previously thrown on the real nature of the executive. At the same time, the 1958 Constitution merges at least two of the previously examined traditions: the one in which the head of state is independent from the houses, the other in which the cabinet derives its legitimacy from the houses. The fifth republic is based on the rejection of a third tradition, that of the '*gouvernement d'assemblée*' of which De Gaulle had been very critical in his 1946 blueprint for an alternative constitution (the 'Bayeux' discourse). As far as legitimacy is concerned, therefore, the notion that the executive should be an agent of Parliament was set aside in 1958. But, as we have seen, as far as legality is concerned, it is still alive.

Since 1962, the President has been elected 'by universal suffrage' (the formula by which some democratic societies hypostasize the electorate by naming it after the rule which defines its legal boundaries). To the 'people', another name given to the electorate, thus belongs the power to choose the President. This does not mean that the 'head of state' is unaccountable. In fact, direct popular designation of the President has been understood as creating a direct relationship between President and people. What the people does when it elects a President, the people cannot undo except at the next election, since there is no recall procedure in the 1958 Constitution. Neither is the President accountable to Parliament. But the President is master of his own fate: he can decide to test his legitimacy through different means. He can seek the electorate's confidence by running for another term. This is an instance of what some theorists have called 'electoral accountability', in order to distinguish it from parliamentary responsibility. But this is not the only one: De Gaulle developed a practice of threatening to resign in case the electorate voted negatively in the referendums he summoned. French referendums are binding: the people are empowered by Article 11 of the Constitution to enact statutes instead of Parliament in a limited number of areas. Only the President can summon such a referendum, and De Gaulle considered that his legitimacy was at stake in each of them. He resigned in 1969 just a few hours after the electorate had turned down a bill reforming the Senate and introducing ambitious economic reform. De Gaulle's followers have not done the same. They have consistently refused to make their stay in office depend on the results of any vote other than the Presidential election. The result is that

François Mitterrand did not feel compelled to resign as a consequence of the majority change at the 1986 general election. This generated a new constitutional situation: the coexistence between a right-wing cabinet, relying on a parliamentary majority, and of a left-wing President, designated at an earlier date by the universal suffrage. To sum up, the President is not politically accountable, except when he decides to become so.

The fifth republic is *also* a parliamentary regime. Very conspicuous in the constitutional enactment are the defining features of such a regime, notably cabinet accountability to parliament, Articles 20, 49, and 50. The link between government and accountability is made visible in Article 20:

[T]he *gouvernement* determines and conducts the nation's policy. It has authority over the *administration* and the armed forces. It is accountable to parliament.

Article 49 creates four procedures: the fourth one empowers the Prime Minister to request from the Senate, the second chamber, a vote on a motion of 'general policy'. The Senate can thereby express its confidence in the ministry, or lack thereof, but this vote will be deprived of any consequence. Article 50, unlike the three other procedures involving the National Assembly, does not make resignation compulsory. Conversely, defiance based on the three other procedures compels the *gouvernement* to resign. Article 49(1) allows the Prime Minister to request the confidence of the National Assembly on the government's programme or on a declaration of general policy. Article 49(2) gives to at least one tenth of MPs the reciprocal power to put down a motion of no confidence. It will only be passed if it is voted by a majority of all MPs, knowing that only votes against the government are counted in support of the motion (abstentions being counted as implicitly expressing confidence). Despite the imbalance in favour of the ministry, which is a feature of the type of rationalization embodied in the 1958 Constitution, these are classical features of a parliamentary regime. More original is the procedure of Article 49(3): the Prime Minister can stake the house's confidence on a bill. The bill is considered as adopted if a motion of no confidence is not laid down in the following twenty-four hours and voted in accordance with the conditions in Article 49(2). This is considered to be a means of forcing a reluctant majority to vote for a measure: the ministry threatens to resign if the bill is not passed.

Through Article 49 the cabinet's legitimacy is derived at least in part from the confidence of the National Assembly. But, and here lies the difference with a more traditional parliamentary regime, Parliament has lost the monopoly of political representation in the regime. In the fifth republic, the President is the incarnation of a superior type of legitimacy. The legitimacy of Parliament has been weakened: its enactments only express, says the *Conseil Constitutionnel*, the general will when they are pursuant to the Constitution. Since 1958, the existence of constitutional judicial review, something new in the French context, is a manifestation of this loss of symbolic value. As a result, there are at least two channels through which legitimacy is communicated to the *gouvernement*. On the one hand, there is a President designated by universal suffrage and entrusted with large constitutional prerogatives, amongst which is a power to designate the Prime Minister and the other cabinet members, and a customary power to replace them at will (even if, as in 1972, the Prime Minister had very recently enjoyed a vote of confidence in Parliament). On the other hand, there is a democratically elected house and a ministry, embodying the ordinary relationship between such institutions in any parliamentary regime. The Constitution does not choose between these two options. The analysis of the different possibilities generated by this state of affairs would involve a study of the relations between the President on one hand and the *gouvernement*/parliamentary majority on the other. At some periods, the power of the President has been paramount and has oriented in his favour the construction of the constitutional clauses. At other periods, those of *cohabitation*, the parliamentary nature of the regime has come back to the forefront, and Presidential authority has been curtailed.

8

The Growth of the Italian Executive

*Giacinto della Cananea**

1. The executive in Italy: insufficient or excessive power?

By the end of the 1970s, the weakness of the Italian executive was becoming increasingly evident. Economic difficulties (oil crises and high inflation), the launch of the new fifteen regions (with bodies elected twenty-two years after the Constitution of 1948) and serious political tensions created by the social conflict and terrorism of those years all resulted in a singular form of government by assembly. The strong Communist party's exclusion from government was compensated for by a tendency to include it in decision-making by way of parliamentary negotiations and compromises.[1] Such a method was applied, above all, in relation to the bills approving increased or new forms of spending, often financed by the creation of new debt. Such a state of affairs gave rise, among constitutional lawyers and political scientists, to the notion of Parliament's 'centrality'. It also led some North American political scientists to wonder whether a government actually existed in Italy.[2]

Some twenty-five years later, many observers share quite the opposite concern. Since 1994, the new electoral rules have strengthened the executive's constitutional position vis à vis Parliament. The number of rules enacted either by the Council of Ministers or by individual ministers has seen a spectacular rise since the end of the 1980s, particularly during the last ten years. Since the reforms carried out in 1992–93 by the Amato government in fields such as health, social security and the civil service, their political importance has grown, too.[3] At the same time, European integration has enhanced the role of both members of the

---

* I wish to thank Sabino Cassese and Gaetano D'Auria for their helpful comments on a earlier draft of this paper. Catharine De Rienzo translated a first draft of the text. Any errors and omissions are, however, mine.

[1] See A. Predieri (ed.), *Il Parlamento nel sistema politico italiano* (Comunità, 1975).

[2] For a critical discussion of this thesis, see S. Cassese, *Is there a Government in Italy? Politics and Administration at the Top*, in R. Rose and E. Suleiman (eds.), *Presidents and Prime Minister* (AEI, 1980), 171.

[3] G. della Cananea, 'Reforming the State: The Policy of Administrative Reform in Italy under the Ciampi Government' (1996) 19 *West European Politics* 321.

Council of Ministers and senior civil servants, all of whom are included in European Union (EU) decision-making procedures.

There is thus a growing concern amongst public lawyers that the constitutional balance of powers between Parliament and the executive has been altered. This opinion reflects the dominant tradition in legal and political studies of Italian institutions which is based on the idea that Parliament is (almost) omnipotent insofar as it is vested with popular sovereignty. The legitimacy of all other institutions is, in contrast, indirect since it is drawn from Parliament. Every departure from such a model represents a violation of the Constitution. A different point of view emphasizes that the actions of public institutions are not established once and for all by law but are inevitably marked by conflict. The ups and downs of more traditional parliamentary power to decide the budget provide the best support for such an approach. Whilst the first cultural tradition has received considerably more attention from legal academics, this chapter intends to develop certain aspects inspired by the second.[4] As a result, this chapter will not only focus on the relationship between Parliament and the executive, but it will also consider the wider institutional framework, including the evolution of the relationship between central and decentralized government.

2. The decline of the executive after 1948

When considering the executive's powers from an historical perspective, it soon becomes evident that Italy has experienced different variations in the balance of power in different periods. The country's political unification in 1861 was achieved on the basis of a model of public administration that was dominated by a centralized machine subordinate to the executive, rather than one entrusted to Parliament and the courts, such as in England until the Victorian era. The institutional framework was thus Napoleonic in its derivation, though its distinguishing feature was a proliferation of derogations for particular public bodies. Already present during the era of Cavour and his successors, the executive's supremacy over other powers became more marked under Francesco Crispi around 1890.[5] It was necessary to wait until the first fifteen years of the twentieth century (dominated by the figure of Giovanni Giolitti) to see Parliament make a partial come-back. This process was interrupted, however, by the First World War and then by Fascism, which set up a 'Prime Minister's regime'.[6]

The most prominent feature of the democratic Constitution adopted in 1948 is a reaction to that involution of parliamentary government. With the aim of

---

[4] A seminal contribution on academics' positions is that of N. Bobbio, *Ideological Profile of Twentieth Century Italy* (Princeton University Press, transl. by L.C. Cochrane, 1995).

[5] S. Cassese, *Lo Stato introvabile* (Donzelli, 1997), 22 and 'Toward a European Model of Public Administration', in D.S. Clark (ed.), *Comparative and Private International Law. Essays in Honor of John Henry Merryman* (Duncker & Humblot, 1990), 355.

[6] S. Romano, *Corso di diritto costituzionale* (Cedam, 1940), 213.

preventing Caesarism, the Constitution not only established the Regions (to allow a distribution of legislative and administrative powers), but also gave Parliament a position of pre-eminence. The Chambers give their vote of confidence or no-confidence in the government and receive the results of the checks carried out by the Court of Auditors on government actions. Perhaps the most striking feature of the Italian Constitution, in this respect, is the differentiated way in which the traditional functions of the state are defined. While legislative and judicial powers are identified and clearly attributed to Parliament and the courts, the executive's jurisdiction is neither identified nor attributed. Rather, it is a residual concept. Not even one of the executive's most characteristic powers, namely, that of issuing regulations (roughly corresponding to UK statutory instruments), is expressly attributed to the government. It is only mentioned incidentally, by the provision in the Constitution that attributes the signing of such regulations to the President of the Republic, Article 87.

Parliament's pre-eminence became more marked with effect from the 1960s. The shift of decision-making power to Parliament resulted in excessive law-making. This, in turn, generated a vicious circle since, constitutionally, a new law is required to modify (or, at worst, repeal) every law.[7] From the 1960s onwards, numerous spending laws with long-term effect for the financing of education, health and, particularly, social security entitlement programmes have weakened the executive's control over spending.[8]

As noted earlier, all these factors led some American observers to emphasize the executive's weakness. In fact, a more accurate analysis might have permitted the observation that the short life of successive individual governments did not necessarily lead to changes in fundamental political choices, in the political majority that expressed them, or in the identity of the main ministers. Moreover, parliamentary omnipotence in the field of legislation was belied for two reasons.

On the one hand, most laws were developed in ministerial offices, with the result that it would be necessary to re-read the relationship between ministerial bureaucrats and Parliament in a sense that recalls the '*gesta Francorum per Deum*' rather than the '*gesta Dei per Francos*'. On the other hand, the government was the '*dominus*' of any statute's implementation once it had been approved. Quite frequently, it applied statutes only partially and after delays, thereby provoking further reaction from Parliament in the form of new legislation aimed at limiting the executive's discretionary power.

---

[7] See S. Cassese, 'L'inflation législative et réglementaire en Italie', in C. Debbasch (sous la direction de), *L'inflation législative et réglémentaire en Europe* (C.N.R.S., 1986), 17.

[8] V. Onida, 'The Historical and Constitutional Foundations of the Budgetary System in Italy' and S. Cassese, 'Special Problems of Budgetary Decision-Making in Italy', in D. Coombes (ed.), *The Power of the Purse. The Role of European Parliaments in Budgetary Decisions* (P.E.P., 1975), 215 and 254. On the changes of the 1990s see M. Bull and M. Rhodes, 'Between Crisis and Transition: Italian Politics in the 1990s', in M. Bull and M. Rhodes (eds.), *Crisis and Transition in Italian Politics* (1997) 20 *West European Politics, Special Issue* 1–14.

There nevertheless resulted a singular confusion over legislative and executive power. Weak governments appeared as the child of Parliament (or, indeed, of the political parties it represented), but were still capable of paralysing its political choices. This was particularly so as regards the management of public spending. Not even the grafting of democracy by referendum onto the praxis of government by assembly brought any relief. Twenty-six referenda have taken place in Italy during the period 1974–93, as against two in the United Kingdom. These referenda (others have been excluded by the Constitutional Court),[9] have dealt, first, with civil rights, such as divorce and abortion in the 1970s; secondly, with political rights, especially in the case of the rules for the election of the Chamber of Deputies in 1993; thirdly, with the organization and functioning of public administrations, especially in 1993, when the statutes establishing two central departments were abolished by the electorate.[10] During this period, it is correct to say that referenda have allowed certain decisions to be referred to the electorate who had been deprived of the possibility of having an impact on the choice of government. However, democracy by referendum has also reinforced the political system's Rousseauan component, at the expense of the division of powers following Locke and Montesquieu.

3. The changing role of the executive during the last twenty years

(a) From indirect to direct legitimacy

The situation described above began to change in the 1980s, when the executive's capacity to make decisions and take action autonomously regained ground. In 1980 the Minister of the Treasury decided to restore the autonomy of the central bank (*Banca d'Italia*), which was no longer obliged to support deficit spending policies. Three years later, the executive abolished the mechanism for increasing salaries in line with inflation, obtaining unforeseen support from the electorate in the referendum subsequently requested by the opposition. Some

---

[9] Art. 75 of the Constitution provides that: '1. A popular referendum shall be held to abrogate, totally or partially, a law or an act having the force of law, when requested by five hundred thousand electors or five regional councils. 2. A referendum is not permitted in the case of tax, budget, amnesty and pardon law, in authorization or ratification of international treaties' (unofficial translation provided by the Secretariat general of the Chamber of Deputies, *Costituzione della Repubblica italiana* Rome, 1990). Not only have the limits stemming from the second paragraph been widely interpreted by the Constitutional Court, for example as regards laws different from the budget, but having financial implications, but the Court has also introduced other limits, by way of standards of clarity and coherence of the questions proposed by the committees promoting the referendum. There is certainly no lack of studies on referenda, though many of them are mainly descriptive. See G.M. Salerno, *Il referendum* (Cedam, 1992).

[10] The results of the referenda are illustrated in (1993) 16 *West European Politics* 607–15. For a fuller account, see G. della Cananea, 'Paradoxes of Administrative Reforms in Italy', in J.J. Hesse, C. Hood and B.G. Peters (eds.), *Paradoxes in Public Sector Reform* (Duncker & Humblot, 2003), 273–87.

military operations were conducted abroad (Lebanon in the 1980s, Iraq in 1991) despite strong opposition in both Houses of Parliament.[11]

A more profound transformation was produced by the electorate's decision in the referendum on the electoral system (1993). The latter repealed the laws providing for the election of deputies on a proportional basis and thus made changes in the electoral law necessary. Such changes were carried out by Parliament during the XI legislature (1992–94). Under the new system, since 1994,[12] a three-fourths majoritarian and one fourth proportional system, the electorate tends to choose not only the members of Parliament who represent it but also the highest levels of the executive that govern it. The trend has been accentuated by the decision taken during the XIII legislature (1996–2001) to allow ballot papers to indicate the name of the candidate for the premiership together with those of the parties. Such developments have created a tension with the laws of the 1948 Constitution, which is still in force.

First of all, the Constitution presupposed a proportional system through which it tempered the strength of the parliamentary majority. This is no longer the case. For this reason, the electoral majority (which may be a minority of the population) gives greater weight both to the parliamentary majority and to the government that it supports.

Secondly, some constitutional conventions developed during the period when Parliament was conceived as the place representing all the forces present in society. For example, according to one such convention, no amendment of the Constitution was possible without a vote greatly exceeding the absolute majority required by Article 138. Furthermore, the parliamentary majority abstained from electing its own representatives as speakers of both Chambers, leaving one Chamber to a representative of one of the opposition parties. Once the constitutional premise of the proportional electoral system no longer existed, both conventions fell into disuse: the second, the day after the first election held on the majority basis and the first on the eve of the third round of voting.[13]

Last but not least, there exists strong tension between majoritarian democracy and the 1948 Constitution as regards the power to dissolve the Chambers. The Italian Constitution, unlike the British one, does not attribute this power to the Prime Minister but, rather, to the President of the Republic. The latter can also appoint a government backed by a majority other than the one that won the election, as occurred in 1994. Clearly, the existence of such presidential power is

---

[11] P. Furlong, 'Parliament in Italian Politics' (1990) 13 *West European Politics* 62.

[12] On this point, see F. Sidoti, 'The Significance of Italian Elections' (1994) 29 *Government and Opposition* 336–7.

[13] Curiously enough, for more than twelve years all political parties debated constitutional reforms in ad hoc committees, but large majorities have not been reached or even attempted since 1994. Although constitutional conventions were legally relevant, there has been a lack of studies after the book of G.U. Rescigno, *Le convenzioni costituzionali* (Cedam, 1972), which probably reveals the prevailing positivist attitude of Italian public lawyers.

not in issue.[14] It is, rather, a question of observing the conflict that may derive from the referendum choice to deprive Parliament and the political parties of the power to choose the government.[15] The transformation brought about by the new method for choosing members of Parliament is all the more important in that its impact has not just been felt at a national level. Indeed, the new national law was preceded by the issue of a new electoral law governing town councils (once again, spurred by a referendum result). Thanks to this law, mayors are elected directly, on a vote that is separate even from supporting parties and movements. More recently, provision has been made for the direct election of regional Presidents (1999).[16]

Other forms of legitimacy have also been added or have reinforced the confidence the Chambers accord the executive. One such is legitimation deriving from results (not even the empires of the past would have been able to keep going by brute force alone). This has long been neglected in Italy, but matters have recently changed. As noticed earlier, the electorate has had some influence by expressing its negative opinion through the referendum request to repeal the laws founding a series of public offices. A less rudimentary technique for expressing opinions was introduced in 1994 by way of charters for public utilities, following the model of the British *Citizen's Charter*. These charters allow users to express their vote and, in some cases, permit the reimbursement of expenses sustained.

The constitutional position of the executive has also been strengthened by the need to respect the EU criteria for the reduction of both public debt and deficit. Since the main political goal of the 1990s was financial recovery, especially when Carlo Azeglio Ciampi was Minister of the Treasury, the executive succeeded in imposing unprecedented reductions in the financial resources transferred to local government, universities, and public enterprises, as well as in the sums of money spent in the health sector. These unpopular decisions were taken following ordinary budgetary procedure, naturally. However, they were taken on the basis of standards which were no longer established by Parliament but, rather, by the Ecofin council. Even before the electoral system was modified, therefore, the foundations were laid for depriving Parliament of a fundamental decision, i.e. the size of the deficit.

Another form of legitimacy to which the legal order is attaching growing importance is that based on procedures. The basic law on Government,

---

[14] However, the Berlusconi government is trying to modify the Constitution in that respect: for a critical examination of this project, see P. Calderisi, F. Cintioli and G. Pitruzzella (eds.), *La Costituzione promessa* (Soveria Mannelli, Rubbettino, 2004).

[15] For further comments on this point, see S. Cassese, *Maggioranza e minoranza. Il problema della democrazia in Italia* (Garzanti, 1995); A. Manzella, 'La transition institutionnelle', in S. Cassese (sous la direction de), *Portrait de l'Italie actuelle* (La documentation française, 2001), 55.

[16] Among those who argue that the new electoral systems enhance the constitutional role of the electorate, see T.E. Frosini, *Forme di governo e partecipazione popolare* (Giappichelli, 2002). But see also, G. Pasquino, 'The Government, the Opposition and the President of the Republic' [2003] *Journal of Modern Italian Studies* 498.

No. 400/1988, took an important first step in this direction. This law established that all regulations (whether governmental, ministerial or inter-ministerial) must bear the name 'regulation'. Moreover, no regulation can enter into force unless it has previously been submitted to the Council of State, the opinion of which is rarely disregarded by the Council of Ministers.[17] Legitimacy based on procedure is thereby reinforced although, in principle, there is no provision for the hearing of interested parties.

This kind of procedural legitimacy has become increasingly important with the advent of the majoritarian system. The majoritarian system allows those governing to make decisions without having either to negotiate their content with the parliamentary opposition or to listen to minority interests. At the same time, however, the need to hear and consult parties representing other (environmental, social, and cultural) interests is becoming increasingly urgent. In contrast, something may be learned from the failure of important political initiatives taken by governments enjoying comfortable majorities simply because they were not preceded by adequate negotiations and agreements with social and economic forces, the regions or local authorities. For example, Law No. 443/2001 and its implementing rules entrust government with the power to approve plans for works that constitute strategic infrastructures of significant national interest. However, in the case where the works are also of regional interest, the state decision cannot disregard the consent of the region in whose territory the work is to be carried out. The decision is otherwise unlawful, as has recently been established by the Constitutional Court.[18]

A more sophisticated procedural regime is that of regulatory authorities set up since the late 1970s. Their rules are in continual expansion, albeit known by various names (guidelines, standards, etc.) and they not only concern the economy, but the social sphere as well. The problem of their legitimacy has consequently arisen, since they do not act under the direction of elected politicians. Several steps have been taken by legislation, accordingly, to strengthen their procedural legitimacy (*legitimation durch verfahren*). However, regulatory authorities, such as the CONSOB (*Commissione nazionale per le società e la borsa*, set up in 1979) in the field of financial services and the AGCOM (*Autorità per le garanzie nelle comunicazioni*, set up in 1997) for telecommunications and television, are not bound by the detailed rules established by Law No. 241/1990 in order to enhance the right to be heard.[19] Indeed they must only respect the broad principles of openness and transparency of that law, but at the same time they must adopt their own regulations. These regulations provide that before adopting new rules or changing the old ones, the authorities must publish (both

---

[17] S. Cassese, 'L'attività consultiva del Consiglio di Stato in materia di norme', in G. Paleologo (ed.), *I Consigli di Stato di Francia e d'Italie* (Giuffrè, 1998), 87.

[18] Constitutional Court, judgment No. 233/2004, available at the site www.cortecostituzionale.it.

[19] See M. D'Alberti, 'La 'visione' e la 'voce': le garanzie di partecipazione ai procedimenti amministrativi' (2000) 49 *Rivista trimestrale di diritto pubblico* 179.

in their bulletins and in their web site) a document explaining the broad policy guidelines which they intend to follow. Only the gas and energy regulator (AEEG), however, has constantly followed the *notice and comment*'s requirements, publishing both the draft document and the comments received from private parties. A less satisfactory record is that of the AGCOM. For example, after beginning the open consultation in view of adopting a regulation on rights of way for the building of new infrastructures, not only has it refrained from adopting it, but it has failed to provide any justification for doing so. This explains, by the way, why legislation has changed, in order to entrust government with the power to adopt that regulation.[20]

(b) The executive's powers

This brings us to the question of the powers enjoyed by the national government. These powers include making political choices about individual and collective interests, enacting rules, adopting other decisions, such as appointment of higher civil servants and members of state-owned companies.

The entrenchment of the executive's powers involves, first of all, the exercise of sovereignty abroad. Until a few years ago it could be said that sovereignty (in the strict sense) had been exercised only twice during the period of the Republic: first through membership of NATO and then by participation in the European Community (now the European Union). The strategic decision to install new defence weapons (the so-called Euro-missiles) during the 1980s may be considered an application of the first, just as adherence to the European Monetary System was an application of the second. Subsequently, however, with the two Iraqi conflicts, the decision was taken to participate in armed intervention beyond the confines of the countries belonging to NATO. Unlike in other situations, in both these cases Parliament and the country were sharply divided. Furthermore, there emerged uncertainty regarding entitlement to command the armed forces. This was resolved at the beginning of the 1990s in the sense that formally this power lies with the President of the Republic, aided by a specific collegial body, the Supreme Defence Council. Another military intervention outside NATO borders is worth mentioning, since parliamentary debate took place while Italian airplanes were already targeting Serbian forces.

Another line of development regarding government powers involves a series of decisions concerning specific policies. Emergency powers, always part of the executive's arsenal, are one example. These powers have been extended by the laws on environmental protection and civil defence. An Act of Parliament, for example, provides that the President of the Council of Ministers' orders dealing with an environmental crisis may derogate from all legislative rules.[21] At the

[20] See the decree No. 259/2003, which implements EC directives No. 19, 20, 21 and 22/2002.
[21] Article 5, law No. 225/1992. For a restrictive interpretation, see Consiglio di Stato, judgment of 13 November 2002, No. 6280, *Giornale di diritto amministrativo*, 2003, 1157.

same time, in an economic context, when European directives abolished public utilities' monopolies, the government reserved itself a golden share along British lines and in conflict with the European laws that safeguard the free movement of capital.[22]

During the same period there has been an unprecedented rise of governmental legislation, although in a strict sense, the executive has no legislative function. In accordance with Articles 76 and 77 of the Constitution, it may assume such a function in only two eventualities. The first concerns decree laws, the other delegated legislation. Decree laws lay down necessary and urgent norms, have the status of primary legislation, and expire if they are not converted into law within sixty days. Although this is a derogation from the general rule that legislation is reserved to the Chambers (Article 70), the situation is different in actual fact. Well before the 1990s the Council of Ministers issued a vast number of decrees having force of law (*decreti-legge*) and these governed areas extending almost as far as those covered by ordinary laws.[23] They have even been renewed more than once in cases where they have not been ratified. This abuse has been at least partly ended in 1996, due to a judgment of the Constitutional Court which held renewal to be illegal.[24] Accordingly, the number of *decreti-legge* decreased: while the Prodi government enacted an average of eight each month, those led by D'Alema and Amato limited themselves to three. The Berlusconi government is currently adopting almost four *decreti-legge* each month.[25]

There has nevertheless been a remarkable increase in governmental rules. In the first twenty-nine months of activity, the Prodi government (1996–9) adopted 407 acts having force of law (*decreti-legge* and delegated legislation) and 158 regulations, whilst the Berlusconi government (2001–4) has adopted 244 acts having force of law and 144 regulations. However, the latter has also adopted 1,188 acts containing secondary rules (average 40 per month) against the 1,005 of the former (thirty-five each month).[26]

Meanwhile, several other rules are adopted by way of administrative decrees with regard to both the organization and functioning of public administration and the relations between private parties. An interesting example is offered by a recent decree. Under the new Article 117 of the Constitution, the state has an exclusive competence with regard to the adoption of statutes laying down basic standards concerning the protection of civil and social rights. In the field of

[22] Case C-58/99, *European Commission v. Italy* [2000] ECR I-3811 holding that the golden share infringes Arts. 52 and 59 EC.

[23] See A. Celotto, *L'abuso; del decreto-legge*, (Cedam, 1997).

[24] Constitutional Court, judgment No. 360/1996, available at the web site www.cortecostituzionale.it.

[25] The data are taken from an analysis carried out twice a year: G. Napolitano (ed.), 'L'attività normativa del Governo: luglio-dicembre 2003' (2003) *Rivista trimestrale di diritto pubblico* 478–9. On the years 1994–98, see G. Vesperini (ed.), *I governi del maggioritario* (Donzelli, 1998).

[26] These acts include decrees of the President of the Republic, governmental regulations, decrees and directives of the President of the Council of Ministers, and his orders of a normative nature *ordinanze*). These data, too, are taken from G. Napolitano, n. 25, 475–7.

health, however, the statute simply gave the government broad discretionary power to decide these standards. The governmental decree (not having the nature of regulation, but of an administrative act) was thus challenged before administrative courts, but Parliament gave legislative force to the decree with an *ex post* statute. As a result, the administrative court of appeal dismissed the action.[27]

The growing volume of governmental rules has two main causes. The first is European integration. The steady increase in the number of directives approved by the EC Council of Ministers for the purpose of achieving the Single Market has allowed the executive to free itself from Parliament's supremacy in the legislative process. Since 1989, moreover, Parliament approves a yearly bill (*la legge comunitaria*) to ratify directives which are subsequently implemented by the executive either in the form of delegated legislation or as regulations. The other cause is the need to reform the organization and functioning of most public institutions and the legal framework for the delivery of public services. Although Parliament approved the administrative reforms of the 1990s, it has increasingly limited itself to stating objectives and referring implementation to a series of delegated legislative decrees.

As a result of the growth of the executive's rule-making powers, not only have the procedures for enacting rules been modified (as noted earlier) but their publicity has also been improved. The consolidated rules adopted by the government under Decree No. 1092 in 1985 provided that not only all primary rules adopted by Parliament, but also all secondary and tertiary rules adopted by the executive should be published.[28] Law No. 241/1990 then established that all general measures regarding the public administration's organization and procedures must be published.[29]

Despite the fact that it is quicker and simpler for the government to enact its own rules, the volume of statute law itself originating from the executive is also increasing. A few years ago it was calculated that the bills drawn up on Parliament's initiative represented approximately three quarters of those put before the Chambers, yet only one tenth became law as against between 80–90 per cent of the bills prepared by the government.[30] More recently, in the first two years of its activity, the Berlusconi government presented 241 bills to Parliament (as compared to the 423 of the Prodi government). Together with the *decreti-legge*, however, these constitute the source of more than 90 per cent of the spending laws. It may therefore be said that primary legislation is largely governmental.

---

[27] Consiglio di Stato, section IV, judgment of 4 February 2004, n. 398.
[28] L. Paladin, *Le fonti del diritto italiano* (Cedam, 1996), 45.
[29] For a detailed analysis, see D. Sorace, 'Administrative Law', in S. Lena and U. Mattei (eds.), *Introduction to Italian Law* (Kluwer, 2002), 133.
[30] G. D'Auria, 'La 'funzione legislativa' dell'amministrazione' (1995) *Rivista trimestrale di diritto pubblico* 705.

(c) The executive's resources: money and staff

The executive's power depends not only on the elements examined above, but also results from the tighter control being exercised over two resources that are fundamental for public action: money and staff. Three factors converge in the financial system to reinforce the executive's position of pre-eminence.

The first, already indicated, is the EU. Since it is the Council, on the Commission's proposal, which decides about public debt and deficit, the government recovers a fraction of the power ceded by the state to the EU and restricts the decisions lying with Parliament.

The second factor regards the Finance Act which, since 1978, exists in addition to the Budget Act. The Finance Act is the main politically driven measure in the economic field. It is preceded by a governmental paper, the economic and financial planning document, which indicates the net balance to be financed. Once the Chambers have approved this during the summer budgetary session, they are bound by it when they approve the Finance Act. The latter, moreover, allows the government to modulate the financing of spending laws previously issued. Lastly, the amount of expenditure fixed by the Finance Act cannot be varied by individual spending laws. The Finance Act is therefore a powerful instrument for limiting parliamentary choices.

The third factor is the executive's capacity to have a determining influence on the Budget's implementation. Indeed, the Budget requires a certain number of actions to be taken either by individual ministers or by the committees in which they participate. A central responsibility lies with the Ministry of Economy and Finance. Recently, a new Act of Parliament consolidated the long-exercised power to suspend disbursements when their related funds have been or are about to be exhausted (the so-called 'spending cuts').[31]

The executive's other power concerns the choice of top civil servants. Until 1972, top civil servants lacked a specific status. Even after that, for twenty years they had no powers of their own that were distinct from those enjoyed by politicians. Autonomous powers for senior civil servants were provided for only in 1993, together with changes in the recruitment system in line with the principles of impartiality and sound administration established by the Constitution.[32] In 1998, a new statute (proposed by the Prodi government) was passed by the Parliament, introducing instead what is considered as a sort of 'spoils system'. It was subsequently reinforced in 2001 by the Berlusconi government (Law No. 145/2002).

The new legislative framework provides that the sixty top ranking civil servants are appointed by each government. When the latter changes, the former

---

[31] Although some observers criticized these provisions, they are not 'anomalous' from a comparative point of view: see R. Perez (ed.), *Le limitazioni governative della spesa* (Giuffrè, 2003).

[32] S. Battini, 'Administration et politique en Italie: des logiques contradictoires' (1998) 86 *Revue française d'administration publique*, 205.

must be re-appointed or replaced. Also the approximately 6,000 second-ranking senior officials are appointed for a maximum of three years. At the end of this period, they may be replaced without any obligation to give reasons for such a decision. After one further year, they may lose their position if the government does not re-appoint them. Such a result is, according to several observers, in contrast with the principles of impartiality and efficiency laid down by the Constitution. It is not at all surprising, accordingly, that both the new legal framework and the decisions based on it have been challenged before the courts. Administrative courts have sought to interpret the new legislative rules in accordance with constitutional principles, in accordance with the judicial policy of preserving legislation if there is at least one way to reconcile it with those principles. The results, however, are far from being fully satisfactory, particularly the attempt by a lower administrative court to qualify the relationship between politicians and senior officials in terms of 'technical reliance'.[33] The only serious way to verify it is to carry out the checks provided by legislation, but these checks are never carried out. As a consequence, the judgment is based only on other factors, sometimes of arbitrary nature.

If we look at the actual meaning and effects of this legislative framework, it becomes evident that it infringes the constitutional requirement of impartiality. It is not necessary to support the old system in order to realize that the current one is doubly unacceptable. In the first place, it subjects not only the top bureaucrats but also a great number of second-ranking senior officials to the constraints resulting from political and even trade-union power. Furthermore, this result, which is incompatible with constitutional principles, is even more undesirable in a prevalently majoritarian electoral system. Not only is the competence and impartiality of the administration at stake, but also the proper functioning of majoritarian democracy, which exceeds its own constitutional limits.[34] For these reasons, it was a gross mistake of the Constitutional Court to underestimate the conflict between this law and principles in the Constitution.[35]

(d) A weak corrective: decentralization

In modern structures of government, a corrective to the majoritarian principle consists of balancing one majority against another majority in different parts of the national territory. The institution of the regions in the 1970s permitted forces that were a minority at national level to govern important regions,

---

[33] Tribunale amministrativo regionale per il Lazio, judgment of 21 maggio 2003, n. 3277 *Giornale di diritto amministrativo*, 2003, 1141.

[34] S. Cassese, *Merit System and Spoils System: US and Italy Compared*, unpublished paper, 2003 and 'Il nuovo regime dei dirigenti pubblici italiani: una modificazione costituzionale' (2003) *Giornale di diritto amministrativo* 1342; S. Battini, 'Il personale' (2004) *Giornale di diritto amministrativo* 787.

[35] Constitutional Court, judgment No. 313/1996, available at the web site www.cortecostituzionale.it.

thereby contributing to the formation of an administrative culture. The direct election of Mayors has worked in the same direction, contributing to a renewal in political management.

The importance of this type of corrective[36] is apparently heightened by the much-debated constitutional reform approved in 2001. This substituted the whole of Title V of the second part of the Constitution which deals with the regions and local authorities. It inverted the criterion for dividing legislative competence between central and local government in the sense that the former enjoys only those exclusive and concurrent competences[37] expressly attributed to it, whereas the regions enjoy both those attributed to them and all residual ones as well. Furthermore, the constitutional reform, in principle, assigned administrative competences to local authorities, except in the cases where the need for a unitary exercise of power justified the attribution of competence to national authorities. The protection of competition constitutes one such example. Lastly, state monitoring of the regions and the local authorities has been abolished, with the exception of the overall financial costs to be examined by the Court of Auditors.

The effectiveness of the corrective provided by decentralization has been undermined by two contrasting obstacles: the reformers' excesses and the difficulty created by central government over ceding a part of its powers. The reform of the Constitution has carried decentralization to levels that were unrealistic, given numerous small-scale councils' limited ability to govern complex issues, or incongruous, when concurrent legislative competences have been provided for.[38] Consider, for example, the regulation of telecommunications and energy sources. On the one hand, the choice to allow the regions to dictate differentiated laws for activities that require uniform rules (such as the construction of infrastructures) is controversial, since it can lead to different rules governing the same administrative procedures and costs for private enterprises. On the other, since the inclusion of these sectors amongst those covered by concurrent legislation leads to a prohibition against state-issued regulations, one may ask whether the prohibition also holds for the regulatory authorities whose responsibility it is to implement the Community laws.

The other difficulty has revealed itself in two ways. The first is the inertia of the central majority. This phenomenon is similar to the one that became

---

[36] In this sense, see S. Cassese, 'Pouvoir local, Région, Fédéralisme: leur contribution à une démocratie pluraliste en Italie', in J. De Lanversin (sous la direction de), *Démocratie et aménagement* (L.G.D.J., 1996), 113–19; S. Cassese and L. Torchia, 'The Meso Level in Italy', in L.J. Sharpe (ed.), *The Rise of Meso Government in Europe* (Sage, 1993), 91, 114.

[37] The areas for exclusive state legislation include, in particular, defence, law and order, justice and financial equalization. Health, education, the professions, the regulation of telecommunications, big infrastructures and energy sources are amongst the subjects for concurrent legislation.

[38] In contrast with modern theories of federal or quasi-federal governments (W. Oates, 'An Essay on Fiscal Federalism' (1999) *Journal of Economic Literature* 1120), shared competences include some twenty broad areas.

manifest after the Constitution came into force in 1948. Indeed, the new constitutional rules require a series of laws and decrees for their implementation. For example, in matters of concurrent legislation, the state is responsible for deciding the fundamental principles whereas the regions are to issue the detailed laws. The central government has nevertheless refrained from establishing the fundamental principles and, when some of the regions issued their own laws, turned to the Constitutional Court seeking their annulment. The Court did not accept the argument that the state's prior intervention is indispensable because that would have prevented the regions from making laws. In other judgments, however, it has interpreted state legislative and, above all, administrative power in a broad sense. It has established, in particular, that if the state enjoys administrative competences in a given sector, it may make tertiary rules for their exercise, forestalling the issue of differentiated laws by the regions.[39]

The other way in which the central government controls local government is through the power of the purse strings. In a situation of marked economic dualism, as is the case in Italy, it is inevitable that the Constitution attributes to the state a duty to equalize financial resources. Were this not so, numerous regional and local governments would not be able to provide primary services the cost of which they cannot sustain, especially in the health sector. Yet the central government that finances local governments also constitutes a limit to the autonomy of the regions and the local authorities that are capable of being self-financing. Moreover, it often ends up intervening in the running of subsidized activities. In other words, there is nothing surprising about a decisive financial backer also wanting to make the decisions. This explains why the regions and the local authorities carry on acting like lobbies through organizations such as the National Association of Italian Town Councils (Anci—*l'Associazione nazionale dei comuni d'Italia*) and the Union of Italian Provinces (Upi—*l'Unione delle province italiane*), seeking greater transfer of money and powers in favour of decentralized government.

(e) Disregard for legislative limits circumscribing the executive

The problem created by the imbalance between the increased ambitions of central governments and their weak constitutional checks during the difficult transition from proportional to majoritarian democracy becomes more evident if two other aspects are considered: the restrictions placed on the assumption of public office and the limits deriving from the jurisdiction attributed to independent regulatory authorities.

Within the first category fall numerous statutes that, according to the individual case, prescribe particular requirements governing eligibility for public

---

[39] Constitutional Court, judgement No. 303/2003, available at the web site www.cortecostituzionale.it.

appointments or office. Other statutes forbid the permanence of the appointment or limit either the actions of the person holding office or acceptance of further public posts. These stratagems differ in their practical implications, ineligibility, in the first case and incompatibility, in the second.[40] They nevertheless pursue the same goal: only apparently paradoxically, they intend to limit democracy so as to protect it from its own excesses. They are extremely important in the Italian institutional framework for two reasons. Firstly, according to the Constitution, sovereignty belongs to the people, rather than Parliament, as in England, but is exercised in ways established by law, (Article 1). Even the power of the people, therefore, is subject to limits and conditions. Secondly, since the majoritarian principle accentuates that power, those limits and conditions have to be re-defined.

Yet it was only on the eve of the first election under the majoritarian system that it was noted that the Italian law of 1953 was rudimentary and inadequate. It took it for granted that the members of the government were members of Parliament, whereas they might or might not be. The 'technical' ministers, that is to say those who have not been elected, but chosen by the President of the Council of Ministers either for their personal prestige or for their capacities (academics, professionals, members of administrative elites), for example, are not. Moreover, by a further paradox, the few limits to which the members of government are subject are narrower in their scope than those applicable to the professional civil servants working under them. The prohibition against the licensee of public television services assuming any public office issuing the licences was not applied immediately after the 1994 election, nor subsequently.[41] The current state of affairs is therefore far from satisfactory.

To remedy the matter and after a long and controversial debate, Parliament has just approved a law aimed at avoiding the creation of a conflict of interests. Law No. 215/2004 works on three levels. In the first place, it forbids those in government posts to hold other public or private offices which may give rise to a conflict of interest. For example, belonging to a company's board of directors or practising as a lawyer is prohibited. In the second place, it puts the holders of government posts under a series of duties to provide information. In the third place, it attributes tasks of surveillance and powers to impose sanctions on two independent authorities: the antitrust authority and the television and telecommunications regulator (AGCOM). However, the law defines the conflict of interests as the action of the person in charge of a public office, who takes illicit profit from it, therefore failing to resolve the underlying problem arising

---

[40] S. Cassese—B.G. Mattarella (eds.), *Democrazia e cariche pubbliche* (Il Mulino, 1996).

[41] See A. Pace, 'Ineleggibilità, incompatibilità e conflitto d'interessi dei parlamentari e dei titolari di organi di governo', in S. Cassese—B.G. Mattarella (eds.), n. 40, 53–72 and 'La proprietà di emittenti televisive determina ineleggibilità parlamentare, non solo incompatibilità nelle cariche di governo', in www.associazionedeicostituzionalisti.it/dibattiti/conflitto/pace.htm (for the thesis that the lack of the legal requirements does not merely produce the duty to design after the elections, but is an obstacle to the election).

not from the action or inaction, but from the inherent conflict between individual and collective interests.[42]

Moreover, the independent authorities face serious difficulties starting with the modalities of appointment and the limited human resources at their disposal. As far as the electronic communications sector is concerned, there is considerable doubt regarding the authorities' actual independence from vested interests. Although Law No. 249/1997 establishes that the existence of a dominant position (without the additional element of its abuse) is sufficient for the regulating authority to be obliged to issue orders and sanctions, the telecommunications regulator has refrained from doing so. The fact that it felt that it could justify its behaviour with the debatable argument that the increased percentage of the market held by the two oligopolist operators was the fruit of a 'spontaneous' market trend was only further proof of the difficulty of getting neutral powers to take root.

What is more, the executive has sought to limit their authority in various ways. A recent example concerns one of the regulatory bodies just mentioned, the television and telecommunications regulator. Whilst, in accordance with Community directives, its institutive law gave the authority the task of issuing licences for radio and television broadcasting over the airspace (a limited public good), a subsequent law gave it back to the government. In the same way, the new consolidated rules adopted by the Ministry of Telecommunications give it jurisdiction that, on the basis of EC law, lies with an authority that is independent of vested interests.[43] This is not an isolated problem, as is demonstrated by the recent government's plan to suppress another regulator, that for electricity and gas. Eventually, the plan was abandoned. If it had not been dropped the violation of European laws would have been even more flagrant.

4. Accountability: political and legal

(a) Parliament's ineffective scrutiny of the executive

One of the negative consequences of government by assembly existing less recently in Italy was the lack of interest in monitoring shown by MPs. This was particularly manifest in the financial field. What both the majority and the opposition MPs were really interested in was deciding expenditure rather than verifying its correct management. Confirmation of this fact may be found in

---

[42] B. Mattarella, 'Conflitto di interessi: quello che le norme non dicono' (2004) *Giornale di diritto amministrativo* 1285 (for the thesis that the problem does not lie in the illicit advantages that a given politician may obtain, but in the influence which may be played on the electorate).

[43] For a comparison with other regulators in Europe, see M. Thatcher, 'Regulation after Delegation: Independent Regulatory Agencies in Europe' (2002) 9 *JEPP* 954, 960. The problem of independence has been raised, for example, by the President of ISTAT, the Italian statistical office: see the interview given to *Il Sole—24 Ore*, 10 March 2005, 2.

repeated breaches of the constitutional law providing for the annual approval of the closing balances or statements of account, (Article 81, first sub-section).

The situation could have changed as a result of the application of the majoritarian principle to parliamentary elections, since this principle allows the elected majority to make all the decisions. For this reason, several external observers, including the present author, hypothesized that the minorities would lose the power to co-decide and, as a consequence, would have an interest in checking the way power was exercised, so as to inform citizens in view of new elections. The monitoring carried out by other public offices on Parliament's behalf should therefore have been reinforced and the opposition should have chaired the control committees.

Ten years later, the result is far from comforting, however, both as regards the controls carried out on the initiative of MPs and those that ought to be carried out on the basis of the reports made by numerous public offices. In the first case, Parliamentary questioning and interpellation are gone through as a weary ritual, arousing little or no interest in institutions or in the nation. Not even the inquiries provided for by parliamentary decisions have proved effective for carrying out controls, as has been seen in the case of the one on the use and abuse of funds set aside for reconstructing the parts of the *Mezzogiorno* involved in the 1980 earthquake. The introduction of 'question-time', along British lines, has brought a limited improvement but there remains much ground to cover if a new constitutional status of the opposition is to be perfected.[44]

The situation is decidedly worse as regards the monitoring Parliament carries out on the basis of reports prepared by other public offices. Important reforms were approved in this field during the last decade of the twentieth century. These first reduced and then eliminated the state's *ex ante* checks on the regions and local authorities. They provided that all public offices should set up their own internal control systems and that the Court of Auditors should supervise their proper functioning. They reduced the preventive checks that the Court of Auditors carries out on government rules and decisions and strengthened subsequent checks on financial management and on individual policies (e.g. health and employment).

If we look at the concrete reality, however, the changes have been modest. The internal control offices are still missing in some parts of public administration, whilst in some others (regional ones, above all) they perform their tasks only formalistically.[45] Once the *ex ante* checks lying with the Court of Auditors had been reduced, the central budget offices increased their own. However, the preventive checks entrusted to the *Ragioneria generale dello Stato*, one of

[44] A recent survey shows that only rarely is the President of the Council of Ministers in both Houses of Parliament during question-time: see G. Rivosecchi, 'Quali rimedi all'inattuazione del 'Premier question time'?, in www.forumcostituzionale.it/contributi/prospettive/htm.

[45] See G. della Cananea and L. Fiorentino (eds.), *Le gestioni finanziarie pubbliche* (Ministero dell'economia e delle finanze, 2003.)

the Italian Treasury departments, constitute one such inconsistency: on the admission of its head, they are very costly and not very useful. As for the Court of Auditors, it lies at the centre of the system of renewed controls but struggles to adapt its role to its new tasks. Indeed, it tends to fill its monitoring of management with matters proper to the monitoring of legality to which it dedicated itself in the past. Not by chance, it has not availed itself of the option to employ not only lawyers but experts from various other disciplines as well.

For its part, Parliament pays little or no attention to the work carried out by other offices. Some cases may serve to demonstrate this. For example, the law requires the Minister for the Civil Service to present a report on the overall state of public administration. After years of omission, such a report was prepared in 1993 and taken as the basis for a series of government initiatives on reorganisation. There has been no Parliamentary 'follow-up' in subsequent years, however. The laws on the preventive verification of legality exercised by the Court of Auditors over the executive's administrative actions (dating back to Cavour, in the mid nineteenth century) constitute another example. Where the Court deems the action illegal, it refuses to record it but the government can request its qualified registration. In this case, the Court must carry out such a registration but informs the Chambers. The Court's check therefore does not aim at preventing the executive from acting but, rather, at placing it under Parliament's control. Actually, this has not happened. Like the studies carried out a few years ago the more recent ones reveal that the Court of Auditor's reports sent to parliamentary committees are the subject neither of discussion nor of further action.[46] The same fate is suffered by other reports drawn up by the Court which, notwithstanding a number of defects, supply precious information regarding management of the state's budget, the running of subsidized bodies and the realisation of important spending programmes. Despite their value, few MPs read them and even fewer make any use of them. In other words, the legal (constitutional and legislative) framework is largely ineffective and this does not depend anymore on the scarcity of information provided by the Court of Auditors or on the delay with which it is made public, as happened thirty years ago.[47]

What are the reasons for all this? A possible explanation is that further reform is needed in order to cope with the inadequacy of controls inspired by the 'police patrol' model (i.e. wide-ranging, systematic and inevitably expensive). Given that they do not work, it would be useful to pass to the so-called 'fire-alarm' model, whereby controls are activated only upon the observation of anomalies and are, for this reason, less ambitious but also less expensive and more effective.[48] Another

---

[46] See C. Tucciarelli, 'Parlamento e controlli: come risponde il Parlamento', in U. Allegretti (ed.), *I controlli amministrativi* (Il Mulino, 1994), 219–69; G. D'Auria, 'I controlli', in S. Cassese (ed.), *Trattato di diritto amministrativo. Diritto amministrativo generale* (Giuffrè, 2003), Vol II, 1528. [47] S. Cassese, *Burocrazia ed economia pubblica* (Il Mulino, 1974), 51.

[48] S. Cassese, 'Conclusioni', in *I controlli sulle gestioni finanziarie pubbliche* (Banca d'Italia, 1998), 509.

explanation is that, in spite of all legislative reforms, there is a sort of stickiness about the old control culture. The bodies that ought to be carrying out management controls, such as the Court of Auditors, are struggling to abandon the techniques employed until now inspired by jurisdiction. The executive, which ought to take the Court's reports as a starting point for changing its functional and organizational criteria, only takes an occasional interest. For its part, Parliament, despite being more and better informed than in the past, does not use the information to monitor the executive. Quite the contrary, it has been suggested that that the MPs elected with the majoritarian system have an even lesser interest in critically evaluating the action of governments.[49]

(b) Accountability through the courts

Recognition of the persisting weakness of forms of control over the executive helps to explain the growing importance of judicial review. In other words, there is an increasing demand for justice. Differentiation in the supply of judicial remedies available to the Constitutional Court, on the one hand, and the ordinary judges on the other, has also had an influence, however.

For several reasons, the control exercised by the Constitutional Court is, as it has been in the past, occasional. Article 134 of the Constitution provides that the Court must verify the constitutional legality of laws and acts having force of law. The Court has consistently excluded regulations from this definition, despite the opinion of the greatest twentieth century constitutional lawyer, Costantino Mortati, that they should be included. The Court could, at least, have criticized the inadequacy of the legislative provisions in the cases where the Constitution provides for a *'réserve de loi'* that prevents the executive from issuing primary rules. This it has not done, however, preferring to specify limits by way of interpretation.

The Constitutional Court has exercised a sort of self-restraint when evaluating the legality of delegated legislation as well. Considering the number of vague and defective pieces of delegated legislation, the cases in which they have been declared unconstitutional are, all in all, very few. The Court's reluctance to examine political issues tied to the guidelines set by the Chambers has had its influence, first of all. Another influence is undoubtedly the doctrine of the connection between delegating and delegated legislation, which implies a concept of widely discretionary powers at the executive's disposal when acting under the delegation.[50] The other type of case which the Constitutional Court is required to decide concerns disputes between different state institutions over the attribution of jurisdiction. Here, too, there have been many cases where it has avoided declaring illegal the central government's interventions in areas which fall to the regional governments.

[49] D'Auria, n. 46.   [50] For this line of argument, see Paladin, n. 28, 214.

In contrast, there has recently been increasing intervention on the part of the ordinary judges and the criminal judges, in particular.[51] The criminal courts' jurisdiction is limited according to the following criteria: parties (i.e. holders of public posts, whether or not they are professionals—the heads of organizations governed by private law are usually excluded), subject matter (i.e. issues related to offences committed against the public administration), and the question to be decided, (i.e. lawfulness). Criminal judges have nevertheless interpreted the parameters of their jurisdiction regarding parties broadly, even indicting professionals for opinions given to public officials. They have stretched their interpretation of criminal laws to the point of equating criminal unlawfulness with actions that are ultra vires. For example, the question of whether a decision is ultra vires may be ascertained by the administrative court which would accordingly declare the decision null and void. Such a court could not however prosecute the author. Statutes constitute only one source of law: suffice it to think of the Constitution, general legal principles, and tertiary rules. As far as the mass media and public opinion are concerned, judgments given by the criminal judges have greater weight than others, particularly if they impact on politicians and managers, because they involve areas such as personal freedom that are most intensely protected by the order. In reality, their impact on administrative activity is doubly limited: criminal judges decide individual cases which are concentrated primarily in certain sectors, public contracts, state subsidies etc., and they intervene by methods that are repressive in nature. It is a real pity that the sometimes very accurate knowledge of the public prosecutors and judges has not been put to good use for amending the laws underlying administrative action and enriching the codes of conduct introduced since 1994.

For the reasons just given, the most important supervision of administrative action remains that carried out by the civil and administrative judges.[52] On the basis of the 1865 law, civil judges have always had jurisdiction over all issues concerning the rights of private parties in relation to the public administration. Administrative judges, on the other hand, have had jurisdiction over issues relating to legitimate interests since 1890. Legitimate interests are those that the legal order protects less vigorously. In concrete terms, administrative acts that violate laws or regulations are quashed, but no award of damages is made. During the last thirty years, however, this distinction has lost some of its force for two reasons.

In the first place, there has been a great increase in the number of laws attributing jurisdiction to one or other type of judge as regards a whole group of subjects.[53] However, the Constitutional Court has twice struck down statutes

---

[51] See C. Franchini, *Giudice penale e pubblica amministrazione* (Cedam, 1999).

[52] The initial features of the Italian system and its recent transformation are examined by Sorace, n. 29, 138–48.

[53] Constitutional Court, judgment No. 204/2004, in www.cortecostituzionale.it.

aiming at transferring to administrative courts all disputes concerning 'public services' In the second place, there has been a reinforcement of the administrative judges' powers to acquire evidence, employ interim measures not provided for by law (partly through the influence of EU law), and establish the award of damages. The justice available at the hands of the administrative judges is therefore no longer inferior to that dispensed by the civil judges. On the contrary, it is preferable for the greater speed of the interim measures, as well as on the merits.

The implications for private parties are neither few, nor unimportant. The courts have extended *locus standi:* an increasing number of people have been given leave to take action, against, for example, measures limiting the circulation of motor vehicles. Recognition of the legal capacity to sue has been given to environmentalists' groups and, finally, to consumers' associations taking action to enforce application of the EC laws requiring those in charge to pay the sanctions provided for violation of production limits in relation to quotas and milk. The earlier laws excluding the possibility of challenging political acts before an administrative judge have been interpreted narrowly, in line with Article 113 of the Constitution. A case of particular importance concerned the order for the extradition of an Italian citizen accused of murder in the United States of America. The civil judges had found in favour of the extradition application. In contrast, the administrative judge suspended the effect of the order, referring the issue of the legality of the national law allowing extradition to a country endorsing capital punishment (where the applicant authority had not expressly excluded it) to the Constitutional Court. The latter accepted the reference and held the legislative rules allowing extradition to be invalid.[54]

Despite such progress, there are at least two weak areas so far as administrative justice and accountability are concerned. Although there is growing support even amongst the institutions for the argument that the government has no legitimate power to appoint judges to the Council of State or the Court of Auditors, its own watchdogs, in actual fact this power has been exercised in a measured and occasional fashion over the last thirty years. If anything, the administrative courts' self-restraint regarding policy choices expressed in tertiary rules is more worrying, since the latter often represent the foundation for individual decisions. The other problem concerns the persistent weakness of the procedures for alternative dispute resolution (ADR). At present, these are used only for telecommunications. During the last decade, not only has the executive failed to put forward proposals of this kind, but it has also abstained from issuing regulations implementing laws providing for conciliation and arbitration before the electricity and gas regulator.

---

[54] See Constitutional Court, judgment No. 226/96, in *Giornale di diritto amministrativo,* 1997, 1, 30.

(c) The President of the Republic

The weakness of both parliamentary controls and those carried out by the Constitutional Court explains why the control exercised by the President of the Republic has, most recently, acquired significance.

Truth to tell, the powers at his disposal under the Constitution are limited. Apart from appointing the person charged to form the Council of Ministers and the ministers that the latter proposes (Article 92), the President of the Republic also appoints the top civil servants on the basis of a ministerial proposal. He signs the legislative and administrative acts that the ministers issue individually or jointly (Article 89). He can ask Parliament to modify a law, if he considers that such law infringes the Constitution. However, if the houses approve it again, it 'must be promulgated' (Article 74). Since no act of the President is valid unless it is signed by a minister, who assumes responsibility for it, the question arose whether there were decisions which fell exclusively within his powers. A positive answer has been given for the appointment of the five constitutional judges that Article 135 of the Constitution provides must be chosen by the President. A similar conclusion has been reached as far as the power of granting pardons (Article 87), although the actual Minister of Justice seems to disagree.

That said, it ought to be added that exercise of the powers conferred by the Constitution has allowed the President of the Republic to play a much stronger role in political and administrative life. Thus when Francesco Cossiga was President, in 1991, he sent to Parliament a controversial document in which broad institutional reform was suggested. His successor, Scalfaro, in 1994 succeeded in avoiding making ministerial appointments in cases where there were strong grounds for suspecting a conflict of interest. He also gave the presidential signature to some bills and decree laws only after the appending of certain corrective measures. Perhaps the most important example has been the modification, on a couple of occasions, of the Finance Bill by way of eliminating or mitigating substantive rules not aimed at financial regulation. More recently, on two occasions, concerning the televisions market and the reform of the judiciary approved by Parliament, Carlo Azeglio Ciampi has requested a new debate and approval. However, the role of the President of the Republic is that of a sort of *pouvoir neutre* (to use Benjamin Constant's famous concept) which must be used with discretion.[55] It is one unsuited to over-frequent, or everyday, intervention.

Partly for this reason, the weakness that, from a comparative point of view, is revealed by the other forms of control is all the more serious. It has already been noted that parliamentary inquiries have obtained modest results. The fate of the Inquiry Committees has been no better. Apart from anything else, these have recently undergone a sort of transformation insofar as they are now set up by majority vote and are presided over by majority MPs. Nor is there any public

---

[55] See C. Esposito, *Capo dello Stato—Controfirma ministeriale* (Giuffrè, 1962).

office similar to the Parliamentary ombudsman. The only existing type of ombudsman is envisaged in a local context in the form of a local government ombudsman (*difensore civico*). He receives the claims and complaints brought by private parties against local administrations and can ask for documents and make findings and recommendations. The *difensore civico* has not been provided for by all the municipal charters, however, and even where his role exists, he is rarely an effective form of control.

(d) The increasing importance of international and supranational institutions

From a comparative perspective, the limits placed on governmental powers by the standards set by international and supranational institutions have acquired considerable importance. The reason is that they are not subject to decisions taken by the majority. The most important example is certainly control over excessive public deficits, provided for by the EU Treaty and reinforced by the controversial Stability Pact. This type of control deprives majority governments of both the power to establish the amount of public spending to be financed via the deficit and the power to check that it is respected. The effectiveness of this type of control must be examined not only in the light of the most recent events (i.e. Ecofin's decision regarding the French and German governments). The very existence of common standards for debt and deficit as well as of checks issuing from an independent institution such as the Commission has reinforced the position of the few 'Guardians of the Treasury' (the Ministry of Economy and Finance, the *Banca d'Italia* and the Court of Auditors) against the countless 'spending advocates'. It has thus led to results unrivalled within the Union: public debt has been reduced from 124 to 106 per cent of the gross domestic product and the deficit from 11 to 2 per cent,[56] although the latter has begun to rise again more recently, particularly as a consequence of increased expenses made by regional and local authorities. The question thus arises whether, and to what extent, in the new constitutional framework, EC rules strengthen the legal foundation for national laws imposing limits and controls on both regions and local authorities.

5. Concluding remarks

Three conclusions may be drawn from the above analysis. The first is that a profound transformation has occurred as regards the balance of powers established by the 1948 Constitution and the way in which it developed until twenty years

---

[56] For further details, see G. della Cananea, 'The reforms of finance and administration in Italy: contrasting achievements', in M. Bull and M. Rhodes (eds), *Crisis and transition in Italian Politics* (Frank Cass, 1997), 195–210.

ago. Such transformation has had both internal and external causes and has affected the forms of legitimation, the powers of the executive, and the main resources (i.e. top management and money) the latter has at its disposal for achieving its objectives.

Meanwhile, however, the Constitution has remained unaltered. It has not been adapted in line with the greater decision-making power that the majority has assumed in the meantime. For example, thanks to the constitutional convention mentioned earlier by which a representative of the opposition parties was Speaker in one of the Chambers, such parties contributed to the decisions regarding the composition of certain independent authorities and the governing board of the public Italian Radio and Television Corporation (RAI). Once the constitutional convention died, the RAI has been managed on a 'spoils-system' basis, to the detriment of the public interest. Furthermore, it has increased its quota in the advertising market to equal that of the other oligopolist, without the sector regulator intervening. If one takes account of the other difficulties indicated above (violation of the few laws governing conflict of interest and the grand-scale application of the spoils-system to the posts of senior public officials), it may be concluded that constitutional reform is incomplete as far as the central institutions are concerned.

The institutional framework is also unsatisfactory as regards relations between central and local government. In complex and differentiated societies such as the Italian one, it certainly might not be thought that a single institution could make decisions on its own in a large number of different sectors. It is therefore right that the actions of the Executive are limited and that there are institutions capable of ensuring those limits are respected. The constitutional reform of 2001 has extended concurrent jurisdiction beyond measure, however, creating uncertainty and overlapping areas, as has been demonstrated by the increase in litigation before the Constitutional Court. The danger is that not only accountability, but also the overall efficiency of the political and administrative system are jeopardized.

Partly for these reasons, partly for the interests of political parties, Parliament has just approved a new and broader constitutional reform, the main pillars of which are the transformation of the role of the President of the Council of Ministers and a new division of tasks between the state and regions. The role of the former would be enhanced, by the new form of government, which is based on the idea of a strong premier, who would appoint ministers and dissolve Parliament, in case new elections appear to be necessary. The regional competences would be strengthened in some areas, concerning health and education, and reduced in others that require uniform legislation, such as telecommunications and infrastructures. Moreover, the concept of national interest would be re-introduced. While the advocates of this reform hold that it is necessary both to make the Constitution fit with the new electoral system and to cope with the weaknesses of the reform adopted in 2001, opponents claim that this reform would infringe the basic principles of the Constitution, parliamentary democracy and unity of the Republic.

That said, exactly as happened in 2001, the constitutional reform has been approved by absolute majority, but without the qualified one (two thirds), which presupposes an agreement between majority and opposition (or part of it) and prevents the holding of a referendum. As a result, provided that the constitutional bill is approved also in the second voting, as is required by Article 138 of the Constitution, the lack of the qualified majority will make it very likely that a new referendum will be requested by the opposition, which has much more than the one fifth of the members of one of the Houses. While these results cannot be predicted, one thing is sure: the majoritarian conception of government is producing an outcome which is hardly in the interest of the country, that is to say the instability of the Constitution.

9

The Scope and Accountability of Executive Power in Germany

Eberhard Schmidt-Aßmann* and Christoph Möllers**

1. The scope of executive power

(a) The unitary notion of executive power

German constitutional law adopts a unitary notion of executive power. The cardinal provision of the German Constitution or *Grundgesetz*, Article 20(2), distinguishes the two other powers—those of the legislature and the judiciary—from the executive. In Article 20 the *Grundgesetz* sets its face against any distinction between political government on the one hand and public administration executing the laws on the other.[1] There are historical reasons for the avoidance of this distinction: the autonomy of the government was often suggested in German constitutional history as enabling the acts of a monarch to be exempted from legal consequences,[2] while the need for the government to be free was promoted in national socialist law as an argument against any sort of judicial control. Subjecting both the political and the administrative parts of the executive to the law was a principal goal of the authors of the 1949 Constitution.

Despite this, there is no satisfactory definition of executive power in either German constitutional case law or scholarship. Efforts to develop such a definition have emanated primarily from doctrines of administrative law.[3] However, until recently they have stimulated barely any scholarly or practical interest. This can be attributed to the fact that the delimitation of acts of the executive from those of other powers, necessary as it is in practice, does not in fact cause many problems. Cases in which there is an ambiguity with regard to the classification of a state act under a certain power are rare. In practice, acts of the executive can be defined without presupposing an elaborate theoretical

---

* Professor of Public Law, University of Heidelberg, Director of the Institute for German and European Administrative Law.   ** Professor of Public Law, University of Münster.

[1] See comparison by A. v. Bogdandy, *Gubernative Rechtsetzung* (Mohr Siebeck, 2000).
[2] W. Frotscher, *Regierung als Rechtsbegriff* (Duncker & Humblot, 1975).
[3] References on this point by C. Möllers, *Gewaltengliederung*, 2005 (forthcoming).

framework. This is a context in which one could echo the words of Potter J that: 'I shall not today attempt further to define ... but I know it when I see it.'[4]

As we shall see, the fact that executive power is regarded as a unitary concept does not mean that it should be understood in German law as a monolithic or pyramid organization. But it does mean that certain constitutional dictates are on the whole to be uniformly applied to the executive. The unity of the executive power, which is merely implied in Article 20(2), is in this respect normatively coupled with other constitutional provisions that apply equally to the authorities of the federal states.[5] Article 1(3) of the *Grundgesetz* provides for a uniform obligation on the executive to respect the basic rights provisions of the Constitution.[6] The importance of this provision should not be underestimated in terms of the competences and structure of the executive: the scope of basic rights, which is comparatively comprehensive in Germany,[7] circumscribes the exercise of power by all executive organs, whether they are politically accountable, subordinate, or under public or private legal form.[8] This is of immense practical importance because in German law basic rights have a normative effect on almost all other areas of law.[9] Due to the guarantee of legal protection provided for by Article 19(4) of the *Grundgesetz*, the obligation of the executive to abide by the Constitution is to a significant extent subject to judicial control and establishes in principle a non-restricted scope of judicial review of the executive.[10] Duties promoting uniformity may also be said to arise from the organizational legal principles of democracy[11] and the rule of law.[12]

(b) The organizational diversity of executive power

Despite the unitary concept of the executive in German constitutional law, German government has a complex organizational structure. This is for many reasons, some particular to Germany and others related to the structure of modern public administration in general. The first cause has to do with the diversity of tasks and functions that is characteristic of executive power in western constitutional states.[13] Executive authorities perform the most diverse

---

[4] *Jacobellis v. Ohio*, 378 US 184 (1964).
[5] H. Dreier, *Hierarchische Verwaltung im demokratischen Staat* (Mohr Siebeck, 1991).
[6] The original formulation was changed, in order to make clearer the obligation of the armed forces to respect basic rights.
[7] R. Wahl, 'Die objektiv-rechtliche Dimension der Grundrechte im internationalen Vergleich', in D. Merten and H.-J. Papier (eds.), *Handbuch der Grundrechte*, (C.F. Müller, Vol. 1, 2004).
[8] D. Ehlers, *Verwaltung in Privatrechtsform* (Duncker & Humblot, 1984).
[9] G.F. Schuppert and C. Bumke, *Die Konstitutionalisierung der Rechtsordnung* (Nomos, 2000).
[10] See further below, pp. 285–7.
[11] E. Schmidt-Aßmann, 'Verwaltungslegitimation als Rechtsbegriff' (1991) 116 *Archiv des öffentlichen Rechts* (AöR) 329.
[12] E. Schmidt-Aßmann, 'Der Rechtsstaat', in J. Isensee and P. Kirchhof (eds), *Handbuch des Staatsrechts*, (C.F. Müller, 3rd edn., 2004), § 24.
[13] G. F. Schuppert, *Verwaltungswissenschaft* (Nomos, 2000).

tasks by means of a variety of legal forms and upon consideration of a multiplicity of legal provisions. Government ranges from big, central ministries, whose functions involve *agenda setting* and *rule making*, to municipal registry offices, which simply deal with individual cases.

A second reason for the organizational complexity of the executive derives from Germany's federal structure. The separation of powers is an important principle at both the federal level and in the states (*Länder*). As such, there exist in Germany seventeen widely differentiated structures of executive authority. Only in a few cases does the federal level have at its disposal a complete hierarchical structure of authorities ranging from central ministries to subordinate public authorities that have unique decision-making powers vis-à-vis the citizen. On the contrary, the laws of the federal state are generally executed by the *Länder*.[14] Regional administrations are organizationally varied and employ a greater number of civil servants. Citizens normally encounter the executive power of the federal state in its function as political actor in the framework of legislative procedure and only rarely in its function as the source of individual decisions that affect their rights. That said, there is one area of executive power where the administration of the federal state has become more important in recent years: the police. The federal police, called Federal Border Guard ('*Bundesgrenzschutz*'), which initially confined itself to the security of borders and traffic routes, has recently been upgraded to an entire police force—principally in the context of the fight against terrorism—that may in the future bear the name of Federal Police Force ('*Bundespolizei*'). Apart from this important exception, it is the executive authorities of the *Länder* who are entrusted with the majority of executive functions in Germany.

A third reason for the organizational diversity of executive power in German law arises from the structure of autonomous self-administration. This term applies to forms of administration that are more or less independent of the government. The cardinal form of self-administration guaranteed in Article 28 of the *Grundgesetz* is municipal self-administration,[15] which guarantees that certain functions be conferred upon municipalities and other territorial corporate entities. This is the form of administration that citizens encounter most frequently. Although the design of the organization of municipalities is a matter for the legislatures of the *Länder*, the municipalities are, from an organizational point of view, similarly structured to one another. Self-administration is legitimized through two distinct notions. First, it is justified by the obligation to obey the law, as well as from its control by superior authorities (that is, a top-down legitimation). Secondly, it is justified by virtue of the opportunities for popular participation that exist at this level (that is, a bottom-up legitimation).

---

[14] Art. 83 of the Grundgesetz.
[15] BVerfGE 79, 127. On this decision: F. Schoch 'Zur Situation der kommunalen Selbstverwaltung nach der Rastede-Entscheidung des Bundesverfassungsgerichts' (1990) 81 *Verwaltungs-Archiv (VerwArch.)* 18.

Independent agencies, which are widely used in American and English law, where they are entrusted with matters relating to the regulation of the economy,[16] play only a marginal role in German administration. Newly founded administrative authorities, such as those for telecommunications and postal services[17] or for the supervision of financial services[18] are generally subordinate to a competent ministry and are to a large extent subject to the ministry's instructions. It has to be said, however, that there are numerous tendencies towards rendering these authorities more autonomous vis-à-vis the government. The administration of telecommunications, for example, requires expertise and is difficult for ministers or judges to supervise effectively.[19] As well as the argument for expertise, ideological pressures towards privatization and the influence of EU law also push in the direction of establishing greater independence for regulatory agencies.[20] In conclusion, the executive in Germany cannot be described as a self-contained, pyramid or uniform organization. It comprises a number of forms of organization, which are structured along the two federal levels. Questions pertaining to the uniformity of the administration are not satisfactorily answered from the point of view of organization but, rather, from the examination of executive accountability.[21]

(c) **Executive prerogatives and emergency powers**

Executive prerogatives are competences that the government can, in principle, administer without authorization and/or without judicial control. Such prerogatives are largely alien to German law. The historical experience, especially the erosion of the parliamentary system of the 1919 Constitution by the emergency laws of the period at the end of the Weimar Republic, prompted the drafters of the *Grundgesetz* to exclude such competences. Only in 1968 were provisions for emergency situations inserted into the constitution. The provisions implemented during the Cold War pertain mainly to an attack on German national territory by a foreign power and to the emergence of situations similar to civil war. They secure for these circumstances parliamentary control over the government, through a common committee of the Lower House of the German

---

[16] On the relation between politics and administration, see V. Mehde, 'Responsibility and Accountability in the European Commission' (2003) 40 *CMLRev* 423.
[17] K. Oertel, *Die Unabhängigkeit der Regulierungsbehörde nach §§ 66 ff. TKG* (Duncker & Humblot, 2000). [18] See www.bafin.de.
[19] On that point: H.-H. Trute, 'Regulierung—am Beispiel des Telekommunikationsrechts', in C.-E. Eberle (ed.), *Festschrift für Winfried Brohm zum 70. Geburtstag* (C.H. Beck, 2002), 169.
[20] See R. Wahl, 'Privatorganisationsrecht als Steuerungsinstrument bei der Wahrnehmung öffentlicher Aufgaben', in E. Schmidt-Aßmann and W. Hoffmann-Riem (eds), *Verwaltungsorganisationsrecht als Steuerungsressource*, (Nomos, 1997), 301 and C. Möllers, 'Die auswärtige Verselbständigung nachgeordneter Behörden' (2005) 65 *Zeitschrift für ausländisches öffentliches Recht und Völkerrecht (ZaöRV)*, forthcoming.
[21] G. Haverkate, 'Die Einheit der Verwaltung als Rechtsproblem' (1988) 46 *Veröffentlichungen der Vereinigung der deutschen Staatsrechtslehrer (VVDStRL)*, 181, 217, 221–2.

Parliament (*Bundestag*) and the Federal Council of Germany (*Bundesrat*).[22] Most of these provisions are not really suitable for more recent problems relating to national security, such as the threat from terrorism. Other constitutional provisions pertain to problems that arise from Germany's federal structure, such as provisions on the joint commitment of police forces to the federal government and to the *Länder* and, in certain circumstances, of the armed forces in the event of serious accidents (Article 35 of the *Grundgesetz*).[23]

Article 10(2) of the Constitution is a provision that is of particular significance at the moment. It concerns the secrecy of mail and telecommunications. The provision was introduced in connection with the 1968 emergency provisions but it is not restricted to these cases. It provides that all interceptions of mail and telecommunications require parliamentary authorization. However, when the interception serves to protect the democratic order, that is to say the core existence of the constitution, the law can provide that the fact of the interception will not be disclosed to those concerned. In such cases judicial control is not possible. It is replaced by a parliamentary control commission that reviews the procedure. This highly controversial provision has been repeatedly scrutinized by the Federal Constitutional Court ('*Bundesverfassungsgericht*'). In its landmark decision of 15 December 1970 the Court established that the replacement of judicial control by the parliamentary commission is compatible with the rule of law. The principle of proportionality requires that those concerned be informed subsequently, when the purpose of the surveillance is no longer jeopardized by the disclosure.[24]

This area of law has been adapted to the dangers arising from international crime and terrorist threats. Surveillance of telephone communications may be ordered today when there exist indications that someone is planning to commit, commits, or has committed serious criminal offences as specified in the Code of Criminal Procedure ('*Strafprozessordnung*'). The same applies when there exists suspicion that someone is a member of a terrorist group. Strategic restrictions also allow for international telecommunications as far as they serve the purpose of collection of information, knowledge of which is essential in order to discover and respond to dangers of international terrorist attacks. The Federal Constitutional Court again addressed the problems of Article 10(2) of the *Grundgesetz* in its decision of 14 July 1999. It regarded these wide restrictions on the secrecy of telecommunications to be permissible as a matter of principle.[25] Such interferences with the private sphere do not correspond to the traditional model of intrusions aiming to avert concrete dangers or to prosecute on suspicion that an offence has been committed. Anyone could become subject to surveillance.

---

[22] Art. 115 of the *Grundgesetz*.

[23] Art. 35 of the *Grundgesetz*. See also the new law on the new regulation of duties for air security (*Gesetz zur Neuregelung von Luftsicherheitsaufgaben*), passed by the Lower House of the German Parliament on 24 September 2004.   [24] BVerfGE 30, 1, 20, 25.

[25] BVerfGE 100, 313, 382.

International intelligence is, however, important in order to defend superior common goods against new forms of international crime.

A parallel development appears in the context of another basic right, the right to sanctity of the home (Article 13 of the *Grundgesetz*). In this context Germany has written into its constitution extensive powers of surveillance. These are not always judicially reviewable. In its decision of 3 March 2004[26] the Federal Constitutional Court interpreted these provisions restrictively. It referred to the inviolability of the right to human dignity in Article 1 of the *Grundgesetz* and restricted powers of surveillance to certain forms of communication and to particular, serious offences. However, it is disputed in legal scholarship whether these restrictions will lead to rights being effectively protected.

The laws on Articles 10 and 13 of the Constitution are for the time being symptomatic: the new security and emergency laws have not established any general executive prerogatives or privileges. Everything has developed in the context of the law and remains in this respect the responsibility of Parliament. In the case of some of these measures, the government is obliged to obtain the agreement of the relevant parliamentary control body. Consequently, criticism should be directed less at the fact that executive powers have been enlarged and more at the expansion of state interference with basic rights, interference which is permitted not only for defence against external dangers but also as a precaution in the interests of security.[27] The tendency to say 'Farewell to the police law (*'Polizeirecht'*) of the liberal constitutional state,'[28] previously only fragmentary, has been reinforced by the so-called anti-terrorist laws that have been enacted in Germany since the 11 September attacks in the USA.[29] The weakening of the imperative of separation and the strengthening of preventive powers are marked. Police authorities, law enforcement authorities, and intelligence services now work closely together. The former principle of 'dividing powers within the administration'[30] has receded. This principle had previously been considered to be important as a restriction on the activities of the security services.[31] Not only did it allocate competences to the various services, but it also delimited the extent of their co-operation with the police. The anti-terrorist laws now allow for a closer co-operation between these authorities, especially on issues pertaining to

---

[26] BVerfGE 109, 279.

[27] M. Albers, *Die Determination polizeilicher Tätigkeit in den Bereichen der Straftatenverhütung und der Verfolgungsvorsorge* (Duncker & Humblot, 2001).

[28] That was the title of an article by F. Schoch, (2004) 43 *Der Staat*, 347. On the same problem, see: H. Trute, 'Gefahr und Prävention in der Rechtsprechung zum Polizei- und Ordnungsrecht' (2003) 36 *DV* 501.

[29] M. Rau, 'Country Report on Germany', in Ch. Walter, S. Vöneky, V. Röben and F. Schorkopf (eds.), *Terrorism as a Challenge for National and International Law: Security versus Liberty?*, (Springer, 2004), 311.

[30] W. Leisner, 'Gewaltenteilung innerhalb der Gewalten', in H. Spanner (ed.) *Festgabe für Theodor Maunz zum 70. Geburtstag* (C.H. Beck, 1971), 267.

[31] K. Nehm, 'Das nachrichtendienstliche Trennungsgebot und die neue Sicherheitsarchitektur' (2004) 57 *Neue Juristische Wochenzeitschrift (NJW)* 3289.

the collection of information and investigation methods. What has been created is a new, unitary 'architecture of security' ('*Sicherheitsarchitektur*') that acts on the principles of precaution and prevention. Schoch has described the new situation in the following terms:[32]

A comprehensive planning for the gathering of information, which overrides the knowledge of individual cases and requires structural understanding, appears to be essential. The threshold of danger, the hallmark of traditional police law, loses its importance. In the 'danger society' ('*Risikogesellschaft*') it is sufficient for the strengthening of the functions of the administration that there is a concern regarding the emergence of future dangers. It is not only potential trouble-makers who are affected by such measures. Most importantly the measures can be addressed to practically everybody. This is shown from criminal investigations, video surveillance of public places and the dragnet controls.

It seems, however, premature to speak of a 'farewell' to the police law of the liberal constitutional state. Freedom and security have been balanced against each other as police functions have been delineated. For sure, it is difficult to find a new balance. Many worry about permanent losses for basic rights.[33] We should remember, however, that the state is not only obliged to respect the rights of its citizens, but also to safeguard their protection. The state must, therefore, be in the position to respond to new challenges. The legislature is pre-eminently responsible. The executive cannot act if Parliament does not lay down principles. Parliament's laws set the framework within which the executive has competence to act. Such laws must take into account the imperatives of the rule of law and legal certainty. This was already the case with regard to criminal and police law. Today it is equally important where executive powers are authorized in order to prevent dangers. Yet even here rules must be accompanied by discretion—the law must place at the disposal of the administration 'adequately clear standards' for the exercise of its discretion.[34] All measures must be devised according to the principle of proportionality.[35] Where it is necessary to include in police operations significant numbers of uninvolved people, as occurs in the case of dragnet controls, additional procedural guarantees should be integrated in order to compensate for the extensive police measures. There are examples for this: some of the instruments referred to above may be ordered only by a judge. Such 'clauses in favour of the judiciary' ('*Richtervorbehalte*') traditionally exist for arrest and search warrants.[36] The clauses have now been introduced into the new police law as well. But some courts have nonetheless insisted that, in the case of

---

[32] F. Schoch, n. 28, 354.
[33] O. Lepsius, 'The relationship between security and civil liberties in the Federal Republic of Germany after September 11', in P. Gewirtz and J.K. Cogan (eds.), *Global Constitutionalism* (Yale Law School, 2002), III7–III24, V95–V103 with more references.
[34] Federal Constitutional Court, Decision of 3 March 2004 in (2004) 57 *NJW*, 2213, 2216.
[35] Th. Groß, 'Terrorbekämpfung und Grundrechte' (2002) 35 *Kritische Justiz* 1.
[36] Arts. 104 and 13 of the *Grundgesetz*.

police controls not based on reasonable suspicion, the administration must prepare in advance an alternative test that lays down criteria for state intervention. In this way, arbitrary actions may be prevented. The rule of law and the guarantee of security should not be regarded as absolutes, but there is a need for legal imagination in order to establish a new balance between these requirements and the need for adequate executive powers.[37]

2. The accountability of the executive

Parliaments, courts, and other controlling or supervising organs are, of course, important instruments in ensuring executive accountability. Equally important, however, or so we will argue, is a well-structured administrative law that pre-emptively controls the operation of the administration and guarantees its accountability from the outset. To this end it is necessary to follow firm legal forms.

(a) Legal forms and executive functions

From a *practical* point of view, the executive has numerous means by which it may perform its duties. It may give orders, impose bans, conclude contracts, offer goods and services, issue warnings, recommendations or directives, impose taxes, pay subsidies, and publish reports. From a *legal* point of view, the instruments must be structured and—as in Article 249 EC—take a legal form. The forms are construed so that they protect the citizen from the administration, while at the same time making it possible for the government to perform its tasks and duties efficiently. In the agitated sea of administrative activities legal forms build islands of stability. The *two-fold mission of administrative law*, ('*Doppelauftrag des Verwaltungsrechts*') to guarantee protection and effectiveness, arises particularly clearly in the theory of legal forms.[38] As such, it supplements older perspectives on public administration, which place judicial control at the heart of administrative law.[39]

The most important legal forms are, for the purposes of rule-making, the regulation (*Verordnung*), the ordinance (*Satzung*), and the administrative instruction and, for the purposes of adjudication, the administrative act (*Verwaltungsakt*) and the administrative contract (*Verwaltungsvertrag*). These forms are not *numerus clausus*. Still, they set crystallization points for the operation of executive power. Constitutional law, case law and more specialized,

---

[37] W. Hoffmann-Riem, 'Freiheit und Sicherheit im Angesicht terroristischer Anschläge' (2002) 35 *Zeitschrift für Rechtspolitik (ZRP)* 497; W. Brugger, 'Rasterfahndung im Rechtstaat', in H.-P. Mansel u.a. (eds), *Festschrift für Erik Jayme* (C.H. Beck, 2004), 1037.

[38] Schmidt-Aßmann, *Das allgemeine Verwaltungsrecht als Ordnungsidee* (Springer, 2nd edn., 2004), 16–18.

[39] One can see here a parallel to the English red- and green-light theories. For more: A. Tomkins, 'In Defence of the Political Constitution' (2002) 22 *OJLS* 157, 158–61.

technical law (such as urban planning law) determine the rules that the executive must observe in the rule-making process. The 1976 Administrative Procedure Act (VwVgG) sets the rules for the administrative act and the administrative contract. This is the most important codification of German administrative law. At the time of its drafting the usual objections against codification were voiced but today it is viewed positively. Officials and lawyers dealing with administrative cases find in the Act important rules on orderly decisions, compulsory hearings, the right to access records, the obligations of secrecy and neutrality, as well as provisions on the reasons for and notification of administrative acts. Judicial decisions focus on the interpretation of particular provisions of the Act and are easily traced in the commentaries on the respective provisions.[40] The codification does not preclude further development of the law; it rather renders possible its systematic evolution. In this way, for example, provisions pertaining to e-communication were introduced into the Act in 2002.

(i) Legal forms of rule-making

German law (unlike common law systems[41]), distinguishes between two forms of executive rule-making. Statutory regulations, issued in accordance with express legal authorization, are rules that render general laws more concrete; in this way they can establish citizens' rights and obligations. Administrative directives are, on the other hand, intra-administrative rules that are supposed internally to harmonize the application of the laws but, according to classical doctrine, they cannot create legal effects outside the administration. Administrative directives are therefore, in principle, general instructions or guidelines of a superior authority to a subordinate one or instructions given by a director of an authority to his or her staff.

Both types of rule are provided for in constitutional law, albeit to different degrees of exactness. Article 80 of the *Grundgesetz* provides for procedural requirements for the enactment of statutory regulations and requires the legislature to implement clearly defined authorization rules, on the basis of which statutory regulations can then be issued. Administrative directives are mentioned in the Constitution, which provides, for example, when they can be enacted between the federal state and the *Länder*, without, however, the Constitution regulating their legal form as such.

Traditionally, legal scholarship has emphasized the differences between these two legal forms, accentuating the distinction between 'internal' and 'external' administrative procedures. More recent scholarly debate has focused on what they have in common.[42] The first noticeable feature shared in common is the

---

[40] Compare: P. Stelkens, H.J. Bonk and M. Sachs, *Verwaltungsverfahrensgesetz, Kommentar* (C.H. Beck, 6th edn., 2001); H.J. Knack, *Verwaltungsverfahrensgesetz, Kommentar* (Heymanns, 8th edn., 2004).

[41] R. Baldwin, *Rules and Government* (Clarendon Press, 1995); compare Bogdandy, n. 1.

[42] K. Lange, 'Innenrecht und Außenrecht', in W. Hoffmann-Riem, G. F. Schuppert and E. Schmidt-Aßmann (eds.), *Reform des Allgemeinen Verwaltungsrechts* (Nomos, Baden-Baden, 1993), 307.

relatively marginal role of the rule-making procedures involved. This is especially the case for those potentially affected by the rule, who do not normally enjoy any enforceable procedural protection.[43] This tendency has started to change in recent years. An increasing number of statutory regulations and administrative directives have been enacted in procedures set up by law that commit the authorities to enable those affected by the measures to participate actively in their making. This has occurred particularly in the field of environmental law.[44] Still, such procedures remain the exception, as there is no constitutional requirement to use them.

A second common feature concerns the binding effect of the two legal forms. Even if external legal effects are not traditionally attributed to administrative acts, they may still have several indirect effects: the enactment of administrative acts amounts to self-commitment ('*Selbstbindung*') of the administration, from which it may not deviate without infringing judicially reviewable law. Owing to its self-commitment, the administration guarantees on the one hand a certain degree of equal treatment of addressees while, on the other hand, ensuring the rationality of its decisions. Both factors may be judicially reviewed—at least indirectly. The significance of administrative self-commitment is increased in contexts of broad legal powers, for example in police law, and where facts are particularly complicated, for example in technical law, where exhaustive judicial control is rendered difficult. The same factors favour stronger rule-making structures. Especially in view of the wide-reaching powers of the police, this aspect of executive rule-making has become more important. When legal authorization to the administration is formulated in such a way that judicial control derives only from the general character of the law, it is important that the executive delineates its own functions and tasks according to clear standards and makes them comprehensible.

(ii) *Legal forms of adjudication*

The Administrative Procedure Act provides for two legal forms that the administration can use for the adjudication of individual cases: the administrative act and the administrative contract.

The notion of administrative act is used in a specific sense. It is an instrument that unilaterally imposes rules on the citizen. Administrative acts can have either an encumbering or a beneficial content, or both. Even today, the administrative act is the most important instrument of executive power. This legal form dominates in the fields of tax law, social security law, police law, and environmental law. The executive can use this instrument when it is authorized to do so on the basis of public law. The executive may enforce administrative acts without

---

[43] Th. Th. Ziamou, *Rulemaking, Participation and the Limits of Public Law in the USA and Europe* (Ashgate, 2001).
[44] J. Saurer, 'Die Mitwirkung des Bundestages an der Verordnungsgebung nach §48b BImSchG' (2003) 22 *Neue Zeitschrift für Verwaltungsrecht (NVwZ)* 1176.

recourse to the courts. 'Administrative act' is defined in the 1976 Administrative Procedure Act, which also establishes the form (oral, in writing, and latterly also electronically), in which administrative acts are to be enacted and the requirements that are to be met for grounding them. Especially important is the binding force of the administrative act ('*Bestandskraft*'): once an administrative act has been enacted, it remains effective for as long as and to the extent that it is not revoked, withdrawn, or annulled.

The Administrative Procedure Act provides that administrative acts are void *ab initio* only when they suffer from a serious defect that is obvious. For all other administrative acts, it is the task of the addressee to defend himself with a legal action against an administrative act. This action is, however, subject to time limits.[45] If the action is filed on time and the objection of illegality is admissible, the court may set aside an administrative act, with the consequence that it will not create any binding effect. If the addressee does not file his action on time or his action is unsuccessful, he is deprived of a later objection that the administration decided unlawfully. The binding force of administrative acts also binds the executive. This is important, especially for beneficial administrative acts (such as those which allocate subsidies or grant planning permission). The administration may revoke such administrative acts only within certain time limits and after having considered the interests of the beneficiary. Under certain circumstances it must pay compensation. All in all, the administrative act can be described as a legal form with sharp contours. It stands at the border between procedural and material law, as the administrative/operational perspective and the judicial/controlling perspective are combined within it.

In order to understand administrative contracts, one must bear in mind that the executive may conclude contracts in German law not only under the regime of public law but also under private law. The executive may conclude private law contracts when it buys or sells services in the market. The most important example is in public procurement. Even in private law the executive does not enjoy complete freedom of contract: it must respect basic human rights, especially the principle of equality and the prohibition of arbitrariness. In the case of public law administrative contracts there are stricter obligations. Public law contracts are the instruments used to perform typically public tasks, such as urban development and environmental protection. For a time there was some doubt about whether public law contracts were lawful. The Administrative Procedure Act settled the issue. Under its provisions the administration may conclude public law contracts where this is not expressly prohibited, but they must be concluded in writing and they must meet certain criteria as to their content. Provisions of the Act offer specific procedural protections to individuals who conclude contracts with the executive.

---

[45] One month upon notification, when there was an instruction for filing a legal remedy included in the administrative act, otherwise one year.

(iii) Informal administrative action

Many administrative tasks do not fit within the forms of administrative law; they are operated informally. This does not mean that they are irrelevant in a legal sense. For a long time, informal administrative action was ignored by administrative law. More recently it has been regarded with a certain skepticism.[46] That said, the perception has been established that informal action is normal even where public administration is formally structured by law, and that, in principle, the general standards of democratic legitimacy and the obligation to respect basic rights apply to informal action as well.[47] However, informal forms of action generate specific dangers, to which administrative law needs to react. These derive mainly from the fact that agreements between private parties and the administration proceed at the expense of third parties. The informal consensus reached between industry and the federal government in the context of nuclear power in Germany, from which the competent *Länder* authorities were excluded, is a good example.[48] There is also an issue concerning the information and warnings that may be issued by the executive, where such information could interfere with basic rights. While much scholarly literature has demanded the application of general standards in such cases, the federal constitutional court has, thus far, developed a less strict regime.[49]

(b) Parliamentary accountability

The basis for parliamentary accountability of the executive in German law is the fact that the head of government in both the federal state and the *Länder* is elected by and from within Parliament. Just as the heads of government are elected by their Parliaments, so too may the Parliaments deselect them.[50] In the *Grundgesetz* the Federal Chancellor ('*Bundeskanzler*') is directly dependent on the Parliament as the head of government. The destiny of all other ministers follows that of the Chancellor. In this way, German constitutional law organizes the relationship between government and Parliament in accordance with the paradigm of the British parliamentary system. The difference between the two is that in the British system there is a more substantial integration of the majority party members within the government, whereas this does not apply to the same extent in Germany. With the introduction of the office of the parliamentary secretary of state ('*Parlamentarischer Staatssekretär*'), a personal connection between the Parliament and the executive was created, which transcends the head of government and the ministers. The closeness of the working relations between

---

[46] H. Dreier, 'Informales Verwaltungshandeln' (1993) 4 *Staatswissenschaft und Staatspraxis (SuS)* 647.   [47] M. Schulte, *Schlichtes Verwaltungshandeln* (Mohr Siebeck, 1995).
[48] BVerfGE 104, 249.   [49] BVerfGE 105, 253, 279.
[50] H. Dreier, 'Verantwortung im demokratischen Verfassungsstaat', in U. Neumann and L. Schulz (eds), *Verantwortung in Recht und Moral* (Steiner, 2000), 9.

government and Parliament is still not fully accepted by German legal scholars who see a violation of the separation of powers in the co-operation between the political party of the majority and the ministerial bureaucracy. But the criterion against which this assessment is made is not the *Grundgesetz* but an ideal situation, derived from the constitutional traditions of the USA and of the former German empire, where all constitutional connections between government and Parliament were deliberately and strictly limited.[51] Under the Westminster model there is close co-operation, especially in the context of law-making, between the majority party and the government itself. As such, the parliamentary accountability of the government may be less apparent in Parliament's power to select a new head of government than it is in the cooperation between the government and the majority party on new legislation when they are aiming at obtaining a majority.[52]

What forms of parliamentary accountability can the opposition avail itself of in this system? Parliamentary accountability vis-à-vis the opposition becomes manifest in the rights of inquiry and questioning and of investigation/examination that constitutional law grants to parliamentary minorities. It is possible for both single committees and individual members to call government ministers to plenary session of Parliament and publicly to ask them questions. The inquiry committee constitutes perhaps the most significant constitutional instrument for securing the accountability of the government vis-à-vis the opposition. Its appointment can be demanded by one quarter of the members of the Lower House of the German Parliament.[53] Parliamentary inquiry committees hold their meetings in accordance with criminal procedures. They serve the purpose of elucidating relevant facts and they produce reports.

More generally, numerous constitutional provisions, especially its human rights provisions, impose requirements of legal certainty. Such requirements compel the legislature to regulate certain matters and not to leave them to the executive. The constitutional insistence upon statute is one of the most important parameters of the executive's accountability to Parliament. This is explored further below.

(c) Accountability within the administration

Although the executive is bound by the laws as a whole, the structures of accountability do not cease to apply with the enactment of a law. Nor is accountability limited to parliamentary accountability. On the contrary, the internal organization of the executive is another component of its accountability.

---

[51] C. Schönberger, 'Die überholte Parlamentarisierung, Einflussgewinn und fehlende Machtfähigkeit im sich demokratisierenden Kaiserreich' (2001) 272 *Historische Zeitschrift (HZ)* 623.

[52] H. Schulze-Fielitz, *Theorie und Praxis parlamentarischer Gesetzgebung* (Duncker & Humblot, 1988); K. v. Beyme, *Der Gesetzgeber* (Westdeutscher Verlag, 1997).

[53] Art. 44(1) of the *Grundgesetz*.

The traditional view was that the accountability of the executive manifested itself through the hierarchical organization of the administration. The minister is responsible to the Parliament as the director of an executive agency and, in the same way, his subordinates are accountable to him through his ability to issue them with instructions. The legal ground for this view is premised on the democratic principle in Article 20 of the Constitution. However, the relationship between 'democratic principle' and 'hierarchical organization' is a matter of some controversy in Germany, as it is elsewhere.[54] The Federal Constitutional Court has continually relied on the connection in its case law,[55] even if one can detect some revisionism in a more recent decision.[56]

Numerous arguments have been advanced against this view. The first question is to whom subordinate parts of the executive should be responsible—to the minister at the top, remote as he may sometimes be, or to directly affected citizens? If the latter, this argues against a hierarchical construction and in favour of an autonomous construction entailing appropriate participatory administrative procedures for those directly affected. Two counter-arguments have been suggested: first, participation and rights to co-decision cannot be equated. The right to an adequate administrative procedure, in which citizens are heard, is self-evident, but it can only complement democratic legitimacy; it cannot replace it.[57] Secondly, if legitimacy mechanisms are fragmented, the danger arises that decisions of certain administrative units will be made at the expense of people who have not participated in the decision-making. In this respect, a more general legislative procedure would serve to prevent administrative decisions being made on the basis of particular interests—this is the problem generally known as *agency capture*.

In Germany, this problem clearly arises in structures of functional self-administration. In the field of social security, for example, the self-administrative structures of doctors and public health insurers are entrusted with decision-making powers that affect all patients in the public health sector.[58] There are similar problems within certain professional associations, which often interfere with the basic rights of their own members in such a way that is not covered by their limited legal mandate.[59] Both examples show the problems regarding the way in which certain administrative units become autonomous, a process that has its roots in the corporatist tradition. Alongside the democratic critique of the hierarchical nature of public administration stands the critique of its efficiency. The question is to what extent the head of an authority is in the position to control the actions of the organization as a whole. The answers to this question

---

[54] P. Craig, *Public Law and Democracy in the United Kingdom and the United States of America* (Clarendon, 1990); R.B. Stewart, 'The Reformation of American Administrative Law' (1975) 88 *Harvard L Rev* 1669.   [55] BVerfGE 93, 37.
[56] BVerfGE 107, 59.   [57] C. Möllers, n. 3.
[58] E. Schmidt-Aßmann, *Grundrechtspositionen und Legitimationsfragen im öffentlichen Gesundheitswesen* (de Gruyter, 2001).   [59] For many decisions, see: BVerfGE 106, 181.

are not uniform in the scholarly debate in administrative law. It is by no means the case that all scholarly contributions in the field of organizations conclude that hierarchies are obsolete.[60]

Academic discussion of the accountability structures within public administration will continue. The hierarchical organization of executive power that was for so long considered as self-evident has, in recent years, been put under pressure both in scholarly criticism and through a greater legislative willingness to re-shape it. This does not mean that the forms of hierarchical organization are necessarily obsolete: they remain a central component of both public and private organizations. It must be recognized that the federal structure of German executive power and the protection of municipal self-administration limit the extent to which accountability can be reconstructed completely non-hierarchically.[61] It should also be observed that non-hierarchical forms of administration have, for their part, massive problems not only from a constitutional perspective but also from a purely functional perspective.

Before we leave this section, the question of how the correlation between democratic government and subordinate levels of public administration should be organized needs to be considered in more detail. In particular, we should ask whether the concept of hierarchical organization ought to be maintained, albeit in a modified form.[62] It may be argued that a hierarchical organization of public administration helps to concretize legal requirements. The upper parts of the executive create law of wide material scope in the form of *rules*. These rules define and limit the margin of decision of other parts of the administration. The vertical structure of hierarchy guarantees both a progressive concreteness from top to bottom and the legalization of executive decisions. The hierarchy serves the purpose of organizing the commitment of the executive to its legislative prescriptions and the accountability of the hierarchical top vis-à-vis the general democratic process,[63] and requires normative efficiency to concretize actions through internal rules. At the top of the hierarchy stand those organs of executive power that emanate from a democratic political process and that in co-operation with the legislature instigate law with a high degree of generality. At the bottom of the hierarchy stand decisions of minor generality with comparatively higher binding force that resemble judicial decisions. While the concept of a strict hierarchical executive organization, in which potentially every decision can be vertically determined, is neither practically easy to achieve,[64] nor required from a

---

[60] H.A. Simon, *Administrative Behaviour* (Free Press, 4th edn., 1997), 7–9, F.W. Scharpf, *Games Real Actors Play* (Westview Press, 1997), 171–93.
[61] H.-C. Röhl, *Der Wissenschaftsrat* (Nomos, 1994), 138–9.
[62] On that point, see: C. Möllers, n. 3.   [63] H. Dreier, n. 50, 12–13.
[64] For a critic in the German legal scholarship, see: V. Mehde, *Demokratieprinzip und Neues Steuerungsmodell* (Duncker & Humblot, 2000), 446–70; H.-H. Trute, 'Funktionen der Organisation und ihre Abbildung im Recht', in E. Schmidt-Aßmann and W. Hoffmann-Riem (eds.), *Verwaltungsorganisationsrecht als Steuerungsressource*, (Nomos, 1997), 249, 264–9. For comparison with the United States, see also: U. Haltern, F. Mayer and C. Möllers, 'Wesentlichkeitstheorie und

theoretical point of view some notion of hierarchy is nonetheless valuable. It connects,[65] even if only loosely, the political process in Parliament with rule-making by the judiciary.[66]

(d) Federal segmentation of executive accountability

The German constitutional system is generally characterized as one of executive federalism.[67] With this term one specifies the condition that in most cases, the execution of federal law is incumbent on the *Länder*, and that this separation of competences renders essential the participation of the executive authorities of the *Länder* in the law-making procedure of the federal state. This has weighty repercussions for both parliamentary and internal administrative accountability.

The participation of the *Länder* in federal law-making is guaranteed in German constitutional law through the fact that laws which directly affect the administrations of the *Länder* require the approval of the Federal Council of Germany ('*Bundesrat*'), which represents the *Länder*. This design, even though explicitly required by constitutional law, poses some problems because (as with the Council of Ministers in the EU) it means that an executive organ is taking part in law-making. The *Bundesrat* is not a parliament, in that its discussions are directed towards neither the public nor to political parties. However, it frequently reaches decisions along party-political lines, even though its members do not have any particular mandate for federal political issues.[68] Given that the political majorities of the Lower House of the German Parliament ('*Bundestag*') and the Federal Council ('*Bundesrat*') often diverge, the former must in many cases retreat from its political line, so that a consensus with the *Bundesrat* is possible. Such compromises are developed in private meetings of the conciliation committee. The integration of the *Länders*' executive authorities in the law-making process interferes more with the democratic correlations of accountability than it furthers them, exacerbating, as it does, the need for all-inclusive coalition politics.[69]

This structure of comprehensive co-operation is echoed in the context of rule-making at subordinate levels. For almost all of the political fields that are administered by the *Länder*, organs have emerged in which the competent

---

Grundrechte, Zur institutionellen Kritik des Gesetzesvorbehalts' (1997) 30 *Die Verwaltung* (DV) 51, with more references.

[65] On the notion, see, K.E. Weick, *Der Prozeß des Organisierens* (Suhrkamp, 1985), 163–4.

[66] For a solution of coordination problems through hierarchy, see: G.J. Miller, *Managerial Dilemmas, The Political Economy of Hierarchy* (Cambridge University Press, 1992), 217.

[67] G. Lehmbruch, *Parteienwettbewerb im Bundesstaat* (Westdeutscher Verlag, 3rd edn., 2000). For insightful parallels with EC law, see: P. Dann, 'European Parliament and Executive Federalism: Approaching a Parliament in a Semi-Parliamentary Democracy' (2003) 9 *ELJ* 527.

[68] C. Möllers, 'Der parlamentarische Bundesstaat', in J. Aulehner u. a. (eds.), *Föderalismus–Zukunft oder Auflösung der Staatlichkeit* (Boorberg, 1998), 81.

[69] E.-W. Böckenförde, 'Sozialer Bundesstaat und parlamentarische Demokratie', in *Politik als gelebte Verfassung, Festschrift für Rudolf Schäfer* (Westdeutscher Verlag, 1980), 182.

ministries co-ordinate with each other and harmonize their actions. This results in such homogeneous government that the question arises why one actually requires a variety of local authorities. It also results, in some cases at least, in decisions of the states' legislatures being so exhaustively prepared at an intergovernmental level that the Parliaments of the *Länder* have no choice but to 'ratify' the guidelines as if they were law. The classic problems of parliamentary participation in the area of foreign affairs repeat themselves here within the federal state. Moreover one can recognize in professionally specialized executive committee systems, a structure very similar to the much-criticized European comitology system.[70]

Federal authorities do not intervene in the enforcement by the *Länder* of federal law. States' authorities are not hierarchically dependent on the federal government when they enforce federal laws. Theoretically, federal authorities may control the legality of the enforcement of federal law, but this almost never occurs in practice. The obligation on states' authorities to abide by federal law is guaranteed by the courts—and depends upon legal actions being filed by affected citizens, not by the federal state. The only exception lies in certain politically controversial areas, where the federal state enjoys broad competences to issue directives. The supervision of nuclear facilities has generated a series of constitutional disputes before the courts between the federal state and the *Länder* on this issue. All these disputes have ultimately been won by the federal state.[71] However, this sits uncomfortably with structures of government accountability. Even where federal instructions leave the *Länder* no real choices, it is the *Länder* that remain politically and legally accountable for these decisions.

The German structure of federal administrative enforcement has parallels to the organization of executive power in the European Union. In both cases, rules are normally legislated at the upper level and enforced at the lower level.[72] This similar starting point does not lead to an identical system of legal relationships, however. While the influence of the federal executive on the *Länder* is the exception, European influence on member state governments is much more common. Although EC law acknowledges the institutional autonomy of national administrations,[73] this autonomy does not limit the particular rules of secondary EC law, which may give to the Commission extensive rights of control and intervention. The European enforcement structure presents a confusingly varied structure that is differently designed in each field of law whereby the correlations of cooperation and control between the Commission and national administrations are regulated in different ways. This results in unclear correlations as regards both democratic accountability and legal protection.[74] Despite the fact that it is always problematic

---

[70] For parallels with Europe: G. Haibach, 'Komitologie nach Amsterdam—Die Übertragung von Rechtssetzungsbefugnissen im Rechtsvergleich' (1999) 90 *VerwArch* 98.
[71] BVerfGE 81, 310.   [72] For this comparison: C. Möllers, n. 3.
[73] Case 205-215/82, *Deutsche Milchkontor v. Bundesrepublik* [1983] ECR 2633.
[74] On the last point: J. Hofmann, *Rechtsschutz und Haftung im Europäischen Verwaltungsverbund* (Duncker & Humblot, 2004).

to compare national and supranational levels, the German model of control on enforcement being carried out exclusively by courts may be one from which European administrative law could learn in the future.

(e) Judicial accountability and legal protection

What power does the judiciary possess to hold the exercise of executive power to account? The courts are regarded in Germany as the most important resource for securing accountability. They are the corner stone—as it has been expressed—of the architecture of the rule of law. The 1949 Constitution incorporated an older tradition and built upon it. It provides in Article 19(4): 'Should any person's rights be violated by a public authority, legal recourse shall be open to him.' Neither government nor Parliament may restrict this constitutional guarantee. The only exceptions are the aforementioned controls on correspondence and telephone communications, which are referred to in the Constitution as exceptions.

The legal recourse mentioned in Article 19(4) is, of course, recourse to the courts. In most cases this will be the administrative courts. Together with the civil and criminal courts these constitute the 'third power.' All courts are distinct from the executive as far as their organization, personnel, and functions are concerned. The Constitution prescribes for their independence and neutrality along the same lines as those found in Article 6 ECHR. The administrative courts conduct themselves according to procedures that are stipulated in the relevant Order of 1960 (the '*Verwaltungsgerichtsordnung*'). This Order, along with the Administrative Procedure Act is the second, complementary codification of the principles and institutions of German administrative law.

All government actions—that is, not only administrative acts but also warnings, recommendations, and other communications, can be challenged before the courts. This is known as the doctrine of 'comprehensive legal protection.' If the administration does not grant to the claimant a service or benefit that he applied for, the claimant may raise a claim to require the administration to act upon his petition, while if the administration has not responded to his application, he may raise a claim for a failure act. Legal actions for injunctive relief are also admissible. Instruments of interim legal protection further guarantee legal protection: the courts may award interim remedies and may stay the enforcement of administrative decisions. The most important claim that can be raised against an administrative act (avoidance claim) has a suspending effect. That is to say, the act cannot be executed until the court has decided the case.

The intensity of judicial control is high.[75] According to prevailing opinion, Article 19(4) of the Constitution requires that the courts fully control administrative acts from both a factual and a legal point of view. This is known

---

[75] From a comparative law perspective: R. Brinktrine, *Verwaltungsermessen in Deutschland und England* (C.F. Müller, 1998).

as the doctrine of 'thorough judicial control.' The courts are not bound by the administration's findings of fact, but are required to control the facts of the case for themselves.[76] This applies to notions used in laws, which are vague to a great extent because of their prognostic or valuing content. Here too, the courts have the last word where there is a dispute. For example, courts will thoroughly scrutinize whether in a particular situation there is a danger to public security and order and whether the police are authorized to intervene. Only exceptionally may the legislature entitle the executive to decide in the last resort. Even in these exceptional cases, the courts may control whether the administration has made a justifiable decision.[77] Judicial control examines whether the margin of appreciation set by the law has been observed and whether the authorities have used their powers according to the purpose of the authorizing act. The principle of proportionality is employed in the context of assessing the margin of appreciation. This requires the court to review the suitability, necessity, and adequacy of an executive measure. This principle is central to the German conception of the rule of law. It forms 'a sensible adjustment factor for the balancing between freedom and intervention and for the juxtaposition between common welfare and individual interests.'[78] The various components of the principle of proportionality are thoroughly scrutinized by the courts. This has resulted in the courts often casting light on the discretion of the administration in a very precise way—sometimes even, too precisely. In some cases courts have imposed themselves on areas which are, according to the separation of powers, the responsibility of the administration. This tendency has rightly been criticized. When it is said of the English courts that they have been reluctant to embrace the principle of proportionality,[79] this is not necessarily a bad thing when the German experience is borne in mind. All in all, however, the strong position of the courts vis-à-vis the administration stands the test. Not only do the courts protect individual freedoms, but they also stabilize administrative action by trusting and accepting it. Finally, they guarantee a uniform execution inside the federal structure of divided executive power.

There is one issue on which German administrative law lags behind the legal protection of most other European countries: namely, standing to sue. An action can be filed only by someone who asserts that their rights are violated. The courts have interpreted this notion reasonably broadly. Even third parties may have the right to sue under certain circumstances, such as when they are neighbours or competitors. A mere sufficient interest, however, will not generally suffice—that is, not unless it has been specifically provided for. Thus, actions filed by

---

[76] M. Kaufmann, *Untersuchungsgrundsatz und Verwaltungsgerichtsbarkeit* (Mohr Siebeck, 2002).
[77] E. Schmidt-Aßmann, 'Die Kontrolldichte der Verwaltungsgerichte: Verfassungsgerichtliche Vorgaben und Perspektiven' (1997) 112 *DVBl* 281.
[78] Ch. Knill and F. Becker, 'Divergenz trotz Diffusion, Rechtsvergleichende Aspekte des Verhältnismäßigkeitsprinzips in Deutschland, Großbritannien und der Europäischen Union' (2003) 36 *DV* 447, 463.   [79] *Ibid.*, 475.

associations or interested parties are permitted in some consumer protection law. Generally, however, the courts are reluctant to expand the law of standing, although this could be challenged in the future in the field of environmental law as a result of the Aarhus Convention.[80]

The legitimacy of judicial review is strengthened by the fact that the procedure takes place in public. In legal proceedings, administrative procedures become visible to everyone. The claimant has a right of access to all relevant administrative files, which derives from his constitutional right to a fair trial (in Article 103(1) of the *Grundgesetz*). Given that, for his part, the claimant is not bound by a duty of nondisclosure and that the oral hearing is, as a rule, public, the subject-matter of the proceedings is also rendered public. However, the public nature of administrative legal protection has recently come under pressure from two developments. First, through the increasing number of sensitive administrative procedures in police and secret service matters and, secondly, through the right that has evolved in the context of privatization, in which context the judicial review of a regulatory measure might entail the communication of business secrets. German administrative law suggests that non-public administrative procedures would not, in principle, infringe the Constitution. The continued publicity of the administrative process represents a significant challenge in the praxis and legitimacy of contemporary judicial review.

(f) Other forms of accountability

Most recent changes have taken place, as the issue of actions filed by associations shows, in the field of administrative jurisdiction. In view of the vigorous position of Germany's administrative courts, there is little need for the construction of new instruments of accountability in addition to those that already exist. A traditional instrument is the right of petition. According to Article 17 of the Constitution, everyone has the right to address written requests or complaints to competent authorities and representative assemblies. The Parliaments have their own committees of petitions. These committees are entitled to hear witnesses and experts and to require the administration to submit files and disclose information. It is occasionally argued that some committees—that for asylum affairs, for instance—'interfere' too much. However, only a small proportion of petitions are successful.[81]

There is no tradition of ombudsmen in Germany. There are nonetheless a few commissioners who perform particular tasks similar to those of ombudsmen.[82] Examples include the federal and regional commissioners for the protection of

---

[80] See S. Schlacke, 'Rechtsschutz durch Verbandsklage, Zum Fortentwicklungsbedarf des umweltbezogenen Rechtsschutzsystems' (2004) 26 *Natur und Recht (NuR)* 629.

[81] See on that the report of the committee for petitions of the German Lower House of Parliament for the year 2003, dated 5 May 2004 (BT-Drucks. 15/3150), 12.

[82] See V. Mehde, 'Rechtliche und rechtspolitische Potentiale von Petitionsrecht und Ombudsmanneinrichtungen' (2001) 16 *Zeitschrift für Gesetzgebung (ZG)* 145, including also a comparative perspective with regard to England.

data.[83] They are appointed by their respective Parliaments, are independent in the exercise of their duties and are, of course, subject to the law. Anyone may turn to them when they believe that a public authority has violated its obligations while processing data that pertains to them. In addition, the commissioners for the protection of data have objective controlling tasks vis-à-vis the government: all administrative authorities are obliged to give them information and facilitate their access to files, as well as to permit them to enter their offices. The progress reports that are published every two years are an efficient instrument of review and scrutiny.

Currently there is much discussion in Germany as to how far there should be a general right of access to administrative files.[84] According to the traditional view, only the parties involved in an administrative procedure have such a right. But EC law has brought about a change as far as environmental information is concerned. In the meantime, several *Länder* have introduced a general right of access to their administrative files. Plans to create a similar right at the federal level were put on hold in the light of the new security situation post 11 September 2001.

Accountability has become a newly prominent theme in German debates about the relationship between the individual and the state. Two inter-connected sets of observations may be made in this regard. First, there is increasing scholarly interest in individuals' participation in processes of government. Secondly, there is considerable interest in the idea that the forms of administrative action no longer correspond to the classic model of bureaucratic decisions being unilaterally imposed on individuals.[85]

These issues have gained in importance as a result of EU initiatives, such the privatization of state companies like the postal service and the railways, both of which provoked extensive discussion about the splitting of accountability[86] between the public and private sectors, especially in the context of the performance of ostensibly public duties. There are other fields of law too, such as environmental law, where a variety of regulatory techniques that incorporate the private sector are employed. It is evident that the state no longer delivers many services itself, but rather stands as some sort of guarantor in case the private

---

[83] D. Zöllner, *Der Datenschutzbeauftragte im Verfassungssystem* (Duncker & Humblot, 1995).

[84] F. Schoch and M. Kloepfer, *Informationsfreiheitsgesetz. Entwurf eines Informationsfreiheitsgesetzes für die Bundesrepublik Deutschland* (Duncker & Humblot, 2002).

[85] One may ask oneself whether the notion of accountability is well chosen in this regard because it threatens to blur the basic distinction between individual freedom and state action. See H. C. Röhl, 'Verwaltungsverantwortung als dogmatischer Begriff?' (1999) 32 Beiheft 2 *DV* 33. The debate on administrative law has ignored this question for some time. It has developed instead a variety of different types of more or less intensive involvement of individuals in the accountability of the executive power. See H. Bauer, 'Privatisierung von Verwaltungsaufgaben' (1995) 54 *VVDStRL*, 243, 277ff; G.F. Schuppert, 'Rückzug des Staates?' (1995) 48 *Die öffentliche Verwaltung (DÖV)* 761, 768.

[86] H.-H. Trute, 'Die Verwaltung und das Verwaltungsrecht zwischen gesellschaftlicher Selbstregulierung und staatlicher Steuerung' (1996) 111 *Deutsches Verwaltungsblatt (DVBl.)* 950.

corporations that offer public services should collapse.[87] In the fields of telecommunications, postal, and railway services this form of public responsibility is guaranteed by the Constitution.[88] It is also to be found, however, in other areas that are not regulated by constitutional law, such as the energy market.[89] The constitutional provisions that deal with co-operation between the administration and individuals cannot really solve the problems that arise: on the contrary, it seems that German constitutional law presupposes a clear differentiation between state and private action. These norms lose much of their practical efficacy in structures where accountability is split. Standards of democratic legitimacy and the obligation to respect basic rights cannot be automatically applied to structures in which the state and the private sector act together.

Against this background, administrative law is confronted with the challenge of developing mechanisms that can compensate for the dilution of constitutional law requirements. It is all about developing structures on the level of ordinary laws that do not divorce the different contributions of public administration and the private sector, while on the other hand continuing to differentiate between their divergent rationales. This is perhaps the principal challenge of executive accountability in the early twenty-first century.

---

[87] A. Voßkuhle, 'Beteiligung Privater an der Wahrnehmung öffentlicher Aufgaben und staatliche Verantwortung' (2003) 62 *VVDStRL* 266.

[88] M. Eifert, *Grundversorgung mit Telekommunikationsleistungen im Gewährleistungsstaat* (Nomos, 1998).

[89] For a comparison with the UK: J.-P. Schneider, *Liberalisierung der Stromwirtschaft durch regulative Marktorganisation* (Nomos, 1999).

10

The Executive and the Law in Spain

Daniel Sarmiento*

1. The Spanish Constitution and the role of the executive

In 1978, Spanish politics and public law experienced a dramatic change, both in scope and content. After a dictatorship under General Franco spanning forty years in the aftermath of a cruel civil war, Spain returned to the path of democracy, recovering its constitutional values. The most visible and obvious symptom of this change was the 1978 Constitution, which proclaimed the establishment of a parliamentary monarchy with the King of Spain acting as Head of State, an exhaustive bill of rights, a highly decentralized territorial landscape and an open door towards European integration. After forty years of an unrestricted totalitarian executive, public law became, once again, the leading force on the Spanish political stage.

However, some areas of Spanish public law were surprisingly well developed during Franco's regime. Although constitutional law was at the time a mere list of values and principles designed by the military establishment headed by the *Caudillo*, administrative law proved to be a rather well-established area of the Spanish legal system. During the second half of Franco's regime, a technocratic school of thought flourished inside the executive and brought Spanish administrative law in line with its European counterparts.[1] It was evidently a partial and specific development, but nevertheless it provided Spanish law with efficient and technically well-designed institutions and concepts such as administrative procedures, compulsory purchases, public procurement, public properties, and state

---

* Ph.D., Complutense University of Madrid. Advisor at the Spanish Ministry of the Presidency.

[1] In the late 1950s young scholars and members of the civil service such as Eduardo García de Enterría, Manuel Alonso Olea, Fernando Garrido Falla and Jose Luis Villar Palasí developed a new perspective in the study and practice of administrative law, deeply influenced by the German, French, and Italian experience. The new doctrine was consolidated through a periodical, the *Revista de Administración Pública* (RAP), and its members were lately known as 'the RAP generation'. On the history of this generation and its major works, see E. García de Enterría, 'Para una historia interna de la RAP' (2002) 150 *Revista de Administración Pública* 611; C. Chinchilla Marín, 'Dos grandes momentos en cien años de Derecho administrativo: la década de los cincuenta y la Constitución de 1978', in *El Derecho español en el siglo XX* (Garrigues—Marcial Pons, 2000), 33.

liability.[2] Further, due to the establishment of specialized administrative courts in the late 1950s,[3] Spanish administrative law became a major element of its legal system, despite the lack of a constitutional framework and, above all, democratic governance.

The Constitution of 1978 drastically changed the concept of public law in Spain, but mostly with regard to issues foreign to administrative law. The backbone of administrative law had been developed in the 1960s and early 1970s, and the Constitution confirmed some elements designed and implemented prior to 1978. Thus, the Constitution proved more of a *political* and *structural* change as far as public law was concerned, its legal novelties being limited to the area of constitutional law.

However limited in appearance, the transformation in administrative law was spectacular. From 1978 onwards, Spain became a parliamentary monarchy under the rule of law,[4] with seventeen Autonomous Communities with devolved powers,[5] an independent judiciary, and a major interpreter of the Constitution: the Constitutional Court.[6] The King of Spain is the Head of State and holds representative powers, although previously countersigned by a member of government. He is 'the symbol of [the] unity and permanence' of the Spanish State, he 'arbitrates and moderates the regular working of the institutions, assumes the highest representation of the Spanish State in international relations', and 'performs the functions expressly conferred on him by the Constitution and the law'.[7] The King is inviolable and cannot be held accountable, either legally or politically. But despite his immunity, he holds no executive powers. The source of executive power thus lies with the government. Government acts subject to the political and legal control of Parliament (the *Cortes Generales*) and the courts, respectively. Article 93 of the Constitution enabled Spain to accede to the European Communities, and was put into action in 1986 with Spanish incorporation in the process of European integration.[8]

According to Article 97 of the Constitution, the executive conducts both domestic and foreign policy, directs the operation of the Public Administration

---

[2] The major pieces of legislation were the following: *Ley del Régimen Jurídico de la Administración del Estado* of 26 July 1957; *Ley de Procedimiento Administrativo* of July 17th 1958; *Ley de Expropiación Forzosa* of 16 December 1954 and *Ley del Patimonio del Estado* of 15 April 1964.

[3] The *Ley Reguladora de la Jurisdiccion Contencioso-Administrativa*, of 26 December 1956, thoroughly examined by J.R. Fernández Torres, *Jurisdicción administrativa revisora y tutela judicial efectiva* (Civitas, 1998). [4] See Arts. 56 to 65 of the Constitution.

[5] Andalusia, Aragón, Asturias, Balearic Islands, Canary Islands, Cantabria, Castile—La Mancha, Castile—León, Catalonia, Extremadura, Galicia, La Rioja, Madrid, Murcia, Navarre, Basque Country, and Valencia. Also, the towns of Ceuta and Melilla are established as 'autonomous cities', situated in the north of Africa. See Arts. 137 to 158 of the Constitution.

[6] Arts. 117 to 127 and 159 to 165 of the Constitution. [7] Art. 56 of the Constitution.

[8] Art. 93 states that 'by means of an organic law, authorization may be established for the conclusion of treaties which attribute to an international organization or institution the exercise of competences derived from the Constitution. It is the responsibility of the Parliament or the Government, as the case may be, to guarantee compliance with these treaties and the resolutions emanating from the international or supranational organizations which have been entitled by this cession'.

and guarantees the defence of the state. The executive acts in accordance with the Constitution and the law,[9] and is thus scrutinized by both the ordinary courts and the Constitutional Court. Ordinary courts conduct reviews of administrative issues, mainly through one of the judiciary's specialized jurisdictions: the *contencioso-administrativo* jurisdiction. On the other hand, the Constitutional Court holds competence on territorial conflicts among central and regional powers, although it also has jurisdiction to hear direct action brought by citizens to guarantee their fundamental rights: the *recurso de amparo*.

As may be observed, it is important to underline the major role played by the law in the Spanish constitutional framework. Government was subject, even in Franco's day, to some form of legal scrutiny. However, in 1978, government and all public authorities became strictly subject to the law. Administrative law was no longer the only source of legal scrutiny, and public law as a whole, as a structured and all-embracing system of rules and principles intended to check public power, expanded and helped to consolidate the rule of law. The scope and intensity of this framework will be explained below.

2. The executive through law

(a) The executive as a legal concept

According to Article 97 of the Constitution, the executive is the sum of two distinct but connected organizations: government ('*el Gobierno*') and administration. The government, as a collective body chaired by the President, represents the political face of the executive and thus assumes all political responsibilities. The President is in charge of directing government action and 'co-ordinating the functions of the other members thereof'.[10] On the other hand, the administration is a bureaucratic structure directed by the government, each individual minister being in charge of specific departments. This two-fold structure of the executive helps to distinguish between political and legal responsibilities, but also contributes to assuring a certain degree of continuity in administrative issues. However, the main consequence of the partition lies in the scope of the law and the limits of legal scrutiny. As will be shown in section three of this chapter, the division has contributed to the executive being exempt from certain forms of legal control, particularly judicial control, and helps to trace a line between the political and legal landscape of public affairs.

No matter how well defined the division between government and administration, the Constitution has designed a strict notion of 'legality' as a source of governmental action. Following a century-long tradition in continental Europe, the Spanish executive is bound by the law and acts only when the law so

---

[9] Arts 9.1, 97 and 103 of the Constitution. [10] Art. 98.2 of the Constitution.

provides. The Constitution implicitly provides that all governmental action must be previously authorized by an Act of Parliament, and this requirement applies to every act of the executive. Thus, Spanish public law has made use of a strict version of the principle of legality, although the extent of such principle is currently under consideration. Indeed, the Constitutional Court has made a rigorous use of the principle of legality, while allowing certain areas of governmental action besides legal mandates. Such is the case of executive power in the area of internal administrative organization, or matters that have a positive impact in the legal sphere of citizens.[11] Thus, the executive is empowered exclusively by Acts of Parliament and is therefore bound by the provisions thereof, but in certain areas it will be free to make decisions if, and only if, the consequences of these decisions are not restrictive on individuals. This rather abstract version of the principle of legality, along with the formal definition of the executive in Article 97, provide us with an account of what the law portrays as the executive in Spain. However formalistic, it is a first but essential step in the development of the entire framework of Spanish public law.

(b) The executive and Parliament

Despite the legal definition provided by the Constitution, executive powers can often blend with the role of the legislature, either in cooperative or intrusive terms. Cooperation from the executive is requested by Parliament in cases of severe necessity, extreme technical complexity, or in relation to issues requiring some form of 'codification' or legal ordering. In contrast, the executive holds rule-making powers that often clash with the competence of the *Cortes*, and several constitutional and statutory restrictions have been instituted to avoid such intrusions. Thus, the executive must make use of its rule-making powers subject to the principle of legality, under the conditions mentioned above.

Cooperative participation by the executive often takes place through express delegations from Parliament. When issues are of a technical nature or need some legal codification, Parliament authorizes the executive to draft a complete regulation that will ultimately have the same effects as an Act of the *Cortes*. As long as the executive remains within the conditions of the delegation, its rules will constitute statutes and not administrative decrees. The executive becomes an indirect legislature, and it will make use of these powers to flesh out abstract mandates into concrete provisions. This type of norm, known as *Decretos Legislativos*,[12] is expressly provided by the Constitution and is frequently used by Parliament, although not as often as it might be expected.

---

[11] Arguing for a strict implementation of the principle of legality, see E. García de Enterría and T.-R. Fernández, *Curso de Derecho Administrativo* (Thomson-Civitas, 8th edn., 2002). In more nuanced terms, and following established case-law and administrative practice, see M. Beladiez Rojo, 'La vinculación de la Administración al Derecho' (2000) 153 *Revista de Administración Pública* 315.   [12] Arts. 82 to 85 of the Constitution.

In contrast with the *Decretos Legislativos*, the executive can make use of *Decretos Leyes* in cases of 'extraordinary and urgent necessity',[13] without any prior consent from Parliament. Due to the special circumstances surrounding such norms, the executive will make use of its pseudo-legislative powers and then apply to the *Cortes* to validate the government's decision. The *Decreto Ley* is precluded from areas such as fundamental rights, basic institutions of the state, and territorial and electoral issues, but the Constitutional Court has tended to construe Article 86 of the Constitution, in which the conditions of 'extraordinary and urgent necessity' are stated,[14] both broadly and generously. Thus, the executive has employed this rule-making instrument to liberalize strategic markets, to derogate from previous Parliamentary Acts approved by former parliamentary majorities, or to enforce decisions of the Courts. Due to the slow pace of parliamentary activities compared with the urgencies of daily governance, the executive has at times abused its constitutional powers in this particular area. In 2002, ten *Decretos Leyes* were brought into force, and seven in 2003. Even though these numbers are not excessively high, the circumstances in which the instruments were used could not always be described as 'extraordinary or urgent'.

Despite these cooperative relations, the executive will often collide with the *Cortes* whenever it makes use of its rule-making powers in the implementation of Acts of Parliament. The executive holds such rule-making powers ('*potestad reglamentaria*', as stated by Article 97 of the Constitution), but strictly subject to the provisions laid down by Parliament. The executive will frequently issue regulations in accordance with the provisions of statutes, and the former are often essential to render the latter operative. However, regulations can also enter into areas where Parliament has remained silent. In these cases, the principle of legality comes into play and restricts executive action to areas previously authorized by Parliament. Nevertheless, as previously indicated, legal scholars and case law have agreed on a few exceptions to this strict version of the principle of legality, and currently approve the exercise of governmental regulations in areas with purely internal or organizational consequences.[15] If these conditions are met, the executive holds an inherent and non-delegated rule-making power, but unlike a *Decreto Legislativo* or a *Decreto Ley* (that hold the same status as an Act of Parliament, although issued by the executive), these independent regulations are subordinated to the Constitution and parliamentary acts.

These cases of cooperation and collision hide, however, the real practice of everyday governance. The executive, or rather its political branch (*el Gobierno*), is the result of a parliamentary majority that will ultimately support governmental action. *Decretos Leyes* will be approved by Parliament without hindrance, as the executive is the result of the same parliamentary majorities that will ultimately confirm its decisions. Spanish political parties scrutinize their members closely,

---

[13] Art. 86 of the Constitution.
[14] See Cases 29/1982 (31 May 1982) and 111/1983 (2 December 1983).
[15] See Beladiez, n. 11.

especially their congressmen and senators, and party-discipline has contributed to the blurring of executive and legislative tasks.[16] The law has become an instrumental requirement in any action by government, and constitutional conditions, such as the principle of legality, are seen more as formalistic obstacles than democratic guarantees. But overall, the executive's activities have been rationalized due to conditions established in the law. By setting strict competences in which the executive is allowed to act, and strict conditions for the exercise of these powers, the law has set regular and relatively rigid patterns of conduct that citizens may expect. Also, the courts have played a decisive role in ensuring that the government remains within the confines of its powers, and we shall see in section three of this chapter how intense the degree of judicial review is at present.

(c) The executive, the regions and local government

An outstanding feature of the Spanish constitutional framework is its highly decentralized territorial structure, made up of three levels of power: central, regional, and local authorities. The Constitution guarantees legislative and executive powers to the Autonomous Communities and executive powers to local authorities, but the precise definition of regional and local governance is left to a constant and open-ended process of devolution, to be designed and negotiated by all central, regional, and local authorities. The Constitution establishes a fixed set of competences held exclusively by central authorities (e.g. nationality, immigration, international relations, defence and the Armed Forces, Administration of Justice, commercial, civil, labour, criminal and procedural legislation, monetary system, etc.),[17] followed by a list of competences that Autonomous Communities can assume voluntarily and include in their respective *Estatutos de Autonomía*.[18] During the early 1980s most Autonomous Communities assumed in their *Estatutos* a wide list of competences, both legislative and executive in nature, which were increased significantly in the following years due to legislative transfers of power approved by the *Cortes*. Each Autonomous Community assumes its competences in the terms and conditions individually agreed vis-à-vis the central authorities. As a result, Spain's different regions currently enjoy a varied and asymmetric degree of decentralization.

---

[16] See M. Presno Linera, *Los partidos y las distorsiones jurídicas de la democracia* (Ariel, 2000).
[17] Art. 149 of the Constitution.
[18] Art. 148 includes a non-exhaustive list of competences that may be assumed by Autonomous Communities in their *Estatutos de Autonomía*. Among others, the Communities had the power to assume legislative and executive competences over the organization of their institutions, town and country planning, railways and roads whose routes lie exclusively within the territory of the Autonomous Community, recreation ports and airports, agriculture, forestry, environmental protection management, local fairs, promotion of culture, sports, social assistance, health and hygiene. All the regions have gone way beyond the list of Art. 148 in their *Estatutos*, and they will undergo changes in the near future to assume further competences, although limited by the exclusive competences held by central authorities listed in Art. 149 of the Constitution.

As a consequence of the nature of the competences assumed by the Autonomous Communities, each region has a representative chamber and a regional executive. Conflicts of competence and jurisdiction between central and regional authorities fall under the jurisdiction of the Constitutional Court, but the ordinary courts also deal with a growing number of cases concerning regional and central disputes. According to Article 153 of the Constitution, 'central-Law', or 'state-Law' as it is commonly known, is a subsidiary source in areas covered by regional competence.

With this legal background and despite the centralized structure of the state during the years prior to 1978, regional governments have assumed an extraordinary role in Spain.[19] Most Autonomous Communities have historical, linguistic, and political roots that reinforce the existence of a regional polity,[20] and the past twenty years have borne witness to impressive development in this level of governance. Furthermore, the law has attained higher standards of legitimacy (particularly regional law), but there has also been greater conflict than hitherto. The Constitutional Court has devised solid case law regarding the division of competences among central and regional authorities, but its precedents are still too attached to concrete cases and specific competences. Whenever a doubt arises as to who has competence, the conflict is barely negotiated and tends to be placed directly into the hands of the Constitutional Court. A form of institutional litigation becomes the norm, and issues concerning specific competences become legal issues to be solved in judicial rather than political terms.

A similar portrait can be drawn at a local level. Spain has over eight thousand local municipalities, and the Constitution guarantees their autonomy vis-à-vis central and regional authorities.[21] However, the main structures of local governments are not designed by the Constitution itself, a task left to the *Cortes* and regional Parliaments. The *Cortes* defines the 'basic' elements of local governments, and the regions develop these common structural features in order to adapt local authorities to the peculiarities of each Autonomous Community.[22] Along with these 'basic' and regional features, both central and regional authorities can devolve powers in specific matters to the local authorities through Parliamentary Acts. Therefore, municipalities in Catalonia can be far more independent than municipalities in Andalusia, should the Catalonian Parliament deem it appropriate, but only in those areas over which Catalonia holds competence.

Therefore, Spain has developed a complex and multi-layered system of governance, with three different authorities acting as a result of three different

---

[19] E. Aja, *El Estado Autonómico. Federalismo y hechos diferenciales* (Alianza Editorial, 2nd edn., 2003).

[20] Particularly the Balearic Islands, the Basque Country, Catalonia, Galicia, and Valencia for linguistic reasons.   [21] Art. 140 of the Constitution.

[22] The 'basic' provisions were enacted by Parliament in 1985, through the *Ley reguladora de las Bases del Régimen Local*, of 2 April. Currently most Autonomous Communities have their 'Local Government Act', covering those areas left open by the 'basic' 1985 Act. See L. Morell Ocaña, *El régimen local español* (Civitas, 1988).

electoral processes. Democratic legitimacy is thus evident in the three levels of government and the law is a consequence of this complex but democratically enhanced design.

(d) The executive and the EU

The process of European integration has added further sophistication to the Spanish territorial framework. Along with the devolution of powers from central to regional and local governments, Spain has also attributed some of its sovereign competences to the European Union. The state is represented in the Council and European Council by the central executive, and thus the regions and local governments barely have a voice in Brussels. Efforts have been made in the past to assure some form of regional participation, although results have been modest and the process is currently under consideration.[23]

Nevertheless, however deficient this participation may be, both the regions and municipalities have significant competence with regard to the implementation of EU law. The regions have competences in areas such as the environment, employment, and commerce, and are thus involved in major areas of European policy. Regional and local implementation can take place either through regulations or administrative action, but in both cases this requires coordination with the *Cortes* and central government.[24] Therefore, EU law has become an important element of Spanish public law and has also contributed in reinforcing Spain's devolution process. The European decision-making process requires coherent positions from each Member State, and hence forces regions and central authorities to speak with a single voice. Although the current coordination method still fails to provide the regions with full guarantees of representation, it has nevertheless forced agreements and common policies among central and regional authorities in ways that are hard to imagine in purely domestic issues.

(e) The executive in times of emergency: extraordinary powers and the role of Parliament

The executive can issue three different declarations in cases of emergency, each depending on the gravity of the circumstances. The 'state of emergency' requires no parliamentary intervention, and would be issued in cases akin to natural disasters, health emergencies, and other similar contingencies. Conversely, a 'state of exception' and a 'state of siege' require the prior approval of Parliament,

---

[23] Cooperation between the state and the regions is currently articulated through the Conference for European Affairs Act 1997. See a critical analysis by legal scholars in P. Pérez Tremps, *La participación europea y la acción exterior de las Comunidades Autónomas* (Institut d'Estudis Autonòmics, 1997).

[24] A.M. Moreno Molina, *La ejecución administrativa del Derecho comunitario: régimen europeo y español* (Marcial Pons, 1998).

and are provided only in cases of extreme urgency. As a consequence of any of the above declarations, the executive is enabled to restrict several fundamental rights, particularly the right of persons to free movement (including deprivations of liberty), privacy, or assembly.[25]

However relevant the role of Parliament might be, all decisions made by the executive in these circumstances are subject to judicial review. This is provided in Article 3 of the State of Emergency, Exception and Siege Act, followed by the recognition of the right of all individuals to claim for damages despite the circumstances in which the executive's decisions were made. This rule carries important consequences from a legal standpoint.

First, Article 3 reinforces the right to an effective remedy provided in Article 24 of the Constitution, and thus implies a stricter degree of scrutiny by the courts.[26] This conclusion is reinforced by the contents of the Act, which require the executive to make decisions strictly adhering to the requirements of the principle of proportionality.[27] Thus, the extraordinary powers assumed by the executive in these circumstances are proportional to the intensity of the review to be exercised by the courts.

Second, parliamentary scrutiny plays an accessory role once the declarations have been made, and review of executive action becomes a strictly legal issue. In practice, the burden of control lies in the hands of the courts, and the *Cortes* assume the role of a mere witness. This may even be dramatically so in cases where Parliament is unable to form, as occurred on 23 February 1981 when a frustrated *coup d'etat* took over the *Cortes* for several hours, and no parliamentary decision could be taken during such time.

3. Accountability and the law

(a) Accountability through Parliament

Constituted as a parliamentary monarchy, Spain's political system has a strict separation of powers in which Parliament plays an essential role in the election, scrutiny, and fall of the executive. The *Cortes* 'represent the Spanish people and consist of the Congress of Deputies and the Senate'.[28] The Congress of Deputies invests the President of the Spanish Government with its confidence by vote of the absolute majority of its members, and both chambers are responsible for parliamentary scrutiny over the executive. As the President of the Government is a member of Parliament and the trustee of a parliamentary majority, the *Cortes*

---

[25] See Arts. 55 and 116 of the Constitution.

[26] P. Cruz Villalón, *Estados excepcionales y suspensión de garantías* (Tecnos, 1984).

[27] See Art. 1.2 of the State of Emergency, Exception and Siege Act 1981. See also, D. Sarmiento, *El control de proporcionalidad de la actividad administrativa* (Tirant lo Blanch, 2004).

[28] See Art. 66.1 of the Constitution.

play a relevant role in everyday politics, particularly when the government holds a small majority either in Congress or the Senate.

The Autonomous Communities have also instituted governments dependant upon the majority of their regional Parliament, and this form of political accountability is almost identical to the mechanisms designed by the Constitution for the *Cortes* and the central government. Despite the gap in the Constitution on this matter, the regions have always looked upon the example of central Parliament and government in the definition and regulation of their democratic institutions.

Parliamentary accountability is the expression of political control over the government's action. The law plays an ancillary role in the actions of Parliament, mostly aimed at the organization and rationalization of debates and decision-making.[29] Political scrutiny occurs through oral and written questioning,[30] parliamentary inquiries, and reports,[31] and oral hearings with the intervention of members of government.[32] These activities attract a significant amount of attention in the media, and Parliament thus becomes the main stage of political discussion, both in central and regional decision-making. But the degree of attention has been conditioned in the past by the nature of parliamentary majorities, and the levels of support achieved by each government. This feature is a consequence of electoral outcomes and it is hardly associated with the role of the law in the course of everyday parliamentary activities. Nevertheless, it is obvious that weak governments have been highly dependant on the logic of parliamentary accountability and the support of its political allies in the *Cortes*, while other periods of Spanish political history, in which governments ruled with an absolute majority both in Congress and the Senate, show a considerable decrease of Parliament's influence on governmental scrutiny.[33] On these occasions, accountability can become an eminently judicial task, and the courts have taken over the role of Parliament due to the latter's limited capacity to assure strict control over the executive's actions, particularly in sensitive or notorious cases in which political scrutiny has proved to be inefficient. Of course this exchange of roles between Parliament and the courts only occurs under extreme circumstances, and will also be influenced by the reticence of high officials to assume responsibilities and therefore resign.

This exchange of roles between Parliament and the courts proves how malleable political scrutiny can sometimes be, and highlights the subsidiary task of the courts when Parliament's powers are weakened. However, whenever the courts have assumed these stronger responsibilities, the executive's attention has

---

[29] Besides the constitutional provisions regulating the *Cortes*, both Congress and Senate have their respective regulations (Regulations of the Congress of Deputies, of 10 February 1982 and Regulations of the Senate, of 3 May 1994). Regional Parliaments also have their own Regulations, as approved by the Chambers in the exercise of their autonomy.
[30] Arts. 109 and 111 of the Constitution. [31] Art. 76 of the Constitution.
[32] Art. 111 of the Constitution.
[33] This was the case in the periods 1982–86, 1986–89, 1989–93 and 2000–04.

obviously turned towards the judiciary, in the hope of affecting future judgments through a policy of politically-aimed appointments to the bench. In practice, the executive's efforts have mostly been in vain in Spain, and the courts, particularly the administrative courts, continuously show a high degree of independence. Of course the courts are obviously involved in the game of politics, but their interests are mostly based on their own autonomy with respect to the executive. Judicial politics have been mostly attached to the professional demands of the judiciary or to issues that conditioned their independence with other powers of the state. This exceptional role of the judiciary in the political arena has, however, empowered its jurisdiction in the review of governmental action, as will now be explained.

(b) Accountability through the courts

However decentralized Spain may be, the devolution of powers has not affected the judiciary. The Autonomous Communities hold competences over the administrative tasks pertaining to the courts (bailiffs, Court secretaries, services such as the provision of official state paper, etc.), but not much more.[34] The judiciary is governed by its own representative institution, the General Council of the Judiciary (*'Consejo General del Poder Judicial'*).[35] The Supreme Court (*'Tribunal Supremo'*)[36] operates pursuant to an internal division of tasks based on the subject matter involved: civil, criminal, administrative, and labour courts. The executive's actions come under the competence of the administrative courts, but their jurisdiction is not exclusive, for public officials and governmental activities can, and usually do, become the centre of a civil, criminal, or labour dispute before other courts competent in their relevant jurisdictions. However, the vast majority of public law cases are adjudicated in the administrative courts, whose jurisdiction extends to the review of administrative action and inaction.[37] They also review administrative regulations and *Decretos Legislativos* that have exceeded the delegation they are based upon.[38] The administrative courts' jurisdiction extends not only over all public authorities, central, regional, and local, but also over independent agencies and regulatory bodies using public powers.[39] Their jurisdiction even includes the judicial review of 'administrative issues'

---

[34] Art. 149.1.5 of the Constitution and the Constitutional Court judgments 56/1990 and 62/90, where the competences of the regions over the 'administration of justice' were confirmed.

[35] Art. 122.2 of the Constitution and Arts. 107 to 148 of the Judiciary Act 1985.

[36] Art. 123 of the Constitution.

[37] Besides the general provisions included in the Judiciary Act 1985, the administrative courts are regulated under the Administrative Jurisdiction Act 1998. Art. 25 of the Act states that the courts are competent to judge administrative decrees and acts, both express or tacit. The courts are also empowered to review the legality of administrative inaction, and 'material actions that may constitute a *vía de hecho*'. The latter are understood as administrative actions lacking of all legal formalities, both procedural and substantive.

[38] Art. 1, section 1 of the Administrative Jurisdiction Act.

[39] Art. 1, section 2 of the Administrative Jurisdiction Act.

arising in 'constitutional organs', that is, the *Cortes*, the Constitutional Court, the General Council of the Judiciary, the Court of Auditors, and the Ombudsman.[40] Standing requirements are extremely generous due to an ample construction of the fundamental right to an effective legal remedy in Article 24 of the Constitution, and individuals as well as organizations have access to the courts whenever their 'rights' or 'legitimate interests' are in question.[41] Full access is thus guaranteed.

The scope of judicial review is therefore wide and ample, and the executive is subject to legal scrutiny in practically all its expressions. Even when governmental delegations provide public powers to private corporations or associations, the administrative courts have been zealous in the implementation of their jurisdiction, and no matter how private the activity may be, if public powers are involved they are subject to judicial review by the administrative courts. This has been so in the case of sports law, where most decisions by private sport federations come under the scrutiny of administrative courts.[42] Recent privatizations of state-owned corporations have also been made subject to the administrative courts whenever public officials or state funds are involved in their activities.[43]

However generous the *scope* of the courts' jurisdiction, the *intensity* of review is also a matter of constant debate. No matter how wide the notion of 'public powers' and standing requirements, judicial review in Spain is also conditioned by the concept of administrative discretion, its precise meaning and the dividing lines between judicial, administrative, and political tasks. As I will now show in this chapter, past years have been witness to a lively debate over these crucial matters.

(i) Clearing the ground: political or administrative action?

A major feature of public law during Franco's regime was the surprising scope and intensity of judicial review. Despite being a military dictatorship, during the 1950s and 1960s Spanish public law achieved a considerable degree of judicial scrutiny over the executive's decisions.[44] But no matter how generous the military establishment tried to show itself, the rules applicable to judicial review kept several safeguards with the sole purpose of restricting judicial scrutiny over

---

[40] Art. 1, section 3 of the Administrative Jurisdiction Act.

[41] J.R. Fernández Torres, 'La legitimación corporativa en la jurisdicción contencioso-administrativa y el derecho a la tutela judicial efectiva', in *La protección jurídica del ciudadano. Estudios en homenaje al profesor Jesús González Pérez* (Civitas, 1997), 1379.

[42] G. Real Ferrer, *Derecho público del deporte* (Civitas, 1991), and J. Bermejo Vera, *Constitución y deporte* (Tecnos, 1998).

[43] S. González-Varas Ibáñez, *El Derecho Administrativo privado* (Montecorvo, 1996), 113–27.

[44] Access to the bench was based on an exam, but the appointment to strategic posts of the judiciary was strictly under the control of the regime. The administrative courts were highly technical and at first glance administrative cases were better left in the hands of specialized judges. As a consequence, the members of the administrative courts were not necessarily the most reactionary members of the judiciary. Also, they proved to be more receptive to scholarly contributions, and this explains the influence of the works of García de Enterría.

sensitive issues. The Administrative Jurisdiction Act 1956 therefore included an ouster clause to be considered whenever the challenged administrative decision was of a 'political' nature.[45] This rule gave birth to the doctrine of 'political acts' as a source of governmental immunity from judicial review. The notion of 'political acts' was left in the hands of the administrative courts, but achieved the contrary effect to that expected by the regime: administrative courts struggled to restrict the contents of 'political acts', and gradually established a reasonably ample case law expanding the areas of executive action subject to judicial review.

The doctrine of 'political acts' survived after the enactment of the 1978 Constitution. This was probably due to the positive role of the administrative courts during the latter years of Franco's regime, but the doctrine proved deficient shortly after democracy was restored to Spain. Absolute judicial immunity from administrative action had to be rejected when it collided with the respect for fundamental rights. No matter how restrictive the judicial construction of 'political acts' had been, the doctrine clashed with the Constitution and particularly with the fundamental right to an effective remedy. In the seminal case of the *CESID documents*,[46] the administrative chamber of the Supreme Court ruled that the doctrine of 'political acts' could not apply where it would preclude an individual's right to a fair trial. In the course of judicial investigations over the counter-terrorist activities approved by the Ministry of the Interior in the late 1980s, several documents of the secret services, classified as confidential, were requested by the judge in charge of the case. The government denied all access, and when its decision was appealed before the *Tribunal Supremo* it argued that such a decision was immune from judicial review, as it was to be considered a 'political act'. The Supreme Court dismissed the argument and set a series of conditions governing the executive's use of the doctrine. The Court's main concern was based on the protection of fundamental rights, and thus stated that 'Articles 9 and 24.1 of the Constitution require judicial scrutiny whenever the legislature has defined legal boundaries through judicially feasible concepts. In such case, the Courts must review eventual excesses or breaches of previous legal requirements in which the Government might have incurred'.[47]

In its judgment regarding the *CESID documents*, the Supreme Court anticipated the Administrative Jurisdiction Act 1997. The doctrine of 'political acts' was indirectly incorporated in the Act, but in considerably nuanced terms. Article 2, section (a) establishes the administrative courts' jurisdiction in cases pertaining to the judicial protection of fundamental rights, regulatory-based elements, and state liability, in regard to all acts issued by the central and regional governments, 'whatever the nature of such acts'. The new regulation is an important contribution to judicial review for the following reasons.

---

[45] Art. 2, section (a) of the former Administrative Jurisdiction Act.
[46] Cases 602, 634 and 726/1996.
[47] *Ibid.*, para. 8. See B. Lozano, *La desclasificación de los secretos de Estado* (Civitas, 1998).

First, it eradicates the ouster clause provided in the 1956 Act and tacitly recognizes a scope of immunity in the decisions of *the government*, but not of the administration. The distinction previously made in section two of this chapter now becomes crucial in determining the scope of judicial review. Article 2 of the 1997 Act therefore restricts judicial immunity to decisions of a clear and evident political nature, such as the design of governmental policies. Second, it redirects the debate over 'political acts' back to the terrain of discretion, from which it never should have moved. As we will now see, the debate over political decisions is not different from the discussion over how much discretion a public official has. Third, no matter how political an act may be, it will always be subject to judicial review if it violates fundamental rights or breaches clear and unconditional statutory provisions. Also, the state will be liable for the damages inflicted in the making of political decisions. The scope of judicial review is therefore considerably increased, and the courts will always have a word to say no matter how political in nature a decision is. Along with the case law concerning discretionary powers, the role of public law and administrative courts thus becomes central.

(ii) The real debate: discretion, interpretation and substitutive powers of the courts

Since the notion of 'political acts' has been driven into the province of administrative discretion, the Spanish administrative courts have been more concerned with the scope of discretionary powers and the limits of judicial review. The terms of the debate are not conditioned by the existence of 'political' or 'non-political' issues, for these matters have been severely restricted by the Administrative Jurisdiction Act 1997. The real debate over discretionary powers and judicial review is now discussed in terms familiar to other European legal systems, particularly the French and German. Thus, judicial review of the executive's discretionary actions has currently been based on three grounds of review: breach of legal indeterminate concepts, clear and unconditional statutory provisions, and principles of law.[48] The entire construction of discretionary powers and its limits is a creation of the courts, first developed in the latter years of the Franco regime, and thoroughly developed after the enactment of the Constitution. The legislature has accepted this doctrine in the past, and most of the courts' contributions can now be found in the provisions of the Administrative Jurisdiction Act 1997, as a consequence of lively and productive feedback between the courts and Parliament.

'Legal indeterminate concepts' are open-ended terms contained in statutory provisions. This doctrine was first established in German administrative law and later transplanted into Spanish public law in the late 1960s with considerable

---

[48] E. García de Enterría and T.-R. Fernández, *Curso de Derecho Administrativo* (Thomson-Civitas, 8th edn., 2002), 444–73.

success.[49] According to its supporters, legal indeterminate concepts are terms whose constructions are solely in the hands of the courts. Only the courts can provide legally valid interpretative criteria over the content and scope of terms such as 'general interest', 'objective justification', 'necessary means', or 'reasonable time-limit'. The aim behind this doctrine is obvious, that is, an interpretative monopoly held by the courts over terms that may require the 'will of Parliament' to determine their proper meaning. The Spanish administrative courts thus ignore any reference to legislative intention in the construction of statutes, and base their reasoning on self-sufficient criteria, particularly previous case law. As a consequence of this doctrine the courts have given themselves considerable power, constructing their own concept of legal provisions, and even avoiding the contents of statutory provisions, no matter how clear they may be.

Judicial review of discretionary action will also be available when the administration has breached clear und unconditional provisions that regulate the exercise of such powers. These provisions, such as an age requirement or the ownership of a product, will usually require no interpretation by the court and thus restrict the margin of action originally granted by a discretionary power.

Furthermore, judicial scrutiny will also take place when the administration violates general principles of law, such as proportionality, legitimate expectations, equality, or transparency. The importance of principles in Spanish public law will be developed in the following section.

The consequence of the doctrine of discretion and legal indeterminate concepts is a fully empowered administrative jurisdiction. However, the way in which the courts initially made use of their powers was deferential to the administration. Despite the margin of interpretation placed in the hands of the courts, their scrutiny has depended upon several criteria, particularly the 'normative density' of a specific area of the law, the technical difficulties of the case, and the intensity of the breach of individual rights, mostly when the case deals with fundamental rights. Depending on the presence or absence of these factors, the administrative courts will vary the intensity of review, thus creating a substantive model of judicial review that is somewhat nuanced in actual practice.[50]

---

[49] The first complete work on this issue was F. Sáinz Moreno, *Conceptos jurídicos, interpretación y discrecionalidad administrativa* (Civitas, 1976), later followed by the Supreme Court and, finally, established case law. The doctrine has been severely criticized in recent years by M. Bacigalupo, *La discrecionalidad administrativa. Estructura normativa, control judicial y límites constitucionales de su atribución* (Marcial Pons, 1997), 125 and M. Beltran de Felipe, *Discrecionalidad administrativa y Constitución* (Tecnos, 1995), 235–61.

[50] In the 1990s, several administrative lawyers held an important debate over the scope and intensity of judicial review of discretionary action. The defenders of an intense and exhaustive scrutiny, such as Eduardo García de Enterría and Tomás-Ramón Fernández, had to admit that several areas of administrative action were immune to scrutiny, or required nuanced approaches. On the other hand, authors such as Luciano Parejo and Miguel Sánchez Morón supported a deference-oriented perspective to judicial review, but also recognized that discretion was a legal concept, and therefore a matter to be solved exclusively by the Courts. Overall, the debate proved that both camps agreed on the main features of a substantive type of judicial review over administrative discretion, and this perspective is currently upheld by the practice of the courts.

Another relevant feature of judicial review of discretionary action deals with the substitutive powers of the courts. Substitution of administrative decisions takes place when the plaintiff claims the full restoration of his or her legal situation, which may imply the adoption of a new administrative act. The courts have traditionally devolved these matters to the competent administration, but the Administrative Jurisdiction Act 1998 empowers the courts to grant 'full reparation' to the plaintiff, thus including substitution of administrative decisions.[51] A typical case of substitution is found in the judicial review of denied licences, once the court finds that the law imposes no objection to such licences being granted. The court is then empowered either to order the competent authority to issue a new licence, or it may issue the licence itself. The latter will take place only if the law can be specified in clear and unconditional terms, and if the plaintiff proves that he or she is entitled to the license. If these conditions are met, the court will substitute the administration's previous decision and resolve the case by itself. However, if the court has to exercise a margin of discretion in the substitution of the decisions, it is most probable that the case will be referred to the administration so that the decision is taken by the executive.[52]

(iii) Judicial review and beyond: principles of law and the role of European law

Legal scrutiny of the executive's action has gradually evolved from formalistic methods of review towards substantive standards of scrutiny. The doctrine of discretion and legal indeterminate concepts proved an adequate first step in the evolution of administrative law during the 1960s and 1970s, and thus laid a framework of judicial review by the time the Constitution was approved. But probably the most outstanding sign of substantive judicial review has developed through the doctrine of general principles of law.

Principles of law, understood as 'optimizing commands' that demand argumentation,[53] are open-ended norms that empower the court to apply a balance test that will ultimately solve a particular legal question. In most legal systems, principles are a source of judicial discretion, rather than an answer to the issue of administrative discretion. However, the Spanish Constitution and its legislature

---

See, E. García de Enterría, *Democracia, jueces y control de la Administración* (Civitas, 4th edn., 2000); T.-R., Fernández, *De la arbitrariedad de la Administración* (Civitas, 3rd edn., 1999); L. Parejo Alfonso, *Administrar y juzgar: dos funciones constitucionales distintas y complementarias* (Tecnos, 1993); M. Sánchez Morón, *Discrecionalidad administrativa y control judicial* (Tecnos, 1994). On the terms of this debate, see M. Atienza, 'Sobre el control de discrecionalidad administrativa: Comentarios a una polémica' (1995) 85 *Revista Española de Derecho Administrativo* 5.

[51] Art. 31, section 2 of the Administrative Jurisdiction Act.

[52] M. Beltrán de Felipe, *El poder de sustitución en la ejecución de las sentencias condenatorias de la Administración* (Civitas, 1995).

[53] Robert Alexy's terminology of principles, conceptualized as 'optimization requirements', has been accepted in Spanish public law. Authors such as J. M Rodríguez de Santiago, F. Velasco, and F. Rubio Llorente have contributed to the usage of the term, and it is quite common that the concept of principles is linked to Alexy's work.

have both frequently turned to principles as binding norms, thus leaving the final construction of each principle in the hands of the courts. The Constitution has expressed several principles of law that flesh out the basic structure of Spanish constitutional and administrative law: legality, equality, legal certainty, proportionality, etc. Even the charter of fundamental rights, contained in Articles 14 to 52 of the Constitution, can be understood as a list of principles expressed in the language of rights.[54] In fact, the European Court of Justice has categorized fundamental rights 'as an integral part of the general principles of law the observance of which the Court ensures',[55] and the Spanish courts, including the Constitutional Court, have also endorsed this conception, although applied to the rights guaranteed by the Spanish Constitution.

Along with the Constitution, legal provisions have also made reference to binding principles of law, thus conditioning the executive's action, and ultimately empowering administrative courts. Spanish legislation will frequently begin with a statement of principles directly applicable to its subject matter.[56] These principles will also have interpretative consequences, for the courts will often construct other legal provisions in the light of general principles, mostly when these principles have been previously defined in the same statutory body. Therefore, principles can serve as fully-fledged norms that will give a complete answer to a specific case, but also as interpretative tools for the solution of legal gaps and statutory construction. And despite the fact that Spanish public law is mostly made up of statutory provisions, the courts tend to make frequent use of both written and unwritten principles.

The doctrine of principles was developed by García de Enterría in the mid-1960s with extraordinary success.[57] Influenced by the French *Conseil d'Etat*'s case law and the academic works of Viehweg, Enterría proposed a serious approach to principles of administrative law, later to be followed by the Supreme Court. The entry into force of the Constitution reinforced Enterría's substantive conception of public law, invigorating the use of principles by the courts, but also, as it was said, by Parliament.

Since Spain's entry into the European Communities, the principles of EC Law have reinforced the use of such norms by the courts. Direct effect and supremacy of EC law enable national courts to implement EC principles, despite the contents of national law.[58] The nature of EC law thus provides a 'parallel' list of principles, both national and European, to be implemented depending on the existence of a European link. When certain EC principles proved to have higher

---

[54] F. Rubio Llorente (ed.), *Derechos fundamentales y principios constitucionales* (Ariel, 1995), xiv–xvi.   [55] Case 11/70, *Internationale Handelsgesellschaft* [1970] ECR 1125, para. 4.

[56] This is the case with important pieces of legislation such as the Coastal Areas Act 1988, the Citizen's Security Act 1992, the Health System Act 1986, as well as a vast majority of environmental Acts.

[57] E. García de Enterría, 'Reflexiones sobre la Ley y los principios generales del Derecho en el Derecho administrativo' (1965) 40 *Revista de Administración Pública* 124.

[58] T. Tridimas, *The General Principles of EC Law* (Oxford University Press, 2000), 19–23.

standards of protection, the Spanish courts were forced to equate such divergent degrees of control, and it ultimately had, inevitably, a spill-over effect onto national law. EC law thus contributed to the strengthening of substantive review by the courts, but also expanded its contents into areas foreign to Spanish national law. In order to avoid dual and parallel regimes depending on the existence or not of a European link, the courts (as well as the legislature) have expanded the contents of EC law into the province of Spanish public law, and this process has been particularly fruitful in the case of EC principles.

Such was the case of the principle of legitimate expectations, once imported from German administrative law into the case law of the ECJ, but completely foreign to the Spanish public law tradition.[59] However, the fact that the Spanish courts were making frequent use of it whenever a case bore an EC law link, forced Parliament to incorporate the principle as a general principle of administrative law, so stating in section 3 of the Legal Regime of Public Administrations Act. From then onwards, legitimate expectations have become an important feature of Spanish administrative law, and judicial review has increased its degree of protection in comparison with previous case law, before the principle was fully incorporated into Spanish law.[60]

Principles of law are one further instrument in the creation of a substantive conception of the rule of law. The development of a complete system of judicial review requires normative criteria, and these elements sometimes require an individual answer to an individual case. Such solutions can only be previously laid through open-ended norms, such as principles, and a considerable degree of judicial discretion. Although principles can prove to be a dangerous weapon in the hands of non-elected authorities, such as judges, the case law proves that the courts have made a careful and fully reasoned use of such norms.[61] Legal argumentation by the courts has proven to be a crucial element in the implementation of principles, for it shows the logical procedure through which a judge applies the law to a specific case. A theory of legal reasoning therefore becomes an important tool in the practice and scrutiny of judicial review, as it shows the limits of legal discourse, or at least it points to the weaknesses of a court's decision.

This feature of theories of legal reasoning explains why in recent years Spanish public lawyers have become interested in the works of legal theorists, such as

---

[59] J. García Luengo, *El principio de protección de la confianza en el Derecho administrativo* (Civitas, 2002); E. Arana García, *La alegación de la propia torpeza y su aplicación al Derecho Administrativo* (Comares, 2003); J. González Pérez, *El principio de la buena fe en el Derecho administrativo* (Civitas, 4th edn., 2004).

[60] In particular, see the Supreme Court's judgement in Case 495/1998, para. 1.

[61] For example, in areas of wide administrative discretion, proportionality is implemented only in cases of extreme unreasonableness. If the courts accept to quash an administrative decision on the grounds of proportionality, they will give exhaustive reasons in a way that is not common in other judgments. Overall, balancing tests are the result of a careful analysis of multiple conditions, supported by thorough argumentation by the court.

Alexy or MacCormick.[62] This convergent vision of public law and legal theory, along with the growing influence of European law, has led to a wider perspective being taken by lawyers that ultimately has enriched a substantive conception of judicial review. As I pointed out above, the courts have made a cautious use of substantive standards of review, and Parliament has contributed to confirming this type of scrutiny.[63] Social scientists have still to prove if this framework is efficient and contributes to reinforce the authority of the executive, but at the present time it appears to be the outcome of a gradual process in which the courts and Parliament have upheld a substantive perspective towards Spanish public law.

(iv) State liability as a means of control

The Spanish courts will undertake substantive judicial review, and the final judgment can go beyond the formal annulment of an administrative act or regulation. Under Spanish public law the executive is bound by the law, and it must also bear the cost of the damages it causes on individuals. State liability is a parallel form of legal protection that can accompany the plaintiff's claim. It has become a major feature of administrative law and is applicable to damage caused by all public authorities, including Parliament and the courts. In fact, damages can be claimed either with or without fault in the executive's actions, and this has caused an extraordinary degree of protection for the individual, but with considerable economic consequences for the Treasury. Absence of fault in the executive's actions implies that mere damages will suffice to grant compensation, without regard to the authorities' negligence, will, or intention. This form of liability, commonly known as 'objective liability', is currently the cause of profound reconsideration among legal scholars and the courts.[64]

However, state liability is a guaranteed right provided in Article 106.2 of the Spanish Constitution, and it can hardly be avoided by the courts or Parliament.[65] As a common denominator to all forms of state liability, individuals can

---

[62] There is an evident impact of these theories on the works of administrative lawyers such as T.-R. Fernández, n. 50, 223, L. Arroyo Jiménez, *Libre empresa y títulos habilitantes* (Centro de Estudios Políticos y Constitucionales, 2004); E. Desdentado Daroca, *Discrecionalidad administrativa y planeamiento urbanístico. Construcción teórica y análisis jurisprudencial* (Aranzadi, 2nd edn., 1999); L. Moral Soriano, *El precedente judicial* (Marcial Pons, 2003); J. M. Rodríguez de Santiago, *La ponderación de bienes e intereses en el Derecho administrativo* (Marcial Pons, 2000).

[63] For example, the Health System Act 1986 includes in Title I, Chapter I, a list of 'general principles' including 'promotion of health', 'promotion of individual, family and social interests in the establishment of adequate sanitary measures', 'sanitary assistance in all cases', etc.

[64] See F. Pantaleón Prieto, *Responsabilidad médica y responsabilidad de la Administración (Hacia una revision del sistema de responsabilidad patrimonial de las Administraciones Públicas)* (Civitas, 1995); O. Mir Puigpelat, *La responsabilidad patrimonial de la Administración. Hacia un Nuevo sistema* (Civitas, 2002).

[65] According to Art. 106, section 2, 'Private individuals shall, under the terms established by law, be entitled to compensation for any loss that they may suffer to their property or rights, except in cases of *force majeure*, whenever such loss is the result of the operation of public services.'

claim for damages if three conditions are met: first, that the plaintiff has suffered a loss that he or she was not supposed to assume, secondly the damage must be considered to be real and effective, and third, a causal link must be established among the first two elements. Irrespective of the degree of negligence in the authorities' action, the state will be judged liable and the individual will be entitled to claim his or her compensation. The only exception to these conditions arises in the event that extraordinary or unforeseeable circumstances justify the state's damaging actions. The existence of *force majeure* is a condition that the executive will have to prove in court, for the burden of proof is borne by the executive, in favour of the individual who has suffered the loss. This sole exception is provided in Article 106.2 of the Constitution, and current legislation has not developed any further exempting circumstances in favour of the executive.

This approach to state liability appears to be extremely generous to the individual. Furthermore, despite the fact that its doctrinal foundations have been the subject of significant criticism,[66] the courts have expanded its contents to other authorities besides the executive. In the late 1990s, the Supreme Court found against a regional Parliament for the enactment of an environmental Bill imposing harsh restrictions on property rights.[67] The plaintiff argued that the regional authorities had never mentioned that such measures would be adopted, and their previous policies even proved to be exactly the opposite to that which the regional Parliament finally decided. Property owners were without warning and with no previous information whatsoever deprived of property rights by an Act of Parliament, being entitled to no compensation. The Supreme Court held that state liability applied to all forms of public action, particularly when the individual suffered a substantive restriction of rights. If such a restriction should be compensated under ordinary expropriatory rules, there was no reason why an Act of Parliament should mean that the state could avoid paying compensation for such restriction. When Parliament caused damage of such kind, the individual had a right to claim for the loss under the ordinary procedures provided for the executive's liability.

The rationale behind this judgment equates the role of Parliament with the role of the executive, and does not differentiate between the restrictions that the legislature may enact and those adopted by the executive. This analogy has driven the courts to impose state liability irrespective of whomever the authority might be, or whatever role the Constitution previously allocated to such authority. However, the courts seem willing to confirm this case law and recent years have borne witness to further judgments in which parliamentary Acts have constituted a breach, giving rise to state liability. Recently, this has been the case in relation to statutory provisions declared unconstitutional by the

[66] n. 64.   [67] Case 7217/1995.

Constitutional Court, which will automatically enable individuals to claim for damages.[68]

Although EC law has contributed to the evolution of state liability in several Member States, this has not been the case in Spain. The highly protective conditions in favour of the individual are considered to surpass the *Francovich, Brasserie* and *Factortame* case law laid by the European Court of Justice in case of breaches of EC law.[69] In fact, the main features of the Spanish regime were embedded in the law before incorporation into the Communities in 1986.

State liability has proven to be an effective mechanism for controlling the executive. At present, the administration's actions are carefully designed in the light of the mentioned case law in order to avoid costly compensation imposed by the courts. However, as an alternative to judicial review, state liability does not appear to be an efficient way to repair rights. Extraordinarily high compensation is not followed by disciplinary actions against liable civil servants and officials, and this indifference encourages further breaches by public authorities, for a sense of immunity develops inside the executive. A positive consequence of this framework is that the law manages to ensure that the executive's actions remain *intra vires*. A negative consequence is that it appears all too costly to be considered efficient.

(c) Alternative sources of scrutiny

Although the courts play a central role in the scrutiny of executive action, Spain has developed alternative sources of scrutiny that act as a complement to legal review. The most significant authority in this regard is the Ombudsman ('*Defensor del Pueblo*'), provided in Article 54 of the Constitution as a 'high commissioner of the *Cortes*' in the protection and guarantee of fundamental rights. The Ombudsman has no tradition in Spanish constitutional law, but it has proved to be an efficient source of governmental control, particularly in sensitive areas of policy such as immigration, social protection, minorities, or consumer rights. The Ombudsman submits an annual report before the *Cortes*, reviewing its activities and pointing to governmental deficiencies and breaches of rights.[70] His independence is guaranteed by a direct appointment from Parliament for a five-year period, although renewal is not excluded. In the course of his activities, he may open a special enquiry, whether at his own discretion or at a citizen's request, over cases of maladministration in which central, regional, or local authorities may have been involved. He holds no judicial powers, and his

---

[68] Legal scholars have been fiercely critical of this case law. Among others, see E. García de Enterría, 'El principio de protección de la confianza legítima como supuesto título justificativo de la responsabilidad patrimonial del Estado legislador' (2002) 159 *Revista de Administración Pública* 173; L. Martín Rebollo, 'Responsabilidad patrimonial por actos legislativos: una discutible elaboración jurisprudencial en expansión' (2002) 556 *Actualidad Jurídica Aranzadi* 8.

[69] Cases C-46 and 48/93 *Brasserie du Pêcheur and Factortame* [1996] ECR I-1029.

[70] See Art. 54 of the Constitution and the Ombudsman Act 1981.

opinions are not binding. His activities sometimes coincide with the activities of the courts over certain areas (for example in the analysis of immigration policies, that may also come under the scrutiny of the administrative courts), but his decisions are mere recommendations dealing with the way in which the administration exercises its powers. Unlike the decisions of the courts, the Ombudsman's opinions are not based upon legal arguments, but on criteria more closely linked to administrative efficiency and management.

The Ombudsman, as an institution, has been extended to the Autonomous Communities, and most Spanish regions currently have their own '*Defensor del Pueblo*', with authority within the territories of the region in question.[71] Although regional Ombudsmen could often clash with the activities of the 'central' Ombudsman mentioned in Article 54 of the Constitution, experience has shown a peaceful coexistence among these different authorities, and their activities have exerted further pressure on administrative practices. There are no rigorous studies that show the impact of the Ombudsmen over the Spanish administrations, but the Annual Reports show that the citizens' trust in the institution has grown significantly in recent years.[72]

Budgetary control also plays an important role in the scrutiny of executive action. The national Court of Auditors is an independent authority guaranteed by the Constitution, although several regions have instituted their own regional Courts of Auditors as alternative sources of budgetary and financial control.[73] The Court of Auditors acts as an external authority in respect of the executive, but most administrations also have their own internal auditing authorities, commonly known as 'inspectors of services', with powers not only restricted to budgetary or financial issues. Disciplinary actions against civil servants are usually initiated by these authorities, and they currently have an important role in the internal structure of every administrative department.

Probably the most relevant source of alternative control lies in the executives themselves, and the mutual pressures that central and regional executives exert over each other. The Spanish distribution of competences among central and regional authorities is open-ended and leaves an important role to interpretation. This role is mostly in the hands of the Constitutional Court, as the ultimate adjudicating body over such issues. However, procedures before the Constitutional Court currently take approximately five to seven years, and conflicts of competence are usually resolved in arenas foreign to the Court. As a consequence, the Autonomous Communities will usually exert pressure on the central executive with the aim of achieving further transfers of competence, or changes in

---

[71] The Autonomous Communities of Andalusia, Aragon, Canary Islands, Castile—La Mancha, Castile—León, Catalonia, Valencia, Galicia, Navarre and Basque Country have currently their regional Ombudsman.
[72] According to the Ombudsman's 2003 annual report, individual complaints grew from 13,365 to 17,389 between years 2001 and 2003.
[73] Art. 136 of the Constitution and the Court of Auditors Act 1982.

current legislation. In this context, the Spanish central executive will make use of its controlling powers over the regions to achieve other aims, or in order to neutralize pressures from the regions. The overall result is a complex and multilayered system of control among the different executives, but displayed by the executives themselves with the initial aim of protecting or amplifying competences.

A similar phenomenon arises when the executive's actions are scrutinized by European Institutions, particularly when the Commission or the ECJ make use of their powers of enforcement against a Member State. This situation can become highly complex when a breach of EU law is the consequence of regional or local activities. According to well-established case law, the Member state itself is liable vis-à-vis the EU, no matter which public authority was responsible for the breach of EU law.[74] Pressure from EU institutions is thus exerted over the Spanish state as a whole, and it is the task of the central executive to respond before Brussels on behalf of its regions, local authorities, or independent agencies. Control over executive action when EU obligations are at stake operates therefore as an additional mechanism for holding public officials to account, and the foundation for this control lies in EU Law.

4. Conclusions

This brief summary of Spanish public law shows how the executive appears as a dual body: government and administration. The executive as a whole, either through governmental or administrative actions, is bound to the Constitution and the law. This feature was reinforced after the enactment of the Constitution of 1978, when the immunity of executive action to the law became a thing of the past. However, it took some time after 1978 before the unconditional submission of the executive to the law was achieved. In this chapter it has been shown how the courts gradually submitted the executive to a strict rule of law. This result, and particularly the intensity of such scrutiny, remains a matter of discussion to this day.

Overall, Spanish public law shows a considerable degree of normative intensity in the definition of the executive and in the conditions for its appropriate action. The executive can only act if a parliamentary Act has previously authorized it, subject to the few exceptions in which an inherent normative authority has been admitted, as previously mentioned, and statute law tends to implement exhaustive regulations over most areas of executive action. Bearing in mind the important role played by the courts, particularly the administrative courts, in the exercise of complete judicial review of governmental and administrative action, Spanish public law proves to be a 'dense' or 'thick' legal system

---

[74] Cases C-46 and 48/93 *Brasserie du Pêcheur and Factortame* [1996] ECR I-1029, para. 37.

over matters concerning the executive. The executive thus becomes a creature of the law, and this accentuates the importance of public law in everyday legal affairs.

The executive is also a complex structure, made up of central, regional, and local authorities. Adjudication over competences has become a common feature of contemporary Spanish public law, and the precise content and scope of such competences is open-textured, due to the generality in which the Constitution and statute law have regulated these matters. As a consequence, the executive is not only bound to the law in the terms explained in the previous paragraph, but also in the light of a highly 'legalized' landscape of territorial powers. The European Communities and the European Union add to the complexity of public competences. As a consequence, public law and the courts tend to absorb what could commonly be solved through ordinary political decision-making procedures.

In descriptive terms, if we had to diagnose the main features of Spanish public law, it could be easily said that it responds to a traditional control-oriented, or 'red-light' approach. The extreme degree of regulatory density is due to a strict version of the principle of legality, but is also an indirect consequence of the role played by the courts. Citizens demand a precise and detailed regulation over executive competences, and the courts have added to this vision by requiring 'dense' regulation over issues that involve executive action. A tendency to litigate becomes inevitable as a result, and ultimately the system revolves around the courts' case law. It must be recognized that the courts have exercised a policy of deference and self-restriction when it comes to scrutinize administrative action, but the last word still lies with the courts. The Constitutional Court has contributed towards reinforcing this 'red-light' approach to public law, in as much as Parliament is bound by its judgments, and the line between 'constitutional' and 'non-constitutional' issues is still not firmly defined by the Court.

However, this 'red-light' conception of public law has contributed to reinforcing the individual's role in the executive's actions. Legislation tends to be previously agreed with private parties to avoid litigation, and thus associations have acquired an important role in Spanish political life. This must be judged in positive terms, particularly in a country where public deliberation over legislative affairs had been eradicated during the Franco regime. A 'consensual' method of rule-making has also extended to administrative regulations, and thus the courts have even imposed, in certain areas, a mandatory rule upon the administration to consult with private parties during the drafting of such regulations.

However, it is still too early to make an overall judgment on the nature of Spanish public law. A new constitutional regime has been introduced in the short time-period of twenty-five years, and the remnants of a military dictatorship are still present in Spanish life, including the law. Many citizens still associate public administration with arbitrary decision-makers, and this may explain why the courts continue to play a major role in the implementation of public law. 'Green light' approaches based on informal or soft-law procedures, arbitration among authorities and citizens, open courses of information, and transparency, etc., may become acceptable sooner or later, but at the present time public law is still the domain of the courts, and thus a continuous process of adjudication among parties.

11

The Locus and Accountability of the Executive in the European Union

Paul Craig[*]

1. Introduction

Locating executive power and determining the mechanisms by which it is held to account is important within any polity. This is especially so given the more general concerns about democracy and legitimacy within the EU.

The task of locating executive power and determining its scope is particularly difficult within the EU. The Rome Treaty as amended contains no neat legal category with the appellation 'executive', nor does the Constitutional Treaty. It will be seen that the legal and political reality is that executive power is shared within the EU. The Commission, the Council, and the European Council all exercise such power to varying degrees, and the manner of the division differs depending upon the particular type of executive power under consideration. The primary focus within the first half of the chapter will therefore be on the identification of different facets of executive power within the EU, and an analysis *de jure* and *de facto* as to how this power is shared between the primary players. This analysis will be undertaken primarily in relation to the Rome Treaty as amended, but consideration will also be given to the position under the Constitutional Treaty.

The discussion in the second half of this chapter turns to the different techniques for securing accountability for the exercise of executive power. This inquiry requires consideration of the extent to which the European Parliament has power to hold the executive to account, and the way in which this is used. We shall consider the roles played respectively by the Ombudsman and the Court of Auditors. The Community courts have developed principles of judicial review and these constitute a further mechanism for enforcing accountability. The analysis will also reveal the importance of constitutional principles of good administration that are enshrined within Community legislation, especially the Financial Regulation.

[*] Professor of English Law, St. John's College, Oxford.

2. The location and scope of executive power in the EU: the framework for analysis

(a) Preliminaries

This chapter is concerned with executive power in the EU on the basis of the Rome Treaty as modified by later Treaty amendments up to the Treaty of Nice 2000. The locus of executive power under the Constitutional Treaty is a complex topic in its own right. It will be dealt with in the course of this discussion, but fuller treatment can be found elsewhere.[1] In the light of the negative votes in the French and Dutch referenda the Constitutional Treaty has been 'put on hold' and is unlikely to be revived. Some discussion of the relevant provisions of the Constitutional Treaty nonetheless seems warranted in this chapter. The problems concerning matters such as the tenure of the European Council President, the internal organization of the Commission and the Council formations will not go away. The 'solutions' to these issues embodied in the Constitutional Treaty will at the least serve as a repository of ideas that may be drawn on in future reform exercises.

Identifying the locus of executive power in the Rome Treaty as amended is a challenging task. The nature of this challenge should be made apparent at the outset. Most nation states will have a written constitution, which will contain provisions naming the executive and stating with varying degrees of precision its powers. This will still of course leave a plethora of issues to be resolved such as the meaning of the constitutional provisions, and the extent to which they capture the reality of executive power within that state in the light of the fact that there may be agencies and the like that exercise such power.

Identifying the locus of executive power in the EU is considerably more difficult. The Rome Treaty as amended does not contain any chapter or title on the 'Executive', nor for that matter does the Constitutional Treaty. What we have in both instances are Treaty provisions dealing with the Community institutions. These Treaty articles coupled with others enable one to get a pretty good idea of the disposition of legislative power within the EU, and this is so even though there are various ways in which legislation can be made. It is therefore possible to identify the six ways in which legislation can be enacted, the respective contributions of the Council, European Parliament,[2] and the circumstances in which the different methods will be used. The formal Treaty provisions dealing with institutions provide much less indication of the locus of executive power, and that is before we even factor in the reality of how the system

---

[1] P. Craig, 'The Constitutional Treaty: Legislative and Executive Power in the Emerging Constitutional Order' (EUI Working Paper Law No. 2004/7); P. Craig, 'European Governance: Executive and Administrative Powers under the New Constitutional Settlement' (Jean Monnet Working Paper No. 5/04, 2004).   [2] Hereafter EP.

works or the existence of other Community bodies that possess a degree of executive authority.

We shall see that executive power in the EU is shared both *de jure* and *de facto*, and that the power sharing differs in relation to different aspects of the executive function. The Treaty articles must nonetheless be our starting point, before moving on to consider the reality of executive power within the EU.

(b) The Treaty articles

The major institutional players that are relevant for present purposes are the European Council, the Council, and the Commission. The bare Treaty articles concerning the functions of each of these institutions give little help for one who is on quest to locate executive power within the EU.

The European Council comprises the heads of the Member States assisted by their foreign ministers, and the Commission President assisted by a member of the Commission. Article 4 TEU provides that the European Council shall provide the EU with the necessary impetus for its development and shall define the general political guidelines thereof. Article 202 EC states that the Council, consisting of a representative of each Member State at ministerial level, shall ensure coordination of the economic policies of the Member States, has power to take decisions, and can confer implementing powers on the Commission. We are told by Article 211 EC that in order to ensure the proper functioning and development of the common market the Commission shall: ensure that the Treaty and norms made thereunder are applied; formulate recommendations or opinions when instructed by the Treaty or when it considers it necessary; have its own power of decision and participate in the shaping of measures taken by the Council and the EP in the manner provided for in the Treaty; and exercise the powers conferred on it by the Council for the implementation of the rules laid down by the latter.

(c) The structure of the analysis

It is clear that the bare Treaty articles do not take us very far in locating executive power in the EU. Read by themselves they address little of direct relevance for the topic at hand, although as we shall see they are not irrelevant. It is therefore necessary to broach the subject from a somewhat different angle. The ensuing analysis will consider the locus of executive power, both legally and factually, in relation to different facets of the executive function. This might be thought to beg the question of what the executive function actually is, and it can be accepted that this varies between nation states. We can nonetheless identify a core set of tasks that are commonly undertaken by the executive branch of government. The executive will usually play a central role in setting the overall priorities and agenda for legislation. It will develop the policy choices. The executive will have responsibility for the effective implementation of agreed policy initiatives and legislation. It will normally have principal responsibility for foreign affairs and defence. The executive will have an important say in the structure and allocation of the budget. We can therefore focus on each of these issues in turn and identify which institution or institutions within the EU exercise this power.

3. The locus and scope of executive power: specific aspects

(a) Establishing priorities and planning the legislative agenda

The establishment of the EU's priorities and the planning of the legislative agenda exemplify the regime of shared executive power within the EU, with the Commission the Council, and the European Council all playing important roles.

The Commission produces its annual work programme in the autumn of the year before it is to take effect. While this programme is designed, *inter alia*, to influence the EU's policy agenda the extent to which it achieves this goal should not, as Nugent states, be exaggerated.[3] This is in part because the work programme is determined by pre-existing commitments, and in part because Council Presidencies have their own work programme/priorities that influence the Commission agenda. The Council will establish its own annual work programme at the beginning of each year, although as Hayes-Renshaw and Wallace note this will be influenced by the Commission programme, and by external events.[4] The Council has, since the Seville European Council,[5] developed a multi-annual programme. The first such programme was produced in 2003,[6] and the process is regulated by the Council's Rules of Procedure. These rules provide that the General Affairs Council recommends to the European Council a multi-annual programme for the next three years, which is based on a joint proposal drawn up by the Presidencies concerned in consultation with the Commission.[7] In the light of this multi-annual programme, it is for the two Presidencies that hold office in the following year to submit jointly a draft annual programme for that year.[8] The importance of the European Council in this process should not be underestimated, notwithstanding the paucity of Treaty references to it, or the fact that it lacks formal legal powers. It will react to the proposals submitted by the General Affairs Council concerning the multi-annual agenda, and it will also be proactive in shaping what appears on that agenda. The reality is that no developments of genuine importance for the Community's overall priorities will occur without having passed through one or more summit

[3] N. Nugent, *The European Commission* (MacMillan, 2001), 223–4.
[4] F. Hayes-Renshaw and H. Wallace, *The Council of Ministers* (MacMillan, 1997), 185–6.
[5] POLGEN 52, 13463/02, *Seville European Council*, Annex II, Brussels 24 October 2002, 23–4.
[6] POLGEN 76, 15047/03, *Multi-annual Strategic Programme*, Brussels 20 November 2003.
[7] Council Decision of 22 July 2002 adopting the Council's Rules of Procedure, Dec. 2002/682, [2002] OJ L230/7, Art. 2(4).   [8] *Ibid.*, Art. 2(5).

meetings. The European Council's role in this respect has been enhanced by the fact that the reports from its meetings have tended over the years to be longer, more detailed, and prescriptive.

The significance of the role played by the European Council in the planning of priorities for the EU can be exemplified by the initiation and development of the Open Method of Coordination, OMC. The OMC did not 'begin' with the Lisbon Summit in March 2000.[9] Its intellectual origins can be traced to the strategy for dealing with Economic and Monetary Union post Maastricht, and to the European Employment Strategy developed post Amsterdam. The Lisbon Summit was nonetheless important, since the European Council gave its imprimatur to OMC as an approach to be used more generally within EU governance. The European Council assessed the EU's strengths and weaknesses, and concluded that it was necessary to 'undertake economic and social reforms as part of a positive strategy which combines competitiveness and social cohesion'.[10] There was to be a new strategic goal for the coming decade. The EU was 'to become the most competitive and dynamic knowledge-based economy in the world, capable of sustainable economic growth with more and better jobs and greater social cohesion'.[11] The more particular aspects of the plan were in part economic, such as a fully operational internal market, and in part social an active employment policy and the promotion of social inclusion.

The strategy was to be implemented by 'improving the existing processes, introducing a new open method of coordination at all levels, coupled with a stronger guiding and coordinating role for the European Council to ensure more coherent and strategic direction and effective monitoring of progress'.[12] The general features of OMC were said to be:[13] fixing guidelines for the EU combined with specific timetables for achieving the goals; establishing quantitative and qualitative indicators and benchmarks as a means of comparing best practice; translating these European guidelines into national policies by setting specific targets and adopting measures, taking into account national and regional differences; and periodic monitoring, evaluation, and peer review organized as mutual learning processes. The Lisbon approach was developed at the Nice European Council in December 2000.[14] The Commission, sectoral Council formations and the Member States were instructed or requested to take steps to fulfil the objectives set out.[15] Thus the Commission was 'requested' to take the OMC forward by developing indicators against which employment policy or social exclusion could be judged, and to present an annual report to the European Council, detailing its initiatives and the contributions of the other actors to attaining the objectives of the social model. The Employment and Social Policy Council was 'instructed' to implement the social agenda, including in this respect the setting of benchmarks and indicators as part of the OMC process.

---

[9] Lisbon European Council, 23–24 March 2000.   [10] *Ibid.*, para. 4.
[11] *Ibid.*, para. 5.   [12] *Ibid.*, para. 7.   [13] *Ibid.*, para. 37.
[14] Nice European Council, 7–9 December 2000.   [15] *Ibid.*, Annex I, para. 32.

The discussion thus far has focused on the Rome Treaty as amended. The Constitutional Treaty[16] contains important provisions relating to the locus of executive power concerning priorities and agenda-setting for the EU. The regime of shared executive power is readily apparent.

Article I-21 of the Constitution modifies Article 4 TEU by providing that the European Council shall define the EU's priorities, as well as defining its general political directions. This language is mandatory, and the additional task of defining the EU's priorities is not expressly qualified by the adjective 'general'.[17] This is a classic example of law catching up with political reality, given that the European Council has been playing an important role in relation to priorities for some considerable time. The connection between the extended tasks of the European Council and the President's role is obvious: the President must, *inter alia*, chair the European Council and drive forward its work.[18] The work of the European Council now includes setting priorities for the EU, and hence the President will have the obligation to drive this forward. The very fact that the President of the European Council is to hold the office for two and half years renewable once means moreover that the incumbent of the office will have time to develop a vision for the EU that was simply not possible under the previous six-monthly rotation system.

It is however clear that power in this respect is shared with the Commission. Article I-26(1) provides, *inter alia*, that the Commission shall initiate the EU's annual and multi-annual programming with a view to achieving inter-institutional agreements. Thus while the Commission is accorded a general right to initiate particular pieces of Union legislation,[19] it also has the right and duty to initiate the Union's more general programming strategy. The language of Article I-26(1) serves to reinforce the sense of shared executive power: the Commission initiates the Union's annual and multi-annual programming with a view to achieving inter-institutional agreement.

(b) The development of policy choices

It might be thought that once priorities have been settled and the agenda set then we move from the realm of executive power to that of legislative power. Legislation will be enacted in accord with the established legislative procedure, which will normally be co-decision, with the Commission having the right of legislative initiative under the Rome Treaty as amended, this being affirmed by Article I-26(2) of the Constitutional Treaty. Matters are not however that simple. This picture is based on the assumption that once the agenda has been

---

[16] *Treaty Establishing a Constitution for Europe* CIG 87/04, Brussels 6 August 2004.
[17] Art. I-21(1): the operative phrase is 'shall define the general political directions and priorities thereof'. [18] Art. I-22(2).
[19] Art. I-26(2).

agreed then we move straight to the legislative process, with the consequence that the holders of executive power have no influence on the development of the agreed choices. A moment's reflection will reveal that this is not how matters work even in many national systems, since the executive will commonly exert considerable influence over the development of more detailed initiatives. This is certainly true in the EU, both under the Rome Treaty as amended and the Constitutional Treaty.

Under the Rome Treaty, the General Affairs and External Relations Council, GAERC, has the obligation to prepare the European Council meetings *and* to ensure that they are followed-up. This obligation is embodied in the Council's Rules of Procedure.[20] The agenda for the European Council is drawn up by the GAERC on a proposal from the Presidency,[21] and the Presidency would normally also submit position papers on the key issues placed on the agenda.[22] This regime was incorporated in Article I-22(2) of the Constitutional Treaty. The position of the President of the European Council has been further strengthened by Article I-24(2), which provides that the General Affairs Council shall prepare and ensure follow-up to meetings of the European Council in liaison with the President of the European Council and the Commission. The follow-up to meetings of the European Council may often require work by the other sectoral Councils. The President of the European Council, when liaising with the GAC, will therefore be able to exert influence over the detailed initiatives required to carry European Council policy into action. It should be remembered that a significant number of legislative initiatives have their origin in suggestions from the Council, which are then routed to the Commission via Article 208 EC, or Article III-345.[23] The President of the European Council, reinforced by the constitutional obligation on the GAC to ensure follow up to meetings of the European Council, will be in a strong position to press other Council formations to take the necessary steps to carry through the detail of European Council policy.

(c) Implementation of legislation and policy

When legislation has been enacted or policy initiatives have been agreed they must be carried out. Implementation will normally fall to the executive branch of government, backed up by the established bureaucracy. Thus it will be common for departments dealing with different subject-matter areas to have responsibility for implementation of legislation that falls within their purview, and such departments will normally be headed by a minister who is a member of the executive and who takes ultimate responsibility for such matters. This paradigm can of course be qualified or modified by the existence of agencies and the like

---

[20] Council's Rules of Procedure, n. 7, Art. 2(2)(a).
[21] *Ibid.*, Art. 2(3)(a).
[22] *Seville European Council*, n. 5, Annex 1, para. 4.
[23] Ex Art. 152.

who are accorded responsibility for the oversight and execution of policy within particular areas.

In the EU it is the Commission that has the primary executive responsibility for implementation of Community legislation. Article 211 EC provides that the Commission shall ensure that the provisions of the Treaty and the measures taken by the institutions pursuant thereto are applied. This power is reaffirmed by Article I-26(1) of the Constitutional Treaty which provides, *inter alia*, that the Commission shall ensure the application of the Constitution and measures adopted by the institutions pursuant to the Constitution; that it shall execute the budget and manage programmes; and that it shall exercise coordinating, executive, and management functions as laid down in the Constitution.

If one stopped there one might conclude that executive power in relation to implementation of legislation lies squarely with the Commission, and that in this respect such power is not shared within the EU. This conclusion does not however comport with reality. The position is more complex. The Commission plays a major role when it comes to implementing Community norms, but executive power is shared, and it is shared in many different ways. This is a difficult subject and more detailed treatment can be found elsewhere.[24] Four brief examples serve to demonstrate the different ways in which implementing power is shared between the Commission and other players.

(i) Delegated rule-making

The first concerns power over the content and passage of secondary or implementing rules. This takes us into the world of Comitology, where implementing power is shared between the Commission and the Member States, with some input from the EP.[25] Comitology was born in the context of the Common Agricultural Policy.[26] It became clear that the administration of the CAP would require detailed rules in ever changing market circumstances. Recourse to primary legislation was impracticable. It was equally apparent that the Member States were wary of according the Commission a blank cheque over the making of implementing rules, especially given that power once delegated would

---

[24] P. Craig, *Law, Administration and Administrative Law in the EU* (forthcoming).

[25] R. Pedler and G.F. Schaefer (eds.), *Shaping European Law and Policy: The Role of Committees and Comitology in the Political Process* (European Institute of Public Administration, 1996); C. Joerges, K.-H. Ladeur and E. Vos (eds.), *Integrating Scientific Expertise into Regulatory Decision-Making: National Traditions and European Innovations* (Nomos, 1997); C. Joerges and E. Vos (eds.), *EU Committees: Social Regulation, Law and Politics* (Hart, 1999); *Third Report of the House of Lords' Select Committee on European Legislation: Delegation of Powers to the Commission: Reforming Comitology* (HL 23; 1999); E. Vos, *Institutional Frameworks of Community Health and Safety Legislation: Committees, Agencies and Private Bodies* (Hart, 1999); M. Andenas and A. Turk (eds.), *Delegated Legislation and the Role of Committees in the EC* (Kluwer Law International, 2000); C. Bergstrom, *Comitology, Delegation of Powers in the European Union and the Committee System* (Oxford University Press, 2005); Craig, n. 24, Chap. 4.

[26] C. Bertram, 'Decision-Making in the EEC: The Management Committee Procedure' (1967–68) 5 *CMLRev* 246; P. Schindler, 'The Problems of Decision-Making by Way of the Management Committee Procedure in the EEC' (1971) 8 *CMLRev* 184; Bergstrom, n. 25, Chap. 2.

generate legally binding rules without further possibility of Council oversight. This wariness was heightened by the tensions between the Council and the Commission in the mid-1960s leading to the Luxembourg Crisis and subsequent Accords. It would however be mistaken to see the birth of the committee system solely in terms of Council distrust of Commission. It was also conceived as a way of dealing with disagreements between the Member States themselves. It is readily apparent that Member States might agree on the general regulatory principles for a particular area, but disagree on the more detailed ramifications thereof. Involvement in the making of the implementing rules served moreover to facilitate interaction between national administrators who would be responsible for the application of the rules at national level. The net result was the birth of the management committee procedure, embodied in the early agricultural regulations. The committee composed of national representatives, normally those with expertise or understanding of the relevant area, would be directly involved with the Commission in the deliberations concerning the secondary regulations or directives. The secondary measure would be immediately applicable, subject to the caveat that it could be sent back to the Council if it was not in accord with the committee's opinion. It was then open to the Council to take a different decision by qualified majority within one month.[27]

The committee methodology spread rapidly to other areas, and became a standard feature attached to the delegation of power to the Commission. It was moreover not long before the more restrictive version, known as the regulatory committee procedure, was created in the context of the common commercial policy.[28] On this version of the committee procedure, if the committee failed to deliver an opinion, or if it gave an opinion contrary to the recommended measure, the Commission would have to submit the proposal to the Council, which could then act by qualified majority. There was a safety net or *filet*, such that if the Council had not acted within three months of the measure being submitted to it, then the proposed provisions could be adopted by the Commission. The desire for greater political control reached its apotheosis in the modified version of the regulatory committee procedure, which embodied what became known as the *contre-filet*: the normal regulatory committee procedure applied, subject to the caveat that the Council could by simple majority prevent the Commission from acting even after the expiry of the prescribed period.

The Comitology regime gave rise to major battles over the years involving the Commission, Council, and EP. Some greater regularity was instilled through Community Decisions that attempted to systematize the process.[29] The apposite

---

[27] See, e.g. Council Regulation 19/62, *On the Progressive Establishment of a Common Organisation of the Market in Cereals* [1962] OJ 30/933, Arts. 25–26.

[28] See, e.g. Council Regulation 802/68, *On the Common Definition of the Concept of the Origin of Goods* [1968] OJ L148/1, Arts. 12–14.

[29] Council Decision 87/373, *Laying Down the Procedures for the Exercise of Implementing Powers Conferred on the Commission* [1987] OJ L197/33; Council Decision 99/468, *Laying Down the Procedures for the Exercise of Implementing Powers Conferred on the Commission* [1999] OJ L184/23.

point for present purposes is that these Decisions preserved Member State input into the making of implementing rules. Power over implementation continued to be shared between the Commission and the Member States, with some increase in the influence of the EP.

It remains to be seen whether the Constitutional Treaty alters this. It does not in terms abolish or downgrade the Comitology committees, although it is clear that this is the Commission's objective. The Constitution provides for what are termed non-legislative acts.[30] The Commission is empowered to enact delegated regulations to 'supplement or amend certain non-essential elements of the law or framework law'.[31] The objectives, content, scope, and duration of the delegation must be defined in the laws and framework laws, and the delegation may not cover the essential elements of the subject matter, which is reserved for the law or framework law. The European Parliament or the Council may decide to revoke the delegation; or the delegated regulation may enter into force only if no objection has been expressed by the European Parliament or the Council within a period set by the law or framework law.[32] The Commission's constitutional strategy has been to regard delegated regulations as a species of executive power exercised by the Commission, subject to the constraints above. It hopes that the new category of delegated regulations will lead to the demise of Comitology, or at least the removal of the management and regulatory committees. The idea is therefore for the Commission in its executive capacity to be able to enact the relevant regulations, subject to the possibility of call back by the Council or EP.

(ii) Shared management

The Committee of Independent Experts was a body established to consider allegations of fraud and mismanagement in the EU. Its initial report led to the downfall of the Santer Commission. In a second report it looked more broadly at the ways in which Community policy was delivered and provided a helpful definition of shared management. It connoted,[33]

[M]anagement of those Community programmes where the Commission and the Member States have distinct administrative tasks which are inter-dependent and set down in legislation and where both the Commission and the national administrations need to discharge their respective tasks for the Community policy to be implemented successfully.

The administration of the CAP is shared in the sense that the various forms of price support payments are administered jointly by the Commission and the Member States.[34] This is done through the European Agricultural Guidance and Guarantee Fund (EAGGF). The Guidance section deals with EC expenditure relating to agricultural structures; the Guarantee section covers payments relating

---

[30] Art. I-33(1).   [31] Art. I-36.   [32] Art. I-36(2).
[33] Committee of Independent Experts, *Second Report on Reform of the Commission, Analysis of Current Practice and Proposals for Tackling Mismanagement, Irregularities and Fraud* (10 September 1999), Vol. I, para. 3.2.2. (Hereafter Second CIE).   [34] Second CIE, n. 33, Vol. I, para. 3.6.3.

directly to the regulation of agricultural markets, refunds on exports, and intervention payments.

Structural Fund also operates through shared management, which applies in different ways to project and programme selection, and to implementation and monitoring of selected projects and programmes. Shared management applies therefore both with respect to the input stage and the output stage. A number of principles run through Structural Fund regime, including partnership connoting the idea that Community operations shall be established through close consultations between the Commission, the Member State concerned, and the competent authorities designated by the latter at national, regional, local, or other level with each party acting as a partner in pursuit of a common goal. The partnership covers preparation, financing, monitoring, and assessment of the operations. More recent Community legislation has delegated greater responsibility to the Member States for the implementation and monitoring of particular programmes.[35]

(iii) Administration of the open method of coordination

The administration of the programmes covered by the Open Method of Coordination varies, the constant theme being that multiple actors are involved. Consider by way of example the way in which coordination operates within the European Employment Strategy (EES).[36]

The European Council each year considers the employment situation in the Community and adopts conclusions based on the joint report from the Commission and the Council. The conclusions reached by the European Council then form the basis for the Council, acting by qualified majority on a proposal from the Commission, and after consulting the EP, ECOSOC, the Committee of the Regions, and the Employment Committee, to draw up guidelines which the Member States shall take into account in their employment policies. It is then for each Member State to provide the Council and the Commission with an annual report on the principal measures taken to implement its employment policy in the light of these guidelines. The Council considers these reports and the opinion of the Employment Committee and forms a view on the implementation of the guidelines at national level. It is open to the Council acting on a recommendation from the Commission to decide to make recommendations to a particular Member State. Having completed their examination of the reports from the Member States, the Council and the Commission make their joint report to the European Council on the employment situation in the Community and the implementation of the guidelines for employment. The annual process then begins once again. The Employment Committee assists in this process.[37] It is composed of two persons from each Member State, plus two members of the Commission. It acts in an advisory capacity to promote coordination between

[35] Craig, n. 24, Chap. 3.   [36] Art. 128 EC.   [37] Art. 130 EC.

the Member States on employment and labour market policies and more particularly to monitor the employment situation and policies in the Member States and in the Community, and to formulate opinions to contribute to the preparation of the Council proceedings described above. In fulfilling its mandate the Employment Committee is instructed to consult management and labour.

(iv) Agencies

The EU has also begun to make greater use of agencies for the administration of Community policy. Two agencies were established in 1975, and there are currently sixteen.[38] They possess legal personality; have management boards on which Member State influence predominates, although there is some supranational representation; they operate outside the Commission and Council; and they were normally established by a regulation made under Article 308.[39] Some of the agencies are concerned with the collation and dissemination of information, while others have de facto executive/regulatory powers in relation to matters such as Community trademarks and plant variety rights. In formal terms, the degree of agency autonomy is constrained by ECJ jurisprudence which limits the delegation of power to bodies which are not mentioned in the constituent Treaties.[40] In substantive terms, the degree of autonomy possessed by each agency varies considerably, depending upon the composition of its governing board, its financing, and the subject matter with which it deals.[41]

(d) Foreign and security policy

The conduct of foreign policy and defence are quintessential features associated with executive power. It is clear that so far as the EU has competence in these areas it is the European Council and the Council that possess the power.

The relevant provisions are contained in the Treaty on European Union, Title V of which contains the provisions on Common Foreign and Security Policy, CFSP. It is the European Council that defines the principles and general guidelines for the CFSP, and it is the European Council that decides on common strategies to be implemented by the EU where the Member States have

---

[38] European Centre for the Development of Vocational Training, European Foundation for the Improvement of Living and Working Conditions, European Environment Agency, European Training Foundation, European Monitoring Centre For Drugs and Drug Addiction, European Medicines Agency, Office for Harmonization in the Internal Market, European Agency for Safety and Health at Work, Community Plant Variety Office, European Translation Centre for Bodies of the EU, European Monitoring Centre on Racism and Xenophobia, European Agency for Reconstruction, European Food Safety Authority, European Maritime Agency, European Aviation Safety Agency, European Network and Information Security Agency.

[39] A. Kreher, 'Agencies in the European Community—A Step Towards Administrative Integration in Europe' (1997) 4 *JEPP* 225.

[40] K. Lenaerts, 'Regulating the Regulatory Process: 'Delegation of Powers' in the European Community' (1993) 18 *ELRev* 23; M. Everson, 'Independent Agencies: Hierarchy Beaters?' (1995) 1 *ELJ* 180.

[41] Kreher, n. 39, 238.

important interests in common.[42] It is the Council that takes the decisions necessary for defining and implementing the CFSP on the basis of the general guidelines defined by the European Council.[43] It is the Council that makes recommendations as to common strategies to the European Council, and implements them, in particular through adopting joint actions and common positions.[44] Joint actions address specific situations where operational action by the EU is required. The terms of the joint action will lay down its objectives, scope, and the means available to the EU.[45] Common positions define the EU's approach to a particular matter of a geographical or thematic nature, and Member States are to ensure that their national policies conform to the common positions.[46] The prominence of the European Council is even more marked in relation to defence policy.[47]

The Member State that holds the Presidency of the Council also chairs the meetings of the European Council.[48] The Presidency represents the EU in matters coming within the CFSP, and has the responsibility for implementing decisions under the CFSP Title.[49] The Presidency is assisted by the Secretary-General of the Council who exercises the function of High Representative for the CFSP.[50] The High Representative assists the Council through contributing to the formulation, preparation, and implementation of policy decisions.[51]

The reins of power are therefore firmly in the hands of the Member States as represented in the European Council and the Council. The Commission is however to be 'fully associated' with the Presidency's tasks,[52] and more generally with the work carried out in the CFSP field.[53] The EP must be consulted by the Presidency on the 'main aspects and basic choices' of the CFSP, the Presidency must ensure that the EP's views are duly taken into consideration, and the EP can ask a question of the Council or make recommendations to it.[54]

It is clear that under the Constitutional Treaty executive authority continues to reside with the European Council and the Council. It is the European Council that identifies the strategic interests and determines the objectives of the CFSP through strategic guidelines.[55] It is primarily the Council that adopts the decisions to implement the strategic guidelines of the European Council.[56] It is the Council that adopts decisions that define the EU's approach to a particular matter of a geographical or thematic nature.[57] The primacy of place accorded to the European Council is even more marked in relation to defence.[58] Executive authority within the EU in relation to CFSP continues to rest primarily with institutions of an intergovernmental nature, the European Council and the Council. This must however be qualified to some extent because the principal constitutional innovation in this area is the creation of the post of EU Minister

---

[42] Art. 13(1)-(2) TEU.   [43] Art. 13(3) TEU.   [44] Arts 13(3), 14, 15 TEU.
[45] Art. 14(1) TEU.   [46] Art. 15 TEU.   [47] Art. 17 TEU.   [48] Art. 4 TEU.
[49] Art. 18 TEU.   [50] Art. 18(3) TEU.   [51] Art. 26 TEU.   [52] Art. 18(4) TEU.
[53] Art. 27 TEU.   [54] Art. 21 TEU.   [55] Art. I-40(2) and Art. III-295(1).
[56] Art. I-40(3) and Art. III-295(2).   [57] Arts. III-297–298.   [58] Art. I-41.

for Foreign Affairs, who is to 'conduct' the Union's common foreign and security policy.[59] The idea that executive power within the Union is divided between the European Council and the Commission is personified in this post. The Minister for Foreign Affairs is appointed by the European Council by qualified majority, with the agreement of the Commission President.[60] The EU Foreign Minister is one of the Vice Presidents of the Commission, and is responsible for handling external relations and for co-ordinating other aspects of the Union's external action.[61] The EU Foreign Minister therefore wears a 'shared hat'. The holder of the office takes part in the work of the European Council,[62] chairs the Foreign Affairs Council,[63] and is also a Vice-President of the Commission.

(e) Resources and budget

The direction of EU policy is not wholly dependent on money. The EU is rightly regarded as a regulatory state, and many initiatives do not require expenditure from EU funds. This can be readily accepted, while at the same time acknowledging that control over the EU's resources and its budget are also matters of importance.

In relation to resources, Article 269 EC provides that the budget shall be financed wholly from the EU's own resources. The system for the EU's resources is laid down in provisions made by the Council, acting unanimously on a proposal from the Commission, and after consulting the EP. These provisions are then recommended for adoption by the Member States in accord with their constitutional requirements. The Constitutional Treaty largely preserves this position.[64]

In relation to the budget, Article 272 EC stipulates the procedure to be applied for the annual budget. The procedure is complex, but in effect it is a modification of the co-decision procedure, with a proposal coming from the Commission and input from the Council and the EP. Implementation of the budget is for the Commission,[65] which is to act in accord with more detailed financial regulations.[66] The EP, acting on a recommendation from the Council, has the power to give discharge to the Commission for its implementation of the budget, and the EP can question the Commission in this regard, having considered the accounts in the light of the report by the Court of Auditors.[67]

The provisions of the Constitutional Treaty in relation to the budget distinguish between the multi-annual financial framework and the annual budget. The multi-annual financial framework, which is to be established for a period of at least five years, is designed to ensure that EU expenditure develops in an

---

[59] Art. I-28. [60] Art. I-28(1). [61] Art. I-28(4). [62] Art. I-21(2).
[63] Art. I-28(4). [64] Art. I-54(3). [65] Art. 274 EC.
[66] Art. 279 EC; Council Regulation 1605/2002, *on the Financial Regulation Applicable to the General Budget of the European Communities* [2002] OJ L248/1. [67] Art. 276 EC.

orderly manner and within the limits of its resources.[68] It determines the amounts of the annual ceilings for commitment and payment appropriations. This framework is laid down in a European law made by the Council acting unanimously after obtaining the consent of the EP.[69] The European Council acting unanimously may adopt a European decision allowing the Council to act by qualified majority when adopting subsequent multi-annual frameworks.[70] The annual budget must comply with the multi-annual financial framework.[71] Executive power in relation to setting of the financial framework is therefore shared between the Commission, Council, and the EP, since the European law made by the Council will be based on a proposal from the Commission.[72] The annual budget is made through a European law jointly by the EP and the Council on a proposal from the Commission.[73] The procedure is a modification of the ordinary legislative procedure, the successor to the co-decision procedure. The EP's powers have been increased because the distinction between 'compulsory' and 'non-compulsory' expenditure has been abolished.

4. Executive power and accountability in the EU

(a) Executive power and accountability to the legislature

It is common within national political systems that the legislature will exercise some control over the executive. The way in which this control is structured will vary as between different systems, as will its effectiveness. Indeed the very meaning of the word control can connote different things in the context of legislative-executive relations in different political systems. This issue is especially complex within the EU, because legislative power is divided between the Commission, EP, and the Council, and executive power is shared between the Commission, Council, and European Council. Notwithstanding these complexities there are a number of ways in which the EP in its capacity as legislature exercises control over the Commission when the latter exercises executive power. These controls vary, but they are all provided for in the Treaty.

The EP has the 'nuclear strike weapon' whereby it can dismiss the Commission. This is provided in Article 201 EC, which stipulates that if a two-thirds majority of the votes cast vote in favour of a censure motion tabled against the Commission then the Members of the Commission shall resign as a body. This is by its nature an extreme weapon. The threat that it would be exercised was however part of the reason why the Santer Commission resigned in 1999. There had been concern for some considerable time about fraud, and mismanagement, as revealed by, *inter alia*, the Court of Auditors. The European Parliament repeatedly expressed its dissatisfaction with the management of the Community's

---

[68] Art. I-55(1) and Art. III-402(1).   [69] Art. I-55(2).   [70] Art. I-55(4).
[71] Art. I-55(3).   [72] Art. I-26(2).   [73] Art. I-56 and Art. III-404.

financial resources. This culminated in a resolution of 14 January 1999 which called for a Committee of Independent Experts to be convened under the auspices of the European Parliament and the Commission with a mandate to detect and deal with fraud, mismanagement, and nepotism. It was for the Committee to decide how far the Commission as a body, or individual Commissioners, had responsibility for such matters. The Committee was also to conduct a fundamental review of the Commission's practices in the award of all financial contracts. The Committee produced its first report within two months, by March 15 1999.[74] Exigencies of time meant that the Committee could investigate only a limited number of Community policies. It nonetheless produced a 146-page report by the stipulated date, which was highly critical of the way in which the Commission exercised its executive power in relation to the implementation of Community policy and programmes. This had an immediate, dramatic effect: the Commission resigned en bloc. It 'jumped' before it could be 'pushed' by a censure motion from the EP.

The EP also has more finely-tuned tools to investigate particular instances of maladministration. It has the power to establish a temporary Committee of Inquiry to investigate alleged contraventions or maladministration in the implementation of Community law, except where the alleged facts are being examined before a court and while the case is still subject to legal proceedings.[75] Committees of Inquiry were established in relation to matters such as the Community transit system and the BSE crisis. Corbett, Jacobs, and Shackleton are of the view that these committees were a success and had a visible impact on the work of the institutions investigated, in particular the Commission: 'the committees served to show that the Parliament could serve as a focus for public concern on issues transcending national boundaries and could organise the obtaining of evidence from witnesses across Europe in a way that few, if any, national institutions or parliaments could hope to match'.[76] They were however mindful of weaknesses in the powers of such committees.

The EP can receive petitions from a Community citizen on a matter that comes within the Community's field of activity where the matter affects the citizen directly.[77] Such petitions will commonly be lodged by citizens affected by Community administration. They are deemed admissible if they are formally in order and if they fall within the Union's sphere of activities. Petitions have since 1987 been dealt with by a special committee established for this purpose. The Committee of Petitions can 'draw up reports on matters referred to it, organise hearings, send MEPs to investigate on the spot, or request information or action from the Commission and, to a more limited extent, the Member States'.[78]

---

[74] Committee of Independent Experts, *First Report on Allegations regarding Fraud, Mismanagement and Nepotism in the European Commission* (15 March 1999).   [75] Art. 193 EC.
[76] R. Corbett, F. Jacobs and M. Shackleton, *The European Parliament* (John Harper Publishing, 4th edn., 2000), 264.   [77] Art. 194 EC.
[78] Corbett, Jacobs and Shackleton, *The European Parliament*, n. 76, 276.

The Committee prepares an annual report for debate in plenary session.[79] The number of petitions submitted varies, but it is around 1,300 per annum. The majority of petitions are concerned either with expressions of view on particular policy issues, where there will commonly be many signatories, or with the redress of grievances, where there will normally be one petitioner. There may however be little that the Committee can do in relation to the former, and the European Ombudsman will now often be preferred if the matter concerns individual grievance.

The EP also has important power over the discharge of the budget. We have already seen that the EP plays a role in the approval of the budget and that this has been increased under the Constitutional Treaty. Implementation of the budget is the Commission's responsibility. The EC Treaty accords the EP important power over the discharge of the budget. The accounts must be submitted to the Council and the EP, and the EP acting on a recommendation from the Council gives discharge over the budget. It has the power to examine the Commission over aspects of budgetary implementation. The EP has used this power to put pressure on the Commission concerning the manner in which the latter has implemented the budget, more especially when there has been an adverse report from the Court of Auditors. It was pressure exerted by the EP in this manner that led to the establishment of the Committee of Independent Experts, whose report led to the downfall of the Santer Commission.

(b) Executive power and accountability through the Ombudsman

The European Ombudsman plays an important role in controlling the exercise of executive power in the EU. The Ombudsman is appointed by the EP after each election for the duration of its term of office. The holder of the post is eligible for reappointment,[80] and is to be completely independent in the performance of his duties, taking no instructions from any body.[81]

The Ombudsman can receive complaints from any EU citizen or natural or legal person residing or having its registered office in a Member State. The complaints must relate to instances of maladministration in the activities of the Community institutions and bodies, with the exception of the Community courts acting in their judicial role.[82] The Ombudsman has power to conduct inquiries on his own initiative, or he can deal with matters referred by a MEP, but he cannot investigate matters that are or have been subject to legal proceedings. Where maladministration has been found the Ombudsman refers the matter to the relevant institution, which has three months in which to respond. The Ombudsman then forwards a report to the EP and the institution concerned, and the complainant is informed of the outcome of the proceedings. The

---

[79] *Report on the Deliberations of the Petitions Committee during the Parliamentary Year 2003–2004* A6-0040/2005.   [80] Art. 195(2) EC.
[81] Art. 195(3) EC.   [82] Art. 195(1) EC.

Ombudsman must also submit an annual report to the EP on the outcome of the inquiries.

The complaints will often relate to the activities of the Commission concerned with the implementation of EU policy, and therefore the Ombudsman is a valuable additional mechanism for ensuring accountability in the exercise of executive power in the EU. This is particularly so given that from the perspective of the private individual a complaint to the Ombudsman will be less daunting than the initiation of formal legal proceedings.

Limits of space preclude detailed analysis of the contribution made by the European Ombudsman. Suffice it to say for the present that the office is important in three related respects. Firstly, and most obviously, it functions as a mechanism for the resolution of individual grievances without recourse to court. Secondly, investigation into individual complaints will not infrequently lead to the publication of special reports in which the European Ombudsman will recommend a change of rule or policy by the Commission or Council that gave rise to the initial problem. Thirdly, the European Ombudsman has published a Code of Good Administrative Behaviour designed to flesh out the meaning of the right to good administration contained in Article 41 of the Charter of Fundamental Rights.

(c) Executive power and accountability through the Court of Auditors

The Court of Auditors is another institution that provides a check on executive power in the EU, more especially in relation to financial matters. The members of the Court of Auditors must be those who have expertise in matters of audit and they will normally have belonged to audit bodies within their Member State.[83] They are appointed for six years by the Council after consulting the EP. The members are eligible for reappointment,[84] and they, like the Ombudsman, must be completely independent in the performance of their duties and must not seek or take instructions from any other body.[85] The Court of Auditors helps to foster executive accountability in two ways.

The Court has a *general duty to examine the accounts for all revenue and expenditure for the EU*. We have already seen that it is the Commission that has the general duty to implement the EU's budget. The Court of Auditors' duty amounts therefore to an audit on the way in which the Commission has implemented Community policies in that year. The Court of Auditors must provide the EP and the Council with a statement of assurance as to the regularity of the accounts, and the legality and regularity of the underlying transactions.[86] To this end the Court of Auditors examines whether all revenue and expenditure

[83] Art. 247(1) EC. [84] Art. 247(3) EC. [85] Art. 247(4) EC.
[86] Art. 248(1) EC.

has been incurred in a lawful and regular manner and whether financial management has been sound, and it must report on cases of irregularity. The audit must be carried out before the closure of the accounts for the relevant year.[87] The Court of Auditors will normally undertake these duties on the basis of written records, but it also has the power to conduct on the spot investigations in other Community institutions, and in Member State institutions that manage revenue or expenditure on behalf of the Community.[88] The Court of Auditors will draw up an annual report at the close of each financial year.

The Court of Auditors' general duty to examine revenue and expenditure for the EU has been a powerful tool. It has not been uncommon for the Court to refuse to give the Council and the EP an assurance as to the reliability of the accounts and the legality and regularity of the underlying transactions where it forms the view that this is not warranted by the records. It has been common for the Court's annual report to be highly critical of aspects of Community administration. A succession of such critical reports was an important factor in the establishment of the Committee of Independent Experts that led to the downfall of the Santer Commission. It should however also be noted that the succession of adverse reports from the Court of Auditors did not suffice in itself to secure reform in the Commission. This only occurred after the fall of the Santer Commission precipitated by the first report of the Committee of Independent Experts.

The Court of Auditors also *has the power to make special reports on particular topics.*[89] The Court makes regular use of this power. The reports bring a more laser-like scrutiny to bear on an issue, which will often be one about which the Court has expressed concern in its annual report on the EU's accounts. The reports are instructive and go beyond mere financial regularity. They will commonly take the form of wider-ranging administrative audits designed to highlight shortcomings in the administration of a particular policy, coupled with recommendations for improvement. The power to make special reports can be especially significant when the Court returns to the same topic in subsequent years to determine whether improvements that it has recommended have been implemented.[90]

(d) Executive power and legal accountability: judicial review

Judicial review provides an important mechanism for holding executive power to account. It can be used to challenge any Community act that has legal effect.

---

[87] Art. 248(2) EC.   [88] Art. 248(3) EC.   [89] Art. 248(4) EC.
[90] See, e.g., Court of Auditors, Special Report 21/98, *Concerning the Accreditation and Certification Procedures as Applied to the 1996 Clearance of Accounts for EAGGF—Guarantee Expenditure* [1998] OJ C389/1; Court of Auditors, Special Report 22/2000, *On Evaluation of the Reformed Clearance of Accounts Procedure* [2000] OJ C69/1.

This covers regulations, decisions, and directives, which are listed in Article 249. The ECJ has, however, also held that this list is not exhaustive, and that other acts which are *sui generis* can also be reviewed, provided that they have binding force or produce legal effects.[91] Applicants can seek judicial review of Community action either directly or indirectly.

(i) Direct and indirect actions

The *direct action* for judicial review is based on Article 230 EC.[92] This provides the substantive criteria for review and also delineates the rules of standing that apply in the context of direct actions.

The Court of Justice shall review the legality of acts adopted jointly by the European Parliament and the Council, of acts of the Council, of the Commission, and of the ECB other than recommendations and opinions, and acts of the European Parliament intended to produce legal effects vis-à-vis third parties.

It shall for this purpose have jurisdiction in actions brought by a Member State, the European Parliament, the Council or the Commission on the grounds of lack of competence, infringement of an essential procedural requirement, infringement of this Treaty or of any rule of law relating to its application, or misuse of powers.

The Court shall have jurisdiction under the same conditions in actions brought by the Court of Auditors and by the ECB for the purpose of protecting their prerogatives.

Any natural or legal person may, under the same conditions, institute proceedings against a decision addressed to that person or against a decision which, although in the form of a regulation or decision addressed to another person, is of direct and individual concern to the former.

The proceedings provided for in this Article shall be instituted within two months of the publication of the measure, or of its notification to the plaintiff, or, in the absence thereof, of the day on which it came to the knowledge of the latter, as the case may be.

Article 230 has been preserved in the Constitutional Treaty as Article III-365. It has been modified to make it clear that it is applicable against EU agencies and bodies and also against the European Council. The other significant change concerns the rules of standing provided for in Article 365(4), which have been liberalized to a limited extent such that it will no longer be necessary to show individual concern in relation to regulatory acts that do not require implementing measures.

Indirect challenge to the legality of Community action is through Article 234 EC. This Article establishes a mechanism whereby a national court can seek a preliminary ruling on a point of Community law where that is necessary for the resolution of the case. Article 234 reads as follows.

---

[91] Case 22/70, *Commission v. Council* [1971] ECR 263; Case 60/81, *International Business Machines Corporation v. Commission* [1981] ECR 2639; Case C-39/93P, *Syndicat Français de l'Express International (SFEI) v. Commission* [1994] ECR I-2681; Case C-57/95, *France v. Commission (Re Pension Funds Communication)* [1997] ECR I-1627.

[92] There is also an action for failure to act, Art. 232 EC.

The Court of Justice shall have jurisdiction to give preliminary rulings concerning:

(a) the interpretation of the Treaty;
(b) the validity and interpretation of acts of the institutions of the Community and of the ECB;
(c) the interpretation of the statutes of bodies established by an act of the Council, where those statutes so provide.

Where such a question is raised before any court or tribunal of a Member State, that court or tribunal may, if it considers that a decision on the question is necessary to enable it to give judgment, request the Court of Justice to give a ruling thereon.

Where any such question is raised in a case pending before a court or tribunal of a Member State, against whose decision there is no judicial remedy under national law, that court or tribunal shall bring the matter before the Court of Justice.

It is for the national court to decide whether to seek a preliminary ruling, and in that sense, Article 234 creates a reference system, not an appellate one. The individual has no right to take the case to the ECJ from the national court, should the latter refuse to make a reference. Preliminary rulings are important as a method of indirect challenge to the legality of Community action. Article 234(1)(b) allows national courts to refer to the ECJ questions concerning the 'validity and interpretation of acts of the institutions of the Community'. This provision has assumed an increased importance for private applicants because of the Court's narrow construction of the standing criteria under Article 230.[93] This has meant that a reference under Article 234 is often the only mechanism whereby such parties may contest the legality of Community norms. It may be helpful to set out a paradigm case in order to understand how Article 234 is used in this context. A common situation is of a Common Agricultural Policy (CAP) regulation, which cannot be contested under Article 230, either because the applicant lacks standing, or because of the time limit. The regulations will normally be applied at national level by a national intervention agency. A regulation may, for example, require in certain circumstances the forfeiture of a deposit that has been given by a trader. The trader believes that this forfeiture and the regulation are contrary to Community law, because it is disproportionate, or discriminatory. If the security is forfeited the trader may then institute judicial review proceedings in the national court, claiming that the regulation is invalid.[94] It will be for the national court to decide whether to refer the matter to the ECJ under Article 234(1)(b). An alternative way in which the action can arise is where there is a regulation, under which a trader is liable to pay a levy, which it believes to be in breach of EU law. The trader might decide to resist payment, be sued by the national agency, and then raise the alleged invalidity of the regulation

---

[93] P. Craig and G. de Burca, *EU Law, Text, Cases and Materials* (Oxford University Press, 3rd edn., 2002), Chap. 12; Case C–50/2000 P, *Union de Pequenos Agricultores v. Council* [2002] ECR I–6677; Case C–263/02 P, *Commission v. Jego-Quere & Cie SA* [2004] ECR I–000.

[94] See, e.g., Case 181/84, *R v. Intervention Board for Agricultural Produce, ex p. E. D. & F. Man (Sugar) Ltd* [1985] ECR 2889.

on which the demand is based by way of defence. It would then be for the national court to decide whether to refer the matter to the ECJ.

(ii) The principles of judicial review

The principles of judicial review applied by the ECJ and the CFI are eclectic. They are derived from the Treaty, Community legislation, the jurisprudence of the Community courts, and soft law. These will be considered in turn.

The *EC Treaty* contains certain Articles that deal with principles, both procedural and substantive, that are directly relevant for judicial review. Thus, for example, Article 253 EC establishes a duty to give reasons that applies to regulations, decisions, and directives adopted either by the Council, Commission, and Parliament, or by the Council and Commission alone. It is noteworthy that Article 253 imposes a duty to give reasons not only for administrative decisions, but also for legislative norms, such as regulations or directives. Article 255 EC deals with access to information. It provides that any citizen of the Union, and any natural or legal person residing or having their registered office in a Member State, shall have a right of access to European Parliament, Council, and Commission documents, subject to certain principles and conditions. Non-discrimination provides an example of a substantive principle within the Treaty that is of direct relevance for judicial review. Thus Article 12 contains a general proscription of discrimination on the grounds of nationality, and this same proscription is to be found in the specific Treaty articles dealing with free movement of workers, freedom of establishment, and the provision of services. Non-discrimination on the grounds of gender is dealt with by Articles 137 and 141 EC. There are also provisions dealing with non-discrimination as between producers or consumers in the field of agriculture, Article 34(2), and specific provisions such as Article 90, prohibiting discriminatory taxation.

Community legislation made pursuant to the Treaty may also deal with the principles of judicial review. This legislation may flesh out a principle contained in a Treaty article. This was the case in relation to the legislation adopted pursuant to Article 255 EC, dealing with access to information.[95] Community legislation may also establish a code of administrative procedure that is to apply in a particular area, as exemplified in the context of EC competition policy.

It has however been the *Community courts* that have made the major contribution to the development of a set of administrative law principles that are to govern the legality of Community decision-making. The ECJ and the CFI have read principles such as proportionality, fundamental rights, legal certainty, legitimate expectations, equality, and procedural justice into the Treaty, and used them as the foundation for judicial review, under Articles 230 or 234. It is important at this juncture to understand in juridical terms how these principles

---

[95] S. Peers, 'The New Regulation on Access to Documents: A Critical Analysis' (2002) 21 *YBEL* 385.

were read into the Treaty. The ECJ used the 'window' of Article 230(2). This sets out in general terms the grounds of judicial review. The administrative law principles adumbrated above were read into the Treaty more specifically through the provision in Article 230(2) that allows for review on the ground of infringement of any rule of law relating to the application of the Treaty. This open textured provision allowed the Community courts to fashion a detailed administrative law jurisprudence that it had lacked hitherto. In developing these principles the Community courts drew upon administrative law doctrine from the Member States. The ECJ and CFI did not systematically trawl through the legal systems of each of the Member States in order to find principles that they had in common, which could then be transferred to the Community context. Their approach was rather to consider principles found in the major legal systems of the Member States, to use those that were felt to be best developed and to fashion them to suit the Community's own needs. German law was perhaps the most influential in this regard. It was German jurisprudence on, for example, proportionality and legitimate expectations that was of principal significance for the development of Community law in these areas.

It should also be recognized that *soft law* has played a role in the evolution of the principles of Community administrative law. This is exemplified by Inter-Institutional Agreements, which are agreements between the Council, Commission, and the Parliament. Such agreements have been made on topics of constitutional significance such as subsidiarity, transparency, and participation rights.

(iii) Intensity of judicial review

The Community courts apply the principles of judicial review with varying degrees of intensity. The intensity of review may be evident at different stages of judicial review.

It can be apparent in relation to the *jurisdictional conditions* that apply to the exercise of the relevant power. The initial decision-maker, which will normally be the Commission, will be accorded power to do certain things on certain conditions. The conditional grant of power may be contained in a Treaty article, or in Community legislation. A claimant will contend that the Commission has committed an error in the interpretation of the conditions that establish its jurisdiction over the relevant topic. It will be for the Community courts to decide on the existence of this error, and it will be for the Community courts to decide on the appropriate test for review to be used in such circumstances. Courts may apply a correctness test, whereby they substitute judgment on the meaning of the contested term. They can alternatively apply a less intrusive test, framed in terms of rationality, and only overturn the contested decision if it fails to meet this criterion. There is, in EU law, no case equivalent to *Chevron*[96] in the

---

[96] *Chevron USA Inc v. NRDC* 467 US 837 (1984).

USA, in which the ECJ has articulated a general approach to problems of this kind. A reading of the case law makes it clear nonetheless that the ECJ has in fact adopted a variable test for review when dealing with cases of this kind. In some situations it will simply substitute judgment on the matter at hand, specifying the interpretation that the contested words must have, and striking down the measure if it fails to accord with that interpretation. In other situations the ECJ has however adopted a test for review that is equivalent to rationality scrutiny. It has moreover done so for the same type of reasons that have influenced national courts in this respect. The subject matter, the relative expertise of the initial decision-maker, and the specificity of the jurisdictional condition have been of particular importance in this respect.

This can be exemplified by the case law on state aids. The basic principle is that state aid is contrary to EU law, since it distorts the ideal of a level playing field between competitors in different Member States. The Commission is however afforded power to authorize state aid in certain circumstances. Thus Article 87(3)(a) provides that 'aid to promote the economic development of areas where the standard of living is abnormally low or where there is serious under-employment' may be considered to be compatible with the common market. The meaning of this provision came before the ECJ in the *Philip Morris Holland* case.[97] The Dutch government gave aid to a tobacco manufacturer. The Commission found that the aid did not come within Article 87(3)(a), and this was challenged by the applicant. It argued, *inter alia*, that the Commission was wrong to hold that the standard of living in the relevant area was not 'abnormally low', and was wrong to conclude that the area did not suffer serious 'under employment' within the meaning of Article 87(3)(a). The ECJ rejected the argument. It held that in the assessment of what was a jurisdictional condition the Commission had a discretion, the exercise of which involved economic and social assessments that had to be made in a Community context.[98] The Commission had advanced good reasons for assessing the standard of living and serious under-employment in the relevant area, not with reference to the national average in the Netherlands but in relation to the Community level. The same judicial approach is evident in other decisions concerning state aids.[99]

The *relative intensity of judicial review is also apparent in the jurisprudence on proportionality*. It is a general principle of Community law, which has been brought into the Community legal order in the manner explicated above. The principle is also enshrined in Article 5 EC, which provides that action by the

---

[97] Case 730/79, *Philip Morris Holland BV v. Commission* [1980] ECR 2671.
[98] *Ibid.*, para. 24.
[99] Cases 62 and 72/87, *Executif Régional Wallon and Glaverbel SA v. Commission* [1988] ECR 1573; see also in the context of the Common Agricultural Policy, Case 74/74, *CNTA SA v. Commission* [1975] ECR 533; Case 78/74, *Deuka, Deutsche Kraftfutter GmbH, B. J. Stolp v. Einfuhr-und Vorratsstelle für Getreide und Futtermittel* [1975] ECR 421, 432. See also Case 57/72, *Westzucker GmbH v. Einfuhr-und Vorratsstelle für Zucker* [1973] ECR 321; Case 98/78, *Firma A. Racke v. Hauptzollamt Mainz* [1979] ECR 69.

Community shall not go beyond what is necessary to achieve the objectives of the Treaty, and its requirements are further fleshed out in a protocol to the Treaty. Proportionality can be used to challenge Community action, and the legality of state action that falls within the sphere of application of Community law. The proportionality inquiry will normally require the Court to decide whether the measure was suitable to achieve the desired end; whether it was necessary to achieve the desired end; and whether the measure imposed a burden on the individual that was excessive in relation to the objective sought to be achieved, (proportionality *stricto sensu*). The ECJ may apply all three steps of the inquiry. It will not do so where the case can be resolved at one of the earlier stages. Moreover, in some cases the ECJ may distinguish stages two and three of the inquiry, in others it may in effect 'fold' stage three of the inquiry back into stage two. The ECJ will decide how intensively to apply the proportionality test. As de Burca states, 'the way the proportionality principle is applied by the Court of Justice covers a spectrum ranging from a very deferential approach, to quite a rigorous and searching examination of the justification for a measure which has been challenged'.[100] The courts express this deference through a number of juridical devices.[101]

The ways in which a court may defer in such circumstances range from deeming the measure to be non-justiciable, to refusing to look closely at the justification for the restrictive effects of the measure, to placing the onus of proof on the challenger who is claiming that the measure is disproportionate. Courts tend to be deferential in their review in cases which highlight the non-representative nature of the judiciary, the limited evidentiary and procedural processes of adjudication, and the difficulty of providing a defined individual remedy in contexts which involve complex political and economic policies.

Three broad types of case can be distinguished, and the intensity of proportionality review differs in these types of case.

There are cases concerning rights, which prompt the most intensive scrutiny. In *Hauer*[102] the applicant challenged a Community regulation that placed limitations on the planting of new vines. The Court found that this did not, in itself, constitute an invalid restriction on property rights. It then considered whether the planting restrictions were disproportionate, 'impinging upon the very substance of the right to property'.[103] The Court found that they were not, but it carefully examined the purpose of the general scheme within which the contested regulation fell. The objects of this scheme were to attain a balanced wine market, with fair prices for consumers and a fair return for producers; the eradication of surpluses; and an improvement in the quality of wine. The disputed regulation, which prohibited new plantings, was part of this overall plan.

---

[100] G. de Búrca, 'The Principle of Proportionality and its Application in EC Law' (1993) 13 YBEL 105, 111.   [101] *Ibid.*, 112.
[102] Case 44/79, *Hauer v. Land Rheinland-Pfalz* [1979] ECR 3727.   [103] *Ibid.*, para. 23.

It was not disproportionate in the light of the legitimate, general Community policy for this area. This policy was designed to deal with an immediate problem of surpluses, while at the same time laying the foundation for more permanent measures to facilitate a balanced wine market. In *Hautala*[104] an MEP sought access to a Council document concerning arms exports. The Council refused to grant access, on the ground that this could be harmful to the EU's relations with third countries, and sought to justify this under Article 4(1) of Decision 93/731,[105] governing access to Council documentation. The ECJ held that the right of access to documents was to be broadly construed so as to include access to information contained in the document, not just the document itself. The principle of proportionality required the Council to consider partial access to a document that contained information the disclosure of which could endanger one of the interests protected by Article 4(1). Proportionality also required that derogation from the right of access be limited to what was appropriate and necessary for achieving the aim in view.

There are cases where the attack is on the penalty imposed, the claim being that it is excessive. The Community courts are reasonably searching in this type of case too, since they can normally strike down a particular penalty without thereby undermining the entirety of the administrative policy with which it is connected. In *Man (Sugar)*[106] the applicant was required to give a security deposit to the Board when seeking a licence to export sugar outside the Community. The applicant was then late, but only by four hours, in completing the relevant paperwork. The Board, acting pursuant to a Community regulation, declared the entire deposit of £1,670,370 to be forfeit. The Court held that the automatic forfeiture of the entire deposit in the event of any failure to fulfil the time requirement was too drastic, given the function performed by the system of export licences.

The third type of case is where the individual argues that the policy choice made by the administration is disproportionate, because, for example, the costs are excessive in relation to the benefits, or because the measure is not suitable or necessary to achieve the end in view. The Community courts will often be more circumspect in this type of case, especially where the contested measure relates to social and economic regulatory policy.[107] Proportionality still applies in such instances, but the judicial tendency is only to overturn the policy choice if it is clearly or manifestly disproportionate. This is exemplified by the *Fedesa* case.[108]

---

[104] Case C-353/99P, *Council v. Hautala* [2001] ECR I-9565.   [105] [1993] OJ L340/43.
[106] Case 181/84, *Man Sugar*, n. 94. See also Case C-365/99, *Portugal v. Commission* [2001] ECR I-5645.
[107] C. Vajda, 'Some Aspects of Judicial Review within the Common Agricultural Policy—Part II' (1979) 4 *ELRev* 341, 347–8; T. Tridimas, *The General Principles of EC Law* (Oxford University Press, 1999), Chap. 3.
[108] Case C-331/88, *R v. Minister for Agriculture, Fisheries and Food, ex parte Fedesa* [1990] ECR 4023.

The applicants were manufacturers and distributors of veterinary medicine who challenged the validity of national legislative measure implementing a Directive that prohibited the use in livestock farming of certain hormonal substances. They argued that the Directive infringed, *inter alia*, the principle of proportionality. The applicants contended, more specifically, that the prohibition on the hormones was inappropriate to attain the declared objectives, since it would be impossible to apply in practice and would lead to the creation of a dangerous black market. They argued further that the prohibition was not necessary, because consumer anxieties could be allayed by the dissemination of information and advice. In relation to the third part of the proportionality inquiry, the applicants contended that the prohibition entailed excessive disadvantages to the concerned traders, who would suffer considerable financial loss, and that this outweighed the alleged benefits to the general Court acknowledged that proportionality was one of the general principles of Community law. The lawfulness of the prohibition of an economic activity was therefore subject to the condition that the prohibitory measures were appropriate and necessary in order to achieve the objectives legitimately pursued by the legislation. When there was a choice between several appropriate measures recourse must be had to the least onerous, and the disadvantages caused must not be disproportionate to the aims pursued. The ECJ then continued in the following vein.[109]

However, with regard to judicial review of compliance with those conditions it must be stated that in matters concerning the common agricultural policy the Community legislature has a discretionary power which corresponds to the political responsibilities given to it by ... the Treaty. Consequently, the legality of a measure adopted in that sphere can be affected only if the measure is manifestly inappropriate having regard to the objective which the competent institution is seeking to pursue.

The applicants had therefore to show that the measure was manifestly inappropriate and the Court concluded that they had not discharged this burden.[110] The prohibition, even though it might have caused financial loss to some traders, could not be regarded as manifestly inappropriate. A similar judicial reluctance to engage in intensive review is also apparent in other areas in which the Commission is possessed of discretionary power requiring it to make complex evaluative choices, as in the case of state aids,[111] dumping,[112] and safeguard measures.[113]

---

[109] *Ibid.*, para. 14.
[110] See also, e.g., Case C-8/89, *Vincenzo Zardi v. Consorzio Agrario Provinciale di Ferrara* [1990] ECR I-2515, 2532-3; Case T-30/99, *Bocchi Food Trade International GmbH v. Commission* [2001] ECR II-943, para. 92.
[111] Case T-380/94, *AIUFFASS v. Commission* [1996] ECR II-2169; Case T-358/94, *Compagnie Nationale Air France v. Commission* [1996] ECR II-2109.
[112] Case T-118/96, *Thai Bicycle Industry Co Ltd v. Council* [1998] ECR II-2991.
[113] Case C-390/95P, *Antillean Rice Mills NV v. Commission* [1999] ECR I-769, para. 48.

(e) Executive power and accountability through principles for the exercise of Community administration

The principles of judicial review are not the only mechanism for holding the executive to account. There are also principles contained in the new Financial Regulation, which are significant for the present discussion in two ways.[114]

The Financial Regulation *established a constitutional framework for Community administration of the kind that had not existed hitherto*, and contains important provisions concerning the way that Community programmes are implemented and administered. The previous Financial Regulation was enacted in 1977, and had been amended on many occasions.[115] The new Financial Regulation 2002[116] provides a legal framework for the structure of Community administration.

This is dealt with in Title IV, Implementation of the Budget, Chapter 2 of which is concerned with Methods of Implementation. Article 53(1) of the Financial Regulation provides that the Commission shall implement the budget either on a centralized basis, or by shared or decentralized management, or by joint management with international organizations.

Centralized management covers those instances where the Commission implements the budget directly through its departments, or indirectly.[117] The principles concerning indirect centralized implementation are set out in Article 54. The Commission is not allowed to entrust its executive powers to third parties where they involve a large measure of discretion implying political choices. The implementing tasks delegated must be clearly defined and fully supervised.[118] There will clearly be problems in deciding whether the task allocated to third parties is *ultra vires*, in the sense that it involves 'a large measure of discretion implying political choices', within the meaning of Article 54(1). Within these limits the Commission can entrust tasks to the new breed of executive agencies, or Community bodies that can receive grants.[119] It can also, within the limits of Article 54(1), entrust tasks to national public-sector bodies, or bodies governed by private law with a public service mission guaranteed by the state.[120] These national bodies can only be entrusted with budget implementation if the basic act concerning the programme provides for the possibility of delegation, and lays down the criteria for the selection of such bodies. It is also a condition that the delegation to national bodies is a response to the requirements of sound financial management, and is non-discriminatory. The delegation of executive tasks to these bodies must be transparent, and the procurement

---

[114] P. Craig, 'The Constitutionalisation of Community Administration' (2003) 28 *ELRev* 840.
[115] *Financial Regulation of 21 December 1977 Applicable to the General Budget of the European Communities* [1977] OJ L356/1.
[116] Council Regulation 1605/2002, *on the Financial Regulation Applicable to the General Budget of the European Communities* [2002] OJ L248/1.   [117] *Ibid.*, Art. 53(2).
[118] *Ibid.*, Art. 54(1).   [119] *Ibid.*, Art. 54(2)(a) and (b).   [120] *Ibid.*, Art. 54(2)(c).

procedure must be non-discriminatory and prevent any conflict of interest. There must be an effective internal control system for management operations, proper accounting arrangements, and an external audit.[121] The Commission is not allowed to entrust implementation of funds from the budget, in particular payment and recovery, to external private-sector bodies, other than those which have a public service mission guaranteed by the state.[122] The Commission is however empowered to entrust such private-sector entities with tasks involving technical expertise, and administrative, preparatory, or ancillary tasks involving neither the exercise of public authority, nor the use of discretionary judgment.[123]

Where aspects of the budget are implemented by shared management tasks are entrusted to the Member States in accordance with specific provisions of the new Financial Regulation concerning the European Agricultural Guidance and Guarantee Fund (EAGGF), Guarantee Section, and the Structural Funds.[124]

Cases of decentralized management cover those instances where funds are intended for third country beneficiaries. These funds can be disbursed directly by the Commission, or by the authorities of the beneficiary state.[125] In the latter instance the rules of the new Financial Regulation concerning separation of function between authorizing and accounting officers, internal and external audit, and procurement procedures are applicable.

The *Financial Regulation also contains the detailed rules concerning the budget.* The Treaty stipulates that financial regulations shall be made specifying the procedure to be adopted for establishing and implementing the budget and for presenting and auditing the accounts.[126] These rules are contained in the Financial Regulation, which also sets out more general principles to be observed in the pursuit of budgetary rectitude.

5. Conclusion

It may be helpful by way of conclusion to reflect more generally on political and legal accountability in relation to executive power within the EU.

(a) Political accountability

It can be accepted that political accountability within a regime of shared executive power will be more complex than in those systems where such power is concentrated within 'the executive'. A regime of shared executive power will not by definition have a single line of executive accountability.

---

[121] *Ibid.*, Art. 56(1). [122] *Ibid.*, Art. 57(1). [123] *Ibid.*, Art. 57(2).
[124] *Ibid.*, Arts. 149–60. [125] *Ibid.*, Arts. 163–71. [126] Art. 279 EC.

This means that in relation to *accountability for the overall political agenda* it is not be possible for the voters to express their dislike and put another party into office with a different agenda. The fact that executive power over agenda setting is shared between the Commission, Council, and European Council prevents such direct transmission of voter preferences. The multi-annual agenda is the result of a discourse between the major institutional players. This is the case under the Rome Treaty as amended and it remains so under the Constitutional Treaty. This discourse will incorporate voter preferences partly through consultation with the EP and under the Constitutional Treaty partly through the Commission President who will be indirectly elected.[127] The discourse will also include state interests as mediated through the European Council and the Council. The dialogue fostered by shared executive power can be healthy in making actors re-think their own pre-conceived positions concerning the direction of EU development. This process may be 'messier' than that in states with a single executive power. Such systems can foster electoral accountability, in the sense that the electorate can throw out the party whose policies they dislike. It should however also be recognized that systems with strong, unitary executive power can often lead to problems of political accountability between elections. Thus commentators in the UK have referred to the system as one of 'elective autocracy', in which a government elected with a reasonable majority has very considerable power and the legislature has little influence.

Political accountability in relation to the implementation and execution of policy choices raises a number of issues that must be disaggregated. The annual and multi-annual agenda will be developed in part through regulations and directives, henceforth to be European laws and framework laws under the Constitutional Treaty, which are commonly legitimated through the co-decision procedure initiated by the Commission. Secondary regulations, the new-style delegated regulations under the Constitutional Treaty, will also be used. There are problems in this latter respect, which are reflective of the difficulty of rendering secondary rule-making both workable and legitimate. In relation to accountability for the implementation/execution of agreed policy choices, the Commission is subject to a plethora of differing constraints. The EP can exercise control through a Committee of Inquiry, through scrutiny by its regular committees, with the long stop of forcing the entire Commission out. The Ombudsman can investigate cases of maladministration. The Commission is moreover subject to the important rules contained in the new Financial Regulation, which covers matters such as fiscal and policy responsibility, audit, delegation, contracting out, and the like.

---

[127] Under the Constitutional Treaty the Commission President is elected by the EP and the European Council must take account of the election results in deciding which person to put forward to the EP as Commission President. Thus, if the electorate dislike the direction of EU policy they can express this through a change in the EP, which will have some impact on the European Council's decision as to the candidate for Commission President.

(b) Legal accountability

Judicial review as applied by the Community courts covers the great majority of instances where policy is implemented by the Commission, whether this is in the form of individual determinations or secondary rules. The Community courts are however largely excluded from the CFSP. The Constitutional Treaty left the general structure of the courts' powers unchanged. The European Council has however been made subject to judicial review in relation to acts that are intended to produce legal effects vis-à-vis third parties,[128] with a similar amendment concerning failure to act.[129] It is clear that binding acts of the European Council could also be challenged indirectly through national courts via the preliminary ruling procedure. Inter-institutional disputes concerning the disposition of executive power might also end up before the ECJ. It should also be recognized that the detailed rules laid down in the new Financial Regulation concerning the way in which Community administration must be conducted will be enforceable through the courts, and this constitutes a further important element in legal accountability for executive power within the EU.

[128] Art. III-365(1).   [129] Art. III-367.

Index

Aarhus Convention, 287
accountability,
  see also judicial review, ombudsman
  Australia and, *see* Australia, executive power in,
  Britain, government accountability in
    legal: doctrine of the rule of law, 41; doctrine of ultra vires, 41; judicial review, mechanism of executive accountability, 42–8; Parliament, sovereignty of, 41
    other mechanisms: audit, 48–50; ombudsman, 48–50; public inquiries, 48–50
    political: constitutional conventions, rules of responsibility, 37; collective ministerial responsibility, 37–8; individual ministerial responsibility, 37–8; maintaining majority support in Parliament, 38; Ministerial Code, 39; Questions of Procedure for Ministers, 39; select committees,
  Canada and, *see* Canada, executive power in,
  European Union and, *see* European Union, executive in the
  France and, *see* France, executive power in,
  Germany, *see* Germany, executive power in,
  Italy and, *see* Italian executive, growth of,
  New Zealand and, *see* New Zealand, New Public Management,
  Scotland, *see* Scotland, domesticated executive
  Spain, *see* Spain, the executive and the law,
  United States and, *see* United States, executive power in,
Administrative Appeal Tribunal,
  accountability mechanism in Australia, 119
AEEG,
  gas and energy regulator, 250
AGCOM,
  television and telecommunications regulator, 249, 250, 257–8
alternative dispute resolution,
  telecommunications in Italy, 263
Amato Government, 243
anticorruption commissions,
  accountability mechanism in Australia, 122
anti-terrorist laws,
  Germany and, 273

audit,
  Comptroller and Auditor General, 48
  National Audit Office, 48–9
  Public Accounts Committee, 49
  value-for-money, 23, 48
Auditor General,
  Australia and, 105
  Canada and, 77–8
  New Zealand and, 158–9
  Scotland and, 206–12
Australia, executive power in,
  accountability, other mechanisms,
    Administrative Appeal Tribunal, 119
    anticorruption commissions, 122
    Freedom of Information Act 1982, 120–1
    independent merits review, 119–20
    ombudsman, 121–2
    specialist merits review tribunals, 120
    whistle-blowing legislation at federal level, 122
  accountability through courts,
    Administrative Decisions (Judicial Review) Act 1977, 116–18
    judicial review under statute for Commonwealth decisions, 116–18
    judicial review under the Constitution, 112–16
    limits on the scope of judicial review, 118
    remedies under the Constitution, 112
    rule of law influence on judicial review, 114–15
    separation of powers doctrine and, 112
  accountability through Parliament,
    Certain Maritime Incident (CMI) Report, 109–12
    committees, 104–7
    document production, 107
    government-at-arm's-length, 108–19
    government business enterprises, 108
    individual ministerial responsibility, 101–3
    joined up government, 111–12
    ministerial advisers, 109
    obstacles to, 107–12
    outsourcing to contractors, 108, 121
    Question Time, 103–4
  Additional Estimates Statements, 105
  Budget Statements, 105
  responsible government system,
    Australian Constitution, 89

Australia, executive power in, (*cont.*):
  conventions, 90
  Governor-General, 89–90
  principles of, 90
  scope of executive authority,
    division between Commonwealth and State, 91
    federal division of executive power, 91
  scope of powers,
    constitutional powers conferred on the executive, 91–3
    prerogative powers of the executive, 91, 93–5
    state and territory level, 99–101
    statutory powers and constitutional constraints, 91, 96–9
Australian Children Overboard affair, 109–12
Australian Constitution, 90
Australian Law Reform Commission and Administrative Review Council, report on Freedom of Information Act 1995, 121
Australian National Audit Office, 105

Barthélémy J, 225
Berlusconi government, 251–3
Blackstone,
  Commentaries on the king's power, 218, 221
Blair Tony, 18–19, 21
  growth of political authority of prime minister's office under, 50
  resignation if Commons failed to support war policy, 38
  Scotland and, 215
Britain, delimiting executive power in,
  accountability,
    legal, 41–8
    other mechanisms of, 48–50
    political, 37–40
  advisers, 22–3
  audit, 48–9
  cabinet, 18–22
  civil servants, 22–3
  Comptroller and Auditor General, 48
  constitution,
    tripartite separation of powers and the, 25
  core executive, 18–22
  diplomacy, legal accountability and, 46–7
  foreign affairs, legal accountability and, 46–7
  functions of the executive,
    general principle, 24–5
    judicial functions and 26–37
    legislative functions and, 25–6
  government policy, courts cannot review, 47
  judicial review, grounds for
    illegality, 42–3
    irrationality, 42–4
    procedural impropriety, 42, 44
    statutory, 44–5
  judicial review, remedies for, 45–6
  military matters, legal accountability and, 46–7
  National Audit Office, 48–9
  national security, legal accountability and, 47
  ombudsman, 49–50
  Prime Minister, 18–22
  public inquiries, 49
  rule of law doctrine, 41
  sovereignty of parliament, 41–2
  ultra vires doctrine, 41

cabinet,
  Canadian, 68–74
  collective decision making and, 16, 18
  core executive, 21
  French, 226
  functions of, 20
  individual prime ministerial diktat and, 16, 18
  ministers appointed by Queen on advice of Prime Minister, 18
  Scottish, 202
Canada, executive power in,
  ambivalent nature of, 52–88
  boundaries of the,
    'freedom of expression' of civil servants under the Charter, 73
    independence of administrative tribunals, 74–7
    interdependence of cabinet and civil service, 68–74
    'whistle-blower' legislation, 72
  checks on,
    Auditors General, 77–8
    federalism, 86–8
    Information and Privacy Commissioners, 78
    judicial review, 78–86
    Ombudsman, 78
    public inquiries, 78
    self-regulatory role of the civil service, 77
  scope of executive authority,
    cabinet controlled legislative power, 55–7, 68
    Charter of Rights and Freedom, 52, 55, 58, 60
    civil service, 56, 68
    Constitution Act 1867, 53, 55, 56, 58
    Constitution Act 1982, 54, 55, 58
    'constitutional monarchy', 52, 54, 55
    'executive power' defined in the constitution, 54–7
    constitutional monarchy, 53, 55

Governor General powers, 54–5
independent judiciary, 52, 54, 65, 75
ministerial responsibility, 56, 60
power of executive, 52, 57
prime minister, 55–7
responsible government principle, 55–6
royal prerogative, Crown deriving power through, 57
separation of powers doctrine,
dynamic of the administrative state, 58, 60–3: Canadian Human Rights Commission, 61–2; Charter and 'courts of competent jurisdiction', 60, 63; mutually reinforcing relationship between the legislative and executive branches, 60; judicial functions vested in tribunals, 60; judicial review availability, 63
dynamic of judicial independence, 58, 64–8: Charter, 65; Constitution Act 1867 provisions, 64; Constitution Act 1982, 65; independence of the judiciary, 64
dynamic of the parliamentary system: entanglement between the legislative and executive branches, 59; sovereignty of Parliament, 59
emerging facet of, 57–8
Canada Labour Law, 82
Canadian Charter of Rights and Freedom, 55, 58, 60, 63, 65–6, 77, 82–3
Canadian Constitution Act 1867, 53, 55, 56, 58, 64, 86–7
Canadian Constitution Act 1982, 54, 55, 58, 65–6
Canadian Human Rights Commission, 61–2
Certain Maritime Incident (CMI) Report, Australian Children Overboard affair, 109–12
Cheffins R.I., 53–4
civil servants, 16
Canada,
scope of the executive, 56
self-regulatory role of, 77
Civil Service Code, 23
not party political, 22
'next steps' agencies, 23
role of, 22
servants of the Crown, 23
service delivery, 22
Clinton President, 181
Code of Good Administrative Behaviour, European Ombudsman, 332
collective ministerial responsibility, 37–8
Common Agricultural Policy (CAP), 324, 335

Common Foreign and Security Policy (CFSP), 326–7, 345
Comptroller and Auditor General, 48
CONSOB,
financial services regulator, 249
constitutional convention,
collective responsibility, 18
core executive,
agencies comprising, 21
joined-up government, 21
Cossiga Francesco, 264
Court of Auditors,
European, 315, 329, 332–3
Italy and, 255, 259–60
Spain, 301, 311
Court of First Instance, 337

Daintith T, 69
Department for Constitutional Affairs, 18
devolved government in Scotland and Wales,
powers and function of police, security and secret intelligence services, 16

Ecofin council, 248, 265
European Agricultural Guidance and Guarantee Fund (EAGGF), 324
European Court of Justice, 335–7
European Union, executive in the,
accountability.
Court of Auditors, 332–3
legal, 345
legislature, to the, 329
ombudsman, 331–2
political, 343–4
Comitology regime, 323
Committee of Independent Experts, 324, 333
Constitutional Treaty, 315–16, 320–1, 324
Council President, 316
Court of Auditors, 315, 329, 332–3
Employment and Social Policy Council, 319
European Employment Strategy, 319, 325
General Affairs Council, 318
judicial review, 333–41
ombudsman, 315, 332
Open Method of Coordination, 319
President of the European Council, 320–1, 327
resources and budget, 328–9
Rome Treaty, 315–16, 320–1
Santer Commission, 324, 329, 333
Treaty on European Union, 317, 320, 326
executive power,
see also under individual country headings
ministers of the Crown, 16
secretaries of state, 16

Federal Chancellor, 279
federalism,
  Canada and checks on executive
      authority, 86–8
  collaboration between central and regional
      governments, 87–8
France, and executive power in,
  'Bayeux' discourse, 240
  definition and scope of,
    executive as administration, 222–5
    executive in the constitution, 225–9
    nation as bearer of political will, 219
    'nation' as sovereign, 219
    revolutionary France, sovereignty and
        government, 218–22
  Conseil Constitutionnel, 237
  Conseil d'Etat, 224, 230, 233–6
  control of executive action,
    criminal liability of executive
        authorities, 238
    constitutional review of executive
        action, 236–8
    defining executive powers in the context
        of judicial review, 233–6
    judicial review, 229–30
    political accountability, 239–42
    theory of 'actes de gouvernement', 230–3
  criminal liability of executive authorities,
    Constitution and, 238
    status of the President, 238
    Treaty of Rome and, 239
  executive decisions,
    'actes de gouvernement', 230–2
    'actes adminstratifs', 231–2
    'decrets', 230
    'ordonnances', 230, 233
  judicial review, 233–9, 241
  juridictions judiciaires, 232
  nuclear weapons,
    President and, 228
  political accountability,
    cabinet accountability to parliament, 241
    'electoral accountability', 240
    President and, 240–2
    Prime Minister and, 241–2
  'pouvoir d'organisation du service' 235
  prerogative of pardon, 228, 231
  President,
    Constitutional powers of
        the, 227–9, 234
    nuclear weapons and the, 228
    power to dissolve national assembly, 228
    Prime Minister nominated by, 227
    referendum and the, 228
  Prime Minister,
    Constitutional powers of the, 227–9
  referenda, 228, 240

revolutionary France, sovereignty and
    government, 218–22
separation of powers and, 217–20
Freedom of Information Act 1982,
  accountability mechanism in Australia,
    correction of records, 121
    enforceable rights of access to
        document, 120
    outsourcing arrangements and, 108, 121
    publishing of information of government
        agencies, 120
French Constitution of 1791, 220
French Constitution of 1958, 227
functions of the executive, in Britain
  judicial functions and,
    growth in constitutional authority of
        judiciary, 26
    judicial review in the context of executive
        decisions, 27
    judicial review of executive decisions in
        the context of criminal
        sentencing, 27
    mandatory life prisoners, 31–7
    planning laws, 27–31
  legislative functions and,
    overlap between, 25–6
  no general principle, 24
  powers conferred by statute, 25
  prerogative powers,
    exercisable by the monarch, 24
    powers exercised by government
        ministers, 24

General Affairs and External Council
    (GAERC), 321
German Constitution (Grundgesetz) 1949,
    268–73, 276, 279–81, 285,
    287, 289
German Constitution 1919, 271
Germany, executive power in,
  accountability,
    administration and, 280–3
    federal segmentation of executive, 283–5
    judicial 285–7
    legal forms and executive
        functions, 275–9
    other forms, 287–9
    parliamentary, 279–80
  agency capture, 281
  anti-terrorist laws, 273
  'architecture of security', 274
  autonomous self-administration, 270
  central ministries, 270
  'comprehensive legal protection'
      doctrine, 285
  dragnet controls, 274
  emergency powers, 271

executive power,
    organizational diversity of, 269–71
    unitary notion of, 268–9
executive prerogatives, 271
Federal Chancellor, 279
Federal Constitutional Court, 272
Federal Council of Germany, 271, 283
Länder, 270, 276, 279, 283–4
mail interceptions, 272, 285
municipal registry, 270
ombudsman, 287
Parliament, 271, 283
police,
    Federal Border Guard, 270
    Federal Police Force, 270
private law, 278
proportionality principle, 274, 286
public law, 278
right to sanctity at the home, 273
rights of inquiry and questioning, 280
right of petition, 287
separation of powers, 270
statutory regulations, 276
telecommunications interceptions, 272, 285
'thorough judicial control' doctrine, 285–6
Giolitti Giovanni, 244
Greenpeace,
    judicial review of government decisions, 45
government accountability, in Britain
    legal,
        doctrine of the rule of law, 41
        doctrine of ultra vires, 41
        judicial review, mechanism of executive accountability, 42–8
        sovereignty of Parliament, 41
    other mechanisms,
        audit, 48–50
        ombudsmen, 48–50
        public inquiries, 48–50
    political,
        constitutional conventions, rules of responsibility, 37
        collective ministerial responsibility, 37–8
        individual ministerial responsibility, 37–8
        maintaining majority support in Parliament, 38
        Ministerial Code, 39
        Questions of Procedure for Ministers, 39
        select committees, 40, 49, 157
government departments,
    creatures of law, 18
    mergers of, 18
    secretaries of state, 18
Governor General,
    Australia, 89–90
    Canada, 54–5

habeas corpus, writ of,
    detention of suspected terrorists, 183, 190
Hansard,
    parliamentary questions, 40
Hogg PW, 54, 83
House of Commons,
    conventions enforced by, 17
    holding ministers to account, 40
Human Rights Act 1998,
    accountability to the courts,
        'slopping out' in Scottish prisons, 210
    reforms effected by,
        judicial review and, 44

independent merits review tribunal,
    mechanism for accountability in Australia, 119
individual ministerial responsibility,
    dual nature of, 39
    generally, 37–8
    means of holding ministers to account,
        asking of parliamentary questions, 40
        select committees, 40
        staging of parliamentary debates, 40
Information and Privacy Commissioners,
    checks on executive powers in Canada, 78
Italian Constitution of 1948, 244–5, 247
Italian executive, growth of,
    accountability,
        courts and, 261–4
        international and supranational institutions, importance of, 265
        Parliament's ineffective scrutiny of the executive, 258–61
        President of the Republic and, 264–5
        'Question Time', 259
    alternative dispute resolution,
        telecommunications and, 263
    'centrality' of Parliament, 244
    changing role,
        antitrust authority, 257
        conflict of interests, avoiding the creation of, 257–8
        decentralization, 254–6
        disregard for legislative limits, 256–8
        executive's powers, 250–2
        executive's resources: money and staff, 253–4
        indirect to direct legitimacy, 246–50
        television and telecommunications regulator, 257
    charters for public utilities, 248
    civil servants appointments, 250, 253–4
    Court of Auditors, 245, 259–60
    decentralization, 254–6
    decline of the executive after 1948, 244–6
    delegated legislation, 251

Italian executive, growth of, (*cont.*):
  executive powers, 250–2
  Finance Act and, 253
  governmental legislation, growth of,
    decree laws, 251.
    decreti-legge, 251–2
  impartiality, constitutional requirement
    of, 254
  introduction to, 243–4
  judicial review,
    remedies available in Constitutional
      Court, 261–3
    remedies available through the judges, 261
  majoritarian system, 249, 254, 256–7, 259
  ombudsman, 265
  President of the Republic
    accountability and the, 264–5
    power to dissolve the Chambers, 247
    role of, 264
  referendum on the electoral system, 247
  regional Presidents, 248
  regulatory authorities, 249–50, 257
  Stability Pact, 265
  state-owned companies and
    appointments, 250
Italian Radio and Television Corporation, 266

Johnson PA, 54
judicial review,
  applicants seeking,
    'sufficient interest' in the matter, 45
  Australia,
    judicial review under statute for
      Commonwealth decisions, 116–8
    judicial review under the
      Constitution, 112–6
  Britain and, 42–6
  Canada and, 78–86
  European Union and, 333–41
  exercise of government power, decisions
    beyond scope of,
    diplomacy, 46
    foreign affairs, 46
    military matters, 46
  France and, 229–30, 233–9
  Germany and, 285–7
  grounds of review,
    Human Rights Act 1998, supplement
      to, 42
    illegality, doctrine of, 42
    irrationality, doctrine of, 42
    procedural impropriety, 42
  illegality, doctrine of,
    ambiguity or openness of legislative
      language, 43
    subjective discretion, 42
  irrationality, doctrine of,
    'accepted moral standards', 43
    definition from Wednesbury case, 43
    Lord Diplock's definition, 43
  Italy and, 261–3
  limitations in holding the exercise of
    executive power to account, 48
  New Zealand and, 131
  procedural impropriety,
    duty to act fairly, 44
    rule against bias, 44
  reforms effected by Human Rights Act 1998,
    section 6, 44
  test of proportionality, 45
  remedies for,
    award of damages not generally available
      in public law, 46
    declaration, 46
    discretionary nature, 45
    order to prohibit an unlawful decision
      from being made, 46
    order to quash an unlawful decision, 46
    order to require duty to be performed, 46
  Scotland and, 210
  Spain and, 301–8
  United States and, 189–91

Kernaghan, 56
King of Spain, 290–1

Lisbon Summit, 319
Locke, 220, 246
Lord Chancellor's Department,
  replacement of, 18
Luxembourg Crisis, 323

Machiavelli, 220
Madison J, 58, 162
Major government, 40
Ministerial Code,
  rules of ministerial responsibility, 39
Mixed Member Proportional Electoral System,
  New Zealand and the, 135
Montesquieu, 162, 218, 220, 246
Mortati C, 261

National Association of Italian Town
  Councils, 256
NATO, 181, 250
New Zealand, New Public Management,
  Bill of Rights 1990, 125, 130–1, 136, 142,
    148–9, 151
  corporate methods of accountability, 140
  Crown Entities Act 2004,
    autonomous crown entities, 129
    crown agents, 129
    crown entity companies, 129

crown entity subsidiaries, 129
independent crown entities, 129
executive,
  Chief Executives, 127
  Her Majesty in Right of
    New Zealand, 126
  judicial definitions of the, 130–1
  legal definitions of the, 127–30
  Ministers of the Crown, 126
financial accountability and control, 152–5
judicial accountability regimes,
  Bill of Rights application, 136–40, 148–9
  contract law, 150–1
  international treaties, 146–8
  judicial review, 131–5, 142–5
  Maori custom, 145–6
  private regulatory bodies, 135–6
  regulations, 149–50
Maori custom,
  constraint on executive power, 145–6
Ngai Tahu Claims Settlement, 128, 145
other forms of audit and investigation,
  Auditor-General, 158–9
  Ombudsman, 159
  Public Audit Act, 159
  Public Finance Act, 155
political accountability,
  Chief Executives, 156
  ministers' relationship with the Civil
    Service, 155–8
  State Sector Act 1988, 156
  Treaty of Waitangi 1840, 125, 127, 131,
    133–4, 137, 142, 145, 151
  ultra vires transactions, 139–40
Ngai Tahu Claims Settlement, 128, 145
Nixon President Richard, 181

ombudsman,
  Australia and, 121–2
  Canadian, 78
  European, 315, 332
  Germany and, 287
  Italy and, 265
  maladministration, subject to scrutiny of, 50–1
  New Zealand, 159
  goals of, 50
  Parliamentary, 49
  Scotland and the, 211–2
outsourcing arrangements,
  access to documents of contractors in
    Australia, 121
  obstacles to accountability through
    Parliament in Australia, 108

Parliament,
  ownership of rules of ministerial
    responsibility, 39

resolutions contained in Ministerial
  Code, 39
People Smuggling Taskforce (PST), 111
police,
  Germany and the, 270
political advisers, 22
prerogative of pardon,
  France and the, 228, 231
prerogative power to exclude and expel aliens,
  Australia and, 94–5
President,
  France and the, 224–9
  Italy and the, 245, 247, 250, 264–5
primary legislation,
  government and, 41
Prime Minister,
  appointment by Queen, 17
  nominated by President, 227
  office of, 16, 17
Prodi government, 251–2
proportionality principle,
  Germany and, 274, 286
  Spain and, 298
proportionality, test of,
  judicial review,
    reforms effected by Human Rights
      Act 1998, 44
public inquiries,
  Canada and, 78
  mechanism of government
    accountability, 48–50
  reports containing recommendations for
    reform, 49

Queen, the,
  Australia, executive power vested
    in, 89–90
  Canada, executive power vested in, 53
  Scotland and, 197
'Question time',
  accountability and, 259
  Australian accountability through
    parliament, 103–4
  Italy and, 259
Questions of Procedure for Ministers,
  rules of ministerial responsibility, 39

referenda,
  Dutch, 316
  France and, 228, 240, 316
  Italy and, 246–7
regulatory authorities,
  AEEG, 250
  AGCOM, 249, 257
  CONSOB, 249
Rehnquist Court, 189

royal prerogative authority,
  British government and, 41
  Canada, Crown deriving power through, 57

Savoie D, 68
Scotland, domesticated executive,
  Auditor General, 206, 212
  accountability,
    Courts, 210–11
    judicial review, 210
    ombudsmen and others, 211–12
    relationship with Whitehall, 212–15
    Scottish Parliament and, 203–10
  Carltona principle, 195, 211
  concordats, 214–15
  Consultative Steering Group principles, 204, 207–9
  First Minister, 197, 205
  (Fraser) Holyrood Inquiry, 207
  Law Officers,
    Lord Advocate, 197, 210
    Solicitor-General for Scotland, 197
  'memorandum of understanding', 214
  MSPs,
    constituency members, 204
    generally, 206, 209, 212
    lack of filter between citizen and ombudsman, 212
    regional members, 204
  Parliament's fixed term, 204
  powers for the Scottish Executive, 194–203
    Carltona principle, 195, 211
    generally, 194–203
    non-statutory powers, 200–2
    prerogative based powers, 200
    prerogative of mercy, 201
    role of the Queen, 196
    supply arms to the police forces, 201
    'Westminster model', 195
  proportional representation, 204
  Public Petitions Committee, 208
  Queen, the, and, 197
  Scottish Cabinet, 202
  Scottish Executive,
    principal institution created by the Scotland Act, 197
  Sewel motion, 199, 201, 210
  SNP, 204
secondary legislation,
  powers exercisable by government conferred by, 41
secretaries of state, 16
select committees,
  composition of, 40
  means of holding ministers to account, 40
separation of powers,
  Australia and, 112
  Britain and, 25
  Canada and, 58–68
  France and, 217–20
  Germany and, 270
  United States and, 162–4, 187–91
Sewel motion, 199, 201, 210
Spain, the executive and the law,
  accountability,
    budgetary control, 311–12
    central and regional executive pressure, 311–12
    courts and, 300–8
    ombudsman, 301, 310–11
    Parliament and, 298–300
    state liability as a means of control, 308–10
  Autonomous Communities, 291, 295–6, 300, 311
  Congress of Deputies, 298
  Constitution, 290–6, 306, 309–10
  Cortes Generales, 291, 293, 295–6, 298–9, 301, 310
  Court of Auditors, 301, 311
  Decretos Legislativos, 293–4, 300
  Decretos Leyes, 294
  executive,
    European Union and the, 297
    legal concept, 292
    local government and the, 295–7
    Parliament and the, 293–5
    regions and the, 295–7
    role of the, 290–2
    'state of emergency' and the, 297
  judicial review, 301–8
  King of Spain, 290–1
  parliamentary monarchy, 298
  ombudsman, 301, 310–11
  'political acts' doctrine, 302–3
  President, 292
  proportionality principle, 298
  Senate, 298
  sports law, 301
  'state of exception', 297
  'state of siege', 297
Spanish Constitution of 1978, 290–6, 306, 309–10
specialist merits review tribunals,
  accountability mechanism in Australia, 120

terrorists,
  indefinite detention without trial of suspected, 47, 183

Thatcher government, 22–3, 40
Thatcher Margaret, 19, 20–1, 50
Thiers Adolphe, 225
Treaty of Waitangi 1840, 125, 127, 131, 133–4, 137, 142, 145
Truman President Harry S., 166–7

ultra vires doctrine,
  legal accountability and, 41
  New Zealand and, 139–40
Union of Italian Provinces, 256
United States Constitution, 164–8, 174, 178, 186, 188
  comparison with Canada's separation of powers, 58
United States, executive power in,
accountability,
  delegated authority control, 176–8
  executive detention of suspected terrorists, 183–7, 190
  judicial mechanisms, 173–5,
  legislative mechanisms, 171–3
  political mechanisms, 175–6
  war power control, 178–83

executive authority,
  Congress enumerated and residual powers, 164–5
  delegation of powers, 168–9
  President enumerated and residual powers, 164–5
  privileges and immunities,
judicial review, 189–91
separation of powers,
  checks and balances and, 163–4, 187–91
  historical background, 162–4
  President and the, 163
  Senate and the, 163
War Powers Resolution, 181

Weimar Republic, 271
'whistle-blower' legislation,
  legal protection of civil servants in Canada, 72
  accountability mechanism in Australia, 122
Willis J, 68
World Development Movement,
  judicial review of government decisions and, 45